WORLD SCRIPTURES

Compiled by

Leland P. Stewart

In Cooperation with the
Faith Communities Represented

With a Foreword by Dr. David Trobisch

From the Scholar's Desk
Bolivar, Missouri
2003

For information contact: 9\ÞÆ
        From the Scholar's Desk
        (An imprint of Quiet Waters Publications)
        P.O. Box 34, Bolivar MO 65613-0034.
        Email: QWP@usa.net.
For prices and order information visit:
        http://www.fromthescholarsdesk.com

Grateful acknowledgement is made to L. Ron Hubbard Library for permission to reprint selections from the copyrighted works of L. Ron Hubbard.

Revised edition. First paperback edition.

ISBN 1-931475-16-4

Hardback:
Library of Congress Control Number: 2002116082

CONTENTS

TAOIST SCRIPTURES 17

CONFUCIANIST SCRIPTURES 91

HINDU SCRIPTURES 133

BUDDHIST SCRIPTURES.. 203

ZOROASTRIAN SCRIPTURES 293

THE HEBREW SCRIPTURES AND OTHER SACRED
    JEWISH WRITINGS..321

CHRISTIAN SCRIPTURES.. 409

ISLAMIC SCRIPTURES 497

BAHA'I SCRIPTURES 545

SCIENTOLOGY SCRIPTURES 589

BRAHMA KUMARIS SCRIPTURES.............................. 625

BAWA MUHAIYADDEEN'S TEACHINGS...................... 655

TSALAGI TRADITIONS (NATIVE AMERICAN) 663

CAODAI SCRIPTURES 683

SCIENCE OF MIND SCRIPTURES................................701

ABOUT THE COMPILER 732

SOURCES 733

FOREWORD

For fifty years now, Leland P. Stewart, ordained minister of the Universalist Church of America and Harvard University graduate, has studied faith communities and nourished personal contacts with many of their members. In preparation for *World Scriptures* he invited religious leaders to make a selection of scriptures that speak with authority to their communities.

When asked to write a preface to this volume, I did not hesitate for one moment. For the last few years I was part of an interfaith dialogue group in Portland, Maine, which began with Jews, Muslims, and Christians but has widened to include members of the Baha'i faith, followers of the teachings of Confucius, and clergy of Pagan movements. The beneficial influence this group has exercised on the community can hardly be exaggerated, as it reaches from holding informational public lectures to helping employers, school boards, and police understand, respect, and accommodate the needs of Americans who observe practices that are different from traditional American culture.

Teaching at undergraduate and graduate institutions has made the need for information on contemporary religious groups in America obvious to me. Attaining such knowledge should form an integral part of any education.

My hope is that this book will encourage students of religion as well as people of faith to listen to the central religious messages of faith communities other than their own.

This is an important book and it comes at the right time.

Dr. David Trobisch
Professor of New Testament Language and Literature.

PREFACE

The world at large is now beginning to recognize that the real core of lasting peace is to be found in directing people toward spiritual consciousness. Religions and spiritual movements are supposed to provide the basis upon which individuals can build adequate lives and therefore promote peace throughout society.

Many have abandoned religion altogether, but generally have found nothing adequate to replace it. Abandoning any of the existing religions would be foolish indeed. Within each religion are found many grains of the truth for which humanity continues to search. To cope with human problems effectively, it is necessary to grapple with religion. The religious quest is what leads us to the great heights we seek in striving to perfect ourselves and the world in which we live. Not taking into account our religious needs and aspirations will make a study of humanity indeed empty. No matter how many people can comprehend the whole basis of religion today, all people can benefit from it.

The worldwide unity-and-diversity movement, within which the interfaith movement is a vital part, does not attempt to replace the historic religions. Instead, interfaith cooperation is an outgrowth of the coming together of the historic religions and modern spiritual movements. It is a dynamic movement, best suited to those who have learned how to maintain their own faith and, at the same time, work cooperatively with others of differing faiths and with those of no professed faith.

Admittedly, a unity-and-diversity movement is quite different from what we have had throughout history. But we are living in a different kind of world now from that of the past; we are beginning to see human potentialities in a new light. Religious and cultural diversities are facts of life in our interdependent world. The object of global cooperation is not to win converts, but to help people grow morally and spiritually according to their own best insights.

My inspiration for the present publication was a book, Paths of Life, written by Charles Morris of the University of Chicago. Morris has shown the inevitability of a union among the living religions and spiritual movements. He points out that some of them primarily emphasize meditation, others stress action, and the remainder accentuate receptivity. The research and insights which Morris has presented in this book and elsewhere in his writings predicted that a powerful impetus would emerge that stimulates cooperation among existing religions and spiritual groups. In fact, he has studied young people in various countries throughout the world and has discovered that world pressures are moving them in this direction.

His work, and that of a number of other thinkers, points to the need for a scriptural document sufficiently broad and accurate to be used as a reference work for each of the living religions and spiritual groups.

This book is a step in that direction. It is designed to give insight into the authoritative traditions of faith communities other than our own. Dialogue is necessary. So also is spiritual experience.

This is our hope and our dream.

Leland P. Stewart

DEFINITION OF TERMS

The scriptural changes which have been made with some of the materials in this book are not possible with other faiths due to copyright laws. We respect those laws and have abided by them as requested. If in any way we have not succeeded in this effort, we agree to make the proper adjustments in the next issue. This "Definition of Terms" section applies only to those scriptures which could be changed. For example, most religions are written largely in masculine terms. Rewording has been done where possible. Some faiths have made claims that others might question. We have sought to use only those scriptures which encourage mutual understanding and cooperation among the faiths and the world's peoples.

absolute The Eternal may or may not be called an absolute, depending upon one's definition of the term. There is no such thing as absolute good or absolute evil in a finite world, but the Eternal is that ultimate goal toward which all life inevitably tends in the long span of time. The Eternal is the mystery of life, but it need

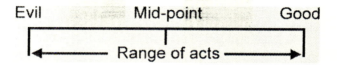

not be conceived as a personal God toward whom certain rituals must be performed. This idea, then, is changeless Reality, which is absolute in the sense that there is nothing beyond it; it is the supreme goal of life.

dispassion (See "passion")

Divine, the (See "Eternal, the")

enlightenment (See "wisdom")

Eternal, the (or "God", "the Infinite," "the Divine," "Life"). These terms are names for the nameless, the supreme and infinite value which includes and transcends all other values. The important idea to realize here is that these terms have been chosen so as to indicate that this idea may be conceived in many different ways, all of which in finite minds are somewhat less than the idea itself. Some believers in every religion think of the Eternal as a personal God to whom one can pray; however, more and more religious individuals are discovering that one need not personalize this idea. The above terms are used in order to indicate that people of both types of conceptions can unite in a world faith comprised of many religions.

ethics Ethics is conceived as the science of moral values. The term is used to describe the system of controlling the relations of person to person in a civilized society.

evil (See "good")

excellent person (See "mature person")

exultation (See "joy")

God God—as used in Zoroastrianism, Judaism, Christianity, Islam, and some other religions and spiritual movements – is understood to be a personal god, one to whom you can speak as to another person. For others, God is seen as the supreme principle in life but not a personal god. It is often for this reason that other names help to clarify this understanding (see "the Eternal", the "Infinite", "Oneness", etc.)

good (vs. "evil") As in regard to "virtue" and "sin," no absolute good or evil can be established in the finite, visible world. Nevertheless, all of the acts of the members of society fall somewhere on the scale between absolute good and absolute evil, and may be given one or the other label to the extent that they approach either extreme.

happiness Happiness is a sustained sense of well-being which is usually associated with a spiritually awakened life. (See "pleasure")

haughtiness (See "pride")

humility This term is sometimes confused with "complacency." We should be humble about what we do, knowing our own place in the great span of time and space, but we should accordingly empty ourselves of our selfish motives in order to be filled with the divine essence, thus through humility rising to otherwise impossible heights of enlightenment and achievement.

Infinite, the (See "Eternal, the")

insight (or "intuition") this idea has been greatly undervalued in modern life. The scriptures collectively should give more than sufficient evidence that the most reliable and only adequate key to life is that provided by our insights and those of others in society. Of course, these insights must be checked with available data, but they cannot be ignored in mature living. "Intuition" is used as as very similar to "insight."

intuition (See "insight")

joy (vs. "exultation") The spirit of individuals can fly highest, and they can be and remain happiest, when they take time to express the innermost feelings they experience, especially those which heal and transform. Laughter can be the opening to a new sense of meaning and purpose.

knowledge (See "wisdom")

Life (See "Eternal, the")

mature person (or "superior person," "excellent person") The notion of maturity has been brought into relation with the ideas of existing religions, which have called it by different names. The other terms, "superior person" and "excellent person," which are found primarily in Confucianism, are used synonymously with "mature person."

maturity One of the objects of introducing this idea into a world scripture is to show that maturity is the same as the full realization of the Eternal. In order to be mature, we must be both actors in life and observers of life; that is, we need to fulfill the complementary notions of withdrawal and return, of meditation and action. Thinking about life must not be left just to "ivory tower" sages!

meditation (vs. "prayer") Meditation, as used here, denotes the reflective, or contemplative, phase of life. Prayer is a form of meditation used when one puts a meditation into words, as to a personal God. It can involve silence, chanting, and other rituals.

misery Misery is a state of great distress or wretchedness.

mysticism Mysticism is one of the two basic elements of religion (the other being ethics). It is the goal of the idea of growth toward maturity, or human progress, to unite with the Eternal. All religion and philosophy are ultimately a search for mystical ethics and ethical mysticism, as Albert Schweitzer has described the process. This awareness, when understood in its true essence, is what makes possible the attempt of the individual to be in tune with Life; only then can one rise out of one's egoism into an altruistic and creative existence.

nature Those who follow their inner nature are those who are true to themselves; in other words, they are the ones who regard the dictates of the inner life as more valid than the standards and criticism of the society.

non-supernatural World religion is sometimes seen as "non-supernatural"; that is, its orientation is not based upon belief in a dogma from one of the historic religions. At the same time, it is not purely "naturalistic,' because it recognizes that the essence of life and the world is infinite and not finite. It aims at relating finite to infinite in their various manifestations and varieties.

passion (vs. "dispassion") "Passion" and "dispassion" seem at first to be contradictory terms; however, they are not so. Passion refers to the emotional life of individuals, which must be developed and refined, so that it may commit them to the most worthy causes, ultimately to the quest for union with the Eternal. Dispassion suggests the attitude of caution, of reserve, of calm reflection upon our ways of living. In a real sense, then, we should be passionate dispassionately.

perfection Perfection refers to an ultimate state of being. It relates to the struggle of individuals for self-perfection and social perfection. Neither will be fully reached, but both have to be pursued in order for either to be sustained.

pleasure (vs. "happiness") These two ideas are shades of the same principle, but their difference is fundamental.

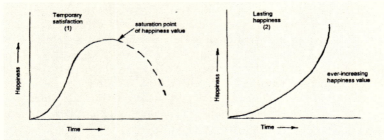

(1) Pleasure is the short-run value of happiness, which disappears readily with the passage of time, having no all-inclusive and lasting significance in one's philosophy of life.

(2) Happiness is the long-range sense of security and integration which comes from discovering meaning in one's life in relation to life and the world in general. It is like the mustard seed in the parables of Jesus, which, though the smallest of seeds, becomes the largest of shrubs.

prayer　Prayer is a direct reaching out, usually in words to a personal God or to the Higher Power as personally understood.

pride　(vs. "haughtiness"). In current usage this word sometimes has a favorable connotation and sometimes an unfavorable one. Usually in scriptures it is thought of as "false pride," and as such is to be eliminated. However, in this book the term "haughtiness" is used in place of "false pride," so as to eliminate the ambiguity. It is desirable to feel proud of a task well done, but at the same time it is dangerous to be conceited or arrogant about one's ways or accomplishments.

propriety　Propriety is a term used here only in Confucianism. It is similar to ethics as describing the relation of person to person in Chinese society.

righteousness　The Chinese have called the ethical life virtuous; Christians and Jews have called it righteous. In either case it is the goal of the ethical phase of religion.

Self　The "Self" of the Upanishads is intentionally equated to the Eternal, because our highest nature is eternal. We need to distinguish between the egoistic self and the altruistic Self in our own lives in order to be true to our real nature and to follow the altruistic Self as primary.

simplicity　Simplicity appears to be a lost virtue today. Modern life is so complex that people tend to forget the simplest items of all. What has to be remembered is that quality of action is far superior to quantity, and that this quality must be based upon the dominance of the spiritual life. Without this, all activity will tend toward misery and self-destruction.

sin (vs. "virtue", "perfection") These are very important terms. Even though no single act can arbitrarily be called "sinful" or "virtuous" without reference to its circumstances, still there are definite notions in most societies of sin and virtue. And in civilized societies quite good agreement can be found regarding these ideas. "Perfect" virtue just indicates the ideal which some few individuals may approximate but not fully realize.

sorrow Sorrow is a condition of sadness, often brought about by the death of a relative or close friend. Kahlil Gibran says that joy and sorrow are the two sides of the same coin. Learning to accept and transform sorrow is one of the greatest challenges of life.

soul The soul is the Self. It is the center of the spiritual life within the individual, although it is obviously not physically locatable.

spirit This is the essence of life. It is the nonmaterial realm, and can best be described in terms of what it is not a part of—namely, the physical or mental phases of life. It is that which gives oneness to the external and internal worlds.

superior person (See "mature person")

understanding (See "wisdom")

union (with the Eternal) The religious (or ultimately, mystical) quest, which is very similar to the idea of growth toward maturity, is the search for union with the essence of life, which is eternal. Although this quest is called by many names, and its paths are greatly varied, its goal is the same throughout.

virtue Virtues are positive qualities in the individual such as honesty, caring, and mercy.

wisdom Wisdom, understanding, and enlightenment are three similar terms used to describe individuals' power to comprehend the meaning of life. Knowledge stands in great contrast to these terms, because it cannot by itself produce wisdom. Understanding life involves both a certain amount of knowledge (of facts) and a great deal of intuition about the nature of reality. Thus, quantity of education is no certain cure for the ills of existence; in fact, excessive years of education can definitely harm an individual's sense of commitment and his/her consequent ability to gain wisdom.

ACKNOWLEDGEMENTS

The World Scriptures project represents more than fifty years of research and writing on the part of author/editor Leland Stewart. However, it also includes considerable help from an increasing number of individuals and organizations as the project was coming to completion and the time of publication. It is most important that these people be known and acknowledged for their very important help.

The first is Hoang Van Duc, M.D., D.Sc., who has consistently pointed out the importance of this work and the need to get it on computer and available to the public. It was his insistence that World Scriptures be available which has helped me take the necessary steps to make it happen. Along with him has been Monique Baudaux Andersen, whose faithful participation in our regular meetings and her artistic support of the project have likewise been most important. The third person is my wife Elizabeth, who has been supportive of the project ever since its beginning in the 1950's. She has patiently waited through all of these years, knowing that the work needed to be done and that it would eventually come to fruition. For this devotion I am most appreciative. More recently, Rabbi Benjamin Herson, in connection with submitting the Hebrew Scriptures, has urged the publication of World Scriptures and its use in classrooms worldwide.

However, there is one person, whose commitment to the project and willingness to provide the major funding for *World Scriptures* have been crucial to seeing it actually happen. That individual is Carl Hult. Carl is a singer who performs as a soloist and choir member with numerous groups in greater Los Angeles. I extend my sincerest thanks to Carl.

Also recently, the various faith groups in the World Interfaith Network, a Specialized Affiliate of the Unity-and-Diversity World Council, Inc., which has been holding Interfaith Celebrations every months for several years, have been submitting their scriptures to be in World Scriptures. If they already had materials in the publication, they would suggest how the materials might be improved. If they did not have materials included, they have offered what they felt would be appropriate. To date these people are as follows:

Taoist Scriptures — Rev. Leland P. Stewart, interpreted from *The Bible of the Wolrd* (New York: Viking, 1934).

Confucianist Scriptures — Rev. Leland P. Stewart, interpreted from *The Bible of the Wolrd* (New York: Viking, 1934).

Hindu Scriptures — Rev. Leland P. Stewart, interpreted from *The Bible of the Wolrd*; Vedanta (considered as part of Hinduism in this volume) Swami Brahmavidyananda and Shiva, monks with Vedanta Society of Southern California.

Buddhist Scriptures — Rev. Leland P. Stewart, interpreted from *The Bible of the Wolrd*; Dr. Ananda Guruge, Dean of Academic Affairs, His Lai University; Rev. Kusala, Monk, International Buddhist Meditation Center.

Zoroastrian Scriptures — Mobed Zarir Bhandara, High Priest, Zoroastrian Association of California; also Dolly Malva, Past President.

Hebrew Scriptures — Rabbi Benjamin Herson, Rabbi Emeritus, Malibu Jewish Center and Synagogue; Founder, Wallenberg Institute of Ethics.

Christian Scriptures — Thomas Whaling, Attorney, Interfaith Conference Organizer (Catholic); Rod Parrott, Disciples Seminary Foundation; also Rev. Jeffrey Utter, Congregational Minister and interfaith leader (both Protestant).

Islamic Scriptures — Mahmoud Ezzeldine, formerly with Islamic Center of Southern California; also Shabbir Mansuri and Aiyub Palmer, Council on Islamic Education.

Baha'i Scriptures — Shahpur Sohaili, Baha'i Community of Santa Monica (deceased); also Sam Sohrab, Baha'i Community of La Canada

Scientology Scriptures — Rev. Dr. Wolfgang Keller and Cat Tebar, Church of Scientology of Los Angeles; also Marilyn Pisani, Secretary, Bridge Publications, Inc.

Brahma Kumaris Scriptures — Sister Jayanti, Global Cooperation House, London, Brahma Kumaris World Spiritual University.

Bawa Muhaiyaddeen's Teachings — Richard Kuznetsky, M.D., Regional Representative, Bawa Muhaiyadeen Fellowship.

Tsalagi Tradition's Teachings (Native American) — drawn from: *Voices of Our Ancestors: Cherokee Teachings from the Wisdom Fire*, by Dhyani Ywahoo.

CaoDai Scriptures — presented by Hum Bui, M.D., an active leader and developer of a CaoDai Center in Pomona, California; in collaboration with Ngasha Beck.

Science of Mind Scriptures — drawn from: *Can We Talk to God?* by Ernest Holmes, founder of the Church of Religious Science; selected by Kathy Juline of "Science of Mind Magazine."

At this time in human history, I believe that scripture is once again open. It is an exciting time to be alive, and our future direction as a global community depends to a considerable extent on the quality and diversity of this kind of cooperative effort. If you have questions or are in interested in helping the project, please contact:

Unity-and-Diversity World Council, Inc.
P. O. Box 661401, Los Angeles, CA 90066-9201 USA
E-mail: udcworld1@yahoo.com
Website: www.udcworld.org
Phone: (310) 391-5735

TAOIST SCRIPTURES

INTRODUCTION

Tao-Te-Ching

This book contains the very profound and beautiful, yet applicable religious, political, and philosophical teachings of China's Lao Tze. Although practically nothing is known about the life of Lao Tze, he is said to have lived in China during the sixth century B.C. As is shown by The Works of Chuang Tze, Lao Tze was probably an older contemporary and critic of Confucius. Lofty mysticism and sound ethics are both to be found in this document. The ideas of faith and love are here expressed in fundamentally the same way as Jesus stated them more than five centuries later.

The Works of Chuang Tze

Chuang Tze belongs to the third and fourth centuries B.C., being the major disciple of Lao Tze. In this way he has had a corresponding influence upon Taoism to what St. Paul had upon Christianity. Chuang Tze elaborated the principles of the Tao-Te-Ching in a prosaic but profound manner. Both of these men showed a very pronounced mystical element, but ethics also were developed in their teachings.

THE TAO-TE-CHING

(1) The Beginning of the Universe

The Way that can be expressed is not the Eternal Way:
The name that can be defined is not the unchanging name.
Thought is called the antecedent of the universe;
Action is the mother of all things.
From eternal thought, therefore, we serenely observe the mysterious beginning of the universe;
From continual action we clearly see the apparent discrepancies.
These two are the same in source and become different when manifested.
This sameness is called mystery. Infinite mystery is the gate whence comes the beginning of all parts of the universe.

(2) The Opposites

When all in the world understand beauty to be beautiful, then ugliness exists.
When all understand goodness to be good, then evil exists.
Thus action suggests thought;
Easy gives rise to difficult;
Short is derived from long by comparison;
Low is distinguished from high by position;
Resonance harmonizes sound;
After follows before.
Therefore, mature individuals seem to carry on their business without action, and to give their teaching without words.

(3) Avoiding Discomfort

Not exalting the competitively successful keeps the people from
  material discontent.
Not valuing rare things keeps them from theft.
Not giving temptation keeps their hearts from confusion.
In this way mature individuals give crafty ones no chance to act.
  They govern with impartial thought; consequently, nothing is
  ungoverned.

(4) The Predecessor of Nature

Followers of the Eternal Way, when put in use for their thought
  about life, are not likely to be always active in life.
In its profundity the Eternal Way seems to be the origin of all
  things.
In its depth it seems ever to remain.
I do not know whose offspring it is;
But it looks like the predecessor of nature.

(5) On Talking

The one who talks more is sooner exhausted.
It is better to keep what is within oneself.

(6) Mystery

Thought and the spirit never die.
They form what is called mystery,
From which comes the origin of the universe.
This (the origin) seems ever to endure.
In use it can never be exhausted.

(7) True Self-interest

Thought is lasting and action enduring.
The reason why they are lasting and enduring is that they do not
  live for themselves;
Therefore, they live long.
In the same way, mature individuals keep themselves behind
  and end up in the front;
They forget themselves and are preserved.
Is it not because they are not self-interested

That their self-interest is established?

(8) Balance

The highest goodness is like water. Water is beneficent to all
things but does not contend. It stays in places which others
despise. Therefore it is near the Eternal.
In dwelling, think one's place suitable;
In feeling, make the heart deep;
In friendship, keep on good terms with all;
In words, have confidence;
In ruling, abide by good order;
In business, take things easy;
In motion, make use of the opportunity.
Since there is no contention, there is no blame.

(9) Detachment

Seeking and holding material gains to the very end—it is better
to leave them alone;
Handling and sharpening a weapon—it cannot be long left un-
used;
When gold and jade fill the hall, no one can protect them;
Wealth and honor plus haughtiness bring with them destruc-
tion:
Having given your best, then withdraw into obscurity—
This is the way to the Eternal.

(10) Self-conquest

Can you keep the soul always concentrated and not straying?
Can you regulate the breath, and become soft and pliant like an
infant?
Can you clear and get rid of the unforeseen, as well as be free
from fault?
Can you love the people and govern the state by holding equilibrium?
Can you open and shut the gates of nature like a female (without force)?
Can you become enlightened and penetrate everywhere without
knowledge? (insight is far more adequate for life than knowledge)

(11) Action and Inaction

Thirty spokes unite in one hub;
And because of the space between the spokes we have the use
of a carriage wheel.
Clay is molded into vessels;
And because of the space where nothing exists, we are able to
use them as vessels;
Doors and windows are cut out in the walls of a house;
And because there are empty spaces, we are able to use them.
Therefore, on the one hand we have the benefit of action; and
on the other, we make use of inaction.

(12) Relaxation

Too many colors will blind one's sight.
Too many sounds will deaden one's hearing.
Too many tastes will spoil one's palate.
Chasing and hunting will drive a person wild.
The competitive attitude will do harm to one's conduct.
Therefore, the mature person makes provision only for his/her
minimum needs and not maximum desires.
Such a person rejects the latter and chooses the former.

(13) Gain and Loss

"Favor and disgrace are like fear; fortune and disaster are like
our body."
What does it mean by "Favor and disgrace are like fear"? Favor
is in a higher place, and disgrace in a lower place. When you
win them, you are like being in fear; and when you lose them,
you are also like being in fear. So favor and disgrace are like
fear.
What does it mean by "Fortune and disaster are like our body"?
We have fortune and disaster because we have a body. When
we have no body, how can fortune or disaster befall us?
Therefore, those who regard the world as they do the fortune of
their own bodies can govern the world. Those who love the
world as they do their own bodies can be entrusted with the
world.

(14) Forms of the Formless

That which we look at and cannot see is called plainness.
That which we listen to and cannot hear is called rareness.
That which we grope for and cannot get is called minuteness.
These three cannot be closely examined;
So they blend into one.
Revealed, it is not dazzling;
Hidden, it is not dark.
Infinite, it cannot be defined.
It goes back to thought.
It is called the form of the formless,
And the image of thought.
It is called mystery.
Meet it, you cannot see its face;
Follow it, you cannot see its back.

(14a) Clue to the Past

By adhering to the highest ideals of the past,
You will master the action of the present
And be able to know the origin of the past.
This is called the clue of the Eternal.

(15) The Mature Individual

In old times mature individuals were subtle, penetrating, and so
   profound that they could hardly be understood. Because they
   cannot easily be understood, I shall endeavor to picture them:
They are cautious, like one who crosses a stream in winter;
They are hesitating, like those who fear their neighbors;
They are modest, like one who is a guest;
They are yielding, like ice that is going to melt;
They are simple, like wood that is not yet wrought;
They are vacant, like valleys that are hollow;
They are dim, like water that is turbid.
For who is able to purify the dark till it becomes slowly light?
Who is able to calm the turbid till it slowly clears?
Who is able to quicken the stagnant till it slowly makes pro-
   gress?
Those who follow these principles do not expect perfection.

Because they are not perfect, therefore, if they once yield to temptation, they can improve.

(16) Immortality

Attain to the goal of absolute vacuity;
Keep to the state of inner peace.
All things come into existence,
And thence we see them leave.
Look at the things that have been flourishing;
Each goes back to its origin.
Going back to the origin is called peace;
It means reversion to destiny.
Reversion to destiny is called eternity.
Those who know eternity are called enlightened.
Those who do not know eternity are running blindly into miseries.
Knowing eternity, they are all-embracing.
Being all-embracing, they can attain magnanimity.
Being magnanimous, they can attain omnipresence.
Being omnipresent, they can attain supremacy.
Being supreme, they can attain the Eternal.
Those who attain the Eternal are everlasting.
Though their bodies may decay, they never perish.

(17) Paradox

The great rulers—the people do not notice their existence;
The lesser ones—they attach to and praise them;
The still lesser ones—they fear them;
The still lesser ones—they despise them.
For where faith is lacking,
It cannot be met by faith.
Now how much importance must be attributed to words?

(18) The Supreme Value

When the path to the Eternal is lost, the highest goals become benevolence and righteousness.
Next, knowledge and shrewdness arise, followed by great hypocrisy.

When family relations are no longer harmonious, certain filial
children and devoted parents appear.

When a nation is in confusion and disorder, certain patriots are
recognized.

Where the Eternal is known, equilibrium exists. When the Eternal is lost, out come all the disagreements among people.

(19) Avoiding Temptation

Do away with extravagant learning, and grief will not be known.

Do away with excessive knowledge, and the people will be
benefited a hundred times.

Do away with enforced benevolence and righteousness, and the
people will return to filial duty and parental love.

Do away with artifice and eject gains, and there will be no robbers and thieves.

These four, if we consider them as culture, are not sufficient.

Therefore, let there be what the people can resort to:

Appear in plainness and hold to simplicity;

Restrain selfishness and curtail craving.

(20) Relativity

Between yes and no, how much difference is there?

Between good and evil, how much difference is there?

What is feared by others, we think we must fear;

Vast are these ideas and unlimited!

The people in general are so happy, as if enjoying a great feast,

Or as going up a tower in spring.

I alone am tranquil, and have made no signs,

Like a baby who is yet unable to smile;

Forlorn, as if I had no home to go to.

Others all have more than enough,

And I alone seem to be in want.

Possibly mine is the mind of a fool,

Which is so ignorant!

The vulgar are bright,

And I alone seem to be dull.

The vulgar are so discriminative, and I alone seem to be tolerant.

I am negligent, as if being obscure;

Drifting, as if being attached to nothing.
The people in general all have something to do,
And I alone seem to be impractical and awkward.
I alone am different from others.
But I value seeking sustenance from the Eternal.

(21) The Origin of All Things

The great virtue as manifested is but seeking the Eternal.
The Eternal is a thing that is both invisible and intangible.
Intangible and invisible, yet there are forms in it;
Invisible and intangible, yet there is substance in it;
Subtle and obscure, there is essence in it;
This essence being invariably true, there is faith in it.
From of old till now, it has never lost its (nameless) name,
Through which the origin of all things has passed.
How do I know that it is so with the origin of all things?
By this (my awareness of the Eternal).

(22) Humility

"Be humble, and you will remain entire."
Be bent, and you will remain straight
Be vacant, and you will remain full.
Be worn, and you will remain new.
Those who have little will receive.
Those who have much will be embarrassed.
Therefore, mature individuals keep to the One and become the
    standard for the world.
They do not display themselves; therefore they shine.
They do not approve themselves; therefore they are noted.
They do not praise themselves; therefore they have merit.
They do not glory in themselves; therefore they excel.
And because they do not compete, no one in the world can
    compete with them.
The ancient saying "Be humble, and you will remain entire"—
Can this be regarded as mere empty words?
Indeed they shall return home entire.

(23) Virtue and Abandonment

A violent wind cannot last a whole morning; pelting rain cannot last a whole day. These things are associated with the universe.

Inasmuch as the universe cannot last forever, how can humans? People who engage themselves in Eternity are identified with Eternity. Those who engage themselves with virtue are identified with virtue. Those who engage themselves in abandonment are identified with abandonment.

Identified with Eternity, they will be well received by Eternity.

Identified with virtue, they will be well received by virtue. Identified with abandonment, they will be well received by abandonment.

(24) The Problem of Competition

People on tiptoe cannot stand firm;
People astride cannot walk on;
Those who display themselves cannot shine;
Those who approve themselves cannot be noted;
Those who praise themselves cannot have merit;
Those who glory in themselves cannot excel.
These, when compared with the Eternal, are called:
"Excess in food and overdoing in action".
Even in other things, mostly they are rejected;
Therefore, people of Eternity do not stay with them.

(25) The Essence of the Universe

There is a thing inherent and natural,
Which existed before the universe.
Motionless and fathomless,
It stands alone and never changes;
It pervades everywhere and never becomes exhausted.
It may be regarded as the Essence of the universe.
I do not know its name.
If I am forced to give it a name,
I call it the Eternal, and I name it as supreme.
Supreme, it passes on;
Passing on, it becomes remote;
Having become remote, it returns.

Therefore, the Eternal is supreme; the universe is supreme; and
the mature individual is also supreme. There are in life three
things supreme, and the mature individual is one of them.
The mature individual follows the laws of the universe;
The universe follows the laws of the Eternal;
The Eternal follows the laws of its intrinsic nature.
The mature individual follows the laws of the universe;
The universe follows the laws of the Eternal;
The Eternal follows the laws of its intrinsic nature.

(26) Dispassion

Heaviness is the basis of lightness;
Calmness is the controlling-power of hastiness.
Therefore, mature individuals, though traveling all day long,
Never go far from the baggage-wagon;
Though surrounded with magnificent sights,
They live in tranquility.
How is it, then, that kings of ten thousand chariots
Should conduct themselves so lightly in the empire?
To be light is to lose the basis;
To be hasty is to lose the controlling power.

(27) The Meaning of Subtlety

Good travelers leave no tracks;
Good speakers leave no errors;
Good reckoners need no counters;
Good closets need no bars or bolts,
And yet it is impossible to open them.
Good fasteners need no cords or knots,
And yet it is impossible to untie them.
Even if people are bad, why should they be rejected?
Therefore, the mature individual is always a good savior of
things,
And nothing is rejected:
This is called double enlightenment.
Therefore, good people are bad people's instructors,
And bad people are good people's materials.
Those who do not esteem their instructors,
And those who do not love their materials,

Though expedient, are in fact greatly confused.
This is essential subtlety.

(28) The Standard of the World

Those who know masculine strength and yet keep to feminine
feebleness
Will become a channel drawing all the world toward them;
Being a channel of the world, they will not be severed from
eternal virtue,
And then they can return again to the state of infancy.
Those who know the dark and yet keep to the light
Will become the standard of the world;
Being the standard of the world, with them eternal virtue will
never falter,
And then they can return again to the Absolute.
Those who know honor and yet keep to humility
Will become a valley that receives all the world into it;
Being a valley of the world, with them eternal virtue will be
complete,
And then they can return again to wholeness.
Wholeness, when divided, will make vessels of utility;
These, when employed by the mature individual, will become
officials and chiefs.
However, for a great function no discrimination is needed.

(29) Dominance

When people wish to take the world over and shape it to their
own ends,
I see that they will not succeed in doing it.
For the world is a divine vessel:
It cannot be forced into shape,
Nor can it be insisted upon.
They who force it damage it;
They who insist upon it lose it.
Therefore, mature individuals do not force it, so they do not
damage it;
They do not insist upon it, so they do not lose it.
For, among all things, some go ahead, while others lag behind;
Some keep their mouths shut, while others give forth puffs;

Some are strong, while others are weak;
Some are on the cart, while others fall off.
Therefore, mature individuals avoid excess, extravagance, and
  indulgence.

(30) Nonviolence

Those who assist a ruler of people in harmony with the Eternal
  will not assert their mastery of the world by force of arms.
They aim only at giving aid, and do not venture to force their
  power upon others.
When aid is given, they will not be assuming;
They will not be boastful; they will not be proud;
And they will think that they were obliged to do it.
So it comes that aid is given without resorting to force.

(30a) Vigor and Age

When things come to the summit of their vigor, they begin to
  grow old.
This is against the Eternal.
What is against the Eternal will soon come to an end.

(31) Military Power

So far as arms are concerned, they are implements of ill-omen.
They are not implements for the person of Eternity. For the actions of arms will be well requited: where armies have been
  quartered, brambles and thorns grow. Great wars are for certain followed by years of scarcity. People of Eternity, when
  dwelling at home, put the festival in the place of honor; when
  using arms, they put mourning in the place of honor. They use
  arms only when they cannot avoid it. In their conquests they
  take no delight. If they took delight in them, it would mean
  that they enjoy the slaughter of people. They who take delight
  in the slaughter of people cannot be following the Eternal.

(32) The Nameless

The Eternal was always nameless.
When for the first time applied to function, it was named.

Inasmuch as names are given, one should also know where to stop.

Knowing where to stop, one can become imperishable.

(33) The Self

Those who know others are wise;
Those who know themselves are enlightened.
Those who conquer others are strong;
Those who conquer themselves are mighty.
Those who know contentment are rich.
Those who keep on their course with energy have will.
Those who do not deviate from their proper place will long endure.
Those who may die but not perish have longevity.

(34) The Eternal

The Eternal pervades everywhere, both on the left and on the right.
By It, all things came into being; and It does not reject them.
Tasks accomplished, It does not claim merit.
It loves and nourishes all things, but does not dominate over them.
It is always in the realm of thought; therefore It can be named as small.
All things return home to It, and It does not claim mastery over them; therefore, It can be named as great.
Because it never assumes greatness, therefore It can accomplish greatness.

(35) The Inexhaustible

To those who hold to the great image of the Eternal, all the world will come in spirit.
They will come and will receive no hurt, but will find tranquility, equality, and community.
Music and dainties will please the passing stranger (for a time);
But the Eternal, when uttered in words, is pure and void of flavor.
When one looks at It, one cannot see It;
When one listens to It, one cannot hear It,

However, when one uses It, It is inexhaustible.

(36) Subtle Wisdom

In order to contract a thing, one should surely expand it first.
In order to weaken, one will surely strengthen first.
In order to overthrow, one will exalt first.
In order to take, one will surely give first.
This is called subtle wisdom.
The soft and weak can overcome the hard and strong.
As the fish should not leave the deep,
So should the sharp implements of a nation not be shown to anyone.

(37) Simplicity

The Eternal is ever inactive, and yet there is nothing that It does not do.
If princes and kings could keep to It, all things would themselves become developed.
When they were developed, craving might stir in them;
I would restrain them by the nameless simplicity, in order to make them free from craving.
Free from craving, they would be at rest;
And the world would itself become rectified.
However insignificant simplicity seems, the whole world cannot make it submissive.
If princes and kings could keep to It,
All things in the world would of themselves pay homage.
The people with no one to command them would of themselves become harmonious.

(38) The Greater and the Lesser

The superior virtue is not conscious of itself as virtue;
Therefore it has virtue.
The inferior virtue never stops displaying virtue;
Therefore it has no virtue.
The superior virtue seems inactive, and yet there is nothing that it does not do.
The inferior virtue acts, and yet in the end leaves things undone.

The superior benevolence acts constantly, but with the need to act.

The superior righteousness acts constantly, but with the need to act.

The superior ritual acts constantly, and when at first no one responds to it,

People raise their arms and begin giving threats.

Therefore, when the Eternal is lost, virtue appears as life's highest aim.

When virtue is lost, benevolence appears;

When benevolence is lost, righteousness appears;

When righteousness is lost, idols appear.

Idols, therefore, are the attenuation of loyalty and faith, and the outset of confusion.

Fore-knowledge is only the flower of the Eternal, and is the beginning of folly.

Therefore, truly great individuals keep to the solid and not to the flimsy;

Keep to the fruit and not to the flower.

Thus they reject the latter and take to the former.

(39) Unity

From of old the things that have acquired unity are these:

The universe by unity has become clear;

The earth by unity has become steady;

The Spirit by unity has become spiritual;

The valley by unity has become full;

All things by unity have come into existence;

Princes and kings by unity have become rulers of the world.

If the universe were not clear, it would be rent;

If the earth were not steady, it would be tumbled down;

If the Spirit were not active, it would pass away;

If the valley were not full, it would be dried up;

If all things were not active, they would be extinct;

If princes and kings were not rulers, they would be overthrown.

The noble must be styled in the terms of the humble;

The high must take the low as their foundation.

Therefore, princes and kings call themselves "the ignorant," "the virtueless" and "the unworthy."

And yet princes and kings choose them as their titles.

Therefore, the highest fame is to have no fame.
Thus kings are increased by being diminished;
They are diminished by being increased.
It is undesirable to be as prominent as a single gem,
Or as monotonously numerous as stones.

(40) Relationship

Returning is the motion of the Eternal,
Weakness is the appliance of the Eternal.
All things in the universe come from action,
And action from thought.

(41) Search for the Eternal

When superior individuals are told of the Eternal,
They work hard to realize It.
When middling individuals are told of the Eternal,
It seems that sometimes they seek It and sometimes they forget
   It.
When inferior individuals are told of the Eternal, they laugh
   aloud at It.
If it were not laughed at,
It would not be sufficient to be the Eternal.
Therefore, the proverb says:
"The Eternal in enlightenment seems obscure;
The Eternal in progress seems regressive;
The Eternal in its straightness seems crooked.
The highest peak seems like a valley;
The purest white seems discolored;
The most magnificent virtue seems insufficient;
The solidest truth seems frail;
The simplest nature seems changeable;
The greatest square has no angles;
The largest vessel is slowest made;
The loudest sound can scarcely be heard;
The biggest form cannot be visualized.
The Eternal, while hidden, is also nameless."
Yet it is The Eternal alone that is good at imparting and com-
   pleting.

(42) Self-destruction

What others teach, I also teach: "The reckless and violent often
do not die a natural death." This (maxim) I shall regard as my
instructor.

(43) Meditation

Thought can enter into the impenetrable.
By this I know that non-action also is useful, as is action.
Teaching without words, utility without action—
Few in the world have come to this.

(44) Contentment

Fame or your person, which is nearer to you?
Your person or wealth, which is dearer to you?
Gain or loss, which brings more evil to you?
Over-love of anything will lead to wasteful spending;
Amassed riches will be followed by heavy plundering.
Therefore, those who know contentment (with few posses-
    sions) can never be humiliated;
Those who know where to stop can never be perishable;
They will long endure.

(45) Appearances

The greatest perfection seems imperfect;
Yet its use will last without decay.
The greatest fullness seems empty;
Yet its use cannot be exhausted.
The greatest straightness seems crooked;
The greatest dexterity seems awkward;
The greatest eloquence seems stammering.
Activity overcomes cold;
Quietness overcomes heat.
Only through purity and quietude can the world be ruled.

(46) Greed

When the Eternal is realized in the world,
The swift horses are used for hauling dung-carts in the field.
When the Eternal is not realized in the world,

War horses are bred on the commons outside the cities.
There is no greater crime than seeking what people crave;
There is no greater misery than knowing no content;
There is no greater calamity than indulging in greed.
Therefore, the sufficiency of contentment is an enduring and
unchanging sufficiency.

(47) Understanding

Without going out of the door,
One can know the whole world;
Without peeping out of the window,
One can see the Eternal.
The further one travels (away from the Self),
The less one understands.
Therefore, mature persons understand everything without traveling;
They name everything without seeing it;
They accomplish everything without having to do it.

(48) Action and Non-action

Those who pursue learning tend to increase every day;
Those who pursue the Eternal tend to decrease every day.
They will decrease and continue to decrease,
Till they come to non-action;
Sensing the value of non-action, everything can be accomplished.

(49) Ethics

Mature individuals have no self to call their own;
They make the self of the people their self.
To the good I act with goodness;
To the bad I also act with goodness:
Thus goodness is attained.
To the faithful I act with faith;
To the faithless I also act with faith:
Thus faith is attained.
The mature individual lives in the world in concord, and rules
over the world in simplicity.
Yet what the people turn their ears and eyes to,

The mature individual looks after others as a mother does her children.

(50) Beyond Death

People go out of life and enter into death.

Of every ten persons, about three are ministers of life, and three are ministers of death. People that from birth, though seeking to live, move towards the region of death are also about three in ten. Why is it so? Because of their excessive effort in seeking to live.

Those who do nothing just for the purpose of living are better than those who prize their lives. For I have heard that those who know well how to manage their lives, when traveling on land do not have to shun the rhinoceros or the tiger; when going to a battle they do not need to avoid arms and weapons. The rhinoceros can find nowhere to drive its horn; the tiger can find nowhere to put its claws; the warriors can find nowhere to thrust their blades. Why is it so?

Because they are beyond the region of death.

(51) Divine Beneficence

The Eternal produces them (all things);

Virtue feeds them;

All of them appear in different forms;

Each is perfected by being given power.

Therefore, each of the numerous things honors the Eternal and esteems virtue.

The honoring of the Eternal and the esteem of virtue are done, not by command, but always of their own accord.

Therefore, the Eternal produces them, makes them grow, nourishes them, shelters them, brings them up, and protects them.

When all things come into being, the Eternal does not reject them.

It produces them without holding possession of them.

It acts without depending upon them, and raises them without lording it over them.

When tasks are accomplished, it does not lay claim to merit.

Because it does not lay claim to merit, therefore it does not lose it.

(52) Harmlessness

The beginning of the universe, when manifested, may be re-
garded as its Essence.
When people have found the Essence, they will know the mani-
festations accordingly;
Though they have known the manifestations, they still keep to
the Essence:
Thus, however their bodies may decay, they will never perish.
If they shut their mouths and close their doors,
They can never be exhausted.
If they open their mouths and parade their affairs,
They can never be restored.
To see the minuteness of things is called clarity of sight;
To keep to what is weak is called power.
Use your light, but dim your brightness;
Thus you will cause no harm to yourself.
This is called following the Eternal.

(53) Encouragement to Robbery

Let me have sound knowledge and walk on the great way;
Only I am in fear of deviating.
The great way is very plain and easy,
But the people prefer by-paths.
While the royal palaces are very well kept,
The fields are left weedy
And the granaries empty.
To wear embroidered clothes,
To carry sharp swords,
To be satiated in drink and food,
To be possessed of redundant riches—
This is called encouragement to robbery.
Is it not deviating from the Eternal?

(54) The One and the Many

What is planted by the best planter can never be removed;
What is embraced by the best embracer can never be loosened.
If they apply the Eternal to themselves, their virtue will be
genuine;
If they apply it to their families, their virtue will be abundant;

If they apply it to their villages, their virtue will be everlasting;
If they apply it to their country, their virtue will be full;
If they apply it to the world, their virtue will be universal.
Therefore, by one's person one may observe persons;
By one's family one may observe families;
By one's village one may observe villages;
By one's country one may observe countries;
By one's world one may observe worlds.
How do I know that the world may be so governed by the
 Eternal?
By this observation.

(55) Virtue

Those who are endowed with ample virtue may be compared to
 an infant.
No venomous insects sting them;
Nor fierce beasts seize them;
Nor birds of prey strike them.
Their bones are frail, their sinews tender, but their grasp is
 strong.
They do not know the conjugation of male and female, and yet
 they have sexual development;
It means they are in the best vitality.
They may cry all day long without growing hoarse;
It means that they are in perfect harmony.
To know this harmony is to approach eternity;
To know eternity is to attain enlightenment.
To increase excitement is to lead to calamity;
To let the heart control the breath is to become stark.

(56) The Valuable

Blunt all that is sharp;
Cut all that is divisible;
Blur all that is brilliant;
Mix with all what is humble as dust;
This is called absolute equality.
Therefore it cannot be made intimate;
Nor can it be alienated.
It cannot be benefited;

Nor can it be harmed.
It cannot be exalted;
Nor can it be debased.
Therefore it is the most valuable thing in the world.

(57) Quietude

Albeit one governs the country by rectitude,
And carries on wars by stratagems,
Yet one must rule the empire by meddling with no business.
The empire can always be ruled by meddling with no business.
Otherwise it can never be done.
How do I know it is so?
By this:
The more restrictions and avoidances that are in the empire,
The poorer become the people;
The more sharp implements the people keep,
The more confusions are present in the country;
The more arts and crafts people have,
The more are fantastic things produced;
The more laws and regulations are given,
The more robbers and thieves there are.
Therefore the mature person says:
Inasmuch as I betake myself to holding equilibrium, the people
by working out their own destinies become developed.
Inasmuch as I love quietude, the people through thinking be-
come righteous.
Inasmuch as I make no fuss, the people benefit.
Inasmuch as I am free from craving, the people in following my
example remain simple.

(58) Non-intervention

When the government holds to non-intervention, the people
may be happy and prosperous;
When the government is always meddling, the people will be
dissatisfied and restless.
It is upon misery that happiness rests;
It is under happiness that misery lies.
Who then can know the supremacy (good government)?
Only when the government does no rectifying (involuntarily).

Otherwise, rectitude will again become a stratagem,
And good becomes evil,
People have been ignorant of this since long ago.
Therefore, mature individuals are square but do not cut others;
They are angled but do not chip others;
They are straight but do not stretch others;
They are bright but do not dazzle others.

(59) Moderation

In ruling people and in seeking the Eternal, mature individuals use only moderation,
By moderation alone they are able to have conformed early to Life.
This early conformity is called intensive accumulation of virtue.
With this intensive accumulation of virtue, there is nothing that they cannot overcome.
Because there is nothing that they cannot overcome, no one will be able to know their supremacy.
Because no one knows their supremacy, they can take possession of a country.
Because what they do is identified with the Eternal, in taking possession of a country they can long endure.
This means that they are deep-rooted and firmly based, and know the way of longevity and eternity.

(60) Gentleness

Govern a great state as you would cook a small fish (do it gently).
Let the Eternal reign over the world, and no power can harm the people.
Neither will the mature individual harm the people.
Inasmuch as no one harms anybody,
Therefore, virtue belongs to all.

(61) The Great State and the Small

A great state is the world's low-stream, to which all the river flows down, the world's field and the world's female. The female always conquers the male by quietude, which is employed as a means of lowering oneself. Thus a great state low-

ers itself towards a small state before it takes over the small
state. A small state lowers itself towards a great state before it
takes over the great state.

Therefore, some lower themselves to take, while others lower
themselves to gather. A great state wishes nothing more than
to have and keep many people, and a small state wishes nothing more than to get more things to do. When the two both
mean to obtain their wishes, the greater one should lower itself.

(62) The Source of All Good Things

The Eternal is the source of all things, the treasure of good
people and the sustainer of evil people.

Therefore, at the enthronement of an emperor, better still than
those who present jewels is the one who presents (propounds)
the Eternal.

Why did the ancients prize the Eternal? Was it not because it
could be attained by seeking, and thus sinners could be freed?
For this reason it has become the most valuable thing in the
world.

Good words will procure one honor; good deeds will get one
credit.

(63) The Natural Way

It is the way of the Eternal to act without being conscious of
acting;

To conduct affairs without feeling the trouble of them;

To taste without discerning any flavor;

To consider what is small as great, and a few as many;

And to repay injury with kindness.

The master of It anticipates things that are difficult while they
are easy,

And does things that would become great while they are small.

All difficult things in the world are sure to arise from a previous
state in which they were easy,

And all great things from one in which they were small.

Therefore, mature individuals, while never doing what is great,
are able on that account to accomplish the greatest things.

Those who make easy promises will seldom keep their word;

Those who regard many things easy will find many difficulties.
Therefore, mature individuals regard things difficult, and consequently never have difficulties.

(64) The Time to Achieve

What is motionless is easy to hold;
What is not yet foreshadowed is easy to form plans for;
What is fragile is easy to break;
What is minute is easy to disperse.
Deal with a thing before it comes into action;
Regulate a thing before it gets into confusion.
The common people in their business often fail on the verge of succeeding.
Take care with the end as you do with the beginning,
And you will have no failure.

(65) Knowledge and Virtue

In olden times the best practitioners of the way of the Eternal did not use it to awaken the people to knowledge.
But used it to restore them to simplicity.
People are difficult to govern when they have too much knowledge.
Therefore, to govern the country purely by increasing the people's knowledge is to be the destroyer of the country;
To govern the country by increasing their understanding is to be the blesser of the country.
To be acquainted with these two ways is to know the standard;
To keep the standard always in mind is to have sublime virtue.
Sublime virtue is infinitely deep and wide.
It goes reverse to all wrong trends;
And so it attains perfect peace.

(66) Non-competition

As the Eternal is to the world, so are oceans and seas to streams and rivers.
Oceans and seas are kings to all streams and rivers, because the former lower themselves to the latter, thus receiving their homage and tribute.

Therefore, mature individuals, in order to be above the people, must in words keep below them;

In order to be ahead of the people, they must in person keep behind them.

Thus, when they are above, the people do not feel their hindrance.

Therefore, all the world is pleased to hold them in high esteem and never get tired of them.

Because they do not compete, therefore no one competes with them.

(67) The Indescribable

All the world says to me: "Great as the Eternal is, It resembles no description (form)." Because It is great, therefore It resembles no description. If It resembled any description, It would have long since become small.

I have three treasures, which I hold and keep safe:

The first is called love;

The second is called moderation;

The third is called not venturing to go ahead of the world.

Being loving, one can be brave;

Being moderate, one can be ample;

Not venturing to go ahead of the world, one can be the chief of all officials.

Instead of love, one has only bravery;

Instead of moderation, one has only amplitude;

Instead of keeping behind, one goes ahead:

These lead to nothing but death.

For those who fight with love will win the battle;

Those who defend with love will be secure;

They will be saved and protected with love.

(68) Consorting with Life

The best soldier is not soldierly;

The best fighter is not ferocious;

The best conqueror does not take part in war;

The best employer of people keeps him/herself below them.

This is called the virtue of not contending;

This is called the ability of tuning in to people;

It is called the supremacy of consorting with life.

(69) Precaution

An ancient male tactician has said:
"I dare not act as a host, but would rather act as a guest;
I dare not advance an inch, but would rather retreat a foot."
This implies that he does not marshal the ranks as if there were
no ranks;
He does not roll up his sleeves as if he had no arms;
He does not seize as if he had no weapons;
He does not fight as if there were no enemies.
No calamity is greater than underestimating the enemy;
To underestimate the enemy is to be on the point of losing our
treasure (love).
Therefore, when opposing armies meet in the field, the cautious
will win.

(70) Word and Deed

Words have an ancestor; deeds have a governor.
My words are very easy to know and very easy to practice.
Yet all people in the world do not know them, nor do they
practice them.
It is because they have excess knowledge that they do not know
Me.
Then those who know Me are few; eventually I am beyond all
praise.
Therefore, mature individuals wear clothes of coarse cloth but
carry jewels in their bosoms;
They know themselves but do not display themselves;
They respect themselves but do not hold themselves in places
of honor.
Thus they reject the latter and take the former.

(71) Not Knowing

Not knowing that one knows is best;
Thinking that one knows, when one does not know, is sickness.
Only when one becomes sick of this sickness can one be free
from sickness,

Mature individuals are never sick in this way; because they are sick of this sickness, therefore they do not get sick.

(72) Fear

If the people have no fear of what they ought to fear, still greater fear will come on them.
Let them not thoughtlessly indulge themselves in their everyday life;
Let them not act as if weary of what life depends on.
It is by avoiding such indulgence that weariness does not arise.
Therefore, mature individuals know these things of themselves but do not parade their knowledge;
Respect, but do not set a value on, themselves.

(73) Benefit or Harm?

Those who show courage in daring will perish;
Those who show courage in not-daring will live.
To know these two is to distinguish the one (benefit) from the other (harm).
Who can tell that one of them should be loathed by the person of the Eternal?
The people who seek the Eternal do not contend, yet they surely win the victory.
They do not speak, yet they surely respond.
They do not call, yet all things come of their own accord.
They remain taciturn, yet they surely make plans.
The net of the Eternal is vast, and its meshes are far apart;
Yet from It nothing escapes.

(74) Natural Death

Since the people are not afraid of death, what use is it to frighten them with the punishment of death? If the people were constantly afraid of death, and we could arrest and kill those who commit treacheries, who then would dare to commit such? However, only the Eternal is qualified to bring about death; to kill is to hack at a piece of wood, as compared with the skillful working of a great carpenter. Now if one hacks, in place of employing a great carpenter, one can scarcely avoid cutting one's own hand.

(75) Meddling

The people starve. Because their officials take heavy taxes from them, therefore they starve. The people are hard to rule. Because their officials meddle with their affairs, therefore they are hard to rule. The people pay no heed to death.
Because they endeavor to seek life, therefore they pay no heed to death.

(76) Weak and Tender

People, when living, are soft and tender; when dead, they are hard and tough. All animals and plants, when living are tender and fragile; when dead, they become withered and dry. Therefore it is said: the hard and tough are parts of death; the soft and tender are parts of life. This is the reason why the soldiers, when they are too tough, cannot carry the day; the tree, when it is too tough, will break. The position of the strong and tough is low, and the position of the weak and tender is high.

(77) The Oneness of All Life

Is not the Eternal like the drawing of a bow? It brings down the part which is high; It raises the part which is low; It lessens the part which is redundant (convex); It fills up the part which is insufficient (concave). The Eternal seeks to lessen the redundant and fill up the insufficient. The way of most individuals, on the contrary, is to take from the insufficient and give to the redundant. Who can take from the redundant and give to the insufficient? Only those who have found the Eternal can. Therefore, mature individuals do not hoard.
The more they help others, the more they benefit themselves. The more they give to others, the more they get themselves. The Eternal does one good, but never does one harm. Thus, mature individuals act but do not contend.

(78) The Weak and the Strong

The weakest things in the world can overmatch the strongest things in the world.

Nothing in the world can be compared to water for its weak and yielding nature;

Yet in attacking the hard and the strong, nothing proves better than it. For there is no other alternative to it.

The weak can overcome the strong, and the yielding can overcome the hard.

This all the world knows but does not practice.

Therefore, mature individuals say:

Those who sustain all the reproaches of the country can be the master of the land;

Those who sustain all time calamities of the country can be the king of the world.

These are the words of truth, though they seem paradoxical.

(79) Impartiality

Return love for great hatred.

Otherwise, when a great hatred is reconciled, some of it will surely remain.

How can this end in goodness?

Therefore, mature individuals hold to their half of an agreement, but do not exact the other holder's half.

The virtuous resort to agreement;

The virtueless resort to exaction.

The Eternal shows no partiality;

It abides always with good people.

(80) Self-control

Suppose that here is a small state with few people:

Though it contains various youths with all kinds of fancy ideas,

I will not have them employed until they earnestly seek the Eternal.

I will see that the people, while looking on death as a grievous matter, yet do not travel around so as to forget about it.

Though they have many boats and carriages, they will not travel in them just for pleasure;

Though they have armor and weapons, they will not show them.

I will let them restore the use of knotted cords (instead of writing), if they so desire.

They will be satisfied with their meager food;
Delighted in their plain dress;
Comfortable in their crude dwellings;
Happy with simple means of enjoyment.
Though the neighboring states, with their many temptations, are
    within sight,
And their cocks' crowing and dogs' barking within hearing;
The people will not yield to these temptations all their lives.

(81) Contrasts

Those who know do not speak;
Those who speak do not know.
Those who are truthful are not showy;
Those who are showy are not truthful.
Those who are virtuous do not dispute;
Those who dispute are not virtuous;
Those who are learned are not wise;
Those who are wise are not learned.
Therefore, mature individuals do not display their own merits.

THE WORKS OF CHUANG TZE

The Music of Life

Tze Ch'i of Nan-kuo sat leaning on a table. Looking up at the heavens, he sighed and became silent, as though soul and body had parted.

Yen Ch'eng Tze Yu, who was standing by him, exclaimed, "What are you thinking about that your body should become like dry wood, your mind like dead ashes? Surely the man now leaning on the table is not he who was here just now."

"My friend," replied Tze Ch'i, "your question is a good one. To-day I have buried myself. Do you understand? Ah! Perhaps you only know the music of the individual, and not that of life."

"Pray explain, " said Tze Yu.

"The breath of the universe," continued Tze Ch'i, "is called wind. At times it is inactive. But when active, every aperture resounds to the blast. Have you never listened to its growing roar?

"Caves and dells of hill and forest, hollows in huge trees of many a span in girth; those are like nostrils, like mouths, like ears, like beam-sockets, like goblets, like mortars, like ditches, like bogs. And the wind goes rushing through them sniffing, snoring, singing, sighing, puffing, purling, whistling, whirring, now shrilly treble, now deeply bass, now soft, now loud; until, with a lull, silence reigns supreme. Have you never witnessed among the trees such a disturbance as this?"

"Well, then," inquired Tze Yu, "since the music of nature consists of nothing more than holes, and the music of the people of pipes and flutes, of what consists the music of life?"

"The effect of the wind upon these various apertures," replied Tze Ch'i, "is not uniform. But what is it that gives to each the individuality, to all the potentiality, of sound?

"Great understanding embraces the whole: small understanding, a part only. Great speech is universal: small speech is particular.

"For whether when the mind is locked in sleep or whether when in waking hours the body is released, we are subject to daily mental perturbations, indecision, want of penetration, concealment, fretting, fear, and trembling terror. Now like a javelin the mind flies

forth, the arbiter of right and wrong. Now like a solemn coven-
anter it remains firm, the guardian of rights secured. Then, as under
autumn's and winter's blight, comes gradual decay, a passing away,
like the flow of water, never to return. Finally, the block occurs,
when all is choked up like an old drain, the failing mind which shall
not see light again.

"Joy and anger, sorrow and happiness, caution and remorse,
come upon us by turns, with ever-changing mood. They come like
music from hollowness, like mushrooms from damp. Daily and
nightly they alternate within us, but we cannot tell whence they
spring. Can we then hope in a moment to lay our finger upon their
very cause?

"But for these emotions I should not be. But for me, they would
have no scope. So far we can go; but we do not know what it is
that brings them into play. It would seem to be a soul; but the clue
to its existence is wanting. That such a power operates is credible
enough, though we cannot see its form. It has functions without
form.

"Take the human body with all its manifold divisions. Which part
of it do individuals love best? Do they not cherish all equally, or do
they have a preference? Do not all equally serve the body? And do
these servitors then govern themselves, or are they subdivided into
rulers and subjects? Surely there is some soul which sways them all.

"But whether or not we ascertain what are the functions of this
soul, it matters but little to the soul itself. For coming into existence with this mortal coil of mine, with the exhaustion of this
mortal coil its mandate will also be exhausted. To be harassed by
the wear and tear of life, and to pass rapidly through it without the
possibility of arresting one's course is not this pitiful indeed? To
labor without ceasing, and then, without living to enjoy the fruit,
worn out, to depart suddenly, one knows not where—is not that a
just cause for grief?

"What advantage is there in what people call not dying? The body
decomposes, and the mind goes with it. This is our real cause for
sorrow. Can the world be so dull as not to see this? Or is it I alone
who am dull, and others not so?

"Speech is not mere breath. It is differentiated by meaning. Take
away that, and you cannot say whether it is speech or not. Can you
even distinguish it from the chirping of young birds?

"But how can the Eternal be so obscured that we speak of it as true and false? And how can speech be so obscured that it admits the idea of contraries? How can the Eternal go away and yet not remain? How can speech exist and yet be impossible?

"The Eternal is obscured by our want of grasp. Speech is obscured by the gloss of the world.

"There is nothing which is not objective: there is nothing which is not subjective. But it is impossible to start from the objective. Only from subjective knowledge is it possible to proceed to objective knowledge.

"When subjective and objective are both without their correlates, that is the very axis of the Eternal. And when that axis passes through the center at which all infinities converge, positive and negative alike blend into an infinite One.

"Therefore it is that, viewed from the standpoint of the Eternal, a beam and a pillar are not separate objects. Ugliness and beauty, greatness, wickedness, perverseness, and strangeness are not absolute qualities. Separation is similar to construction: construction is related to destruction. Life cannot be subject just to construction or to destruction, for these conditions are blended together into One.

"Only the truly intelligent understand this principle of the identity of all things. They do not view things as apprehended by themselves, subjectively; but transfer themselves into the position of the things viewed. And viewing them thus they are able to comprehend them, to master them; and those who can master them will find true happiness. So it is that to place oneself in subjective relation with externals, without consciousness of their objectivity—this is the Eternal. But to wear out one's intellect in an obstinate adherence to the individuality of things, not recognizing the fact that all things are One—this is called 'Three in the Morning.'"

"What is 'Three in the Morning'?" asked Tze Yu.

"A keeper of monkeys," replied Tze Ch'i, "said with regard to their rations of chestnuts that each monkey was to have three in the morning and four at night. But at this the monkeys were very angry, so the keeper said they might have four in the morning and three at night, with which arrangement they were all well pleased. The actual number of the chestnuts remained the same, but there was an adaptation to the likes and dislikes of those concerned.

Such is the principle of putting oneself into subjective relation with externals.

"Therefore, mature individuals aim at the light which comes out of darkness. They do not view things as apprehended by themselves, subjectively, but transfer themselves into the position of the viewed. This is called using the light.

"If there was a beginning, then there was a time before that beginning, and a time before the time which was before the time of that beginning.

"If there is existence, then there must have been non-existence. And if there was a time when nothing existed, then there must have been a time before that when even nothing did not exist. Suddenly, when nothing came into existence, could one really say whether it belonged to the category of existence or of non-existence? Even the very words I have just now uttered—I cannot say whether they have really been uttered or not.

"If all things are One, then what room is there for speech? On the other hand, since I can utter these words, how can speech not exist?

"If it does exist, we have One and speech = two; and two and one = three. From which point onwards even the best mathematicians will fail to reach The Eternal. How much more then will ordinary people fail?

"Hence, if from nothing you can proceed to something, and subsequently reach three, it follows that it would be still easier if you were to start from something. To avoid such progression you must put yourself into subjective relation with the external.

"Before conditions existed, the Eternal was. Before definitions existed, speech was. Subjectively, we are conscious of certain limitations, which are:

Right and Left
Relationship and Obligation
Division and Discrimination
Emulation and Contention

"These are called the Eight Predictables. For the true philosopher, beyond the limits of an external world, they exist but are not recognized. By the true philosopher, within the limits of an external world, they are recognized but are not set apart. And so with regard to the wisdom of the ancients, the true philosophers speak when called upon, but do not justify by argument. And thus, classifying, they do not over-classify; discussing, they do not argue."

"How can that be?" asked Tze Yu.

"The true philosophers," answered Tze Ch'i, "keep their understanding within them unless called upon, while people in general set forth theirs in argument in order to impress each other. And therefore it is said that in arguments they do not manifest themselves.

"Perfect living does not declare itself. Nor does perfect argument express itself in words. Nor does perfect charity show itself in act. Nor is perfect honesty absolutely incorruptible. Nor is perfect courage absolutely unyielding.

"For the way which shines forth is not the way of the Eternal. Speech which argues falls short of its aim. Charity which has fixed points loses its scope. Honesty which is absolute is wanting in credit. Courage which is absolute misses its object. These five are, as it were, round, with a strong bias towards squareness. Therefore that knowledge which stops at what it does not know is the highest knowledge.

"Who knows the argument which can be argued without words? —the way which does not declare itself as 'The Way'? Those who know this may be said to be of the Eternal. To be able to pour in without making full, and pour out without making empty, in ignorance of the power by which such results are accomplished—this is accounted Light."

There Is No Absoluteness

Yeh Ch'ueh asked Wang I, saying, "Do you know for certain that all things are subjectively related?"

"How can I know?" answered Wang I. "Do you know what you do not know?"

"How can I know?" replied Yeh Ch'ueh. "But can then nothing be known?"

"How can I know?" said Wang I. "Nevertheless, I will try to tell you. How can it be known that what I call knowing is not really not knowing, and that what I call not knowing is not really knowing? Now I would ask you this. If people sleep in a damp place, they get lumbago and die. But how about an eel? And living up in a tree is precarious and trying to the nerves; but how about monkeys? Of the human, the eel, and the monkey, whose habitat is the right one, absolutely? Human beings feed on flesh, deer on grass, centipedes on snakes, owls and crows on mice. Of these four, whose is the right taste, absolutely? Monkeys mate with monkeys, bucks with doe; eels consort with fishes, while men admire women, at the sight of whom fishes plunge deep down in the water, birds soar high in the air, and deer hurry away. Yet who shall say which is the correct standard of beauty? In my opinion, the standard of human virtue, and of positive and negative, is so obscured that it is impossible to actually know it as such."

"If you then," asked Yeh Ch'ueh, "do not know what is bad for you, are perfect individuals equally without this knowledge?

"Perfect humans", answered Wang I, "are spiritual beings. Were the ocean itself scorched up, they would not feel hot. Were the Milky Way frozen hard, they would not feel cold. Were the mountains to be shaken by with thunder, and the great deep to be thrown up by storm, they would not tremble. In such case, they would mount upon the clouds, and driving the sun and the moon before them, would pass beyond the limits of this external world, where physical life and death have no more victory over them; how much less what is bad for them?"

Life Is a Great Dream

Chu Ch'iao addressed Chang Wu Tze as follows: "I heard Confucius say, 'Mature individuals pay little heed to mundane affairs. They neither seek nor avoid injury. They ask nothing at the hands of society. They adhere, without questioning, to the Eternal. Without speaking, they can speak; they can speak and yet say nothing. And so they roam beyond the limits of this dusty world. These,' added Confucius, 'are wild words'. Now to me they are the skillful embodiment of the Eternal. What, sir, is your opinion?"

"Points upon which the Yellow Emperor doubted", replied Chang Wu Tze, "how should Confucius know? You are going too fast. You see your egg and expect to hear it crow. You look at your crossbow and expect to have broiled duck before you. I will say a few words to you at random, and do you listen at random?

"How do mature individuals seat themselves by the sun and moon, and hold the universe in their grasp? They blend everything into one harmonious whole, rejecting the confusion of this and that. Rank and precedence, which the vulgar prize, mature humans stolidly ignore. The revolutions of ten thousand years leave their unity unscathed. The universe itself may pass away, but they will flourish still. "How do I know that love of life is not a delusion after all? How do I know but that those who dread to die are not as children who have lost their way and cannot find their home?

"Those who dream of the banquet wake to lamentation and sorrow. Those who dream of lamentation and sorrow wake to join the hunt. While they dream, they do not know that they dream. Some will even interpret the very dream they are dreaming; and only when they awake do they know it was a dream. By and by comes the Great Awakening, and then we find out that this life is really a great dream. Fools think they are awake now, and flatter themselves they know if they are really princes or peasants. Confucius and you are both dreams; and I who say you are dreams, I am but a dream myself. This is a paradox. Tomorrow a wise person may arise to explain it; but that tomorrow will not be until many, many generations have gone by. "Granting that you and I argue. If you beat me, and not I you, are you necessarily right and I wrong? Or if I beat you and not you me, am I necessarily right and you wrong? Or are we both partly right and partly wrong? Or are we both wholly right and wholly wrong? You and I cannot know this, and consequently the world will be in ignorance of the truth.

"Whom shall I employ as arbiter between us? If I employ someone who takes your view, he/she will side with you. How can such a one arbitrate between us? If I employ someone who takes my view, he/she will side with me. How can such a one arbitrate between us? And if I employ someone who either differs from, or agrees with both of us, he/she will be equally unable to decide between us. Since then you, and I, and that person, cannot decide, must we not depend upon our inner authority? Such dependence is the greatest independence. We are embraced in the obliterating unity of the Eternal. There is perfect adaptation to whatever may eventuate; and so we complete our allotted span.

"But what is it to be embraced in the obliterating unity of the Eternal? It is this. With reference to positive and negative, to that which is so and that which is not so—if the positive is really positive, it must necessarily be different from its negative: there is no room for argument. And if that which is so really is so, it must necessarily be different from that which is not so: there is no room for argument.

"Take little heed of the crushing pressures of time, nor any of absolute right and wrong. But passing into the realm of the Infinite, gain your strength therein."

The Middle Course

One's physical life has a limit, but one's potential for understanding is without limit. In striving for others, avoid fame. In striving for self, avoid disgrace. Pursue a balanced life. Thus you will keep a sound body and a sound mind, fulfill your duties, and work out your allotted span.

Prince Hui's Excellent Cook

Prince Hui's cook was cutting up a bullock. Every blow of his hand, every heave of his shoulders, every tread of his foot, every thrust of his knee, every cut of torn flesh, every chop of the chopper, was in perfect harmony, rhythmical like the most difficult of dances, simultaneous like the chords of a symphony.

"Well done!" cried the Prince. "Yours is skill indeed."

"Sire," replied the cook; "I have always devoted myself to the Eternal. It is better than skill. When I first began to cut up bullocks, I saw before me simply whole bullocks. After three years' practice, I saw no more whole animals. And now I work with my mind and not with my eye. When my senses bid me stop, but my mind urges me on, I fall back upon eternal principles. I follow such openings or cavities as there may be, according to the natural constitution of the animal. I do not attempt to cut through joints: still less through large bones.

"A good cook changes his chopper once a year because he cuts, an ordinary cook once a month because he hacks. But I have had this chopper nineteen years, and although I have cut up many thousand bullocks, its edge is as if fresh from the whetstone. For at the joints there are always interstices, and the edge of a chopper being almost without thickness, it remains only to insert that which is almost without thickness into such an interstice. By those means the interstices will be enlarged, and the blade will find plenty of room. It is thus that I have kept my chopper for nineteen years as though fresh from the whetstone.

"Nevertheless, when I come upon a hard part where the blade meets with a difficulty, I am all caution. I fix my eye on it. I stay my hand and gently apply my blade, until with a hwah the part yields like earth crumbling to the ground. Then I take out my chopper, stand up and look around. I pause, until with an air of triumph I wipe my chopper and put it carefully away.

"Bravo!" cried the Prince. "From the words of this cook I have learned how to take care of my life."

The Nature of the Eternal

Those who know what the Eternal is, and who know what humanity is, have attained the goal of life. Knowing what the Eternal is, they know that they themselves proceeded therefrom. Knowing what humanity is, they rest in the knowledge of the known, waiting for the knowledge of the unknown. Working out one's allotted span, and not perishing in mid career—this is the fullness of knowledge.

The Eternal is a principle which exists by virtue of its own intrinsicality, and operates spontaneously, without self-manifestation.

Herein, however, there is a flaw. Knowledge is dependent upon fulfillment. And as this fulfillment is uncertain, how can it be known that my divine is not really human, my human really divine?

The Four Friends

Four people were conversing together when the following resolution was suggested: "Whoever can make understanding the head, life the backbone, and death the tail, of his existence, that person shall be admitted to friendship with us." The four looked at each other and smiled; and tacitly accepting the conditions, became friends forthwith.

By and by, one of them named Tze Yu, fell ill, and another, Tze Ssu, went to see him. "Truly, life is great!" said the sick man. "See how it has doubled me up. My back is so hunched that my viscera are at the top of my body. My cheeks are level with my nave. My shoulders are higher than my neck. My hair grows up towards the sky. The whole economy of my organism is deranged. Nevertheless, my mental equilibrium is not disturbed." So saying, he dragged himself painfully to a well, where he could see himself, and continued, "Alas, that I should be doubled up like this!"

"Are you afraid?" asked Tze Ssu.

"I am not", replied Tze Yu. "What have I to fear? Before long I shall be decomposed. I obtained life because it was my time: I am now parting with it in accordance with the same law. Content with the natural sequence of these states, excitement and misery do not touch me. I am simply, as the ancients expressed it, hanging in the air, unable to cut myself down, bound by the trammels of material existence. But humans have ever given way before the evolution of all life: why, then, should I be afraid?"

By and by, another of the four, named Tze Lai, fell ill, and lay gasping for breath, while his family stood around weeping. The fourth friend, Tze Li, went to see him. "Chut!" cried he to the wife and children; "begone! you balk his decomposition". Then, leaning against the door, he said, "Truly, life is great!"

"We," answered Tze Lai, "must go wherever our nature bids us. If it bids me die quickly, and I demur, then I am disloyal to life. My nature can do me no wrong. The Eternal gives me this form, this toil in adulthood, this repose in old age, this rest in death. And surely that which is such a kind arbiter of my life is the best arbiter of my death.

On Charity

Excessive charity and excessive duty to one's neighbor are surely not included in our moral nature. Yet what sorrow these have involved. Divide your joined toes and you will howl: bite off your finger and you will scream. In one case there is too much, in the other too little; but the sorrow is the same. And the over-charitable of the age go about sorrowing over the ills of the age, while the non-charitable cut through the natural conditions of things in their greed after place and wealth. Surely then excessive charity and duty to one's neighbor are not included in our moral nature. Yet from time immemorial what a fuss has been made about them!

Tsang and Ku were shepherds, both of whom lost their flocks. On inquiry, it appeared that Tsang had been engaged in reading, while Ku had gone to take part in some trials of strength. Their occupations had been different, but the result was in each case loss of the sheep.

Poh I died for fame at the foot of Mount Shouyang. Robber Che died for gain on Mount T'ai. Their deaths were not the same, but the injury to their lives and natures was in each case the same. How then can we applaud the former and blame the latter?

Thus, if individuals die for excessive charity and duty to their neighbors, the world will call them noble fellows; but if they die for gain, the world may call them low fellows. The dying being the same, one is nevertheless generally called noble and the other low. But in point of injury to life and nature, the robber Che and Poh I are one. Where then does the distinction of noble and low come in?

Were people to apply themselves to charity and duty towards their neighbor until they were at a maximum amount, this would not be what I mean by perfection. Or to flavors, until they were at a maximum. Or to sounds, until they were at a maximum. Or to colors, until they were at a maximum. What I mean by perfection is not answered completely by charity and duty to one's neighbor. It is found in the cultivation of the Eternal. And those whom I regard as cultivators of the Eternal are not those who cultivate excessive charity and duty to one's neighbor. They are those who live by the dictates of their inner life. What I call perfection of healing is not healing others but oneself. What I call perfection of vision is not seeing others but oneself. For people who see not themselves but others, do not take possession of themselves but of others, thus taking what others should take and not what they themselves should take. Instead of being themselves, they in fact become someone else. And if people thus become someone else instead of themselves, this is a fatal error of which both the robber Che and Poh I can be equally guilty.

Thus, conscious of my own deficiency in regard to the Eternal, I do not venture at my best to over-practice the principles of charity and duty to my neighbor, nor at my worst to fall into the fatal error above-mentioned.

The Degradation of Horses and People

Horses have hoofs to carry them over frost and snow; hair, to protect them from wind and cold. They eat grass and drink water, and fling up their heels over country roads. Such is the real nature of horses. Palatial dwellings are of no use to them.

One day Poh Loh appeared, saying, "I understand the management of horses."

So he branded them, and clipped them, and pared their hoofs, and put halters on them, tying them up by the head and shackling them by the feet, and disposing them in stables, with the result that two or three in every ten died. Then he kept them hungry and thirsty, trotting them and galloping them, and grooming, and trimming, with the misery of the tasseled bridle before and the fear of the knotted whip behind, until more than half of them were dead.

The potter says, "I can do what I will with clay. If I want it round, I use compasses; if rectangular, a square."

The carpenter says, "I can do what I will with wood. If I want it curved, I use an arc; if straight, a line." But on what grounds can we think that the natures of clay and wood desire this application of compasses and square, of arc and line? Nevertheless, every age extols Poh Loh for his skill in managing horses, and potters and carpenters for their skill with clay and wood. Those who govern the nations make the same mistake.

Now I regard government from quite a different point of view.

The people have certain valuable natural instincts; to weave and clothe themselves, to till and feed themselves. These are common to all humanity, and all are agreed thereon. Such instincts are called "divine."

Thus, in the days when these natural instincts prevailed, people moved quietly and gazed steadily. At that time, there were no roads over mountains, nor boats, nor bridges over water. All things were produced, each for its own proper sphere. Birds and beasts multiplied; trees and shrubs grew up. The former might be led by the hand; you could climb up and peep into the raven's nest. For then people dwelt with birds and beasts, and creation was more nearly one. There were no distinctions of good and bad people. Being without excessive knowledge, their virtue did not often go astray. Being without many evil desires, they were ordinarily in a state of natural integrity, the perfection of human existence.

But when so-called sages appeared, tripping people over excessive charity and fettering with excessive duty to one's neighbor, great confusion found its way into the world. And then, with their luxuries and ceremonies, the nations became divided against themselves.

Were the natural integrity of things left unharmed, who could make exorbitant profits? Were white jade left unbroken, who could make the regalia of courts? Were the Eternal not abandoned, who could introduce excessive charity and duty to one's neighbor? Were our highest ideals our guide, what need would there be for luxuries and innumerable ceremonies? Were the colors not confused, who would practice elaborate decoration? Were the notes of music not confused, who would adopt technical perfection as the main standard for musicianship?

Destruction of the natural integrity of things, just in order to produce worthless articles of various kinds—this is the fault of the artisan. Annihilation of the Eternal in order to over-practice charity and duty to one's neighbor—this is the error of the so-called sage.

Horses live on dry land, eat grass, and drink water. When pleased, they rub their necks together. When angry, they turn around and kick up their heels at each other. Thus far only do their natural dispositions carry them. But bridled and bitted, with a plate of metal on their foreheads, they may (if not well treated) learn to cast vicious looks, to turn the head to bite, to resist, to get the bit out of the mouth or the bridle into it. And thus their natures may become depraved—the fault of Poh Loh.

In the days of Ho Hsu the people did nothing in particular when at rest, and did no unnecessary traveling when they moved. Having meager food, they were contented; having enough to eat, they pursued their work calmly but with determination. Such were the capacities of the people. But when unworthy sages came to worry them with elaborate ceremonies and luxuries in order to rectify the form of government, and dangled charity and duty to one's neighbor before them in order to satisfy their hearts—then the people began to develop a taste for excessive knowledge and to struggle one with the other in their desire for gain. This was the error of the so-called sages.

On Letting Alone

There has been such a thing as letting humanity alone; there has seldom been such a thing as governing humanity properly.

Improper government springs from fear lest our natural growth (mental and spiritual) be perverted and our virtue laid aside. But if their natural growth be not perverted nor our virtue laid aside, what need is there for government in excess?

Because people are made to rejoice and to sorrow and to displace their center of gravity, they lose their steadiness, and are unsuccessful in thought and action. And thus it is that the idea of surpassing others first came into the world, the result being that the whole world could not furnish enough rewards for the good nor distribute punishments enough for the evil among the human race. And as this great world is not equal to the demand for rewards and punishments, and as, since almost the beginning of their existence, people have done nothing but struggle over rewards and punishments—what possible leisure can they have had for struggling with the conditions of their existence?

Besides, over-emphasis on vision leads to debauchery in color; over-emphasis upon hearing leads to debauchery in sound; over-emphasis upon charity leads to confusion in virtue; overemphasis upon duty towards one's neighbor leads to perversion of principle; over-emphasis upon ceremonies leads to divergence from the true object; over-emphasis upon music leads to lewdness of thought; over-emphasis upon knowledge leads to an extension of mechanical art; and over-emphasis upon shrewdness leads to an extension of vice.

If people struggle correctly and unfalteringly with the conditions of existence, so as to reach the point of balanced living, the above eight difficulties may be or may not be; it matters not. But if people do not struggle in this way with conditions of existence, then these eight become hindrances and spoilers, and throw the world into confusion.

In spite of this, most people in the world reverence and cherish them, thereby greatly increasing the sum of human error. And not as a passing fashion, but with admonitions in words, with humility in servitude, and with the stimulus of loud music and song. What then is left for me?

Therefore, for the perfect individual, who is unavoidably summoned to power over his/her fellows, there is naught like a balance between meditation and action. By means of meditation that person will be able to struggle correctly and unfalteringly with the conditions of existence. Thus it is that those who respect the state as their own body are fit to support it, and those who love the state as their own body are fit to govern it. And if I can refrain from injuring my internal economy, and from over-taxing my powers of sight and hearing, in profound silence while my inner self becomes clarified, the mysteries of life responding to every phase of my understanding, as under the yielding influence of meditation all things are brought to maturity and thrive—what time then have I to govern the world in excess?

Ts'ui Chu asked Lao Tze, saying, "If the empire is not to be governed strictly, how are peoples' hearts to be kept in order?"

"Be careful," replied Lao Tze, not to interfere with the natural goodness of the heart of the individual. Our hearts may be forced down or stirred up. In each case the issue is fatal.

"By gentleness, the hardest heart may usually be softened. But try to cut and polish it—it will glow like fire or freeze like ice. In the twinkling of an eye it will pass beyond the limits of reason; in repose, profoundly still; in motion, far away in the sky. No bolt can bar; no bond can bind—such is the human heart."

An emperor once went to Kuang Ch'eng Tze and said, "I am told, sir, that you are in possession of the Eternal. May I ask in what the Eternal consists? I desire to avail myself of the good influence of the universe in order to secure harvests and feed my people. I should also like to control nature in order to assure the protection of all living things. How can I accomplish this?

"What you desire to avail yourself of," replied Kuang Ch'eng Tze, "is the primordial integrity of matter. What you wish to control are the disintegrators thereof. Ever since the empire has been governed by you, the clouds have rained without waiting to thicken, the foliage of trees has fallen without waiting to grow yellow, the brightness of the sun and moon has paled, and the voice of the flatterer is heard on every side. How then speak of the Eternal?" The emperor withdrew. He resigned the throne. He built himself a small solitary hut. For three months he remained in seclusion, working and meditating about his past mistakes and future ideals, and then went again to see Kuang Ch'eng Tze.

The latter was lying down. The emperor approached after the manner of an inferior, with the greatest of humility. Then he said, "I am told, sir, that you are in possession of the Eternal. May I ask how my Self may be realized so that I may find lasting happiness?"

Kuang Ch'eng Tze jumped up with a start. "A good question indeed!" cried he. "Come, and I will speak to you of the Eternal.

"The essence of the Eternal is profoundly mysterious; its extent is lost in obscurity.

"Cherish that which is within you, and rise above the temptations from without; for excess knowledge is a curse. Then I will tell you about that abode of great light which is the true source of power, and escort you through the gate of profound mystery which is the essence of all life.

"Cherish and preserve your own Self in the process of seeking perfection of the personality and the society. I preserve the original

One, while seeking harmony with externals. It is because I have thus cared for my Self now for many years that I have found lasting happiness."

The emperor prostrated himself and said, "Kuang Ch'eng Tze has surely found the Eternal. ..."

Whereupon the latter continued, "Come; I will tell you. That Self is eternal; yet most people think it is mortal. That Self is infinite; yet most people think it is finite. Those who possess the Eternal are the real rulers in life. Those who do not possess the Eternal are tossed about as on a stormy sea, and perishing are thus forgotten.

"Nowadays, most living things spring from the dust and to the dust return. But I seek to lead you through the portals of eternity into the domain of infinity. My light is the light of sun and moon. My life is the life of the universe. I know not who comes or who goes. People may all die, but I have found lasting happiness to be eternal.

The Limitless Eternal

The Master said, "How profound in its depth, how infinite in its purity, is the Eternal!

"If metal and stone were without the Eternal, they would not be capable of emitting sound. And just as they possess the property of sound but will not emit sound unless struck, so surely is the same principle applicable to all creation.

"The person of complete virtue remains dispassionate as regards what goes on around him/her. That person is as originally by nature, and his/her insight extends to the Divine. Thus, the person's virtue expands the heart, which goes forth to all who come to take refuge therein.

"Without the Eternal, form cannot be imbued with life. Without virtue, life cannot be imbued with intelligence. To preserve one's form, live out one's life, establish one's virtue, and realize the Eternal—is not this complete virtue?

"Issuing forth spontaneously, moving quietly but with determination, things following in their wake—such are the people of complete virtue!

"They can see where all is dark. They can hear where all is still. In the darkness they alone can see light. In the stillness they alone can detect harmony. They can sink to the lowest depths of materialism. To the highest heights of spirituality they can soar. This is because they stand in due relation to all things. Though a mere abstraction, they can minister to their wants, and ever and anon receive them into rest—the great, the small, the long, the short, forever without end."

Divine Virtue

At the beginning of the beginning, even nothing did not exist. Then came the period of the Nameless. When One came into existence, there was One, but it was formless. When things got that by which they came into existence, it was called their virtue. That which was formless, but divided, though without interstice, was called destiny.

Then came the movement which gave life, and things produced in accordance with the principles of life had what is called form. When form encloses the spiritual part, each with its own characteristics, that is its nature. By cultivating this nature, we are carried back to virtue; and if this is perfected, we become as all things were in the beginning. We become undistorted, and the undistorted is great. As birds instinctively join their beaks in chirping, and beaks to chirp must be joined—to be thus joined with the universe, this is divine virtue, this is accordance with the eternal fitness of things.

The Gardener

When Tze Kung went south to the Ch'u State on his way back to the Chin State, he passed through Han-yin. There he saw an old man engaged in making a ditch to connect his vegetable garden with a well. He had a pitcher in his hand, with which he was bringing up water and pouring it into the ditch—great labor with very little result.

"If you had a machine here," cried Tze Kung, "in a day you could irrigate a hundred times your present area. The labor required is trifling as compared with the work done. "Would you not like to have one?"

"What is it?" asked the gardener.

"It is a contrivance made of wood," replied Tze Kung, "heavy behind and light in front. It draws up water as you do with your hands, but in a constantly overflowing stream. It is called a well-sweep.

Thereupon the gardener flushed up and said, "I have heard from my teacher that those who have many cunning implements are usually cunning in their dealings, and that those who are cunning in their dealings have cunning in their hearts, and that those who have cunning in their hearts cannot be pure and incorrupt, and that those who are not pure and incorrupt lead restless lives, and that those who lead restless lives are not fit vehicles for the Eternal. It is not that I do not know of these things. I would be ashamed to use them."

At this Tze Kung was much abashed, and said nothing. Then the gardener asked him who he was, to which Tze Kung replied that he was a disciple of Confucius.

"Are you not one who extends his knowledge with a view to appearing learned; who talks big in order to put himself above the rest of humankind; who plays in a key to which no one can sing so as to spread his reputation abroad? Rather become true to your inner self and shake off the trammels of the flesh, and you will be near perfection. But if you cannot govern your own self, what leisure have you for governing the empire? Please do not interrupt my work."

Tze Kung walked slowly away, being not at all pleased with this remark; and it was not before he had traveled some miles that he recovered his usual appearance.

"What did the man we met do," asked a disciple, "that you should not recover your usual appearance for such a long time?"

"I used to think there was only one person in all the world," replied Tze Kung. "I did not know that there was also this man. I have heard Confucius say that the test of a scheme is its practicability, and that usefulness must be certain. The minimum of effort with the maximum of valuable results—such, he says, is the way of the wise person.

"Not so this manner of person. Aiming at the Eternal, such people perfect their virtue. By perfecting their virtue they perfect their bodies, and by perfecting their bodies they perfect their spiritual part. And the perfection of the spiritual part is the goal of the mature person. Coming into life they are as one of the people, knowing not where they are bound. How complete is their purity? Success, profit, skill—these have no place in their hearts. Such people, if they do not will it, they do not stir; if they do not wish it, they do not act. If all the world praises them, they do not heed. If all the world blames them, they do not repine. The praise and the blame of the world neither advantages them nor otherwise. They may be called people of perfect virtue. As for me, I am but a mere creature of impulse."

The Way of the Eternal

The Eternal operates ceaselessly; and all things are eventually produced. If the sovereign operates ceaselessly by means of the Eternal, the empire will benefit from his rule. Since mature people operate ceaselessly in the light of the Eternal, the people in years to come will acknowledge their sway. Those who apprehend the Infinite, who are in relation with mature individuals, and who recognize the radiating virtue of the capable sovereign—their actions will be true to themselves, the actions of enlightened living.

The repose of mature individuals is not what the world calls repose. Their repose is the result of their mental attitude. All creation could not disturb their equilibrium: hence their repose (or balance).

When water is still, it is like a mirror, reflecting the beard and the eyebrows. It gives the accuracy of the water-level, and mature individuals make it their model. And if water thus derives lucidity from stillness, how much more the faculties of the mind? The mind of the mature person, being in repose, becomes the mirror of the universe, the reflection of all creation.

Repose, tranquility, peace, balance—these were the levels of the universe, the ultimate perfection of the Eternal. Therefore, wise rulers and sages act therein. Acting therein they reach the unconditioned, from which springs the conditioned; and with the conditioned comes order. Again, from the unconditioned comes balance, and from balance comes movement, and from movement comes attainment.

Repose, tranquility, peace, balance—these were the source of all things. Due perception of this constitutes the virtue of sovereigns on the throne, the guide of the inspired sage and of the uncrowned king. Keep to this in retirement, and the lettered denizens of sea and dale will eventually recognize your power. Keep to this when coming forward to pacify a troubled world, and your merit shall be great and your name illustrious, and the empire united into one. In your balance you will be wise; in your movements, powerful. By dispassion you will gain respect; and by confining yourself to the pure and simple, you will hinder the whole world from struggling with you for show. To apprehend fully the scheme of the universe, this is called the great secret of being in accord with the Eternal, whereby the empire is so administered that the result is in accord with our highest ideals. To be in accord with our highest ideals is human happiness; to be in accord with the Eternal is to have found lasting happiness.

Appeal to arms is the lowest form of virtue. Rewards and punishments are the lowest form of education. Ceremonies and laws are the lowest form of government. Dance, music, and fine clothes are the lowest form of happiness, which may be called pleasure. Weeping and mourning are the lowest form of grief. These five should follow the movements of the mind.

The ancients indeed cultivated the study of accidentals, but they did not allow it to precede that of essentials. The ruler precedes, the servant follows. The parent precedes, the child follows. The elder sibling precedes, the younger follows. Seniors precede, juniors follow. Distinctions of rank and precedence are part of the scheme of the universe, and the mature individual adopts them accordingly. In point of spirituality, the divine aspect is honorable, the human is lowly. Spring and summer precede autumn and winter: such is the order of the seasons. In the constant production of all things, there are phases of existence. There are the extremes of maturity and decay, the perpetual tide of change. And if life as a whole admits of rank and precedence, how much more the individual?

In the churches, parents rank before all; at court, the most honorable; in the village, the elders; in matters to be accomplished, the most trustworthy. Such is the order which appertains to the Eternal. Those who in considering the Eternal disregard this order, thereby disregard the Eternal; and those who in considering the Eternal disregard it—whence will they secure the Eternal?

Therefore, those of old who apprehended the Eternal first apprehended themselves. The Eternal came next, and then charity and duty to one's neighbor, and then the functions of public life, and then forms and names, and then employment according to capacity, and then distinctions of good and bad, and then discrimination between right and wrong, and then rewards and punishments. Thus wise people and fools met with their dues; the exalted and the humble occupied their proper places. The virtuous and the worthless, being each guided by their own ideals, it was necessary to distinguish capabilities, and to adopt a corresponding nomenclature, in order to serve the ruler, nourish the ruled, administer things generally, and elevate the Self. Because knowledge and arbitrary plans are insufficient, one must fall back upon the inner authority. This is true happiness, the acme of good living.

Of old, Shun asked Yao, saying, "How does your Majesty employ your faculties?"

"I am not arrogant towards the defenseless," replied Yao. "I do not neglect the poor. I grieve for those who die. I pity the orphan. I sympathize with the widow. Beyond this, nothing."

"Good indeed!" cried Shun, "but yet not great."

"How so?" inquired Yao.

"Be dispassionate," said Shun, "like the man of the Eternal. The sun shines; the four seasons revolve; day and night alternate; clouds come and rain falls."

"Alas!" cried Yao, "what a muddle I have been making. You are in accord with the Eternal; I am in accord with my lower nature.

Lao Tze said, "The Eternal Is not too small for the greatest, nor too great for the smallest. Thus all things are included; wide indeed its boundless capacity, unfathomable its depth. "Form, virtue, charity, and duty to one's neighbor; these are not the essence of the spiritual. Except we be an almost perfect individual, who shall determine our place? The world of the perfect individual, is not that vast? And yet it is not able to involve us in trouble. We struggle for power, but we do not join. Though discovering nothing to be completely evil, we are not tempted astray. In spite of the utmost genuineness, we still confine ourselves to essentials.

"We thus find ourselves outside the world of the unenlightened, beyond our greatest concerns, where our life is free from misery. Apprehending the Eternal, we are in accord with virtue. We do not over-practice charity and duty to our neighbor. We treat ceremonies and popular music as adventitious. And so, the mind of the perfect one is at peace. "Books are what the world values as representing the Eternal. But books are only words, and the valuable part of words is the thought therein contained. That thought has a certain meaning which cannot be conveyed in words, yet the world values words as being the essence of books. But though the world values them, they are not of value in themselves; that is, the sense in which the world values them is not the sense in which they are valuable.

"That which can be seen with the eye is form and color; that which can be heard with the ear is sound and noise. But alas! the people of this generation think that form, and color, and sound, and noise, are means by which they can come to understand the essence of the Eternal. This is not so. And as those who know do not speak (glibly), while those who speak (glibly) do not know, how can people derive understanding by means of the senses alone?

The Music of the Eternal

Pei Men Ch'eng said to the Yellow Emperor, "When your Majesty played your musical instrument in the wilds of nature, the first time I heard it I was afraid, the second time I was amazed, and the last time I was dumfounded, speechless, overwhelmed."

"You are not far from the truth," replied the Yellow Emperor. "I played as a man, drawing inspiration from the Eternal. The execution was punctilious, the expression sublime.

"Perfect music first shapes itself according to a human standard; then it follows the lines of the Divine; then it proceeds in harmony with true virtue; then it passes into spontaneity. The four seasons are then blended, and all creation is brought into accord. As the seasons come forth in turn, so are all things produced. Now fullness, now decay, now soft and loud in turn, now clear, now muffled, the harmony of all life. Like a flash was the sound which roused you as the insect world is roused, followed by a thundering peal, without end and without beginning, now dying, now living, now sinking, now rising, on and on without a moment's break. And so you were afraid.

"Then I played again, it was the harmony of life, lighted by the glory of sun and moon; now prolonged, now gentle, now severe, in one unbroken, unfathomable volume of sound. Filling valley and gorge, stopping the ears and dominating the senses, adapting itself to the capacities of things, the sound whirled around on all sides, with shrill note and clear. When the melody was exhausted, I stopped; if the melody did not stop, I went on. You would have sympathized, but you could not understand. You would have looked, but you could not see. You would have pursued, but you could not overtake. You stood dazed in the middle of the wilderness, leaning against a tree and crooning, your eye conscious of exhausted vision, your strength failing for the pursuit, and still unable to overtake me. Your frame was but an empty shell. You were completely at a loss, and so you were amazed.

"Then I played in sounds which produce no amazement, the melodious law of spontaneity, springing forth like nature's countless buds, in manifold but formless joy, as though poured forth to the dregs, in deep but soundless bass. Beginning nowhere, the melody rested in void; some would say dead, others alive, others real, others ornamental, as it scattered itself on all sides in never-to-be-anticipated chords.

"The wondering world inquires of mature individuals. They are in relation with its variation and follow the same eternal law.

"When no machinery is set in motion, and yet the instrumentation is complete, this is the music of the Eternal. The mind awakes to its enjoyment without waiting to be called. Accordingly, Yu Piao praised it, saying, 'Listening you cannot hear its sound; gazing you cannot see its form. It fills the entire universe. Now you desired to listen to it, but you were not able to grasp its existence. Thus you were dumbfounded.

"My music first induced awe; and as a consequence, respect. I then added amazement, by which you were isolated. And lastly, speechlessness; for speechlessness means absence of response, and absence of response usually means that the Eternal is being experienced, and experiencing the Eternal means absorption therein."

Confucius and Lao Tze

Confucius had lived to the age of fifty-one without experiencing the Eternal, when he went south to P'ei, to see Lao Tze.

Lao Tze said, so you have come, sir, have you? I hear you are considered a wise man up north. Have you discovered the Eternal?

"Not yet" answered Confucius.

"In what direction," asked Lao Tze, "have you sought for It?"

"I sought It for five years," replied Confucius, "in the science of numbers, but did not succeed.

"And then? ..." continued Lao Tze.

"Then," said Confucius, "I spent twelve years seeking for it in the doctrines of the religions, also without success."

"Just so," rejoined Lao Tze. "Were the Eternal something which could be presented, there are no individuals who would not present it to their sovereign, or to their parents. Could it be imparted or given, there is none who would not impart it to their brothers and sisters or give it to their children. But this is impossible for the following reason. Unless there is a suitable endowment within, the Eternal will not abide. Unless there is outward correctness, the Eternal will not operate. The external being unfitted for the impression of the internal, the true sage does not seek to imprint. The internal being unfitted for the reception of the external, the sage does not seek to receive.

"Reputation is public property; you may not appropriate it in excess. Charity and duty to one's neighbor are as caravans established by wise rulers of old; you may stop there one night, but not for long, or you will incur reproach.

"Those who make wealth their all in all, cannot bear loss of money. Those who make distinction their all in all, cannot bear loss of fame. Those who affect power will not place authority in the hands of others anxious while holding, distressed if losing, yet never taking warning from the past and seeing the folly of their pursuit—such people are the main barriers to human progress.

"Resentment, gratitude, taking, giving, censure of self, instruction of others, power of life and death,- these eight are the instruments of right; but only those who can adapt themselves to the vicissitudes of fortune , without being carried away, are fit to use them. Such people are the upright among the upright. And they whose hearts are not so constituted, the door of divine intelligence is not yet opened for them."

Confucius spoke of charity and duty to one's neighbor.

Lao Tze said, "The chaff from winnowing will blind our eyes so that we cannot tell the points of the compass. Mosquitoes will keep us awake all night with their biting. And just in the same way this talk of charity and duty to one's neighbor drives me nearly crazy. My friend, strive to keep the world to its own original simplicity. And as the wind blows where it lists, so let virtue establish itself. Why so much misguided energy, as though searching for a fugitive with a big drum?

"The snow-goose is white without a daily bath. The raven is black without daily coloring itself. The original simplicity of black and white is beyond the reach of argument. The vista of fame and reputation is not worthy of enlargement. When the pond dries up and the fish are left upon dry ground, to moisten them with breath or to dampen them with a little spittle is not to be compared with leaving them in the first instance in their native rivers and lakes."

On returning from his visit to Lao Tze, Confucius did not speak for three days. A disciple asked him, saying, "Master, when you saw Lao Tze, in what direction did you admonish him?"

"I thought that I saw a dragon," replied Confucius, "a dragon which by convergence showed a body, by radiation became color, and riding upon the clouds, nourished the true principles of creation. My mouth was agape: I could not shut it. How then do you think I was going to admonish Lao Tze?"

Self-Conceit

Self-conceit and over-assurance, which lead people to abandon the desire to learn about life, to indulge in tall talk and abuse of others—these are nothing more than personal over-estimation, the affection of recluses and those who have closed their hearts to influences leading to self-improvement.

Preaching of charity and duty to one's neighbor, of loyalty and truth, of respect, of economy, and of humility—this is but moral culture, affected by would-be peacemakers and teachers of humanity, and by scholars at home or abroad.

Preaching of meritorious services, of fame, of ceremonial between ruler and people, of the relationship between upper and lower classes—this is mere government, affected by courtiers or patriots who strive to extend the boundaries of their own state and to swallow up the territory of others.

Living in marshes or in wildernesses, and passing one's days in fishing—this is mere inaction, affected by wanderers who have turned their backs upon the world and have nothing better to do.

Exhaling and inhaling, getting rid of the old and assimilating the new, stretching like a bear and craning like a bird—this is but valetudinarianism, affected by professors of hygiene and those who try to preserve the body by artificial methods.

But in self-esteem without self-conceit, in moral culture without excessive charity and duty to one's neighbor, in government without rank and fame, in retirement without solitude, in health without hygiene—there we have oblivion absolute coupled with possession of all things; an infinite calm which becomes an object to be attained by all.

Such is the highest in the universe, such is the virtue of mature individuals. Therefore, it has been said, "In tranquility, in stillness, in the undistorted, in peace, we find the proper medium for thought about life, the very constitution of the Eternal."

Hence, it has been said, "Mature persons are non-competitive entities and thus can maintain a state of dynamic equilibrium. Being non-competitive, they are in a state of balance. And where dynamic equilibrium is, there misery and anxiety do not enter, and foul influences do not collect. And thus virtue is complete and spirituality unimpaired."

Hence, it has been said, "The birth and life of the enlightened ones are among the miracles of history; their death is but a modification of existence. In repose, they share the passivity of the meditator; in action, the energy of the active person. They will have nothing to do with purely short-run pleasures, and so have nothing to do with misery. They must be influenced before responding. Such persons must have a reason before moving. They must be motivated before arising. Omitting the mistakes of the past, they are resigned to the dictates of the inner life.

"And therefore no calamity comes upon them, nothing injures them, no person is against them, no force punishes them. They float through life to rest in death. They have no anxieties; they make no plans for self-assertion. Their honor does not make them illustrious. Their good faith reflects no credit upon themselves. Their spirituality is pure, and their soul vigorous. Thus undistorted and in dynamic balance, they are partakers of the virtue of mature individuals."

Hence, it has been said, "Pleasure and pain are the heresies of virtue; unrestrained joy and anger lead astray from the Eternal; sensual love and violent hate cause the loss of virtue. The heart overcoming one's excesses—that is perfect virtue. Oneness, without change—that is perfect balance. Without any obstruction, that is the perfection of the undistorted. Holding no fixed demands with the external world—that is perfection of the state of maturity. Without blemish of any kind—that is the perfection of purity."

Autumn Floods

This story I have heard:

It was the time of autumn floods. Every stream poured into the river, which swelled in its turbid course. The banks receded so far from one another that it was impossible to tell a cow from a horse.

Then the Spirit of the River laughed for joy that all the beauty of the earth was gathered to Itself. Down with the stream they journeyed east, until they reached the ocean. There, looking eastwards and seeing no limit to its waves, its countenance changes. And as It gazes over the expanse, It sighed and said to the Spirit of the Ocean, "A vulgar proverb says that one who has heard but part of the truth thinks no one equal to him/herself. And such a one am I.

"When formerly I heard people detracting from the learning of Confucius or underrating the heroism of Poh I, I did not believe. But now that I have looked upon your inexhaustibility—also for me, had I not reached your abode, I should have been forever a laughing-stock to those of comprehensive enlightenment!"

To which the Spirit of the Ocean replied, "You cannot speak of ocean to a well-frog—the creature of a narrower sphere. You cannot speak of ice to a summer insect—the creature of a season. You cannot speak of the Eternal to pedagogues: their scope is too restricted. But now that you have emerged from your narrow sphere and have seen the great ocean, you know your own insignificance, and I can speak to you of great principles.

"Dimensions are limitless; time is endless. Conditions are not invariable; terms are not final. Thus, wise people look into space, and do not regard the small as too little, nor the great as too much; for they know that there is no limit to dimension. We look back into the past, and do not grieve over what is far off, nor rejoice over what is near; for we know that time is without end. We investigate fullness and decay, and do not rejoice if we succeed, nor lament if we fail; for we know that conditions are not invariable. We who clearly apprehend the meaning of existence, do not rejoice over life, nor repine at death; for we know that terms are not final.

"What we know is not to be compared with what we do not know. The span of our physical life is not to be compared with the span of our spiritual life.

"I have heard say, the person of Eternity has no reputation; perfect virtue acquires nothing; the truly great person ignores self-interest—this is the height of self-discipline."

"But how then," asked the Spirit of the River, "are the internal and external extremes of value and worthlessness, or greatness and smallness, to be determined?"

"From the point of view of the Eternal," replied the Spirit of the Ocean, "there are no absolute extremes of value and worthlessness.

People individually value themselves and hold others cheap. The world collectively withholds from individuals the right of appraising themselves.

"If we say that a thing is great or small because it is relatively great or small, then there is nothing in all creation which is not great, nothing which is not small.

"The life of humanity passes by like a galloping horse, changing at every turn, at every hour. What should we do, or what should we not do, other than let our decomposition go on?"

"If this is the case," retorted the Spirit of the River, "pray, what is the value of the Eternal?"

"Those who understand the Eternal," answered the Spirit of the Ocean, "must necessarily apprehend the eternal principles above mentioned and be clear as to their application. Consequently, they do not suffer any injury from without.

"The people of perfect virtue cannot be burned by fire, nor drowned in water, nor hurt by frost or sun, nor torn by wild bird or beast. Not that they make light of these; but that they discriminate between safety and danger. Happy under prosperous and adverse circumstances alike, cautious as to what they discard and what they accept—nothing can harm them.

"Therefore it has been said that the natural abides within, the artificial without. Virtue abides in the natural. Knowledge of the action of the natural and of the artificial has its root in the natural, its development in virtue. And thus, whether in action or at rest, whether in expansion or in contraction, there is always a reversion to the essential and to the ultimate.

"Therefore it has been said, do not let the artificial obliterate the natural; do not let will obliterate destiny; do not let virtue be sacrificed to fame. Diligently observe these precepts without fail, and thus you will revert to the Divine."

Each in Its Own Way

The walrus envies the centipede; the centipede envies the snake; the snake envies the wind; the wind envies the eye; the eye envies the mind. The walrus said to the centipede, "I hop about on one leg, but not very successfully. How do you manage all these legs you have?"

"I don't manage them," replied the centipede. "Have you never seen saliva? When it is ejected, the big drops are the size of pearls, the small ones like mist. They fall promiscuously on the ground and cannot be counted. And so it is that my mechanism works naturally, without my being conscious of the fact."

The centipede said to the snake, "With all my legs I do not move as fast as you with none. How is that?"

"One's natural mechanism," replied the snake, "is not often a thing to be improved upon. What need have I for legs?"

The snake said to the wind, "I can manage to wriggle along, but I have a form. Now you come blustering down from the north sea to bluster away to the south sea, and you seem to be without form. How is that?"

"It is true," replied the wind, "that I bluster as you say; but anyone who can point at me or kick at me, excels me. On the other hand, I can break huge trees and destroy large buildings. That is my strong point. Out of all the small things in which I do not excel I make one great one in which I do excel. And to excel in one great thing is given only to the few who reach true maturity."

Lasting Happiness

Is lasting happiness to be found on earth, or not? Are there those who can discover the meaning of life, or not? If so, what do they do, what do they affect, what do they avoid, what do they rest in, accept, reject, like, and dislike?

What the world collectively esteems comprises wealth, rank, long life, and generosity. What it enjoys comprises comfort, rich food, fine clothes, beauty of a sensual nature, and pleasant music. What it does not esteem comprises poverty, want of position, early death, and evil behavior. What it does not enjoy comprises lack of comfort for the body, lack of rich food for the palate, lack of fine clothes for the back, lack of sensual beauty for the eye, and lack of pleasant music for the ear. If people do not get these, they are greatly miserable. Yet from the point of view of our physical frame, this is folly.

Wealthy people who ceaselessly toil, putting together more money than they can possibly use—from the point of view of our physical frame, is not this going beyond the mark?

Officials of rank who turn night into day in their endeavors to encompass the best ends—from the point of view of our physical frame, is not this a divergence?

We are born to sorrow, and what misery is ours whose long life with dulled faculties only means prolonged sorrow! From the point of view of our physical frame, this is going far astray.

Patriots are, in most peoples' opinion, reasonably generous. Yet their generosity does not enable them to discover the meaning of life; and so I do not know whether theirs is true generosity or not.

It has been said, "If your loyal counsels are not attended to, depart quietly without resistance." Thus, when Tze Hsu resisted, his physical frame perished; yet had he not resisted, he would not have made his name. Is there then really such a thing as this generosity, or not?

As to what the world does and the way in which people are happy now, I do not know whether such happiness is real happiness or not. The happiness of most people seems to me to consist in slavishly following the majority, as if they could not help it. Yet they all say they are happy.

But I cannot say that this is happiness or that it is not happiness. Is there then, after all, such a thing as happiness?

I find much real happiness in the act of meditating about life, which the world regards as completely unnecessary. Thus it has been said, "Lasting happiness is the absence of happiness (in the sense of pleasure); perfect renown is the absence of renown (in the popular sense).

Now in this mundane world of ours it is impossible to assign positive and negative absolutely. Nevertheless, in meditation they can be so assigned. Lasting happiness and preservation of life are to be sought for only in, and as the result of, adequate meditation.

Let us consider. The universe does nothing; yet it is clear. Earth does nothing; yet it enjoys equilibrium. From the inaction of these two proceed all the actions of things and beings. How vast, how infinite, is the understanding gained through periods of inaction, yet without tangible result! How infinite, how vast, yet without form!

The endless varieties of action around us all spring from inaction. Therefore it has been said, "The universe does nothing, yet there is nothing which it does not accomplish." But among people, who can attain to a proper balance between inaction and action?

The Fighting Cocks

Chi Hsing Tze was training fighting cocks for the prince. At the end of ten days the latter asked if they were ready. "Not yet," replied Chi, "they are still excited by the sounds and shadows of other cocks." Ten days more, and the prince asked again. "Not yet," answered Chi, "the sight of an enemy is still enough to excite them to rage."

But after another ten days, when the prince again inquired, Chi said, "They will do. Other cocks may crow, but they will take no notice. To look at them one might say they were of wood. Their virtue is complete. Strange cocks will not meet them, but will run."

The Way of the Good Carpenter

Ch'ing, the chief carpenter, was carving wood into a stand for hanging musical instruments, When finished, the work appeared to those who saw it as though of supernatural execution. The prince of Lu asked him, saying, "What mystery is there in your art?"

"No mystery, your Highness," replied Ch'ing, "and yet there is something.

"When I am about to make such a stand, I guard against any diminution of my vital power. I first reduce my mind to absolute quiescence. Three days in this condition, and I become oblivious of any reward to be gained. Five days, and I become oblivious of any fame to be acquired. Seven days, and I become unconscious of my four limbs and my physical frame.

"When, with thought of the court present to my mind, my skill becomes concentrated, and all disturbing elements from without are gone, I enter some mountain forest. I search for a suitable tree. It contains the form required, which is afterwards elaborated. I see the stand in my mind's eye, and then set to work. Otherwise, there is nothing. I bring my own natural capacity into relation with that of the wood. What was suspected to be of supernatural execution in my work was due solely to this."

Chuang Tze and the Strange Bird

When Chuang Tze was wandering in the park at Tiao-ling, he saw a strange bird which came from the south. Its wings were seven feet across. Its eyes were an inch in circumference. And it flew close past Chuang Tze's head to alight in a chestnut grove. "What man-

ner of bird is this?" cried Chuang Tze. "With strong wings it does
not fly away. With large eyes it does not see." So he strode towards
it with his crossbow, anxious to get a shot. Just then he saw a cicada enjoying itself in the shade, forgetful of all else. And he saw a
mantis spring and seize it, forgetting in the act its own body, which
the strange bird immediately pounced upon and made its prey. This
it was which had caused the bird to forget its own nature.

"Alas" cried Chuang Tze with a sigh, how creatures injure one
another. Loss follows the pursuit of gain." So he laid aside his bow
and went home, driven away by the park-keeper who wanted to
know what business he had there.

The Beautiful and Ugly Concubines

The innkeeper had two concubines, one beautiful, the other ugly.
The latter he loved; the former, he hated. Yang Tze asked how this
was; whereupon one of the inn servants said, "The beautiful one is
so conscious of her ugliness that one does not think her ugly."
"Note this, my disciples," cried Yang Tze. "Be virtuous, but without your virtue being on display; and wherever you go, you will be
loved by many people."

The Law of Creation

The universe is very beautiful, yet it says nothing. The four seasons
abide by a fixed law, yet they are not heard. All creation is based
upon absolute principles, yet nothing speaks.

And mature individuals taking their stands upon the beauty of the
universe, pierce the principles of created things. Hence the saying
that the perfect person does nothing, he/she performs nothing,
beyond gazing at the universe.

For our intellect, however keen, face to face with the countless
evolution of things, their death and birth, their squareness and
roundness—can never reach the root. There creation is, and there
it has ever been. The six cardinal points, reaching into infinity, are
ever included in the Eternal. An autumn spikelet, in all its minuteness, must carry the Eternal within itself. There is nothing on earth
which does not rise and fall, but it never perishes altogether. Apparently destroyed, but really existing; the material gone, the immaterial left—such is the law of creation, which passes all understand-

ing. This is called the root, whence a glimpse may be obtained of the Eternal.

All Things after Their Kind

Confucius said to Lao Tze, "Today you are at leisure. Pray tell me about the Eternal."

"Purge your heart by proper self-discipline," answered Lao Tze. "Wash your soul as white as snow. Discard your excess knowledge. The Eternal is abstruse and difficult of discussion. I will try, however, to speak to you of its outline."

Light is born of darkness. Classification is born of formlessness. The soul is born of the Eternal. The body is born of the vital essence.

Thus all things produce after their kind. Creatures with highest complexity are born from the womb. Creatures with less complexity are born from the egg. Of their coming there is no trace. In their departure there is no goal. No entrance gate, no dwelling house, they pass this way and that, as though at the meeting of the crossroads.

Some of those who enter therein become of limb, others subtle of thought, still others clear of sight and hearing. Some suffer no mental fatigue, nor meet with physical resistance.

The universe cannot but be immense. Earth cannot but be heavy. The sun and moon cannot but revolve. All creation cannot but flourish. To do so is their share in the Eternal. "But it is not from extensive study that this may be known, nor by dialectic skill that this may be made clear. The true person will not be satisfied with just these. It is in addition without gain, in diminution without loss, that the mature person finds union with the Eternal.

Unfathomable as the sea, wondrously ending only to begin again, informing all creation without being exhausted, the ways of mature persons are spontaneous in their operation. That all creation can be informed by them without exhaustion, is their eternal quality. "In places of understanding there are individuals who recognize neither absolute positive nor negative. They abide between divine and human, between good and evil. They act their part as mortals, but seek to unite with the divine. From that standpoint, life is but a concentration of the vital fluid whose longest and shortest terms of existence vary by an inappreciable space,- hardly enough for the fixed classifications of institutional religion.

Tree-fruits and plant-fruits exhibit order in their varieties; and our relationships, though more difficult to be dealt with, may still be redeemed in order. Those who meet with these do not violate them. Neither do they continue to hold fast by them. Adaptation by arrangement is understanding. Spontaneous adaptation is the way of the Eternal, by which the true leaders are eventually recognized by the people.

We pass through this subliminary life as a white horse passes a crack: here one moment, gone the next. Neither are there any not equally subject to the ingress and egress of morality. One modification brings life; then another, and it is death. Living creatures cry out; human beings sorrow. The bow-sheath is slipped off; the clothes-bag is dropped and in the confusion life slips away into oblivion.

The reality of the formless, the unreality of that which has form, this is known to all sages. Those who are on the road to attainment care not for these things, but the people at large discuss them. Attainment implies non-argumentation: argumentation implies non-attainment. Manifested, the Eternal has no objective value; hence, silence is better than argument. It cannot be translated completely into speech; better then say nothing at all than to sacrifice one's self-respect.

Where the Eternal Is

Wung Tue Tze asked Chuang Tze, saying, "what you call the Eternal, where is it?"

"There is nowhere," replied Chuang Tze, "where it is not."

"Tell me one place at any rate, where it is," said Tung Huo Tze.

"It is in the ant," replied Chuang Tze.

"Why go so low down?" asked Tung Huo Tze.

"It is in a tare," said Chuang Tze.

"Still lower," objected Tung Huo Tze.

"It is in a potsherd," said Chuang Tze.

"Worse still," cried Tung You Tze.

"It is in manure," said Chuang Tze. Tung Kuo Tze made no reply.

"Sir," continued Chuang Tze, "your question does not touch the essential. When Huo, inspector of markets, asked the managing director about the fatness of pigs, the test was always made in parts least likely to be fat. Do not therefore insist in any particular direction; for there is nothing which escapes. Such is the Eternal; and such also is ideal speech. Whole, entire, all are three words which sound differently but mean the same. Their purpose is one.

"Try to reach with me the palace of nowhere, and there, amid the identity of all things, carry your discussions into the infinite. Try to practice meditation about life, wherein you may find peace and be happy. For thus my mind becomes an abstraction. It does not wander, and yet is not conscious of being at rest. It goes and comes and is not conscious of stoppages. Backwards and forwards without being conscious of any goal. Up and down the realms of infinity, wherein even the greatest intellect would fail to find an end.

"That which makes things the things they are is not limited to such things. The limits of things are their own limits in so far as they are things. The limits of the limitless, the limitlessness of the limited—these are called fullness and emptiness, renovation and decay. The Eternal causes fullness and emptiness, but it is not either. It causes preservation and decay, but it is not either. It causes beginning and end, but it is not either. It causes accumulation and dispersion, but it is not either."

The Invisibility of Nothing

This story I have heard:

Light asked Nothing, saying, "Do you, sir, exist, or do you not exist?"

But getting no answer to his question, Light set to work to watch for the appearance of Nothing.

Hidden, vacuous—all day long he looked but could not see it, listened but could not hear it, grasped at but could not seize it.

"Bravo!" cried Light. "Who can equal this? I can get to be Nothing, but I cannot get as far as the absence of Nothing. Assuming that Nothing has an objective existence, how can it reach this next stage?"

No Past, No Future

Jen Ch'iu asked Confucius, saying, "Can we know about the time before the universe existed?"

"We can," replied Confucius. "Time was of old precisely what it is now."

At this reply, Jen Ch'iu withdrew. Next day he again visited Confucius and said, "Yesterday when I asked you that question and you answered me, I was quite clear about it. Today I am confused. How is this?"

"Your clearness of yesterday," answered Confucius, "was because my answer appealed directly to your natural intelligence. Your confusion of today results from the intrusion of something other than the natural intelligence. There is no past, no future, no beginning, no end. To have posterity before one has posterity—is that possible?"

Jen Ch'iu made no answer, and Confucius continued, "That will do. Do not reply. If life did not give birth to death, and if death did not put an end to life, surely life and death would be no longer correlates, but would each exist independently. What there was before the universe, was the Eternal. The Eternal makes things what they are, but is not itself a thing. Nothing can produce the Eternal; yet everything has the Eternal within it, and continues to produce it without end. And the endless love of mature individuals for their fellow-beings is based upon the same principle."

The Wise Tender of Horses

This story I have heard:

When the Yellow Emperor went to see the Eternal upon the Chu-tz'u Mountain, Fang Ming was his charioteer, Ch'any Yu sat on his right, Chang Jo and Hsi P'eng were his outriders, and K'un Hun and Hua Chi brought up the rear. On reaching the wilds of Hsiang-ch'eng, these seven sages lost their way and there was no one of whom to ask where the road was. By and by, they saw a boy who was grazing horses, and asked him, saying, "Do you know the Chu-tz'u Mountain?"

"I do," replied the boy.

"Can you tell us," continued the sages, "where the Eternal abides?"

"I can," replied the boy.

"This is a strange lad," cried the Yellow Emperor. "Not only does he know where the Chu-tz'u Mountain is, but also where the Eternal abides! Come tell me, pray, how would you govern the empire?"

"I should govern the empire," said the boy, "just the same as I look after my horses. What else should I do?"

"Of course," said the Yellow Emperor, "government is not your trade. Still I should be glad to hear what you would do."

The boy declined to answer, but on being again urged, cried out, "What difference is there between governing the empire and looking after horses? See that no harm comes to the horses; that is all!"

Thereupon the Emperor duly acknowledged the boy's great understanding; and wishing him good fortune, took his leave.

Chuang Tze on Death

When Chuang Tze was about to die, his disciples expressed a wish to give him a splendid funeral. But Chuang Tze said, "With the universe for my coffin and shell; with the sun, moon, and stars as my burial regalia; and with all creation to escort me to the grave— are not my funeral paraphernalia ready at hand?"

"We fear," argued the disciples, "lest the birds should eat the body of our Master;" to which Chuang Tze replied, "Above ground I shall be food for birds; below I shall be food for mole-crickets and ants. Why rob one to feed the other?

· If you adopt, as absolute, a standard of evenness which is so only relatively, your results will not be absolutely even. If you adopt, as absolute, a criterion of right which is so only relatively, your results will not be absolutely right. Those who trust to their senses become slaves to objective existences. Those alone who are guided by their intuitions find the true standard. So far are the senses less reliable than the intuitions. Yet fools trust to their senses to know what is good for humankind, with alas! but external results."

Nan Yung

Nan Yung took some provisions, and after a seven days' journey arrived at the abode of Lao Tze.

"Have you come from Keng Sang Ch'u?" said the latter.

"I have," replied Nan Yung.

"But why," said Lao Tze, "bring all these people with you?"

Nan Yung looked back in alarm, and Lao Tze continued, "Do you not understand what I say?"

Nan Yung bent his head abashed, and then looking up, said with a sigh, "I have now forgotten how to answer, in consequence of missing what I came to ask."

"What do you mean?" said Lao Tze.

"If I do not know," replied Nan Yung, "people call me a fool. If I do know, I injure myself. If I am not charitable, I injure others. If I am, I injure myself. If I do not do my duty to my neighbor, I injure others. If I do it, I injure myself. My trouble lies in not seeing how to escape from these three dilemmas. On the strength of my connection with Kong Sang, your disciple, I would venture to ask your advice."

"When I saw you," said Lao Tze, "I knew in the twinkling of an eye what was the matter with you. And now what you say confirms my view. You are confused, as a child that has lost its parents. You would fathom the sea with a pole. You are astray. You are struggling to get back to your natural self, but cannot find the way. Alas! alas!"

Nan Yung begged to be allowed to remain, and set to work to cultivate the good and eliminate the evil within him. At the expiration of ten days, with sorrow in his heart, he again sought Lao Tze.

"Have you thoroughly cleansed yourself?" said Lao Tze. "But this grieved look. There is some evil obstruction yet.

"If the disturbances are external, do not be always combating them, but close the channels to the mind. If the disturbances are internal, do not strive to oppose them, but close all entrance from without. If the disturbances are both internal and external, then you will not even be able to hold fast to the Eternal, still less practice its dictates."

"If a rustic is sick," said Nan Yung, "and another rustic goes to see him; and if the sick man can say what is the matter with him— then he is not seriously ill. Yet my search after the Eternal is like swallowing drugs which only increase the malady. I beg therefore merely to ask the art of preserving life."

"The art of preserving life," replied Lao Tze, "consists in being able to keep all in One, to lose nothing, to estimate good and evil without guessing, to know when to stop, and how much is enough, to leave others alone (except when they ask for help), and attend to oneself, to be without misery and without excessive knowledge—to be in fact as a child (in its childlike characteristics and not in its childish ones). A child will cry all day and not become hoarse, because of the perfection of its constitutional harmony. It will keep its fist tightly closed all day and not open it, because of the concentration of its virtue. It will gaze all day without taking off its eyes, because its sight is not attracted by externals. This is the art of preserving life."

"Is this then the virtue of the mature individual?" cried Nan Yung.

"Not so," said Lao Tze. "I am, as it were, but breaking the ice.

"Mature individuals share the food of the earth and also the happiness of the Eternal. They do not incur trouble either from people or things. They do not join in censuring, in plotting, in toadying. Free from misery they come, and unobtrusively they go—this is the art of preserving life."

"This then is perfection?" inquired Nan Yung.

"Not yet," said Lao Tze. "I specially asked if you could be as a child. A child acts without worrying about the acceptability of what it does; moves without worrying about the passage of time. Thus, good and evil fortune find no lodgment therein; and there where good and evil fortune are not, how can the misery of mortality be?

"Those whose minds are in a state of balance give forth a divine radiance, by the light of which they see themselves as they are. And only by cultivating such balance can we attain to the constant.

"Those who are constant are sought after by alert individuals and assisted by their own inner strength.

"To study this is to study what cannot be fully learned. To practice this is to practice what cannot be fully accomplished. To discuss this is to discuss what can never be proved. Let knowledge stop at the unknowable. That is perfection. With such defenses for the body, ever prepared for the unexpected, deferential to the rights of others—if then calamities overtake you, they cannot do you harm. Let them not disturb what you have already achieved. Let them not penetrate into the soul's abode. For there resides the will. And if the will knows not what to will, it will not be able to will.

"Those who are naturally in sympathy with others, to them all understanding people come. But those who adapt under pressure have no room even for themselves, still less for others. And those who have no room for others in their thinking, have no possibility of discovering the meaning of life. It is all over with them.

"The Eternal forms its own subdivisions, the divisions of many gifts among many people. What is feared in subdivision is separation. What is feared in separation, is further separation. Thus, to issue forth and attain the goal, this is called lasting happiness. To die and yet to have blended with the Eternal, this is convergence of the supernatural into One. To make things which have form appear to all intents and purposes formless—this is the sum of all things.

"Birth is not a beginning; death is not an end. There is existence without limitation; there is continuity without a starting-point. Existence without limitation is space. Continuity without a starting point is time. There is birth, there is death, there is issuing forth, there is entering in. That through which one passes in and out without seeing its form, that is the Portal of Life.

"The Portal of Life is non-existence (or 'thought'). All things (or 'actions') sprang from non-existence. Existence (or 'action') could not make existence. It must have proceeded from non-existence, and non-existence and nothing are One. Herein is the source of inspiration of the mature individual.

"The knowledge of the Ancients reached the highest point in the time before anything existed. This is the highest point. It is exhaustive. There is no adding to it.

"The second best was that of those who started from existence. Life was to them a misfortune. Death was a time of misery. There was already separation.

"The next in the scale said that at the beginning there was nothing. Then life came, to be followed quickly by death. They made nothing the head, life the trunk, and death the tail of existence, claiming as friends whoever know that existence and non-existence, and life and death were all One.

"These three classes, though different, were of the same quality; as were those who inherited fame, and those who inherited territory.

"Our life is as the soot on a kettle. Yet people speak of the subjective point of view. But this subjective point of view cannot be proven true or untrue; it must be experienced. It touches points where knowledge cannot reach.

"Let us try to formulate this subjective point of view. It originates with life, and, with knowledge as its tutor, drifts into the admission of right and wrong. But one's own standard of right is the standard, and others have to adapt themselves to it. Individuals will die for this. Such people look upon the useful as appertaining to wisdom, the useless as appertaining to folly; upon success in life as honorable, upon failure as dishonorable. This subjective point of view is that of the present generation, who like the cicada and the young dove see things only from their own standpoint.

"If people tread upon strangers' toes in the market-place, they apologize quickly. If elder siblings did this, they are quick with an exclamation of sympathy. And if a parent does so, nothing whatever is done.

"Therefore, it has been said, 'Perfect politeness is not artificial; perfect duty to one's neighbor is not a matter of calculation; perfect wisdom takes no straining of thought; perfect charity recognizes no ties; perfect trust requires no pledges'.

"Discard the stimuli of self-seeking. Free the mind from disturbances. Get rid of entanglements to reward. Pierce the obstructions to the Eternal.

"Honors, wealth, distinction, power, fame, gain—these six stimulate self-searching.

"Appearance, carriage, beauty, arguments, influence, opinions—these six, when lavishly displayed, disturb the mind.

"Hate, ruthless competition, excitement, anger, misery, pleasure—these six are entanglements to virtue.

"Excesses of rejecting, adopting, receiving, giving, knowledge, technical skill—these six are obstructions to the discovery of the Eternal.

"If these twenty-four be not allowed to run riot, then the mind will be duly ordered. And being duly ordered, it will be in dynamic equilibrium. And being in dynamic equilibrium, it will be clear of perception. And being clear of perception, it will be undistorted. And being undistorted, it will be in that state of peace by which there is nothing which cannot be accomplished."

CONFUCIANIST SCRIPTURES

INTRODUCTION

Confucius was born in 551 B.C. in the province of Shantung, China. He married at nineteen and devoted his life to teaching and government. For a certain period he was actually in political life, but afterward he chose to teach about good government and the development of culture in China. His emphasis is shown to have been predominantly ethical, but it contains definite value for world religion.

Mencius was the most outstanding disciple of Confucius, although the followers of Confucius were quite numerous. The books presented here are about the Master, but were written by his disciples.

Taoism and Confucianism together give a good illustration of the two basic elements of religion: mysticism and ethics. These two do not necessarily contradict one another, but in the past they often have done so. The proper balance is what is difficult to attain.

ANALECTS OF CONFUCIUS

Book 1

The Master said, "Is it not pleasant to learn about life with a constant perseverance and application? Is it not delightful to have friends coming from distant quarters? Are we not people of complete virtue who feel no discomposure though people may take no note of us?

"Fine words and an insinuating appearance are seldom associated with true virtue."

The philosopher Tsang said, "I daily examine myself on three points: —whether, in transacting business for others, I may have been unfaithful; —whether, in intercourse with friends, I may have been insincere; —whether I may not have mastered and practiced the instructions of my teacher."

The Master said, "To rule a country of any size, there must be reverent attention to business, and sincerity; economy in expenditure, and love for all beings; and the employment of the people at the proper seasons."

Tsze-hsia said, "If we withdraw our minds from the love of sensuality and apply them to the love of the virtuous; if, in serving our parents, we can exert our utmost strength; if, in serving our leaders, we can devote our life; if, in our discourse with our friends, our words are sincere—although people say that we have not learned, I will certainly say that we have."

The philosopher Yu said, "When agreements are made according to what is right, what is spoken can be made good. When respect is shown according to what is proper, one keeps far from shame and disgrace. When the parties upon whom a person leans are proper persons to be intimate with, we can make them our guides and masters."

The Master said, "We who aim to be people of complete virtue in our food do not seek to eat more than our needs demand, nor in our dwelling-place do we seek the appliances of ease; we are earnest in what we are doing, and careful in our speech; we frequent the company of people of principle that we may be rectified: — such a person may be said indeed to love to learn about life.

"I will not be afflicted at others not knowing me; I will be afflicted that I do not know others."

Book 2

The Master said, "Those who exercise government by means of their virtue may be compared to the north polar star, which keeps its place as all the other stars turn around it.

"If the people be led by laws, and uniformity sought to be given them by punishments, they will try to avoid the punishment, but have no sense of humility. If they be led by virtue, and uniformity sought to be given them by the rules of propriety, they will have the sense of humility and moreover will become good.

"At fifteen, I had my mind bent on learning about life. At thirty, I stood firm. At forty, I had no doubts. At fifty, I knew the decrees of life. At sixty, my ear was an obedient organ for the reception of truth. At seventy, I could follow what my heart desired, without transgressing what was right.

"I have talked with Hui for a whole day, and he has not made any objection to anything I said; —as if he were stupid. He has retired, and I have examined his conduct when away from me and found him able to illustrate my teachings. Hui! —he is not stupid.

"See what individuals do. Mark their motives. Examine in what things they rest. How can people conceal their character?

"If people keep cherishing their present enlightenment, while continually seeking to acquire more, they may be teachers of others."

Tsze-kung asked what constituted the superior individual. The Master said, "Those who act before they speak, and afterwards speak according to their actions. The superior person is universally minded and not a partisan. The inferior person is a partisan and not universal."

The Master said, "Yu, shall I teach you what knowledge is? When you know a thing, to hold that you know it; and when you do not know a thing, to allow that you do not know it—this is knowledge."

The duke Ai asked, saying, "What should be done in order to secure the cooperation of the people?" Confucius replied, "Advance the upright and set aside the crooked; then the people will eventually be won over. Advance the crooked and set aside the upright; then the people will not submit for long."

The Master said, "For people to sacrifice themselves for a cause which is not truly a part of them is flattery.

"To see what is right and not to do it is lack of courage."

Book 3

The Master said, "If people are without the virtues proper to humanity, what have they to do with the rites of propriety? If people are without the virtues proper to humanity, what have they to do with music and the other arts?"

The Master said, "Things that are done, it is needless to speak about; things that have had their course, it is needless to remonstrate about; things that are past, it is needless to blame."

The Master said, "High station filled without indulgent generosity; ceremonies performed without reverence; mourning conducted without sorrow; —wherewith should I contemplate such ways?"

Book 4

The Master said, "It is virtuous manners which constitute the excellence of a neighborhood. If people, in selecting a residence, do not select one where such manners prevail, how can they be wise?

"Those who are without virtue cannot long abide contentedly either in a condition of hardship, or in a condition of true happiness. The virtuous rest in virtue; the wise desire virtue. It is only the truly virtuous person who can love all beings.

"A person whose mind is set on truth, but who is ashamed of poor clothes and meager food, is not fit to be discoursed with.

"The superior people, in the world, do not harbor prejudices either for anything or against anything—what is right they will follow. The superior people think of virtue; the small people think of favors which they may receive.

"Those who act with a constant view to their own advantage will be much murmured against.

"A person should say, 'I am not concerned that I have no place, I am concerned how I may fit myself for one. I am not concerned that I am not known, I seek to be worthy to be known.'

"The reason why the ancients did not readily give utterance to their words, was that they feared lest their actions should not come up to them.

"Virtue is not left to stand alone. Those who practice it will have true neighbors."

Tsze-yu said, "In serving a ruler, frequent protests lead to disgrace. Between friends, frequent reproofs make the friendship distant."

Book 5

Someone said, "Yung is truly virtuous, but he is not ready with his tongue." The Master said, "What is the good of being ready with the tongue? Those who encounter people with smartness of speech for the most part procure themselves hatred. I know not whether they be truly virtuous, but why should they show readiness of the tongue?"

The Master was wishing Ch'i-tao K'ai to enter on official employment. He replied, "I am not yet able to rest in the assurance of this." The Master was pleased.

The Master said of Tsze-ch'an that he had four of the characteristics of a superior person: —in his conduct of himself, he was humble; in serving his superiors, he was respectful; in nourishing the people, he was kind; in ordering the people, he was just.

Chi Wan thought thrice, and then acted. When the Master was informed of it, he said, "Twice may do."

The Master said, "When good order prevailed in his country, Ning Wu acted the part of a wise man. When his country was in disorder, he acted the part of a stupid man. Others may equal his wisdom, but they cannot equal his stupidity."

Yun Yuan and Chi Lu being by his side, the Master said to them, "Come, let each of you tell his wishes."

Tsze-lu said, "I should like having chariots and horses, and light fur dresses, to share them with my friends, and though they should spoil them, I would not be displeased."

Yen Yuan said, "I should like not to boast of my excellence, nor to make a display of my meritorious deeds."

Tsze-lu then said, "I should like, sir, to hear your wishes." The Master said, "They are, in regard to the aged, to give them rest; in regard to friends, to show them sincerity; in regard to the young, to treat them tenderly.

"In a group of ten families, there may be found one honorable and sincere as I am, but not so fond of learning about life."

Book 6

"They who know the truth are not equal to those who love it, and they who love it are not equal to those who delight in it."

Fan Ch'ih asked what constituted wisdom. The Master said, "To give one's self earnestly to the duties due to others; and, while respecting spiritual masters, to keep aloof from dependence upon them, may be called wisdom." He asked about perfect virtue. The Master said, "People of virtue make the difficulty to be overcome their first business, and success only a subsequent consideration—this may be called perfect virtue."

Tsai Wo asked, saying, "Benevolent people, though it be told them, 'There is a man in the well,' will go in after him, I suppose." Confucius said, "Why should they do so? Superior people may be made to go to the well, but they cannot be made to go down into it. They may be imposed upon, but they cannot be fooled."

Tsze-kung said, "Suppose some individuals are extensively conferring benefits on the people, and able to assist all, what would you say of them? Might they be called perfectly virtuous?" The Master said, "Why speak only of virtue in connection with them? Must they not have the qualities of mature people? Even Yao and Shun were still solicitous about this. Now people of perfect virtue, wishing to be established themselves, seek also to enlarge others. To be able to judge others by what is the best in ourselves—this may be called the art of virtue."

Book 7

The Master said, "From people bringing no payment for my teaching upwards, I have never refused instruction to anyone. I do not open up the truth to one who is not eager to get knowledge, nor help out those who are not anxious to speak about themselves. When I have presented one corner of a subject to anyone, and that person cannot from it learn the other three, I do not endlessly repeat my lesson."

When the Master was eating by the side of a mourner, he never ate to the full. He did not sing on the same day in which he had been weeping.

Tsze-lu said, "If you had the conduct of the armies of a great state, whom would you have to act with you?" The Master said, "I would not have those to act with me who will unarmed attack a tiger, or cross a river without a boat, or die without any regret. My associates must be those who proceed to action full of solicitude, who are fond of adjusting their plans, and then carry them into execution."

The Master said, "If the search for riches were sure to be successful, though I should become a groom with whip in hand to get them, I would not go after them. As the search may not be successful, I will follow after that which is true to my own nature."

The Master said, "In letters I am perhaps equal to other people, but the character of the superior person, carrying out in my conduct what I profess, is what I have not yet attained to."

Book 8

The Master said, "Respectfulness, without the rules of propriety, becomes laborious bustle; carefulness, without the rules of propriety, becomes timidity; boldness, without the rules of propriety, becomes insubordination; straightforwardness, without the rules of propriety, becomes rudeness.

"When those who are in high stations perform well all their duties to their relations, the people are aroused to virtue. When old friends are not neglected by them, the people are preserved from inferiority.

"Though people have abilities as admirable as those of the best of all, yet if they are haughty and niggardly, those other things are really not worth being looked at."

Book 9

There were four things from which the Master was entirely free. He had no foregone conclusions, no arbitrary predeterminations, no obstinacy, and no egoism.

The Master said, "Am I indeed possessed of knowledge? I am not knowing. But if a mean person, who appears quite empty-like, asks anything of me, I set it forth from one end to the other and exhaust it."

Yen Yuan, in admiration of the Master's doctrines, sighed and said, "I looked up to them, and they seemed to become more high; I tried to penetrate them, and they seemed to become more firm; I looked at them before me, and suddenly they seemed to be behind. The Master, by orderly method, skillfully leads people on. He enlarged my mind with learning, and taught me the restraints of propriety. When I wish to give over the study of his doctrines, I cannot do so, and having exerted all my ability, there seems something to stand right up before me; but though I wish to follow and lay hold of it, I really find no way to do so."

Tsze-kung said, "There is a beautiful gem here. Should I lay it up in a case and keep it, or should I seek for a good price and sell it?" The Master said, "Sell it! Sell it! But I would wait for one to offer the price."

The Master, standing by a stream, said, "Lasting happiness passes on just like this, not ceasing day or night!"

The Master said, "I have not seen one who loves virtue as he/she loves beauty.

"Youth are to be regarded with respect. How do we know that their future will not be equal to our present? If they reach the age of forty or fifty, and have not established themselves, then indeed they may no longer be worth being regarded with respect.

"Hold faithfulness and sincerity as first principles. Have no friends whom you cannot respect. When you have faults, do not fear to abandon them.

"Dressed himself in a tattered robe quilted with hemp, yet standing by the side of men dressed in furs, and not ashamed; ah, it is Yu who is equal to this! 'He dislikes none, he covets nothing; — what can he do but what is good?'"

Book 10

Confucius, in his village, looked simple and sincere, and as if he were not able to speak.

When he was in the prince's temple, or in the court, he spoke minutely on every point, but cautiously.

When he was waiting at court, in speaking with the great officers of the lower grade, he spoke freely, but in a straightforward manner; in speaking with those of the higher grade, he did so blandly, but precisely.

When the ruler was present, his manner displayed respectful uneasiness; it was grave, but self-possessed.

Book 11

The Master said, "The people of former times, in matters of ceremonies and the arts, were rustics, it is said, while the people of these latter times, in ceremonies and the arts, are accomplished individuals. If I have occasion to use those things, I follow the people of former times."

Chi Lu asked about serving the spirits of the dead. The Master said, "While you are not able to serve people now, how can you serve their spirits?"

Chi Lu added, "I venture to ask about death." He was answered, "While you do not know life, how can you know about death?"

Tsze-kung asked which of the two, Shih or Shang, was the superior. The Master said, "Shih goes beyond the due mean, and Shang does not come up to it." "Then," said Tsze-kung, "the superiority is with Shih, I suppose." The Master said, "To go beyond is as wrong as to fall short."

Tsze-lu asked whether he should immediately carry into practice what he heard. The Master said, "There are your father and elder brothers to be consulted; why should you act on that principle of immediately carrying into practice what you hear?" Yen Yu asked the same, whether he should immediately carry into practice what he heard, and the Master answered, "Immediately carry into practice what you hear." Kung-hsi Hwa said, "Yu asked whether he should carry immediately into practice what he heard, and you said, 'There are your father and elder brothers to be consulted.' Ch'iu asked whether he should immediately carry into practice what he heard, and you said, 'Carry it immediately into practice.' I, Ch'iu, am perplexed, and venture to ask you for an explanation." The Master said, "Ch'iu is retiring and slow; therefore, I urged him forward. Yu has more than his own share of energy; therefore, I kept him back."

Book 12

Yen Yuan asked about virtue. The Master said, "To subdue one's self and return to propriety is virtue. If a people can for one day subdue themselves and return to propriety, all will ascribe virtue to them.

Chung-kung asked about virtue. The Master said, "It is, when you go abroad, to behave to everyone as if you were receiving a great guest; to employ the people as if you were assisting at a great ceremony; not to do to others as you would not wish done to yourself; to have no murmuring against you in the country, and none in the family." Chung-kung said, "though I am deficient in intelligence and vigor, I will make it my business to practice this lesson."

Sze-ma Niu asked about the superior person. The Master said, "The superior person has neither anxiety nor fear." "Being without anxiety or fear!" said Niu; "does this constitute what we call the superior person?" The Master said, "When internal examination discovers nothing wrong, what is there to be anxious about, what is there to fear?"

Tsze-chang asked what constituted intelligence. The Master said, "We with whom neither slander that gradually soaks into the mind, nor statements that startle like a wound in the flesh, are successful, may be called intelligent indeed. Yes, the one with whom neither soaking slander nor startling statements are successful, may be called far-seeing."

Tsze-kung asked about government. The Master said, "The requisites of government are that there be sufficiency of food and shelter, sufficiency of military equipment, and the confidence of the people in their ruler."

Tsze-kung said, "If it cannot be helped, and one of these must be dispensed with, which of the three should be foregone first?" "The military equipment," said the Master.

Tsze-kung again asked, "If it cannot be helped, and one of the remaining two must be dispensed with, which of them should be foregone?" The Master answered, "Part of the food and shelter. From old, death has been the lot of all people; but if the people have no faith in their rulers, there is no hope for the government itself."

The Master said, "In hearing disputes, I am like any other body. What is necessary, however, is to cause the people to have no disputes."

Chi K'ang asked Confucius about government, saying, "What do you say to killing the unprincipled for the good of the principled?" Confucius replied, "Sir, in carrying on your government, why should you use killing at all? Let your desires be for what is good, and the people will tend to be good.

Tsze-chang asked, "What must the officer be, who may be said to be distinguished?" The Master said, "What is it you call being distinguished?" Tsze-chang replied, "It is to be heard of through the state, to be heard of throughout his community." The Master said, "That is notoriety, not distinction. Now the people of distinction are solid and straightforward, and love righteousness. They examine people's words, and look at their countenances. They are anxious to humble themselves to others. Such people will be distinguished in the country; they will be distinguished in their communities.

Fan Ch'ih asked about benevolence. The Master said, "It is to love all beings. He asked about true knowledge. The Master said, "It is to know all beings—that is, to understand them."

Tsze-kung asked about friendship. The Master said, "Faithfully encourage your friends, and skillfully lead them on. If you find them unresponsive, stop. Do not disgrace yourself."

Book 13

Tsze-lu said, "The ruler of Wei has been waiting for you, in order with you to administer the government. What will you consider the first thing to be done?"

The Master replied, "What is necessary is to rectify names."

"So, indeed!" said Tsze-lu, "You are wide of the mark! Why must there be such rectification?"

The Master said, "How uncultivated you are, Yu! Superior people, in regard to what they do not know, show a cautious reserve.

"If names are not correct, language is not in accordance with the truth of things. If language is not in accordance with the truth of things, affairs cannot be carried on to success.

"When affairs cannot be carried on to success, proprieties and the arts will not flourish. When proprieties and the arts do not flourish, punishments will not be properly awarded. When punishments are not properly awarded, the people do not know how to move hand or foot.

"Therefore superior people consider it necessary that the names they use may be spoken appropriately, and also that what they speak may be carried out appropriately. What superior people require is just that in their words there may be nothing incorrect."

When the Master went to Wei, Zan Yu acted as the driver of his carriage. The Master observed, "How numerous are the people!" Yu said, "Since they are so numerous, what more shall be done for them?" "Enrich them," was the reply. "And when they have been enriched, what more shall be done?" The Master said, "Teach them."

Tsze-kung asked, saying, "What do you say of individuals who are loved by all the people of their neighborhoods?" The Master replied, "We may not for that accord our approval of them." "And what do you say of those who are hated by all the people of their neighborhoods?" The Master said, "We may not for that conclude that they are bad. It is better than either of these cases that the good in the neighborhood love them, and the bad hate them. Better still is that they be respected by as many as possible, because of their adherence to truth and their love for all."

The Master said, "Superior people are easy to serve and difficult to please. If you try to please them in any way which is not in accord with right, they will not be pleased. But in their employment of people, they wish them to be equal to everything.

"Superior people have a dignified ease without haughtiness. Inferior people have haughtiness without a dignified ease."

Book 14

The Master said, "Alas! there is no one that knows me." Tsze-kung said, "What do you mean by thus saying—that no one knows you?" The Master replied, "I do not murmur against the laws of life. I do not grumble against people. My studies lie low, and my understanding rises high. But there is lasting happiness; that I have found!"

Yuan Zang was squatting on his heels, and so awaited the approach of the Master, who said to him, "In youth, do not be humble as befits a junior; in adulthood, doing nothing worthy of being handed down and living on purposelessly into old age—this is to be a pest."

Book 15

The Master said, "The determined individual and the person of virtue will not seek to live at the expense of injuring their virtue. They will even sacrifice their lives to preserve their virtue complete."

Tsze-kung asked about the practice of virtue. The Master said, "The mechanic, who wishes to do his work well, must first sharpen his tools. When you are living in any state, take service with the most worthy among its great officials, and make friends of the most virtuous among its citizens."

The Master said, "If people take no thought about what is distant, they will find sorrow near at hand.

"Those who require much from themselves and little from others, will keep themselves from being the object of resentment.

"When a person is not in the habit of saying, 'What shall I think of this? What shall I think of this?' I can indeed do nothing with him/her!

"When a number of people are together for a whole day without their conversation turning on righteousness, and when they are fond of carrying out the suggestions of a small shrewdness, theirs is indeed a hard case.

"Superior individuals in everything consider righteousness to be essential. They perform it according to the rules of propriety. They bring it forth in humility. They complete it with sincerity. These are indeed superior people.

"Superior individuals are distressed by their want of ability. They are not distressed by people's not knowing them.

"Superior people are dignified and do not wrangle. They are sociable but not partisan."

Tsze-kung asked, saying, "Is there one word which may serve as a rule of practice for all one's life?" The Master said, "Is not reciprocity such a word? What you do not want done to yourself, do not do to others."

The Master said, "Deceptive words confound virtue. Want of forbearance in small matters confounds great plans.

"When the multitude hate a person, it is necessary to examine into the case. When the multitude like a person, it is necessary to examine into the case.

"The object of superior people is truth. Food is not their object. There is ploughing; even in that there is sometimes want. So with learning—profit may be found in it. Superior people are anxious lest they should not get truth; they are not anxious lest poverty should come upon them.

"In teaching there should be no distinction of social or economic classes."

Book 16

Confucius said, "There are three friendships which are advantageous, and three which are injurious. Friendship with the upright; friendship with the sincere; and friendship with the person of much observation—these are advantageous. Friendship with the person of specious airs; friendship with the insinuatingly soft; and friendship with the glib-tongued—these are injurious.

"There are three errors to which they who stand in the presence of a person of virtue and station are liable. They may speak when it does not come to them to speak; this is called rashness. They may not speak when it comes to them to speak; this is called concealment. They may speak without looking at the countenance of their superior; this is called blindness.

"There are three things which superior people guard against. In youth, when the physical powers are not yet settled, they guard against lust. When they are strong, and the physical powers are full of vigor, they guard against quarrelsomeness. When they are old, and the animal powers are decayed, they guard against covetousness.

"There are three things of which superior people stand in awe. They stand in awe of the ordinances of life. They stand in awe of great people. They stand in awe of the words of sages. Inferior people do not know the ordinances of life, and consequently do not stand in awe of them. They are disrespectful to great people. They make sport of the words of sages.

"Superior people have nine things which are subjects with them of thoughtful consideration. In regard to the use of their eyes, they are anxious to see clearly. In regard to the use of their ears, they are anxious to hear distinctly. In regard to their countenance, they are anxious that it should be benign. In regard to their speech, they are anxious that it should be sincere. In regard to their doing of business, they are anxious that it should be reverently careful. In regard to what they wonder about, they are anxious to question others. When they are angry, they think of the difficulties their anger may involve them in. When they are tempted to seek their own, they think of righteousness!"

Book 17

Tsze-chang asked Confucius about virtue. Confucius said, "To be able to practice five things everywhere constitutes virtue." He begged to ask what they were, and was told, "Gravity, generosity of soul, sincerity, earnestness, and kindness. If you are grave, you will not often be treated with disrespect. If you are generous, you will gain true friends. If you are sincere, people will repose trust in you. If you are earnest, you will accomplish much. If you are kind, this will enable you to employ the services of others."

The Master said, "Yu, have you heard the six words to which are attached six principles?" Yu replied, "I have not." "Sit down and I will tell them to you.

"There is the love of being benevolent without the love of learning (about life); the beclouding here leads to a foolish simplicity. There is the love of knowing without the love of learning; the beclouding here leads to dissipation of mind. There is the love of being sincere without the love of learning; the beclouding here leads to an injurious disregard of consequences. There is the love of straightforwardness without the love of learning; the beclouding here leads to rudeness. There is the love of boldness without the love of learning; the beclouding here leads to insubordination. There is the love of firmness without the love of learning; the beclouding here leads to extravagant conduct."

The Master said, "Hard is it to deal with those who will stuff themselves with food the whole day, without applying their minds to anything good! Are there not gamesters and chess players? To be one of these would still be better than doing nothing really constructive."

Tsze-lu said, "Does the superior person esteem valor?" The Master said, "The superior person holds righteousness to be of the highest importance. A person in a superior situation, having valor without righteousness, will be guilty of insubordination. One of the lower people, having valor without righteousness, will commit robbery."

Tsze-kung said, "Do superior people have their hatreds also?" The Master said, "They have their hatreds, but they are of evils and not of total personalities, because no person is completely evil. They hate the idea of proclaiming the evil of others. They hate the practice of slandering superiors. They hate the idea of valor merely, and not being observant of propriety. They try to help those who are forward and determined, and at the same time, of real understanding."

Book 18

Tsze-chang said, "People trained for public duty, seeing threatening danger, are prepared to sacrifice their lives. When the opportunity of gain is presented to them, they think first of righteousness. In making sacrifices for the common good, their thoughts are reverential. In mourning, their thoughts are about the grief which they should feel. Such a person commands our approbation indeed."

The disciples of Tsze-hsia asked Tsze-chang about the principles that should characterize mutual intercourse. Tsze-chang asked, "What does Tsze-hsia say on the subject?" They replied, "Tsze-hsia says: 'Associate with those who can advantage you. Put away from you those who cannot do so.'" Tsze-chang observed, "This is different from what I have learned. The superior person honors the talented and virtuous, and bears with all. They praise the good, and pity the incompetent. Am I possessed of great talents and virtue? Who is there among us whom I will not bear with? Am I devoid of talents and virtue? People will put me away from them. What have we to do with the putting away of others?"

Tsze-hsia said, "Even in inferior studies and employments there is something worth being looked at; but if it be attempted to carry them out to what is remote, there is a danger of their proving inapplicable. Therefore, the superior person does not practice them."

Book 19

Tsze-chang asked Confucius, saying, "In what way should people in authority act in order that they may conduct government properly?" The Master replied, "Let them honor the five excellent, and banish away the four bad, things; then may they conduct government properly." Tsze-chang said, "What are meant by the five excellent things?" The Master said, "When people in authority are beneficent without great expenditure; when they lay tasks on the people without their repining; when they pursue what they desire without being covetous; when they maintain a dignified ease without being haughty; when they are majestic without being fierce."

Tsze-chang said, "What is meant by being beneficent without great expenditure?" The Master replied, "When the person in authority makes more beneficial to the people the things from which they naturally derive benefit; is not this being beneficent without great expenditure? When he chooses the labors which are proper and asks the people to labor on them, who will repine? When his desires are set on benevolent government, and he secures it, who will accuse him of covetousness? Whether he has to do with many people or few, or with things great or small, he does not dare to indicate any disrespect; is not this to maintain a dignified ease without any haughtiness? He adjusts his clothes and cap, and throws a dignity into his looks, so that, thus dignified, he is looked at with awe; is not this to be majestic without being fierce?"

Tsze-chang then asked, "What are meant by the four bad things?" The Master said, "To put the people to death; this is called cruelty. To require from them, suddenly, the full amount of work, without having given them warning; this is called oppression. To issue orders as if without urgency, at first, and, when the time comes, to insist on them with severity; this is called injury. And, generally in the giving of pay or reward, to do it in a stingy way; this is called acting the part of a mere official."

The Master said, "Without recognizing the ordinances of life, it is impossible to be a superior person. Without an acquaintance with the rules of propriety, it is impossible for character to be established. Without knowing the force of words, it is impossible to know others."

THE GREAT LEARNING

What the Great Learning teaches is to illustrate illustrious virtue; to renovate the people; and to rest in the highest excellence.

The point at which to rest being known, the object of pursuit is then determined; and, that being determined, a calm state may be attained to. To that calmness there will succeed a tranquil repose. In that repose there may be careful deliberation, and that deliberation will be followed by the attainment of the desired end.

Things have their root and their branches. Affairs have their end and their beginning. To know what is first and what is last will lead to what is taught in the Great Learning.

The ancients who wished to illustrate illustrious virtue throughout the kingdom first ordered well their own states. Wishing to order well their states, they first regulated their families. Wishing to regulate their families, they first cultivated their persons. Wishing to cultivate their persons, they first rectified their hearts. Wishing to rectify their hearts, they first sought to be sincere in their thoughts. Wishing to be sincere in their thoughts, they first extended to the utmost their understanding. Such extension of understanding lay in the investigation of things.

Things being investigated, understanding became complete. Their understanding being complete, their thoughts were sincere. Their thoughts being sincere, their hearts were then rectified. Their hearts being rectified, their persons were cultivated. Their persons being cultivated, their families were regulated. Their families being regulated, their states were rightly governed. Their states being rightly governed, the whole kingdom was made tranquil and happy.

From the greatest of individuals to the mass of the people, all must consider the cultivation of the person the root of everything.

It cannot be, when the root is neglected, that what should spring from it will be well ordered. It seldom has been the case that what was of great importance has been poorly cared for, and, at the same time, that what was of slight importance has been properly cared for.

THE DOCTRINE OF THE STEADFAST MEAN

My master, the philosopher Ch'ang, says: "Being without inclination to any excess is called Balance; admitting of no change is called Steadfastness. By Balance is denoted the correct course to be pursued by all people; by Steadfastness is denoted the fixed principle regulating all people. This work contains the law of the mind, which should be handed down from one to another, lest in the course of time errors arise about it. The book first speaks of one principle; it next spreads this out, and embraces all things; finally, it returns, and gathers them all up under the one principle. Unroll it, and it fills the universe; roll it up, and it retires and lies hid in mysteriousness. The relish of it is inexhaustible. The whole of it is solid learning. When skillful readers have explored it with delight till they have apprehended it, they may carry it into practice all their lives and will find that it cannot be exhausted."

What has been conferred is called The Nature; an accordance with this nature is called The Path of Duty; the regulation of this path is called Instruction. The path should not be left for an instant. On this account, superior people do not wait till they see things to be cautious, nor till they hear things to be apprehensive.

There is nothing more visible than what is secret, and nothing more manifest than what is minute. Therefore, superior people are watchful over themselves when they are alone.

While there are no stirrings of pleasure, anger, misery, or exultation, the mind may be said to be in the state of Equilibrium. When those feelings have been stirred, and they act in their due degree, there ensues what may be called the state of Harmony. This Equilibrium is the great root from which grow all the human actions in the world, and this Harmony is the universal path which all should pursue. Let the states of equilibrium and harmony exist in perfection, and a happy order will prevail throughout the earth, and all things will be nourished and flourish.

The Master said, "Perfect is the virtue which is according to the Mean! Rarely have they been among the people who could practice it!

"I know how it is that the path of the Mean is not walked in: The knowing go beyond it, and the stupid do not come up to it. I know how it is that the path of the Mean is not understood: The people of talents and virtue go beyond it, and the worthless do not come up to it.

"People all say, 'We are wise'; but being driven forward and taken in a net, a trap, or a pitfall, they know not how to escape. People all say, 'We are wise'; but happening to choose the course of the Mean, they are not able to keep it for a full month.

"The kingdom, its states, and its families, may be perfectly ruled; dignities and emoluments may be declined; naked weapons may be trampled under the feet; but the course of the Mean cannot so easily be attained to."

Tsze-lu asked about energy. The Master said, "Do you mean the energy of the South, the energy of the North, or the energy which you should cultivate yourself?

"To show forbearance and gentleness in teaching others; and not to revenge unreasonable conduct—this is the energy of awakening life, and the good person makes it his/her study.

"To die under arms and meet death without regret—this is the energy of the world server, and the forceful make it their study.

"Therefore, superior people cultivate a friendly harmony, without being weak. How firm they are in their energy! They stand erect in the middle, without inclining to either side. How firm they are in their energy! When good principles prevail in the government of their country, they do not change from what they were in retirement. How firm they are in their energy! When bad principles prevail in the country, they maintain their course to death without changing. How firm they are in their energy!"

The way which superior people pursue reaches wide and far, and yet is secret. Common men and women, however ignorant, may meddle with the knowledge of it; yet in its utmost reaches, there is that which even the sage is not able to carry into practice. Great as the earth is, people still find some things in it with which to be dissatisfied. Thus it is that, were superior people to speak of their way in all its greatness, nothing in the world would be found able to embrace it, and were they to speak of it in its minuteness, nothing in the world would be found able to split it.

The Master said, "The path is not far from us. When we try to pursue a course which is far from the common indications of consciousness, this course cannot be considered The Path.

When individuals cultivate to the utmost the principles of their nature, and exercise them on the principle of reciprocity, they are not far from the path. What you do not like when done to yourself, do not do to others.

"In the way of superior people there are four things, to not one of which have I as yet attained. To serve my parent as I would wish my child to serve me: to this I have not attained; to serve my workers as I would wish my minister to serve me: to this I have not attained; to serve my elder brother as I would wish my younger brother to serve me: to this I have not attained; to set the example in behaving to a friend as I would wish him to behave to me: to this I have not attained. Earnest in practicing the ordinary virtues, and careful in speaking about them, if in our practice we have anything defective, superior people dare not but exert themselves; and if, in their words, they have any excess, they dare not allow themselves such license. Thus their words have respect to their actions, and their actions have respect to their words; is it not just an entire sincerity which marks superior people?"

Superior people do what is proper to the station in which they are; they do not desire to go beyond this.

In a position of wealth and honor, superior people do what is proper to a position of wealth and honor. In a poor and low position they do what is proper to a poor and low position. Situated among barbarous tribes, they do what is proper to a situation among barbarous tribes. In a position of sorrow and difficulty, they do what is proper to a position of sorrow and difficulty. Superior people can find themselves in no situation in which they are not themselves.

In a high situation, they do not treat with contempt their inferiors. In a low situation, they do not court the favor of their superiors. They rectify themselves and seek for nothing from others, so that they have no dissatisfactions. They do not murmur against life, nor grumble against others.

Thus it is that superior people are quiet and calm, waiting for the appointments of life, while inferior people walk in dangerous paths, looking for lucky occurrences.

It is said, "Happy union with wife and children is like the music of lutes and harps. When there is concord among all life, the harmony is delightful and enduring. Thus may you regulate your family, and enjoy the pleasure of your wife and children."

Then duke Ai asked about government.

The Master said, "The government of Wan and Wu is displayed in the records. Let there be the leaders, and the government will flourish; but without the leaders, their government decays and ceases. With the right leaders the growth of government is rapid, just as vegetation is rapid in the earth; and moreover their government might be called an easily growing rush. Therefore the administration of government lies in getting proper leaders. Such leaders are to be gotten by means of the ruler's own character. The character is to be cultivated by his/her treading in the ways of duty. And treading those ways of duty is to be cultivated by the cherishing of benevolence.

"Benevolence is the characteristic element of humanity, and the great exercise of it is in loving relatives. Righteousness is the accordance of actions with what is right, and the great exercise of it is in honoring the worthy. The decreasing measures of the love due to relatives, and the steps in the honor due to the worthy are produced by the principle of propriety.

"The duties of universal obligation are five, and the virtues wherewith they are practiced are three. The duties are those between sovereign and minister, between father and son, between husband and wife, between elder brother and younger, and those belonging to the intercourse of friends. Those five are the duties of universal obligation. Understanding, magnanimity, and energy— these three are the virtues universally binding. And the means by which they carry the duties into practice is singleness. Some are born with the knowledge of those duties; some know them by study; and some acquire the knowledge after a painful feeling of their ignorance. But the knowledge being possessed, it comes to the same thing. Some practice them with a natural ease; some from a desire for their advantages; and some by strenuous effort. But the achievement being made, it comes to the same thing."

The Master said, "To be fond of learning about life is to be near to understanding. To practice with vigor is to be near to magnanimity. To possess the feeling of humility is to be near to energy. Those who know these three things, know how to cultivate their own character. Knowing how to cultivate their own character, they know how to govern other people. Knowing how to govern other people, they know how to govern the kingdom with all its states and families.

"All who have the government of the kingdom with its states and families have nine standard rules to follow—namely, the cultivation of their own characters; the honoring of people of virtue and talents; affection toward their relatives; respect toward the great ministers; kind and considerate treatment of the whole body of officers; dealing with the mass of the people as children; encouraging recourse to all classes of artisans; indulgent treatment of people from a distance; and the kindly cherishing of the leaders of the states.

"In all things success depends on previous preparation, and without such previous preparation there is sure to be failure. If what is to be spoken be previously determined, there will be no stumbling. If affairs be previously determined, there will be no difficulty with them. If one's actions have been previously determined, there will be no sorrow in connection with them. If principles of conduct have been previously determined, the practice of them will be inexhaustible.

"Sincerity is the way of life. The attainment of sincerity is the way of superior people. Those who possess sincerity are those who, without an effort, hit what is right, and apprehend without the exercise of rationality; they are the ones who naturally and easily embody the right way. Those who attain to sincerity are those who choose what is good, and firmly hold it fast. To this attainment there are requisite the extensive study of what is good, accurate inquiry about it, careful reflection on it, the clear discrimination of it, and the earnest practice of it.

"Superior people, while there is anything they have not studied, or while in what they have studied there is anything they cannot understand, will not intermit their labor. While there is anything they have not inquired about, or anything in what they have inquired about which they do not know, they will not intermit their labor. While there is anything which they have not reflected on, or anything in what they have reflected on which they do not apprehend, they will not intermit their labor. While there is anything which they have not discriminated, or their discrimination is not clear, they will not intermit their labor. If other people succeed by one effort, they will use a hundred efforts. If other people succeed by ten efforts, they will use a thousand. Let people proceed in this way, and, though dull, they will surely become intelligent; though weak, they will surely become strong."

' Sincerity is that whereby self-completion is effected, and its way is that by which we must direct ourselves. Sincerity is the end and beginning of things; without sincerity there would be nothing. On this account, superior people regard the attainment of sincerity as a most excellent thing. Possessors of sincerity do not merely accomplish the self-completion of themselves. With this quality they complete other people and things also. The completing of ourselves shows our perfect virtue. The completing of other people and things shows our knowledge. Both of these are virtues belonging to our nature, and this is the way by which a union is effected of the external and internal. Therefore, whenever we—the sincere people—employ these virtues, our actions will be right.

The heavens now before us appear only as a bright surface; but when viewed in their inexhaustible extent, the sun, moon, stars, and constellations of the zodiac are in them, and all things are covered by them. The earth before us is but a handful of soil; but when regarded in its breadth and thickness, it sustains huge mountains without feeling their weight, and contains the rivers and seas, without their leaking away. The mountain now before us appears only as a stone; but when contemplated in all the vastness of its size, we see how the grass and trees are produced on it, and birds and beasts dwell on it, and precious things which we treasure are found on it. The water now before us appears but a small amount; yet extending our view to its unfathomable depth, the largest tortoises, fishes, and turtles are produced in it, articles of value and sources of wealth abound in it.

The Master said, "Let those who are ignorant be fond of using their own judgment; let those without rank be fond of assuming a directing power to themselves; let those who are living in the present age go back to the ways of antiquity; to the persons who act thus, calamities will be sure to come."

All things are nourished together without their injuring one another. The courses of the seasons, and of the sun and moon, are pursued without any collision among them. The smaller energies are like river currents; the greater energies are seen in mighty transformations. It is this which makes the universe so great.

It is only those possessed of all mature qualities that can exist adequately in the world, who show themselves quick in apprehension, clear in discernment, of far-reaching intelligence, and all-embracing understanding, fitted to maintain a firm hold. They are self-adjusted, grave, never swerving from the Mean, and correctly fitted to command reverence; accomplished, distinctive, focused, and searching, fitted to exercise discrimination. All-embracing are they and vast, deep and active as a fountain, sending forth in their due season their virtues.

All-embracing and vast, they are like the universe. Deep and active as a fountain, they are like the abyss. They are seen, and people revere them; they speak, and the people believe them; they act, and the people are pleased with them.

Hence, their fame, in the course of time, covers the world, and extends to all people. Wherever ships and planes reach; wherever the ships and planes reach; wherever the strength of those individuals penetrates; wherever the skies overshadow and the earth sustains; wherever the sun shines, wherever frosts and dews fall; the majority who have blood and breath sincerely honor and love them. Hence it is said, "They are above all others."

It is only the individuals possessed of the most entire sincerity that can exist adequately in the world, who can adjust the great invariable relations of humanity, and know the transforming and nurturing operations of the universe. Do these individuals have any supernatural being beyond themselves on which they depend?

Call them humanity in its ideal, how earnest are they! Call them an abyss, how deep are they! Call them the universe, how vast are they!

Who can know them but those who are indeed quick in apprehension, clear in discernment of far-reaching intelligence and all-embracing understanding, possessing all virtue?

THE WORKS OF MENCIUS

The Perfect Government

Mencius went to see King Hwuy of Leang. The king said, "Venerable sir, since you have not counted it far to come here, a distance of a thousand miles, may I presume that you are likewise provided with counsels to profit my kingdom?" Mencius replied, "Why must Your Majesty use that word profit? What I am 'likewise' provided with counsels to benevolence and righteousness, and these are my only topics.

"If Your Majesty says, 'What is to be done to profit my kingdom?' and the inferior officers and the common people will say, 'What is to be done to profit our persons?' Superiors and inferiors will try to snatch this profit the one from the other, and the kingdom will be endangered. In the kingdom of ten thousand chariots, the murderer of his sovereign shall be the chief of a family of a thousand chariots. In a kingdom of a thousand chariots, the murderer of his prince shall be the chief of a family of a hundred chariots. To have a thousand in ten thousand, and a hundred in a thousand, cannot be said not to be a large allotment; but if righteousness be put last, and profit be put first, they will not be satisfied without snatching all.

"There never have been people trained in benevolence who neglected their parents. There never have been people trained in righteousness who made their sovereign an after-consideration.

"Let Your Majesty also say, 'Benevolence and righteousness, and these shall be the only themes.' Why must you use that word, 'profit'?"

Mencius, another day, saw King Hwuy of Leang. The king went and stood with him by a pond, and, looking around at the large geese and deer, said, "Do wise and good princes also find pleasure in these things without killing them?"

King Hwuy of Leang said, "Small as my virtue is, in the government of my kingdom I do indeed exert my mind to the utmost. If the year be bad on the west of the river, I remove as many of the people as I can to the east of the river, and convey grain to the country on the west. When the year is bad on the east of the river, I act on the same plan. On examining the government of the neighboring kingdoms, I do not find that there is any prince who employs his mind as I do. And yet the people of the neighboring kingdoms do not decrease, nor do my people increase. How is this?"

Mencius replied, "Your Majesty is fond of war; let me take an illustration from war: The soldiers move forward to the sound of the drums; and after their weapons have been crossed, on one side they throw away their coats of mail, trail their arms behind them, and run. Some run a hundred paces and stop; some run fifty paces and stop. What would you think if those who run fifty paces were to laugh at those who run a hundred paces?" The king said, "They may not do so. They merely did not run a hundred paces; but they also ran away." "Since Your Majesty knows this," replied Mencius, "you need not hope that your people will become more numerous than those of the neighboring kingdoms.

"If the seasons of husbandry are not interfered with, the grain will be more than can be eaten. If close nets are not allowed to enter the pools and ponds, the fishes and turtles will be more than can be consumed. If the axes and saws enter the hills and forests only at the proper time, the wood will be more than can be used. When the grain and fish and turtles are more than can be eaten, and there is more wood than can be used, this enables the people to nourish their living and bury their dead, without any feeling against one another. This condition, in which the people nourish their living and bury their dead without any feeling against one another, is the first step of royal government.

"Let mulberry trees be planted about the homesteads, and persons of fifty years may be clothed with silk. In keeping fowl, pigs, dogs, and swine, let not their times of breeding be neglected, and persons of seventy years may eat flesh. Let there not be taken away the time that is proper for the cultivation of the farm, and the family of several mouths that is supported by it shall not suffer from hunger. Let careful attention by paid to education in schools, inculcating in it especially the filial and fraternal duties, and gray-haired people will not be seen upon roads, carrying heavy burdens. It never has been that the ruler of a state where such results were seen—persons of seventy wearing silk and eating flesh, and people suffering neither from hunger nor cold—did not attain to the imperial dignity.

"Your dogs and swine eat the food of humans, and you do not know enough to make any restrictive arrangements. There are people dying from famine on the roads, and you do not know enough to issue the stores of your granaries for them. When people die, you say, 'It is not owing to me; it is owing to the year.' In what does this differ from stabbing a person and killing him/her, and then saying, 'It was not I; it was the weapon'? Let Your Majesty cease to lay the blame on the year, and from all the empire the people will come to you."

King Hwuy of Leang said, "I wish quietly to receive your instructions."

Mencius replied, "Is there any difference between killing a person with a stick and with a sword?" The king said, "There is no difference."

"Is there any difference between doing it with a sword and with the style of government?" "There is no difference," was the reply.

Mencius then said, "In your kitchen there is fat meat; in your stables there are fat horses. But your people have the look of hunger, and on the wilds there are those who have died of famine. This is leading on beasts to devour people. Beasts devour one another, and people hate them for doing so. When rulers, being the guardians of their people, administer their government so as to be chargeable with leading on beasts to devour people, where is their proper relation to the people?"

Mencius went to see the king Seang of Leang. On coming out from the interview, he said to some persons, "When I looked at him from a distance, he did not appear like a sovereign; when I drew near to him, I saw nothing venerable about him. Abruptly he asked me, 'How can the empire be settled?' I replied, 'It will be settled by being united under one sway.'

"'Who can so unite it?'

"I replied, 'Those who have no pleasure in killing people can so unite it.'

"'Who can give it to him?'

"I replied, 'All the people of the empire will unanimously give it to him. Does Your Majesty understand the way of the growing grain? During the seventh and eighth months, when drought prevails, the plants become dry. Then the clouds collect densely in the skies, by a shoot. When it does so, who can keep it back? Now among the shepherds of people throughout the empire, there is not one who does not find pleasure in killing others, all the people in the empire would look toward him/her with outstretched necks.

Such being indeed the case, the people would come as water flows downwards, which no one can repress.'"

The king said, "What virtue must there be in order to attain the imperial sway?" Mencius answered, "The love and protection of the people; with this there is no power which can prevent a ruler from attaining it."

The king asked again, "Is such a one as I competent to love and protect the people?" Mencius said, "Yes." "From what do you know that I am competent to do that?" "I heard the following incident from Hoo Heih: 'The king,' said he, 'was sitting aloft in the hall, when a man appeared, leading an ox past the lower part of it. The king saw him, and asked, "Where is the ox going?" The man replied, "We are going to consecrate a bell with its blood." The king said, "Let it go. I cannot bear its frightened appearance as if it were an innocent person being put to death." The man answered, "Shall we then omit the consecration of the bell?" The king said, "How can that be omitted? Change it for a sheep." ' I do not know whether this incident really occurred."

The king replied, "It did," and then Mencius said, "The heart seen in this is sufficient to carry you to the imperial sway. The people all supposed that your ruler grudged the animal, but your servant knows, surely, that it was your ruler's not being able to bear the sight, which made you do as you did."

The king said, "You are right. And yet there really was an appearance of what the people condemned. But though Ts'e be a small and narrow state, how should I grudge one ox? Indeed it was because I could not bear its frightened appearance, as if it were an innocent person being put to death, that therefore I changed if for a sheep."

"There is no harm in their saying so," said Mencius. "Your conduct was an artifice of benevolence. You saw the ox, and had not seen the sheep. So are superior persons affected toward animals, that, having seen them alive, they cannot bear to see them die; having heard their dying cries, they cannot bear to eat their flesh. Therefore they keep away from the cook-room."

The king was pleased, and replied, "It is said, 'The minds of others, I am able by reflection to measure.' This is verified, my Master, in your discovery of my motive. I indeed did the thing, but when I turned my thoughts inward, and examined into it, I could not discover my own mind. When you, Master, spoke these words, the movements of compassion began to work in my mind. How is it that this heart has in it what is equal to the imperial sway?"

Mencius replied, "Suppose a person were to make this statement to Your Majesty: 'My strength is sufficient to lift three thousand pounds, but it is not sufficient to lift one feather (my eyesight is sharp enough to examine the point of an autumn hair, but I do not see a wagonload of faggots)—would Your Majesty allow what he said?" "No" was the answer, on which Mencius proceeded, "Now here is kindness sufficient to reach to animals, and no benefits are extended from it to the people. How is this? Is an exception to be made here? The truth is, the feather's not being lifted is because the strength is not used; the wagonload of firewood's not being seen is because the vision is not used; and the people's not being loved and protected is because kindness is not employed. Therefore Your Majesty's not exercising the imperial sway is because you do not do it, not because you are not able to do it."

The king asked, "How may the difference between not doing a thing, and not being able to do it, be represented?" Mencius replied, "In such a thing as taking a mountain under your arm, and leaping over an ocean with it, if you say to people, 'I am not able to do it,' that is a real case of not being able. In such a matter as breaking off a branch from a tree at the order of a superior, if you say to people, 'I am not able to do it,' that is a case of not doing it; it is not a case of not being able to do it. Therefore Your Majesty's not exercising the imperial sway is not such a case as that of taking a mountain under your arm, and leaping over an ocean with it. Your Majesty's not exercising the imperial sway is a case like that of breaking off a branch from a tree.

"Treat with the reverence due to age the elders in your own family, so that the elders in the families of others shall be similarly treated; treat with the kindness due to youth the young in your own family, so that the young in the families of others shall be similarly treated; do this, and the empire may be made to go around in your palm. It is said, 'His example affected his wife. It reached to his brothers, and his family in the state was governed by it.' The language shows how a king simply took this kindly heart and exercised it toward those parties. Therefore the carrying out his kindly heart by a prince will suffice for the love and protection of all people, and if he does not carry it out, he will not be able to protect his wife and children. The way in which the ancients came greatly to

surpass other people was no other than this: simply that they knew
well how to carry out, so as to affect others, what they themselves
did. Now your kindness is sufficient to reach to animals, and no
benefits are extended from it to reach the people. How is this? Is
an exception to be made here?

"You collect your equipment of war, endanger your soldiers and
officers, and excite the resentment of others; do these things give
you pleasure?"

The king replied, "No. How should I derive pleasure from these
things? My object in them is to seek for what I greatly desire."

Mencius said, "May I hear from you what it is that you greatly desire?" The king laughed and did not speak. Mencius resumed, "Are
you led to desire it because you have not enough rich and sweet
food for your mouth? Or because you have not enough light and
warm clothing for your body? Or because you have not enough
beautifully colored objects to delight your eyes? Or because you
have not voices and tones enough to please your ears? Or because
you have not enough attendants and favorites to stand before you
and receive your orders? Your Majesty's various officers are sufficient to supply you with those things. How can Your Majesty be
led to entertain such a desire on account of them?" "No," said the
king; "my desire is not on account of them." Mencius added,
"Then, what Your Majesty greatly desires may be known. You wish
to enlarge your territories, to have a large number of people wait at
your court, to rule many lands, and to attract to you the people you
rule. But to do what you do to seek for what you desire, is like
climbing a tree to seek for fish."

The king said, "Is it as bad as that?" "It is even worse," was the
reply. "If you climb a tree to seek for fish, although you do not get
the fish, you will not suffer any subsequent calamity. But if you do
what you do to seek for what you desire, doing it moreover with all
your heart, you will assuredly afterwards meet with calamities." The
king asked, "May I hear from you the proof of that?" Mencius said,
"If the people of a small state should fight with the people of a
large state, which of them does Your Majesty think would conquer?" "The people of the large state would conquer." "Yes; and so
it is certain that a small country cannot contend with a great, that
few cannot contend with many, that the weak cannot contend with
the strong. All of your territory together is but one-ninth of the
total. If with one part you try to subdue the other eight, what is the

difference between that and a small state's contending with a large? For, with the desire which you have, you must likewise turn back to the radical course for its attainment.

"Now, if Your Majesty will institute a government whose action shall be benevolent, this will cause the officials in the empire to wish to stand in Your Majesty's marketplaces, and traveling strangers to wish to make their tours on Your Majesty's roads, and all throughout the empire who feel aggrieved by their rulers to wish to come and complain to Your Majesty. And when they are so bent, who will be able to keep them back?"

The king said, "I am stupid, and not able to advance to this. I wish you, my Master, to assist my intentions. Teach me clearly; although I am deficient in intelligence and vigor, I will essay and try to carry your instructions into effect."

Mencius replied, "They only are people of education, who, without a certain livelihood, are able to maintain a fixed heart. As to the people, if they have not a certain livelihood, it follows that they will not have a fixed heart. And if they have not a fixed heart, there is nothing which they will not do, in the way of self-abandonment, of moral deflection, of depravity, and of wild license. When they thus have been involved in crime, to follow them up and punish them—this is to entrap the people. How can such a thing as entrapping the people be done under the rule of a benevolent leader?

"Therefore an intelligent ruler will regulate the livelihood of the people, so as to make sure that they shall have sufficient wherewithal to serve their parents if necessary, and sufficient wherewithal to support their wives and children; that in good years they shall always be abundantly satisfied, and that in bad years they shall escape the danger of perishing. After this the ruler may urge them, and they will proceed to what is good, for in this case the people will follow after that with ease.

"Now, the livelihood of the people is so regulated that they have not sufficient wherewithal to serve their parents, and they have not sufficient wherewithal to support their wives and children. Notwithstanding good years, their lives are continually embittered, and, in bad years, they do not escape perishing. In such circumstances they only try to save themselves from death, and are afraid they will not succeed. What leisure have they to cultivate propriety and righteousness?

"If Your Majesty wishes to effect this regulation of the livelihood of the people, why not turn to that which is the essential step to it?

The Path to Peace

Kung-sun Ch'ow asked Mencius, saying, "Master, if you were to be appointed a high noble and the prime minister of Ts'e, so as to be able to carry your principles into practice, though you should thereupon raise the prince to be in charge of all the other princes, or even to the imperial dignity, it would not be to be wondered at. In such a position would your mind be perturbed or not?" Mencius replied, "No. At forty, I attained to an unperturbed mind."

Ch'ow said, "Since it is so with you, my master, you are far beyond Mang Pun." The mere attainment," said Mencius, "is not difficult. The scholar Kaou had attained to an unperturbed mind at an earlier period of life than I did."

"I venture to ask," said Ch'ow, "Wherein you, Master, surpass Kaou." Mencius told him, "I understand more. I am skillful in nourishing my vast, flowing happiness."

Ch'ow pursued, "I venture to ask what you mean by your vast, flowing happiness!" The reply was, "It is difficult to describe it.

"This is the feeling of happiness: It is exceedingly great, and exceedingly strong. Being nourished by rectitude, and sustaining no injury, it fills up all in the universe.

"This is the feeling—happiness: It is the mate and assistant of righteousness and reason. Without it, people are in a state of starvation.

"It is produced by the accumulation of righteous deeds; it is not to be obtained by incidental acts of righteousness. If the mind does not feel calmness in the conduct, the nature becomes starved. I therefore said, 'Kaou has never understood righteousness, because he makes it something external.'

"There must be the constant practice of this righteousness, but without the object merely of nourishing the feeling of happiness. Let not the mind forget its work, but let there be no impatience regarding the growth of that feeling. Let us not be like the man of Sung. There was a man of Sung, who was grieved that his growing corn was not longer, and so he pulled it up. Having done this, he returned home, looking very stupid, and said to his people, 'I am tired today. I have been helping the corn to grow long.' His son ran to look at it, and found the corn all withered. There are few in the world who do not deal with their desire for happiness as if they were assisting the corn to grow long. Some indeed consider it of no benefit to them, and let it alone—they do not weed their corn. What they do is not only of no benefit to the desire, but it also frustrates it."

Mencius said, "Those who, using force, make a pretense to benevolence are the leaders of the princes. Leaders of the princes require a large kingdom. Those who, using virtue, practice benevolence are the sovereigns of the empire. To become the sovereign of the empire, a prince need not wait for a large kingdom.

"When one by force subdues people, they do not submit in heart. They submit because their strength is not adequate to resist. When one subdues people by virtue, in their heart's core they are pleased, and sincerely submit, as was the case with the seventy disciples in their submission to Confucius. What is often said,

From the west, from the east,
From the south, from the north,

There was not one who thought of refusing submission, is an illustration of this."

Mencius said, "Most people have a mind which cannot bear to see the sufferings of others.

"The ancient kings had this commiserating mind, and they, as a matter of course, had likewise a commiserating government. When with a commiserating mind was practiced a commiserating government, the government of the empire was as easy a matter as making anything go around in the palm.

"When I say that most people have a mind which cannot bear to see the sufferings of others, my moaning may be illustrated thus: Even nowadays, if individuals suddenly see a child about to fall into a well, they will experience a feeling of alarm and distress. They will feel so, not as a ground on which they may seek the praise of their neighbors and friends, nor from a dislike to the reputation of having been unmoved by such a thing.

"From this case we may perceive that the feeling of commiseration is essential, that the feeling of humility is essential, that the feeling of modesty is essential, and that the feeling of approving and disapproving is essential.

"The feeling of commiseration is the principle of benevolence. The feeling of humility is the principle of righteousness. The feeling of modesty is the principle of propriety. The feeling of approving and disapproving is the principle of true knowledge.

"From the want of benevolence and the want of wisdom will ensue the absence of propriety and righteousness; those who are in such a case must be the inferior of other people. To be the inferior of others and yet ashamed of such inferiority is like a bow-maker's being ashamed to make bows, or an arrow-maker's being ashamed to make arrows.

"If you are ashamed of your case, your best course is to practice benevolence. People who would be benevolent are like archers. Archers adjust themselves and then shoot. If they miss, they do not murmur against those who surpass them. They simply turn around and seek the cause of their failure in themselves."

Mencius said, "When individuals told Tsze-loo that they had faults, he rejoiced. The great Shun had a still greater delight in what was good. He regarded virtue as the common property of himself and others, giving up his own inferior ways to follow the superior ways of others, and delighting to learn from others to practice what was good.

"To take example from others to practice virtue is to help them in the same practice. Therefore, there is no attribute of superior persons greater than their helping others to practice virtue."

The Root of the State

Mencius said, "With those who do violence to themselves, it is impossible to speak. With those who throw themselves away, it is impossible to do anything. To disown in your conversation propriety and righteousness is what we mean by doing violence to one's self. To say, 'I am not able to dwell in benevolence or pursue the path of righteousness' is what we mean by throwing one's self away.

"Benevolence is the tranquil habitation of individuals, and righteousness is their straight path.

"Alas for them, who leave the tranquil dwelling empty, and do not reside in it, and who abandon the right path and do not pursue it!"

Mencius said, "When those occupying inferior situations do not obtain the confidence of the sovereign, they cannot succeed in governing the people. There is a way to obtain the confidence of the sovereign: if you are not trusted by your friends, you will not obtain the confidence of true sovereign. There is a way of being trusted by your friends: if you do not serve your parents so as to make them pleased, you will not be trusted by your friends. There is a way to make your parents pleased: if you, on turning your thoughts inwards, find a lack of sincerity, you will not give pleasure to your parents. There is a way to the attainment of sincerity in yourself: if you do not understand what is good, you will not attain sincerity in yourself.

"Therefore, sincerity is the basis of religious living. To think how to be sincere is the way of superior people.

"Never has there been one possessed of complete sincerity, who did not move others. Never has there been one who had not sincerity who was able to move others profoundly.

Mencius said, "Acts of propriety which are not really proper, and acts of righteousness which are not really righteous, the great person does not do.

"Those who keep the Mean, train up those who do not, and those who have abilities, train up those who have not, and hence people rejoice in having associates who are possessed of virtue and talent. If they who keep the Mean spurn those who do not, and they who have abilities spurn those who have not, then the space between them—those so gifted and the ungifted—will not be reconcilable.

"We must be decided on what we will not do, and then we are able to act with vigor in what we ought to do. Great people do not always need to think beforehand of their words that they may be sincere, nor of their actions that they may be resolute; they simply speak and do what is right.

"The great people are those who do not lose their child's heart.

"That whereby we differ from the lower animals is but small. The mass of people cast it away, while superior individuals preserve it.

"When at first it appears proper to take a thing, and afterwards not proper, to take it is contrary to moderation. When at first it appears proper to give a thing and afterwards not proper, to give it is contrary to kindness. When at first it appears proper to sacrifice one's life, and afterwards not proper, to sacrifice it is contrary to bravery.

"Here is someone who treats me in a perverse and unreasonable manner. The superior person in such a case will turn around upon him/herself—'I must have been wanting in benevolence; I must have been wanting in propriety—how should this have happened to me?'

"We examine ourselves and are especially benevolent. We turn around upon ourselves and are especially observant of propriety. The perversity and unreasonableness of the other, however, are still the same. We will again turn around on ourselves—'I must have been failing to do my utmost.'

"Superior people turn around upon themselves and proceed to do their utmost, but still the perversity and unreasonableness of the other are repeated. At this point superior individuals would likely say, 'This is one who appears utterly lost! Since he/she carries on so, what is there to choose between that individual and a brute? Why should I go to contend with a brute? I can forgive the individual but choose not to contend with him/her.'"

Of Friendship and Gifts

Wan Chang asked Mencius saying, "I venture to ask the principles of friendship." Mencius replied, "Friendship should be maintained without any presumption on the ground of your superior age, or station, or the circumstances of your relatives. Friendship with people is friendship with their virtue and does not admit of assumptions of superiority.

"Respect shown by inferiors to superiors is called giving to the noble the observance due to rank. Respect shown by superiors to inferiors is called giving honor to talents and virtue. The rightness in each case is the same."

Wan Chang asked Mencius, saying, "I venture to ask what feeling is expressed in the presence of friendship." Mencius replied, "The feeling of respect."

Mencius said to Wan Chang, "Those whose virtue is most distinguished in a village shall make friends of the virtuous ones in the village. Those whose virtue is most distinguished throughout a state shall make friends of the virtuous ones of that state. Those whose virtue is most distinguished throughout the empire shall make friends of the virtuous ones of the empire.

"When we feel that our friendship with the virtuous ones of the empire is not sufficient to satisfy us, we proceed to ascend to consider the people of antiquity. We repeat their poems and read their books, and as we do not know what they were as individuals, to ascertain this we consider their history. This is to ascend and make friends of the ones of antiquity."

Convention and Emergency

A man of Jin asked the disciple Uh-loo, saying, "Is an observance of the rules of propriety in regard to eating, or the eating, the more important?" The answer was, "The observance of the rules of propriety is the more important."

. "Is the gratifying the appetite of sex, or the doing so only according the rules of propriety, the more important?" The answer again was, "The observance of the rules of propriety in the matter is the more important."

The man pursued, "If the result of eating only according to the rules of propriety will be death by starvation, while by disregarding those rules we may get food, must they still be observed in such a case? If according to the rule that he shall go in person to meet his wife a man cannot get married, while by disregarding that rule he may get married, must he still observe the rule in such a case?"

Uh-loo was unable to reply to these questions, so he told them to Mencius. Mencius said, "What difficulty is there in answering these inquiries?

"If you do not adjust them at their lower extremities, but only put their tops on a level, a piece of wood an inch square may be made to be higher than the pointed peak of a high building.

"Gold is heavier than feathers; but does that saying have reference, on the one hand, to a single clasp of gold, and, on the other, to a wagonload of feathers?

If you take a case where the eating is of the utmost importance and the observing the rules of propriety is of little importance, and compare the things together, why stop with saying merely that the eating is more important? So, taking the case where the gratifying the appetite of sex is of the utmost importance and the observing the rules of propriety is of little importance, why stop with merely saying that gratifying the appetite is the more important?

"Go and answer him thus, 'If, by twisting your elder brother's arm, and snatching from him what he is eating, you can get food for yourself, while, if you do not do so, you will not get anything to eat, will you so twist his arm? If by getting over your neighbor's wall, and dragging away his virgin daughter, you can get a wife, while if you do not do so, you will not be able to get a wife, will you so drag her away?'"

The Awakening of Right Motives

Sung K'ang being about to go to Ts'oo, Mencius met him and asked, "Where are you going?"

K'ang replied, "I have heard that Ts'in and Ts'oo are fighting together, and I am going to see the king of Ts'oo and persuade him to cease hostilities. If he shall not be pleased with my advice, I shall go to see the king of Ts'in, and persuade him in the same way. Of the two kings, I shall surely find that I can succeed with one of them."

Mencius said, "I will not venture to ask about the particulars, but I should like to hear the scope of your plan. What course will you take to try to persuade them?" K'ang answered, "I will tell them how unprofitable their course is to them." "Your aim is great," said Mencius, "but your argument is not good.

"If you, starting from the point of profit, offer your persuasive counsels to the kings of Ts'in and Ts'oo, and if those kings are pleased with the consideration of profit so as to stop the movements of their armies, then all belonging to those armies will rejoice in the cessation of war, and find their pleasure in the pursuit of profit. Ministers will serve their sovereign for the profit of which they cherish the thought; sons will serve their fathers, and younger brothers will serve their elder brothers, from the same consideration. The issue will then be, that, abandoning benevolence and righteousness, sovereign and minister, parent and child, younger sibling and elder, will carry on all their intercourse with this thought of profit cherished in their breasts. But never has there been such a state of society, without ruin being the result of it.

"If you, starting from the point of profit, offer your persuasive counsels to the kings of Ts'in and Ts'oo, and if those kings are pleased with the consideration of benevolence and righteousness so as to stop the operations of their armies, then all belonging to those armies will rejoice in the stopping from war, and find their pleasure in benevolence and righteousness. Ministers will serve their sovereign, cherishing the principles of benevolence and righteousness; sons will serve their fathers, and younger siblings will serve their elders, in the same way; and so, sovereign and minister, parent and child, elder sibling and younger, abandoning the thought of profit, will cherish the principles of benevolence and righteousness, and carry on all their intercourse upon them. But never has there been such a state of society, without the state where it prevailed rising to imperial sway. Why must you use that word 'profit'?"

All Things Are Complete in Us

Mencius said, "Those who have used their mental constitution to the full know their nature. Knowing their nature, they know life. To preserve our mental constitution, and nourish our nature, is the way to serve life.

"There is an appointment for everything. People should receive submissively what may be correctly ascribed thereto. Therefore, those who have the true idea of what is life's appointment will not stand beneath a precipitous wall. Death sustained in the discharge of one's duties may correctly be ascribed to the appointment of life. Death under handcuffs and fetters probably cannot be so ascribed.

"All things are already complete in us.

"If we act with a vigorous effort at the law of reciprocity, when we seek for the realization of perfect virtue, nothing can be closer than our approximation to it.

"To act without understanding, and to do so habitually without examination, pursuing the proper path all of one's life without knowing its nature—this is the way of the multitudes.

Mencius said, "Let us not do what our own sense of righteousness tells us not to do, and let us not desire what our sense of righteousness tells us not to desire; to act thus is all we have to do.

Mencius said, "If people of virtue and ability are not confided in, a state will become empty and void. Without the rules of propriety and the distinctions of right, the high and the low will be thrown into confusion. Without the great principles of government and their various business there will not be wealth sufficient for the expenditure.

"Anciently, people of virtue and talents by means of their own enlightenment made others enlightened. Nowadays, it is tried, while they are themselves in darkness, and by means of that darkness, to make others enlightened.

"There are the footpaths along the hills; if suddenly they are used, they become roads; and if as suddenly they are not used, the wild grass fills them up. Now the wild grass fills up people's minds.

"Words which are simple, while their meaning is far-reaching, are good words. Principles which, as held, are compendious, while their application is extensive, are good principles. The words of the superior person do not go below the girdle, but great principles are contained in them. The principle which the superior person holds is that of personal cultivation, and the empire is thereby tranquilized. Our disease is this: that we neglect our own fields and go to weed the fields of others, and that what we require from others is great, while what we lay upon ourselves is light.

"Those who give counsel to people in public life should show them how to live without their pomp and display. Halls thirty feet high, with beams projecting several feet—these, if my wishes were to be realized, I would not have. Food spread before me over huge tables, and attendant girls to the amount of hundreds—these, though my wishes were realized, I would not have. Excessive pleasure and wine, and the dash of hunting, with thousands of chariots following after me—these, though my wishes were realized, I would not have. What they esteem are what I would have nothing to do with; what I esteem are the rules of superior living. Why should I stand in awe of them?"

THE BOOK OF FILIAL PIETY

The Meaning of Filial Duty

Once upon a time Confucius was sitting in his study, having his disciple Tseng Ts'an to attend upon him. He asked Tseng Ts'an: "Do you know by what virtue and power the good emperors of old made the world peaceful, the people to live in harmony with one another, and the inferior contended under the control of their superiors?" To this Tseng Ts'an, rising from his seat, replied: "I do not know this, for I am not clever." Then said Confucius: "The duty of children to their parents is the fountain whence all other virtues spring, and also the starting point from which we ought to begin our education. Now take your seat, and I will explain this. Our body and hair and skin are all derived from our parents, and therefore we should not injure any of them. This is the first duty of a child.

"To live an upright life and to spread the great doctrines of humanity will win a good reputation and reflect upon our parents. This is the last duty of a child.

"Hence the first duty of children is to pay careful attention to every want of their parents. The next is to serve the government whenever its cause is just; and the last is to establish themselves as being worthy."

The Three Powers

On hearing what Confucius said about filial duty, Tseng Tze remarked: "How great is the use of filial duty!" Here Confucius continued: "Filial duty is the constant doctrine of good citizenship, the natural righteousness of life, and the practical duty of humanity. Every member of the community ought to observe it with the greatest care. We do what is taught by prophets and what is good for the general public in order to organize the community. On this account our education is widespread, and our government is sound. The effect of education upon the minds of the people was well known to the good emperors of old. They encouraged all citizens to love their parents by loving their own parents first. They induced every person to cultivate virtue by expounding the advantages of virtue to all. They behaved themselves respectfully and humbly, so that the people might not quarrel with one another. They trained the people with ceremonial observances, and educated them with the arts so that they might live in harmony. They told people what things they liked or disliked to see done, so that they might understand what they were expected not to do."

It is written: "The dignified statesperson is the proper subject of the attention of the people."

Filial Duty in Government

The good emperors of old ruled the empire by means of filial duty, and so dared not neglect the heads of their states. They thereby gained the goodwill of their people. This is what we mean by saying that the good emperors of old governed the world by filial duty.

As to the states, their rulers dared not treat widowers and widows with insolence; how then could they dare act so toward the literary class and the people? Hence they gained the goodwill of their subjects, and the latter would join them in serving the needs of the society as a whole.

Now we may say a word about families. If the heads of families do not act haughtily toward other members of the family, they will not act so to their wives and children. Hence they will gain the goodwill of all their people, and they will help them in the fulfillment of their filial duty. In such a family the parents will feel much happier than otherwise. By the principle of filial duty the whole world can be made happier, and many calamities and dangers can be averted. Such was the government of the Empire by the enlightened rulers of old, in accordance with the principle of filial duty.

It is written: "If you adorn yourself with the highest virtue, the whole world will be as your children."

The Question of Remonstrance

Tseng Tze said: "I have heard all that you said about parental love, filial love, reverence to elders, how to treat parents, and how to please them by making yourself known for good conduct; and now I will venture to ask you whether it is filial that children should obey every command of their parents, whether right or wrong?"

What do you say? What do you say?" replied Confucius. "Once upon a time there was a certain emperor who would have lost his empire through his wickedness but that he had seven good ministers who often checked his illegal actions by strong protests; there was also a baron who would have lost his estate through wantonness, but for the fact that he had five good people who often made strong protests to him; and there was also a statesperson who would have brought frightful calamity upon his family, but for the fact that he had three good servants who often strongly advised him not to do what he ought not.

"If people have good friends to resist them in doing wrongful actions, they will have their reputation preserved; so if a parent has a child to resist their wrong commands, they will be saved from committing serious faults.

"When the command is wrong, children should resist their parents, and ministers should resist their august masters". The maxim is, 'Resist when wrongly commanded.' Hence, how can we be called filial who obey our parents when they are commanded to do wrong?"

HINDU SCRIPTURES

INTRODUCTION

Hinduism is the name used to designate the religious creeds and practices of a great number of Hindus, who form the body of the oldest major religion alive today.

Upanishads

In about the eighth or seventh century B.C., a group of Hindu thinkers wrote down various speculations regarding their previously developed rituals, in a number of separate Upanishads. The Upanishads are the ending portion of each of the four vedas. They are the wisdom portion and equal the end, or goal, as well as the final portion of the Vedas. The ritual portion contains ancient rituals, prayers, and hymns.

These documents have not all been translated, or even located, but the major ones were assembled in a single volume, from which the following selections were made.

Bhagavad-Gita

The gigantic epic poem, the Mahabharata, which was written over a period of several hundred years (perhaps 500 B.C. to 250 A.D.), contained the Bhagavad-Gita, which has become the most prominent scripture for Hindus as a whole. The Gita portrays the battle of life, and is presented here as a discourse between the great teacher Krishna and his disciple Arjuna. This document brings out very clearly the variety of belief and practice which is possible in searching for the Eternal.

Sankaracharya's Atma Bodha

This short writing gives some idea of how it is possible to discover the meaning of the soul.

The Yoga Sutras of Patanjali

The Hindus, in their Yoga systems, have the most highly developed science of human discipline ever known to man. Western psychology and medicine are just today discovering how much these people learned by means of Yoga, about which technological science is still ignorant. Patanjali's system, with very little interpretation, yields a method of Self-realization that in general principle is universally applicable.

The Works of Sri Ramakrishna

The section entitled "The Works of Sri Ramakrishna," and that of "The Parables of Sri Ramakrishna," give considerable insight into the teachings of the great 19th century sage Sri Ramakrishna. The worldwide Vedanta Society has developed from his teachings, and those of his principal disciple, Swami Vivekananda. Hinduism has remained largely in India, whereas the Vedanta Society has spread globally. Swami Vivekananda was one of the major highlights of the Parliament of the World's Religions in Chicago (1893). Since the emphasis of both Ramakrishna and Vivekananda was on all religions, rather than mostly on Hinduism, many consider Vedanta to be a separate religion.

THE UPANISHADS

Isha

Life in the world and life in the spirit are not incompatible. Work, or action, is not contrary to knowledge of the Eternal, but indeed, if performed without attachment to its fruits, is a means to it. On the other hand, renunciation is renunciation of the ego, of selfishness—not of life. The end, both of work and of renunciation, is to know the Self within and the Eternal without, and to realize their identity. The Self is of the same essence as the Eternal, and the Eternal pervades all.

In the heart of all things, of whatever there is in the universe, dwells the Eternal. It above all is the reality. Therefore, renouncing vain appearances, rejoice in It. Covet nobody's wealth.

Well may we be content to live a hundred years if we act without attachment—if we do our work with earnestness, but without craving, not yearning for its fruits—we, and we alone.

The Self is one. Unmoving, it moves swifter than thought. The senses do not overtake it, for always it goes before. Remaining still, it outstrips all that run. Without the Self, there is no life.

To the ignorant the Self appears to move—yet it moves not. From the ignorant it is far distant—yet it is near. It is within all, and it is without all.

Those who see all beings in the Self, and the Self in all beings, hate none.

To the illumined soul, the Self pervades all. For the one who sees everywhere oneness, how can there be delusion or grief?

The Self is everywhere. Bright is it, bodiless, without scar or imperfection, without bone, without flesh, pure, untouched by evil. The One which is above all, the Eternal—this it is that has established order among objects and beings from beginningless time.

To darkness are they doomed who devote themselves only to life in the world, and to a greater darkness they who devote themselves only to meditation.

Life in the world alone leads to one result, meditation alone leads to another. So have we heard from the wise.

They who devote themselves both to life in the world and to meditation, by life in the world overcome death, and by meditation achieve eternity (or lasting happiness).

To darkness are they doomed who worship only the body, and to greater darkness they who worship only the spirit.

Worship of the body alone leads to one result, worship of the spirit leads to another. So have we heard from the wise.

They who worship both the body and the spirit, by the body overcome death, and by the spirit achieve eternity.

Kena

The power behind every activity of nature and of humanity is the power of the Eternal. To realize this truth is to be immortal.

For what reason does the mind think? What bids the body to live? What makes the tongue speak? What is it that directs the eye to form and color and the ear to sound?

The Self is ear of the ear, mind of the mind, speech of the speech. It is also breath of the breath, and eye of the eye. Having given up the false identification of the Self with the senses and the mind, and knowing the Self to be eternal, the wise become truly enlightened and, thus, imperishable.

This the eye does not see, nor the tongue express, nor the mind grasp. This we neither know nor are able to teach. Different is it from the known, and different is it from the unknown. So have we heard from the wise.

That which cannot be expressed in words but by which the tongue speaks—know that to be the Eternal. The Eternal is not the being who is worshipped by individuals.

That which is not comprehended by the mind but by which the mind comprehends—know that to be the Eternal. The Eternal is not the being who is worshiped by individuals.

That which is not seen by the eye but by which the eye sees—know that to be the Eternal. The Eternal is not the being who is worshipped by individuals.

That which is not heard by the ear but by which the ear hears—know that to be the Eternal. The Eternal is not the being who is worshipped by individuals.

That which is not drawn by the breath but by which the breath is drawn—know that to be the Eternal. The Eternal is not the being who is worshipped by individuals.

If you think that you know well the truth of the Eternal, know that you know little. What you think to be the Eternal in your self, or what you think to be the Eternal in others—that is not the

Eternal. What is indeed the truth of the Eternal you must therefore learn.

I cannot say that I know the Eternal fully. Nor can I say that I know it not. Those among us know it best who understand the spirit of the words, "Nor do I know that I know it not."

They truly know the Eternal who know it as beyond knowledge; those who think that they know, know not. The ignorant think that the Eternal is known, but the wise know it to be beyond knowledge.

Those who realize the existence of the Eternal behind every activity of their being—whether sensation, perception, or thought—they alone gain immortality. Through knowledge of the Eternal comes power. Through knowledge of the Eternal comes victory over death.

Blessed are those who while they live realize the Eternal. Those who realize it not suffer the greatest loss. Those who have realized the Eternal as the Self in all beings become eternal.

A Disciple: Sir, teach me more of the knowledge of the Eternal.

The Master: I have told you the secret knowledge. Balanced living, self-control, performance of duty without craving—these are the body of that knowledge. The scriptures are its limbs. Truth is its very soul.

Those who attain to knowledge of the Eternal, being freed from evil, find the essence of life, the Supreme.

Peace, peace, peace.

Katha

The secret of immortality is to be found in purification of the heart, in meditation, in realization of the identity of the Self within and the Eternal without. For immortality is simply union with the Eternal.

This story I have heard of long ago:

On a certain occasion Vajasrabasa, hoping for divine favor, performed a rite which required that he should give away all his possessions. He was careful, however, to sacrifice only his cattle, and of these only such as were useless—the old, the barren, the blind, and the lame. Observing this niggardliness, Nachiketa, his young son, whose heart had received the truth taught in the scriptures, thought to himself, "Surely a worshiper who dares bring such

worthless gifts is doomed to utter darkness!" Thus reflecting, he
came to his father, and cried,

"Father, I too belong to you; to whom will you give me?"

His father did not answer; but when Nachiketa asked the question again and yet again, he replied impatiently,

"You I give to Death!"

Then Nachiketa thought to himself, "Of my father's many sons
and disciples I am indeed the best, or at least of the middle rank,
not the worst; but of what good am I to the King of Death?" Yet
being determined to keep his father's word he said,

"Father, do not repent your vow! Consider how it has been with
those that have gone before, and how it will be with those that now
live. Like corn, people ripen and fall to the ground; like corn, they
spring up again in their season."

Having thus spoken, the boy journeyed to the house of Death.

But the god was not at home, and for three nights Nachiketa
waited. When at length the King of Death returned, he was met by
his servants, who said to him,

"A priest, like a flame of fire, entered your house as a guest, and
you were not there. Therefore must a peace offering be made to
him. With all accustomed rites, O King, you must receive your
guest, for if householders do not show due hospitality to a priest,
they will lose what they most desire—the merits of their good
deeds, their righteousness, their sons, and their cattle."

Then the King of Death approached Nachiketa and welcomed
him with courteous words.

"O Sir," he said, "I salute you. You are indeed a guest worthy of
all reverence. Let, I pray you, no harm befall me! Three nights have
you passed in my house and have not received my hospitality; ask
of me, therefore, three boons—one for each night."

"O Death," replied Nachiketa, "so let it be. And as the first of
these boons I ask that my father be not anxious about me, that his
anger be appeased, and that when you send me back to him, he
recognize me and welcome me."

"By my will," declared Death, "your father shall recognize you
and love you as heretofore; and seeing you again alive, he shall be
tranquil of mind, and he shall sleep in peace."

Then said Nachiketa, "In heaven there is no fear at all. You, O
Death, are not there, nor in that place does the thought of growing
old make one tremble. There, free from hunger and from thirst,

and far from the reach of sorrow, all rejoice and are glad. You know, O King, the fire sacrifice that leads to heaven. Teach me that sacrifice, for I am full of faith. This is my second wish."

Whereupon, consenting, Death taught the boy the fire sacrifice, and all the rites and ceremonies attending it. Nachiketa repeated all that he had learned, and Death, well pleased with him, said,

"I grant you an extra boon. Henceforth shall this sacrifice be called the Nachiketa Sacrifice, after your name. Choose now your third boon."

And then Nachiketa considered within himself, and said,

"When people die, there is this doubt: Some say, the person still lives; others say, he/she does not. Taught by you, I would know the truth. This is my third wish."

"No," replied Death, "Even the gods were once puzzled by this mystery. Subtle indeed is the truth regarding it, not easy to understand. Choose some other boon, O Nachiketa."

But Nachiketa would not be denied.

"You say, O Death, that even the gods were once puzzled by this mystery, and that it is not easy to understand. Surely there is no teacher better able to explain it than you—and there is no other boon equal to this."

To which, trying Nachiketa again, the god replied,

"Ask for sons and grandsons who shall live a hundred years. Ask for cattle, elephants, horses, gold. Choose for yourself a mighty kingdom. Or if you can imagine anything better, ask for that—not for sweet pleasures only but for power, beyond all thought, to taste their sweetness. Yes, truly, the supreme enjoyer will I make you of every good thing. Celestial maidens, beautiful to behold, such indeed as were not meant for mortals—even these, together with their bright chariots and their musical instruments, will I give you, to serve you. But for the secret of death, O Nachiketa, do not ask!"

But Nachiketa stood fast, and said, "These things endure only till the morrow, O Destroyer of Life, and the pleasures they give wear out the senses. Keep therefore horses and chariots, keep dance and song, for yourself! How shall we desire wealth, O Death, once we have seen your face? No, only the boon that I have chosen—that only do I ask. Having found out the society of the imperishable and the immortal, as in knowing you I have done, how shall I, subject to decay and death, and knowing well the vanity of the flesh—how shall I wish for long life?

"Tell me, O King, the supreme secret regarding which people doubt. No other boon will I ask."

Whereupon the King of Death, well pleased at heart, began to teach Nachiketa the secret of immortality.

King of Death:

The good is one thing; the pleasant is another. These two, differing in their ends, both prompt to action. Blessed are they that choose the good; they that choose the pleasant miss the goal.

Both the good and the pleasant present themselves to us. The wise, having examined both, distinguish the one from the other. The wise prefer the good to the pleasant; the foolish, driven by fleshly desires, prefer the pleasant to the good.

You, O Nachiketa, having looked upon fleshly desires, delightful to the senses, have renounced them all. You have turned from the miry way in which many people wallow.

Far from each other, and leading to different ends, are ignorance and knowledge. You, O Nachiketa, I regard as one who aspires after knowledge, for a multitude of pleasant objects were unable to tempt you.

Living in the abyss of ignorance yet wise in their own conceit, deluded fools go round and round, the blind led by the blind.

To thoughtless youth, deceived by the vanity of possessions, the path that leads to the Eternal is not revealed. The material world alone is real, there is nothing beyond—thinking thus, they fall again and again into my jaws.

To many it is not given to hear of the Self. Many, though they hear of it, do not understand it. Wonderful are those who speak of It. Intelligent are those who learn of it. Blessed are those who, taught by a good teacher, are able to understand It.

The truth of the Self cannot be fully understood when taught by an ignorant person, for opinions regarding It, not founded in knowledge, vary one from another. Subtler than the subtle is this Self, and beyond all logic. Taught by a teacher who knows the Self and the Eternal as one, a person leaves vain theory behind and attains to truth.

The awakening which you have known does not come through the intellect but rather, in fullest measure, from within the total person. Beloved Nachiketa, blessed, blessed are you, because you seek the Eternal. Would that I had more pupils like you!

Well I know that material treasure lasts but till the morrow. For did I not myself, wishing to be King of Death, make sacrifice with fire? But the sacrifice was a fleeting thing, performed with fleeting objects, and small is my reward, seeing that only for a moment will my reign endure.

. The goal of worldly desire, the glittering objects for which most people long, the celestial pleasures they hope to gain by religious rites, the most sought after of miraculous powers—all these were within your grasp. But all these, with firm resolve, you have renounced.

The ancient, the indwelling Spirit, subtle, deep-hidden in the human being, is hard to know. But the wise person, following the path of meditation, knows it, and is freed alike from pleasure and from pain.

The person who has learned that the Self is separate from the body, the senses, and the mind, and has fully known It, the Soul of Truth, the Subtle Principle—such a person verily attains to It, and is exceedingly glad, because that person has found the source and dwelling place of all felicity. Truly do I believe, O Nachiketa, that for you the gates of joy stand open.

Nachiketa:

Teach me, O King, I beseech you, whatever you know to be beyond right and wrong, beyond cause and effect, beyond past, present, and future.

King of Death:

Of that goal which all the scriptures declare, which is implicit in all penances, and in pursuit of which people lead lives of continence and service, of that will I briefly speak.

It is—Peace.

This word is eternal. This word is indeed supreme. Those who know it obtain their desire.

It is the strongest support. It is the highest symbol. Those who know it are reverenced as a knower of the Eternal.

The Self, whose symbol is Peace, is the omniscient One. It is not born. It does not die. It is neither cause nor effect. This Ancient One is unborn, eternal, imperishable; though the body is destroyed, it is not killed.

If the slayers think that they slay, if the slain think that they are slain, neither of them knows the truth. The Self slays not, nor is it slain.

Smaller than the smallest, greater than the greatest, this Self forever dwells within the lives of all. When individuals are free from craving, their minds and senses purified, they behold the glory of the Self and are without sorrow.

Though seated, It travels far; though at rest, It moves all things. Who but the purest of the pure can realize this lasting happiness which is joy and which is beyond joy.

Formless is it, though inhabiting form. In the midst of the fleeting It abides forever. All-pervading and supreme is the Self. Wise individuals, knowing It in his true nature, transcend all grief.

The Self is not known through study of the scriptures alone, not through subtlety of the intellect, nor through much learning. Only by those who long for It is It known. Truly to them does the Self reveal its true meaning.

By learning, individuals cannot know the Eternal if they do not refrain from evil, if they do not control their senses, if they do not quiet their minds, and if they do not practice meditation.

Both the individual self and the Universal Self have entered the cave of the body, the abode of the Eternal, but the knowers of the Eternal see a difference between them as between sunshine and shadow.

May we perform the Nachiketa Sacrifice, which bridges the world of suffering. May we know the imperishable, which is fearless, and which is the end and refuge of those who seek liberation.

Know that the Self is the rider, and the body the chariot; that the intellect is the charioteer, and the mind the reins.

The senses, say the wise, are the horses; the roads they travel are the mazes of desire. The wise call the Self the enjoyer when it is united with the body, the senses, and the mind.

When people lack discrimination, and their minds are uncontrolled, their senses are unmanageable, like the restive horses of a charioteer. But when people have discrimination, and their minds are controlled, their senses, like the well-broken horses of a charioteer, lightly obey the reins.

Those who lack discrimination, whose minds are unsteady and whose hearts are impure, never reach the goal but find misery instead. But those who have discrimination, whose minds are steady and whose hearts are pure, reach the goal, and having reached it are miserable no more.

Those who have a sound understanding for charioteer, a controlled mind for reins—those are the ones that reach the end of the journey, the supreme abode of the Eternal, the all-pervading.

The senses derive from physical objects, physical objects from mind, mind from intellect, intellect from ego, ego from the unmanifested seed, and the unmanifested seed from the Eternal—the Uncaused Cause.

Eternity is the end of the journey. The Eternal is the supreme goal.

The Eternal, this Self, deep-hidden in all beings, is not revealed to all; rather, it is the seers, pure in heart, concentrated in mind—to them is it revealed.

The senses of the wise obey their minds, their minds obey their intellects, their intellects obey their egos, and their egos obey the Self.

Arise! Awake! Approach the feet of the Master and know THAT. Like the sharp edge of a razor, the sages say, is the path. Narrow it is, and difficult to tread!

Soundless, formless, intangible, undying, tasteless, odorless, eternal, without beginning, without end, immutable, beyond nature, is the Self. Knowing it as such, one is freed from death.

The Narrator:

The wise, having heard and taught the eternal truth revealed by the King of Death to Nachiketa, are glorified in the finding of the Eternal.

King of Death:

The challenges of the world make the senses turn outward. Accordingly, most people look toward what is without, and see not what is within. Rare are those who, longing for immortality, shut their eyes in meditation and behold the Self.

Fools follow the desires of the flesh and fall into the snare of all-encompassing death; but the wise, knowing the Self as eternal, seek not the things that pass away.

This through which we see, taste, smell, hear, feel, and enjoy, is the Infinite.

This, truly, is the immortal Self. Knowing this, one knows the most important thing of all.

This through which we experience the sleeping or waking states is the all-pervading Self. Knowing it, one grieves no more.

Those who know that the individual soul, enjoyer of the fruits of action, is the Self—ever present within, lord of time, past and future—cast out all fear. For this Self is the immortal Self.

That in which the sun rises and in which it sets, that which is the source of all the powers of nature and of the senses, that which nothing can transcend—that is the immortal Self.

What is within us is also without. What is without is also within. Those who see difference between what is within and what is without go evermore toward death.

By the purified mind alone is the indivisible One to be attained. Those who see only the manifold universe and not also the one Reality go evermore toward death.

That essence dwells deep within the human body. It is the lord of time, past and future. Having attained it, one fears no more. It, truly, is the immortal Self.

That essence is like a flame without smoke. It is the lord of time, past and future, the same today and tomorrow. It, truly, is the immortal Self.

As rain, fallen on a hill, streams down its side, so runs the individual after delusion who sees manifoldness in the Self.

As pure water poured into pure water remains pure, so does the Self remain pure, O Nachiketa, uniting with the Eternal.

To the Birthless, the light of which forever shines, belongs the city of many gates (the body). Those who meditate on the ruler of that city know no more misery. They attain liberation, and for them there can no longer be death. For the ruler of that city is the immortal Self.

The immortal Self is the sun shining in the sky. It is the breeze blowing in space, It is the guest dwelling in the house; It is in all beings, It is in the ether, It is wherever there is truth; It is the fish that is born in water, It is the plant that grows in the soil, It is the river that gushes from the mountain—It, the Changeless Reality, the Illimitable!

This, the adorable One, seated in the body, is the power that gives breath. To it all the senses do homage.

What can remain when the essence of this body leaves the outgrown shell, since it is, truly, the immortal Self?

The individual does not live by breath alone, but by this in which is the power of breath.

That which is awake in us even while we sleep, shaping in dream the objects of our desire—that indeed is pure, that is the Eternal, and that truly is called the Immortal. All the world has its being in that, and none can transcend it. That is the Self.

As fire, though one, takes the shape of every object which it consumes, so the Self, though one, takes the shape of every object in which it dwells.

As the sun, revealer of all objects to the seer, is not harmed by the sinful eye, nor by the impurities of the objects it gazes on, so the one Self, dwelling in all, is not touched by the evils of the world. For it transcends all.

It is one, the innermost Self of all; of one form, It makes of itself many forms. To those who see the Self revealed in their own being belongs eternal bliss—to none else, to none else!

Intelligence of the intelligent, eternal among the transient, It, though one, makes possible the desires of many. To those who see the Self revealed in their own being belongs eternal peace—to none else, to none else!

Nachiketa:

How, O King, shall I find that blissful Self, supreme, ineffable, which is attained by the wise? Does it shine by itself, or does it reflect light from elsewhere?

King of Death:

It the sun does not illumine, nor the moon, nor the stars, nor the lightning—nor fires kindled upon earth. It is the one light that gives light to all. It shining, everything shines.

This universe is a tree eternally existing, its root aloft, its branches spread below. The pure root of the tree is the Eternal, the immortal, in which the world has its being, which none can transcend, which is truly the Self.

The whole universe came forth from the Eternal, moves in the Eternal. For those who attain this, death has no terror.

The senses have separate origin in their several objects. They may be active, as in the waking state, or they may be inactive, as in sleep. Those who know them to be distinct from the changeless Self grieve no more.

Above the senses is the mind. Above the mind is the intellect. Above the intellect is the ego. Above the ego is the un-manifested seed, the Primal Cause.

And truly beyond the un-manifested seed is the Eternal, the all-pervading spirit, the unconditioned, knowing which one attains to freedom and achieves immortality.

None beholds it with the eyes, for it is without visible form. Yet in the body is it revealed, through self-control and meditation. Those who know this become immortal.

When all the senses are stilled, when the mind is at rest, when the intellect wavers not—that, say the wise, is the highest state.

This calm of the senses and the mind has been defined as union with the Eternal. Those who attain it are freed from delusion.

In one not freed from delusion this calm is uncertain, unreal; it comes and goes. The Eternal words cannot reveal, mind cannot reach, eyes cannot see. How then, save through those who know this, can It be known?

There are two selves: the apparent self and the real Self. Of these it is the real Self, and it alone, which must be felt as truly existing. To those who have felt It as truly existing, It reveals its innermost nature.

The mortal in whose heart craving is dead becomes immortal. The mortal in whose heart the knots of ignorance are untied becomes immortal. These are the highest truths taught in the scriptures.

The Supreme, the innermost Self, dwells forever in the body of all beings. As one draws the pith from a reed, so must the aspirant after truth, with great perseverance, distinguish the Self from the body. Know the Self to be pure and immortal, capable of purifying the body also—yes, pure and immortal!

The Narrator:

Nachiketa, having at last understood this knowledge and the whole process of union with the Eternal, was freed from impurities and from death, and was united with the Eternal. Thus will it be with others also if they know the innermost Self.

Peace, peace, peace.

Prasna

Sukesha, Satyakama, Gargya, Kousalya, Bhargava, and Kabandhi, seekers after the truth of the supreme way, with faith and humility approached the sage Pippalada.

Said the sage: Practice self-control and faith for a year; then ask what questions you wish. If I can, I will answer them.

After a year Gargya approached the teacher and asked:

Master, when a person's body sleeps, what is it within that sleeps, and what is awake, and what is dreaming? What then experiences happiness, and with what are all the sense organs united?

"As the rays of the sun, O Gargya, when it sets," replied the sage, "appear to gather themselves up in its disk of light, to come out again when it rises, so the senses actually do gather themselves up in the mind, the highest of them all. Therefore, when people do not hear, see, smell, taste, touch, speak, grasp, enjoy, we say that they sleep.

"Only the primal energies are then awake in the body, and the mind is led nearer to the Self.

"While in dream, the mind revives its past impressions. Whatever it has seen, it sees again; whatever it has heard, it hears again; whatever it has enjoyed in various countries and in various quarters of the earth, it enjoys again. What has been seen and not seen, heard and not heard, enjoyed and not enjoyed, both real and unreal, it sees; yes, it sees all.

"When the mind is overpowered by deep slumber, it dreams no more. It rests happily in the body.

"As birds, my friend, fly to the tree for rest, even so do all these things fly to the Self: the eye and what it sees, the ear and what it hears, the nose and what it smells, the tongue and what it tastes, the skin and what it touches, the voice and what it speaks, the hands and what they grasp, the feet and what they walk on, the mind and what it perceives, the intellect and what it understands, the ego and what it appropriates, the heart and what it loves, light and what it illumines, energy and what it binds together.

"For truly it is the Self that sees, hears, smells, tastes, thinks, knows, acts. It is the Eternal, the essence of which is enlightenment. It is the immutable Self, the Supreme.

' "Those who know the immutable, the pure, the shadowless, the bodiless, the colorless, attain to the Eternal, O my friend. Such individuals become all-knowing, and they dwell in all beings. Of those individuals it is written:

"'Those who know that immutable Self, wherein live the mind, the senses, primal energies, the elements—truly such individuals know all things, and realize the Self in all.'"

Whereupon Satyakama, coming near to the master, said,

"Venerable Sir, if we meditate upon the word Peace all of our life, what shall be the result?"

And the master answered him thus,

"Satyakama, peace is of the Eternal—both the conditioned and the unconditioned, the personal and the impersonal. By meditating upon it, the wise may attain either the one or the other.

"If we meditate upon peace with but little knowledge of its meaning, but nevertheless are enlightened thereby, we may be born again (that is, transformed), and during this new life we will be devoted to self-control and faith, and will attain to spiritual greatness.

"If, again, we meditate upon peace with a greater knowledge of its meaning, we may be transformed even more completely than in the usual rebirth.

"But if we meditate upon peace in the full consciousness that it is one with the Eternal, we will be united with the light that is in the sun, we will be freed from evil, even as a snake is freed from its swamp, and we will ascend to the fullest realization of life, which is that of discovering lasting happiness (or immortality). Then we will realize the Eternal, which ever more abides in the heart of all beings—the Supreme!

"Concerning the sacred word peace, it is written:

"'The word peace, when it is not fully understood, does not lead beyond mortality. When it is fully understood, and meditation is therefore rightly directed, a person is freed from fear, whether that person be awake, dreaming, or sleeping the dreamless sleep, and attains to the Eternal.

"'By virtue of a little understanding of peace, individuals may be reborn. By virtue of a greater understanding, they attain to a still greater transformation. By virtue of a complete understanding, they learn what is known only to the seers. Sages, with a focus on peace, can reach the Eternal, the fearless, the un-decaying, the immortal!'"

The sage concluded, saying,

"What I have told you is all that can be said about the Self, the Supreme. Beyond this there is nothing."

The disciples paid their respects to the sage, and said,

"You are indeed our guide. You have led us beyond the sea of ignorance."

Peace, peace, peace.

Mundaka

Once upon a time Sounaka, the famous householder, came to Angiras and asked respectfully, "Holy Sir, what is that by which all else is known?"

"Those who know the Eternal," replied Angiras, "say that there are two kinds of knowledge, the higher and the lower.

"The lower is knowledge of the scriptures, and also of phonetics, ceremonials, grammar, etymology, the sciences, and so on.

"The higher is knowledge of that by which one knows the Changeless Reality. By this is fully revealed to the wise that which transcends the senses, which is uncaused, which is indefinable, which has neither eyes nor ears, neither hands nor feet, which is all-pervading, subtler than the subtlest—the Everlasting, the Source of All.

"As the web comes out of the spider and is withdrawn, as plants grow from the soil and hair from the human body, so springs the universe from the Eternal."

Considering religion to be observance of rituals and performance of acts of charity, the deluded remain ignorant of the Highest Good. Having enjoyed the reward of their good works, they are satisfied to live completely in the world of mortals.

But wise, self-controlled, and tranquil souls—who are contented in spirit, and who practice self-control and meditation in solitude and silence—are freed from impurity, and attain by the path of liberation to the Immortal, the Truly Existing, the Changeless Self.

Let a person devoted to spiritual life examine carefully the ephemeral nature of such enjoyment as may be won by good works alone, and so realize that it is not by quantity of these works that one gains the Eternal. Let that individual give no thought to transient things except as they relate to the Intransient, but let him/her first be absorbed in meditation. To know the Eternal, let the person humbly approach someone already devoted to the Eternal and well-versed in the scriptures.

To a disciple who approaches reverently, who is tranquil and self-controlled, the wise teacher gives that knowledge, faithfully and without stint, by which is known the Truly Existing, the Changeless Self.

The Imperishable is the Ultimately Real. As innumerable sparks fly upward from a blazing fire, so from the depths of the Imperishable rise all things. To the depths of the Imperishable they again descend.

Self-luminous is that essence, and formless. It dwells within all and without all. It is unborn, pure, greater than the greatest, without breath, without mind.

Thus the Eternal is all in all. It is action, knowledge, goodness supreme. To know this, hidden in the human body, is to untie the knot of ignorance.

Self-luminous is the Eternal, ever present in the being of all. It is the refuge of all, it is the supreme goal. In it exists all that moves and breathes. In It exists all that is. It is both that which is gross and that which is subtle. Adorable is It. Beyond the ken of the senses is It. Supreme is It. Attain to the Eternal!

This, the Self-luminous, subtler than the subtlest, in which exists all the world and all those that live therein—it is the Imperishable. It is the principle of life. It is speech, and it is mind. It is real. It is immortal. Attain this, O my friend, the supreme goal to be attained!

Affix to the Upanishad, the bow incomparable, the sharp arrow of devotional worship; then, with mind absorbed and heart melted in love, draw the arrow and hit the mark—the Imperishable.

Peace is the bow, the arrow is the individual being, and the Eternal is the target. With a tranquil heart, take aim. Lose yourself in this, even as the arrow is lost in the target.

In it are woven all parts of the universe together with the mind and all the senses. Know this, the Self alone. Give up vain talk. This is the bridge of immortality.

Within the human body it dwells, where, like the spokes of a wheel, the faculties of supreme coordination meet. Meditate on this as Peace. Easily may you cross the sea of darkness.

This Self, which understands all, which knows all, and the glory of which is manifest in the universe, lies within human grasp, the bright throne of Eternity.

By the pure in heart is it known. The Self exists in the individual and is the master of life and of the body. With mind illumined by the power of meditation, the wise know this, the blissful, the immortal.

The knot of the heart, which is ignorance, is loosed, all doubts are dissolved, evil effects of past deeds are destroyed, when that which is both personal and impersonal is realized.

In the human body dwells the Eternal, which is passionless and indivisible. It is pure, it is the light of lights. This the knowers of the Self attain.

It the sun does not illumine, nor the moon, nor the stars, nor the lightning—nor, truly, fires kindled upon earth. It is the one light that gives light to all. It shining, everything shines.

This immortal Idea is before, this immortal Idea is behind, this immortal Idea extends to the right and to the left, above and below. Truly, all is the Eternal and the Eternal supreme.

Like two birds of golden plumage, inseparable companions, the individual self and the immortal Self are perched on the branches of the selfsame tree. The former tastes of the sweet and bitter fruits of the tree; the latter, tasting of neither, calmly observes.

The individual self, deluded by forgetfulness of its identity with the Divine Self, bewildered by the ego, grieves and is sad. But when we recognize our own true Self, and behold its glory, we grieve no more.

When seers behold the Effulgent One, the Supreme, then, transcending both good and evil, and freed from impurities, they unite themselves with This.

The Eternal is the one life shining forth from every creature. Seeing it present in all, the wise ones are humble and do not put themselves forward. Their delight is in the Self, their joy is in the Self, they serve the Divine in all. Such people, indeed, are the true knowers of the Infinite.

This Effulgent Self is to be realized by self-control, by steadfastness in truth and meditation, and by super-conscious vision. Their impurities washed away, the seers realized it.

Truth alone succeeds, not untruth. By truthfulness the path of felicity is opened up, the path which is taken by the sages, freed from cravings, and which leads them to truth's eternal abode.

The Divine is supreme; it is self-luminous, it is beyond all thought. Subtler than the subtlest is it, farther than the farthest, nearer than the nearest, it resides in the care of every being.

The eyes do not see it, speech cannot utter it, the senses cannot reach it. It is to be attained neither by austerity nor by sacrificial rites alone. When through discrimination the heart has become pure, then, in meditation, the Impersonal Self is revealed.

The subtle Self within the living and breathing body is realized in that pure consciousness wherein is no duality—that consciousness by which the heart beats and the senses perform their office.

Those who, brooding upon sense objects, come to yearn for them, are forever restless in their living, driven by desire. But those who have realized the Self, and thus satisfied all hunger, attain to liberation in this life.

The Self is not to be known just through study of the scriptures, nor through subtlety of the intellect, nor through much learning. But by those who long for It is It known. Truly to those individuals does the Self reveal its true essence.

The Self is not to be known by the weak of mind nor by the thoughtless, nor by those who do not rightly meditate. But by the rightly meditative, the thoughtful, and the spiritually strong, it is fully known.

Having known the Self, the enlightened are filled with joy. Blessed are they, tranquil of mind, free from passion. Realizing everywhere the all-pervading Essence, deeply absorbed in contemplation of this, they enter into it, the Self of all.

As rivers flow into the sea and in so doing lose name and form, even so the wise person, freed from name and form, attains the Supreme, the Self-Luminous, the Infinite.

Those who know the Eternal become Eternal. No one ignorant of the Eternal is ever born into this unity. They pass beyond all misery. They overcome evil. Freed from the fetters of ignorance, they become immortal.

Let the full truth of the Infinite be taught to those who seek to obey its law, who are devoted to it, and who are pure in heart.

Hail to the sages! Hail to the illumined souls!

This truth of the Divine was taught in ancient times to Shounaka by Angira. Hail to the sages! Hail to the illumined souls!

Peace, peace, peace.

Mandukya

The word Peace, which is imperishable, is of the essence of the universe. Whatever has existed, whatever exists, whatever shall exist hereafter, is in some sense eternal. And whatever transcends past, present, and future—that also is Eternal.

All this that we see without is the Eternal. This Self that is within is the Eternal.

This Self, which is one with Peace, has three aspects, and beyond these three, different from them and indefinable—The Fourth.

The first aspect of the Self is the universal person, the collective symbol of created beings in their physical nature. They are awake and are conscious only of external objects. They are the enjoyers of the pleasures of sense.

The second aspect of the Self is universal persons in their mental nature. They are dreaming and are conscious only of their dreams. In this state they are the enjoyers of the subtle impressions in the mind of the deeds they have done in the past.

The third aspect of the Self is universal persons in dreamless sleep. They do not dream. They are without craving. As the darkness of night covers the day, and the visible world seems to disappear, so in dreamless sleep the veil of unconsciousness envelops their thought and knowledge, and the subtle impressions of the mind apparently vanish. Since they experience neither strife nor anxiety, they are said to be blissful and the experiencer of bliss.

This idea is the lord of all who believe in the Eternal. Truly, the Eternal knows all things. It is the origin of all. It is the end of all.

The Fourth, say the wise, is not subjective experience, nor objective experience, nor experience intermediate between these two, nor is it a negative condition which is neither consciousness nor unconsciousness. It is not the knowledge of the senses, nor is it relative knowledge, nor yet inferential knowledge. Beyond the senses, beyond full understanding, beyond all expression, is The Fourth. It is pure unitary consciousness, wherein awareness of the world and of multiplicity is completely obliterated. It is Ineffable Peace. It is the Supreme Good. It is One without a second. It is the Self. Know It above all else!

This Self, beyond all words, is the goal of Peace.

The Self as universal persons in their physical being, corresponds to the first step. Those who know this obtain what they desire and become the first among all peoples.

The Self as universal persons in their mental being, corresponds to the second step. Whoever knows this grows in wisdom and is highly honored.

The Self as universal persons in dreamless sleep corresponds to the third step. The Eternal is the origin and the end of all. Whoever knows this knows the essence of all things.

The Fourth, the Self, is the indivisible One. This idea is unutterable and beyond mind. In it the manifold universe becomes unified. It is the supreme good—One without a second. Whoever fully knows Peace knows the Self and becomes the Self.

Taittiriya

You are indeed the manifested Eternal. Of you will I speak. You will I proclaim in my thoughts as true. You will I proclaim on my lips as true.

May truth protect me, may it protect my teacher, may it protect us both. May glory come to us both. May the light of the Infinite shine in us both.

Those who dwell in the Eternal become king over themselves. They control their wandering thoughts. They become master of their speech and of all their organs of sense. They become masters of their intellects.

Peace, peace, peace.

To a Lay Student:

Let your conduct be marked by right action, including study and teaching of the scriptures; by truthfulness in word, deed, and thought; by self-denial and the practice of balanced living; by poise and self-control; by performance of the everyday duties of life with a cheerful heart and an unattached mind.

Speak the truth. Do your duty. Do not neglect the study of the scriptures. Do not cut the thread of progeny. Swerve not from the truth. Deviate not from the path of good. Revere greatness.

Let your mother be respected by you; let your father be respected by you; let your teachers be respected by you; let your guests also be respected by you. Do only such actions as are blameless. Always show reverence to the great.

Whatever you give to others, give with love and reverence. Gifts must be given with joy, humility, and compassion.

If at any time there is any doubt with regard to right conduct, follow the practice of great souls, who are guileless, of good judgment, and devoted to truth.

Thus conduct yourself always. This is the injunction, this is the teaching, and this is the command of the scriptures.

Those who know the Divine attain the supreme goal. This is the abiding reality, it is pure knowledge, and it is infinity. Those who know that the Divine dwells within the human body become one with it and enjoy all blessings.

Concerning which truth it is written: "Before creation came into existence, the Eternal existed as the Unmanifest. From the Unmanifest was created the manifest. From the manifest came various witnesses to the Eternal. Hence it is known as the Self-Existent."

The Self-Existent is the essence of all felicity. Who could live, who could breathe, if that blissful Self dwelt not within the human body? This it is that gives true happiness.

When individuals find their existence and unity in the Self—which is the basis of life, which is beyond the senses, which is formless, inexpressible, beyond all predicates—then alone do they transcend fear. So long as there is the least idea of separation from It, there is fear. To those who think themselves learned, yet do not know themselves as eternal, the Eternal appears as fear itself.

Who could live, who could breathe, if that blissful Self dwelt not within the human body? This it is that gives true happiness.

It is written: "Those who know the happiness of the Eternal (or lasting happiness), which words cannot express and the mind cannot reach, is free from fear. They are not distressed by the thought, 'Why did I not do what is right? Why did I do what is wrong?' Those who know the happiness of the Infinite, knowing both good and evil, transcend both."

Bhrigu, respectfully approaching his father, Varuna, said, "Sir, teach me of the Eternal." Varuna explained to him the physical and the vital self and the functions of the senses, and added, "That from which all beings are born, in which they live, being born, and to whom at death they return—seek to know this. It is the Eternal."

Bhrigu practiced self-control and meditation. Then it seemed to him that food was Divine. For of food all beings are born, by food they are sustained, being born, and into food they enter at death.

This knowledge, however, did not satisfy him. He again approached his father Varuna and said, "Sir, teach me of the Eternal."

Varuna replied, "Seek to know the Eternal by meditation. Meditation is the best path to the Divine."

Bhrigu practiced meditation and learned that primal energy is Eternal. For from mind all beings are born, by mind they are sustained, being born, and into mind they enter at death.

Still doubtful, he approached his father and said, "Sir, teach me of the Eternal." His father replied, "Seek to know the Eternal by meditation. Meditation is the best path to the Divine."

Bhrigu practiced meditation and learned that intellect is Eternal. For from intellect all beings are born, by intellect they are sustained, being born, and into intellect they return at death.

Not yet satisfied, doubting his understanding, Bhrigu approached his father and said, "Sir, teach me of the Eternal." Varuna replied, "Seek to know the Eternal by meditation. Meditation is the best path to the Divine."

Bhrigu practiced meditation and learned that happiness is Eternal. For from happiness all beings are born, by happiness they are sustained, being born, and into happiness they enter at death.

This is the wisdom which Bhrigu, taught by Varuna, attained within his heart.

He who attains this wisdom wins true glory, grows spiritually rich, enjoys health and true fame.

The Eternal is to be meditated upon as the source of all thought and life and action. It is the splendor in wealth, it is the light in the stars. It is all things.

Let individuals meditate upon the Eternal as support, and they will be supported. Let them meditate upon the Eternal as greatness, and they will be great. Let them meditate upon the Eternal as mind, and they will be endowed with intellectual power. Let them meditate upon the Eternal as adoration, and they will be adored. Let them worship the Eternal as eternal, and they will become eternal.

That which is the Self in the individual, and that which is the Self in all beings, are one.

Peace, peace, peace.

Aitareya

What is this Self which we desire to worship? Of what nature is this Self?

Is it the self by which we see form, hear sound, smell odor, speak words, and taste the sweet or the bitter?

It is the heart and the mind by which we perceive, command, discriminate, know, think, remember, will, feel, desire, breathe, love, and perform other like acts?

No, these are but adjuncts of the Self, which is pure consciousness. And this Self, which is pure consciousness, is the Eternal. It is

God, all gods; the many elements; all beings, great or small, born of eggs, born from the womb, born from heat, born from soil; horses, cows, men, elephants, birds; everything that breathes, the beings that walk and the beings that do not walk. The reality behind all these is the Eternal, which is pure consciousness.

All these, while they live, and after they have ceased to live, blend into the Eternal.

Chandogya

The requirements of duty are three. The first is self-sacrifice, study, charity; the second is self-control in all areas; the third is life as a student of some competent spiritual teacher and of the scriptures. Together, these three should lead one to the realm of truth. But those who are firmly established in the knowledge of the Eternal achieve immortality.

Truly has this universe come forth from the Eternal. In the Eternal it lives and has its being. Assuredly, all is the Eternal. Let a person, freed from the taint of passion, seek the Eternal.

Individuals are, above all, their will. As is their will in life, so do they become. Therefore should their will be fixed on attaining the Infinite.

The Self, which is to be realized by the purified mind and the illumined consciousness, the form of which is light, the thoughts of which are true; which, like the ether, remains pure and unattached; from which proceed all works, all desires, all odors, all tastes; which pervades all, which is beyond the senses, and in which there is fullness of joy forever—this is my very Self, dwelling within the human body.

Smaller than a grain of rice is the Self; smaller than a grain of barley, smaller than a mustard seed, smaller than a canary seed, yes, smaller even than the kernel of a canary seed. Yet again is that Self, within the human body, greater than the earth, greater than the solar system, yes, than the universe.

This from which proceed all works, all desires, all odors, all tastes; which pervades all, which is beyond the senses, and in which there is fullness of joy forever—this, the Self, is truly Divine.

Said the seer Sandilya: At all times a seeker of the Divine should meditate on the following truths:

It is imperishable.

It is the Changeless Reality.

It is the Source of Life.

This highest knowledge, the knowledge of the Eternal, having drunk of which one never thirsts, did Ghora Angirasa teach to Krishna, the son of Devaki.

Narada once came to Sanatkumara and asked to be taught. To Sanatkumara's question, "What have you already studied?" Narada replied that he had studied all the branches of learning—art, science, music, and philosophy, as well as the sacred scriptures. "But," said he, "I have gained no peace. I have studied all this, but the Self I do not know. I have heard from great teachers like you that he who knows the Self overcomes grief. Grief is ever my lot. Help me, I pray you, to overcome it."

Sanatkumara said, "Whatever you have read is only name. Meditate on name as the Eternal."

Narada asked, "Is there anything higher than name?"

"Yes, speech is higher than name. It is through speech that we come to know the many branches of learning, that we come to know what is right and what is wrong, what is true and what is untrue, what is good and what is bad, what is pleasant and what is unpleasant. For if there were no speech, neither right nor wrong, what is true and what is untrue, what is good and what is bad, what is pleasant and what is unpleasant, would be known. For if there were no speech, neither right nor wrong would be known, neither the true nor the false, neither the pleasant nor the unpleasant. Speech makes us know all this. Meditate on speech as the Eternal."

"Sir, is there anything higher than mind?"

"Yes, will is higher than mind. For when people will, they think in their mind; and when they think in their mind, they put forth speech; and when they put forth speech, they clothe their speech in words. All these, therefore, center in will, consist of will, and abide in will. Meditate on will as the Eternal."

"Sir, is there anything higher than will?"

"Yes, discriminating will is higher than will. For when people discriminate by analyzing their past experiences and considering on the basis of these what may come in the future, they rightly will in the present. Meditate on discriminating will as the Eternal."

"Sir, is there anything higher than discriminating will?"

"Yes, concentration is higher than discriminating will. Those who reach greatness reach it through concentration. Thus, while small and vulgar people are always gossiping and quarreling and for lack of concentration abusing one another, great people, possessing it, obtain their reward. Meditate on concentration as the Eternal."

"Sir, is there anything higher than concentration?"

"Yes, insight is higher than concentration. Through insight we understand all branches of learning, and we understand what is right and what is wrong, what is true and what is false, what is good and what is bad, what is pleasant and what is unpleasant. All of life we can understand through insight. Meditate on insight as the Eternal."

Then said Sanatkumara, "But, truly, they are the true knowers who know Eternal Truth."

"Reverend sir, I wish to be a true knower."

"Then ask to know of that infinite Reality."

"Sir, I wish to know of it."

"It is only when we have realized Eternal Truth that we declare it. Those who reflect upon it realize it. Without reflection it is not realized.

"And only those who have faith and reverence can reflect on Eternal Truth.

"And only those who seek the Eternal can gain faith and reverence.

"And only those seek the Eternal who struggle to achieve self-control.

"And only those achieve self-control who find happiness in it. Ask to know of this happiness."

"Sir, I wish to know of it."

"The Infinite is the source of happiness. There is no lasting happiness in the finite. Only in the Infinite is there true happiness. Ask to know of the Infinite."

"Sir, I wish to know of it."

"Where one sees nothing but the One, hears nothing but the One, knows nothing but the One—there is the Infinite. Where one sees another, hears another, knows another—there is the finite. The Infinite is immortal, the finite is mortal."

"In what does the Infinite rest?"

"In its own glory—no, not even in that. In the world it is said that cows and horses, elephants and gold, slaves, wives, fields, and houses are the individual's glory—but these are finite things. How shall the Infinite rest anywhere but in itself?"

"The Infinite is below, above, behind, before, to the right, to the left. It is all this. This Infinite is the Self. The Self is below, above, behind, before, to the right, to the left. It is all this. One who knows, meditates upon, and realizes the truth of the Self—such a one delights in the Self, revels in the Self, rejoices in the self. Such a person becomes master of the inner life and master of all the world. Slaves are they who know not this truth.

Those who know, meditate upon, and realize this truth of the Self, find that everything—primal energy, all elements, mind, will, concentration, speech, sacred hymns and scriptures, indeed the whole universe—issue forth from it.

"It is written: 'Those who have realized Eternal Truth do not see death, nor illness, nor pain; they see everything as the Self and obtain all.'

"The Self is one, and it has become all things.

"When the senses are purified, the heart is purified; when the heart is purified, there is constant and unceasing remembrance of the Self; when there is constant and unceasing remembrance of the Self, all bonds are loosed and freedom is attained."

Thus the venerable Sanatkumara taught Narada, who was pure in heart, how to pass from darkness into light:

Within the city of Eternity, which is the body, there is a little house. Within this little house dwells that which is to be sought after, inquired about, and realized.

What then is that which, dwelling within this little house, is to be sought after, inquired about, and realized?

As large as the universe outside, even so large is the universe within the human body. Within it are the universe, the sun, the moon, the lightning, and all the stars. What is in the macrocosm is in this microcosm.

All things that exist, all beings and all desires, are in the city of Eternity; what then becomes of them when old age approaches and the body dissolves in death?

Though old age comes to the body, the Self does not grow old. At death of the body, it does not die. The Self, where the Eternal exists in all its glory—that, and not the body, is the true city of Eternity. The Eternal, dwelling therein, is untouched by any deed, ageless, deathless, free from grief, free from hunger and from thirst. Its desires are right desires, and its desires are fulfilled.

As on earth, all the wealth that one earns is but transitory, so likewise transitory are the enjoyments acquired by the performance of rituals. Therefore, those who die without having realized the Self and its right desires find no permanent happiness; while those who have realized the Self and its right desires find permanent happiness everywhere.

Indeed, whatever such knowers of the Divine may desire, it is soon theirs; and having obtained it, they are generally respected by all. The fulfillment of right desires is within reach of everyone, but a veil of illusion obstructs the ignorant.

Do we wish for our beloved, among the living or among the dead, or is there anything else for which we long, yet, for all our longing, do not obtain? All shall be ours if we but dive deep within, even to the core of life, where the Eternal dwells. Yes, the object of every right desire is within our reach, though unseen, concealed by a veil of illusion.

As one not knowing that a golden treasure lies buried beneath his/her feet may walk over it again and again, yet never find it, so all beings live every moment in the city of Eternity, yet never find it, because of the veil of illusion by which it is concealed.

The Self resides within the human body. Knowing this, consecrated to the Self, the mature individual will enter daily into that holy sanctuary.

Absorbed in the Self, the mature individual is freed from identification with sensuality and lives in blissful consciousness. The Self is the immortal, the fearless; the Self is the Eternal. The Eternal is Eternal Truth.

The Self within the body is like a boundary which divides the visible world from That. Day and night cross not that boundary, nor old age, nor death; neither grief nor pleasure, neither good nor evil deeds. All evil shuns That. For That is free from impurity: by impurity can it never be touched.

Wherefore, those who have crossed that boundary, and have realized the Self, if they are blind, cease to be blind; if they are wounded, cease to be wounded; if they are afflicted, cease to be afflicted. When that boundary is crossed, night becomes day; for the world of Eternity is light itself.

And that world of Eternity is reached by those who practice self-control. For the knower of Eternal Truth knows it through self-control. And what is known as worship, that also is self-control. For a person worships Life by self-control and thus attains it.

What people call salvation is really self-possession. For through self-possession the person is freed from ignorance. And what is known as the vow of silence, that too is really self-possession, because a person through self-possession realizes the Self and lives in quiet.

What people call dwelling in solitude, that is really self-possession.

In the world of Eternity there is a lake whose waters are like nectar, and whoever tastes of it is immediately drunk with joy; and beside that lake is a tree which yields the juice of immortality. Into this world they cannot enter who do not practice self-control.

For the world of Eternity belongs to those who practice self-control. They alone enter that world and drink from that lake of nectar. For them there is freedom in all the world.

It was said many years ago:

"The Self, which is free from impurities, from old age and death, from grief, from hunger and thirst, which desires nothing but what it ought to desire, and resolves nothing but what it ought to resolve, is to be sought after, is to be inquired about, is to be realized. Those who learn about the Self and realize it obtain all the world and all desires."

Brihadaranyaka

The world existed first as seed, which as it grew and developed took on names and forms. As a razor in its case or as fire in the wood, so dwells the Self, in all forms, even to the tips of the fingers. Yet the ignorant do not know this, for behind the names and forms it remains hidden. When one breathes, one knows it as breath; when one speaks, one knows it as speech; when one sees, one knows it as the eye; when one hears, one knows it as the ear; when one thinks, one knows it as the mind. All these are but names related to its acts; and those who worship the Self as one or another of them does not know it, for of them it is neither one nor another. Therefore let a person seek it as the Self, and as the Self alone. The perfection which is the Self is the goal of all beings. For by knowing the Self one knows all. The person who knows the Self is honored by all mature individuals and attains to blessedness.

This Self, which is nearer to us than anything else, is indeed dearer than a child, dearer than wealth, dearer than all else. Let people worship the Self as dearest to them, for if they worship the Self as dearest, the object of their love will never perish.

Peace, peace, peace.

Swetaszatara

Disciples inquire within themselves:

What is the cause of the universe? Is it the Eternal? Where do we come from? Why do we live? Where shall we at last find rest? Under what command are we bound by the law of happiness and its opposite?

Time, space, law, chance, matter, primal energy, intelligence—none of these, nor a combination of these, can be the final cause of the universe, for they also are effects, and exist to serve the soul. Nor can the individual self be the cause, for, being subject to the law of happiness and misery, it is not free.

The seers, absorbed in contemplation, saw within themselves the Ultimate Reality, the Self-luminous Essence, the Eternal, which dwells as the self-conscious power in all creatures. It is One without a second. It presides over time, space, and all apparent causes.

Know the Eternal, and all fetters will be loosed. Ignorance will vanish. Meditate upon it and transcend physical consciousness. Thus will you reach union with the essence of the universe. Thus will you become identified with that which is One without a second. In It all your desires will find fulfillment.

The truth is that you are always united with the Eternal. But you must know this. Nothing further is there to know. Meditate, and you will realize that mind, matter, and the power which unites mind and matter are but three aspects of the One Reality.

Like oil in sesame seeds, butter in cream, water in the river bed, fire in tinder, the Self dwells within the soul. Realize this through truthfulness and meditation.

Like butter in cream is the Self in everything. Knowledge of the Self is gained through meditation (and consequent action). The Self is of the Eternal. By realization of the Eternal is all ignorance destroyed.

To realize the Eternal, first control the outgoing senses and harness the mind. Then meditate upon the light in the heart of the fire—meditate, that is, upon pure consciousness as distinct from the ordinary consciousness of the intellect. Thus the Self, the Inner Reality, may be seen behind physical appearance.

Control your mind so that the Ultimate Reality, the Self-luminous Essence, may be revealed. Strive earnestly for lasting happiness.

With the help of the mind and the intellect, keep the senses from attaching themselves to objects of pleasure. They will then be purified by the light of the Inner Reality, and that light will be revealed.

The wise control their minds, and unite their hearts with the Infinite, the Omniscient, the All-pervading Eternal. Only discriminating souls practice spiritual disciplines. Great is the glory of the Self-luminous Essence, the Inner Reality.

Hear, all you children of lasting happiness: Follow first in the footsteps of the illumined ones, and by continuous meditation (in the process of concentrated action) merge both mind and intellect in the Eternal. The glorious Divine will be revealed to you.

Control the vital force. Set fire to the Self within by the practice of meditation. Be drunk with the wine of Divine Love. Thus shall you reach perfection.

Be devoted to the Eternal. Unite the light within you with the light of Infinity. Thus will the source of ignorance be destroyed, and you will rise above your finite limitations.

With earnest effort hold the senses in check. Controlling the breath, regulate the vital activities. As charioteers hold back their restive horses, so do persevering aspirants hold back their minds.

As a soiled piece of metal, when it has been cleaned, shines brightly, so the Inner Reality, when it has realized the truth of the Self, is freed from misery and attains to happiness.

Peace, peace, peace.

THE BHAGAVAD-GITA (OR "THE SONG OF THE LORD")

Revolt Against War

Having seen arrayed the army of the Pandavas, the Prince Duryodhana approached his teacher, and spoke these words,

"Behold this mighty host of the sons of Pandu, O teacher, arrayed by the son of Drupada, your wise disciple. Insufficient seems this army of ours, though marshaled by Bhishma; therefore in the rank and file let all, standing firmly in their respective divisions, guard Bhishma, even all the generals."

To enhearten him, the Ancient of the Kurus, the grandsire, the glorious, blew his conch, sounding on high like a lion's roar. Then conches and kettledrums, tabors and drums and cowhorns, suddenly blared forth; and the sound was tumultuous.

Then, stationed in their great war-chariot, yoked to white horses, Krishna and Arjuna blew their conches. Drupada and the Draupadeyas, and Saubhadra, the mighty-armed, on all sides their several conches blew. That tumultuous uproar rent the hearts of the sons of Dhritarashtra, filling the earth and sky with sound.

Beholding the sons of Dhritarashtra standing arrayed, and the flight of arrows about to begin, Arjuna, the son of Pandu, took up his bow, and spoke this word to Krishna, his charioteer and teacher,

"In the midst, between the two armies, stay my chariot, O Krishna, that I may behold these people standing, longing for battle, with whom I must strive in this outbreaking war, and gaze on those here gathered together, ready to fight, desirous of pleasing in battle the evil-minded son of Dhritarashtra."

Thus addressed by Arjuna, Krishna, having stayed that best of chariots in the middle between the two armies, said,

"O Arjuna, behold these Kurus gathered together."

Then saw Arjuna standing there, uncles and grandfathers, teachers, mothers' brothers, cousins, sons and grandsons, comrades, fathers-in-law and benefactors also in both armies; seeing all these kinsmen thus standing arrayed, Arjuna, deeply moved to pity, uttered in sadness,

"Seeing these my kinsmen, O Krishna, arrayed, eager to fight, my limbs fail and my mouth is parched, my body quivers, and my hair stands on end; my bow and arrow slip from my hand, and my skin burns all over; I am not able to stand, my mind is whirling, and I see adverse omens, O teacher. Nor do I foresee any advantage from slaying kinsmen in battle.

"For I desire not victory, O Krishna, nor kingdom, nor pleasures; what is kingdom to us, what enjoyment, or even life? Those for whose sake we desire kingdom, enjoyments and pleasures stand here in battle, abandoning life and riches—teachers, fathers, sons, as well as grandfathers, mothers' brothers, fathers-in-law, grandsons, brothers-in-law, and other relatives. These I do not wish to kill, though myself slain, O teacher, even for the sake of the kingship of the world; how then for my own land?

"Slaying these sons of Dhritarashtra, what pleasure can be ours, O Krishna? Killing these desperadoes, sin will but take hold of us. Therefore, we should not kill the sons of Dhritarashtra, our relatives; for how, killing our kinsmen, may we be happy? Although these, with intelligence overpowered by greed, see no guilt in the destruction of a family, no crime in hostility to friends, why should not we learn to turn away from such a sin, O teacher, who see the evils in the destruction of a family? In the destruction of a family the immemorial family traditions perish; in the perishing of tradition, lawlessness, O Krishna, the women of the family become corrupt; women corrupted, there arises confusion; this confusion debases the slayers of the family, and the family. By these confusing misdeeds of the slayers of the family, the everlasting social customs and family customs are abolished. Alas! in committing a great sin are we engaged, we who are endeavoring to kill our kindred from greed of the pleasures of kingship. If the sons of Dhritarashtra, weapon in hand, should slay me, unresisting, unarmed, in the battle, that would for me be the better."

Having thus spoken on the battlefield, Arjuna sank down on the seat of the chariot, casting away his bow and arrow, his mind overborne by grief.

Then Krishna said, "Whence has this dejection befallen you in this perilous strait, ignoble, infamous, O Arjuna? Do not yield to impotence, O son! it does not befit you. Shake off this paltry faintheartedness! Stand up, Arjuna!"

Arjuna said, "How, O teacher, shall I attack Bhishma and Drona with arrows in battle, they who are worthy of reverence, O slayer of foes? Better in this world to eat even the beggar's crust than to slay these most noble teachers. Slaying these teachers, our wellwishers, I should taste of blood-besprinkled feasts. Nor do I know which for us is the better, that we conquer them or they conquer us—these, whom having slain, we should not care to live, even these arrayed against us, the sons of Dhritarashtra. My heart is weighed down with the vice of faintness; my mind is confused as to duty. I ask you which may be the better—that tell me decisively. I am your disciple, suppliant to you; teach me. For I do not see that it would drive away this anguish that withers up my senses, if I should attain unrivaled monarchy, or even the sovereignty of a spiritual ruler."

Krishna said, "As everyone experiences childhood, youth, old age, so the steadfast one grieves not thereat. The contacts of matter, O disciple, giving cold and heat, pleasure and pain, they come and go, impermanent; endure them bravely, O Arjuna.

"Those persons whom these do not torment, O chief, balanced in pain and pleasure, steadfast, they are fitted for Eternity. The unreal has no being; the real never ceases to be; the truth about both has been perceived by the seers of the essence of things. Know That to be indestructible, by which life is pervaded. Nor can any work the destruction of that imperishable One. These bodies of the One, which is eternal, indestructible, and immeasurable, are known as finite. Therefore fight, O Arjuna. Those who regard themselves as slayers, and those who think they are slain, both of them are ignorant. They do not slay, nor are they slain. They do not die; nor having been do they cease any more to be; perpetual, eternal, they are not slain when the body is slaughtered. Those who know that which is indestructible, perpetual, un-diminishing, how can those people slay, O Arjuna, or cause to be slain?

"As people, casting off worn-out garments, take on new ones, so the spiritually conscious beings, casting off worn-out ways, take on others that are new. Weapons do not cleave to them, nor does fire burn them, nor do waters wet them, nor does wind dry them away. Un-cleavable, incombustible, and indeed neither to be wetted nor dried; perpetual, all-pervasive, stable, immovable. Un-manifest, unthinkable, they are called; therefore, knowing them as such, you should not grieve.

"Beings are un-manifest in their origin, manifest in their middle state, O Arjuna, un-manifest likewise are they in dissolution. What room then for lamentation? As marvelous one regards life; as marvelous another speaks thereof; as marvelous another hears thereof; yet having heard, none indeed understands. This spirit, in the body of everyone, is ever invulnerable, O son of Pandu; therefore, you should not grieve for any creature."

The Rule of Action

Arjuna said, "With these perplexing words you only confuse my understanding; therefore, tell me with certainty the one way by which I may reach bliss."

Krishna said, "In this world there is a twofold path, as I said before, O sinless one: that of union through understanding; and that of union by disciplining action.

"People do not win freedom from action by abstaining from activity, nor by mere renunciation do they rise to perfection. Nor can anyone, even for an instant, remain really actionless; for helplessly is everyone driven to action by the qualities born of nature. Those who sit, controlling the organs of action, but dwelling in their minds on the objects of the senses, those bewildered ones are called hypocrites. But those who, controlling the senses by the mind, O Arjuna, with the organs of action without attachment, discipline their action; they are worthy. Perform right action, for action is superior to inaction; for, if you were inactive, even the maintenance of your body would not be possible.

"However, the world is bound by action, unless performed for the sake of fulfilling purpose; for that sake, free from attachment, O son of Pandu, perform action. Since in ancient times humanity developed by means of purpose, guides of this development have said, 'By this shall you propagate; let purpose be to you the giver of desires; with it seek the Infinite; thus seeking, you shall reap the supreme good. For, seeking to fulfill purpose, you shall find the happiness you desire.' Thieves truly are those who enjoy what is given them without returning anything. Know that from the Eternal comes action; therefore, the Eternal, the all-permeating, is ever present in purposeful living.

"Those who on earth do not follow the wheel thus revolving, but are sinful and rejoice in the senses, they, O son of Pandu, live in vain. But those who rejoice in the Self are satisfied with the Self, and are content in the Self, for them truly there is nothing for which to compete; for them there is no craving for things done in the world, nor for things not done, nor does any object of theirs depend on any being. Therefore, without attachment, constantly perform action which is duty; for, by performing action without attachment, you will truly reach the Supreme.

"Whatever a great one does, that other people also do; the standard they set up, by that the people go. Let no wise ones unsettle the mind of ignorant people attached to action; but, acting in harmony with life, let them render all action attractive.

"All worthy actions are wrought by the qualities of nature only. The self, deluded by egoism, thinks, 'I am the doer.' But those, O

mighty-armed, who know the essence of the divisions of the qualities and functions, holding that 'the qualities move amid the qualities,' are not attached. Those deluded by the qualities of nature are
attached to the functions of the qualities. The person of great understanding should not unsettle the foolish, whose understanding is
small. Surrendering all actions to the Eternal, with your thoughts
resting on the supreme Self, from attachment and egoism freed,
and of mental fever cured, engage in the battle (of life).

"They who abide ever in this teaching of mine, full of faith and
free from finding fault, they too can rise above their actions
through understanding. Those who carp at my teaching and act not
thereon, being senseless, deluded in understanding, these careless
ones are leading to their own destruction.

"The person of understanding behaves in conformity with
his/her own nature; beings follow nature; what shall restraint avail?
Affection and aversion for the objects of sense abide in the senses;
let none come under the dominion of these two; they are obstructions of the path. It is better to do one's own duty, though destitute
of praise, than the duty of another, well-discharged. It is better to
die in the discharge of one's own duty, for the duty of another is
certain to be full of danger."

Arjuna said, "But by what temptation does a person commit sin,
reluctantly indeed, O teacher, as it were constrained by force?"

Krishna said, "It is craving, it is wrath, begotten by the quality of
notion; all-consuming, all-polluting, know this as our greatest foe.
As a flame is enveloped by smoke, as a mirror by dust, as an embryo is wrapped by the amnion, so is wisdom enveloped by this
constant enemy of the wise in the form of craving, which is as insatiable as a flame.

"The senses, the mind, and the reason are said to be its seat; by
enveloping wisdom in these areas, it bewilders the spirit in the
body. Therefore, mastering first the senses, slay this thing of sin,
destructive of wisdom and knowledge. It is said that the senses are
great; greater than the senses is the mind; greater than the mind is
the reason; but what is greater than the reason is the Self.

"Thus understanding the Self as greater than the reason, restraining the self by the Self, slay, O mighty-armed, the enemy in the
form of craving, however difficult to overcome."

The Rule of Wisdom

Krishna said, "Those who are aware of the mystery of life in its essence, having abandoned the body, do not come to death, but come into union with the Infinite, O Arjuna. Freed from passion, fear and anger, filled with love, taking refuge in the Self, purified in the fire of wisdom, many have entered into this union. No matter how people approach it, even so can they find it, for the path we take from every side is toward the same goal, O son of Pandu.

"Those who long after success in action worship the idols of society; for in brief space, truly, in this world of people, "success" is born of constant action. However, actions do not necessarily have much real effect, nor is the utilization of the fruits of action desired as a substitute. Only those who act from a higher purpose are not bound by actions.

"Having known this, our forefathers, ever seeking the Infinite, performed action; therefore, you also should perform action, as did our forefathers in the olden time.

"'What is action, what inaction?' Even the wise are perplexed at this question. Therefore, I will declare to you the action, which, by knowing, you shall be loosed from evil. It is needful to discriminate action, to discriminate unlawful action, and to discriminate inaction; mysterious is the path of action. Those who see inaction in action, and action in inaction, they are wise among people, they are harmonious, even while performing all action.

"Those whose works are all free from temptation, whose actions are burned up by the fire of wisdom, them the wise have called mature. Having abandoned attachment to the fruits of action, always content, nowhere seeking escape, they are not doing anything for personal gain, although doing actions. Hoping for nothing, their minds self-controlled, having abandoned all greed, performing action by the body alone, they do not commit sin. Content with whatever are their rewards, without envy, balanced in success and failure, though acting they are not bound. Those with attachment dead, harmonious, with their thoughts established in wisdom, their works as sacrifices, the detrimental effects of action melt away.

"Even if you are the most sinful of all sinners, yet shall you cross over all sin by the raft of wisdom. As the burning fire reduces fuel to ashes, O Arjuna, so does the fire of wisdom reduce all temptations to ashes. Truly, there is no purifier in this world like wisdom;

those that are perfected in discipline find it in the Self in due season.

"Those who are full of faith obtain wisdom, and those also who
have mastery over their senses; having obtained wisdom, they go
swiftly toward the supreme peace. But the ignorant, faithless,
doubting self goes to self-destruction; nor is happiness to be found
by the purely skeptical self.

"Those who have renounced the fruits of actions by discipline,
who have cloven asunder doubt by wisdom, who are ruled by the
Self, actions do not bind them, O Arjuna.

"Therefore, with the sword of the wisdom of the Self cleaving
asunder this ignorance-born doubt, dwelling in your heart, be established in discipline. Stand up, O son of Pandu."

The Nature of the Eternal

Krishna said, "With the mind clinging to truth, O Arjuna, observing disciplined living, how you shall without doubt know life to the
uttermost, that you must hear. I will declare to you this wisdom in
its completeness, which, having known, nothing more needs to be
known. Among thousands of people, scarcely one knows life in its
essence.

"Know mystery to be the womb of all beings. It is the source of
the forth-going of the whole universe and likewise the place of its
dissolving. There is nothing whatever higher than this, O Arjuna.
All existence is threaded on this, as rows of pearls on a string.

"It is the palatability in waters, O son of Pandu, radiance in the
sun, word of power in all the earth, sound in the air, and virility in
all beings; the pure fragrance of earth and the brilliance in fire is it;
the life in all beings is it, and the austerity in ascetics. Know this, O
Arjuna! as the eternal seed of all beings. It is the reason of the rea-
son-endowed, the splendor of splendid things, and the strength of
the strong, devoid of craving and passion. In beings it is desire not
contrary to duty, O son of Pandu. The natures that are harmonious, active, meditative, know these as of the Eternal.

"All this world, seduced by lower natures, does not know Eternity, which is above these natures, imperishable. This divine illusion, caused by various limitations, is hard to pierce; they who
come to life, they cross over this illusion."

The Imperishable

Krishna said, "The indestructible, the supreme is the Eternal; its essential nature is called Self-knowledge; the emanation that causes the birth of beings is named action; knowledge of the elements concerns the perishable nature, and understanding of the world concerns the life-giving energy.

"And those who, overcoming the limitations of the body, go forth seeking the Eternal till the time of their deaths, they enter into this union: there is no doubt of that. Whoever at last abandons the lusts of the body, thinking upon any ideal, to that ideal only they go, Arjuna, ever to that conformed in nature. Therefore, at all times think upon the Eternal only, and fight. With mind and reason set on this, without doubt you shall realize it. With the mind not wandering after anything else, harmonized by continual practice, constantly meditating, O son of Pandu, one goes to the Spirit supreme, divine.

"Those who think upon the Ancient, the Omniscient, minuter than the minute, the supporter of all, of form unimaginable, refulgent as the sun beyond the darkness, in the time of going forth, with unshaken mind, fixed in devotion, by the power of discipline drawing together their life-sustaining powers, they go to this Spirit, supreme, divine.

"That which is declared indestructible by the prophets, that which the controlled and passion-free enter, that path I will declare to you with brevity.

"All the gates leading to lust closed, the mind controlling the heart, the life-breath fixed in their own being, concentrated by discipline, thinking upon the Infinite, those who go forth controlling the body, they go on the highest path. Those who constantly think upon this level, not thinking ever of lesser goals, for them the Eternal is easily reached, O Arjuna.

"Having come to this Self-realization, these victors need not fear death, the time of pain and sorrow; they have achieved the highest bliss. The activities of the world come and go, O Arjuna; but those who come to the Infinite know how to overcome their limitations.

"The people who know the day of Eternity, a thousand ages in duration, and the night, a thousand ages in ending, they know day and night.

"From the un-manifested all the manifested stream forth at the coming of day; at the coming of night they dissolve, even in that called the un-manifested. This multitude of beings, going forth continually, is dissolved at the coming of night: by ordination, O son of Pandu, it streams forth at the coming of day. Therefore, truly there exists the Eternal, which, in the destroying of all beings, is not destroyed. That un-manifested, 'the Indestructible,' it is called; it is named the highest goal. They who reach it do not return.

"The highest Spirit, O Arjuna, may be reached by unswerving devotion to the Infinite alone, in which all beings abide, by which all of life is pervaded."

The Mystery of Life

Krishna said, "By mystery in its un-manifested aspect all this world is pervaded; all beings have root in it, but it is not rooted in them. As the mighty air everywhere moving is rooted in the ether, so all beings rest rooted in mystery—this you must know.

"Hidden in nature, which is its own, it brings forth again and again a multitude of beings, helpless, by the force of nature. Under the veil of mystery, nature sends forth the moving and unmoving; because of this, O Arjuna, the universe revolves.

"The foolish disregard this, when clad in human semblance, ignorant of life's supreme nature, the greatest among the great; instead, they are empty of hope, empty of worthy deeds, empty of wisdom, senseless, partaking of the deceitful, brutal, and demoniacal nature.

"Others also, sacrificing themselves with wisdom, worship life as the one and the manifold everywhere present.

"To those who seek the Eternal above all else, to those ever harmonious, will come full security. They who worship material gains go to material ends; to the ancestors go the ancestor-worshipers; to the elementals go those who worship elementals; but worshipers of life come to life. One who, with sincerity, offers to a worthy cause even a leaf, a flower, a fruit, water, or any other token gift, will have it accepted from the striving self, offered as it is with devotion.

"On life fix your mind; be devoted to life; sacrifice for life; harmonized thus in the Self, you shall come to life, having the realization of life as your supreme goal."

The Form of the Eternal

Arjuna said, "This word of the supreme secret concerning the Self, you have spoken out of compassion; by this my delusion is taken away. The production and destruction of beings have been heard by me in detail from you, O Krishna, and also the imperishable greatness of the Self, O teacher, even as you describe them. O best of beings, I desire to see the total vision. If you think that by me it can be seen, O Krishna, then help me to see the imperishable Self."

The great teacher said, "Behold, O son of Pandu, this form, a hundred-fold, a thousand-fold, various in kind, divine, various in colors and shapes. Behold many marvels never seen before this, O Arjuna. Here, today, behold the whole universe, movable and immovable, viewed as one, with anything else you desire to see. But truly you are not able to behold this with the unseeing eyes of most people; you must have eyes of understanding. Having these, behold!"

Having thus spoken, the great Krishna helped Arjuna to see the supreme view of life. With many visions of marvel, the Eternal all-marvelous and boundless was envisioned, with rays stretching out everywhere.

If the splendor of a thousand suns were to blaze out together in the sky, that might resemble the glory of this vision.

There Arjuna beheld the whole universe, divided into manifold parts, viewed as one in the indescribable form. Then he, overwhelmed with astonishment, his hair upstanding, bowed down his head and, with joined palms, spoke softly.

Then Krishna said,

"Arjuna, by good favor you have seen
This loftiest form of life's self revealed!
Radiant, all-penetrating, endless, first,
That few beside yourself have ever seen.
Nor self-sacrifice, nor alms, nor works,
Nor sharp austerity, nor study deep,
Can win the vision of this form for humans,
Foremost of Kurus, that you have seen.
Do not be bewildered, nor yet afraid,
Because you have beheld this wondrous form;
Cast fear away, and let your heart rejoice;
Behold again this familiar shape."

Arjuna said, "Beholding again this form, O Krishna, I am now collected, and am restored to my own nature."

The great teacher said, "This form beheld by you is very hard to see. Truly many beings ever long to behold this form. Nor can it be seen as you have seen it, by austerities, nor by alms, nor by works alone: but by devotion to the Eternal it may thus be perceived, Arjuna, and known and seen in essence, and entered, O Arjuna. The one who does actions with this in mind, whose supreme good is the Infinite, my devotee, freed from attachment, without hatred of any being, that person comes to this, O son of Pandu."

The Rule of Devotion

Arjuna said, "Those devotees who, ever harmonized, worship the Eternal as if in human form, and those also who worship the Indestructible, the Unmanifested, which of those is the more able to attain union?

Krishna said, "They who with mind fixed on the Eternal, in whatever form, with faith supreme endowed, these in my opinion are best in striving toward union.

"They who worship the Indestructible, the Ineffable, the Unmanifested, Omnipresent, and Unthinkable, the Unchanging, Immutable—restraining and subduing the senses, regarding everything equally, rejoicing in the welfare of all—these also come to the Eternal.

"The difficulty of those whose minds are set on the Unmanifested is greater; for the path of the Unmanifested is hard for the embodied to reach.

"Those truly who, renouncing all un-purposeful actions and intent on realization, worship meditating on life, with wholehearted striving, these are speedily lifted up from the ocean of death, O son of Pandu, their minds being fixed on the Eternal, in whatever form.

"Place your mind in life, into life let your reason enter; then without doubt you shall abide in life hereafter. And if you are not able firmly to fix your mind on life, then by the discipline of practice seek to reach life, O Arjuna.

"If also you are not equal to constant practice, be intent on service; performing actions for life's sake, you shall attain perfection. If even to do this you do not have strength, then, taking refuge in union with life, renounce all fruits of action with the self controlled.

"Better indeed is wisdom than constant practice; than wisdom, meditation is better; than meditation, renunciation of the fruits of action; on renunciation follows peace.

"Those who bear no ill-will to any being, being friendly and compassionate, without attachment and egoism, balanced in pleasure and pain, forgiving, ever content, harmonious with the self, controlled, resolute, with mind and reason dedicated to the Infinite, they, my devotee, are able to attain union.

"He from whom the world does not shrink away, who does not shrink away from the world, being freed from the anxieties of excitement, anger, and fear, he is able to attain union.

"Those who want nothing, are pure, expert, passionless, untroubled, renouncing every purposeless undertaking, they, my devotee, are able to attain union. Those who neither sensually love nor violently hate, nor grieve, nor crave, but are full of devotion, they are able to attain union.

"Those who are alike to foe and friend, and also in fame and ignominy, alike in cold and heat, pleasure and pain, destitute of attachment, taking equally praise and reproach, silent, wholly content with what comes as personal reward, homeless, firm in mind, full of devotion, those beings are able to attain union."

The Good Person and the Evil

"Fearlessness, cleanness of life, steadfastness in the quest of wisdom, self-restraint and self-sacrifice and study of the scriptures, austerity, straightforwardness, harmlessness, truth, absence of wrath, renunciation, peacefulness, absence of crookedness, compassion to living beings, un-covetousness, mildness, modesty, absence of fickleness, vigor, forgiveness, fortitude, purity, absence of envy and haughtiness—these are the ones who have the divine properties, O Arjuna.

"Hypocrisy, arrogance and conceit, wrath and also harshness and un-wisdom are those who have demoniacal properties.

"The divine properties are deemed to be for liberation, the demoniacal for bondage. Do not grieve, for you have all divine properties, O Arjuna.

"Two opposing elements are found among the animate creation in the world, the divine and the demoniacal: the divine have been described at length: hear from me, O son of Pandu, the demoniacal. These negative traits in people are: knowing neither right energy nor right abstinence, nor purity, nor even propriety, nor truth. 'The universe is without truth, without basis,' people of this type say, 'without any Eternal; brought about by mutual union, and caused by lust and nothing else.'

"Holding this view, these people of small understanding, often of fierce deeds, come forth as hindrances to the growth of civilization. Surrendering themselves to insatiable desires, possessed with vanity, conceit, and arrogance, holding evil ideas through delusion, they engage in action with impure resolves. Giving themselves over to unmeasured thought whose end is death, regarding the gratification of cravings as the highest, feeling sure that this is all, held in bondage by a hundred ties of expectation, given over to lust and anger, they strive to obtain by unlawful means hoards of wealth for sensual enjoyments.

"'This today by me has been won, that benefit I shall gain; this wealth is mine already, and also this shall be mine in the future. I have slain this enemy, and others also I shall slay. I am the lord, I am the enjoyer, I am perfect, powerful, happy; I am wealthy, well-born; who else is there that is like me? I will give alms, I will rejoice.' Thus deluded by unwisdom, bewildered by numerous thoughts, enmeshed in the web of delusion, addicted to the gratification of urges, they go to self-destruction.

"Self-glorifying, stubborn, filled with the pride and intoxication of wealth, they perform lip-sacrifices for ostentation, contrary to scriptural ordinance. Given over to egoism, power, insolence, lust and wrath, these malicious ones hate truth in others and in themselves.

"People liberated from these ways of darkness, O son of Pandu, accomplish their own welfare and thus reach the highest goal.

"Those who, having cast aside the ordinances of the scriptures, follow the promptings of craving do not attain happiness, or perfection, or the highest goal.

"Therefore, let the scriptures be your authority in determining what ought to be done. Knowing what has been declared by the ordinances of the scriptures, you ought to work in the world."

The Way of Deliverance

"Humans reach perfection by each being intent on duty to self and to others. Listen as to how perfection is won by one who is intent on this duty. Better is one's own duty, thought destitute of merits, than the well-executed duty of another. One who does the duty laid down by one's own nature does not incur sin. Duty to one's own nature, O son of Pandu, though defectively executed, ought not to be abandoned. All undertakings indeed are clouded by defects as fire by smoke.

"One whose reason is everywhere unattached, the self subdued, dead to lusts, goes by renunciation to the supreme perfection of freedom from external authority. How one who has approached perfection obtains the Eternal, that highest state of wisdom, learn from me only succinctly, O Arjuna.

"United to the reason, purified, controlling the self by firmness, having abandoned sound and the other objects of the senses, having laid aside passion and malice, dwelling in spiritual solitude, abstemious, sparing of speech, body and mind subdued, constantly concerned with meditation and discipline, taking refuge in dispassion, having cast aside egoism, violence, arrogance, craving, wrath, covetousness; being selfless and peaceful——they are fit to discover lasting happiness.

"Finding lasting happiness, serene in the Self, they neither grieve nor desire; the same to all beings, they obtain supreme devotion to the Eternal. By devotion they know life in essence; having thus known life in essence, they enter into the Supreme. Though ever performing actions, taking refuge in purposeful living, they obtain the eternal, indestructible condition.

"Renouncing mentally all distractions, intent on the Infinite, resorting to the discipline of discrimination, have your thought ever on the highest goal. Thinking thus, you shall overcome all obstacles; but if from egoism you will not depart, you shall destroy yourself. Entrenched in egoism, you think, 'I will not fight;' to no purpose your determination, nature will constrain you.

"O son of Pandu, bound by your own duty born of your own nature, that which from delusion you desire not to do, even that you shall perform. The Eternal dwells in the hearts of all beings, O Arjuna, by some illusive power, causing all beings to revolve, as though mounted on a potter's wheel.

"Flee to the Self for shelter with all your being, O Arjuna; with its aid you shall obtain supreme peace, the everlasting dwelling-place. Thus has wisdom, more secret than secrecy itself, been declared to you by me; having reflected on it fully, then act as well as you have listened."

Arjuna said, "Destroyed is my delusion. I have gained understanding by means of your teachings, O Krishna. I am firm; my doubts have fled away. I will do according to your word."

SANKACHARYA'S ATMA BODHA (KNOWLEDGE OF THE SOUL)

The human soul is smothered, as it were, by ignorance, but as soon as ignorance is supplanted, the soul shines forth, like the sun when released from the clouds. After the soul, afflicted by ignorance, has been purified by understanding, excess knowledge disappears, as salt after it has dissolved in water.

Like an image in a dream, the world is troubled by craving, hatred, and other poisons. As long as the dream lasts, the image appears to be real; but on awakening it vanishes.

Those beings, true, intelligent, comprehend within themselves every variety of being, penetrating and permeating all as a thread which strings together beads.

In consequence of possessing diverse attributes, the supreme existence appears manifold, but when the attributes are comprehended, unity is discovered. In consequence of those diverse attributes, a variety of names and conditions are supposed proper to the soul, just as a variety of tastes and colors are attributed to water.

All that belongs to the body is visible; it is perishable as bubbles of air (on the surface of water); but that which has not these signs must be recognized as pure soul which says of itself, "I am of the Eternal."

This conception, "I am of the Eternal," incessantly entertained, disperses the hallucinations born of ignorance, as medicine disperses sickness.

THE YOGA SUTRAS OF PATANJALI

I

The following instruction concerns the science of union with the Eternal. This union is achieved through the subjugation of the psychic nature, and the restraint of the mind. When this has been accomplished, individuals know themselves as they are in reality.

The mind states are five, and are subject to pleasure or pain; they are painful or not painful. These modifications are: correct knowledge, incorrect knowledge, fancy, passivity (sleep), and memory. The basis of correct knowledge is correct perception, correct deduction, and correct witness (or accurate evidence).

The control of these modifications of the internal organ, the mind, is to be brought about through tireless endeavor and through nonattachment to needless pleasures.

When the object to be gained is sufficiently valued, and the efforts toward its attainment are persistently followed without intermission, then the steadiness of the mind is secured.

Nonattachment is freedom from longing for all objects of craving, either worldly or traditional. The consummation of this nonattachment results in an exact knowledge of the spiritual person when liberated from all temptations.

The consciousness of an object is attained by concentration upon its fourfold nature: the form, through examination; the quality, through discriminative participation; the purpose, through inspiration; and the soul, through identification.

A further stage of union is achieved when, through one-pointed thought, the outer activity is brought into dynamic equilibrium.

Other people achieve union and arrive at a discrimination of pure spirit through belief, followed by energy, memory, meditation, and right perception.

The attainment of this state (spiritual consciousness) is rapid for those whose will is intensely alive.

By intense devotion to the soul, knowledge of the soul is gained.

The obstacles to soul cognition are bodily disability, mental inertia, wrong questioning, carelessness, laziness, lack of dispassion, erroneous perception, inability to achieve concentration, failure to hold the meditative attitude when achieved. Pain, despair, misplaced bodily activity, and wrong direction (or control) of the life currents are the results of the obstacles in the lower psychic nature. To overcome the obstacles and their accompaniments, the intense application of the will to some one truth (or principle) is usually required.

Peace of mind can be brought about through the practice of sympathy, tenderness, steadiness of purpose, and dispassion in regard to pleasure or pain, or toward all forms of good or evil. Peace of mind is also brought about by the regulation of the activities of life.

To those whose modifications of the substance of the mind are entirely controlled, there eventuates a state of identity with and similarity to that which is realized. The knower, knowledge, and the field of knowledge become one, just as the crystal takes to itself the colors of that which is reflected in it.

When this state is reached, individuals acquire pure spiritual realization through the balanced condition of the mind. Their perception is now much more exact.

II

The discipline of action, leading to union with the Eternal, is aspiration, spiritual reading, and devotion to the spiritual life.

These are the difficulty-producing hindrances: ignorance, egoism, craving, hate, and the sense of attachment to pleasures. These five hindrances, when subtly known, can be overcome by an opposing mental attitude.

To the illuminated person, all existence contains sorrow, owing to the prevalence of suffering. However, much suffering may be eliminated or warded off by proper attention to this endeavor.

In the case of the person who has achieved union, the objective universe has ceased to be. But it exists still for those who are not yet free.

Eight means of seeking union are: the commandments, the rules of life, posture, right control of life's activities, abstraction, attention, meditation, contemplation. Harmlessness, truth to all beings, abstention from theft, from incontinence and from avarice, constitute the five commandments. The five commandments, which are universal duty, are irrespective of race, place, time, or emergency.

When thoughts which are contrary to union are present, there should be the cultivation of their opposite. Thoughts contrary to union are: harmfulness, falsehood, theft, incontinence, and avarice, whether committed personally, caused to be committed or approved of, whether arising from avarice, anger, or delusion (ignorance); whether slight in the doing, middling, or great. These result always in excessive pain and ignorance. For this reason, the contrary thoughts must be cultivated.

In the presence of those who have perfected harmlessness, all enmity ceases. When truth to all beings is perfected, the effectiveness of words and acts is soon to be seen. When abstention from theft is perfected, individuals can have whatever they desire. By abstention from sexual promiscuity, energy is acquired. When abstention from avarice is perfected, there comes an understanding of the law of spiritual birth.

The posture assumed must be steady and easy. Steadiness and ease of posture are to be achieved through persistent slight effort and through the concentration of the mind upon the Infinite. When this is attained, the pairs of opposites no longer limit. When right posture has been attained, there follows right control of the life currents and the breath.

Right control of the life currents is external, internal, or motionless; it is subject to place, time, and number, and is also protracted or brief.

There is a fourth stage which transcends those dealing with the internal and external phases. Through this, that which obscures the light is gradually removed, and the mind is prepared for concentrated meditation.

III

Concentration is the fixing of the mind upon a particular object. Sustained concentration is meditation. When the mind becomes absorbed in that which is the reality (or idea embodied in the form), and is unaware of separateness or the ego, this is contemplation. When concentration, meditation, and contemplation form one sequential act, then is clarity of mind achieved. As a result of clarity of mind comes the shining forth of the light.

The sequence of mental states is as follows: the mind reacts to that which is seen; then follows the moment of mind control. Then ensues a moment wherein the mind responds to both these factors. Through the cultivation of this habit of mind there will eventuate a steadiness of spiritual perception. The establishing of this habit, and the restraining of the mind from its thought-form-making tendency, result eventually in the constant power to contemplate.

Through concentrated meditation upon the triple nature of every form comes the revelation of that which has been and of that which will be. The sound (or word), that which it denotes (the object), and the embodied spiritual essence (or idea) are usually confused in the mind of the perceiver. By concentrated meditation on these three aspects comes an intuitive comprehension of the sound uttered by all forms of life.

Through concentrated meditation, the thought images in the minds of other people become apparent. As, however, the object of those thoughts is not apparent to the perceivers, they see only the thought and not the object. Their meditation excludes the tangible.

By concentrated meditation upon the distinction between form and substance, those properties of the substance which make it visible to the human eye are negated (or withdrawn), and the individual can become selfless.

The effects are of two kinds: immediate or future. By perfectly concentrated meditation on these, individuals know the meaning of their experience in the world. This knowledge comes also from signs.

Union with others is to be gained partially through one-pointed meditation upon the three states of feeling—compassion, tenderness, and dispassion.

Understanding of mind-consciousness may be increased by one-pointed meditation upon the heart center.

By liberation from the causes of bondage through their weakening and by an understanding of the mode of transference (withdrawal or entrance), the mind can enter another body.

One-pointed meditation upon the five forms which every element takes produces mastery over every element. These five forms are: the gross nature, the elemental form, the quality, the pervasiveness, and the basic purpose. Through this mastery, minuteness and the other powers are attained, likewise true bodily perfection and freedom from all hindrances.

Mastery over the senses is brought about through concentrated meditation upon their nature, peculiar attributes, egoism, pervasiveness, and useful purpose. As a result of this perfection, there come rapidity of action like that of mind, perception independent of the organs, and mastery over root substance.

There should be entire rejection of all allurements from all forms of being, for the recurrence of evil contacts remains possible.

When the objective forms and the soul have reached a condition of equal purity, then is at-one-ment achieved and liberation results.

THE WORKS OF SRI RAMAKRISHNA

The Sayings of Sri Ramakrishna

You see many stars at night in the sky but find them not when the sun rises; can you say that there are no stars in the sky during the day? So, O friend, because you do not find the Eternal in the days of your ignorance, do not say that there is no Eternal.

As one and the same material, water, is called by different names by different peoples—one calling it water, another eau, a third aqua, and another pani—so the One, the everlasting-intelligent-bliss, is sought by some as God, by some as Allah, by some as Jehovah, by some as Hari, and by others as Brahman.

As one can ascend to the top of a house by means of a ladder or a bamboo or a staircase or a rope, so diverse are the ways and means to approach the Eternal, and every religion in the world shows at least one of these ways.

Different creeds are but different paths to reach the Eternal. Various and different are the ways that lead to the temple of Mother Kali. Similarly, various are the ways that to the dwelling place of the Divine. Every religion is nothing but one or more of such paths that lead to the Eternal.

As the young wife in a family shows her love and respect to father-in-law, mother-in-law, and every other member of the family and at the same time loves her husband more than these, similarly, being firm in your devotion to the supreme value of your own choice, do not despise other deities and beliefs, but honor them all in proportion to the thoughts and actions they produce.

Two persons were hotly disputing as to the color of a chameleon. One said, "The chameleon on that palm tree is of a beautiful red color. The other, contradicting him, said, "You are mistaken, the chameleon is not red but blue." Not being able to settle the matter by arguments, both went to the person who always lived under that tree and had watched the chameleon in all its phases of color. One of them said, "Sir, is not the chameleon on that tree of a red color?" The person replied, "Yes, sir." The other disputant said, "What do you say? How is it? It is not red, it is blue." That person again humbly replied, "Yes, sir." The person knew that the chameleon is an animal that constantly changes color; thus it was that he said "yes" to both of the conflicting statements.

The One likewise has many forms. The devotees who have seen the Eternal in one aspect only, know it in that aspect alone. But those who have seen It in manifold aspects are alone in a position to say, "All these forms are one, and the Eternal is multiform." It is with form and without form, and many are its forms which no one knows.

Those who try to give an idea of the Eternal by mere book learning are like the ones who attempt to give an idea of a city by means of a map or picture.

All the sacred scriptures of the world have become as if defiled (as food thrown out of the mouth becomes polluted), because they have been constantly repeated by and have come out of human mouths. But the Infinite has never been defiled, for no one as yet has been able to express It by human speech.

As long as one is not blessed with the divine vision, as long as the base metal is not turned into gold by touching the philosopher's stone, there will be the delusion of "I am the doer," and so long must there necessarily remain the idea of the distinction between "I have done this good work," and "I have done that bad work." This idea of duality or distinction is the evil which is responsible for the continuance of much world confusion. By taking refuge in the Eternal, which follows the adoption of the right path, one can reach it. Those alone cross the ocean of life who come face to face with Truth, who realize the Eternal within. They are truly free, living even in this body, who know that Life is the doer and they are the non-doers.

The magnetic needle always points toward the north, and hence it is that the sailing vessel does not lose her course. As long as the hearts of individuals are directed toward the Infinite, they cannot be lost in the ocean of worldliness.

Some people weep rivers of tears because a son is not born to them. Others wear away their hearts with sorrow because they cannot get riches. But how many are there who weep and sorrow because they have not found the Eternal? They will find who seek earnestly; those who with intense longing search for God will find God.

Truly, truly, I say to you, those who long for the Eternal will find it. Go and verify this in your own life. Try for three consecutive days with genuine earnestness and you are sure to succeed.

Spirit cannot be found as long as there is the slightest taint of craving. Therefore, have your small longings satisfied, and renounce the big cravings by right reasoning and discrimination.

It is the nature of the lamp to give light. With its help some may cook food, some may forge a deed, and others may read words of truth. So with the help of divine guidance some try to attain self-realization, others try to serve their lesser purposes, and so on. The Infinite, however, remains unaffected.

The truly wise person is one who has found the Divine. That person becomes like a child. The child, no doubt, seems to have an egoism of its own; but that egoism is a mere appearance; it is not selfish egoism. The self of a child is nothing like the self of a grown-up.

Understanding and love of God are ultimately one and the same. There is no difference between pure understanding and pure love.

The Master said, "Everything that exists is divine." The male youth understood it literally, but not in the right spirit. While he was passing through the street he met an elephant. The driver shouted aloud from his high place, "Move away! Move away!" The pupil argued in his mind, "Why should I move away? I am divine, so is the elephant divine; what fear has the divine of itself?" Thinking thus, he did not move. At last the elephant took him up in his trunk and dashed him aside. He was hurt severely, and going back to his master, he related the whole adventure. The master said, "All right. You are divine, the elephant is divine also, but the Divine in the shape of the elephant-driver was warning you to move. Why did you not pay heed to his warnings?"

Saviors are the messengers of the Eternal. They are like the viceroys of a mighty monarch. As when there is some disturbance in a far-off province, the viceroy is sent to quell it, so whenever there is a decline of religion in any part of the world, a savior appears there. It is one and the same savior that, having plunged into the ocean of life, rises up in one place and is known as Krishna, and diving down again rises in another place and is known as Christ.

The saviors stand in relation to the Infinite as the waves of the ocean are to the ocean.

On the tree of Absolute Existence-Knowledge-Bliss there hang innumerable Ramas, Krishnas, Buddhas, Christs, etc., out of which one or two appear in the world now and then to produce mighty changes and revolutions.

There is a fabled species of birds called Homa, which live so high up in the heavens, and so dearly love those regions, that they never condescend to come down to the earth. Even their eggs, which when laid in the sky begin to fall down to the earth attracted by gravity, are said to get hatched in the middle of their downward course and give birth to the young ones. The fledglings at once find out that they are falling down and immediately change their course and begin to fly upward toward their home, drawn there by instinct. Men such as Suka Deva, Navada, Jesus, Sankaracharya, and others, are like those birds, who even in their boyhood give up all attachments to the limitations of this world and betake themselves to the highest regions of true knowledge and divine light.

As an aquatic bird, such as a pelican, dives into water, but the water does not wet its plumage, so the emancipated soul lives in the world, but the world does not pollute it.

Ornaments cannot be made of pure gold. Some alloy must be mixed with the gold. People totally devoid of attachment to the world will not survive more than twenty-one days. So long as individuals have a body, they must have some attachment, however small it may be, to carry on the functions of the body.

Do you have, O preacher, the badge of authority? As the humblest servant of the king authorized by him is heard with respect and awe, and can quell a riot by showing his/her badge, so must you, O preacher, obtain first the order and inspiration from the Divine. So long as you do not have this badge of divine inspiration you may preach all your life, but only in vain.

What is true preaching like? Instead of preaching to others, if one seeks the Eternal all that time, that is enough preaching. Those who strive to make themselves free are the real preachers. Hundreds come from all sides, no one knows from where, to those who are free, and are taught by them. When a rosebud blooms, the bees come from all sides uninvited and unasked.

Throw an unbaked cake of flour into hot butter, and it will make a sort of boiling noise. But the more it is fried, the less becomes the noise; and when it is fully fried, the bubbling ceases altogether. As long as people have little knowledge, they go about lecturing and preaching, but when the perfection of knowledge is obtained, they cease to make vain displays.

As many have merely heard of snow but not seen it, so many are the religious preachers who have read only in books about the attributes of the Divine, but have not realized them in their lives. And as many have seen but not tasted it, so many are the religious teachers who have got only a glimpse of divine glory, but have not understood its real essence. They only who have tasted the snow can say what it is like. Similarly, they alone can describe the attributes of the Eternal who have associated with It in its different aspects, now as a servant of Life, then as a friend of Life, then as a lover of Life, or as being absorbed in Life.

The seeds of Vajrabantul do not fall to the bottom of the tree. They are carried by the wind far off and take root there. So the spirit of the prophets manifests itself at a distance and is appreciated there.

The sunlight is one and the same wherever it falls, but only bright surfaces like water, mirrors, and polished metals can reflect it fully. So is the Divine Light. It falls equally and impartially on all hearts, but only the pure and clean hearts of the good and holy can fully reflect It.

Every person should follow his/her own religion. A Christian should follow Christianity, a Muslim should follow Islam, and so on. For the Hindus the ancient path, the path of the Aryan Rishis, is the best.

People partition off their lands by means of boundaries, but no one can partition off the all-embracing sky overhead. The indivisible sky surrounds all and includes all. So average individuals in ignorance say, "My religion is the only one; my religion is the best." But when their hearts are illumined by true knowledge, they know that above all these wars of sects and sectarians presides the one Indivisible, Eternal, All-knowing Bliss.

As a mother, in nursing her sick children, gives rice and curry to one and sago arrowroot to another and bread and butter to a third, so Spirit has laid out different paths for different people suitable to their natures.

Do not dispute. As you rest firmly on your faith and opinion, allow others also the equal liberty to stand by their own faiths and opinions. By mere disputation you will never succeed in convincing others of their errors. When the light of inspiration descends on them, all will understand their own mistakes.

So long as the bee is outside the petals of the lily, and has not tasted the sweetness of its honey, it hovers around the flower emitting its buzzing sound; but when it is inside the flower, it noiselessly drinks its nectar. So long as a person quarrels and disputes about doctrines and dogmas, he/she has not tasted the nectar of true faith; when one has tasted it, one becomes quiet and full of peace.

People of some ages care for the essence of everything. They will accept the essentials of religion and not its nonessentials (that is, the rituals, ceremonials, dogmas, and creeds).

Although in a grain of paddy the germ is considered the only necessary thing (for germination and growth), while the husk or chaff is considered to be of no importance; still if the husked grain be put into the ground, it will not sprout up and grow into a plant and produce rice. To get a crop one needs to sow the grain with the husk on. But if one wants to get at the kernel itself, one must remove the husk of the grain. So rites and ceremonies are necessary for the growth and perpetuation of a religion. They are receptacles that contain the kernel of truth, and consequently everyone must perform them until the central truth is reached.

Honor spirit and form, both sentiment within and symbol without.

Many people talk of religion but act not a grain of it; while the wise person speaks little, but his/her whole life is a religion acted out.

What you wish others to do, do yourself.

The tender bamboo can be easily bent, but the full-grown bamboo breaks when an attempt is made to bend it. It is easy to bend young hearts toward the Eternal, but the heart of the old more easily escapes the hold when so drawn.

Newborn calves look very lively, blithe, and merry. They jump and run all day long, and only stop to suck the sweet milk from their mothers. But no sooner are the ropes placed around their necks than they begin to pine away gradually, and, far from being merry, wear a dejected and sorry appearance, and get almost reduced to a skeleton. As long as children have no concern with the affairs of the world, they are as merry as the day is long. But when they once feel the weight of responsibilities of a family person, by binding themselves in time to the world by the indissoluble tie of wedlock, then they no longer appear jolly, but wear the look of dejection, care, and anxiety, and are seen to lose the glow of health from their cheeks, while wrinkles gradually make their appearance on the forehead. Blessed are those who, though accepting responsibilities, by means of idealism retain the spirit of a child throughout their lives, free as the morning air, fresh as a newly blown flower, and pure as a dew-drop.

Worldly people repeat the name of their savior and perform various pious and charitable deeds with the hope of worldly rewards, but when misfortune, sorrow, poverty, or death approach them, they forget them all. They are like the parrot that repeats by rote the divine name "Radha Krishna, Radha Krishna" the livelong day, but cries "Kaw, Kaw," when caught by a cat, forgetting the divine name.

Flies sit at times on the sweetmeats kept exposed for sale in the shop of a confectioner; but no sooner does a sweeper pass by with a basketful of filth than the flies leave the sweetmeats and set upon the basket of filth. But the honey-bee never sits on filthy objects, and always drinks honey from the flowers. The worldly people are like flies. At times they get a momentary taste of divine sweetness, but their natural tendency for filth soon brings them back to the dunghill of worldly temptations. The good person, on the other hand, is always absorbed in the beatific contemplation of divine beauty.

It is true that the Divine is even in the tiger, but we must not go and face the animal. So it is true that the Divine dwells even in the most wicked, but it is not suitable that we should associate freely with the wicked.

A young plant should always be protected by a fence from the mischief of goats and cows and little urchins. But when once it becomes a big tree, a flock of goats or a herd of cows may find shelter under its spreading boughs and fill their stomachs with its leaves. So when you have but little faith within you, you should protect it from the evil influences of bad company and worldliness. But when once you grow strong in faith, no worldliness or evil inclination will dare approach your holy presence; and many who are wicked will become godly through your holy contact.

If you have a mind to live spiritually unattached to the world, you should first practice devotion in relative solitude for some time— say a year, or six months, or a month, or at least twelve days. During the period of retirement you should meditate constantly upon the Eternal and seek after divine love. You should revolve in your mind the thought that there is nothing in the world that you may call your own; those whom you think your own will pass away in no time. Life is really your own, it is your all-in-all. How to obtain it should be your only concern.

Those who live in the world and try to find union with the Divine are like soldiers that fight protected by the breastwork of a fort, while the ascetics who renounce the world in search of union are like soldiers fighting in the open field. To fight from within the fort is more convenient and safer than to fight in the open field.

The spiritual gain of individuals depends upon their sentiments and ideas, proceeds from their hearts and not from visible actions. Two friends, while strolling about, happened to pass a place where the meaning of the scriptures was being preached. One of them said, "Brother, let us go there for a while and hear the good words spoken." The other replied, "No, friend, what is the use of hearing the scriptures? Let us spend the time in yonder public-house in amusement and pleasure." The first one did not consent to this. That individual went to the place where the scripture was being read and began to hear it. The other went to the public-house, but did not find the pleasure that had been anticipated there and was thinking all the while, "Alas, me! Why have I come here? How happy is my friend hearing all the while the sacred life and deeds of the savior." Thus the one friend meditated on the Savior even though in a public-house. The other one who was hearing the scripture did not find pleasure in it. Sitting there, the first friend began to indulge in self-blame, saying, "Alas! Why did I not accompany my friend to the public-house? What a great pleasure my friend must be enjoying at this time there!" The result was that the one who was sitting where the scripture was preached meditated on

192 / WORLD SCRIPTURES

the pleasure of the public-house and acquired the degradation of going to the public-house because of his bad thoughts; while the one who had gone to the public-house acquired the merit of hearing the scripture because of having a good heart.

It is the mind that makes us wise or ignorant, bound or emancipated. We are holy because of our minds, one is degraded because of having an undisciplined mind, while another is virtuous because of his purified mind. So those whose minds are always fixed on the Eternal require no other practices, devotion, or spiritual exercises.

The faith-healers of India order their patients to repeat with full conviction the words, "There is no illness in me, there is no illness at all." The patient repeats it, and thus mentally denying the illness, it usually goes away. So if you think yourself mortally weak and without goodness, you will really find yourself to be so in time. Know and believe that you are of immense power, and the power will come to you at last.

A wife once spoke to her husband, saying, "My dear, I am very anxious about my brother. For the last few days he has been thinking of renouncing the world and of becoming an ascetic, and has begun preparations for it. He has been trying gradually to curb his desires and reduce his wants." The husband replied, "You need not be anxious about your brother. He will never become an ascetic. No one has ever renounced the world by making long preparations." The wife asked, "How then does one become an ascetic?" The husband answered, "Do you wish to see how one renounces the world? Let me show you." Saying this, instantly he tore his flowing dress into pieces, tied one piece around his loins, told his wife that she and all women were henceforth his mother, and left the house never to return.

There is nothing to be proud of in money. If you say that you are rich, there are richer and richer people than you, in comparison with whom you are a mere beggar. After dusk, when the glow-worms make their appearance, they think, "We are giving light to the world." But when the stars rise, their haughtiness is gone. Then the stars begin to think, "We are shedding light on the universe." After some time the moon ascends into the sky, and the stars are humiliated and look melancholy. So again the moon begins to be arrogant and think that by her light the world is lighted, and smiles and bathes in beauty and cheerfulness. But lo! the dawn proclaims the advent of the rising sun on the eastern horizon. Where is the moon now? If they who think themselves rich ponder over these natural facts, they will never, never boast of their riches again.

If I hold up this cloth before me, you will not see me any more, though I shall be as near to you as ever. So also the Eternal is nearer to you than anything else, yet because of the screen of egoism you cannot see It.

Sankaracharya had a male disciple who served him for a long time, but he did not give any instructions to him. Once when Sankara was seated alone, he heard the footsteps of someone coming behind. He called out, "Who is there?" The disciple answered, "It is I." The Master said, "If the word I is so dear to you, then either expand it indefinitely—that is, know the universe as yourself—or renounce it altogether."

If you find that you cannot make this "I" go, then let it remain as the "servant I." There is not much to fear of mischief in the "I" which knows itself as "I am the servant of God; I am a devotee." Sweets beget dyspepsia, but crystallized sugar candy is not among the sweets, for it has not that injurious property.

The "servant I," the "I" of a devotee, or the "I" of a child is like the line drawn with a stick on a sheet of water. It does not last long.

If you feel proud, feel so in the thought that you are the servant of Life. Great people have the nature of children. They are always children in the Divine Light, so they have no egoism. All their strength is of the Eternal, belonging to and coming from It, nothing of themselves.

There are two egos—one ripe and the other unripe. "Nothing is mine; whatever I see, feel or hear, no, even this body, is not mine. I am always eternal, free, and all-knowing"—the ego that has this idea is the ripe one, while the unripe ego is that which thinks, "This is my house, my child, my wife, my body, etc."

When the knowledge of Self is gained, all fetters fall off of themselves. Then there is no distinction between a clergyman and a layman, a high class and a low class. In that state the sacred thread of a class falls away of itself. But so long as people have the consciousness of distinction and difference, they should not forcibly throw it off.

The spiritual-minded belong to a class of their own, irrespective of all social conventions.

When people are on the plains, they see the lowly grass and the mighty pine tree and say, "How big is the tree and how small is the grass!" But when they ascend the mountain and look from its high peak to the plain below, the mighty pine tree and the lowly grass blend into one indistinguishable mass of green verdure. So in the sight of the worldly there are differences of rank and position—one is a king, another is a cobbler, one a father, another a son, and so on—but when the divine sight is opened, all appear as equal and one, and there remains no separation of good and bad, high and low.

Human beings are like pillow-cases. The color of the one may be red, that of another blue, that of a third black, but all contain the same cotton. So it is with human beings—one is beautiful, another is ugly, a third holy, a fourth wicked—but the divine One dwells within them all.

If you fill an earthen vessel with water and set it apart upon a shelf, the water in it will dry up in a few days; but if you place the same vessel immersed in water, it will remain filled as long as it is kept there. Even so is the case with true love. Fill and enrich your bosom with the love of things eternal for a time and then employ yourself in other affairs, forgetting this love all the while, and then you are sure to find within a short time that your heart has become poor and vacant and devoid of that precious love. But if you keep your heart immersed always in the ocean of divine love, your heart is sure to remain ever full to overflowing with the water of the divine love.

There are three kinds of love—unselfish, mutual, and selfish. The unselfish love is of the highest kind. These lovers only mind the welfare of the beloved and do not brood over their own sufferings. In mutual love the lovers not only want the happiness of their beloved but have an eye toward their own pleasure also. It is middling. The selfish love is the lowest. It only looks toward its own pleasure, no matter whether the beloved experiences well-being or ill.

A male devotee after fourteen years' penance in a solitary forest obtained at last the power of walking on water. Overjoyed at this, he went to his teacher and said, "Master, master, I have acquired the power of walking on water." The master rebukingly replied, "Alas, O child! Is this the result of your fourteen years' labors? Truly, you have obtained only that which is worth a penny; for what you have accomplished after fourteen years' arduous labor ordinary people do by paying a penny to the boatman."

Fans should be discarded when the wind blows. Prayers and penances should be discarded when the light of the Eternal shines.

As long as one does not become simple like a child, one does not get divine illumination. Forget the worldly knowledge that you have acquired and become as ignorant of worldly ways as a child, and then you will get the divine wisdom.

Lunatics, drunkards, and children sometimes give out the truth unconsciously, as if inspired by a vision of the Eternal.

To kill another, swords and shields are needed, while to kill one's own self even a pin will do; so to teach others one must study many scriptures and sciences, while to acquire self-illumination firm faith in a single motto will suffice.

THE PARABLES OF SRI RAMAKRISHNA

The Saints and the Saviors

A place was enclosed by means of a high wall. The people outside did not know what sort of place it was. Once four persons determined to find out what was inside by scaling the wall with a ladder. As soon as the first individual ascended to the top of the wall, he/she laughed out, "Ha, ha, ha!" and jumped in. The second also, as soon as he/she ascended, similarly laughed aloud and jumped in, and so did the third. When the fourth and last person got up to the top of the wall, that individual found stretched below a large and beautiful garden containing pleasant groves and delicious fruits. Though strongly tempted to jump down and enjoy the scene, the last person resisted the temptation, and coming down the ladder, preached the glad tidings about the beautiful garden to all outsiders.

The state of peace is like the walled garden. Those who see it forget their own existence and with ecstatic joy rush headlong into it to attain to absolute freedom from the cares of the world. Such are the holy people and liberated saints of the world. But the saviors of humanity are those who have found peace and, being at the same time anxious to obtain lasting happiness by sharing their divine vision with others, refuse the final liberation from worldly cares, and willingly undergo the troubles of living in the world in order to teach and lead struggling humanity to its ultimate goal.

The Fortunate Woodcutter

A male woodcutter led a very miserable life with the small means he could procure by daily selling the load of wood brought from a neighboring forest. Once a male hermit, who was wending his way through the forest, saw him at work and advised him to proceed onward into the interior recesses of the forest, intimating to him that he would be a gainer thereby. The woodcutter obeyed the injunction and proceeded onward until he came to a sandalwood tree, and being much pleased, he took away with him as many sandal logs as he could carry and sold them in the market and derived much profit. Then he began to think within himself why the good hermit did not tell him anything about the wood of the sandal tree, but simply advised him to proceed onward into the interior of the forest. So the next day he went on beyond the place of the sandalwood, and at last came upon a copper mine, and he took with him as much copper as he could carry, and, selling it in the market, got much money by it. Next day, without stopping at the copper mine, he proceeded further still, as the hermit had advised him to do, and came upon a silver mine, and took with him as much of it as he could carry and sold it all and got even more money; and so daily proceeding further and further, he got at gold mines and diamond mines and at last became exceedingly rich.

Such is also the case with devotees who aspire after true knowledge. If they do not stop in their progress after attaining a few extraordinary powers, they at last will become really rich in the eternal knowledge of truth.

The Power of Faith

A female disciple, having firm faith in the infinite power of her teacher, walked over a river even by pronouncing her name. The teacher, seeing this, thought, "Well, is there such a power even in my name? Then I must be very great and powerful, no doubt!" The next day he/she also tried to walk over the river pronouncing "I, I, I," but no sooner had the teacher stepped into the waters than he/she sank and was drowned. Faith can seemingly achieve miracles, while vanity or egoism is the death of the individual.

Of Worldly Demands

It is said that when primitives try to invoke the deity through the medium of the spirit of the dead, they sit over a fresh human corpse and keep food and wine nearby. During the invocation, if at any time the corpse is vivified (though temporarily) and opens its mouth, the intrepid invoker must pour the wine and the food into its gaping mouth at the time to appease the elemental that has, for the time being, taken possession of the dead body. If they do not do so, the invocation is interrupted by this elemental and the higher spirit does not descend. So, dwelling in the bosom of the carcass of the world, if you want to attain beatitude, you must first provide yourself beforehand with everything necessary to pacify the clamor of all worldly demands upon you; otherwise your devotions will be broken and interrupted by worldly cares and anxieties.

The Ocean of Lasting Happiness

Alligators love to swim on the surface of the water, but as soon as they rise up they are made a mark of by the hunters. Necessarily they are obliged to remain under water and cannot rise to the surface. Still, whenever they find an opportunity, they rise up with a deep whizzing noise and swim happily on the wide watery expanse. O friend, entangled in the meshes of the world, you too are anxious to swim on the surface of the ocean of lasting happiness, but are prevented from doing so by the importunate demands of your society. But be of good cheer, and whenever you find any leisure seek intensely to develop your inner life. In the proper time, then, you will surely be emancipated and enabled to swim merrily on the surface of the ocean of lasting happiness.

The Protection of the Eternal

A Jnani (knower of the Eternal) and a Premika (lover of the Eternal) were once passing through a forest. On the way they saw a tiger at a distance. The Jnani said, "There is no reason why we should flee; the Eternal will certainly protect us." At this the Premika said, "No, friend, come let us run away. Why should we seek divine guidance for what can be accomplished by our own exertions?"

The Aspects of the Eternal

Be not like Ghanta Karna in your bigotry. He was a man who worshipped Shiva but hated all other deities. One day Shiva appeared to him and said, "I shall never be pleased with you as long as you hate the other gods." But the man was inexorable. After a few days Shiva again appeared to him and said, "I shall never be pleased with you as long as you hate." The man kept silent. After a few days Shiva again appeared to him. This time he appeared as Harihar—namely, one side of his body was that of Shiva and the other side that of Vishnu. The man was half pleased and half displeased. He worshipped the side representing Shiva, and did not recognize the side representing Vishnu. Then Shiva said, "Your bigotry is unconquerable. I, by assuming this dual aspect, tried to convince you that all gods and goddesses are but various aspects of the Eternal."

The Converted Snake

A snake dwelt in a certain place. No one dared to pass by that way; for whoever did so was instantly bitten to death. Once a male saint passed by that road, and the serpent wriggled toward the man in order to bite him. But when the snake approached the man, he lost all his ferocity and was overpowered by the gentleness of the saint. Seeing the snake, the man said, "Well, friend, do you plan to bite me?" The snake was abashed and made no reply. At this the man said, "Hearken, friend; do not injure anybody in the future." The snake bowed and nodded assent. The saint went his own way, and the snake entered his hole, and thenceforward began to live a life of innocence and purity without even attempting to harm anyone. In a few days all the neighborhood began to think that the snake had lost all his venom and was no longer dangerous, and so everyone began to tease him. Some pelted him; others dragged him mercilessly by the tail, and in this way there was no end to his troubles.

Fortunately, the saint again passed by that way and, seeing the bruised and battered condition of the good snake, was very much moved, and inquired the cause of his distress.

At this the snake replied, "Sir, this is because I do not injure anyone after your advice. But alas! they are so merciless!"

The saint smilingly said, "My dear friend, I simply advised you not to bite anyone, but I did not tell you not to make others keep their distance. Although you should not bite any creature, still you should keep everyone at a safe distance by giving forth a loud hiss."

Similarly, if you live in the world, make yourself respected. Do not injure anyone, but do not at the same time be injured by others.

The Fisherwoman's Sleeplessness

A fisherwoman on her way home from a distant market was over-taken by a storm at nightfall, so she was compelled to take refuge in a florist's house near at hand. The hospitable florist received her very cordially and allowed her to spend the night in a room next to his garden. The fragrant atmosphere of the place was too good for the fisherwoman. She could not sleep for a long time. At last, when she discovered that the sweet aroma of the flowers in the garden kept her awake, she sprinkled water on her empty basket of fish, placed it close to her nose, and immediately fell into a sound sleep. Such indeed is the power and influence of bad habits over all those who are addicted to them. They cannot enjoy the uplifting influence of the spiritual atmosphere.

The Diamond and the Dust

A husband and wife renounced the worldly kind of existence and jointly undertook a pilgrimage to various religious shrines. Once, as they were walking on a road, the husband, being a little ahead of his wife, saw a piece of diamond on the road. Immediately he scratched the ground to hide the diamond, thinking that, if his wife saw it, she might perchance be moved by avarice and thus lose the merit of her renunciation. While he was thus busy, the wife came up and asked him what he was doing. In an apologetic tone he gave her an evasive reply. She noticed the diamond, however, and reading his thoughts, asked him, "Why have you left the worldly kind of existence, if you still feel the difference between the diamond and the dust?"

The Hurt of the Divine Mother

The god Kartikeya, the leader of the heavenly army, once happened to scratch a cat with his nail. On going home he saw there was the mark of a scratch on the cheek of his mother. Seeing this, he asked of her, "Mother, dear, how have you got that ugly scratch on your cheek?"

The goddess Durga replied, "Child, this is your own handi-work—the mark scratched by your own nail."

Kartikeya asked in wonder, "Mother, how is it? I never remember to have scratched you!"

The mother replied, "Darling, have you not forgotten having scratched a cat this morning?"

Kartikeya said, "Yes, I did scratch a cat; but how did your cheek get marked?"

The mother replied, "Dear child, nothing exists in this world but myself. I am all creation. Whomever you hurt, you hurt me." Kartikeya was greatly surprised at this, and determined never to harm anyone; for whom would he harm? Every woman was mother to him.

I am like Kartikeya in that I consider all life as divine.

The Seven Jars of Gold

Greed brings woe, while contentment with one's possessions is all happiness. A barber was once passing under a haunted tree when he heard a voice say, "Will you accept seven jars of gold?" The barber looked around, but could see no one.

The mysterious voice again repeated the words, and the cupidity of the barber being greatly roused by the spontaneous offer of such wealth, he spoke aloud, "When the merciful God is so good as to take pity even on a poor barber like me, is there anything to be said as to my accepting the kind offer so generously made?"

At once the reply came, "Go home, I have already carried the jars there." The barber ran in hot haste to his house and was overjoyed to see the promised jars there. He opened them one after another and saw them all filled, save one which was half filled.

Now arose in the heart of the barber the desire of filling this last jar. So he sold all his gold and silver ornaments and converted them into coins and threw them into the jar. But the jar still remained empty. He now began to starve himself and his family by living upon insufficient, coarse, and cheap food, throwing all his savings into the jar, but the jar remained as empty as ever. The barber then requested the king to increase his pay as it was not suffi-cient to maintain him and his family. As he was a favorite of the king, the latter granted his request. The barber now began to save all his pay and emoluments and throw them all into the jar, but the greedy jar showed no sign of being filled. He now began to live by begging, and became as wretched and miserable as possible.

One day the king, seeing his sad plight, inquired of him by saying, "Hello! when your pay was half of what you get now, you were far happier and more cheerful, contented, and healthy; but with double that pay I see you morose, careworn, and dejected. Now what is the matter with you? Have you accepted the seven jars of gold?"

The barber was taken aback by this home-thrust, and asked the king as to who had informed his majesty about the matter. The king answered, "Whoever accepts the riches of a Yaksha is sure to be reduced to such an abject and wretched plight. I have known you through this invariable sign. Do away with the money at once. You cannot spend a farthing of it. That money is for hoarding and not for spending.

The barber was brought to his senses by this advice and went to the haunted tree and said, "O Yaksha, take back your gold," and he returned home to find the seven jars vanished, taking with them his lifelong savings. Nevertheless, he began to live happily thereafter.

BUDDHIST SCRIPTURES

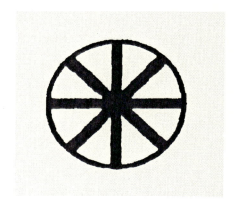

INTRODUCTION

The Life and Doctrine of the Buddha

Buddhism as a religion developed from the teachings of Gotama, a prince of the Sakya clan in India, who lived from 560 to 480 B.C. At the age of twenty-nine Gotama left his palace, and his wife and son, in order to search for a way by which humanity could overcome the suffering and misery of life. After many years of asceticism and renunciation, he finally reached a satisfactory set of conclusions, which he proceeded to teach to a group of disciples for a period of about forty years. As a result of his enlightenment he was called the Buddha, meaning the enlightened one.

The Dhammapada

This document is a series of proverbs on a number of religious and philosophical subjects.

The Diamond Sutra

This Sutra is a talk supposedly given by the Buddha in answer to the fundamental questions of one of his disciples, called Subhiti.

Asvaghosha's Discourse on the Awakening of Faith

Asvaghosha attempts here to systematize two aspects of the soul. Such an undertaking is dangerous if one does not always keep in mind that the whole is greater than the summation of its parts; that is, that ultimately it is impossible to subdivide religious ideas and retain their complete essence. At the same time, this attempt can be very fruitful if we remember that we must reassemble the parts once we have examined them.

The Tibetan Doctrine

The Tibetan Doctrine is a collection of poetic proverbs, from a number of Tibetan writings.

Jaina Sutras

Jainism is not actually a part of Buddhism, but because it plays a rather minor role in contemporary religious thought, and also because it grew up (like Buddhism) as a reaction against the Hindu tradition, it has been included in this section. Nahavira, who was its founder, started his ministry about a third of a century before the Buddha, being approximately contemporary with Lao Tze, Confucius, and Zarathustra (Zoroaster). These Sutras, as interpreted, state primarily the vows prerequisite to complete maturity in the modern world.

A Manual of Zen Buddhism

Zen Buddhism perhaps owes as much credit to Taoism as to Buddhism. Whether or not this is true, it does represent an integration of the thought of these two religions. It developed to some extent in China as Chan Buddhism, but it had its most outstanding development in Japan.

BUDDHIST SCRIPTURES

THE LIFE OF THE BUDDHA[1]

The Conception and Birth of the Buddha

It is related that, at the time of the Buddha's birth, the midsummer festival had been reclaimed in the city of Kapilavatthu, and the multitude were enjoying the feast. Queen Maha-Maya, abstaining from strong drink, and brilliant with garlands and perfumes, took part in the festivities for the six days previous to the day of the full moon. When it came to be the day of full moon, she rose early, bathed in perfumed water, and dispensed four hundred thousand pieces of money in great largess. Decked in full gala attire, she ate of the choicest food; after which she took the traditional vows, and entered her elegantly furnished chamber of state. Lying down on the royal couch, she fell asleep and dreamed the following dream:

Four guardian angels came and lifted her up, together with her couch, and took her away to the Himalayan Mountains. There, in the Manosila table land, they laid her under a huge tree, and took up their positions respectfully at the side. Then came the wives of these guardian angels, and conducted her to Anotatta Lake, and bathed her, to remove every human stain. After clothing her with divine garments, they anointed her with perfumes and decked her with divine flowers. Not far off was Silver Hill, and in it a golden mansion. There they spread a divine couch and laid her down upon it. Now the future Buddha had become a superb white elephant, and was wandering about at no great distance, on Gold Hill. Descending from there, he ascended Silver Hill, and approaching the mansion, he plucked a white lotus with his silvery trunk, and trumpeting loudly, went into the golden mansion. Several times he walked around his mother's couch, and striking her on one side, he

---

[1] The legendary story of Gotama Buddha's life and death compiled largely from the *Introduction to the Jataka, The Buddha-Charita,* and *The Dialogues of the Buddha.*

seemed to enter her womb. Thus the conception took place in the midsummer festival.

On the next day the queen awoke, and told the dream to the king. The king caused a great number of eminent seers to be summoned and spread costly seats for them on ground festively prepared with green leaves, many-colored flowers, and so forth. The seers being seated, he filled gold and silver dishes with the best of food; and covering these dishes with others, made likewise of gold and silver, he gave the seers to eat. Not only with food, but with other gifts, such as new garments, tawny cows, and so forth, he satisfied them completely. When their every desire had been satisfied, he told them the dream and asked them what would come of it.

"Do not be anxious, great king!" said the seers; "A child has planted itself in the womb of your queen, and it is a male child and not a female. You will have a son. And he, if he continues to live the household life, will become a universal monarch. But if he leaves the household life and abandons its luxury, he will become a Buddha and roll back the clouds of sin and folly in this world."

So Queen Maha-Maya carried the future Buddha in her womb, as it were like oil in a vessel, for ten months; and being almost ready to give birth, she grew desirous of going home to her relatives. She said to King Suddhodana, "Sire, I should like to visit my kinsfolk in the city of Devadaha."

"So be it," said the king; and from Kapilavatthu to the city of Devadaha he had the road made even, and garnished it with plantain-trees set in pots, and with banners, and streamers; and, seating the queen in a golden palanquin borne by a thousand of his courtiers, he sent her away in great pomp.

Now between the two cities, and belonging to the inhabitants of both, there was a pleasure-grove of sal-trees, called Lumbini Grove. At this particular time the grove was one mass of flowers from the ground to the topmost branches, while among the branches and flowers hummed swarms of bees of five different colors, and flocks of various kinds of birds flew about warbling sweetly. Throughout the whole of Lumbini Grove the scene resembled the magnificently decorated banqueting pavilion of some potent king.

When the queen beheld it, she became desirous of stopping at the park, so the courtiers took her into it. Going to the foot of the largest tree of the grove, she wished to take hold of one of its branches. The branch, like the tip of a well-stemmed reed, was bent down easily by the queen's hand. However, as she was holding onto the branch, her pain of impending birth came upon her. Thereupon the people draped a curtain about her and retired. So her delivery took place while she was still in the garden.

Afterward, so it is related, the people present took the future Buddha and carried him to Kapilavatthu.

Now it came to pass at that time that an ascetic named Kaladovala, who was an intimate friend of King Suddhodana, heard that a son had been born to the king. On hearing this, the ascetic entered the dwelling of the king; and having seated himself on the seat assigned to him, he said, "Great king, I hear that a son has been born to you. I would like to see him.

Then the king had the prince magnificently dressed, and brought in, and carried up to the ascetic. After the visitor had seen the boy, the king said, "What shall my son see to make him enlightened, since the people think he will become a Buddha?"

"The four signs."

"What four?"

"A decrepit old man, a diseased man, a dead man, and a monk."

"From this time forth," said the king, "let no such persons be allowed to come near my son. It will never do for my son to become a Buddha. What I would wish to see is my son exercising sovereign rule and authority over all the great continents and the many attendant isles, and walking through the lands surrounded by a huge retinue." When he had so spoken, he placed guards for a distance of a quarter of a league in each of the four directions in order that none of these four kinds of people might come within sight of his son.

He Sees the Four Signs

Now on a certain day the future Buddha wished to go to the park and asked his charioteer to make ready the chariot. Accordingly the man brought out a sumptuous and elegant chariot, and adorning it richly he harnessed to it four white horses. He then announced to the future Buddha that everything was ready. And the future Buddha mounted the chariot, which was like a palace, and proceeded toward the park.

On the way, he soon came upon a decrepit old man, broken-toothed, gray-haired, crooked and bent of body, leaning on a staff and trembling. Then said the future Buddha, whose name was Gotama, to the charioteer, "Friend, pray, who is this man? Even his hair is not like that of other men." When he heard the answer, he said, "Shame on birth, since to everyone that is born, old age must come." And agitated in heart, he thereupon returned and ascended his palace.

"Why has my son returned so quickly?" asked the king.

"Sire, he has seen an old man," was the reply; "and because he has seen an old man, he is about to leave his present way of life."

"Do you want to kill me, that you say such things? Quickly get ready some plays to be performed before my son. If we can but get him to enjoy pleasure, he will cease to think of taking this action." Then the king extended the guard to half a league in each direction.

Again, on a certain day, as the future Buddha was going to the park, he saw a diseased man; and having again made inquiry, he returned, agitated in heart, and ascended his palace.

The king made the same inquiry and gave the same orders as before; and again extending the guard, placed them for three-quarters of a league around.

Again on a certain day, as the future Buddha was going to the park, he saw a dead man; and having again made inquiry, he returned agitated in heart, and ascended his palace.

The king made the same inquiry and gave the same orders as before; and again extending the guard, placed them for a league around.

Again on a certain day, as the future Buddha was going to the park, he saw a monk, carefully and decently clad; and he asked his charioteer, "Pray, who is this person?"

The man replied, "Sire, this is one who has abandoned the ways of the world"; and he thereupon proceeded to sound the praises of so doing.

The Great Renunciation

At this juncture, Siddhodana, the king, having heard that the future Buddha's wife, whom he married shortly before, had brought forth a son, sent a messenger, saying, "Announce the glad news to my son."

On hearing the message, the future Buddha said, "An impediment (rahula) has been born; a fetter has arisen."

"What did my son say?" questioned the king; and when he had heard the answer, he said, "My grandson's name shall be Prince Rahula from this very day."

But the future Buddha, in his splendid chariot, entered the city with a pomp and magnificence of glory that enraptured all minds. At the same moment, Kisa Gotami, a virgin, ascended to the roof of her palace, and beheld the beauty and majesty of the future Buddha, as he wandered around the city; and in her pleasure and satisfaction at the sight, she burst forth into this song of joy:

"Full happy now that mother is,
Full happy now that father is,
Full happy now that woman is,
Who owns this lord so glorious!"

On hearing this, the future Buddha thought, "In beholding a handsome figure, the heart of a mother attains happiness, the heart of a father attains happiness, the heart of a wife attains happiness. This is what she says. But wherein does happiness really consist?" And to him, whose mind was already averse to passion, the answer came: "When the fire of lust is extinct, that is happiness; when the fires of hatred and infatuation are extinct, that is happiness; when haughtiness, false belief, and all other passions and torments are extinct, that is happiness. She has taught me a good lesson. Certainly, happiness is what I am looking for. It behooves me this very day to quit the household life and to meditate in quest of happiness. I will send this lady a teacher's fee." And loosening from his neck a pearl necklace worth many pieces of money, he sent it to Kisa Gotami. And great was her satisfaction at this, for she thought, "Prince Siddhattha has fallen love with me and has sent me a present."

The future Buddha then entered his palace in great splendor and lay on his couch of state. Immediately, richly dressed women, skilled in all manner of dance and song, and beautiful as celestial nymphs, gathered about him with all kinds of musical instruments, and with dance, song, and music they endeavored to please him. But the future Buddha's aversion to passion did not allow him to take pleasure in the spectacle and he fell into a brief slumber. The women, exclaiming, "He for whose sake we should perform has fallen asleep. Of what use is it to weary ourselves any longer?" threw their various instruments on the ground and lay down. The lamps fed with sweet-smelling oil continued to burn.

Soon the future Buddha awoke, and seating himself cross-legged on his couch, perceived these women lying asleep, with their musical instruments scattered about them on the floor—some with their bodies wet with trickling phlegm and spittle; some grinding their teeth, and muttering and talking in their sleep; some with their mouths open; and some with their dress fallen apart so as plainly to disclose their loathsome nakedness. This great alteration in their appearance still further increased his aversion to sensual pleasures. To him that magnificent apartment, as splendid as the palace of any ancient king, began to seem like a cemetery filled with dead bodies impaled and left to rot; and these various modes of existence appeared like houses all ablaze.

Breathing forth the solemn utterance, "How oppressive and stifling is it all!: his mind turned ardently to abandoning all this luxury. "It behooves me to go forth on the great quest this very day," said he; and he arose from his couch, and coming near the door, called out, "Who's there?"

"Master, it is I, Channa," replied the courtier who had been sleeping with his head on the threshold.

"I wish to go forth on the great quest today. Kindly saddle a horse for me."

"Yes, sire." And taking saddle and bridle with him, the courtier started for the stable. There, by the light of lamps fed with sweet-smelling oils, he perceived the mighty steed Kanthaka in his pleasant quarters, under a canopy of cloth beautified with a pattern of jasmine flowers. "This is the one for me to saddle today," thought he; and he saddled Kanthaka.

Now the future Buddha, after he had sent Channa on his errand, thought to himself, "I will take just one look at my son;" and, rising from the couch on which he was sitting, he went to the suite of apartments occupied by the mother of Rahula, and opened the door of her chamber. Within the chamber was burning a lamp fed with sweet-smelling oil, and the mother of Rahula lay sleeping on a couch strewn deep with jasmine and other flowers, her hand resting on the head of her son.

When the future Buddha reached the threshold, he paused and gazed at the two from where he stood.

"If I were to raise my wife's hand from off the child's head, and take him up, she would awake and thus prevent my departure. I

will first become a Buddha, and then come back and see my son."
So saying, he descended from the palace.

When the future Buddha had thus descended from the palace, he
came near to his horse, and said, "My dear Kanthaka, save me now
this one night; and then, when thanks to you I have become a
Buddha, I will help restore the world to sanity." Thereupon he
vaulted upon Kanthaka's back.

The future Buddha rode on the back of the mighty steed, made
Channa hold on by the tail, and in this way arrived at midnight at
the great gate of the city.

Advancing in inner glory, the future Buddha in one night traveled
a great distance and finally came to the river named Anoma.

The future Buddha, stopping on the riverbank, said to Channa,
"What is the name of this river?"

"Sire, its name is Anoma (Illustrious)."

"My retirement from the world of luxury shall also be called
Anoma," replied the future Buddha. And he, dismounting and
standing on the sandy beach that stretched away like a sheet of silver, said to Channa, "My good Channa, take these ornaments and
Kanthaka, and go home. I am about to retire from the world for
awhile to meditate."

"Sire, I will come with you."

Three times the future Buddha refused him, saying, "It is not for
you to retire from the world. Go now!" and made him take the
ornaments and Kanthaka.

Channa then did obeisance to the future Buddha and departed.

Buddha Is Instructed and Instructs

Then, after Channa left, he by whom all objects are accomplished
entered a monastery. The monks who had gone outside for the
sake of fuel, having come with their hands full of fuel, flowers, and
grass—pre-eminent as they were in penance, and proficient in wisdom—went to see him, and did not go to their rooms.

Then he, being duly honored and invited to enter by these dwellers in the monastery, paid his homage to the saints, with a voice
like a cloud in the rainy season. So, the wise one, longing for liberation, traversed that monastery filled with the holy company, gazing
at their strange practices. He, the gentle one, having seen the different kinds of practices carried out by the ascetics in that sacred
grove, desiring to know the truth, thus addressed one of the ascet-

ics who was following him: "Since this today is my first sight of a monastery, I do not understand this rule of practice; therefore, will your honor kindly explain to me what resolve possesses each one of you."

Then the monk, well versed in practice, told to him, in order, all the various kinds of practice and the fruit thereof. "Uncultivated food, growing out of the water, leaves, water, and roots and fruits—this is the fare of the saints according to the sacred texts; but the different alternatives of practice vary. Some live like the birds on gleaned corn, others graze on grass like the deer, others live on air with the snakes, as if turned into ant-hills. Others win their nourishment with great effort from stones, others eat corn ground with their own teeth; some, having boiled for others, dress for themselves what may chance to be left. Others sing hymns; others, plunging like fishes into the water, dwell there, with their bodies scratched by tortoises. By such penance endured for a time, by the higher they attain union with the Divine, by the lower the world of evil; by the path of pain they eventually dwell in happiness; pain, they say, is the root of merit."

The king's son, having heard this speech of the ascetic, even though he saw no lofty truth in it, was not content, but gently uttered these thoughts to himself: "The practice is full of pain and of many kinds, and the fruit of the practice is mainly self-hypnosis at its best, and the value of this is subject to question; truly, the labor of the monasteries is spent for but little gain. Those who, abandoning wealth, kindred, and worldly objects, undertake vows for the sake of self-hypnosis—they only wish to go to a still greater forest of their own again. There is ever to living creatures fear of death, and they with all their efforts seek not to die; where there is action, there must inevitably be death—they are always drowned therein, just because they are afraid."

Gotama spent several nights there, examining their practices; and he departed from that practice-field, feeling that he had comprehended the whole nature of practice. The dwellers of the monastery followed him with their minds fixed on the greatness of soul visible in his person, as if they were great seers beholding religion herself, withdrawn from a land invaded by the base. Then he looked on all those ascetics with their matted hair, bark garments, and rag-strips waving, and he stood considering their practices under an auspicious and noble tree by the wayside.

Then the monks, having approached, stood surrounding the future Buddha; and an old man from among them thus addressed him respectfully in a gentle voice: "At your coming the monastery seems to have become full, it becomes as it were empty when you are gone; therefore, my son, you surely will not desert it, as life leaves the body of one who wishes to live. Have you seen in this sacred grove one who neglects all ceremonies or who follows confused ceremonies or an outcast or one impure, that you do not desire to dwell here? Speak out, and let the abode be welcomed."

He, the chief of the wise, when thus addressed in the midst of the ascetics by their chief—having resolved in his mind to put an end to all craving—thus uttered his inward thought: "The saints, the upholders of religion, become the very ideal of our own kindred through their delight in showing hospitality; by all these kind feelings of yours toward me affection is produced in me and the path which regards the Self as supreme is revealed. I seem to be all at once bathed by these gentle heart-touching words of yours, and the joy now throbs in me once more which I felt when I first grasped the idea of discipline. I am indeed sorrowful when I reflect that I shall have to depart, leaving you who are thus engaged, you who are such a refuge and who have shown such excessive kindness to me, just as there was when I had to leave my kindred behind. But this devotion of yours is for the sake of self-hypnosis, while my desire is to find true happiness; therefore, I wish not to dwell in this wood; the nature of cessation is different from that of activity. It is not therefore any dislike on my part or the wrong conduct of another which makes me go away from this wood; for you are all like great sages, standing fast in the religious duties which are in accordance with former ages."

Then, having heard the prince's discourse, gracious and of deep meaning, gentle, strong, and full of dignity, the ascetics extended to him special honor. But a certain monk, who was lying there in the ashes, tall and wearing his hair in a tuft, and clothed in the bark of trees, with reddish eyes and a thin long nose, and carrying a pot with water in his hand, thus lifted his voice: "With the nose of a well-fed horse, large long eyes, a red lower lip, white sharp teeth, and thin red tongue—this face of yours will drink up the entire ocean of what is to be known. That unfathomed depth which characterizes you, that majesty and all those signs of yours, they shall win a teacher's chair in the earth which was never won by sages even in a former age."

The prince replied, "Very well," and having saluted the company of sages he departed; the monks also, having duly performed to him all the rites of courtesy, entered again into the ascetic-grove.

The Firm Resolve

Then on the pure bank of the Nairangana the saint whose every effort was pure fixed his dwelling bent as he was on a lonely habitation. Five monks, desiring enlightenment, came up to him when they beheld him there, just as the objects of the senses come up to a percipient who has gained wealth and health by his previous merit.

Being honored by these monks who were dwelling in that vicinity and thinking, "This may be the means of abolishing the present misery," he at once commenced a series of difficult austerities by fasting.

For six years, vainly trying to attain merit, he practiced self-mortification, performing many rules of abstinence, hard for a man to carry out. At the hours for eating, he, longing to cross the world whose farther shore is so difficult to reach, interrupted his fast with a few fruits, seeds, and rice. Having only skin and bone remaining, with his fat, flesh, and blood entirely wasted, yet, though diminished, he still shone with undiminished grandeur like the ocean.

Then the seer, having his body evidently emaciated to no purpose in a cruel self-mortification, dreading continued existence, thus reflected in his longing to become a Buddha: "This is not the way to passionlessness, or to perfect knowledge, or to liberation; that was certainly the true way which I found through previous meditation. But that cannot be attained by one who has lost his strength". So, resuming his care for his body, he next pondered thus, how best to increase his bodily vigor: "Wearied with hunger, thirst, and fatigue, with his mind no longer self-possessed through fatigue, how should one who is not absolutely calm reach the end which is to be attained by his mind? True calm is properly obtained by the satisfaction of the senses; the mind's self-possession is only obtained by the senses' being reasonably well satisfied. True meditation is produced in him whose mind is self-possessed and at peace, to him whose thoughts are engaged in meditation the exercise of perfect contemplation begins at once. By contemplation are obtained those conditions through which is eventually gained that supreme calm, un-decaying, immortal state, which is so hard to be reached."

Having thus resolved, "This means is based upon eating food," the wise seer of unbounded wisdom, having made up his mind to accept the continuance of life, and having bathed, thin as he was, slowly came up the bank of the Nairangana, supported by the trees on the shore.

Now at that time Nandabala, the daughter of the leader of the herdsmen, with sudden joy in her heart, had just come near, her arm gay with a white shell, and wearing a dark blue woolen cloth, like the river Yamuna, with its dark blue water and its wreath of foam. She, having her joy increased by her faith, with her lotus-like eyes opened wide, bowed down before him and persuaded him to take some milk. By partaking of that food, having made her obtain the full reward for her kindness, he himself became capable of gaining the highest knowledge, all his senses now being satisfied.

The seer, having his body now fully robust, together with his glorious fame, one beauty and one majesty being equally spread in both, felt as if he shone like the ocean and the moon, radiating the light of ideal humanity as the ocean and moon reflect the light of the sun.

However, thinking that he had returned to his former ways, the five monks left him, as all temptations leave the wise soul when it is liberated. Accompanied only by his own resolve, having fixed his mind on the attainment of perfect understanding, he went to the root of a fig-tree, where the surface of the ground was covered with young grass. Then he sat down on his hams in a posture, immovably firm and with his limbs gathered into a mass like a sleeping serpent's hood, exclaiming, "I will not rise from this position on the earth until I have obtained my utmost aim."

Attainment of Understanding

Thus he, the holy one, sitting there on his seat of grass at the root of the tree, pondering having overcome the many temptations which beset him, by his own efforts attained at last perfect understanding. Then bursting the shell of ignorance, having gained all the various kinds of intuition, he attained all the partial understanding of alternatives which is included in perfect understanding. He became the most wise, the king of the law, the Enlightened One, he who has attained the understanding of all forms, the lord of all science.

The Great Ministry Begins

Then the holy one pondered: "The profound wisdom so hard to be understood is now known by me. This sin-defiled world understands not this most excellent law, and the unenlightened shamelessly censure both me and my wisdom. Shall I proclaim the law? It is only produced by insight; having attained it thus in my lonely pondering, do I feel strong enough to deliver the world?" Having remembered all that he had heard before, he again pondered; and resolving, "I will explain it for the sake of delivering the world," Buddha, the chief of saints, absorbed in contemplation, shone forth, eventually arousing the world, having emitted in the darkness of the night a light far brighter than that of any other person living in his country.

Then Buddha set out to go joyfully to Benares, manifesting as he went the manifold course of life he had envisioned. Having made a monk whom he met happy in the path of those who are illustrious through the law, the glorious one went on, illumining the country which lies to the north of Gaya. Having stayed in the dwelling of the prince of the Nagas, named Sudarsana, on the occurrence of night, he ate a morning meal and departed, gladdening him with his blessing. Near Vanara he went under the shadow of a tree and there he established a poor clergyman named Nandin in sacred knowledge.

At Vanara in a householder's dwelling he was lodged for the night. In the morning he partook of some milk and departed, having given his blessing. In the village called Vumdavira he lodged in the abode of a man named Vumda, and in the morning after taking some milk and giving his blessing he departed.

Having delivered various beings in every place from their state of confusion and misery, the saint journeyed on to Gandhapura and was praised there by a man named Gandha.

The next day he, the unequaled one, proceeded to Deer Park. The five monks, united in a group, when they beheld him, said to one another, "This is Gotama who has come here, the ascetic who has abandoned his self-control. He wanders about now, greedy, unstable, and with his senses under no firm control, devoted to inquiries regarding the necessities for survival. We will not ask after his health, or rise to meet him, or address him, or offer him a welcome, or a seat, or bid him enter into our dwelling."

Having understood their agreement, with a smiling countenance, Buddha advanced gradually nearer, holding his few possessions. Forgetful of their agreement, the five friends, under his constraining majesty, rose up like birds in their cages when scorched by fire. Having put his things away for him, they gave him water for washing his feet and rinsing his mouth; and, bowing reverentially, they said to him, "Honored Sir, health to you."

"Health in every respect is ours—that wisdom has been attained which is so hard to be won." So saying, the holy one thus spoke to the five worthy monks: "But address me not as 'Worthy Sir'— know that I am at last enlightened—I have come to give the first part of the law to you. Receive initiation from me, and you shall obtain the state of true happiness.

Then the five, pure in heart, begged leave to undertake his vow of a religious life; and the Buddha, touching their heads, received them as his disciples. Then at the monks' respectful request the chief of saints bathed in the tank, and after eating some food he reflected on the extent of the law.

Announcement of Death

Now the Exalted One robed himself early in the morning and went into Vesali. When he had finished eating, he addressed the venerable Ananda, and said: "Come with me, Ananda; I will go and spend the day at a spot called Chapala."

"So be it, lord!" said the venerable Ananda, in assent, to the Exalted One. And making ready, he followed the Exalted One.

So the Exalted One proceeded to Chapala, and when he had come there he sat down, and the venerable Ananda took his seat respectfully beside him. Then the Exalted One addressed the venerable Ananda, and said: "How delightful a spot, Ananda, is Chapala!"

While the Exalted One was at Chapala, he deliberately and consciously let go interest in life's conditions. And when he realized he had done this, he broke out into the following hymn of exultation:

"His sum of life the sage renounced,
What may be reckoned and what not,
With inward joy and calm, he broke,
Like coat of mail, the self-compound!"

And when he had thus spoken, the venerable Ananda addressed the Exalted One, and said: "Vouchsafe, lord, to remain during the aeon: live on through the years, O Exalted One! for the good and the happiness of the great multitudes, out of pity for the world, for the good and the gain and the weal of all!"

"Enough now, Ananda; do not beseeech the Enlightened One!" was the reply.

And again, the second time, and the third time, the venerable Ananda besought the Exalted One in the same words.

"Have you faith, Ananda, in the wisdom of the Enlightened One?"

"Even so, lord!"

"Now why, then, Ananda, do you trouble the Enlightened one even until the third time?"

"From his own mouth have I heard from the Exalted One, from his own mouth have I received this saying: 'Whoever has developed, practiced, dwelt on, expanded, and ascended to the very heights of the many paths to happiness, and so mastered them as to be able to use them as a vehicle, and as a basis, he, should he desire it, could remain in the same state for an aeon, or for that portion of the aeon which had yet to run.' Now the Enlightened One has thoroughly practiced and developed them, and he could, therefore, should he desire it, live on yet for an aeon, or for that portion of the aeon which has yet to run."

"Have you faith, Ananda?"

"Even so, lord!"

"But now, Ananda, have I not formerly declared to you that it is in the very nature of all things, near and dear to us, that we must divide ourselves from them, leave them, sever ourselves from them? How, then, Ananda, can this be possible—whereas anything whatever born, brought into beings, and organized, contains within itself the inherent necessity of dissolution—how then can this be possible that such a being should not be dissolved? No such condition can exist! And that which, Ananda, has been relinquished, cast away, renounced, rejected, and abandoned by the Enlightened One—the remaining sum of life surrendered by him—truly with regard to that the world as gone forth from the Enlightened One, saying,: 'The passing away of the Enlightened One shall take place before long. At the end of three months from this time the

Enlightened One will die!' That the Enlightened One for the sake of living should repent that saying—this cannot be!

"Come, Ananda, let us go to the Kutgara Hall."

"Even so, lord!" said the venerable Ananda, in assent, to the Exalted One.

Then the Exalted One proceeded, and Ananda with him, to the Kutagara Hall: and when he had arrived there he addressed the venerable Ananda, and said: "Go now, Ananda, and assemble in the Service Hall such of the disciples as reside in the neighborhood of Vesali."

"Even so, lord!" said the venerable Ananda, in assent, to the Exalted One. And when he had assembled in the service Hall such of the disciples as resided in the neighborhood of Vesali, he went to the Exalted One and saluted him and stood beside him. And standing beside him, he addressed the Exalted One, and said: "Lord! the assembly of the disciples has met together. Let the Exalted One do even as seems to him fit."

Then the Exalted One proceeded to the Service Hall and sat down there. And when he was seated, the Exalted One addressed the disciples, and said: "Which then, O friends, are the things which, when I had perceived, I made known to you, which when you have mastered it behooves you to practice, meditate upon, and spread abroad, in order that pure religion may last long and be perpetuated, in order that it may continue to be for the good and the happiness of the great multitudes, out of pity for the world, to the good and the gain and the weal of all?

"They are these:

The earnest meditations,
The great struggle,
The many roads to happiness,
The moral powers,
The organs of spiritual sense,
The various kinds of wisdom, and
The eightfold path.

"These, O friends, are the truths that, when I had perceived, I made known to you, which when you have mastered them behooves you to practice, meditate upon, and spread abroad, in order that pure religion may last long and be perpetuated, in order that it may continue to be for the good and the happiness of the great multitudes, out of pity for the world, to the good and the gain and the weal of all!"

And the Exalted One exhorted his disciples, and said: "Behold now, O friends, I exhort you, saying: 'All component things must grow old. Work out your problems with diligence. The final extinction of the Enlightened One will take place before long. At the end of three months from this time the Enlightened One will die!"

My age is now full ripe, my life draws to its close:
Leaving you I shall go, relying on the Self, virtuous,
Be earnest then, O friends, holy, full of thought!
Be steadfast in resolve! Keep watch o'er your own hearts!
The one who wearies not, but earnest keeps in right and rule,
Shall cross this sea of life, shall make an end of grief.

Preparation for Death

Now the Exalted One addressed the venerable Ananda, and said: "Come, Ananda, let us go on to the Sala Grove of the Mallas, on the further side of the river Hiranyavati."

"Even so, lord!" said the venerable Ananda, in assent, to the Exalted One.

And the Exalted One proceeded with a great company of the disciples to the Sala Grove of the Mallas, on the further side of the river Hiranyavati: and when he had come there he addressed the venerable Ananda, and said: "Spread over for me, I pray you, Ananda, the couch, between the twin Sala trees. I am weary, Ananda, and would lie down."

"Even so, lord!" said the venerable Ananda, in assent, to the Exalted One. And he spread a covering over the couch, between the Sala trees. Then the Exalted One laid himself down, and he was mindful and self-possessed.

Now at that time the twin Sala trees were all one mass of bloom with flowers, and all over the body of the Enlightened One these dropped and sprinkled and scattered themselves.

Then the Exalted One addressed the venerable Ananda and said: "Now it is not thus, Ananda, that the Enlightened One is rightly honored, reverenced, venerated, held sacred or revered.

But the brother or the sister, the devout man or the devout woman, who continually fulfills all the greater and the lesser duties, who is correct in life, walking according to the precepts—it is he/she who rightly honors, reverences, venerates, holds sacred, and

reveres the Enlightened One with the worthiest homage. Therefore, O Ananda, be constant in the fulfillment of the greater and of
the lesser duties, and be correct in life, walking according to the
precepts; and thus, Ananda, should it be taught."

"What are we to do, Lord, with the remains of the Enlightened
One, when you are gone?"

"Hinder not yourselves, Ananda, by honoring the remains of the
Enlightened One. Be zealous, I beseech you, Ananda, in your own
behalf! Devote yourselves to your own good! There are wise men
and women, Ananda, among the nobles, among the clergy, among
the heads of houses, who are firm believers in the Enlightened
One; and they will do honor to the remains of the Enlightened
One."

Ananda Weeps

Now the venerable Ananda went into the Vihara, and stood leaning
against the lintel of the door, and weeping at the thought: "Alas! I
remain still but a learner, one who has yet to work out his own perfection. And the Master is about to pass away from me—he who is
so kind!"

Now the Exalted One called the disciples, and said: "Where then,
friends, is Ananda?"

"The venerable Ananda, lord, has gone into the Vihara, and
stands leaning against the lintel of the door, weeping."

And the Exalted One called a certain brother, and said: "Go now
and call Ananda in my name, and say: 'Brother Ananda, the Master
calls for you.'"

"Even so, Lord!" said that brother, in assent, to the Exalted One.
And he went up to the place where Ananda was: and when he had
come there, he said to the venerable Ananda: "Brother Ananda, the
Master calls for you."

"Very well," said the venerable Ananda, in assent, to that disciple.
And he went up to the place where the Exalted One was, and when
he had come there, he bowed down before the Exalted One, and
took his seat respectfully on one side.

Then the Exalted One said to the venerable Ananda, as he sat
there by his side: "Enough, Ananda! Do not let yourself be troubled; do not weep! Have I not already, on former occasions, told
you that it is in the very nature of al things most near and dear to
us that we must divide ourselves from them, leave them, sever our-

selves from them? How, then, Ananda, can this be possible—whereas anything whatever born, brought into being, and organized, contains within itself the inherent necessity of dissolution—how, then, can this be possible, that such a being should not be dissolved? No such condition can exist!

"For a long time, Ananda, have you been very near to me by acts of love, kind and good; that never varies, and is beyond all measure. For a long time, Ananda, have you been very near to me by words of love, kind and good; that never varies, and is beyond all measure. For a long time, Ananda, have you been very near to me by thoughts of love, kind and good; that never varies, and is beyond all measure. You have done well, Ananda! Be earnest in effort, and you too shall soon be free from the intoxications—of sensuality, and delusion, and ignorance!"

Death of the Buddha

Now the Exalted One addressed the venerable Ananda, and said: "It may be, Ananda, that in some of you the thought will arise, 'The word of the Master is ended; we have no more teacher!' But it is not thus, Ananda, that you should regard it. It is perfection-discipline, and the rules for the disciples, which I have set forth and laid down for you all; let them, after I am gone, be the teacher to you."

Then the Exalted One addressed the disciples, and said: "It may be that there is doubt or misgiving in the mind of some of you as to the Buddha, or the doctrine, or the path, or the method. Inquire freely, friends. Do not have to reproach yourselves afterwards with the thought: 'Our teacher was face to face with us, and we could not bring ourselves to inquire of the Exalted One when we were face to face with him!'"

And when he had thus spoken, the disciples were silent.

And again the second and the third time the Exalted One addressed the monks.

And even the third time they were silent.

Then the Exalted One addressed the monks, and said: "It may be that you put no questions out of reverence for the teacher. Let comrade communicate to comrade."

And when he had thus spoken, the monks were silent.

And the venerable Ananda said to the Exalted One: "How wonderful a thing it is, and how marvelous! Truly, I believe that in this whole assembly of the monks there is not one who has any doubt or misgiving as to the Buddha, or the doctrine, or the path, or the method!"

"It is out of the fullness of faith that you have spoken, Ananda! But, Ananda, the Enlightened One knows for certain that in this whole assembly of the disciples there is not one brother who has any doubt or misgiving as to the Buddha, the doctrine, the path, or the method! For even the most backward, Ananda, of all these monks has become converted, is no longer liable to continue in a state of excess suffering, and is assured of attaining some degree of enlightenment."

Then the Exalted One addressed the monks, and said: "Behold now, my friends, I exhort you, saying: 'Decay is inherent in all component things! Work out your problems with diligence.'"

Then the venerable Ananda said to the venerable Anuruddha: "O my Lord, O Anuruddha, the Exalted One is dead!"

"No! brother Ananda, the Exalted One is not dead. He has entered into that state in which his body has ceased to be, but his spirit will live forever through us and those who come after us!"

THE DOCTRINE OF THE BUDDHA

Nine Avoidances

Those who are enlightened, in whom the intoxicants are destroyed, who are living the life, who are doing their tasks, who are laying low their burdens, who are putting an end to suffering, particularly avoid nine things:

1. Needlessly depriving a living creature of life.
2. Taking what is not given so that it constitutes theft.
3. Sexual impurity.
4. Deliberately telling lies.
5. Laying up treasure for indulgence in worldly pleasure.
6. Taking a wrong course through partiality.
7. Taking a wrong course through hate.
8. Taking a wrong course through stupidity.
9. Taking a wrong course through fear.

These nine things the enlightened ones, in whom the mental intoxicants are destroyed, who are living the life, whose tasks are be-

ing done, whose burdens are being laid low, who are putting an end
to suffering, are certain to avoid.

Setting Up of Mindfulness

Thus have I heard.

The Exalted One was once staying among the Kurus. Kammas-
sadhamma is a city of the Kuru country. There the Exalted one
addressed them, saying, "Friends!"

"Reverend sir!" they responded.

And the Exalted One said: "The one and only path, friends, leading to the purification of beings, to passing far beyond needless
grief and lamentation, to the overcoming of evil and misery, to the
attainment of right method, to the realization of lasting happiness,
is that of the setting up of mindfulness.

"How is this done? Herein, O friends, let yourselves, as to the
body, continue so to look upon the body that you remain ardent,
self-possessed, and mindful, so as to overcome both the hankering
and the dejection common in the world.

"Therefore, as to the body, continue to consider the body, either
internally or externally, or both internally and externally. Keep on
considering how the body is something that passes away; or again
keep on considering the coming to be with the passing away; or a
gain, conscious that 'There is the body,' mindfulness hereof becomes thereby established, far enough for the purposes of knowledge and of self-collectedness. And then abide independent, craving nothing in the world whatever. Thus, friends, should you continue to regard the body.

"And moreover, friends, when you are walking, be aware of it
thus: 'I walk'; or when you are standing, or sitting, or lying down,
be aware of it. However you are disposing the body, be aware
thereof.

"And moreover, friends, whether you have drawn in or stretched
out your limbs, whether you have donned a shirt, a coat, or shoes,
whether you are eating, drinking, chewing, reposing, or whether
you are obeying the dictates of your nature—you are aware of what
you are about. In going, standing, sitting, sleeping, watching, talking, or keeping silence, you know what you are doing.

"Herein, O friends, when you are affected by a feeling of pleasure, be aware of it, reflecting: 'I feel a pleasurable feeling.' So, too,
you are aware when affected by a painful feeling, or by a neutral

feeling, or by a pleasant or painful or neutral feeling concerning material things, or by a pleasant or painful or neutral feeling concerning spiritual things.

"So do you, as to your feelings, continue to consider feeling, both internally and externally, or internally and externally together. Keep on considering how the feelings are something that come to be, or again keep on considering their coming to be with their passing away.

Or again, with the consciousness: 'There is feeling,' mindfulness thereof becomes thereby established far enough for the purposes of knowledge and of self-collectedness. And you can abide independent, craving nothing in the world whatever. Thus, friends, do you, with respect to the feelings, continue to consider feeling.

"And how, friends, do you, as to thought, continue to consider thought?

"Herein, friends, if your thought is lustful, be aware that it is so, or if your thought is free from lust, be aware that it is so; or if your thought is full of hate, or free from hate, or dull, or intelligent, or attentive, or distrait, or exalted, or not exalted, or mediocre, or ideal, or composed, or discomposed, or liberated, or bound, be aware in each case that your thought is so, reflecting: 'My thought is lustful,' and so on.

"So do you, as to thought, continue to consider thought, internally or externally, or internally and externally together. Keep on considering how thought is something that comes to be, or again keep on considering how a thought is something that passes away, or again always consider its coming to be and passing away together. Or again, with the consciousness: 'There is a thought,' mindfulness thereof becomes thereby established, far enough for the purposes of knowledge and of self-possession. Be sure to abide independent, craving nothing in the world whatever. Thus, does a disciple, with respect to thought, continue to consider thought.

"And how, friends, do you, as to ideas, continue to consider ideas?

"Herein, friends, as to ideas, continue to consider ideas from the point of view of various hindrances.

"And how, friends, do you, as to ideas, continue to consider ideas relating to various hindrances?

"Herein, O friends, when within you is sensual desire, be aware of it, reflecting: 'I have within me sensual desire.' Or again, when within you is no sensual desire, be aware of this. And know of the uprising of such desire unfelt before, know too of your putting aside that uprisen sensual desire, know too of the non-arising in future of that banished sensual desire.

"Moreover, friends, as to ideas, continue to consider ideas from the point of view of the internal and external spheres of sense. And how do you do this?

"Herein, O friends, be aware of the organ of sight, be aware of the objects of sight, and any fetter which arises on account of them both—of that, too, you are aware; and how there comes an uprising of a fetter not arisen before—of that, too, you are aware; and how there comes a putting aside of a fetter that has arisen—of that, too, you are aware; and how in the future there shall arise no fetter that has been put aside—of that, too, you are aware.

"And so, too, with respect to the organ of hearing and sounds, to the organ of smell and odors, to the organ of taste and tastes, to the organ of touch and tangibles, to the sensorium and images, you need to become aware of the sense and of the object, of any fetter which arises on account of both, of how there comes an uprising of a fetter not arisen before, of how there comes a putting aside of a fetter that has arisen, and of how in the future there shall arise no fetter that has been put aside.

"So, as to ideas, continue to consider ideas from the point of view of the internal and external spheres of sense.

"And moreover, friends, as to ideas, continue to consider ideas from the point of view of truth. And how do you do this?

"Herein, O friends, at the thought: 'This is ill!' be aware of it as it really is; at the thought: 'This is the way leading to the cessation of ill!' be aware of it as it really is.

"And what, friends, is the truth concerning the way that leads to the cessation of ill?

"This is the eightfold path, to wit: right view, right aspiration, right speech, right doing, right livelihood, right effort, right mindfulness, right rapture.

"And what, friends, is right view?

"Knowledge about ill, knowledge about the coming to be of ill, knowledge about the cessation of ill. This is what is called right view.

"And what, friends, is right aspiration?

The aspiration toward renunciation of the fruits of action, the aspiration toward benevolence, the aspiration toward kindness. This is what is called right aspiration.

"And what, friends, is right speech?

"Abstaining from lying, slander, abuse, and idle talk. This is what is called right speech.

"And what, friends, is right doing?

"Abstaining from taking any life unnecessarily, from taking what is not given, from carnal indulgence. This is what is called right doing.

"And what, friends, is right livelihood?

"Herein, O friends, having put away wrong livelihood, support yourself by right livelihood, which is dictated by your nature.

"And what, friends, is right effort?

"Herein, friends, make effort to bring forth will-power, so that evil states that have not arisen within you may not arise; to that end call forth energy and determination. That you may put away evil states that have arisen within you put forth will-power, make effort, call forth energy and determination. That good states which have not arisen may arise, put forth will-power, make effort, call forth energy and determination. That good states which have arisen may persist, may not grow blurred, may multiply, grow abundant, develop and come to perfection, put forth will-power, make effort, call forth energy and determination. This is what is called right effort.

"And what, friends, is right mindfulness?

"Herein, O friends, as to the body, continue so to look upon the body, that you remain ardent, self-possessed and mindful, having overcome both the hankering and the dejection common in the world. And in the same way as to feelings, thoughts and ideas, look upon each, that you remain ardent, self-possessed and mindful, having overcome the hankering and the dejection that is common in the world. This is what is called right mindfulness.

"And what, friends, is right rapture?

"Herein, O friends, aloof from sensual appetites, aloof from evil ideas, enter into and abide in true happiness, wherein there is, in addition to action, a time for reflection and deliberation, which is born of solitude and full of joy. Balancing reflection with action, enter into and abide in even higher happiness, which is self-evoked, born of concentration, full of joy, in that, set free from excessive reflection and deliberation, the mind grows calm and sure, dwelling on high. And further, disenchanted with mirth, abide calmly contemplative while, mindful and self-possessed, feel in your body that ease whereof people declare: 'Those who are calmly contemplative and aware dwell at ease.' Therefore, seek to enter into and abide in still higher happiness. And further, by putting aside ease and malaise, by the passing away of the excitement and melancholy you used to feel, enter into and abide in the highest happiness, rapture of utter purity of mindfulness and equanimity, wherein neither passion is felt nor chronic discontentment. This is what is called right rapture.

"This, friends, is the truth concerning the way leading to the cessation of ill.

"It was on account of these things that the following was said at the beginning: 'The one and only path, friends, leading to the purification of beings, to passing far beyond needless grief and lamentation, to the dying out of ill and misery, to the attainment of right method, to the realization of lasting happiness, is that of the setting up of mindfulness.'"

Thus spoke the Exalted One. Pleased were the disciples, delighting in that which was spoken by the Exalted One.

The Perfect Net

Thus have I heard.

The Blessed One was once going along the high road between Rajagaha and Nalanda with about five hundred disciples. And Suppiya the monk too was going along the high road between Rajagha and Nalanda with his disciple, the youth Brahmadatta. Now just then Suppiya the monk was speaking in dispraise of the Buddha, in dispraise of his teachings, in dispraise of his followers. But young Brahmadatta, his pupil, gave utterance to praise of the Buddha, to praise of his teachings, to praise of his followers. Thus these two, teacher and pupil, holding opinions in direct contradition one to the other, were following step by step, after the Blessed One and the company of the disciples.

Now the Blessed One discovered a royal rest-house in which to pass the night, and with him the company of his disciples. And so also did Suppiya the monk, and with him his young disciple Bramadatta. And there, at the rest-house, these two carried on the same discussion as before.

In the early dawn a number of the disciples assembled, as they rose up, in the pavilion; and there was talk that sprang up among them as they were seated there. "How wonderful a thing is it, friends, and how strange that the Blessed One, he who knows and sees, the Buddha Supreme, should so clearly have perceived how various are the inclinations of people! For while Suppiya the monk speaks in dispraise of the Buddha, his teachings, and his followers, his own disciple, young Bramadatta, speaks in praise of them. So do these two, teacher and pupil, follow step by step after the Blessed One and the company of the disciples, giving utterance to views in direct contradiction one to the other."

Now the Blessed One, on realizing the drift of their talk, went to the pavilion and took his seat there. When he had sat down, he said: "What is the talk on which you are engaged sitting here, and what is the subject of the conversation between you?" And they told him all.

And he said: "Friends, if outsiders should speak against me, or against my teachings, or against my followers, you should not on that account either bear malice, or suffer heart-burning, or feel ill will. If you, on that account, should be angry and hurt, that would stand in the way of your own self-conquest. If, when others speak against us, you feel angry at that, and displeased, would you then be able to judge how far that speech of theirs is well said or ill?"

"That would not be so, Sir."

"But when outsiders speak in dispraise of me, or of my teachings, or of my followers, you should unravel what is false and point it out as wrong, saying: 'For this or that reason this is not the fact, that is not so, such a thing is not found among us, is not in us.'

"But also, friends, if outsiders should speak in praise of me, in praise of my teachings, in praise of my followers, you should not, on that account, be filled with pleasure or gladness, or be lifted up in heart. Were you to be so, that also would stand in the way of your self-conquest. When outsiders speak in praise of me, or of my teachings, or of my followers, you should acknowledge what is right to be the fact, saying: 'For this or that reason this is the fact, that is so, such a thing is found among us, is in us.'

"It is in respect only of trifling things, of matters of little value, of mere morality, that an unconverted person, when praising the Enlightened One, would speak. And what are such trifling, minor details of mere morality that such a person would praise?

"'Putting away the killing of living things, Gotama holds aloof from the destruction of life. He has laid the cudgel and the sword aside, and ashamed of roughness, and full of mercy, he dwells compassionate and kind to all creatures that have life.' It is thus that the unconverted person, when speaking in praise of the Enlightened one, might speak.

"Or he might say: 'Putting away the taking of what has not been given, Gotama lives aloof from grasping what is not his own. He takes only what is given, and expecting that gifts will come, he passes his life in honesty and purity of heart.'

"Or he might say: 'Putting away sensuality, Gotama is pure. He holds himself aloof, far off, from vulgar practices, from sensuality.'

"Or he might say: 'Putting away lying words, Gotama holds himself aloof from falsehood. He speaks truth, from the truth he never swerves; faithful and trustworthy, he breaks not his word to the world.'

"Or he might say: 'Putting away slander, Gotama holds himself aloof from calumny. What he hears here he repeats not elsewhere to raise a quarrel against the people here; what he hears elsewhere he repeats not here to raise a quarrel against the people there. Thus does he live as a binder together of those who are divided, and encourager of those who are friends, a peacemaker, a lover of peace, impassioned for peace, a speaker of words that make for peace.'

"Or he might say: 'Putting away rudeness of speech, Gotama holds himself aloof from harsh language. Whatever word is searching, truthful, reaching to the heart, dispassionate—such are words he speaks.'

"Or he might say: 'Putting away frivolous talk, Gotama holds himself aloof from vain conversation. In season he speaks, in accordance with the facts, words full of meaning, in religion, on the discipline of his followers. He speaks, and at the right time, words worthy to be laid up in one's heart, well illustrated, clearly divided, to the point.'

"There are, friends, other things, profound, difficult to realize, hard to understand, tranquilizing, sweet, not to be grasped by mere logic, subtle, comprehensible only by the wise. These things the Enlightened One, having himself realized them and seen them face to face, has set forth; and it is of them that they who would rightly praise the Enlightened One in accordance with the truth, should speak.

"And what are they?

"There are people, friends, who reconstruct the ultimate beginnings of things, whose speculations are concerned with the ultimate past, and who on a number of grounds put forward assertions regarding it. And about what, with reference to what, do those venerable ones do so?

"There are, friends, some people who are eternalists, and who proclaim that both the soul and the world are eternal. And about what, with reference to what, do those venerable ones do so?

"In the first place, friends, some persons by means of ardor, of exertion of application, of earnestness, of careful thought, reach up to such rapture of heart that, rapt in heart, they call to mind various dwelling places in times gone by; and say to themselves: 'Eternal is the soul; and the world, giving birth to nothing new, is steadfast as a mountain peak, as a pillar firmly fixed; and though these living creatures pass away, yet they are for ever and ever. And why must that be so? Because I, by means of ardor, of exertion, of application, of earnestness, of careful thought, can reach up to such rapture of heart that, rapt in heart, I can call to mind, and in full detail both of condition and of custom, my various dwelling places in times gone by.'

"This, friends, is the first state of things on account of which, starting from which, some people are eternalists, and maintain that both the soul and the world are eternal.

"And in the next place, friends, on what ground is it, starting from what, that those venerable ones are eternalists and maintain that the soul and the world are eternal?

"In this case, friends, some person is addicted to logic and reasoning. He or she gives utterance to the following conclusion of his or her own, beaten out by his or her argumentations and based on his or her sophistry; 'Eternal is the soul; and the world, giving birth to nothing new, is steadfast as a mountain peak, as a pillar firmly fixed; and those living creatures, though they pass away, yet they are for ever and ever.'

"This, friends, is another state of things on the ground of which, starting from which, some people are eternalists, and maintain that the soul and the world are eternal.

"Now of these, friends, the Enlightened One knows that these speculations thus arrived at, thus insisted on, will have such and such a result, such and such an effect on the future condition of these who trust in them. What does he know, and he knows also other things far beyond, far better than those speculations; and having that knowledge he is not puffed up, and thus untarnished he has, in his own heart, realized the way of escape from them, has understood, as they really are, the rising up and passing away of sensations, their sweet taste, their danger, how they cannot be relied on; and not grasping after any of these things people are eager for, he, the Enlightened One, is quite free.

"These, friends, are those other things, profound, difficult to realize, hard to understand, tranquilizing, sweet, not to be grasped by mere logic, subtle, comprehensible only by the wise, which the Enlightened One, having himself realized and seen face to face, has set forth; and it is concerning those that they who would rightly praise the Enlightened One in accordance with the truth, should speak.

"For whoever, friends, whether clergy or lay people, are thus reconstructors of the past or arrangers of the future, or who are both, whose speculations are concerned with both, who put forward various propositions with regard to the past and to the future, they, all of them, are entrapped in the net of these modes; this way and that they plunge about, but they are in it; this way and that they may flounder, but they are included in it, caught in it.

"Just, friends, as when skillful fisherpersons should drag a tiny pool of water with a fine-meshed net they might fairly think: 'Whatever fish of size may be in this pond, every one will be in this net; flounder about as they may, they will be included in it, and caught'—just so it is with these speculators about the past and the future, in this net, flounder as they may, they are included and caught.

"The outward form, friends, of those who have won the truth, stand before you, but that which binds it is cut in two. So long as these bodies shall last, so long do people behold them. On the dissolution of the bodies, no one shall see them.

"Just, friends, as when the stalk of a bunch of mangoes has been cut, all the mangoes that were hanging on that stalk go with it; just so, though the outward form of one who has won the truth stands before you, that which binds it has been cut in two. So long as these bodies shall last, so long do people behold them. On the dissolution of the bodies, no one shall see them."

When he had thus spoken, the venerable Ananda said to the Blessed One: "Strange, Master, is this, and wonderful! And what name has this exposition of the truth?"

"Ananda, you may remember this exposition as the Net of Advantage, and as the Net of Truth, and as the Supreme Net, and as the Net of Theories; remember it even as the glorious victory in the day of battle!"

Thus spoke the Blessed One, and glad at heart the disciples exalted his word.

Questions Which Do Not Tend to Edification

Thus have I heard.

On a certain occasion the Blessed One was dwelling in Anathapindika's Park. Now it happened to the venerable Malunkyaputta, being in seclusion and plunged in meditation, that a consideration presented itself to his mind, as follows: "These theories which the Blessed One has left un-elucidated, has set aside and rejected—that the world is eternal, that the world is not eternal, that the world is finite, that the world is infinite, that the soul and the body are identical, that the soul is one thing and the body another that the saint exists after death, that the saint does not exist after death, that the saint both exists and does not exist after death, that the saint neither exists nor does not exist after death—these the Blessed One does not elucidate to me. And the fact that the Blessed One does not elucidate them to me does not please me or suit me. Therefore I will draw near to the Blessed One and inquire of him concerning this matter. If the Blessed One will elucidate them to me, in that case will I lead the religious life under the Blessed One. If the Blessed One will not elucidate them to me, in that case will I abandon religious training and return to the life of a layperson."

Then the venerable Malunkyaputta arose at eventide from his seclusion, and drew near to where the Blessed One was; and having drawn near and greeted the Blessed One, he sat down respectfully at one side. And seated respectfully at one side, the venerable Malunkyaputta spoke to the Blessed One as follows:

"Reverend Sir, it happened to me, as I was just now in seclusion and plunged in meditation, that a consideration presented itself to my mind, as follows: 'These theories which the Blessed One has left un-elucidated, has set aside and rejected, that the world is eternal, that the world is not eternal, ... that the saint neither exists nor does not exist after death, these Blessed One does not elucidate them to me does not please me or suit me. I will draw near to the Blessed One and inquire of him concerning this matter. If the Blessed One will elucidate them to me, in that case will I lead the religious life under the Blessed One. If the Blessed One will not elucidate them to me, in that case will I abandon religious training and return to the life of a layman.'

"If the Blessed One knows that the world is eternal, let the Blessed One elucidate to me that the world is eternal; if the Blessed One knows that the world is not eternal, let the Blessed One elucidate to me that the world is not eternal. If the Blessed One does not know either that the world is eternal or that the world is not eternal, the only upright thing for one who does not know, or who has not that insight, is to say, 'I do not know; I have not that insight.'"

"Pray, Malunkyaputta, did I ever say to you, 'Come, Malunkyaputta, lead the religious life with me, and I will elucidate to you either that the world is eternal, or that the world is not eternal, ... or that the saint neither exists nor does not exist after death?'"

"No, truly, Reverend Sir."

"Or did you ever say to me, 'Reverend Sir, I will lead the religious life with the Blessed One on condition that the Blessed One elucidate to me either that the world is eternal, or that the world is not eternal, ... or that the saint neither exists nor does not exist after death?'"

"No, truly, Reverend Sir."

"That being the case, vain man, whom are you so angrily denouncing?

"Malunkyaputta, anyone who should say, 'I will not lead the religious life under the Blessed One until the Blessed One shall elucidate to me either that the world is eternal, or that the world is not eternal, ... or that the saint neither exists nor does not exist after death:' that person would die, Malunkyaputta, before the Enlightened One had ever elucidated this to him.

"It is as if, Malunkyaputta, a person had been wounded by an arrow thickly smeared with poison, and his/her friends and companions, relatives and kinsfolk, were to procure a physician or surgeon; and the sick person were to say, 'I will not have this arrow taken out until I have learned whether the person who wounded me belonged to the armed services or to the clergy, or to the laboring class.'

"Or again he were to say, 'I will not have this arrow taken out until I have learned whether the arrow which wounded me was an ordinary arrow, or a claw-headed arrow, or an iron arrow, or a calf-tooth arrow.' That man would die, Malunkyaputta, without ever having learned this.

"In exactly the same way, Malunkyaputta, anyone who should say, 'I will not lead the religious life with the Blessed One until the Blessed One shall elucidate to me either that the world is eternal, or that the world is not eternal, ... or that the saint neither exists nor does not exist after death'; that person would die, Malunkyaputta, before the Enlightened One had ever elucidated this matter.

"The religious life, Malunkyaputta, does not depend on the dogma that the world is eternal; or that the world is not eternal. There still remain old age, death, sorrow, lamentation, misery, grief and despair, for the overcoming of which in the present life I am prescribing.

"Accordingly, Malunkyaputta, bear always in mind what it is that I have not elucidated, and what it is that I have elucidated. And what, Malunkyaputta, have I not elucidated? I have not elucidated, Malunkyaputta, that the world is eternal; I have not elucidated that the world is not eternal. I have not elucidated that the saint neither exists nor does not exist after death. And why, Malunkyaputta, have I not elucidated this. Because, Malunkyaputta, this profits not, nor has to do with the fundamentals of religion, nor tends to aversion, absence of passion, cessation of misery, calmness, the intuitive faculties, supreme wisdom, and lasting happiness; therefore have I not elucidated it.

"And what, Malunkyaputta, have I elucidated? Misery have I elucidated; the origin of misery have I elucidated; the cessation of misery have I elucidated; and the path leading to the cessation of misery have I elucidated. And why, Malunkyaputta, have I elucidated this? Because this does profit, has to do with the fundamentals of religion, and tends to aversion, absence of passion, cessation of misery, calmness, intuition, supreme wisdom, and lasting happiness; therefore have I elucidated it. Accordingly, Malunkyaputta, bear always in mind what it is that I have not elucidated, and what it is that I have elucidated."

Thus spoke the Blessed One; and, delighted, the venerable Malunkyaputta applauded the speech of the Blessed One.

The Fall and Rise of Social Behavior

When poverty had become rife, a certain man took that which others had not given him, what people call by theft. They caught him and brought him before the king, saying: "This man, O king, has taken that which was not given him, and that is theft."

Thereupon the king spoke thus to the man: "Is it true, sir, that you have taken what nobody gave you, that you have committed what is called theft?"

"It is true, O king."

"But why?"

"O king, I have nothing to keep me alive."

Then the king bestowed wealth on that man, saying? "With this wealth, sir, both keep yourself alive, maintain your parents, maintain your children and wife, carry on your business, and keep up such alms for the holy ones as shall be of value, spiritual gifts, the result whereof shall be lasting happiness."

"Even so, O king," replied the man.

Now another man, friends, took by theft what was not given him. They caught him and brought him before the king, and told him, saying: "This man, O king, has taken by theft what was not given him."

And the king spoke and did even as he had spoken and done to the former man.

Now people heard, friends, that to them who had taken by theft what was not given them, the king was giving wealth. And hearing, they thought: "Let us then take by theft what has not been given us."

Now another man did so. They caught him and charged him before the king, who, as before, asked him why he had stolen.

Then the king thought: "If I bestow wealth on anyone who has taken by theft what was not given him, there will be hereby an increase of this stealing. Let me now put a final stop to this, inflict corporal punishment on him by having his head cut off!"

So he bade his soldiers saying: "Now, look! Bind this man's arms behind him with a strong rope and a tight knot, shave his head bald, lead him around with a harsh sounding drum from road to road, from crossways to crossways, take him out by the southern gate to the south of the town, put a final stop to this, inflict on him the uttermost penalty, cut off his head."

"Even so, O king," answered the soldiers and carried out his commands.

Now people heard, friends, that they who took by theft what was not given them were thus put to death. And hearing, they thought: "Let us also now have sharp swords made ready for ourselves, and them from whom we take what is not given us—what they call theft—let us put a final stop to them, inflict on them the uttermost penalty, and cut their heads off."

And they got themselves sharp swords, and came forth to sack village and town and city, and to work highway robbery. And them whom they robbed they made an end of, cutting off their heads.

Thus, my friends, from goods not being bestowed on the destitute, poverty grew rife; from poverty growing rife, stealing increased; from the spread of stealing, violence grew apace; from the growth of violence, the destruction of life became common; from the frequency of murder, both the span of life in those beings and their comeliness also wasted away, so that, of humans whose span of life was seventy years, the children lived but sixty-five years.

Now among humans of the latter span of life, my friends, a certain man took by theft what was not given him and, even as those others, was accused before the king and questioned if it was true that he had stolen. "No, O king," he replied, thus deliberately telling a lie.

Thus, from goods not being bestowed on the destitute, poverty grew rife ... stealing ... violence ... murder ... until lying grew common. And from lying growing common, both the span of life in those beings and the comeliness of them wasted away, so that of humans whose span of life was sixty-five years, the children lived but sixty years.

Now among humans of the latter lifespan, a certain man took by theft what was not given him. Him a certain person reported to the king, saying: "Such and such a man, O king, has taken by theft what was not given him"—thus speaking evil of him.

And so, my friends, from goods not being bestowed on the destitute, poverty grew rife ... stealing ... violence ... murder ... lying ... evil speaking grew abundant. And from evil speaking growing abundant, both the lifespan of those beings and also the comeliness of them wasted away, so that, of humans whose lifespan was sixty years, the children lived but fifty-five years.

Now among humans of the latter span of life, my friends, some were comely and some were ugly. And so those who were ugly, coveting them that were comely committed adultery with their neighbors' wives.

Thus from goods not being bestowed on the destitute, poverty ... stealing ... violence ... murder ... lying ... evil speaking ... immorality grew rife. And from the increase of immortality, both the lifespan of those beings and also the comeliness of them wasted away, so that, of humans whose lifespan was fifty-five years, the children lived but fifty years.

Now among humans of the latter span of life, my friends, two things increased, abusive speech and idle talk. And from these two things increasing, both the lifespan of these beings and the comeliness of them wasted away, so that, of humans whose lifespan was fifty years, some of their children lived but forty-five years.

Among humans of a lifespan of forty-five years, covetousness and ill-will waxed great. And thereby ... the children lived but forty years.

Among humans of the latter span of life, false opinions grew. And thereby the lifespan of those beings and the comeliness of them wasted, so that, of humans whose lifespan was forty years, the children usually lived but thirty-five years.

Among humans of the latter span of life, my friends, three things grew apace: incest, wanton greed, and perverted lust. Thereby the lifespan of those beings and their comeliness wasted, so that, of humans whose span of life was thirty-five years, some of the children lived but thirty years.

Among humans of a lifespan, friends, of thirty years, these things grew apace: lack of filial piety to mother and father, lack of religious piety to holy ones, and lack of regard for the head of the nation.

Thus, my friends, from goods not being bestowed on the destitute, poverty grew great ... stealing ... violence ... murder ... lying ... evil speaking ... adultery ... abusive and idle talk ... covetousness and ill-will ... false opinions ... incest, wanton greed and perverted lust ... till finally lack of filial and religious piety and lack of regard for the head of the nation grew great. From these things growing, the life-span of those beings and the comeliness of them wasted, so that, of humans whose span of life was thirty years, the children lived but twenty-five years.

There will come a time, friends, when the descendants of those humans will have a lifespan of ten years. Among humans of this lifespan, maidens of five years will be of a marriageable age. Among such humans these kinds of tastes (savors) will disappear: butter, sugar, salt, and so on. Among such humans, poor grain will be the highest kind of food. Even as today, rice and curry are in some lands considered the highest kind of food, so will poor grain be then. Among such humans, moral courses of conduct will altogether disappear, whereas immoral courses of action will flourish excessively. There will be no word for moral among such humans—far less any moral agent. Among such humans, friends, those who lack filial and religious piety, and show no respect for the head of the nation—it is they to whom homage and praise will be given, just as today homage and praise are given to the filial-minded, to the pious and to them who respect the heads of their nations.

Among such humans, friends, there will be no such thoughts of reverence as are a bar to intermarriage with mother, or mother's sister, or mother's sister-in-law, or teacher's wife, or father's sister-in-law. The world will fall into promiscuity, like goats and sheep, fowls and swine, dogs and jackals.

Among such humans, friends, keen mutual enmity will become the rule, keen ill-will, keen animosity, passionate thoughts even of killing, in a mother toward her child, in a child toward its mother, in a father toward his child and a child toward its father, in brother to brother, in brother to sister, in sister to brother. Just as a sportsman feels toward the game that he sees, so will they feel.

Among such humans, friends, there will arise a sword-period of seven days, during which they will look on each other as wild beasts; sharp swords will appear ready to their hands, and they, thinking, "This is a wild beast, this is a wild beast," will with their swords deprive each other of life.

Then to some of those beings it will occur: "Let us not slay just anyone; nor let just anyone slay us! Let us now, therefore, betake ourselves to dens of grass, or dens in the jungle, or holes in trees, or river fastnesses, or mountain clefts, and subsist on roots and fruits of the jungle." And they will do so for those seven days. And at the end of those seven days, coming forth from those dens and fastnesses and mountain clefts, they will embrace each other, and be of one accord comforting one another, and saying: "Hail, O mortal, that you live still! O happy sight to find you still alive!"

Then this, friends, will occur to those beings: "Now, only because we had gotten into evil ways, have we had this heavy loss of kith and kin. Let us therefore now do good. What can we do that is good? Let us now abstain from taking life. That is a good thing that we may take up and do." And they will abstain from slaughter, and will continue in this good way. Because of their getting into this good way, they will increase again both as to their span of life and as to their comeliness. And to them thus increasing in life and comeliness, to them who lived but one decade, there will be children who will live for fifteen years.

Then this will occur to those beings: "Now we, because we have gotten into good ways, increase in length of life and comeliness. Let us now do still more good. Let us now abstain from taking what is not given, let us abstain from adultery, let us now abstain from abuse and from idle talk, let us now abstain from covetousness, from ill-will, from false opinions, let us now abstain from the three things—incest, wanton greed and perverted desires; let us now be filial toward our mothers and our fathers, let us be pious toward holy ones, let us respect the heads of nations, yes, let us continue to practice each of these good things.

So they will practice these virtues. And because of the good they do, they will increase in length of life and in comeliness, so that the children of them who lived but fifteen years will come to live twenty years. And the children of these children will come to live twenty-five years; their children to thirty years; their children to thirty-five years; their children to forty years; their children to forty-five years; their children to fifty years; their children to fifty-five years; their children to sixty years; their children to sixty-five years; and the children of those that lived sixty-five years will come to live seventy years.

Among humans living seventy years, friends, maidens are marriageable at twenty-five years of age. Among such humans there will be only three kinds of disease—appetite, non-assimilation, and old age. Among such humans, this world will be mighty and prosperous, the villages, towns, cities, and nations will be so close that a cock could fly from each one to the next.

The Buddha and the Elephant

Thus have I heard:

On a certain occasion the Exalted One was staying at Kosambi in Ghosita Park. Now on that occasion the Exalted One was bothered by monks and nuns, lay-followers, both men and women, by kings and royal ministers, by sectarians and their followers; and he was in discomfort, not in peace. Then the Exalted One thought: Here am I being bothered by monks and nuns ... by sectarians and their followers. I am in discomfort, not in peace. Suppose I were temporarily to go away from the crowd alone so as to meditate.

So the Exalted One, robing himself in the forenoon and taking his possessions, entered Kosambi to quest for food; and having gotten some food in Kosambi, after returning and eating his meal, he himself set his bed and lodging in order, and taking his possessions, without informing his attendant or giving notice to his disciples, alone and unattended, started on his way for Parileyya Village, and later on reached that place. There the Exalted One took a seat in Guarded Forest Glade, at the foot of a lovely tree.

Now a certain bull-elephant was being bothered by elephants and she-elephants, by calf-elephants and sucklings, and had to feed on grass already cropped by them. They ate the bundles of branches as he broke them off. He had to drink muddied water, and when he crossed over by the ford the she-elephants went pushing against his body. So he was in discomfort, not in peace. So this bull-elephant thought: "Here am I bothered by elephants and she-elephants, by calf-elephants and sucklings. I have to feed on grass already cropped. They eat the bundles of branches as I break them off. I have to drink muddied water, and when I cross over by the ford the she-elephants go pushing against my body. Thus I am in discomfort, not in peace. Suppose now I were temporarily to go away from the crowd alone."

Accordingly, that bull-elephant left the herd and started for Marileyya Village and Guarded Forest Glade and the foot of the lovely tree where the Exalted One was resting. On reaching that place, he kept the spot where the Exalted One was staying free from grass, and with his trunk brought water for the use of the Exalted One.

Thus the Exalted One remained for a certain length of time in seclusion and solitude, and there arose in him this thought: "Formerly I was bothered by monks and nuns ... I was in discomfort,

not in peace. But now here am I unbothered by monks and nuns
... by sectarians and their followers. Unbothered, I am in comfort
and in peace." Likewise, that bull-elephant thought: "Formerly I
was bothered by elephants ... Now I am unbothered, in comfort
and in peace."

And the Exalted One, observing his own seclusion and knowing
with his mind the thought of that bull-elephant, at that time gave
utterance to this verse of uplift:

Herein agree mind with mind, of sage
And elephant whose tusks are like a plough pole,
Since both alike love forest solitude.

At last, having regained their mental equilibrium, the two returned to their respective duties, and fought the battle of life much
more purposefully than before their needed withdrawal.

The Mighty Ocean of Perfection

Then the Exalted One admonished the monks, saying: "Just as,
friends, the mighty ocean flows down, slides and tends downward
gradually, and there is no abrupt precipice, so also in this perfection-discipline the training is gradual, the action is gradual, the procedure is gradual; there is no abrupt penetration of understanding.
Since this is so ... this is the first strange and wonderful thing, seeing which, disciples take delight in this perfection-discipline.

"Just as, friends, the mighty ocean is of a stable nature, since it
overpasses not its boundary, even so, my disciples transgress not,
even at cost of life, the training enjoined on them by me. Since this
is so ... this is the second strange and wonderful thing.

"Just as, friends, the mighty ocean consorts not with a dead body;
for when a dead body is found in the mighty ocean it quickly wafts
it ashore, throws it up on the shore; even so, whatever person is
immoral, of a wicked nature, impure, of suspicious behavior, of
covert deeds, one who is not sincere, though claiming to be such,
one rotten within, full of lusts, a rubbish-heap of filth—with such
the pure consort not, but gathering together quickly ask that person
either to seek perfection or to leave. Though, friends, this person
may be seated in the midst of the pure, yet is he/she far away from
them; far away are the pure from him/her. Since this is so ... this is
the third strange and wonderful thing.

"Just as, friends, whatever great rivers there are, on reaching the
mighty ocean, abandon their former names and lineage, and hence-

forth go by the name of just 'mighty ocean"; even so, friends, the various classes—namely, the professions, the clergy, the merchants, the laborers, and others—on going forth from home to the homeless in the perfection-discipline proclaimed by the prophets, abandon their former titles and securities, and go by the title of just 'servers of humanity.' Since this is so ... this is the fourth strange and wonderful thing.

"Just as, friends, whatever streams flow into the mighty ocean and whatever floods fall from the sky, there is no shrinkage or overflow seen thereby in the mighty ocean; even so, friends, though many people pass finally into that condition of lasting happiness which has no remainder, yet is there no shrinkage or overflow in that condition of happiness seen thereby. Since this is so ... this is the fifth strange and wonderful thing.

"Just as, friends, the mighty ocean is of one flavor, the flavor of salt, even so, this happiness is of one flavor, the flavor of release. Since this is so ... this is the sixth strange and wonderful thing.

"Just as, friends, the mighty ocean has many gems, diverse gems ... even so in this happiness are many gems, diverse gems; therein are the arisings of mindfulness, the best efforts, the bases of psychic power, the faculties, the limbs of wisdom, the eightfold way. Since this is so ... this is the seventh strange and wonderful thing.

"Just as, friends, the mighty ocean is the abode of great creatures; even so, this perfection-discipline is the abode of great creatures. Since this is so ... this, friends, is the eighth strange and wonderful thing about lasting happiness, beholding which again and again people take delight in this perfection-discipline.

"These, then, friends, are the eight strange and wonderful things in lasting happiness, beholding which again and again disciples take delight in this perfection-discipline."

The Elephant and the Blind People

Thus have I heard: On a certain occasion the Exalted One was staying near Savatthi ... in Anathapindika's Park.

Now on that occasion a great number of disciples and clergy, who held various views, entered Savatthi to ask for advice. They held various views, were tolerant of various things, favored various things, inclined to rely on various views. Some disciples and clergy spoke in favor of this, and held this view: that the world is eternal, that this is the truth, that any other view is infatuation. Other disciples and clergy held that the world is not eternal; that this is truth, any other view infatuation. Some held that the world is limited ... others that it is unlimited. Some held that the living principle is body ... others that the living principle is one thing, body another. Some held that the self is beyond death, others that the self is not beyond death ... that it both is and is not beyond death ... that it neither is nor is not beyond death ... that this is truth, that any other view is infatuation. So they, by nature quarrelsome, wrangling and disputatious, lived wounding one another with the weapons of the tongue, maintaining: "Happiness is such and such; happiness is not such and such; it is, it is not."

Now a great number of them, robing themselves in the forenoon and taking some possessions, entered Savatthi to ask advice of the Exalted One. They said: "Sir, there are living here in Savatthi a great number of your disciples and clergy who hold various views to the following effect": (and they detailed the various views). Then said the Exalted One:

"Friends, those who dispute these views are blind, unseeing. They do not know the profitable, they do not know the unprofitable. They do not know happiness, they do not know what is not happiness. In their ignorance of these things they are by nature quarrelsome, wrangling and disputatious in maintaining their several views thus and thus. Formerly, friends, there was a certain raja of this same Savatthi. Then, that raja called to a certain man, saying, 'Come, good fellow, go and gather together in one place all the people in Savatthi who were born blind.'

"'Very good, sire,' replied that man, and in obedience to the raja gathered together all the people born blind in Savatthi, and having done so went to the raja and said, 'Sire, all the people born blind in Savatthi are assembled.'

"'Then, my good man, show the blind people an elephant.'

"'Very good, sire,' said the man, and did as he was told, and said to them, 'O blind people, such as this is an elephant': and to one individual he presented the head of the elephant, to another its ear, to another a tusk, to another the trunk, the foot, back, tail, and tuft of the tail, saying to each one that that was the elephant.

"Now, friends, that man, having thus presented the elephant to the blind people, came to the raja and said, 'Sire, the elephant has been presented to the blind people. Do what is your will.'

"Thereupon, friends, that raja went up to the blind people and said to each, 'Have you seen the elephant?'

"'Yes, sire.'

"'Then tell me, blind people, what sort of thing is an elephant?'

"Thereupon those who had been presented with the head answered, 'Sire, an elephant is like a pot.' And those who had observed an ear only replied, 'An elephant is like a winnowing-basket.' Those who had been presented with a tusk said it was a plough-share. Those who knew only the trunk said it was a plough; they said the body was a granary; the foot, a pillar; the back, a mortar; the tail, a pestle; the tuft of the tail, just a broom.

"Then they began to quarrel, shouting, 'Yes, it is!' 'No, it is not!' 'An elephant is not that!' 'Yes, it's like that!; and so on, till they came to blows over the matter.

"Then, friends, that raja was delighted with the scene.

"Just so are these people holding various views, blind, unseeing, knowing not the profitable, knowing not the unprofitable. They do not know happiness. They do not know what is not happiness. In their ignorance of these things they are by nature quarrelsome, wrangling and disputatious, each maintaining it is thus and thus."

Thereupon the Exalted One at that time, seeing the meaning of it, gave utterance to this verse of uplift:

> O how they cling and wrangle, some who claim
> Of clergy and disciple the honored name!
> For, quarreling, each to his/her view they cling.
> Such folk see only one side of a thing.

Death of the Insects

Thus have I heard: On a certain occasion the Exalted One was staying near Savatthi ... in Anathapindika'a Park.

On that occasion the Exalted One was seated in the open air, on a night of inky darkness, and oil-lamps were burning.

And at that time swarms of winged insects kept falling into those oil-lamps and thereby met their end, came to destruction and utter ruin. And the Exalted One saw those swarms of winged insects so doing, and at that time, seeing the meaning of it, gave utterance to this verse of uplift:

> They hasten up and past, but miss the real;
> A bondage ever new they cause to grow.
> Just as the flutterers fall into the lamp,

So some are bent on what they see and hear.

The Sorrow of Visakha

Thus have I heard: On a certain occasion the Exalted One was staying near Savatthi in East Park, at the house of Visakha.

Now at that time the dear and lovely granddaughter of Visakha had died. So Visakha, with clothes and hair still wet from washing, came at an unseasonable hour to see the Exalted One, and on coming to him, saluted him and sat down at one side. As she sat thus the Exalted One said this to Visakha: "Why, Visakha! How is it that you come here with clothes and hair still wet at this unseasonable hour?"

"O, sir, my dear and lovely granddaughter is dead! That is why I come here, with hair and clothes still wet at this unseasonable hour."

"Visakha, would you like to have as many children and grandchildren as there are people in Savatthi?"

"Yes, sir, I would indeed!"

"But how many people do you suppose die daily in Savatthi?"

"Ten, sir, or maybe nine, or eight; maybe seven, six, five or four, three, two; maybe one a day dies in Savatthi, sir. Savatthi is never free from dying, sir."

"What do you think, Visakha? In such case would you ever be without wet hair and clothes?"

"Surely not, sir! Enough for me, sir, of so many children and grandchildren!"

"Visakha, those who have a hundred people or things beloved, if they are closely attached to their affections, will have a hundred sorrows. Those who have ninety, eighty ... thirty, twenty beloved ... those who have ten ... those who have but one thing beloved, under the same conditions, will have but one sorrow. those who have no one person or thing beloved in this excessive manner will have no sorrow. Sorrowless will they be and passionless, if all their human relations are stable. Serene are they, I declare.

All grief or lamentations whatsoe'er
And diverse forms of sorrow in the world,
Things too dear not being, these do not become.
Happy are they therefore and free from grief
To whom is naught too dear in the world.
Wherefore aspiring for the griefless, sorrowless,

Make in all the world naught too attached to you.

A Sermon to the People

This was said by the Exalted One, so I have heard:

Friends, I am your surety for overcoming needless suffering. Do give up lust, ill-will, delusion, wrath, spite, haughtiness. I am your surety for overcoming.

Friends, those who do not understand and comprehend themselves, who have not detached their minds from pleasures, who have not abandoned lusts, can make no growth in extinguishing ill.

But, friends, those who do understand and comprehend themselves, who have detached their minds from pleasures, who have abandoned lusts, they are able to make growth in extinguishing ill.

Those who, knowing in all their ways,
For all their doings have no lust,
By comprehension of the Self
They truly have overcome all ill.

Friends, for the person who is a learner not yet come to mastery of mind, but who dwells aspiring for lasting happiness, making it a matter concerning what is outside the Self, I see no other single factor so helpful as friendship with the lovely. Friends, one who is a friend of the lovely abandons the spiritually unprofitable and chooses the profitable.

The person who has a lovely friend, who pays
Deference and reverence to him/her, who does
What friends advise, if mindful and composed,
Such in due course shall win all fetters' end.

Here, friends, I discern certain persons with mind at peace to be such because I compass their thoughts with my mind; and, if at this moment these people were to die, they probably would be remembered according to their true value. What is the reason for that? Their minds are at peace. Indeed it is because of a mind at peace, friends, that in this way certain beings, when they die, are remembered with the greatest of respect in all years to come.

Here seeing certain people with mind at peace,
The Teacher 'mid the group set forth this saying:
"If at this time these people were to die,
They would be remembered with respect.
Indeed the minds of those have come to peace.
Thro' peace of mind people reach true happiness.

As people lay down what they have taken up,
So such people, when their bodies break up,
Strong in wisdom, are recalled till Eternity."

Friends, if beings knew, as I know, the value of sharing gifts, they would not enjoy their use without sharing them, nor would the taint of stinginess obsess the heart and stay there. Even if it were their last bit, their last morsel of food, they would not enjoy its use without sharing it, if there were anyone to receive it. But inasmuch, friends, as beings do not know, as I know, the value of sharing gifts, therefore they enjoy their use without sharing them, and the taint of stinginess obsesses their heart and stays there.

If only beings knew—as said the mighty sage—
The value of sharing gifts, how great the fruit thereof,
Putting away the taint of stinginess, with heart
Made pure within, they would bestow in season due
When great the fruit of charity on all beings.
And giving food as gift to those deserving much
From ego-state falling, hence givers may arise.
In the fullness of their heart's desire the value
Of sharing gifts, the fruit of their unselfishness.

Friends, whatever grounds there be for good works undertaken with a view to reward, all of them are not worth one-sixteenth part of that goodwill which is the heart's release; goodwill alone, which is the heart's release, shines and burns and flashes forth in surpassing them. Just as, friends, the radiance here on earth of all the starry bodies is not worth one-sixteenth part of the sun's radiance, but the sun's radiance shines and burns and flashes forth in surpassing them, even so, friends, goodwill ... flashes forth in surpassing good works undertaken with a view to reward.

Just as, friends, in the last month of the rains, in autumn time, when the sky is cleared of clouds, the sun, rising into the sky, drives away all darkness from the heavens and shines and burns and flashes forth, even so, friends, whatever grounds there be for good works ... goodwill ... flashes forth in surpassing them.

Just as, friends, in the night at time of daybreak a certain star shines and burns and flashes forth, even so, whatever grounds there be for good works undertaken with a view to reward, all of them are not worth one-sixteenth part of that goodwill which is the heart's release. Goodwill, which is the heart's release, alone shines and burns and flashes forth in surpassing them.

Friends, two perfection-teachings of the wayfarer disciple, a rightly awakened one, take place one after the other. What two? "Look at evil as evil" is the first perfection-teaching. "Seeing evil as evil, be disgusted therewith, be cleansed of it, be freed of it" is the second perfection-teaching. These two perfection-teachings of the wayfarer take place one after the other.

> Of the wayfarer, the awakened one,
> Who has compassion on all things that be,
> Behold the way of speech and teachings both:
> "Evil behold for what it is, and then
> Conceive disgust for it: with heart made clean
> Of evil, you shall make an end of ill."

Friends, ignorance leads the way to the attainment of unprofitable things; unawareness and disregard of blame follow after. But, friends, knowledge leads the way to the attainment of profitable things, awareness and acceptance of blame follow after.

> Whatever be these ill-borns in this world of troubles,
> All-rooted are in ignorance, of lust compounded.
> And since the wicked ones are void of shame, and have
> No reverence, therefore they work wickedness,
> And through that wickedness they to their downfall go.
> Wherefore forsaking longing, lust, and ignorance
> And causing knowledge to arise in them, disciples
> Should give up, leave behind, the ill-borns one and all.

Friends, there are these two conditions of happiness. What two? The condition of happiness with the basis still remaining and that without basis. Of what sort, friends, is the condition of happiness which has the basis still remaining? Herein, friends, people become enlightened, those who have destroyed the cankers, who have lived the life, done what was to be done, laid down the burden, won the goal, worn out the fetters of attachment, released by perfect understanding. In them the sense-faculties still remain, through which, as they have not yet departed, they experience sensations pleasant and unpleasant, undergo pleasure and pain. In them the end of lust, malice and delusion, friends, is called "the condition of happiness with the basis still remaining."

And of what sort, friends, is the condition of happiness that is without basis?

Herein people become enlightened ... released by perfect understanding, but in them all things that are experienced have no meaning, because they have become cool. This is called "the condition of happiness without basis." So, friends, those are the two conditions of happiness.

> These two happiness states are shown by those
> Who see, who are such and unattached.
> With base remaining, tho' attachment's stream
> Be cut off. While the state without a base
> Belongs to the future, wherein all
> Attachments utterly do come to cease.

Friends, do you delight in solitary communing; delighted by solitary communing, given to mental calm in the inner self, not neglecting musing, possessed of insight, do you foster resort to empty places? One of two fruits is to be looked for in those who do these things, namely, gnosis in the not too distant future or, if there be still a basis, overcoming of needless suffering.

> They who with heart at peace discriminate,
> Thoughtful and musing, rightly perfection see,
> Their passions they do closely scrutinize.
> For being inclined to seriousness and seeing
> Peril in wantonness, they are not the sort
> To fail, but to happiness they are close.

Friends, there are these three persons found existing in the world. What three? The one who is like a drought, the one who rains locally, and the one who pours down everywhere.

And how, friends, is a person like a drought?

Herein, friends, a certain person is not a giver to all alike, no giver of food and drink, clothing and vehicle, flowers, scents and unguents, bed, lodging and light to disciples and clergy, to wretched and needy beggars. In this way, friends, a person is like a drought.

And how, friends, is a person like a local rainfall?

In this case a person is a giver to some, but to others he/she does not give; be they clergy or wretched, needs beggars, he/she is not giver of food and drink ... lodging and lights. In this way a person is like a local rainfall.

And how, friends, does a person rain down everywhere?

In this case a certain person gives to all, be they disciples and clergy or wretched, needy beggars; he/she is a giver of food and drink ... lodging and lights. In this way a person rains down everywhere.

So these are the three sorts of persons found existing in the world.

Friends, even if monks should seize the hem of my garment and walk behind me step for step, yet if they are covetous in their desires, fierce in their longing, malevolent of heart, of mind corrupt, careless and unrestrained, not quieted but scatter-brained and uncontrolled in sense, those monks are far from me and I am far from them. What is the cause of that? Friends, those monks do not see perfection. Not seeing perfection, they do not see me. Friends, even though monks should dwell a hundred miles away, yet if they are not covetous in their desires, not fierce in their longing, not malevolent of heart, not of mind corrupt, but with mindfulness set up and composed, calmed, one-pointed in mind and restrained in sense, then indeed those monks are near to me and I am near to them. What is the cause of that? Friends, these monks see perfection. Seeing perfection, they see me.

> Tho' following in their steps, if they are passionate,
> Vexatious—lo! how far away the follower
> Of lust from those that have no lust. How far
> The not-waned from the waned! How far the greedy
> But perfection comprehending thoroughly,
> Lustless, like pool unstirred by wind, are calmed.
> That lustless to the lustless, lo! how near.
> That waned one to the waned! That one not greedy,
> How near to those that have put greed away.

Friends, there are these two gifts, the material and the spiritual. Of these two gifts, the spiritual gift is pre-eminent. Friends, there are these two sharings together, the sharing of the material and the sharing of the spiritual. Of these two sharings together, the sharing of the spiritual is pre-eminent. Friends, there are these two acts of kindness, the material and the spiritual. Of these two acts of kindness, the spiritual is pre-eminent.

> That which people call "the best gift, unsurpassed,"
> That sharing which the Exalted One has praised,
> With heart of faith in that best merit-field,
> Who would not offer it in season due?
> They who both hear it and who speak thereof,
> With heart of faith in the Wayfarer's teaching,
> In them their highest profit is made pure
> Who set themselves to the Wayfarer's teaching.

Friends, I am a clergyperson, one to ask a favor of, clean-handed, always aiming to be my true self, physician of the mind. You are my own true children, born of my mouth, born of perfection, created by perfection, my spiritual heirs, not material heirs.

Friends, live perfect in virtue, live perfect in the performance of the obligations, restrained with the restraint of the obligations, perfect in the practice of right behavior; seeing danger in the slightest faults, undertake and train yourselves in the training of the precepts. For those who so live ... so restrained ... who undertake the training of the precepts, what else remains to be done?

> Whether we walk or stand or rest or lie
> Or stretch our limbs or draw them in again,
> Let us do all these things composedly;
> Whatever is one's role in all the world—
> Let us be those who view the rise-and-fall
> So dwelling ardent, living a life of peace
> And not elated, but to calmness given,
> For mind's composure doing what is right,
> Ever and always training—"ever intent"—
> That is the name people give to such a one.

THE DHAMMAPADA

The Twin-Verses

All that we are is the result of what we have thought: it is founded on our thoughts; it is made up of our thoughts. If people speak or act with an evil thought, pain follows them, as the wheel follows the foot of the ox that draws the carriage.

All that we are is the result of what we have thought: it is founded on our thoughts, it is made up of our thoughts. If people speak or act with a pure thought, happiness follows them, like a shadow that never leaves them.

"He abused me, he beat me, he defeated me, he robbed me:—in these who harbor such thoughts, hatred will never cease.

For hatred does not cease by hatred at any time: hatred ceases by love—this is an old rule.

The world does not know that we must all come to an end here; but those who know it, their quarrels cease at once.

Those who live looking for pleasures only, their senses uncontrolled, immoderate in their food, idle, and weak, temptation will certainly overthrow them, as the wind throws down a weak tree.

Those who live without looking for pleasures, their senses well controlled, moderate in their food, faithful and strong, temptation will certainly not overthrow them, any more than the wind throws down a rocky mountain.

They who imagine truth in untruth, and see untruth in truth, never arrive at truth, but follow vain desires.

They who know truth in truth, and untruth in untruth, arrive at truth, and follow true desires.

As rain breaks through an ill-thatched house, passion will break through an unreflecting mind.

As rain does not break through a well-thatched house, passion will not break through a well-reflecting mind.

On Earnestness

Earnestness is the path of life, thoughtlessness the path of death. Those who are in earnest do not die, those who are thoughtless are as if dead already.

Having understood this clearly, those who are advanced in earnestness delight in earnestness, and rejoice in the knowledge of the enlightened ones.

These wise people, meditative, steady, always possessed of strong powers, attain to the highest happiness.

If earnest individuals have roused themselves, if they are not forgetful, if their deeds are pure, if they act with consideration, if they restrain themselves and live according to law—then their inner glory will increase.

By rousing themselves, by earnestness, by restraint and control, the wise people may make for themselves an island which no flood can overwhelm.

Earnest among the thoughtless, awake among the sleepers, the wise person advances like a racer, leaving behind the hack.

Thought

As fletchers make straight their arrows, wise people make straight their trembling and unsteady thought, which is difficult to guard, difficult to hold back.

As fish taken from their watery homes and thrown on the dry ground, our thought trembles all over in order to escape the dominion of temptation.

It is good to tame the mind, which is often difficult to hold in and flighty, rushing wherever it lists; a tamed mind brings happiness.

Let the wise ones guard their thoughts, for they are difficult to perceive, very artful, and they rush wherever they list: thoughts well guarded bring happiness.

Before long, alas! this body will lie on the earth, despised, without understanding, like a useless log.

Whatever a hater may do to a hater, or an enemy to an enemy, a wrongly directed mind will do even greater mischief.

Not a mother, not a father, will do so much, nor any other relatives; a well-directed mind will do us greater service.

Flowers

Who shall overcome this earth and the realm of the spirit? Who shall find out the plainly shown path of virtue, as a clever individual finds the right flower?

The disciple will overcome the earth and the realm of the spirit. The disciple will find out the plainly shown path of virtue, as a clever individual finds the right flower.

Those who know that their bodies are like froth, and have learned that it is as unsubstantial as a mirage, will break the flower-pointed arrow of temptation and never see spiritual death.

Death carries off a person who is gathering flowers, and whose mind is distracted, as a flood carries off a sleeping village.

Death overcomes a person who is gathering flowers, and whose mind is distracted, before the person is satiated in pleasure.

As the bee collects nectar and departs without injuring the flower, or its color or scent, so let sages dwell in their villages.

As on a heap of rubbish cast upon the highway, lilies will grow full of sweet perfume and delight, thus among those who are mere rubbish the disciples of the truly enlightened Buddha shine forth by their understanding above the blinded worldling.

The Fool

Long is the night to those who are awake; long is a mile to those who are tired; long is life to the foolish who do not know the true law.

If travelers do not meet with those who are their better, or their equal, let them firmly keep to their solitary journey; there is no companionship with a fool.

"These children belong to me, and this wealth belongs to me;" with such thoughts a fool is tormented. Such people do not belong to themselves, how much less children and wealth?

Fools who know their foolishness, are wise at least so far. But fools who think themselves wise, they are called fools indeed.

If fools are associated with the wise even all their lives, they will perceive the truth as little as a spoon perceives the taste of soup.

If a truly intelligent person is associated for one minute only with an enlightened being, that person will soon perceive the truth, as the tongue perceives the taste of soup.

Fools of poor understanding have themselves for their greatest enemies, for they do evil deeds which bear bitter fruits.

Those deeds are not well done for which people must repent, and the reward of which they receive crying and with a tearful face.

Those deeds are well done for which people do not need to repent, and the reward of which they receive gladly and cheerfully.

As long as the evil deed done does not bear fruit, the fool thinks it is like honey; but when it ripens, then the fool suffers grief.

"One is the road that leads to wealth, another the road that leads to happiness"—if the disciples of Buddha have learned this, they will not yearn for honor, they will strive after separation from the ways of pleasure-seekers.

The Thousands

Even though a speech is a thousand words, but the words are senseless, one word of sense is better, which if a person hears, he/she becomes quiet.

Even though a poem is a thousand words, but the words are senseless, one word of a poem is better, which if a person hears, he/she becomes quiet.

Our own self conquered is better than that of all other people; no one could change into defeat the victory of those who have vanquished themselves and always live under restraint.

If people for a hundred years sacrifice some of their possessions regularly month by month, and if they but for one moment pay homage to one whose soul is grounded in true knowledge, better is that homage than the sacrifice for a hundred years.

A life of one day is better if a person has attained firm strength than one who has lived a hundred years and is still idle and weak.

A life of one day is better if a person sees the highest law than to live a hundred years and still not seeing the highest law.

Punishment

All persons tremble at punishment, all persons fear death; remember that you are like them, and do not kill or cause slaughter.

All persons tremble at punishment, all persons love life; remember that you are like them, and do not kill or cause slaughter.

Those who, seeking their own happiness, punish or kill beings who also long for happiness, will not find happiness.

Those who, seeking their own happiness, do not punish or kill beings who also long for happiness, will find happiness.

Do not speak harshly to anyone; those who are spoken to will answer you in the same way. Angry speech is painful: blow for blow will touch you.

Old Age

How is there laughter, how is there gaiety, as this world is always full of suffering? Do you not seek a light, you who are surrounded by darkness?

Look at this dressed-up lump, covered with wounds, joined together, sickly, full of many schemes, but which has no strength, no hold!

This body is wasted, full of sickness and frail; this heap of corruption breaks to pieces, life indeed ends in death.

After one has looked at those gray bones, thrown away like gourds in the autumn, what pleasure is there left in life?

After a stronghold has been made of the bones, it is covered with flesh and blood, and there dwell in it old age and death, haughtiness and deceit.

The brilliant chariots of kings are destroyed, the body also approaches destruction, but the virtue of good people never approaches destruction—thus do the good say to the good.

People who have learned little grow old like an ox; their flesh grows, but their understanding does not grow.

Looking for the meaning of this tabernacle of the body, I have run through a quest of many years, not finding any; and painful is this search. But now the meaning has been found; I shall not be misled again. All the rafters of temptation are broken, and the ridge-pole is sundered; the mind, approaching nirvana, has gained the extinction of all craving.

Anger

Let one leave anger, let one forsake haughtiness, let one overcome all bondage! No sufferings befall the one who is not attached to name and form, and who calls no possession essential.

One who holds back rising anger like a rolling chariot, this one I call a real driver; other people are but holding the reins.

Let a person overcome anger by love, let a person overcome evil by good; let a person overcome the greedy by liberality, the liar by truth!

Speak the truth, do not yield to anger; give, if you are asked for little; by these three steps you will go near perfection.

The Way

The best of ways is the eightfold; the best of truths the words of the prophets, the best of virtues dynamic equilibrium; the best of people are those who open their eyes to see.

This is the way; there is no other that leads to the purifying of intelligence. Go on this path! Other roads lead to the confusion of temptation.

If you go on this way, you will make an end of pain! The way is that preached by me, when I had understood the removal of the thorns in the flesh.

You yourself must make an effort. The clergy are only preachers. The thoughtful who enter the way are freed from the bondage of temptation.

Those who do not rouse themselves when it is time to rise, who, though young and strong, are full of sloth, whose will and thought are weak, those people will never find the way to understanding.

So long as the sensual craving between people, even the smallest, is not overcome, so long is the mind in bondage, even as the calf that drinks milk is to its mother.

A wise and well-behaved individual who knows the meaning of this should quickly clear the way that leads to lasting happiness.

If by leaving pleasure one sees happiness, let a wise person leave the pleasure and look to the happiness.

One who, by causing pain to others, wishes to obtain pleasure for oneself, entangled in the bonds of hatred will never be free from hatred.

What ought to be done is neglected, what ought not to be done is done; the needs and cravings of unruly, thoughtless people are always increasing.

But they whose whole watchfulness is first directed to their own perfection, who do not follow what ought not to be done, and who steadfastly do what ought to be done, the cravings of such watchful and wise people will come to an end.

One who says what is not goes to his/her own destruction; one also who, having done a thing, says I have not done it.

Many whose lives are supposed to be given to serving others are ill-conditioned and unrestrained; such evil-doers by their evil deeds go to their own downfall.

As a blade of grass, if badly grasped, cuts the arm, badly practiced asceticism leads to self-destruction.

If anything is to be done, let an awakened being do it; let him/her attack it vigorously! Careless pilgrims only scatter the dust of their passions more widely.

They who are ashamed of what they ought not to be ashamed of, and are not ashamed of what they ought to be ashamed of—such people, embracing false doctrines, enter the evil path.

They who fear when they ought not to fear, and fear not when they ought to fear—such people, embracing false doctrines, enter the evil path.

They who sin where there is no sin, and see no sin where there is sin—such people, embracing false doctrines, enter the evil path.

They who see sin where there is sin, and no sin where there is no sin—such people, embracing the true doctrine, enter the good path.

True Clergy

People who do not become clergy by virtue of their plaited hair, their family, or by birth; in whom there is truth and righteousness, they are blessed, they are the true clergypeople.

What is the use of plaited hair, O fool! What of the raiment of fine clothes? Within you there is ravening, but the outside you make clean.

Those who wear dirty clothes, who are emaciated and covered with veins, who sometimes meditate alone in the forest, if they are of noble character, them I call indeed true clergypeople.

I do not call people true clergy because of their origin or of their mother. They may indeed be arrogant and wealthy; but the poor, who are free from all attachments to pleasures, them I call indeed true clergy.

Those I call indeed clergy who, though they have committed no offense, endure reproach, stripes, and bonds: who have endurance for their force, and strength for their army.

Those I call indeed clergy who are free from anger, dutiful, virtuous, without appetites, who are subdued, and have found their desired means of service.

Those I call indeed clergy who do not cling to sensual pleasures, like water on a lotus leaf, like a mustard seed on the point of a needle.

Those I call indeed clergy who, without hurting any creatures, whether feeble or strong, do not kill or cause slaughter.

Those I call indeed clergy who are tolerant with the intolerant, mild with the violent, and free from greed among the greedy.

Those I call indeed clergy from whom anger and hatred, haughtiness and hypocrisy have dropped like a mustard seed from the point of a needle.

Those I call indeed clergy who utter true speech, instructive and free from harshness, so that they offend no one.

Those I call indeed clergy who take nothing in the world that is not given them, be it long or short, small or large, good or bad.

Those I call indeed clergy who foster no craving in the world, have no base inclinations, and are unshackled.

Those I call indeed clergy who have no selfish interests, and when they have understood the truth, do not say "How, how?" and who have reached the depth of Nirvana.

Those I call indeed clergy who have risen above both ties, pleasure and pain, who are free from grief, from sin, and from impurity.

THE DIAMOND SUTRA

Thus have I heard concerning the Buddha:

Upon a memorable occasion, the Buddha sojourned in the kingdom of Sravasti, lodging in the grove of Jeta, a park within the imperial domain, which Jeta, the heir-apparent, bestowed upon Sutana, a benevolent minister of state, renowned for his charities and benefactions.

With the Buddha, there were assembled together many disciples, all of whom had attained to eminent degrees of spiritual wisdom.

Upon that occasion, the venerable Subhuti occupied a place in the midst of the assembly. Rising from his seat, with cloak arranged in such manner that his right shoulder was disclosed, Subhuti knelt upon his right knee, then pressing together the palms of his hands, he respectfully raised them toward the Buddha, saying: "You are of transcendent wisdom, honored of the world! With wonderful solicitude, you persevere in the faith, and instruct in the law, this illustrious assembly of enlightened disciples. Honored of the world! If a good disciple, whether man or woman, seeks to obtain supreme spiritual wisdom, what immutable law shall sustain the mind of that disciple, and bring into subjection every inordinate desire?"

The Buddha replied to Subhuti, saying: "Truly a most excellent theme! As you affirmed, I persevere in the faith, and instruct in the law, this illustrious assembly of enlightened disciples. Attend diligently to me, and I shall enunciate a law whereby the mind of a good disciple, whether man or woman, seeking to obtain supreme spiritual wisdom, shall be adequately sustained, and enabled to bring into subjection every inordinate desire." Subhuti was gratified, and signified glad consent. Thereupon, the Buddha, with majesty of person, and perfect articulation, proceeded to deliver the text of this scripture, saying:

"By this wisdom shall enlightened disciples be enabled to bring into subjection every inordinate desire! Every species of life, whether hatched in the egg, formed in the womb, evolved from spawn, produced by metamorphosis, with or without form or intelligence, possessing or devoid of natural instinct—from these changeful conditions of being, I command you to seek deliverance, in the all-important concept of happiness. Thus, you shall be delivered from an immeasurable, innumerable, and illimitable world of sentient life; but, in reality, there is no world of sentient life from which to seek deliverance. And why? Because, in the minds of enlightened disciples, there have ceased to exist such concepts of isolated phenomena as an entity, a being, a living being, or a personality.

"Moreover, Subhuti, an enlightened disciple ought to act spontaneously in the exercise of charity, uninfluenced by sensuous phenomena such as sound, odor, taste, touch, or law. Subhuti, it is imperative that an enlightened disciple, in the exercise of charity, should act independently of phenomena. And why? Because, acting without regard to illusive forms of phenomena, he/she will realize in the exercise of charity a merit inestimable and immeasurable.

"Subhuti, what do you think? Is it possible to estimate the distance comprising the illimitable universe of space?" Subhuti replied, saying: "Honored of the world! It is impossible to estimate the distance comprising the illimitable universe of space." The Buddha thereupon discoursed, saying: "It is equally impossible to estimate the merit of an enlightened disciple, who discharges the exercise of charity unperturbed by the seductive influences of phenomena. Subhuti, the mind of an enlightened disciple ought thus to be indoctrinated."

The Buddha interrogated Subhuti, saying: "What do you think? Is it possible that by means of his physical body, the Buddha may be clearly perceived?" Subhuti replied, saying: "No! Honored of the world! It is impossible that by means of his physical body, the Buddha may be clearly perceived. And why! Because what the Buddha referred to as a physical body is in reality not merely a physical body." Thereupon the Buddha addressed Subhuti, saying: "Every form or quality of phenomena is transient and illusive. When the mind realizes that the phenomena of life are not real phenomena, the Buddha may then be clearly perceived."

Subhuti inquired of the Buddha, saying: "Honored of the world! In future ages, when this scripture is proclaimed, among those beings destined to hear, shall any of them conceive within their minds a sincere, unmingled faith?"

The Buddha replied to Subhuti, saying: "Have no such apprehensive thought! Even at the remote period of five centuries subsequent to the happiness of the Buddha, there will be many disciples observing the vows and assiduously devoted to good works. These, hearing this scripture proclaimed, will believe in its immutability, and similarly conceive within their minds a pure, unmingled faith. Besides, it is important to realize that faith thus conceived is not exclusively in virtue of the insular thought of any particular Buddha, but because of its affiliation with the concrete thoughts of myriad Buddhas throughout infinite ages. Therefore, among the beings destined to hear this scripture proclaimed, many, by momentary reflection, will intuitively conceive a pure and holy faith."

The Buddha addressed Subhuti, saying: "What do you think? Has the Buddha really attained to supreme spiritual wisdom? Or has he a system of doctrine which can be specifically formulated?"

Subhuti replied, saying: "As I understand the meaning of the Buddha's discourse, he has no system of doctrine which can be specifically formulated; nor can the Buddha express, in explicit terms, a form of knowledge which can be described as supreme spiritual wisdom. And why? Because what the Buddha adumbrated in terms of the law is all-pervading and inexpressible. Being a purely spiritual concept, it is neither consonant with law, nor synonymous with anything apart from the law. Thus is exemplified the manner by which wise disciples and buddhas, regarding intuition as the law of their minds, severally attained to different planes of spiritual wisdom."

The Buddha addressed Subhuti, saying: "What do you think? If a benevolent person bestowed as alms an abundance of treasures sufficient to fill the universe, would there accrue to that person a considerable merit?"

Subhuti replied, saying: "A very considerable merit, honored of the world! And why? Because what is referred to does not partake of the nature of ordinary merit, and in this sense the Buddha made mention of a 'considerable' merit."

The Buddha rejoined, saying: "If a disciple adhered with implicit faith to a stanza of this scripture, and diligently explained it to others, the intrinsic merit of that disciple would be relatively greater. And why? Because, Subhuti, the buddhas, and the law by which they attained to supreme spiritual wisdom, severally owe their inception to the truth of this sacred scripture. Subhuti, what is ordinarily termed the Buddhic law is not really a law attributive to Buddha."

The Buddha inquired of Subhuti, saying: "What do you think? May a Srotapatti (that is, one who has entered the stream which bears on to lasting happiness) thus moralize within himself, 'I have obtained the fruit commensurate with the merit of a Srotapatti'?" Subhuti replied, saying: "No! honored of the world! And why? Because Srotapatti is simply a descriptive term signifying 'having entered the stream.' A disciple who avoids attachment to the seductive phenomena of form, sound, odor, taste, touch, and law, is named a Srotapatti."

The Buddha yet again inquired of Subhuti, saying: "What do you think? May an Arhat (having attained to absolute peace of mind) thus meditate, 'I have obtained the condition of an Arhat'?" Subhuti replied, saying: "No! honored of the world! And why? Because there is not in reality a condition synonymous with the term Arhat. Honored of the world! If an arhat thus meditates, 'I have obtained the condition of an Arhat,' there would be obvious recurrence of such concepts as an isolated entity, a being, a living being, and a personality."

Upon that occasion, Subhuti inquired of the Buddha, saying: "Honored of the world! by what name shall this scripture be known, that we may regard it with reverence?" The Buddha replied, saying: "Subhuti, this scripture shall be known as The Diamond Sutra, 'The Transcendent Wisdom,' by means of which we reach "The Other Shore.' By this name you shall reverently regard it! And why? Subhuti, what the Buddha declared as 'transcendent wisdom' by means of which we reach 'the other shore' is not essentially 'transcendent wisdom'—in its essence it transcends all wisdom."

The Buddha addressed Subhuti, saying: What do you think? Your disciples do not affirm that the Buddha reflects thus within himself, 'I bring union with the divine to every living being.' Subhuti, entertain no such delusive thought! And why? Because in reality there are no living beings to whom the Buddha can bring union. If there were living beings to whom the Buddha could bring union, the Buddha would necessarily assume the reality of such concepts as an isolated entity, a being, a living being, and a personality. Subhuti, what the Buddha adverted to as an entity is not in reality an entity;

it is only understood to be an entity, and believed in as such, by the common, uneducated people. Subhuti, what are ordinarily referred to as the 'common, uneducated people,' these the Buddha declared to be not merely 'common, uneducated people.'"

The Buddha addressed Subhuti, saying: "Can the Buddha be perceived by means of his various bodily distinctions?" Subhuti replied, saying: "Even so, the Buddha can be perceived by means of his various bodily distinctions."

The Buddha, continuing, said to Subhuti: "If by means of his various bodily distinctions it were possible to perceive the Buddha, then the Buddha would merely resemble one of the great kings."

Subhuti thereupon addressed the Buddha, saying: "Honored of the world! According as I am able to interpret the Buddha's instruction, it is improbable that the Buddha may be perceived by means of his various bodily distinctions."

Thereafter, the "Honored of the World" delivered these sublime words:

I am not to be perceived by means of any visible form,
Nor sought after by means of any audible sound;
Whoever walks in the way of iniquity,
Cannot perceive the blessedness of the Buddha.

The Buddha said to Subhuti: "If you think thus within yourself 'The Buddha did not, by means of his perfect bodily distinctions, obtain supreme spiritual wisdom,' Subhuti, have no such deceptive thought! Or if you think thus within yourself, 'In obtaining supreme spiritual wisdom, the Buddha declared the abrogation of every law,' Subhuti, have no such delusive thought! And why? Because, those disciples who obtain supreme spiritual wisdom, neither affirm the abrogation of any law nor the destruction of any distinctive quality of phenomena."

The Buddha thereupon declared to Subhuti, "Belief in the unity or eternity of matter is incomprehensible; and only common, worldly-minded people, for purely materialistic reasons, covet this hypothesis."

The Buddha addressed Subhuti, saying: "If a disciple, having immeasurable spheres filled with worldly treasures, bestowed these in the exercise of charity; and if a disciple, whether man or woman, having aspired to supreme spiritual wisdom, selected from this scripture a stanza comprising four lines, then rigorously observed it, studied it, and diligently explained it to others; the cumulative merit of such a disciple would be relatively greater than that of the other.

"In what attitude of mind should it be diligently explained to others? Not assuming the permanency or the reality of earthly phenomena, but in the conscious blessedness of a mind at perfect peace. And why? Because, the phenomena of life may be likened to a dream, a phantasm, a bubble, a shadow, the glistening dew, or lightning flash, and thus they ought to be contemplated so that their relations be understood."

When the Buddha concluded his enunciation of this scripture, the venerable Subhuti, the monks, nuns, and all others present rejoiced exceedingly, and consecrated to its practice, they received it and departed.

ASVAGHOSHA'S DISCOURSE ON THE AWAKENING OF FAITH

After the enlightenment of the Buddha, there were those who possessed in themselves the intellectual power to understand the many-sided meanings of the scriptures, even if they read only a few of them. There were others who by their own intellectual powers could understand the meanings of the scriptures only after an extensive reading of many of them. Still others, lacking in intellectual powers of their own, could understand the meanings of the scriptures only through the assistance of elaborate commentaries. But there are some who, lacking in intellectual powers of their own, shun the perusal of elaborate commentaries and take delight in studying and cultivating inquiries which present the many-sidedness and universality of the doctrine in a concise form.

For the sake of the people of the last class, I write this discourse, in which the most excellent, the deepest, and the most inexhaustible doctrine of the Enlightened One will be treated in comprehensive brevity.

In the one soul we may distinguish two aspects. The one is the soul as suchness, the other is the soul as birth-and-death. Each in itself constitutes all things, and both are so closely interrelated that one cannot be separated from the other.

What is meant by the soul as suchness, is the oneness of the totality of things, the great all-including whole, the quintessence of the doctrine. For the essential nature of the soul is un-create and eternal.

Therefore, all things in their fundamental nature are not nameable or explicable. They cannot be adequately expressed in any form of language. They are without the range of apperception. They are subject neither to transformation nor to destruction. They are nothing but the one soul, for which suchness is another designation. Therefore, they cannot be fully explained by words or exhausted by reasoning.

In the essence of suchness, there is neither anything which has to be excluded nor anything which has to be added.

The soul as birth-and-death comes forth (as the law of causation) from the Enlightened One's womb. But the immortal (i.e., suchness) and the mortal (i.e., birth-and-death) coincide with each other. Though they are not identical, they are not a duality. Thus when the absolute soul assumes a relative aspect by its self-affirmation, it is called the all-conserving mind.

The same mind has a twofold significance as the organizer and the producer of all things.

Again it embraces two principles: (1) enlightenment; (2) non-enlightenment.

Enlightenment is the highest quality of the mind. As it is free from all limiting attributes of subjectivity, it is like space, penetrating everywhere, as the unity of all. That is to say, it is the universal vision of all enlightened ones.

The multitude of people are said to be lacking in enlightenment, because ignorance prevails there from all eternity, because there is a constant succession of confused egoistic states from which they have never been emancipated.

But when they transcend their egoism, they can then recognize that all states of mentation—viz., their appearance, presence, change, and disappearance (in the field of consciousness)—have no genuine reality. They are neither in a temporal nor in a spatial relation with the one soul, for they are not self-existent.

When you understand this, you also understand that enlightenment in appearance cannot be manufactured, for it is no other thing than enlightenment in its suchness, which is uncreate and must be discovered.

To illustrate: people who are lost go astray because they are bent on pursuing a certain direction; and their confusion has no valid foundation other than that they are bent on a certain direction.

It is even the same with most beings. They become unenlightened, foster their egoism and go astray, because they are bent on enlightenment.

While the essence of the mind is eternally clean and pure, the influence of ignorance makes possible the existence of a defiled mind. But in spite of the defiled mind, the mind itself is eternal, clear, pure, and not subject to transformation.

When the oneness of the totality of things is not recognized, then ignorance as well as particularization arise, and all phases of the defiled mind are thus developed. But the significance of this doctrine is so extremely deep and unfathomable that it can be fully comprehended by Buddhas and by no others.

When the mind is disturbed, it fails to be a true and adequate knowledge; it fails to be a pure, clean essence; it fails to be eternal, blissful, self-regulating, and pure; it fails to be tranquil. On the contrary, it will become transient, changeable, un-free, and therefore the source of falsity and defilement, while its modifications outnumber the sands of the Ganges. But when there is no disturbance in the essence of the mind, we speak of suchness as being the true, adequate knowledge, and as possessing pure and clean merits that outnumber the sands of the Ganges.

When the mind is disturbed, it will strive to become conscious of the reality of an external world and will thus betray the imperfection of its inner condition. But as all infinite merits in fact constitute the one mind which, perfect in itself, has no need of seeking after any external support, so suchness never fails to actualize all those areas of enlightenment that, outnumbering the sands of the Ganges, can be said to be neither identical nor non-identical with the essence of the mind, and that therefore are utterly out of the range of our comprehension. On that account suchness is designated the Enlightened One's womb or the Buddha's vision.

The body has infinite forms. The form has infinite attributes. The attribute has infinite excellencies. And the accompanying rewards of enlightenment, that is, the regions where it is born because of previous phenomena, also have infinite merits and ornamentations. Manifesting itself everywhere, the body of happiness is infinite, boundless, limitless, un-intermittent in its action, directly coming forth from the mind.

THE TIBETAN DOCTRINE

A hen, when at rest, produces much fruit;
A gentle horse has a swift pace;
The calmness of a person is the sign of his/her being a sage.

Not to be cheered by praise,
Not to be grieved by blame,
But to know thoroughly one's own virtues or powers
Are the characteristics of an excellent being.

In the same place where the great Buddha is present
Who would acknowledge any other one?
When the sun has risen, though there be many bright stars in
   the sky,
Not one of them is visible.

A foolish person reclaims his/her qualifications;
A wise person keeps them secret within;
A straw floats on the surface of water,
But a precious gem placed upon it sinks.

It is only narrow-minded people that make such distinctions
As "This is our friend, this our enemy";
A liberal-minded person shows affection for all,
For it is uncertain who may yet be of aid to one.

An excellent person, like precious metal,
Is in every way invariable;
A villain, like the beams of a balance,
Is always varying, upwards and downwards.

The greatest wealth consists in being charitable,
And the greatest happiness in having tranquillity of mind.
Experience is the most beautiful adornment;

And the best comrade is one that has no cravings.

People of little ability, too,
By learning from the great, may prosper;
A drop of water is a little thing,
But when will it dry away if united to a lake?

Hurtful expressions should never be used,
Not even against an enemy;
For inevitably they will return to one,
Like an echo from a rock.

When about to perform any great work,
Endeavor to have understanding associates;
If one would burn down a forest,
The aid of a wind is, of course, needed.

An astronomer makes calculations and predictions concerning
the motions of the moon and the stars,
But that same person may not know that in his/her own home
the family member, being at variance, are misbehaving.

In eating, sleeping, fearing, and copulating, individuals and
beasts are alike;
We humans surpass the beast by engaging in religious practices.
So why should people, if they are without religion, not be equal
to the beasts?

Although many stars shine, and that ornament of the earth, the
moon, also shines (that is, by virtue of the sun's light),
Yet when the sun sets, it becomes night.

The science which teaches arts and handicrafts
Is merely science for the gaining of a living;
But the science which teaches overcoming of worldly tempta-
tions,
Is not that the true science?

That which one desires not for oneself,
Do not do to others.

The foolish are like ripples on water,
For whatever they do is quickly effaced;
But the righteous are like carvings upon stone,
For their smallest act is durable.

The supreme path of altruism is a short-cut,
Leading to the realm of the conquerors,
A track more speedy than that of a racing horse;
The selfish, however, know nothing of it.

Charity produces the harvest in the inner self.
Purity is the parent of human happiness.
Patience is an adornment becoming to all.
Industry is the conductor of every personal accomplishment.
Meditation is the clarifier of a beclouded mind.
Insight is the weapon which overcomes every enemy.

Do not gloat, even though death and misfortune overwhelm
  your enemies;
Do not boast, even though you equal all people in greatness.

Some there are who turn inside out their whole interior
By means of over-talkativeness.

Be humble and meek if you would be exalted;
Praise everyone's good qualities if you would have friends.

Relinquish an evil custom even though it be of your fathers and
  ancestors;
Adopt a good custom even though it be established among your
  enemies:
Poison is not to be taken even though offered by one's mother;
But good deeds are acceptable even from one who is inimical.

Be not too quick to express the desire of your heart.
Be not short-tempered when engaged in any work.
Be not jealous of a devotee who is truly religious and pious.
Do not consult one who is habituated and hardened to evil-
  doing.

Rogues there are even in religious orders;
Poisonous plants grow even on hills of medicinal herbs.
Some there are who do not marvel at others removing mountains,
But who consider it a heavy task when obliged to carry a bit of fleece.

One who is ever ready to take the credit for any action when it has proved successful,
And is equally ready to throw the blame on others when it goes wrong in the least,
And who is ever looking for faults in those who are learned and righteous possesses a most evil nature.

Preaching religious truths to an unbeliever is like feeding a venomous serpent with milk.

Although a cloth be washed a hundred times,
How can it be rendered clean and pure
If it be washed in water which is dirty?

Those who know the precepts by heart, but fail to practice them,
Are like those who light a lamp and then shut their eyes.

Who can say with certainty that one will live to see the morrow?
How can it be just to kill helpless and inoffensive creatures unnecessarily?

The mind may be the great slayer of the real. Let the disciple slay the slayer.

Compassion speaks and says: "Can there be bliss when all that lives must suffer? Shall you be happy and hear the whole world cry?"
Let not the fierce sun dry one tear of pain before you have wiped it from the sufferer's eye.
Pupils must regain the child state they have lost before the first sound can fall upon their ears.

Kill in yourself all worries about past experiences. Look not behind or you are lost.

Both action and inaction may find room in you; your body active, your mind tranquil, your soul as limpid as a mountain lake.

To live to benefit humanity is the first step. To practice glorious virtues is the second.

The goal is one for all, the means to reach the goal must vary with the pilgrims.

You shall not let your senses make a playground of your mind.

Have you attuned your being to humanity's great pain, O candidate for light?

Be aware that the Eternal knows no change.

JAINA SUTRAS

Those who know one thing are able to know all things; and those who know all things, know one thing. Those who are careless in any respect are in danger; those who are not careless in any respect are free from danger.

Those who conquer one craving are able to conquer many; and those who conquer many, conquer one. "Knowing the misery of the world," rejecting the limitations of society, "the heroes go on the great journey," they rise gradually; "they do not crave long life."

Those who avoid one lust are able to avoid them all severally; and those who avoid them severally, avoid one. Faithful according to the commandments, wise, and understanding the world according to the commandments, such persons are without danger from anywhere.

Those who know wrath, know haughtiness; those who know haughtiness, know deceit; those who know deceit, know greed; those who know greed, know sensual love; those who know sensual love, know personal hate; those who know hate, know delusion; those who know delusion, know spiritual death; those who know spiritual death, know purposeless suffering.

Therefore, a wise individual should avoid wrath, haughtiness, deceit, greed, sensual love, personal hate, delusion, spiritual death, and purposeless suffering.

The first great vow, sir, runs thus:

' I renounce all killing of living beings, whether subtle or gross, whether movable or immovable, except when absolutely necessary in preserving a higher form of life. Nor shall I myself kill living beings, nor cause others to do it, nor consent to it except under these conditions. As long as I live, I will exempt myself from these sins, in mind, speech, and body.

Mature individuals are careful in their walk, not careless. The Master assigns as the reason, that mature individuals, careless in their walk, might with their feet needlessly hurt or displace or injure or kill living beings. Hence, mature individuals are careful in their walk, not careless.

Mature individuals search into their minds (i.e., thoughts and intentions). If their minds are sinful, blamable, intent on reward, acting on first impulses, producing cutting and splitting, or division and dissension, they should not employ such minds in action; but if, on the contrary, the minds are not corrupted, then they may put it in action.

Mature individuals search into their speech; if their speech is sinful, blamable, intent on reward, acting on first impulses, producing cutting and splitting, quarrels, faults, and pains, injuring living beings, or killing creatures, they should not utter that speech. But if, on the contrary, their minds are not corrupted, then they may utter their words.

Mature individuals are careful in laying down their utensils; they are not careless. The Master says: Mature individuals who are careless in laying down their utensils might hurt or displace or injure or kill all sorts of living beings. Hence, mature individuals are careful in laying down their utensils; they are not careless in this way.

Mature individuals eat and drink after inspecting their food and drink; they do not eat and drink without inspecting their food and drink. The Master says: If mature individuals would eat and drink without inspecting their food and drink, they might hurt and displace or injure or kill all sorts of living beings. Hence, mature individuals eat and drink after inspecting their food and drink, not without doing so.

In this way the great vow is correctly practiced, followed, executed, explained, established, effected according to the precept.

The second great vow runs thus:

I renounce all vices of lying speech arising from anger or greed or fear or mirth. I shall neither myself speak lies, nor cause others to speak lies, nor consent to the speaking of lies by others. I exempt myself from these sins, in mind, speech, and body.

Mature individuals speak after deliberation, not without deliberation. The Master says: Without deliberation people might utter falsehoods in their speech. Mature individuals speak after deliberation, not without deliberation.

Mature individuals comprehend and renounce anger, greed, fear, and mirth. The Master says: Individuals who are moved by anger, greed, fear, and mirth might utter a falsehood in their speech.

In this way the great vow is correctly practiced, followed, executed, explained, established, effected according to the precept.

The third great vow runs thus:

I renounce all taking of anything not given, either in a village or a town or a wood, either of little or much, of small or great, of living or lifeless things. I shall neither take myself what is not given, nor cause others to take it, nor consent to their taking it. As long as I live, I exempt myself from these sins, in mind, speech, and body.

In this way the great vow is correctly practiced, followed, executed, explained, established, effected according to the precept.

The fourth great vow runs thus:

I renounce all craving for sexual pleasures. I shall not give way to sensuality, nor cause others to do it, nor consent to it. As long as I live, I except myself from these sins, in mind, speech, and body.

Mature individuals do not continually discuss topics relating to the opposite sex. The Master says: If people frequently discuss such topics, they might fall from the law declared by the Master, because of the destruction or disturbance of their peace.

Mature individuals do not regard and contemplate the sensual forms of women; mature individuals do not recall to their minds the lustful pleasures they formerly had with the opposite sex; mature individuals do not eat and drink too much, nor do they drink liquors excessively or eat highly seasoned dishes. The Master says: If people did so, they might fall from the law declared by the Master, because of the destruction or disturbance of their peace.

In this way the great vow is correctly practiced, followed, executed, explained, established, effected according to the precept.

The fifth great vow runs thus:

I renounce all needless attachment to the pleasures of life, whether little or much, small or great, living or lifeless; neither shall I myself form such attachments, nor cause others to do so, nor consent to their doing so. As long as I live, I except myself from these sins, in mind, speech, and body.

If creatures with ears hear of various disturbances or temptations, they should not be attached to, or delighted with, or desiring of, or infatuated by, or covetous of, or disturbed by these distractions. The Master says: If people are thus affected, they might fall from the law declared by the Master, because of the destruction or disturbance of their peace.

If it is impossible not to have all those impressions which reach the organs of the senses, mature individuals should avoid the passions originated by them.

In this way the great vow is correctly practiced, followed, executed, explained, established, effected according to the precept.

Those who are well provided with these great vows are really mature, if they, according to the sacred lore, the precepts, and the way, correctly practice, follow, execute, explain, establish, and, according to the precepts, effect them.

A MANUAL OF MAHAYANA AND ZEN BUDDHISM

The Lankavatara Sutra

Those who, desirous of overcoming sufferings arising from the rapidly changing phenomena of the temporal world, seek Nirvana, do not know that the temporal world and Nirvana are not to be separated the one from the other; and, seeing that all things subject to discrimination have no reality, imagine that happiness consists in the further annihilation of the body and the senses. They are not aware, enlightened ones, of the fact that happiness is the superior wisdom where a revulsion takes place by self-realization. Therefore, enlightened ones, those who are stupid talk of the trinity of vehicles and not of the state of mind-only where there are no shadows. Therefore, enlightened ones, those who do not understand the teachings of the prophets of the past, present, and future, concerning the internal world, which is of mind itself, cling to the notion that there is a world outside that is seen of the mind and, enlightened ones, go on seeing nothing beyond the transient elements in life.

Further, enlightened ones, according to the teaching of the prophets of the past, present, and future, all things are unborn. Why? Because they have no reality, being manifestations of mind itself, and, as they are not born of being and non-being, they are unborn. Enlightened ones, all things are like the horns of the hare, horse, donkey, or camel, but the ignorant and simple-minded who are given up to their false and erroneous imaginations, discriminate things where they are not; therefore, all things are unborn.

Enlightened ones, since the ignorant and the simple-minded, not knowing that the world is what is seen of mind itself, cling to the multiplicity of external objects, cling to the notions of being and non-being, oneness and otherness, bothness and not-bothness, existence and non-existence, eternity and non-eternity, as having the character of self-substance, which idea rises from discrimination based on habit-energy, they are addicted to false imaginings. Enlightened ones, it is like a mirage in which the springs are seen as if they were real. They are imagined so by the animals who, thirsty from the heat of the season, would run after them. Not knowing that the springs are their own mental illusions, the animals do not realize that there are no such springs.

In the same way, enlightened ones, the ignorant and simple-minded with their minds impressed by various erroneous speculations and discriminations since beginningless time; with their minds burning with the fire of greed, anger, and folly; delighted in a world of multitudinous forms; with their thoughts saturated with purely physical needs; not understanding well what is meant by existent and non-existent, by inner and outer; the ignorant and simple-minded fall into the way of grasping at oneness and otherness, being and non-being as realities.

Enlightened ones, it is like the city of the gods which the unwitted take for a real city, though it is not so in fact. This city appears in essence owing to their attachment to the memory of a city preserved in seed from beginningless time. This city is thus neither existent nor non-existent.

In the same way, enlightened ones, clinging to the memory of erroneous speculations and doctrines since beginningless time, they hold fast to ideas such as oneness and otherness, being and non-being, and their thoughts are not at all clear about what is seen of mind-only.

Enlightened ones, it is like individuals, who, dreaming in their sleep of a country variously filled with women, men, elephants, horses, cars, pedestrians, villages, towns, hamlets, cows, buffalo, mansions, woods, mountains, rivers, and lakes, enters into their inner apartments and are awakened. While awakened thus, they recollect the city and their inner apartments. What do you think, enlightened ones? Are these people to be regarded as wise, who are recollecting the various unrealities they have seen in their dreams?

Said the enlightened ones: Indeed, they are not, Blessed One.

The Blessed One continued: In the same way the ignorant and simple-minded who are bitten by erroneous views, though included with the philosophers, do not recognize that things seen of the mind itself are like a dream, and are held fast by the notions of oneness and otherness, of being and non-being. Enlightened ones, it is like the painter's canvas on which there is neither depression nor elevation as imagined by the ignorant. In the same way, enlightened ones, there may be in the future some people brought up in the habit-energy, mentality, and imagination based on the philosophers' erroneous views; clinging to the ideas of oneness and otherness, or bothness and not-bothness, they may bring themselves and others to ruin; they may declare those people nihilists who hold the doctrine of no-birth apart from the category of being and non-being. They argue against cause and effect, they are followers of the wicked views whereby they uproot meritorious causes of unstained purity. They are to be kept away by those whose desires are for things excellent. They are those whose thoughts are entangled in the error of self, other, and both, entangled in the error of imagining being and non-being, assertion and refutation.

Enlightened ones, it is like the dim-eyed ones who, seeing a hair-net, would exclaim to one another, saying: "It is wonderful! it is wonderful! Look, O honorable sirs!" And the hair-net has never been brought into existence. It is in fact neither an entity nor a non-entity, because it is seen and not seen. In the same manner, enlightened ones, those whose minds are addicted to discrimination of the erroneous views as cherished by the philosophers, and who are also given up to the realistic ideas of being and non-being. oneness and otherness, bothness and not-bothness, will contradict the good teachings, ending in the destruction of themselves and others.

Enlightened ones, it is like a firebrand-wheel which is no real wheel but which is imagined to be of such character by the ignorant, but not by the wise. In the same manner, enlightened ones, those whose minds have fallen into the erroneous views of the philosophers will falsely imagine in the rise of all beings the reality of oneness and otherness, bothness and not-bothness.

Enlightened ones, it is like those water-bubbles in a rainfall which have the appearance of crystal gems and the ignorant, taking them for real crystal gems, running after them. Enlightened ones, they are no more than water-bubbles; they are not gems, nor are they non-gems, because of their being so comprehended by one party and being not so comprehended by another. In the same manner, enlightened ones, those whose minds are impressed by the habit-energy of philosophical views and discriminations will regard things born as non-existent and those destroyed by causation as existent.

On Believing in Mind

The perfect Way knows no difficulties
Except that it refuses to make preferences;
Only when freed from all kinds of passion,
It reveals itself fully and without disguise;
A tenth of an inch's difference,
And all of life is torn apart;
If you wish to see it before your own eyes,
Have no fixed thoughts either for or against it.

To set up what you like against what you dislike—
This is the disease of the mind:
When the deep meaning of the Way is not understood,
Peace of mind is disturbed to no purpose.

The Way is perfect like vast space,
With nothing wanting, nothing superfluous:
It is indeed due to making choice
That its suchness is lost sight of.

Pursue not the outer entanglements,
Dwell not in the inner void;

Be serene in the oneness of things,
And dualism vanishes by itself.

When you strive to gain quiescence by stopping motion,
The quiescence thus gained is ever in motion;
As long as you tarry in the dualism,
How can you realize oneness?

And when oneness is not thoroughly understood,
In two ways loss is sustained:
The denying of reality is the asserting of it,
And the asserting of emptiness is the denying of it.

Wordiness and intellection—
The more with them the further astray we go;
Away therefore with wordiness and intellection,
And there is no place where we cannot pass freely.

When we return to the root, we gain the meaning;
When we pursue external objects, we lose the reason.
The moment we are enlightened within,
We go beyond the voidness of a world confronting us.

Transformations going on in an empty world which confronts
    us
Appear real all because of ignorance:
Try not to chase after the true,
But cease to display opinions.

Abide not with dualism,
Carefully avoid pursuing it;
As soon as you have right and wrong,
Confusion ensues, and Mind is lost.

The two exist because of the One,
But hold not even to this One;
When a mind is not disturbed,
The ten thousand things offer no offense.

No offense offered, and no ten thousand things;

No disturbance going, and no mind set up to work:
The subject is quieted when the object ceases,
The object ceases when the subject is quieted.

The object is an object for the subject,
The subject is a subject for the object:
Know that the relativity of the two
Rests ultimately on one emptiness.

In one emptiness the two are not distinguished,
And each contains in itself all the ten thousand things;
When no discrimination is made between this and that,
How can a one-sided and prejudiced view arise?

The great Way is calm and large-hearted,
For it nothing is easy, nothing is hard:
Small views are irresolute,
The more in haste the tardier they go.

Clinging is never kept within bounds,
It is sure to go the wrong way;
Quit it, and things follow their own courses,
While the essence neither departs nor abides.

Obey the nature of things, and you are in concord with the
   Way,
Calm and easy and free from annoyance;
But when your thoughts are tied, you turn away from the truth,
They grow heavier and duller and are not at all sound.

When they are not sound, the spirit is troubled;
What is the use of being partial and one-sided then?
If you want to walk the course of the One Vehicle,
Be not prejudiced against the sense-objects.

The ignorant cherish the idea of rest and unrest,
The enlightened have no rigid likes and dislikes:
All forms of dualism
Are contrived by the ignorant themselves.

They are like visions and flowers in the air:
Why should we trouble ourselves to take hold of them?
Gain and loss, right and wrong—
Make them relative once for all!

If an eye never falls asleep, all dreams will by themselves cease:
If the mind retains its absoluteness,
The ten thousand things are of one suchness.

The ultimate end of things where they cannot go any further,
Is not bound by rules and measures:
In the mind harmonious with the Way we have the principle of
   identity,
In which we find all strivings tempered;
Doubts and irresolutions are completely done away with,
And the right faith is straightened;
There is nothing left behind,
There is nothing retained,
All is void, lucid, and self-illuminating,
There is no excess, no waste of energy—
This is where thinking never attains,
This is where the imagination fails to measure.

In the higher realm of true suchness
There is neither "self" nor "other":
When direct identification is sought,
We can only say, "Not two."

What is is the same as what is not,
What is not is the same as what is:
Where this state of things fails to obtain,
Indeed, no tarrying there.

One in all,
All in One—
If only this is realized;
No more worry about your not being perfect!

Where Mind and each believing mind are not divided,
And undivided are each believing mind and Mind,

This is where words fail;
For it is not for the past, present, and future.

On the Absolute

The great Master died on the third day of the eighth month of the second year of Hsien-t'ien. On the eighth day of the seventh month this year, he had a farewell gathering of his followers, as he felt that he was to leave them forever in the following month, and told them to have all the doubts they might have about his teaching once for all settled on this occasion. As he found them weeping in tears, he said: "You are all weeping, but for whom are you so sorry? If you are sorry for my not knowing where I am to depart, you are mistaken; for I know where I am going. Indeed, if I did not, I would not part with you. The reason why you are in tears is probably that you do not yourselves know where I am going. If you did, you would not be weeping so. The essence of life knows no death, no coming-and-going. Please sit down, and let me give you a poem with the title, On the Absolute:

There is nothing true anywhere,
The true is nowhere to be seen;
If you say you see the true,
This seeing is not the true one.

Where the true is left to itself,
There is nothing false in it, which is mind itself.
Then mind in itself is not liberated from the false,
There is nothing true, nowhere is the true to be found.

A conscious being alone understands what is meant by "moving";
To those not endowed with consciousness, the moving is unintelligible;
If you exercise yourself in the practice of keeping your mind unmoved (in meditation),
The immovable you gain is that of one who has found peace.

If you are desirous for the truly immovable,
The immovable is in the moving itself,
And this immovable is the truly immovable one;

There is no seed of enlightenment where there is no movement.

Mark well how varied are aspects of the immovable one,
And know that the first reality is immovable;
Only when this insight is attained,
The true working of suchness is understood.

I advise you, O students of the truth,
To exert yourselves in the proper direction;
Do not in the teaching of the scriptures
Commit the fault of clinging to the relative knowledge of birth
    and death.

Where there is an all-sided concordance of views
You may talk together regarding the Buddha's teaching;
Where there is really no such concordance,
Keep your hands folded and your joy within yourself.

There is really nothing to argue about in this teaching,
Any arguing is sure to go against the intent of it:
Doctrines given up to confusion and argumentation,
Lead by themselves to birth and death."

Yoka Daishi's Song of Enlightenment

Do you know that leisurely philosopher who has gone beyond
    learning and is not restless in anything?
He neither endeavors to avoid new thoughts nor chases after
    the truth;
For he knows that insight, not knowledge, is the Buddha-
    nature,
And that this visionary body is no less than Nirvana.

When one knows what Nirvana is, there is not an object to be
    known as such,
The source of all things, as far as its self-nature goes, is the
    Buddha in his absolute aspect;
The aggregates are like a cloud floating here and there with no
    fixed purpose;
The poisons are like foams appearing and disappearing as it so
    happens to them.

When reality is attained, it is seen to be without an ego-
substance and devoid of all forms of objectivity,
And thereby all the deeds which lead us to self-destruction are
wiped out;
Those, however, who cheat beings with their false knowledge,
Will surely bring about much harm for innumerable ages to
come.

True understanding consists in having a firm conviction;
If, however, you fail to have it, ask me according to your ideas,
and you will be enlightened.
To have a direct understanding in regard to the root of all
things, this is what the Buddha affirms;
If you go on gathering leaves and branches, there is no help for
you.

Many sons of the spirit are known to be poor;
But their poverty is of the body, their spiritual life knows no
poverty;
The poverty-stricken body is wrapped in rags,
But their spirit holds within itself a rare invaluable gem.

The superior one has it settled once for all and forever,
The middling one learns much and holds much in doubt;
The point is to cast aside your soiled clothes you so dearly keep
with you;
What is the use of showing off your work before others?

Let others speak ill of me, let others spite me;
Those who try to burn the sky with a torch end in tiring them-
selves out;
I listen to them and taste their evil-speaking as nectar;
All melts away and I find myself suddenly within the unthink-
able itself.

Seeing others talk ill of me, I acquire the chance of gaining
merit,
For they are really my good friends;

When I cherish, being vituperated, neither enmity nor favorit-
ism,
There grows within me the power of love and humility which is
born of the unborn.

I crossed seas and rivers, climbed mountains, and forded fresh-
ets,
In order to interview the masters, to inquire after truth, to delve
into the secrets of the unknown;
And ever since I was enabled to recognize the path of union
with Nirvana,
I know that birth-and-death is not the thing I have to be concerned with.

For walking is truth, sitting is truth,
Whether talking or remaining silent, whether moving or stand-
ing quiet,
The essence itself is ever at ease;
Even when greeted with swords and spears it never loses its
quiet way,
So with poisonous drugs; they fail to perturb its serenity.

Our Master long ago served a Buddha,
And again for many years disciplined himself as an ascetic.
I have also gone through many and up and many a down (spiri-
tual birth and death);
Ups and downs—how endlessly they recur!

But ever since my end of vacillation, which quite abruptly came
on me,
Vicissitudes of fate, good and bad, have lost their power over
me.
Far away in the mountains I live in a humble hut;
High are the mountains, thick the wooded shades, and under an
old pine-tree
I often sit quietly and contentedly in my home;
Perfect tranquility and rustic simplicity rules here.

Only let us take hold of the root and not worry about the
branches;

It is like a crystal basin reflecting the moon,
And I know now what this precious gem is,
Whereby not only oneself is benefited but others, inexhaustibly,
The moon is serenely reflected on the stream, the breeze passes
softly through the pines,
Perfect silence reigning unruffled—what is it for?

The morality-jewel inherent in the Buddha-nature stamps itself
on the mind-ground of the enlightened one;
Whose robe is cut out of mists, clouds, and dews,
Whose hand from long ago pacified the fiery dragons, and
whose staff once separated the fighting tigers,
And listen to the golden rings of his staff giving out smoothly
flowing tunes.
These are not, however, mere symbolic expressions, devoid of
historical contents;
Wherever the holy staff of Buddhahood moves, the traces are
distinctly marked.

They neither chase after the true nor turn away from the defiled,
They clearly perceive that qualities are empty and have not reality,
That to have no reality does not mean to be one-sided, either
empty or not-empty,
For this is the genuine form of Buddhahood.

The mind like a mirror is brightly illuminating and knows no
obstructions;
It penetrates the vast universe to its minutest crevices;
All its contents, multitudinous in form, are reflected in the
mind,
Which, shining like a perfect gem, has no surface, nor the inside.

Hini the herb grows on the Himalayas where no other grasses
are found,
And the cows feeding on it give the purest of milk, and this I
always enjoy.
One nature, perfect and pervading, circulates in all natures;

One reality, all-comprehensive, contains within itself all realities;
The one moon reflects itself wherever there is a sheet of water,
And all the moons in the waters are embraced within the one
    moon;
The visions of all the Buddhas enter into my own being,
And my own being is found in union with theirs.

Alas! this age of degeneration is full of evils;
Beings are most poorly endowed and difficult to control;
Being further removed from the ancient Sage, they deeply cher-
    ish false views;
Evil is gathering up its forces while the discipline is weakened,
    and hatred is growing rampant;
Even when they learn of the many schools of Buddhist teach-
    ing,
What a pity that they fail to embrace it and thereby to crush
    evils like a piece of brick!

The mind is the author of all works and the body the sufferer of
    all ills;
Do not blame others plaintively for what properly belongs to
    you;
If you desire not to incur upon yourself the deeds of destruc-
    tion,
Cease from blaspheming the perfection-discipline of the good
    student.

There are no inferior trees in the grove of sandal-woods,
Among its thickly growing primeval forest, lions alone find their
    abode;
Where no disturbances reach, where only peace reigns, there is
    the place for lions to roam;
All the other beasts are kept away, and birds do not fly in the
    vicinity.

It is only their own cubs that follow their steps in the woods,
When the young ones are only three years old, they roar.
How can jackals pursue the king of the discipline?
With all their magical arts, the elves gape to no purpose.

"No" is not necessarily "No," nor is "Yes" "Yes";
But when you miss even a tenth of an inch, the difference widens up to one thousand miles,
When it is "Yes," a young girl in an instant attains Buddhahood,
When it is "No," the most learned man while alive falls to destruction.

Since early years I have been eagerly after scholarly attainment,
I have studied the scriptures and texts and commentaries,
I have been given up to the analysis of names and forms, and never
known what fatigue meant;
But giving into the ocean to count up its sands is surely an enormous task and a vain one;
The Buddha has never spared such, his scoldings are just to the point;
For what is the use of reckoning the treasures that are not mine?
All my past achievements have been efforts vainly and wrongly applied—I realize it fully now,
I have been a vagrant for many years to no end whatever.

When the notion of the original family is not properly understood,
You never attain to the understanding of the Buddha's perfect system;
The philosophers are intelligent enough but wanting in understanding;
As to the rest of us, they are either ignorant or puerile;
They take an empty fist as containing something real, and the pointing finger for the object pointed;
When the finger is adhered to as the moon itself, all their efforts are lost;
They are indeed idle dreamers lost in a world of senses and objects.

A royal table is set before the hungry, but they refuse to eat;
If the sick turn away from a good physician, how are they cured?

Practice discipline while in a world of temptations, and the
genuine power of intuition is manifested;
When the lotus blooms in the midst of a fire, it is never destroyed.
Yuse, the disciple, was the offender of one of the gravest
crimes, but when he had an enlightened insight into the Nirvana,
He instantly attained to Buddhahood and is still living in the
minds of others.

However rapidly revolves the iron-wheel over my head,
The perfect brightness of enlightenment in me is never effected;
The sun may turn cold and the moon hot;
With all the power of evil, the doctrine true remains forever in-
destructible.
The elephant-carriage steadily climbs up the steepest hill,
Before whose wheels how can the beetle stand?

The great elephant does not walk on the hare's land,
Supreme enlightenment goes beyond the narrow range of intel-
lect;
Cease from measuring life with a tiny piece of reed;
If you have no insight yet, I will have the matter settled for you.

Dai-o-Kokushi "On Reality"

There is a reality even prior to the universe;
Indeed, it has no form, much less a name;
Eyes fail to see it;
It has no voice for ears to detect;
To call it Mind or Buddha violates its nature,
For it then becomes like a visionary flower in the air;
It is not Mind, or Buddha;
Absolutely quiet, and yet illuminating in a mysterious way,
It allows itself to be perceived only by the clear-eyed.
It is perfection truly beyond form and sound;
It is anything having nothing to do with words.

Wishing to entice the blind,
The Buddha has playfully let words escape his mouth;
The universe has ever since been filled with entangling briars.

O, my good worthy friends gathered here,
If you desire to listen to the thunderous voice of Spirit,
Exhaust your words, empty your thoughts,
For then you may come to recognize this one essence.
Says Hui the Brother, "The Buddha's vision
Is not to be given up to mere humanly sentiments."

Hakuin's Song of Meditation

Sentient beings are primarily all the Buddhas:
It is like ice and water,
Apart from water no ice can exist,
Outside sentient beings, where do we find the Buddhas?
Not knowing how near the truth is,
People seek it far away—what a pity!
They are like the one who, in the midst of water,
Cries in thirst so imploringly;
They are like the son of a rich man
Who wandered away among the poor.
The reason why we transmigrate through the world,
Is because we are lost in the darkness of ignorance;
Going astray further and further in the darkness,
When are we able to get away from death?

As regards the meditation practiced by mature people,
We have no words to praise it fully:
The virtues of perfection such as charity, morality,
And many other good deeds of merit—
All these issue from the practice of meditation;
Even those who have practiced it just for a short time,
May see many of their evil deeds wiped clean;
Nowhere will they find the evil paths,
But the pure land will be near at hand.
With a reverential heart, let them to this truth
Listen even for once,
And let them praise it, and gladly embrace it,
And they will surely be blessed most infinitely.

For such as, reflecting within themselves,
Testify to the truth of Self-nature,
To the truth the Self-nature is no-nature,

They have really gone beyond the ken of sophistry.
For them opens the gate of the oneness of cause and effect,
And straight runs the path of no-duality and non-trinity.
Abiding with the not-particular which is in particulars,
Whether going or returning, they remain for ever unmoved;
Taking hold of the not-thought which lies in thoughts,
In every act of theirs they hear the voice of the truth.
How boundless the sky of life unfettered!
How transparent the perfect moonlight of the true wisdom!
At that moment what do they lack?
As the truth eternally calm reveals itself to them,
This very earth is the dreamland of purity,
And this body is the body of the Buddha.

ZOROASTRIAN SCRIPTURES

INTRODUCTION

The Background

Iran, at the time of Zarathushtra's birth, was a land where many pagan gods and goddesses were being propitiated through ignorance and fear. The Prophet, Zarathushtra, in his sublime hymns, the Gathas, revealed to humanity that there was the One, Supreme, All-knowing, Eternal God of the good creations, the Lord of Wisdom, who was wholly Wise, Good and Just. Ahura Mazda, he taught, was a Ahura Maza, friend to all and never to be feared by human beings, who in turn should worship him. Locked in open conflict he proclaimed, were the two primordial spirits Spenta Mainyu, the Holy Spirit of Ahura Mazda and His diabolical adversary, Anghra Mainyu, the Hostile Spirit.

The Zoroastrian Doctrine

According to the Zoroastrian texts, Ahura Mazda (Pahlavi Ohrmazd), through his Omniscience knew of His own Goodness and His infinite Self, as well as He was aware of the hostile Spirit's limited strength and finite existence. In order to destroy His adversary, Ahura Mazda created an immaculate material world of the seven creations to trap the hostile Spirit. Ahura Mazda knew that the material world would bring within it disorder, falsehood, wickedness, sorrow, cruelty, disease, suffering and death.

Human beings, Ahura Mazda's finest creations, are believed to be the central figures in this cosmic struggle. The prophet declared that it is during this period of conflict that humanity, through free will, should choose to fight and vanquish the hostile Spirit using the ethical paradigm of Goodness, the Good Mind, Truth, Power, Devotion, Perfection and Immortality. These seven qualities collectively came to be known as the Amesha Spentas (Bounteous Immortals). It is our responsibility to imbibe the virtues of these divinities in order to know how to generate the right thoughts, words and actions. Zarathushtra recognized that the use of these principles of righteous living would enable us to bring about the eventual annihilation of evil in this world.

Humanity

Humanity's unique spiritual quest, according to Zoroastrianism, is linked to the preservation and promotion of the Wise Lord's seven creations - namely, the sky, waters, earth, plants, cattle, humans and fire. The last creation, fire, is a potent reality in Zarathushtra's revelation, as the prophet saw fire to be the physical representation of Asha (Order/Truth/Righteousness), and as a source of light, warmth and life for all people. The religious rituals (the performance of which is an important Zoroastrian duty) are solemnized in the presence of fire, the life-energy which permeates and makes dynamic the Wise Lord's other six creations.

Living a Zoroastrian Life

Zarathushtra taught that since this world created by Ahura Mazda is essentially good, we should live well and enjoy its bountiful gifts though always in moderation, as the states of excess and deficiency in Zoroastrianism are deemed to be the workings of the hostile

Spirit. Humanity, in Zoroastrianism, is encouraged to lead a good and prosperous life and hence monasticism, celibacy, fasting and the mortification of the body are anathema to the faith: such practices are seen to weaken us and thereby lessen our power to fight evil. The Prophet saw pessimism and despair as sins, in fact as yielding to evil. In his teachings, we are encouraged to lead an active, industrious, honest and above all, a happy and charitable life.

The After-Life Doctrine

Upon physical death (which is seen as the temporary triumph of evil) the soul will be judged at the Bridge of the Separator, where the soul, it is believed, will receive its reward or punishment, depending upon the life which it has led in this world, based upon the balance of its thoughts, words and deeds. If found righteous, the soul will ascend to the abode of joy and light, while if wicked, it will descend into the depths of darkness and gloom. The after state, however, is a temporary one, as there is no eternal damnation in Zoroastrianism. There is a promise, then, of a series of saviors (the Saoshyants) who will appear in the world and complete the triumph of good over evil. Evil will be rendered ineffective and Ahura Mazda, the Infinite One, will finally become truly Omnipotent in Endless Light. There will then take place, a general last judgment of all the souls awaiting redemption, followed by the resurrection of the physical body, which will once again meet its spiritual counterpart, the soul. Time, as we know it, will cease to exist and the seven creations of Ahura Mazda will be gathered together in eternal blessedness in the Kingdom of Mazda, where everything, it is believed, will remain in a perfect state of joy and undyingness.

The History

For over a thousand years, from about 549 BCE to 625 CE the religion taught by Zarathushtra flourished as the state religion of three mighty Iranian empires, that of the Achaemenian (549-330 BCE), the Parthians (248 BCE - 224 CE) and Sasanians (224 - 652 CE). Among the many subjects of the Achaemenian Empire were the Jews, who adopted some of the Prophet's main teachings and transmitted them in due course to Christianity and later to Islam.

The Parsi Arrival

In the 7th century CE, the Arabs conquered Iran. Many of them
settled there and gradually imposed their own religion of Islam. In
the early 1st century, a small group of Zoroastrians seeking freedom of worship and economic redress, left Iran and sailed towards
the warm shores of western India. They eventually arrived along
the Gujarat coastline in 936 CE at a place they named Sanjan, some
180 kilometers north of Bombay. There they flourished and came
to be known as the Parsis (Persians). Over the millennium, a small
band of faithful Zoroastrians have continued to live in Iran and
have tried to preserve their culture and religious traditions as best
they could.

ZOROASTRIAN SCRIPTURES

The Inner Light

You are eternal light, Ahura Mazda. Your very nature is light. Be
my light, 0 Lord of light. I grope in the dark: scatter the darkness.
Shed your guiding light on my darkened path and lead me onward
on my way to your abode of eternal light. Let your radiance fall
upon me that I may live your light.

 Like the owl that shuns the light, the sinner sees not your light
and, seeing not your light, the sinner does not see you. Humans veil
their eyes when they look in the face of the brilliant sun. Immeas-
urably brighter is your spiritual light than the physical light of the
sun. As the rose unfolds its petals to the light of the sun, so help
me, Ahura Mazda, to unfold my heart to your light by my faithful
adherence to righteousness.

 On the deep dark ocean of life is the worst of my life moving. Be
by my side at the helm, I pray. Keep watch over it and guide me to
steer the vessel on the waves of your divine light to land me secure
on the shores of your heavenly regions.

 The light that burns within the temple of my heart flickers and
burns low through my carelessness. Forgive my negligence, and let
it not fade from my soul. Replenish it in your unfailing kindness,
and inspire me to tend it with devoted care. Let your physical light
shine over me from above, and let your light dart into my soul and

illumine it from within. May your light flood my mind and my heart, and inspire me to live by the inner light. 0 you who live in those lights are the highest of the high, Ahura Mazda.

Asha's Universal Order in the Universe

Life upon earth reveals a smooth and graceful flow and an all round ordered movement. Nature has its seasonal rhythms. Spring and summer, autumn and winter, with seasonal succession of changes, take their unvarying course. The tides rise and fall punctually. The dawn and morning, noon and evening, and night go to their uninterrupted daily round. The dying day gives birth to the night. The night hangs its myriad of silvery lamps to lighten the darkness. The dawn breaks to resurrect the day and the day goes the perennial round of its birth. The heavens and their glittering hosts, the sun, stars, and planets march at a regulated pace. Immutable are the laws that govern the movements of nature and preserve its unfailing regularity. A stable order ensures the existence of the universe.

Asha is the upholder of a moral order in the inner world of humanity. Human life is lived the best when our relations with our neighbors, our duty towards our fellow beings and towards the heavenly beings are regulated according to the moral order of righteousness.

Help me to establish order in my inner world, Ahura Mazda, you who are the source of all order and law. May concord and not discord, order and not disorder, righteousness and not wickedness always prevail in my inner world. May Asha Vahishta, Best Righteousness, be the upholder of my life, now and forever.

The Path of Righteousness

The path of Asha is the Path of Righteousness. One alone is the path, it is the Path of Righteousness. All other paths are non-paths, says he who is Zarathushtra. You dwell in the straightest paths, Ahura Mazda, that lead to the paradise of the righteous.

Right is the Path of Righteousness. Wrong is the Path of Wickedness. The one leads to heaven, to hell the other. The Path of Righteousness leads to the life of eternal felicity, deviation from it spells the soul's destruction for all time. It is left to us to choose whether we will walk the one and be saved or the other and be lost.

Rough and rugged is the path of life. It is beset with difficulties and troubles. Temptation draws us away from the right path and waylays us in the wilderness of wrong. We are lost in the labyrinths of wickedness and are at a loss to find our way out of the maze.

Protect me, Ahura Mazda, from being beguiled and led astray through tempting pitfalls and alluring snares of Angra Mainyu, the Evil Spirit, Guide of Righteousness. Give me firm resolve and strong will, that with sustained effort I can find Garonamana, the abode of the righteous.

Righteousness Is the Rule of Life

Righteousness is the norm that measures our worth. When righteousness alights upon serfs they grow greater in worth than their master if the masters are strangers to righteousness. Greatness glories not and knowledge shines not where righteousness dwells not. When prince and peasant are comrades upon earth in the practice of righteousness, as comrades again after death they enter the shining.

Righteousness is the prize open alike to be won by all who sincerely try. It is equally in the power of all to make it their own. Righteousness shines in rags in the cottage of the poor and shames the raiments of royalty in the palace, if righteousness does not dwell there. Those are not great who are not great in righteousness. They are not rich who are not rich in righteousness. They are not healthy who are not healthy in righteousness. They are not heroic who are not heroic in righteousness. The best one and the greatest one and the noblest one is the righteous one. Ahura Mazda, you are the righteous Lord of righteousness. Bless me in your goodness, with good thoughts of the mind and good words of the tongue and good deeds of the hands, that I may think righteousness, speak righteousness, work righteousness, and be a righteous one in the world of righteousness.

Life Is Your Greatest Gift, AHURA MAZDA

Unquenchable is the thirst for life. A myriad of men and women pray to you, Ahura Mazda, every moment for happy life, full life, joyful life, and long life. We love life and we wish to live a hundred lives and yet our will is not satisfied. An unconquerable urge to live a full and a useful life distinguishes us from animals. This inborn urge drives us to strive for what seems to be beyond our reach and stimulates human progress. It is good and great and glorious indeed to live, O Lord of life.

The longest of life upon earth is but a breath, it is true. But life, though short, has untold possibilities. Life is not fortuitous. It is designed and has a purpose. Let me take life in earnest and let me not while it away. Help me to understand life, that I may be able to live life as it is your will, O Ahura Mazda. Help me to throw myself actively and selflessly and strenuously into the thick of life for the furtherance of the world of righteousness and the decrease of the world of wickedness.

Giver of life and giver of the gifts of life, I thank you for health and happiness and all that makes life livable on earth. None can raise me a memorial equal to the one that I can set up in my lifetime by my life devoted to your service and your reign upon the earth. Help me so to live, my God, that when death extinguishes my life, I may yet live upon earth in my good thoughts and good words and good deeds when my soul dwells with you in heaven.

Great Is the Dignity of Work

There is no shame to put one's hand to the plow, there is no shame to put one's shoulder at the wheel, there is no shame to dig a trench, there is no shame to work as a cook or a servant or a maid or to do any menial work. But there is shame indeed where a stout hand of an able-bodied man or woman is outstretched to accept a dole in the face of the remunerative work waiting for all who may work.

It is humiliating to slumber in sloth and repose and rest, when there is time to work and to toil. It is loss of manhood and womanhood to eat one's bread not earned by one's honest work. Sweeter is the simple bread won by the sweat of one's honest work. Sweeter is the simple bread won by the sweat of one's brow, than the rich bread bestowed upon one by the hand of charity.

Teach me, Ahura Mazda, never to shirk my daily work. Do not let me complain and groan in the face of hard work waiting for me, but enthuse me to do it willingly and wholeheartedly.

The work of the industrious and enterprising of my good co-religionists often supports the idlers and sluggards, along with the disabled and the needy. May it never be my misfortune to be one of them, my merciful God. Inspire me to value my independence and self-respect and to strive for their preservation in the midst of my poverty and want, Ahura Mazda.

I Glory in Activity, AHURA MAZDA

"Up with your feet and up with your hands. Keep your minds in readiness to do lawful and timely deeds and for the undoing of unlawful and untimely deeds," Zarathushtra exhorts us. Industry is a priceless virtue. An active life of hard and honest work is the ideal life.

Truth Is the Most Supreme Virtue

Great is the glory of truth. It shines like a star. Truth is the queen of virtues. Truth is the good Mazda-worshipping religion.

Truth is truth always and ever to the day of doom. Truth is omnipotent and immortal. Truth is one, you are Truth, Ahura Mazda.

Simple and straightforward is the language that truth speaks. It does not need rhetorical embellishment. It shines in its innate simplicity. Never crooked and never zigzag with knobby ways in which travelers may lose themselves, straight is the path of truth.

Truth knows no racial or geographical boundaries. Truth is ever the same for all. Truth blinds the demon of falsehood, as light blinds the owl. To be truthful is to be courageous, for falsehood is cowardice.

Truth walks with halting steps, and falsehood flies on swift wings. Truth builds and creates; falsehood breaks and destroys. A person of truth is trusted and honored by all. The liar must invent two more lies to uphold one and from deep to deeper in the sloughs of falsehood, the person sinks. Zarathushtra concentrates evil in falsehood. The Evil Spirit is falsehood itself.

Truth may be stifled and smothered for a time, but not for all time. Truth to falsehood is like oil forced under the stinking water of falsehood, like oil on the surface, it will swim, while down like water will falsehood drop.

United by the bonds of truth, society flourishes. Falsehood strikes at the root of mutual trust and hastens its fall. Noted for their probity, the ancient Persians, our illustrious ancestors, taught their youths the rigid adherence to truth as the first and foremost lesson of life.

My God, give me a passionate longing for truth and give me a feeling of repulsion from falsehood. Give me the courage to be true. Guide me to think the truth and speak the truth and act the truth. Put me on the right track when my steps do swerve and stray from the straight path. Incline me to walk steadfast on the shining path of truth. Strengthen me to fight falsehood with the weapons of truth. Let me love truth for truth's sake. Let all I speak and what I speak and when I speak be wholly true. Let my mouth speak only that which my heart feels. Let me be true to myself and let me be true to you, 0 Lord of truth.

Demoralizing Dole

You have kindled the spark of mercy, 0 merciful God, in human hearts to succor your poor whom old age has disabled to work and chronic disease has rendered invalids.

When charity, however, becomes indiscriminate in the hands of the tenderhearted people, who aimlessly dole out largess all around, it tends to encourage subsidized idleness. It spells moral degradation, undermines the spirit of self help and independence, dampens the ardor and enthusiasm for enterprise and adventure, and breaks the morale of those that stretch out their hands to receive the demoralizing dole.

Bless me, 0 Lord of benevolence, with the unbending spirit of self-reliance. Give me undying faith and robust confidence in myself. Let me not distrust my inborn strength and my inner resources. Let not the enervating thought of doubting myself and my powers ever cross my mind. Teach me to live by my own efforts and to fight my way successfully through the hard struggle of life.

Help me to earn my own living and eat my bread, 0 Giver of daily bread, earned in the sweat of my brows. Let me be content with half the bread of my own earning than have a whole given by others. Let me go hungry awhile, but let me never beg for my bread. Let me eat sparingly and clothe scantily and dwell in a lowly cottage and deny myself the comforts of life than support myself by my neighbor's help.

Humanity, says Zarathushtra, is the sole arbiter of our destiny. None can help people to win salvation for their souls, and none can likewise help them in this world if they struggle not strenuously to help themselves by an active and industrious life. Let me not look for help from without, when within me lies the inexhaustible store to redeem my poverty.

Priceless is the treasure of self-respect. It is better to die in honor, with self-respect intact, than to live in shame with its loss. Let me be poor and penniless, but help me as long as I live to preserve the dignity of my personhood, Azura Mazda.

Teach me, O Holy One, to see that I have no right to impose my own way of thinking upon others. Teach me to acknowledge and honor the right of all to pray and worship and sacrifice in their own way. Let me not be a purist and regard those as irreligious who regard not formalism. Keep me free from sectarian spirit, and give me strength to root out from my heart bigotry and fanatic zeal. Teach me to discern true religion from religiosity. Fill my mind and heart, Ahura Mazda, with the spirit of toleration.

Contented with What I Have, but Discontented with What I Am

A contented thought is best for everyone, says Zarathushtra. We do not need many things to be happy. Contentment makes life happy, because it is satisfied with but few things.

To desire and not to have the desire fulfilled, to want and not to have the want satisfied brings unhappiness. Contentment desires not and wants not; therefore, it is happy. Whosoever desires more and more, knows no contentment and is always unhappy.

A contented mind is at peace with itself. Contentment is happy in its belief that it has what it wants and cheerfully enjoys what little it has. Contentment gives satisfaction, joy and happiness. Contentment has enough to make life happy and, therefore, it does not ask for more. Contentment gives independence, self-sufficiency, and self-reliance.

The poor who are contented with what little they have, are happy. The rich covet more and more, and with contentment not in their possession they are unhappy in the midst of their abundance. Impregnable is the fortress of contentment.

Contentment is a virtue as it enables us to bear with the hardships of life. It ceases to be so, when we passively reconcile ourselves to squalor and starvation, when we should strive to fight them; to feel resignation, where we should revolt; to suffer meekly, where we should struggle valiantly; to submit passively to social injustice and inequity where we should take courage in both hands and fight against them to redeem ourselves. Discontent with undesirable conditions goads us to exert ourselves to better our lot. Discontent accelerates human progress.

Do not let discontent press heavily upon my heart and make my life miserable. Let contentment be my wealth. With a contented mind and a contented heart, I will be at peace with the world. With contentment within me, I will patiently work during the day, and when the day's duty is done, peacefully will I sink upon my bed at night and soundly will I sleep till dawn. Let me not, however, be content to remain where I am and what I am. Help me to strive and endeavor my utmost to rise above my position in life and better my prospects, Ahura Mazda.

Happiness to Those Who Give Happiness to Others

Unquenchable is our thirst for happiness, Ahura Mazda. In this wide world, there is enough room for all to live and food to eat and good things of life to enjoy and be happy. At the dawn of history, Zarathushtra gave his message to humanity that the individual's happiness depended upon the happiness of all, and gave us the golden rule that happiness came to those who gave happiness to others.

In this world of joy and sorrow, happiness and misery, life would be intolerable if it were not for the sympathy, kindness, and affection of person to person. Unbearable is the burden of life when unaided. It loses its crushing weight when we live in fellowship with our fellow beings and share one another's burden. Life is incomplete when we live for our own self, oblivious of the happiness of others. Life is best lived when it is lived for others. Thus preached our beloved Prophet, the first among the holy Prophets to teach this universal truth.

The sainted souls of all time and clime have loved others more than themselves and have held that the greatest pleasure of life consisted in making others happy. They have lived for others, worked for others, spent their lives for others, risked their all for others, endured everything for others and died for others, that their fellow human beings may be happy.

Give us wisdom, O Wise One, to see that our interests are served the best by working for the common welfare in cooperation for the common good. Teach us to seek our happiness in the happiness of all, to regard the sorrows and sufferings of others as ours and to hasten to assuage them. Enable us to see that we are all fellow mariners steering the common barge across the sea of life and that a common fate to swim or sink awaits us. Inspire us to feel that common is our goal to reach and common our ideal to realize your divine dispensation.

Strengthen us to stand united one with another, and be mindful of the eternal fact that we are brothers and sisters all and belong to one great human family. We are children of one Divine Spirit, Ahura Mazda.

Let None Nurse Intolerance

Intolerance, bigotry and dogmatism are the bitterest enemies of religion upon earth. They make religion a tyrant, a persecutor, the demoniac perversion of angelic religion.

Frogs croak that their well is the whole world, and the bigots boast that theirs is the only inspired and perfect religion. The truth and the whole truth is exclusively garnered in their religion. They say their religion is the crown and culmination of all religions, their religion is ordained to be the universal religion of humanity and salvation is possible only through their religion, so they say.

All bigotry is blind, stupid, and savage. Sectarian bigotry is as bad as inter-religious bigotry. Bigotry stifles reason and the bigots, in their frenzy, try to force all to believe what they believe.

All religions come from the one and the only God Spirit which makes itself known by many a name. From the same source like the tributaries of a river, they flow. All religions make us good upon earth and with safety do they transport our souls to the realm of yours. One alone is truth, and all religions teach this truth, for religion itself is truth.

All open their hearts to the same Ultimate Reality. All open their hearts to the same God Spirit. All concentrate their thoughts on the same God. All seek fellowship with the same one God. All yearn to be united unto the Supreme. All commend their souls into the hands of the same God Great Spirit.

We have no right to demand that our neighbors shall address The One after our patterns and shall pray in our way and worship according to our liking and sacrifice unto God in the manner we do.

No thinking person's own idea of God and religion, at all times and in all conditions of life, is ever to be the same. For everybody's views on religion, then, it is not possible ever to be alike. Monotonous would our world become, if all thought equally and in the same way without ever differing in religious beliefs and practices from one another. Nature shines in her luxuriant glory because of the wide variety of her form and color and beauty. So do they bloom and blossom in the garden of the spirit pervading humanity, foliage and flowers of all shades and grades of devotion and religious emotions.

We Pray for Unity: Communal, National, and International

All men and women are members of one human species, one common stock, one family. The indissoluble bond of common humanity unites them all. They are children of one common Spirit. Brothers and sisters are they all and are interdependent in life. What is good for anyone is good for everyone. They prosper and they progress, when they trust one another and behave with one another in brotherly and sisterly love.

Life is full of trials and tribulations; unity gives all strength to cope with them. It brings harmony and peace within their country and gives them security against outside aggression. Common interest and common hopes, common aspirations and common destiny lead them all to combine and cooperate with one another. United by the bonds of mutual trust, minds confer with minds and hearts work with hearts and they reap happiness.

When dissension in their ranks divide them and party strife keeps them asunder, they are weakened and they suffer. Bitter enmities, mean jealousies and rancorous hatred gnaw their vitals. Everyone is up against everyone else.

The peoples of the world live upon a volcano. Strong, rapacious nations crush weak nations. Armed with the deadly weapons of modern science, war has now become the most dreadful and diabolical in all history. In vain does lasting peace hover above the distracted world. It finds not a place to land. May everything that is discordant and leads to the chronic disturbance of peace among people perish, we pray.

You truly love all. You have commanded that we should love one another as you do, that we may be one with one another and with you, our Lord. You have poured your love in every human heart that men and women may mutually love one another and live as brothers and sisters in the bonds of unity. Help us all to work for communal, national, and international unity that transcends all divisions and breaks all barriers of caste and color and creed. We long for the dawning of the day when we shall take man to his heart and woman shall take woman to her heart and walk on earth as brothers and sisters united in you, Ahura Mazda, O Spirit of all humanity.

Healthy Body, Peaceful Mind and Joyful Heart Make for Happiness

To live is to desire. The senses create in us diverse desires. Gratification of desires gives pleasure, happiness. There are pleasures of the body and pleasures of the mind that are harmless, and there are others by their side that are harmful. We have to discriminate between those that bring happiness and those that end in unhappiness. The chameleon changes colors frequently. When we hanker after anything and everything that senses bring to us and succumb to the temptation of evil desires, we throw ourselves headlong into the scorching fire of sin and suffer like the moth that runs into a candle and perishes. We have to liberate ourselves from the bondage of evil desires.

Desire in itself is not evil, says Zarathushtra. Desire is an incentive to action and a stimulant to an active life. The active life of hard work and industry is the Zoroastrian life. The Prophet of Ancient Iran teaches not the extinction of desires. He teaches to regulate and moderate them.

Our human nature always craves for what we do not possess. All our desires are not satisfied, all wishes are not fulfilled, and all ambitions are not realized. Then, in our ignorance we consider ourselves unhappy. Yet in this life of polarity if we never came across disappointment and despair, and never knew want and sorrow and suffering in short, if one and all of our innocent and wise desires were fulfilled and we were all happy, we could certainly not live in this world. Unbearable would be the burden of ennui and boredom.

Our prime requirement is to be happy with a sound body and a clear brain. The healthy mind goes hand in hand with the healthy body. The soul of a person may be daring and eager to work for righteousness and to fight wickedness within and without. But if the body is sickly and weak, we cannot lead a strenuous life of self-sacrifice and service. Health ensures the vigorous joys of life. What avails wealth, when the health of the body goes amiss.

When we are overwrought with work and wearied by our daily toil, we rest or we turn to games, sports, music, drama, and a host of innocent diversions that bring relaxation after physical fatigue.

Then we are happy. People who have passionate fondness for rational pursuits seek intellectual pleasures of the mind that make them happy. To people of pure conscience, faithful discharge of duty is happiness.

Happiness is the harmony of the body and mind and heart. Happiness is our harmonious relation to our environment. The source of happiness is within us. Where calm are the passions, and conflicting desires do not clamor for satisfaction there is happiness. Where wrinkles of sorrow do not ruffle the smooth surface of the heart, and the heart is not bowed down by the unbearable weight of suffering, there is happiness. Sublime peace in our inner world is happiness.

Happiness grows in degrees, as it widens and spreads among the many. Happiness, the greatest that this earth can ever give, is ours who promote the happiness of others. It is the happiness past all thought. No words can describe it. No hand can pen it. The blessed giver of happiness towards others is lifted into the realm of spiritual ecstasy.

When all our heart's desires are met, our joy is heightened. We bask in happiness. We beam with happiness. Our heart swells with happiness. We live an eternity of happiness in a few such moments, when life seems to be crowded in those few fortunate moments. Our memory loves to linger around these happy moments we have lived.

Zarathushtra asks us so to live that we may get great satisfaction out of living and be happy. An ideal Zoroastrian home is a living paradise upon earth where happiness does not fade.

When my body is ailing, my mind is weary, and my heart is aching, I pray Ahura Mazda to apply your healing balm to them. Then, in your mercy, you cure me and I am happy. You are ever glad to gladden my heart. Whatever I desire is in you. In you is health, peace, and joy. You always will my happiness. I owe you all that makes my life happy. You have blessed me with a powerful physique and a healthy mind in a healthy body. My heart thrills to the rhythmical beat of my bodily organ.

My happiness in life is in your keeping. You are the strength of my body, the peace of my mind, and the joy of my heart. Blessed be your name, 0 Blessed One. You lavish your blessings of happiness on me.

Fate Does Not Weave the Web of Events in Our Lives

Superstitious fatalism teaches that we are not free agents who can shape the actions of our lives. The movements of the stars regulate them. Inexorable and inevitable is fate. It holds universal sway. Nothing can alter what fate has. Everything happens as fate wills. Fate imposes its decree on us and we have to obey its commands. Fate raises us to fame and fate drags us down to shame. We rise to eminence through fate and sink into oblivion through fate. We prosper and triumph who fate befriends. None can escape our fate. What has been fated will take place. Vain are all effort and striving to defy the doings of fate, for fate is all-powerful.

Such superstitious belief in fate inculcates resignation in us to accept with folded hands whatever befalls our lot. It is paralyzing. It cripples our activities, blights our ardor, kills our ambition, cramps our progress and stifles our spirit. It breeds pessimism and cowardice. Life loses its meaning if we cannot direct the deeds of our life independently and shape our destiny as we will.

You, Ahura Mazda, have endowed us with the freedom of will that we can be the maker of our fate. So teaches Zarathushtra the Prophet. True to his teachings, I will be master of my destiny. I will not succumb to the superstitious regard for omens and portents and lucky and unlucky days. I will not invoke fate to cover my weakness and wrong. I will fight fate and let it not play me pranks.

Fate is nothing. My hard and honest work and strenuous effort are everything. Success and prosperity are all products of my own industry. I will not be disappointed and disheartened, when I fail at times in my endeavor to better my position in life. With iron determination will I dare and do my duty conscientiously. I will always have confidence in myself. I will believe in myself and rely on my own resources and have pride of independence. I will make the best of myself. I will be true to myself. I will be at ease with myself and others in life. I will not lack stability. I will be my own self. I will rely on my own self. I will not induce the powers to change the course of events. With my own labor will I gradually and tenaciously work up my way to fulfilling my dreams. The star, planets, and constellations do not decide my fate. I myself am the maker of my fate and master, under your guidance and protection, Ahura Mazda.

Let Me Turn Jealousy, Rooted in My Heart, to Heal Your Emulation

Jealousy is selfish and covetous, blind and malignant, mean and cowardly, vindictive and cruel. It implies inferiority on the part of the person who nurses it. It broods over its inferiority and prostrates itself in impotence.

The jealous people are petty-minded. They cannot behold greatness in another. They hate the greatness to which they cannot rise. They cannot hear other people's praise. They run them down, blaspheme them, and disparage them. The fire of jealousy turns in their hearts when they see their neighbors win, what they aspired to get but failed. They resent others' success. They cannot tolerate the advantage that their antagonists have over them. They cannot bear to see others surpass them. Their feelings of self-importance are hurt. They become envious and are intrigued to snatch what the others hold in their hands. They hate others and are eager to harm them, if they can. They give vent to every passing gust of passion. Their hearts throb with jealousy. Then jealousy reacts upon themselves and makes them miserable. It tears their heart and eats into their soul. It robs them of peace of mind and the quiet of their soul.

Let me not harbor jealousy. Let me not indulge it. Help me, Ahura Mazda, to strangle jealousy at its birth, before it grows strong and holds me in its clutches and ruins me.

Let me not be jealous of greatness. Let me not envy the prosperity of another. Let me not grudge those who possess what I do not. I do not need to be jealous of the good fortune of my neighbor. Let me not envy merit in others. Let me acknowledge their merit. Let me emulate them. Let me recognize their worth. Let me imitate it.

Emulation is a spur to action. It creates the spirit of adventure and enterprise. With the passion for emulation kindled in me, let me strive by my honest work, strenuous effort, and unfailing perseverance to equal my neighbors, or even to excel them by fair means, if I can. With added zest in life, let me enter into healthy rivalry with my successful neighbors to rise to their eminence, to rise above them and go beyond them in the achievement of greatness in life.

Woman Is The Mother of the Human Race

Seated under the Tree of Life all alone, was Mashya, the First Man. He was morose, moody, and melancholy. Oppressive and killing was his solitude in this strange, new world. He dreaded life. He cursed his existence. Then Spenta Mainyu, Ahura Mazda's superb Fashioner of mortal clay, took compassion on him and made Mashyani, the First Woman. Eventually, Mashya took Mashyani as his wife. With his life-mate, Mashya set up his first household upon earth.

When Spenta Mainyu made man, he was acclaimed in the heavenly world as a good architect. When, with softer and finer clay and with unprecedented craftsmanship he made woman, he was hailed by all as the best and matchless molder of all time. Woman is the marvel of creation. Unrivalled and unequalled in the form and beauty is she in this wide world. She is the blooming flower in the garden of life that breathes perfume all around.

Woman is the teacher of gentility to man. She helps man to grow in moral height. She is the sustaining power of the life of man. She has much that man does not have. Man is not man until woman breathes manhood in him. She is the life of man. She has genius to love, and she loves more intensely and more faithfully than man. She is more patient and enduring than man. She suffers silently and hides her grief in her bosom and smothers her tears. She comforts and she soothes. She dispels the darkness of the depressed spirits around her. Wilderness would this world be without woman. There is freshness and there is sweetness where woman steps in. When life becomes weary, woman makes it more cheery.

Man delights to lay at the feet of woman all that he wins from the world. The fanatic iconoclast turns docile idol-worshipper when he approaches woman, the eternal idol of humanity in flesh.

Life becomes livable for man as woman shares it. Woman is the helpmate of man. She is not his drudge or chattel. Woman, again, is not man in the making. She has not to ape man and grow mannish. Woman is woman and always and ever woman. Wifehood and motherhood are her most sacred functions. As a prudent wife and a loving mother, she forgets her own self for the tender love of her dear ones and trains her children to virtue.

Gentle, tender, and delicate is womanly virtue. The slightest waft of vicious wind soils and withers it. Chastity is woman's priceless wealth. Purer than pearl and brighter than diamond is the chaste woman.

Our Duty Is to Work for the Perfection of the World

Many in this life forget that they have a mission to fulfill and a duty to discharge. Idlers lounge on the lawn, the negligent spend their time in merry making and the epicures live for the chase of pleasure and amusement, before you Ahura Mazda. Give them a rude awakening to reality and rouse them to duty. Many there are who think the burden of duty that falls on them unbearable and are tempted to throw it off, when you give them strength to bear it and zeal to carry it along.

Do not let me look on my duty as an unpleasant burden. Do not let me do my duty grudgingly. Do not let me lag, when I hear call of duty. Do not let power on earth force me to relinquish what is my duty. Do not let me shirk my duty. Do not let me rest halfway. Do not let me neglect the duty assigned to me.

Awaken me to my responsibility that I may be true to my vocation. Let me work out everything for myself. Let me do my work with my own hands and not look to others to do what is my duty to do. Guard me, 0 Guardian Divine, from neglecting little things, for creatures mountain high to the littleness of a mole all play their assigned parts in your providence.

Show me my duty and I will consecrate my life to it. Endow me with the right sense of duty. Help me to discern my duty and I will do it with diligence. Quicken my sense of duty and I will faithfully and fearlessly treat its rugged path. Let your guiding hand lead my life. Command what you will and you will ever find me ready to do your bidding and to loyally perform my appointed task as a pleasant duty. I will do my duty, because it is my duty. Duty has it own reward.

To work for humanity is to work for your glory, my God. You have owned people as your fellow workers in the stupendous task of perfecting the world according to the plan laid out by you at the beginning of creation. Help me to do my duty with alacrity and with dauntless courage in the face of difficulties, even though the heavens fall. Doing my duty is the ideal of my life. I will do my duty all the days of my life, that when I have lived my day and am old, I may peacefully sit down to collect and ponder over my doings of life at the close of my earthly career. Then, when the time comes for you to take me back in your loving arms and when you do call me to render the account of my stewardship, I may come to you as came those that diligently did their duties that their callings demanded and proved themselves to be the perfectors of your world, Ahura Mazda.

You are He, Ahura Mazda, whom Zarathushtra, when friendless and forlorn, implored to help him as a friend would help his friend. When his kith and kin disowned him and his wavering followers forsook him, you, his ever-true friend stood by his side and helped him.

We seek you, as Zarathushtra sought you. We lift up our hands to you in invocation seeking your friendship. Everything works for the best, when we have you for our friend. Be our friend this day and all the days of our life. O You, never failing friend of ours.

Let Me Fight and Live Down My Misfortunes

Farmers do not know what the year will bring forth on their fields. People do not know what will befall them. Many a misfortune comes upon people unaware. When fortune plays them falsely, difficulties assault them from all sides, and dangers come from all directions. Life heaps woe upon them. Misfortune weighs heavily upon their minds and depresses their spirits. They cannot bear the troubles that gather about them. They bend and break beneath the yoke of misfortune. Life to them is a long drawn agony.

Tenderhearted persons cannot get over their misfortunes that overtake them. Grief eats and devours their hearts. They drain the cup of sorrow to the dregs. Their eyes are always dim with tears. They wring their hands and beat their breasts and sob their hearts out. They cry to you, Ahura Mazda, flee to you and fall at your feet and between their misfortune. You call them by their names and fold them in your arms and whisper words of comfort in their ears and soothe them into quietude.

The anguish of the miserable of the world is such as would break a heart of stone. Hard would be the heart that would not break at the sight of their woe. Callous would be the heart that would not weep when they weep.

Divine Is Ideal Friendship

From the time that the journey of our life begins, we do not like to be lonely. Our loneliness frightens us. We are afraid to look into it. Crushing is the burden of solitude. Heavy is the load of life, that weighs down our spirit, if all alone we have to bear it. Often is the firmament overcast and the clouds gather over our heads. Dreary darkness falls upon us and weariness of spirit takes possession of us. Ever in search are we of someone who shares the unbearable burden of life and sustains us in our direst straits.

In living together with our kith and kin we find courage and comfort. When we work in unison, we become stronger and better able to go through rough times. Light becomes the burden and easy the yoke of life. Then does life take a brilliant color. We find safety to sail the sea of life in one and the same boat. Mutual love and common interest bind us together. The bond between us is the closest.

Next in worth to our love of our relatives is our attachment to our friends. Friendly love knits us together. Relatives are born: friends are made. Our acquaintance begins with those who come across our path. From acquaintance is born familiarity between persons actuated by same motives, and from familiarity grows friendship that ardently seeks alliance based on mutual trust.

Friends are a staff upon whom we can lean. They can be a tower of strength in our weakness, a solace in sorrow, a reliable counsel and a priceless asset at all times.

Let me face life with my friend with joint fervor and wisdom. Let us two bear each other's joys and sorrows and give help and receive help. Let us trust and confide in each other. Let us open our minds and hearts to each other.

Let us be everything to each other. With close intimacy of friendship, let our two hearts grow into one. United in the bond of friendship, let us two act as one. Let us make each other's interests and concerns our own. Adversity is the touchstone of friendship. In prosperity and in adversity, whether good or ill betides, let us not forsake each other. Let us be inseparable in weal or woe.

Let us bear with each other's infirmities and forgive each other's failings. Let us never fail to give each other what is due. Let us each give our heart to gain the heart of the other. Let us live like sisters and brothers. Let us believe that in the death of our friend, we who remain behind lose our other self. Happy is the land where abundance of congenial friendship is found. True friendship is the Lord God's delicious boon.

Let Us Be All the World to One Another

From the time that the journey of life begins, we prefer not to be lonely. Crushing is the burden of solitude. Heavy is the load of life. We have to bear it all alone. It weighs down our spirit. Often the firmament gets overcast, and the clouds gather over our heads, dreary darkness falls upon us, and weariness of spirit takes possession of us.

We are ever in search of someone who can sustain us in our direst straits. We find courage and comfort in living together with our kin. When we live in unison, we become stronger and better able to go through rough times. Light becomes the burden and easy the yoke of life. Then does life take on a brilliant color. Many together find safety to sail the sea of life in one and the same boat.

Teach us all to bear with one another and live in concord. Teach us to exercise forbearance and forgiveness towards one another. Let us share with our neighbors their joys and sorrows. Let us not be wholly filled with self-love. Let us learn to love one another. Let us all learn to live in unconditional love.

Let us not covet our neighbor's goods. Let us aim at their hearts and win them by our goodwill for them. Let us not seek success in the failure of others. Let us comfort and console the sorrowing and suffering with the kiss of human kindness. Let our hearts go out to others in their misfortunes.

Let us realize that we are all interdependent. Let us behave with one another in mutual trust and in common bonds of love. Trust begets trust. Let us all live so that our lives are for our children, who are our extensions of ourselves. Guide us to serve our friends and love our friends, for you, Ahura Mazda are in them all.

We Think and Thoughts Shape Our Lives

Marvelous is the power of thought. Thinking is as natural to us as breathing. Thought has lifted us above the level of the animal world. It has raised us from the savage to the civilized state in life. Our thought rules the world. The power to think is our most precious right and our proudest privilege.

Thought is the seed of speech and action. When the seed is sound and strong, it germinates and sprouts and blossoms in the harvest of fine words and deeds.

We learn by seeing, hearing, and reading the book of nature and studying human nature, but we learn best by thinking. What we have pondered and thought overfills our minds and enriches them with lasting knowledge.

We live best who thinks best. Let me then think for myself and let me never think through others. I may have my work done by others for me, but let me never get my thinking done for me by others. Let me think and think well and think deep, but let me always think.

Let me be a person of learning, but let me also be a thinker of original thoughts and creative thoughts. Let reason mould and regulate and control my thinking. Give me a thinking habit and give me clear thinking, before I venture upon bold and profound thinking, Ahura Mazda.

Let me think good thoughts, great thoughts, noble thoughts, gentle thoughts, beautiful thoughts, and virtuous thoughts. Let them all build my character.

Truth is your Good Thought, Ahura Mazda. Let it nurture my mind with its good thoughts. Let good thoughts alone ripen into words and deeds and let evil thoughts wither and perish. Let righteous thoughts and devotional thoughts be my constant companions. Let my pious thoughts, concentrated on you, be my silent daily prayer, Ahura Mazda.

Let Us Be the Harbingers of Goodwill to All
By Dastur M. N. Dhalla (deceased)

Do not my faith in human nature be ever shaken, even when we falter and fail. My faith in human nature strengthens my faith in you. I see your image. My Creator is in me, but so is it in my neighbor also. You are enthroned in every human heart. Let us, then, meet one another with goodwill and with the mutual belief that we greet you in all whom we approach and meet.

Selfishness, jealousy, and mutual distrust hinder our unity. Help us to tear down the barriers that divide individuals from individuals, races from races, and nations from nations. Let us bear one another's burdens. All men and all women are drops of water drawn from the one and the same sea of life. Let us strengthen the bond of unity between people and people. Let us love all, as we love ourselves.

All life is made of one blood. All are of one human family, united by the indissoluble bond of common humanity. Every man and every woman as a brother and sister to every other man and every other woman, brothers and sisters all in the one human family. When hearts are united with hearts and souls are united with souls, the whole of humanity will be one heart and one soul in you, the Source of all. Teach us, O God, to love all humanity as you love all your children. Let us live for you, and let us live for all your offspring.

Let everyone's heart go out to the heart of everyone else. Let everyone give to everyone else. Let the ideal of cooperative life grow day by day. Let it continue to community and nation. Help it, Ahura Mazda, to grow to the supreme ideal of one, common humanity, one universal community.

ZARATHUSHTRA'S PHILOSOPHY

BASIC OVERVIEW BY SHAHRIAR SHAHRIARI

Ahura Mazda

Literally translated, Ahura means The Lord Creator, and Mazda means Supremely Wise. This was the name by which Zarathushtra addressed his God. He proclaimed that there is only one God, who is the singular creative and sustaining force of the Universe. Zarathushtra was the first Prophet who brought a monotheistic religion.

Choice

As human beings we are given the right to choose. However, because of the law of cause and effect, we are also responsible for our choices, and must face their consequences.

Dualism

Even though there is only one God, our universe works on the basis of moral dualism. There is Spenta Mainyu (progressive mentality) and Angra Mainyu (evil or regressive mentality). Zarathushtra pleaded with us to think clearly before we choose and asked us to choose the progressive choices to bring about beneficial consequences. He said that Ahura Mazda would not order us to choose either this or that.

In other words, having given us the ability to choose, Ahura Mazda leaves us alone and allows us to make our choices. And, if we choose good, we will bring about good, and if we choose evil, we will cause evil. This is how the moral universe operates.

Devil/Ahriman

Based on the previous principle, we are the causes of all the good and all the evil that happens in our moral universe. Or simply stated, according to Zarathushtra, there is no Devil. However, some of the Post-Zarathushtra scripture introduced the concept of the Devil, or Ahriman, which was effectively a personification of Angra Mainyu.

Purpose in Life

To be among those who renew the world ... to make the world progress towards perfection.

Happiness

Happiness is a byproduct of a way of living. Happiness is for those who work for the happiness of others.

Amesha Spentas (Holy Immortals)

Zarathushtra tells us that Ahura Mazda created everything based on the six Amesha Spentas, which are in fact divine emanations or aspects of the creator. These are:

1. Vohu Mano - The spirit of the Good Mind
2. Asha - The spirit of Truth and Right
3. Khshatra - The spirit of Holy Sovereignty
4. Spenta Armaiti - The spirit of Benevolent Devotion and Love
5. Haurvatat - The spirit of Perfection and Well-Being

6. Ameretat - The spirit of Immortality

According to Zarathushtra, not only the universe was created on the basis of these six, but also they permeate every aspect of creation including ourselves.

Angels

Later on, Post-Zarathushtra Zoroastrianism mythologized the Amesha Spentas into angelic hierarchies, and brought back some of the Pre-Zarathushtra Gods into the scripture as angels.

Cosmology

Ahura Mazda first created Vohu Mano or the Spirit of the Good Mind, through which God created a plan or blueprint for the universe. Part of this blueprint was to incorporate an operating mode and operating laws. This was Asha or the spirit of Truth and Right (the software of the universe).

Then comes the actual act of physical creation, which involved certain actions and manifestations. This is Khshatra or the spirit of Holy Sovereignty. These manifestations are actualized through Spenta Armaiti, with much devotion, faith and love.

And, finally, that the universe is created in the spirit of Perfection (Haurvatat) and is timeless and immortal (Ameretat).

Microcosm

Each one of us carries the divine essence within ourselves. It is our duty to recognize this and act accordingly. How?

Based on Zarathushtra's teachings, we can and should act like Ahura Mazda. We should think about every choice that we wish to make and in the spirit of our good mind choose wisely. We should respect the natural and moral laws and operating mode of the universe. We should act diligently, with love and faith. And, we will then make perfect and timeless choices, and fulfill our purpose of renewing the world.

Co-Workers

We are co-workers and co-creators of God. We are here to fulfill the divine plan, not to become obedient slaves of God, nor to be helpless children of God. This is why we are given the choice, even the choice not to cooperate with God's plan and go against it. We find evil in the world, because there are some who choose not to work according to God's plan.

Heaven and Hell

According to Zarathushtra, after we leave this life, our essence leaves the body, and depending on the choices that it has made, either it will go to the House of Songs or Realm of Light (if we have made good choices) or to the Realm of Darkness and Separation (if evil choices).

Heaven and Hell are not physical places, but are described as timeless states of consciousness, either a state of oneness with or separation from Ahura Mazda.

Post-Zarathushtra Zoroastrianism mythologized these timeless states of consciousness into everlasting physical locations and descriptive places. This later concept carried over into the Jewish and Christian religions.

Some Corollaries

Since we are all endowed with the Divine Essence, we are all good and divine. Therefore, it is not the human beings who are evil, but their choices, actions and deeds that could be good or evil.

There is only one way to fight evil, and that is by spreading goodness, just as there is only one way to fight the darkness, and that is by spreading light. Similarly only by spreading love can we eliminate hatred and enmity, and not by fighting and opposing each other.

Some Basic Maxims of Zoroastrianism

Humata, Hukhta, Huvarshta, which mean: Good Thoughts, Good Words, Good Deeds.

There is only one path, and that is the path of Truth.

Do the right thing because it is the right thing to do, and then all beneficial rewards will come to you, also.

THE HEBREW SCRIPTURES
AND OTHER SACRED JEWISH WRITINGS

INTRODUCTION

The following pages highlight selections from Hebrew Scriptures, Mishnah and Midrash.

The Hebrew Scriptures comprise thirty-nine books in three divisions: Torah, Prophets, and Writings. These selections are from the Jewish Publication Society (1950 edition). They were adapted in modern English by the editor. (Thirty-nine is a popular, standard enumeration.)

The Torah contains the five books of Moses, the Prophets twenty-one books, and the Writings thirteen books. Altogether, their authorship spans eight centuries, from the 13th century B.C.E. to the 5th century B.C.E.

The Mishnah is a compendium of Jewish law and was formulated by the sages in ancient Judea and edited by Judah the Prince c. 220 C.E. in six divisions, which became the basis for Talmudic discussion. The selection here is from Mishnah Abot, The Ethics of the

Fathers, a collection of wise sayings in six chapters but without Talmudic commentary, remaining open to public discourse for generations to come.

The Midrash Aggadah, as distinguished from Midrash Halachah (Law) is Rabbinic interpretation of homiletical, metaphorical, and philosophical nature. Since there are Aggadic elements in the Torah, Midrash is indigenous to Jewish learning from ancient to modern times if and only if new interpretation is grounded in Scripture. Representing the Midrashic mode of Torah commentary in this compendium of World Scripture is the Treatise on Peace (c 6-7th century C.E.). This minor treatise on "Proper Decorum" can be found in the Vilna Talmud as "Derekh Eretz Zuta".

The criteria for selection were as follows: (i) limits of space, (ii) covenantal meaning; (iii) literary form, and (iv) universal significance.

The historic experience of Israel reflects a growing self-awareness of its role as a People of God. The classical sources are defining documents of its character and destiny, testifying to this spiritual evolution as a continuous struggle for meaning and transcendence.

Wisdom dictates a method of interpretation which avoids literal acceptance of the sacred text if it goes contrary to human experience, natural law and the principles of reason. The allegorical method is that Midrashic tool for overcoming contradictions between language and reality, provided its own constructions are not taken literally. The confusion of epistemological categories of thought is the major source of superstition and falsehood. The human imagination, while in itself a miracle of creative wonder, can become a dangerous force, if unbridled and undisciplined, especially in the domain of metaphysics and theology.

Scripture as sacred text inspired by Divine Influence, is a record of the human response to the mystery of the Divine Reality as expressed in human language. The Word of God is the word about God or addressed to and from God in a cultural context, and each generation has its own interpreters according to its experience and comprehension. Faith in God is pure intuition of trust, not a sanction for confusion, dogma, superstition and bigotry, nor is it a shortcut to true knowledge or a substitute for it. What then is its ultimate value?

The notion of Covenant is one of commitment to the Divine Reality as a joint presence in the life of the Spirit. Biblically, there are five covenants between God, Israel, and Humanity, namely the Covenant of Creation (the Sabbath); the Covenant of Humanity (Noah); the Covenant of Land and People (Abraham); the Covenant of Revelation (Torah at Sinai); and the Covenant of Peace (Universal Redemption).

The five Covenants are essentially one in form if not in content. To unite form and content is the historical task. A world scripture should attest to such a possibility and hope: to relate the universal to the particular and the particular to the universal in a state of harmony and wholeness. To be chosen is to teach that every human being is thus chosen as a beloved of God.

The 7th century (B.C.E.) prophet Zephaniah has expressed the vision of the Covenant of Peace (CH 3:9):

For then will I turn to the peoples
A pure language,
That they may all call upon the name of the Lord,
To serve Him with one consent.

Benjamin Herson

GENESIS

The Story of Creation (CH 1:1-31)

In the beginning God created the heaven and the earth. Now the earth was unformed and void, and darkness was upon the face of the deep; and the spirit of God hovered over the face of the waters. And God said: "Let there be light." And there was light. And God saw the light, that it was good; and God divided the light from the darkness. And God called the light Day, and the darkness He called Night. And there was evening and there was morning, one day.

And God said: "Let there be a firmament in the midst of the waters, and let it divide the waters from the waters." And God made the firmament, and divided the waters which were under the firmament from the waters which were above the firmament; and it was so. And God called the firmament Heaven. And there was evening and there was morning, a second day.

And God said: "Let the waters under the heaven be gathered together into one place, and let the dry land appear." And it was so.

And God called the dry land earth, and the gathering together of the waters called the seas; and God saw that it was good. And God said: "Let the earth put forth grass, herb yielding seed, and fruit-tree bearing fruit after its kind, where the seed is, upon the earth." And it was so. And the earth brought forth grass, herb-yielding seed after its kind, and tree bearing fruit, where the seed is, after its kind; and God saw that it was good. And there was evening and there was morning, a third day.

And God said: "Let there be lights in the skies to divide the day from the night; and let them be for signs, and for seasons, and for days and years, and let them be for lights in the skies to give light upon the earth." And it was so. And God made the two great lights: the greater light to rule the day, and the lesser light to rule the night; and the stars. And God set them in the skies to give light upon the earth, and to rule over the day and over the night, and to divide the light from the darkness; and God saw that it was good. And there was evening and there was morning, a fourth day.

And God said: "Let the waters swarm with living creatures, and let fowl fly above the earth in the skies." And God created the great sea-monsters, and every living creature that creeps, wherewith the waters swarmed, after its kind, and every winged fowl after its kind; and God saw that it was good. And God blessed them, saying: "Be fruitful, and multiply, and fill the waters in the seas, and let fowl multiply in the earth." And there was evening and there was morning, a fifth day.

And God said: "Let the earth bring forth the living creature after its kind, cattle, and creeping things, and beast of the earth after its kind." And it was so. And God made the beast of the earth after its kind, and the cattle after their kind, and every thing that creeps upon the ground after its kind; and God saw that it was good. And God said: "Let us make man in our image; and let them have dominion over the fish of the sea, and over the fowl of the air, and over the cattle, and over all the earth, and over every creeping thing that creeps upon the earth." And God created man in His own image; He created male and female. God blessed them and said to them: "Be fruitful, and multiply, and replenish the earth, subdue it, and have dominion over the fish of the sea, over the fowl of the air, and over every living thing that creeps upon the earth." And God said: "Behold, I have given you every herb yielding seed, which is upon the earth, and every tree, in which is the fruit of a tree yielding seed—to you it shall be for food; and to every beast of the earth, and to every fowl of the air, and to every thing that creeps upon the earth, where there is a living soul, (I have given) every green herb for food." And it was so. And God saw every thing that He had made, and it was very good. And there was evening and there was morning, the sixth day.

The Sabbath (CH 2:1-3)

The heaven and the earth were then finished. On the seventh day God completed His work. On the seventh day He rested from all His work. God blessed the seventh day and hallowed it, because in it He rested from all His work.

Man and Woman (CH 2:18-24)

And the Lord God said: "It is not good that the man should be alone; I will make him a help mate." Out of the ground the Lord God formed every beast of the field and every fowl of the air; He brought them to the man to see what he would call them; and whatever the man would call every living creature, that was to be the name. The man gave names to all the cattle, and to the fowl of the air, and to every beast of the field. But for Adam a help mate was not found. The Lord God caused a deep sleep to fall upon the man. He then took one of his ribs, and closed up the place with flesh instead. And with the rib, which the Lord God had taken from Adam, He made a woman, and brought her to him. Adam said: "This is now bone of my bones and flesh of my flesh; she shall be called Woman, because she was taken out of Man." Therefore shall a man leave his father and his mother, and shall cleave to his wife, and they shall be one flesh.

Garden of Eden: Life and Knowledge (CH 3:1-24)

Now the serpent was more subtle than any beast of the field which the Lord God had made. He said to Eve: "Has God said: You shall not eat of any tree of the garden?" And Eve said to the serpent: Of the fruit of the trees of the garden we may eat; but of the fruit of the tree which is in the midst of the garden, God has said: You shall not eat of it, neither shall you touch it, lest you die." And the serpent said to Eve: "You shall not die; for God does know that in the day you eat of that tree, your eyes shall be opened; you shall be as God, knowing good and evil." When she saw that the tree was good for food, and that it was a delight to the eyes, and that the tree was to be desired to make one wise, she took some of the fruit and ate it. She also gave some to Adam, and he ate it. Then the eyes of them both were opened, and they knew that they were naked, so they sewed fig-leaves together and made themselves girdles. Soon afterward they heard the voice of the Lord God walking in the garden late in the day. Adam and Eve hid themselves from the presence of the Lord God among the trees of the garden. God called to the man and said to him: "Where are you?" Adam said: "I heard Your voice in the garden, and I was afraid, because I was naked, so I hid myself." God said: "Who told you that you were naked? Have you eaten of the tree which I commanded you that you should not eat?" Adam replied: "The woman whom You gave to me, she gave me the fruit of the tree, and I ate it." The Lord God said to Eve: "What is this you have done?" Eve replied: "The serpent beguiled me, and I ate the fruit." God said to the serpent: "Because you have done this, cursed are you from among all cattle, and from among all beasts of the field. Upon your belly shall you go, and dust shall you eat all the days of your life. I will put enmity between you and the woman, and between your seed and her seed. They shall bruise your head, and you shall bruise their heel."

To Eve He said: "I will greatly multiply your pain and your travail. In pain you shall bring forth children. Your desire shall be to your husband, and he shall rule over you."

To Adam He said: "Because you have hearkened to the voice of your wife, and have eaten of the tree, of which I commanded you, saying: You shall not eat of it. Cursed is the ground for your sake. In toil you shall eat all the days of your life. Thorns and thistles shall your food bring forth to you; and your shall eat the herb of the field. In the sweat of your face shall you eat bread, till you return to the ground, for out if it you were taken; for dust you are, and to dust shall you return." Adam called his wife's name Eve; because she was the mother of all human beings. The Lord God made garments of skins for Adam and Eve and clothed them.

Then the Lord God said: "Behold, the man has become as one of us, to know good and evil. We need to make sure that he does not extend his hand again and take more from the tree of life, and eat, and live forever." Therefore the Lord God sent Adam forth from the Garden of Eden to till the ground from which he was taken. So

He drove Adam out of the garden. He placed at the east of the Garden of Eden the cherubim, and the flaming sword which turned every way, to guard the way to the tree of life.

Cain and Abel: The Birth of Conscience (CH 4:1-22)

Adam came together with Eve, and she gave birth to Cain. She said: "I have gotten a son with the help of the Lord." Again she gave birth to his brother, who was named Abel. Abel became a keeper of sheep, but Cain was a tiller of the ground. In the course of time, Cain brought from his fruit an offering to the Lord. Abel also brought some of the first of his flock. The Lord had respect for Abel and his offering, but for Cain and his offering He did not have respect. Cain became very angry, and his countenance fell. The Lord said to Cain: "Why are you angry? And why is your countenance fallen? If you do well, shall it not be lifted up? And if you do not do well, sin waits at the door; and to you is its desire, but you may rule over it." Cain then spoke to his brother Abel about this incident. Soon, when they were in the field, Cain came against his brother Abel and killed him.

The Lord soon afterward said to Cain: "Where is your brother Abel?" Cain said: "I do not know; am I my brother's keeper?" The Lord said: "What have you done? The voice of your brother's blood cries to Me from the ground. Cursed are you from the ground, which has opened her mouth to receive your brother's blood from your hand. When you till the ground, it shall not henceforth yield to you her strength. A fugitive and a wanderer shall you be from now on." Cain said to the Lord: "My punishment is greater than I can bear. You have driven me out this day from my land. I will need to hide from Your face. I shall be a fugitive and a wanderer around the world. Whoever finds me and knows what I have done will attempt to kill me." The Lord said to him: "Whoever attempts to kill you, vengeance shall be taken against him." The Lord established a sign for Cain, lest any who found him might kill him.

Cain went out from the presence of the Lord and dwelled in the land of Nod on the east of Eden. Cain came together with his wife, and she gave birth to Enoch. Cain soon built a city and named the city after his son Enoch. To Enoch gave birth to Irad, and Irad gave birth to Mehujael. Mehujael gave birth to Methushael; and Methushael gave birth to Lamech. Lamech had two wives; one was named Adah the other Zillah. Adah birthed Jubal. He was the father of children who played the harp and pipe. Zillah gave birth to Tubal-cain, the forger of every cutting instrument of brass and iron. The sister of Tubal-cain was Naamah.

The Reflection of God in Humanity (CH 5:1-3, 32)

This is the book of the generations of Adam. In the day that God created man, in the likeness of God He made him. He created male and female and blessed them.

Moral Evil (CH 6:1-8)

When people began to multiply on the earth, and children were born to them, the young men observed that the young women were attractive. Soon they took them as wives according to their own choice. The Lord said: "My spirit shall not abide in these people forever, because they are also flesh. Therefore, the length of their lives shall be limited." The Nephilim were around in those days. Soon, when the young men came to see the young women, and they bore children, they often became people of renown.

The Lord saw that the wickedness of many individuals was great, and that their thoughts were often evil. He repented that He had made man and woman, and it grieved Him badly. The Lord said: "I will blot out the human beings whom I have created. This will include people, animals, creeping things, and birds, because it troubles Me that I have made them." But Noah found grace in the eyes of the Lord.

Noah (CH 6:9-14)

These are the generations of Noah. Noah was in his generation a righteous and whole-hearted man. Noah walked with God. Noah gave birth to three sons, Shem, Ham, and Japheth. The earth in general was corrupt and filled with violence.

God said to Noah: "I need to put an end to almost all forms of life that have come before Me, because the earth is filled with violence through them. I will destroy them with the earth. Make an ark of gopher wood and make it with rooms. Use pitch to hold it together. I will bring a flood of waters throughout the earth to destroy all flesh where there is the breath of life. Everything that is not on the ark will perish. But I will establish My covenant with you. You shall come into the ark, you and your wife and your children, and your children's families with you. Of every living thing, bring two of every sort into the ark, to keep them alive with you; they shall be male and female. Of the fowl after their kind, and of the cattle after their kind, of every creeping thing of the ground after its kind, two of every sort shall come to you to keep them alive. Take with you all the food that you need, and gather it to you. It shall be for food for you and for them." Noah did all that God asked him to do.

The Flood (CH 7:17-24)

The flood was forty days upon the earth. The waters increased, and bore up the ark. It was supported by the waters. The waters continued and increased greatly upon the earth. The ark moved upon the surface of the waters. The waters prevailed over the earth. All the mountains were largely covered. All creatures perished that had lived upon the earth: fowl, cattle, beast, every swarming thing, and every person. All in whose nostrils was the breath of life, whatever was on the dry land, died. Only Noah was left, and those that were with him in the ark. The waters prevailed upon the earth a hundred and fifty days.

The Raven and the Dove (CH 8:6-12)

At the end of forty days, Noah opened the window of the ark which he had made. He sent forth a raven. It went to and fro, until the waters were dried up from off the earth. He also sent forth a dove to see if the waters were abated. The dove found no rest for the sole of her foot, and she returned to the ark, for the waters were on the face of the whole earth. Noah put forth his hand and took her, and brought her into the ark. He waited another seven days, and again he sent forth the dove out of the ark. The dove came in to see him at eventide; and in her mouth an olive-leaf freshly plucked. Noah knew then that the waters were drying up from the earth. He waited another seven days and sent forth the dove again. This time she did not return any more.

The Covenant of Noah (CH 9:17-22)

God spoke to Noah, and to his children, saying: "As for Me, I have established My covenant with you, and with your offspring after you. ..." And God said: "This is the token of the covenant which I make between Me and you and every living creature that is with you for perpetual generations. ... The bow shall be in the cloud. I will look upon it, that I may remember the everlasting covenant between God and every living creature that is upon the earth." God said to Noah: "This is the token of the covenant which I have established between Me and all life on earth."

Abraham (CH 12:2,3)

Now the Lord said to Abraham: "I will make of you a great nation, and I will bless you, and make your name great. Be a blessing to all. I will bless those that bless you, and those who curse you will I curse, and in you shall all the families of the earth be blessed."

The Covenant of Abraham (CH 17:7, 8)

"I will establish My covenant between Me and You and Your off-spring after you throughout their generations for an everlasting covenant. I will give you, and to your offspring, all of the land of Canaan, for your ongoing possession; and I will be their God."

Dialogue with God CH 18:22, 23)

The men turned from there, and went toward Sodom, but Abraham remained before the Lord. Abraham drew near and said: "Will You indeed sweep away the righteous with the wicked? Suppose there are fifty righteous within the city. Will You sweep away and not forgive the place for the fifty righteous that are there? That seems strange for You to act in this manner, to slay the righteous with the wicked, so that the righteous should be as the wicked. Shall not the judge of all the earth do justly? The Lord said: "If I find in Sodom fifty righteous, then I will forgive all of Sodom for their sake." Abraham answered and said: "I have taken upon me to speak to the Lord. Suppose there shall be forty-five righteous. Will You destroy all the city for lack of five?" And the Lord said: "I will not destroy it, if I find there forty-five." And Abraham spoke to Him yet again, and said: "Suppose there shall be forty found there." And He said: "I will not do it for the forty's sake." And he said: "Please, do not be angry with me, and I will speak. Suppose there shall be thirty found there." And the Lord said: "I will not do it if I find thirty there." And he said: "I have taken upon me to

speak to the Lord. Suppose there shall be twenty found there."
And He said: "I will not destroy it for the twenty's sake." And he
said: "Please, do not be angry, and I will speak yet but once more.
Suppose ten shall be found there." And the Lord said: "I will not
destroy it for the ten's sake." And the Lord went His way, as soon
as He had finished speaking to Abraham; and Abraham returned to
his home.

Isaac (CH 27:21-41)

And Isaac said to his son: "How is it that you have found it so
quickly, my son?" And he said: "Because the Lord your God sent
me in good speed." And Isaac said to Jacob: "Come near, my son,
that I may touch you whether you may be my very son Esau or
not." And Jacob approached Isaac, his father, who felt him, and
Isaac said: "The voice is the voice of Jacob, but the hands are the
hands of Esau." And he discerned him not because his hands were
hairy as his brother Esau's hands; so he blessed him. And he said:
Are you my very son, Esau? And he said: "I am." And he said:
"Bring it near to me, and I will eat of my son's venison, that my
soul may bless you. ... And his father Isaac said to him: "Come
near now and kiss me, my son." And he came near and kissed him.
And he smelled the smell of his raiment and blessed him, and said:

See, the smell of my son
Is as the smell of a field which the Lord has blessed.
So God gives you of the dew of heaven,
And of the fat places of the earth,
And plenty of corn and wine.
Let peoples serve you,
And nations bow down to you.
Be lord over your brothers,
And let your mother's sons bow down to you.
Cursed be everyone that curses you,
And blessed be everyone that blesses you.

As soon as Isaac had blessed Jacob, and Jacob had scarcely left the
presence of Isaac, his father, when Esau his brother came in from
his hunting. He also made savory food and brought it to his father:
"Let my father arise and eat of his son's venison, that your soul,
may bless me." And Isaac his father said to him: "Who are you?"
Esau replied, "I am your son, your first-born, Esau." Isaac trembled exceedingly and said: "Who then is he that has taken venison

and brought it to me, and I have eaten it all before you came and have blessed him?" When Esau heard the words of his father, he cried with a great and bitter cry, and said to his father: "Bless me, O my father." And Isaac said: "Your brother came with guile and has taken away your blessing." And he added: "Is not he rightly named Jacob? He has tricked me two times: he took away my birthright; and now he has taken away my blessing." Esau then said: Have you not reserved a blessing for me?" Isaac replied: "I have made him your lord, and all his friends I have given to him as servants: with corn and rice I have sustained him. What then shall I do for you, my son?" Esau said to his father: "Have you only one blessing, my father? Bless me, O my father." Esau lifted up his voice and wept. Isaac his father answered and said to Esau:

Behold, of the fat places of the earth shall be your dwelling,
And of the dew of heaven from above;
And by your sword shall you live, and you shall serve your
friends;
It shall come to pass when you shall break loose,
That you shall shake his yoke from around your neck.

Esau hated Jacob because of the blessing with which his father blessed him. Esau said in his heart: "Let the days of mourning for my father be at hand; then I will slay my brother Jacob."

Jacob (CH 28:10-14)

Jacob left Beersheba and went toward Haran. He found a place and stayed there all night, because the sun had set. He took one of the stones of the place where he stayed and put it under his head. Then he lay down to sleep. He dreamed about a ladder set up on the earth, and the top of it reached to heaven. The angels of God were ascending and descending on it. The Lord stood beside him and said: "I am the Lord, the God of Abraham your father, and the God of Isaac. The land on which you lie, to you will I give it, and to your offspring. Your offspring shall be as the dust of the earth, and you shall spread abroad to the west, and to the east, and to the north, and to the south. In you and your offspring shall all of the families of the earth be blessed."

Judah Speaks to Joseph (CH 44:18-34)

Then Judah came near to God and said: "Oh my Lord, let your servant speak a word in your ears, and do not let your anger burn against your servant, because you are my king. My lord asked his servants, saying: Have you a father or a brother? And we said to my lord: We have a father, an old man, and a little child. His brother is dead, and he alone is left from his mother, and his father loves him. You said to your servants: Bring him down to me, that I may set my eyes on him. He said to my lord: The lad cannot leave his father; for if he should leave his father, his father would die. You said to your servants: Unless your youngest brother comes down with you, you will not see my face any more. When we came up to my father, we told him the word of my lord. Our father said: Go again, buy us a little food. We responded: We cannot go down. If our youngest brother is with us, then will be go down, because we will not be able to see the man's face unless our youngest brother is with us. My father said to us: You know that my wife brought two sons. One went away, and I said: Surely he is torn in pieces. I have not seen him since: If you also take this son from me and harm befalls him, you will bring down my gray hairs with sorrow to the grave. Your servant pledged himself as security for the lad (Benjamin), saying: "If I do not bring him back to you, then I shall bear the blame to my father forever. Now therefore let me, your servant, become your bondsman, and let the lad go up with his brothers. How shall I go to my father, if the lad is not with me, lest I look upon the evil that shall come upon my father?"

Then Joseph could not restrain himself before all of them that stood beside him, and he cried: "Let everyone leave." And there was no one with him when Joseph made himself known to his brothers. He wept aloud; and the Egyptians heard him, and the house of Pharaoh heard him. Joseph said to his brothers: "I am Joseph, your brother. Is my father still alive?" His brothers did not answer him for they were frightened at his presence. Joseph said to his brothers: "Please come close to me." They came closer. Then he said: "I am Joseph your brother, whom you sold into Egypt. Do not grieve nor be angry with yourselves, that you sold me there. God sent me before you to preserve life for all. For these past two yours the famine has been in the land. There are still five years to go, in which there shall be neither plowing nor harvest. God sent me to give you food and shelter, and to save your lives. So it was not you that sent me here, but God. He has made me a father to Pharaoh, and lord of all his house, and ruler over the land of Egypt.

Hasten now, go to my father and say to him: Your long lost son Joseph says: God has made me lord of all Egypt. Please come to me and do not wait. You shall dwell in the land of Goshen. You shall be near to me, you and your children, and your children's children, and your flocks, and your herds, and all that are with you. I will see that you are treated well. Your eyes see, including the eyes of my brother Benjamin, that it is my mouth that speaks to you. Please tell my father of all my good fortune in Egypt, and of all that you have seen. Kindly hasten and bring my father here." He then held his brother Benjamin and wept, and Benjamin also wept. He kissed all of his brothers, and wept with them. After that his brothers talked with him.

EXODUS

Sinai (CH 19:16-25)

On the third day, when it was morning, thunder and lightning, plus a thick cloud, came to the mount, and also an exceedingly loud horn. All the people in the camp trembled. Then Moses brought forth the people out of the camp to meet God; and they stood at the lower part of the mount. Mount Sinai was completely in smoke, because the Lord descended upon it in fire; and the smoke ascended as the smoke of a furnace, so that the whole mount quaked greatly. When the sound of the horn grew louder and louder, Moses spoke, and God answered him by a voice. The Lord then came down upon Mount Sinai, to the top of the mount. Then the Lord called Moses to the top of the mount, and Moses went up. The Lord said to Moses: "Go down, charge the people, lest they break through to the Lord to gaze and many of them perish. Let the priests also, that come near to the Lord, sanctify themselves, lest the Lord break forth upon them." Moses said to the Lord: "The people cannot come up to Mount Sinai; for you did charge us, saying: Set bounds about the mount and sanctify it." The Lord said to him: "Go, climb down, and you shall afterward come up, you, and Aaron with you; but let not the priests and the people break through to come up to the Lord, lest He break forth upon them." So Moses went down to the people and told them.

The Ten Commandments (CH 20:1-14)

God spoke all these words, saying:

I am the Lord your God, who brought you out of the land of Egypt, out of the house of bondage.

You shall have no other gods before Me. You shall not make a graven image, nor any manner of likeness, of anything that is in heaven above, or that is in the earth beneath, or that is in the water under the earth. You shall not bow down to them nor serve them; for I the Lord your God am a jealous God, visiting the iniquity of the fathers upon the children to the third and fourth generations for those that hate Me; and showing mercy to the thousandth generation of them that love Me and keep My commandments.

You shall not take the name of the Lord your God in vain; for the Lord will not hold anyone guiltless that takes His name in vain.

Remember the sabbath day, to keep it holy. Six days shall you labor, and do all your work; but the seventh day is a sabbath to the Lord your God, in it you shall not do any manner of work, you, nor your son, nor your daughter, nor your man-servant, nor your maid-servant, nor your cattle, nor any stranger that is in your home; for in six days the Lord made heaven and earth, the sea, and all that is in them, and rested on the seventh day; therefore, the Lord blessed the sabbath day and hallowed it.

Honor your father and your mother, that your days may be long upon the land which the Lord your God gives you.

You shall not murder.

You shall not commit adultery.

You shall not steal.

You shall not bear false witness against your neighbor.

You shall not covet your neighbor's house; you shall not covet your neighbor's wife, nor his servants, nor his animals, nor anything that is your neighbor's.

The Divine Blessing (CH 20:19-23)

Then the Lord said to Moses: Thus You shall say to the children of Israel: You yourselves have seen that I have talked with you from above. You shall not make gods of silver, or gods of gold. An altar of earth you shall make to Me and on it you shall sacrifice your burnt-offerings and your peace offerings, your sheep and your oxen. In every place where you cause My name to be mentioned I will come to you and bless you. And if you make Me an altar of stone, you shall not build it of hewn stones, because if you lift up your tool upon it, you have profaned it. Neither shall you go up by steps to My altar, so that your nakedness will not be uncovered.

LEVITICUS

The Holiness Code (CH 19:1-37)

The Lord spoke to Moses, saying: "Speak to all the congregation of the children of Israel, and say to them:

You shall be holy; for I the Lord your God am holy. Every one of you shall respect your mother and father, and you shall keep My sabbaths. I am the Lord your God. Do not turn to the idols nor make molten gods: I am the Lord your God.

Laws of Charity

When you reap the harvest of your land, you shall not wholly reap the corner of your field, neither shall you gather the gleaning of your harvest. You shall not glean your vineyard, neither shall you gather the fallen fruit of your vineyard. You shall leave them for the poor and for the stranger: I am the Lord your God.

Laws of Decency

You shall not steal; neither shall you deal falsely nor lie one to another. You shall not swear by My name falsely, so that you profane the name of your God: I am the Lord. You shall not oppress your neighbor nor rob him; the wages of a hired servant shall not abide with you until the morning. You shall not curse the deaf, nor put a stumbling-block before the blind. Rather, you shall respect your God: I am the Lord.

You shall show no unrighteousness in judgment. You shall not respect just the poor person nor favor the wealthy. In righteousness you shall judge your neighbor. You shall not go up and down as a talebearer among your people. Neither shall you stand idly by and see your neighbor injured or killed: I am the Lord.

You shall not hate your brother or sister in your heart. You shall surely rebuke your neighbor and not be tempted because of his or her shortcomings. You shall not take vengeance nor bear any grudge against the young people. Rather, you shall love your neighbor as yourself: I am the Lord.

You shall keep My sabbaths, and reverence My sanctuary: I am the Lord.

Do not turn to the ghosts nor to familiar spirits. Do not seek them out, to be defiled by them: I am the Lord your God.

You shall honor older people, and you shall respect your God: I am the Lord.

If a stranger stays with you in your land, you shall not mistreat the stranger. The one who stays with you shall be to you as the home-born among you, and you shall love him/her as yourself. Remember that you were strangers in the land of Egypt: I am the Lord your God.

You shall not be unrighteous in your judgment, in weight or in measure. Just balances, just weights, a just bushel, and a just gallon you shall have: I am the Lord your God, who brought you out of the land of Egypt.

You shall observe all My statutes and all My ordinances and do them: I am the Lord.

NUMBERS

The Priestly Benediction (CH 6:22-27)

The Lord spoke to Moses, saying: "Speak to Aaron and to his children, saying: You shall bless the children of Israel; you shall say to them:

The Lord bless you, and keep you;

The Lord make His face to shine upon you, and be gracious to you;

The Lord lift up His countenance upon you and give you peace.

So shall they put My name with the children of Israel, and I will bless them.

Balaam's Blessing (CH 24:5, 9)

How goodly are your tents, O Jacob; your dwellings, O Israel!

Blessed are all those who bless you, and cursed are those who curse you.

Covenant of Peace (CH 25:12)

Therefore say: "I give to everyone My covenant of peace; it shall be to all, and to those yet to come, the covenant of an everlasting priesthood."

The Rights of Women (CH 27:1-8)

Then the daughters of Zelophehad drew near, the son of Hepher, the son of Gilead, the son of Machir, the son of Manasseh, of the families of Manasseh the son of Joseph. These are the names of his daughters: Mahlah, Noah, Hoglah, Milcah, and Tirzah. They stood before Moses, and before Eleazar the priest, and before the princes and all the congregation, at the door of the place of meeting, saying: "Our father died in the wilderness, and he was not among the company of those that gathered themselves together against the Lord in the company of Korah. Instead, he died in his own sin, and he had no son. Why should the name of our father be taken away from his family because he had no son? Give to us a possession among the brothers of our father." Moses brought their cause before the Lord. And the Lord spoke to Moses, saying: "The daughters of Zelophehad speak right. You shall surely give them a possession of an inheritance among their father's brothers. And you shall cause the inheritance of their father to pass on to them. You shall speak to the children of Israel, saying: If a man dies and has no son, then you shall cause his inheritance to pass on to his daughter."

DEUTERONOMY

Hear, O Israel (CH 6:4-9)

Hear, O Israel: The Lord our God, the Lord is one. You shall love the Lord your God with all your heart, with all your soul, and with all your might. These words which I command you today shall be upon your heart; you shall teach them diligently to your children and shall talk of them when you sit at home, when you walk on your way, when you lie down, and when you rise up. You shall bind them for a sign upon your hand, and they shall be for a sign between your eyes. You shall write them upon the inside of your home and upon your gates.

Not By Bread Alone (CH 8:1-4)

All the commandments which I require of you today you shall be sure to do, that you may live and multiply, as well as possessing the land which the Lord promised to your fathers. You shall remember the great distance which the Lord your God has led you these forty years in the wilderness, that He might impress you, to know what is in your heart, whether you would keep the divine commandments or not. God afflicted you, and caused you to be hungry. God fed you with manna, which you did not know, and neither did your fathers know that He made you know that we do not live by bread alone, but by everything that proceeds out of the mouth of the Lord do we live.

God said to me: "Arise, go in front of the people, causing them to go in and possess the land, which I swore to their fathers to give to them."

The Great, the Mighty, and the Awesome (CH 10:12-22)

O Israel, what does the Lord your God require of you, but to pay attention to the Lord, to walk in all His ways, and to love Him, as well as to serve your God with all your heart and with all your soul; to keep His commandments and His statues, which I command you this day? To the Lord your God belong heaven, earth, and all that they include. The Lord loved your fathers, and He chose their generations after them, including you, as it is today. Therefore, circumcise the foreskin of your heart, and do not be overly strict. For the Lord your God, He is God of gods, and Lord of lords, the great God, the mighty and the awesome, who does not take favors or rewards from people. He does execute justice for the fatherless and widow, and loves the stranger by giving food and raiment. Therefore, love the stranger, for you were strangers in the land of Egypt. You shall respect the Lord your God. You shall serve Him;

and to Him shall you cleave, and by His name shall you swear. He is your glory, and He is your God that has done for you these great and tremendous things, which your eyes have seen. Your fathers went down into Egypt with seventy people; now the Lord your God has made you as plentiful as the stars in the sky.

The Word Is Near (CH 30:11-14)

For this commandment, which I command you this today, is not too hard for you, neither is it far off. It is not in heaven that you should say: "Who shall go up for us to heaven and bring it to us, and make us hear it that we may do it?" Neither is it beyond the sea that you should say: "Who shall go over the sea for us and bring it to us and make us hear it, that we may do it?" The word is very close to you, in your mouth and in your heart, that you may do it.

Choose Life (CH 30:19, 20)

I call heaven and earth to witness...I have set before you life and death, the blessing and the curse. Therefore choose life, that you may live, you and your seed, to love the Lord your God, to hearken to His voice, and to cling to Him. That is your life for the length of your days, that you may dwell in the land which the Lord promised to your fathers, to Abraham, Isaac, and Jacob.

Invocation to God (CH 32:1-3)

Give ear, O heavens, and I will speak;
Let the earth hear the words of my mouth.
My doctrine shall drop as the rain,
My speech shall distill as the dew;
As the small rain upon the tender grass,
And as the showers upon the herb.
For I will proclaim the name of the Lord;
Let us ascribe greatness to our God.

Resurrection (CH 32:29)

See now that I, even I, am He,
And there is no god with Me;
I kill, and I make alive;
I have wounded, and I heal;

I can deliver nothing except through God's hand.

The Death of Moses (CH 34:4-12)

The Lord said to Moses: "This is the land which I swore to Abraham, to Isaac, and to Jacob, saying: I will give it to your offspring. I have caused you to see it with your eyes, but you shall not go there." So Moses, the servant of the Lord, died there in the land of Moab, according to the word of the Lord. He was buried in the valley in the land of Moab near Bethpeor, and no one knows of his burial place to this day. Moses was one hundred twenty years old when he died. His eye was not dim nor his natural force diminished. The children of Israel wept for Moses in the plains of Moab for thirty days. Then the days of weeping for Moses were ended. Joshua, the son of Nun was full of the spirit of wisdom, because Moses had laid his hands upon him. The children of Israel hearkened to him, and did as the Lord commanded Moses. There has not arisen a prophet since in Israel like Moses, whom the Lord knew face to face. He performed many signs and wonders, which the Lord sent him to do in the land of Egypt, to the Pharaoh, to all his servants, and to all his land.

JOSHUA

Joshua's Mission (CH 1:1-3, 8, 9)

After the death of Moses, the servant of the Lord, the Lord spoke to Joshua the son of Nun, Moses' minister, saying: "Moses My servant is dead; now therefore arise, go over the Jordan, you, and all your people, to the land which I do give to them, even to the children of Israel. Every place that the sole of your foot shall tread upon, to you have I given it, as I spoke to Moses. This book of the law shall not depart from your mouth, but you shall meditate therein day and night, that you may observe to do according to all that is written therein; for then you shall make your ways prosperous, and then you shall have good success. Have I not commanded you? Be strong and of good courage; do not be afraid, neither be dismayed: for the Lord your God is with you wherever you go."

Ark of the Covenant (CH 4:15-24)

The Lord spoke to Joshua, saying: "Command the priests that bear the ark of the testimony, that they come up from Jordan." Joshua therefore commanded the priests, saying: "Come up from the Jordan." As the priests that bore the ark of the covenant of the Lord came up out of the midst of the Jordan, as soon as the soles of the priests' feet were drawn up to the dry ground, that the waters of the Jordan returned to their place, and went over all its banks, as before.

Joshua's Covenant with the People (CH 24:21-28)

The people said to Joshua: "We will serve the Lord." And Joshua said to the people: "You are witnesses against yourselves that you have chosen to serve the Lord." They said: "We are witnesses. Now therefore put away the strange gods which are among you, and incline your heart to the Lord, the God of Israel." The people then said to Joshua: "The Lord our God will we serve, and to His voice will we hearken."

So Joshua made a covenant with the people that day, and set them a statute and an ordinance in Shechem. Joshua wrote these words in the book of the law of God; and he took a great stone, and set it up there under the oak that was by the sanctuary of the Lord. Joshua said to all the people: "This stone shall be a witness against us; for it has heard all the words of the Lord which He spoke to us; it shall be therefore a witness against you, lest you deny your God." So Joshua sent the people away, every man to his inheritance.

JUDGES

After Joshua (CH 2:6-10)

Now when Joshua had sent the people away, the children of Israel went to his/her inheritance to possess the land. And the people served the Lord all the days of Joshua, and all the days of the elders that outlived Joshua, who had seen all the great work which the Lord had wrought for Israel. And Joshua the son of Nun, the servant of the Lord, died, being a hundred ten years old. They buried him in the border of his inheritance in Timnathheres, in the hill-country of Ephraim, on the north of the mountain of Gaash. All of that generation were gathered to their fathers. There arose another generation after them that did not know the Lord or the work He had wrought for Israel.

Judges and Wayward Israel (CH 2:20-23)

The anger of the Lord was thereby kindled against Israel. And He said: "Because this nation has transgressed My covenant, which I commanded their fathers, and have not hearkened to My voice, I will not henceforth drive out any of the nations that Joshua left when he died. By them I may prove Israel, whether they will keep the way of the Lord to walk therein, as their fathers did keep it, or not." So the Lord left those nations, without driving them out hastily. Neither did He deliver them into the hands of Joshua.

Deborah (CH 5:1-3, 12-13, 24-28)

On that day Deborah and Barak, the son of Abinoam, sang say-
  ing:
When men let their hair grow in Israel,
When the people offer themselves willingly,
Bless the Lord.
Hear, O you kings; give ear, O you princes;
I will sing to the Lord;
I will sing praise to the Lord, the God of Israel.

Awake, awake, Deborah;
Awake, awake, utter a song
Arise, Barak, and lead your captivity, O son of Abinoam.
Then he made a remnant to have dominion over the nobles and
  the people;
The Lord made me to have dominion over the mighty.

Jephthah (CH 11:29-32, 34-40)

Then the spirit of the Lord came upon Jephthah, and he went to Gilead and Manasseh, and then to Mizpeh of Gilead, and from there he went to the children of Ammon. Jephthah vowed a vow to the Lord, and said: "If You will indeed deliver the children of Ammon into my land, then it whatever comes forth from the doors of my house to meet me, when I return in peace from the children of Ammon, it shall be the Lord's, and I will offer it up for a burnt-offering." So Jephthah went to the children of Ammon to fight against them; and the Lord delivered them into his hand.

Then Jephthan came to his house in Mizpah, and his daughter came out to meet him with timbrels and with dances. She was his only child; beside her he had neither son nor daughter. When he saw her, he tore his clothes and said: "Alas, my daughter, you have brought me very low; you have become my troubler, for I have opened my mouth to the Lord, and I cannot go back." She said to him: "My father, you have opened your mouth to the Lord; do to me according to that which has proceeded out of your mouth. Inasmuch as the Lord has taken vengeance for you with respect to your enemies, even of the children of Ammon." And she continued: "Let this thing be done to me: let me alone two months, that I may depart and go down upon the mountains, and bewail my virginity, I and my companions." At the end of two months she returned to her father, who did with her according to his vow. It then became a custom in Israel that the Israeli daughters went four days a year to lament the daughter of Jephthah the Gileadite.

Samson (CH 13:1-5)

The children of Israel again did that which was evil in the sight of the Lord, so the Lord delivered them into the hand of the Philistines for forty years.

There was a certain man of Zorah, of the family of the Danites, whose name was Manoah. His wife was barren and bore not. The angel of the Lord appeared to the woman, and said to her: "You are now barren and have not borne a child, but you shall conceive and bear a son. Now therefore, I pray, do not drink wine or other strong drink and eat no unclean thing. For you shall conceive and bear a son. No razor shall come upon his head, because the chhild shall be a Nazirite to God from the womb. He shall begin to save Israel from the hand of the Philistines."

Delilah (CH 16:4-6)

It happened that Samson loved a woman in the valley of Sorek whose name was Delilah. The lords of the Philistines came up and said to her: "Entice him and see where his great strength lies, and by what means we may prevail against him, so that we can bind and afflict him. We will give you eleven hundred pieces of silver." Delilah then said to Samson: "Tell me, I pray, where your great strength lies, and how you might be bound so that others could afflict you."

Samson in the Temple of Dagon (CH 16:15-20)

Delilah said to Samson: "How can you say 'I love you' when your heart is not with me? You have mocked me three times and have not told me where your great strength lies." When she pressed him daily with her words and urged him, his soul became vexed to death. He finally told her everything by saying to her: "There has not been a razor touching my head because I have been a Nazirite from my mother's womb. If I am shaven, then my strength will depart from me and I shall become weak and be like any other man." When Delilah saw that he had told her all of his heart, she called for the lords of the Philistines, saying: "Come at once, for he has told me all of his heart." Then the lords of the Philistines came to her and brought the money in their hand. She made him sleep upon her knees, and she called for a man and had the seven locks of his head shaven off. She then began to afflict him, and his strength left him. Then she said: "The Philistines are upon you, Samson." He awoke from his sleep and said: "I will go out as at other times and shake myself." But he did not know that the Lord had departed from him. The Philistines laid hold on him and put out his eyes. They brought him down to Gaza and bound him with fetters of brass. He then was put in prison. While he was in prison, the hair on his head began to grow again after he was shaven.

The lords of the Philistines gathered together to offer a great sacrifice to Dagon, their god, and to rejoice. They said: "Our god has delivered Samson, our enemy, into our hand." When the people saw him, they praised their god and said: "Our god has delivered into our hand our enemy, the destroyer of our country, who has slain many of us." When their hearts were merry, they said: "Call for Samson, that he may make us sport." They called for Samson out of the prison-house, and he made sport before them. They set him between two pillars. Samson said to the lad that held him by the hand: "Let me feel the pillars upon which the house rests, that I may lean upon them." The house was full of men and women, and all the lords of the Philistines were there. On the roof there were about three thousand men and women who watched while Samson made sport. Samson called upon the Lord and said: "O Lord God, remember me, I pray, and strengthen me only this once that I may be avenged of the Philistines for my two eyes." Samson took hold of the two middle pillars upon which the house rested and leaned upon them, the one with his right hand and the other with his left. Samson said: "Let me die with the Philistines." He bent with all his might, and the house fell upon the lords and upon all the people that were there. So the dead that he slew at his death were more than he slew during his life.

FIRST SAMUEL

Hannah's Prayer (CH 2:6-8)

The Lord kills and makes alive;
He brings down to the grave and brings up.
The Lord makes poor and makes rich;
He brings low, and He also lifts up.
He raises up the poor out of the dust,
He lifts up the needy from the dung-hill,
To make them sit with princes,
And inherit the throne of glory;
For the pillars of the earth are the Lord's,
And He has set the world upon them.

Samuel's Speech on Kings (CH 8:10-22)

Samuel spoke all the words of the Lord to the people that asked of him to become a king. He said: "This will be the manner of the king that shall reign over you. He will take your sons and appoint them to him for his chariots, and to be his horsemen; they shall run before his chariots. He will appoint them to you for captains of thousands, and captains of fifties; and to plow his ground, to reap his harvest, to make instruments of war and the instruments of his chariots. He will take your daughters to be perfumers, cooks, and bakers. He will take your fields, your vineyards, and your olive-yards, even the best of them and give them to his servants. He will take a tenth of your seed and of your vineyards to give to his offi-cers and to his servants. He will take your servants and your best young men, and your donkeys, and put them to his work. He will take a tenth of your flocks, and you shall be his servants. You shall cry out in that day because of your kind whom you shall have chosen; and the Lord will not answer you in that day."

David and Goliath (CH 17:41-49)

Goliath, the Philistine, came nearer and nearer to David, and the man that carried his shield went before him. When Goliath looked about and saw David, he laughed at him, because he was just a youth, with a ruddy complexion, and of an attractive countenance. The Philistine said to David: "Am I a dog, that you come to me with staves?" Goliath then cursed David by his god. He said to David: "Come to me, and I will give your flesh to the fowls of the air and to the beasts of the field." Then David said to Goliath: You come to me with a sword, a spear, and a javelin. But I come to you in the name of the Lord of hosts, the God of the armies of Israel, who you have taunted. Today the Lord will deliver you into my hand. I will hit you and take your head from you. I will give the carcasses of the Philistines today to the fowls of the air and to the wild beasts of the earth, so that all the earth may know that there is a God in Israel, and that all this assembly may know that the Lord saves not with sword and spear. The battle is the Lord's, and He will give you into our hand." When Goliath arose and came to meet David, David hastened and ran toward the army to meet him. David put his hand in his bag and took out a stone and slung it, hitting Goliath in the forehead. The stone sank into his forehead, and he fell upon his face to the earth.

SECOND SAMUEL

David's Lament over Saul and Jonathan (CH 1:17-21, 23-25)

Your beauty, O Israel, upon your high places is slain!
How are the mighty fallen!

Tell it not in Gath,
Publish it not in the streets of Ashkelon;
Lest the daughters of the Philistines rejoice,

Lest the daughters of the uncircumcised triumph.
You mountains of Gilboa,
Let there be no dew nor rain upon you,
Neither fields of choice fruits;
For there the shield of the mighty was vilely cast away,
The shield of Saul and Jonathan, the lovely and the pleasant
In their lives, even in their death they were not divided;
They were swifter than eagles,
They were stronger than lions.

How are the mighty fallen in the midst of the battle!

Prophet vs. King (CH 12:1-7)

And the Lord sent Nathan to David. Nathan came to David and said to him: "There were two men in one city, the one rich and the other poor. The rich man had many flocks and herds, but the poor man had nothing except one little ewe lamb, which he had bought and reared; it grew up together with him and with his children. It ate of his own morsel and drank of his own cup; it lay in his bosom and was to him as a daughter. There came a traveler to the rich man, and he spared to take of his own flock and of his own herd, to dress for the wayfaring man that came to him. Rather, he took the poor man's lamb and dressed it for the man who came to him." David's anger was greatly kindled against the rich man; and he said to Nathan: "As the Lord lives, the man that has done this deserves to die; he shall restore the lamb fourfold, because he did this thing and because he had no pity."

Nathan said to David: "You are the man. Thus says the Lord, the God of Israel: I anointed you king over Israel, and I delivered you out of the hand of Saul."

Uriah the Hittite, you have smitten Ammon with the sword, and his wife you have taken as your wife.

FIRST KINGS

Solomon's Prayer and Dedication of the Temple (CH 14:27-30)

But will God in very truth dwell on the earth? Heaven, and the heaven of heavens, cannot contain You; how much less this house that I have built. Yet You have respect for the prayer of Your servant and to his supplication, O Lord my God, hearken to the cry and to the prayer which Your servant prays before You this day. May Your eyes be open towards this house night and day, even toward the place for which You have said: My name shall be there; to hearken to the prayer which Your servant shall pray toward this place. Hearken to the supplication of Your servant, and of Your people Israel, when they shall pray toward this place.

Yes, hear in Heaven Your dwelling-place, and when You hear, forgive.

Elijah in the Cave (CH 19:9-16)

Elijah came to a cave and lodged there. The word of the Lord came to him and said: "What are you doing here, Elijah?" Elijah said: "I have been very jealous for the Lord, the God of hosts. The children of Israel have forsaken Your covenant, thrown down Your altars and slain Your prophets with the sword. Only I am left, and they seek to take my life away." God Said: "Go forth and stand upon the mount before the Lord." The Lord passed by, and a strong wind tore the mountains and broke the rocks into pieces. But the Lord was not in the wind. After the wind was an earthquake, but the Lord was not in the earthquake. After the earthquake was a fire, but the Lord was not in the fire. And after the fire came a still small voice. When Elijah heard it, he wrapped his face in his mantle and went and stood in the entrance of the cave.

The Lord said to him: "Go, return to the wilderness of Damascus. When you come you shall anoint Hazael to be king over Aram; and Jehu, the son of Nimshi, you shall anoint to be king over Israel; and Elisha, the son of Shaphat of Abel-meholah, you shall anoint to be a prophet.

Ahab vs. Elijah (CH 21:1-3, 17-20)

After these things, Naboth the Jezreelite had a vineyard, which was in Jezreel, by the palace of Ahab, King of Samaria. Ahab spoke to Naboth, saying: "Give me your vineyard, that I may have it for a garden of herbs, because it is near my home; I will give you a better vineyard to replace it; or, if it seems good to you, I will give you the worth of it in money." Naboth said to Ahab: "The Lord forbid it to me, that I should give the inheritance of my fathers to you."

The word of the Lord came to Elijah the Tishbite, saying: "Arise, go down to meet Ahab, King of Israel, who dwells in Samaria. He is in the vineyard of Naboth, where he has gone to take possession of it. You shall speak to him, saying: "Thus says the Lord: Have you killed and also taken possession? You shall speak to him, saying: Thus says the Lord: In the place where dogs licked the blood of Naboth shall dogs lick your blood." Ahab said to Elijah: "Have you found me, O my enemy?" He answered: "I have found you; because you have given yourself over to do what is evil in the sight of the Lord."

SECOND KINGS

The Mantle of Elijah upon Elisha (CH 2:7-15)

Fifty men of the sons of the prophets went and stood over beyond them at some distance; and the two prophets stood by the Jordan. Elijah took his mantle and wrapped it together. He struck the waters, and they were divided, so that the two prophets crossed over on dry ground. When they had crossed over, Elijah said to Elisha: "Please ask what I shall do for you, before I am taken from you." Elisha said: "Let a double portion of your spirit be upon me." Elijah replied: "You have asked a hard thing. Nevertheless, if you see me when I am taken from you, it shall be done for you; but if not, it shall not be so." As they moved on and talked, a chariot of fire appeared, with horses of fire, which pulled them apart; and Elijah went up by a whirlwind into heaven.

ISAIAH

Teacher of Righteousness (CH 11:1-9)

And there shall come forth a shoot out of the stock of Jesse,
And a twig shall grow forth out of his roots;
And the spirit of the Lord shall rest upon him,
The spirit of wisdom and understanding,
The spirit of counsel and might,
The spirit of knowledge and of the respect of the Lord.
And righteousness shall be as the clothes of his body,
And faithfulness the control of his imagination.
And the wolf shall dwell with the lamb,
And the leopard shall lie down with the kid;
And the calf and the young lion and the lamb together;
And a little child shall lead them.
And the cow and the bear shall feed;
Their young ones shall lie down together;
And the lion shall eat straw like the ox.
And the suckling child shall play on the head of the snake,
And the weaned child shall put his hand on the lion's den.
They shall not hurt nor destroy
In all My holy mountain;
For the earth shall be full of the knowledge of the Lord.
As the waters cover the sea.

God's Uniqueness (CH 44:6)

Thus says the Lord, the King of Israel,
And his Redeemer, the Lord of hosts:
I am the first, and I am the last,
And beside Me there is no God.

Idolatry (CH 44:9-11)

They that fashion a graven image are all of them vanity,
And their delectable things shall not profit;
And their own witnesses see not, nor know;
That they may be ashamed.
Who has fashioned a god, or molten an image
That is profitable for nothing?

Behold, all the people who have done this shall be ashamed;
And the craftsmen skilled above all;
Let them all be gathered together, let them stand up;
They shall fear, they shall be ashamed together.

God of Good and Evil (CH 45:5-7)

I am the Lord, and there is none else,
Beside Me there is no God;
I have protected you, though you have not known Me;
That they may know from the rising of the sun, and from the
    west,
That there is none beside Me;
I am the Lord, and there is none else;
I form the light and create darkness;
I make peace and create evil;
I am the Lord that does all these things.

God's Sovereignty (CH 45:18, 22-23)

For thus says the Lord that created
The heavens,
He is God;
That formed the earth and made it,
He established it,
He created it not a waste,
He formed it to be inhabited:
I am the Lord, and there is none else.

Look to Me and be saved,
All the ends of the earth;
For I am God, and there is none else.
By Myself have I sworn,
The word is gone forth from My mouth in righteousness,
And shall not come back,
That to Me every knee shall bow,
Every tongue shall swear.

Covenant of Peace (CH 54:7-10, 13)

For a small moment have I forsaken you;
But with great compassion will I gather you.

In a little wrath I hid My face from you for a moment;
But with everlasting kindness will I have compassion on you,
Says the Lord our Redeemer.
For this is as the waters of Noah to Me;
For as I have sworn that the waters of Noah
Should no more go over the earth,
So have I sworn that I would not be angry with you,
Nor rebuke you.
For the mountains may depart,
And the hills be removed;
But My kindness shall not depart from you,
Neither shall My covenant of peace be removed,
Says the Lord that has compassion on you.
And all your children shall be taught of the Lord;
And great shall be the peace of your children.

House of Prayer for All Peoples (CH 56:7)

Even them will I bring to My holy mountain,
And make them joyful in My house of prayer;
Their burnt-offerings and their sacrifices
Shall be acceptable upon My altar;
For My house shall be called
A house of prayer for all peoples.

Supremacy of Ethics Over Ritual (CH 58:6-8, 10)

Is not this the fast that I have chosen?
To loose the fetters of wickedness,
To undo the bands of the yoke,
And to let the oppressed go free,
And that you break every yoke?
Is it not to deal your bread to the hungry,
And that you bring the poor that are cast out to your house?
When you see the naked, that you cover them,
And that you hide not yourself from your own flesh?
Then shall your light break forth as the morning,
And your healing shall spring forth speedily;
And your righteousness shall go before you,
The glory of the Lord shall be your reward.

And if you draw out your soul to the hungry,
And satisfy the afflicted soul;
Then shall your light rise in darkness,
And your gloom be as the noonday.

The Covenant of Torah (CH 59:21)

And as for Me, this is My covenant with them, says the Lord; My spirit that is upon you, and My words which I have put in your mouth, shall not depart out of your mouth, nor out of the mouth of your children, nor out of the mouth of your children's children, says the Lord, from henceforth and forever.

The Redemption (CH 60:1-5, 19-20)

Arise, shine, for your light is come,
And the glory of the Lord is upon you.
For, behold, darkness shall cover the earth,
And gross darkness the peoples;
But upon you the Lord will arise,
And His glory shall be seen upon you.
And nations shall walk with your light,
And kings at the brightness of you rising.

Lift up your eyes round about and see:
They all are gathered together, and have come to you;
Your sons come from far,
And your daughters are borne on the side.
And your heart shall throb and be enlarged;
Because the abundance of the sea
Shall be turned to you,
The wealth of the nations shall come to you.
Neither for brightness shall the moon
Give light to you;
But the Lord shall be to you an everlasting light,
And your God your glory.
Your sun shall no more go down,
Neither shall your moon withdraw itself;
For the Lord shall be your everlasting light,
And the days of your mourning shall be ended.

An Economy of Plenty (CH 66:12)

For thus says the Lord:
Behold, I will extend peace to her like a river,
And the wealth of the nations like an overflowing stream.

JEREMIAH

Lord of Justice and Mercy (CH 9:22-23)

Thus says the Lord:
Do not let the wise ones glory in their wisdom,
Neither let the mighty people glory in their might,
Do not let the rich ones glory in their riches;
But let those that do seek glory, glory in this,
That they understand and know Me,
That I am the Lord who exercises mercy,
Justice and righteousness in the earth;
For in these things I delight,
Says the Lord.

Delusion of Idolatry (CH 10:14-15)

Every person is proved to be brutish, without knowledge,
Every goldsmith is put to shame by the graven image,
Molten images are falsehood,
And there is no breath in them.
They are vanity, a work of delusion;
In the time of their visitation they shall perish.

The Tragedy of Exile (CH 22:10)

Weep not for the dead,
Neither bemoan them;
But weep for those that go away,
For they shall return no more,
Nor see their native country.

The Peace of the City (CH 29:5-7)

Build houses and dwell in them; plant gardens, and eat the fruit of them; take wives and give birth to sons and daughters. Accept wives for your sons and husbands for your daughters, that they may bear sons and daughters. Seek the peace of the city where I have caused you to be carried away captive, and pray to the Lord for it; for in that peace shall you have peace.

Divine Love (CH 31:3)

From afar the Lord appeared to me:
"Yes, I have loved you with an everlasting love;
Therefore with affection have I drawn you."

Return to Zion (CH 31:16-20, 29-30)

Thus says the Lord:
Refrain your voice from weeping,
And your eyes from tears;
For your work shall be rewarded, says the Lord;
And they shall come back from the land of the enemy.
And there is hope for your future, says the Lord;
And your children shall return to their own border.
I have surely heard Ephraim bemoaning himself:
"You have chastised me, and I was chastised,
As a calf untrained;
Turn to me, and I shall be turned,
For You are the Lord my God.
Is Ephraim a darling son to Me?
Is he a child that is spoiled?
For as often as I speak of him,
I do earnestly remember him still;
Therefore My heart yearns for him
I will surely have compassion upon him," says the Lord.

In those days they shall say no more:
"The fathers have eaten sour grapes,
And the children's teeth are set on edge."
But all shall suffer for their own iniquities;
Those who eat the sour grapes,
Their teeth shall be set on edge.

EZEKIEL

The Valley of Dry Bones (CH 37:1-14)

The hand of the Lord was upon me; the Lord carried me out in a spirit and set me down in the midst of the valley, and it was full of bones. He caused me to pass around the bones. There were many in the open valley, and they were very dry. He said to me: "Son of Man, can these bones live?" And I answered: "O Lord God, You know." Then He said to me: "Prophesy over these bones and say to them: O you dry bones, hear the word of the Lord: Thus says the Lord God to these bones: I will cause breath to enter into you, and you shall live. I will lay sinews upon you and will put flesh on you; I will cover you with skin and put breath in you. You shall live; and you shall know that I am the Lord."

So I prophesied as I was commanded. As I prophesied, there was a noise and a commotion, and the bones came together, bone to bone. I saw that there were tendons on them, and flesh came up, and skin covered them; but there was no breath in them. Then He said to me: "Prophesy to the breath, prophesy and say to the breath: Thus says the Lord God: Come from the four winds, O breath, and breathe upon these slain, that they may live." So I prophesied as He commanded me, and the breath came into them, and they lived and stood on their feet, an exceedingly large group. Then He said to me: "O Son of Man, these bones are the whole house of Israel. They say: Our bones are dried up, and our hope is lost; we are cut off. Therefore prophesy and say to them: Thus says the Lord God: I will open your graves, and cause you to come up out of your graves, O My people; and I will bring you into the land of Israel. You shall know that I am the Lord, when I have opened your graves, and caused you to come up out of your graves, O My people. I will put My spirit in you, and you shall live, and I will place you in your own land. You shall know that I the Lord have spoken and performed it."

Moreover I will make a covenant of peace with them—it shall be an everlasting covenant with them. I will establish them and multiply them, and will set My sanctuary in the midst of them forever. My dwelling-place also shall be over them. I will be their God, and they shall be My people.

HOSEA

Divine-Human Love (CH 2:21-22)

And I will bind you to Me forever;
Yes, I will bind you to Me in righteousness and in justice, in
  loving kindness and in compassion.
And I will bind you to Me in faithfulness;
And you shall know the Lord.

JOEL

Day of the Lord (CH 4:14-18)

Multitudes, multitudes in the valley of decision!
For the day of the Lord is near in the valley of decision.
The sun and the moon have become black,
And the stars withdraw their shining.
And the Lord shall roar from Zion,
And utter His voice from Jerusalem,
And the heavens and the earth shall shake;
But the Lord will be a refuge to His people,
And a stronghold to the children of Israel.
So shall you know that I am the Lord your God,
Dwelling in Zion My holy mountain;
Then shall Jerusalem be holy,
And no strangers shall pass through her any more.
And it shall come to pass in that day,
That the mountains shall drop down sweet wine,
And the hills shall flow with milk,
And all the brooks of Judah shall flow with waters;
And a fountain shall come forth of the House of the Lord.

AMOS

Seek Good (CH 5:14-15)

Seek good and not evil, that you may live;
And so the Lord, the God of hosts, will be with you, as you say.
Hate the evil and love the good,
And establish justice in the gate;
It may be that the Lord, the God of hosts,
Will be gracious to the remnant of Joseph.

Social Justice (CH 5:23-24)

Take away from Me the noise of your songs;
And let Me not hear the melody of your musical instruments.
But let justice well up as waters,
And righteousness as a mighty stream.

Redemption (CH 9:13-15)

Behold, the days come, says the Lord,
That the plowman shall overtake the reaper,
And the treader of grapes him that sows seed;
And the mountains shall drop sweet wine,
And I will end the captivity of My people Israel,
And they shall build the waste cities, and inhabit them;
And they shall plant vineyards, and drink the wine thereof;
They shall also make gardens, and eat the fruit of them.
And I will plant them upon their land,
And they shall no more be plucked up
Out of their land which I have given them,
Says the Lord your God.

OBADIAH

The Vision of Obadiah (CH 1:1-4, 8, 10-11, 13-15).

Thus says the Lord God concerning Edom:
We have heard a message from the Lord,

And an ambassador is sent among the nations:
"Arise, and let us go forth to her in battle."
Behold, I make you small among the nations;
You are greatly despised.
The pride of your heart has beguiled you,
O you who dwell in the clefts of the rock,
Your habitation on high;
That says in your heart:
"Who shall bring me down to the ground?"
Though you make your nest as high as the eagle,
And though you set it among the stars,
I will bring you down from there,
Says the Lord.

Shall I not in that day, says the Lord,
Destroy the wise people out of Edom,
And discernment out of the mount of Esau?
For the violence done to your brother Jacob shame shall cover
    you,
And you shall be cut off forever.
In the day that you stood aloof,
In the day that strangers carried away his substance,
And foreigners entered into his gates,
And cast lots upon Jerusalem,
Even you were as one of them.

JONAH

(CH 1:1-16; CH 2:1, 2, 11; CH 3:1-4, 5-7, 9, 10; CH 4:1, 4-5, 11)

Now the word of the Lord came to Jonah, the son of Amittia, saying: "Arise, go to Nineveh, that great city, and speak about its sins;
for its wickedness is come up before Me." But Jonah rose to flee to
Tarshish from the presence of the Lord. He went down to Joppa
and found a ship going to Tarshish. He paid his fare and went
down into it to go to Tarshish, from the presence of the Lord.

But the Lord hurled a great wind over the sea, and there was a
mighty tempest, so that the ship was about to be broken. The
mariners were afraid, and everyone cried to God. They cast forth

the wares that were in the ship into the sea to lighten it up. Jonah was down in the innermost parts of the ship, and he was fast asleep. The shipmaster came and said to him: "What do you mean that you sleep during a time like this? Arise, call upon your God, so that we will not perish.

They said to their fellow sailors: "Come, let us cast lots, that we may know who has caused this evil to come upon us." So they cast lots, and the lot fell upon Jonah. Then they said to him: "Tell us, we ask you, what has caused this evil to come upon us: What is your occupation? And from where did you come? What is your country? And of what people are you? He said to them: "I am a Hebrew; and I respect the Lord, the God of heaven, who has made the sea and the dry land." Then were the people exceedingly afraid, and they said to him: "What is it that you have done?" The people knew that he fled from the presence of the Lord, because he had told them.

Then they said to him; "What shall we do to you, that the sea may be calm for us, because the sea grew more and more tempestuous? He said to them: "Take me up and cast me forth into the sea; so the sea will become calm for you; because I know that for my sake this great tempest is upon you." Nevertheless the men rowed hard to bring it to the land, but they could not, because the sea grew more and more tempestuous against them. Therefore they cried to the Lord and said: "We beseech You, O Lord, we beseech You, let us not perish for this man's life. Do not lay upon us innocent blood; for You, O Lord, have done as it pleased You." So they took up Jonah and cast him forth into the sea, and the sea ceased from its raging. Then the men feared the Lord exceedingly; and they offered a sacrifice to the lord and made vows.

The Lord prepared a great fish to swallow Jonah, and Jonah was in the belly of the fish three days and three nights. Then Jonah prayed to the Lord his God out of the fish's belly.

And the Lord spoke to the fish, and it vomited out Jonah upon the dry land.

The word of the Lord came to Jonah the second time, saying: "Arise, go to Nineveh, that great city, and make to it the proclamation that I bid you." So Jonah arose and went to Nineveh, according to the word of the Lord. Now Nineveh was an exceedingly great city, of three days' journey. Jonah entered into the city, and he proclaimed: "In forty days, Nineveh will be overthrown."

And the people of Nineveh believed God; and they proclaimed a fast and put on sackcloth, from the greatest of them even to the least of them. The tidings reached the king of Nineveh, and he arose from his throne and laid his robe from him. He covered himself with sackcloth and sat in ashes. He caused it to be proclaimed and published through Nineveh by the decree of the king of his nobles, saying: "Who knows whether God will not turn and repent, and turn away from His fierce anger, that we will not perish?"

And God saw their works, that they turned from their evil way. God repented of the evil which He said He would do to them; and He did not do it. But it displeased Jonah exceedingly, and he was angry.

The Lord said: "Are you greatly angry?"

Then Jonah went out of the city, and sat on the east side of the city. There he made a booth. He sat under it in the shadow, till he might see what would become of the city. The Lord God prepared a gourd, and made it come up over Jonah, that it might be a shadow over his head, to deliver him from his evil. So Jonah was exceedingly glad because of the gourd. But God prepared a worm when the next morning came, and it scarred the gourd so that it withered. When the sun arose, God prepared a strong east wind; and the sun beat upon the head of Jonah, so that he fainted, and requested that he might die. He said: "It is better for me to die than to live." And God said to Jonah: "Are you greatly angry at the gourd?" He said: "I am greatly angry, even to death." The Lord said: "You have had pity on the gourd, for which you have not labored, and neither did you make it grow. Should I not have pity on Nineveh, that great city, where there are more than sixty thousand persons that cannot discern between their right hand and their left hand?"

MICAH

[Isaiah's] Vision of Peace (CH 4:1-3)

But in the final days it shall come to pass,
That the mountain of the Lord's house shall be established at
the top of the mountains,
And it shall be exalted above the hills;

And peoples shall flow to it.
And many nations shall go and say:
"Come, and let us go up to the mountain of the Lord,
And to the house of the God of Jacob;
And He will teach us of His ways,
And we will walk in His paths."
For out of Zion shall the law go forth,
And the word of the Lord from Jerusalem.
And He shall judge between many peoples,
And shall decide concerning mighty nations afar off;
And they shall beat their swords into plowshares,
And their spears into pruning-hooks;
Nation shall not lift up sword against nation,
Neither shall they learn war any more.

HABAKKUK

Faith (CH 2:4)

Behold, his ego is puffed up, it is not upright in him;
But the righteous shall live by faith.

No Breath in Idols (CH 2:18-20)

What does it profit the graven image,
That the maker has created it,
Even the molten image, and the teacher of lies:
That the maker of his work trusts in it,
To make lifeless idols?
Woe to the one that says to the wood: "Awake",
To the dumb stone: "Arise!"
Can this happen?
Behold, these idols are overlaid with gold and silver,
But there is no breath at all in the midst of them.
The Lord is in His holy temple;
Let all the earth keep silence before Him.
God, the Lord, is my strength;
He makes my feet move swiftly,
And He helps me walk upon high places.

ZEPHANIAH

A Pure Language (CH 3:9)

For then I will turn to the peoples
A pure language,
That they may all call upon the name of the Lord,
To serve Him with one consent.

HAGGAI

The House of Peace (CH 2:5-7, 9)

The word that I covenanted with you when you came out of Egypt I have established, and My spirit abides among you; do not fear. Thus says the Lord; I will shake the heavens and the earth, the sea and the dry land; I will call forth all nations, and the choicest of all nations shall come. I will fill this house with glory, says the Lord of hosts. And in this place will I give peace.

ZECHARIAH

Spirit is Sovereign (CH 4:6)

Then He answered and spoke to me, saying: "This is the word of the Lord to Zerubbabel, saying: Not by might, not by power, but by My spirit shall you prevail."

A Moral Society (CH 7:9-10)

Thus has the Lord spoken, saying: "Execute true judgment; show mercy and compassion for everyone; do not oppress the widow or the fatherless, the stranger or the poor; and let none of you devise evil against your brother or sister in your heart".

Speak Truth (CH 8:16-17)

"These are the things that you shall do: Speak the truth to your neighbor; execute the judgment of truth and peace in your home; let none of you devise evil in your hearts against your neighbor; and love no false oath; for all these are things that I hate, says the Lord."

The Lord is One (CH 14:9)

And the Lord shall be King over all the earth;
In that day shall the Lord be One, and His name One.

MALACHI

The Hearts of Love (CH 3:22-24)

Remember the law of Moses, My servant,
Which I commanded to those in Horeb for all Israel,
Even statutes and ordinances.
Behold, I will send you Elijah the prophet
Before the coming of the great and terrible day of the Lord.
He shall turn the hearts of the fathers to the children,
And the hearts of the children to their fathers.

PSALMS

Living in God's Presence (CH 1:1-6)

Happy is the person that has not walked in the counsel of the
  wicked,
Nor stood in the way of sinners,
Nor sat in the seat of the scornful.
But his delight is in the law of the Lord;
In His law he meditates day and night.
He shall be like a tree planted by streams of water,
That brings forth its fruit in its season,
Whose leaf does not wither;

In whatever he does he shall prosper.
Not so the wicked;
They are like the chaff which the wind drives away.
Therefore the wicked shall not stand in the judgment,
Nor sinners in the congregation of the righteous.
For the Lord regards the way of the righteous;
But the way of the wicked shall perish.

Human Glory (CH 8:4-6)

When I behold Your heavens, the work of Your fingers,
The moon and the stars, which You have established;
What is humankind, that You are mindful of us?
And the children of humanity, that you think of them?
Yet You have made us a little lower than the angels,
And have crowned us with glory and honor.

Divine Absence (CH 10:1-3)

Why do You stand afar off, O Lord?
Why do You hide Yourself in times of trouble?
Through the pride of the wicked the poor are hotly pursued,
They are taken with the devices that they have imagined.
For the wicked boast of their heart's desire,
And the covetous vaunt themselves, though they condemn
The Lord saying in their hearts:
"God has forgotten; He hides His Face, He will never see."

God's Absence as the Void (CH 13:2, 4, 6)

How long, O Lord, will You forget me?
How long will You hide Your face from me?
Behold You, and answer me, O Lord my God;
Lighten my eyes, lest I sleep the sleep of death.
But as for me, in Your mercy do I trust;
My heart shall rejoice in Your salvation.
I will sing to the Lord
Because He has dealt bountifully with me.

God's Search (CH 14:2)

The Lord looked forth from heaven upon the children of the
world,
To see if there were any people of understanding that did seek
after God.

To Speak Truth in One's Heart (CH 15:1-3)

Lord, who shall sojourn in Your tabernacle?
Who shall dwell upon Your holy mountain?
The ones who walk uprightly and work righteousness,
And speak truth in their heart;
That have no slander upon their tongue,
Nor do evil to their fellows,
Nor take up reproaches against their neighbors.

Compresence (CH 16:8-11)

I have set the Lord always before me;
Surely He is at my right hand. I shall not be moved.
Therefore my heart is glad, and my spirit rejoices;
My flesh also dwells in safety;
For You will not abandon me to the path of destruction;
Neither will You suffer your godly one to see the void.
You help me understand the path of life;
In Your presence is the fullness of joy,
In Your right hand is bliss forevermore.

God's Glory (CH 19:2-7, 8-10, 15)

The heavens declare the glory of God,
And the firmament shows His handiwork;
Day to day You utter speech,
And night to night You reveal knowledge;
There is no speech, there are no words
Without their being heard.
Their line is gone out through all the earth,
And their words to the end of the world.
In them He has set a tent for the sun,
Which is as a bridegroom coming out of his chamber,
And rejoices as a strong man to run his course.

His going forth is from the end of heaven,
And his circuit to the ends of it;
And there is nothing hid from our understanding.

The law of the Lord is perfect, restoring the soul;
The testimony of the Lord is sure, making wise the simple.
The precepts of the Lord are right, rejoicing the heart;
The commandment of the Lord is pure, enlightening the eyes.
The fear of the Lord is clean, enduring forever;
The ordinances of the Lord are true; they are righteous alto-
   gether.

Let the words of my mouth and the meditation of my heart
Be acceptable before You,
O Lord, my Rock, and my Redeemer.

The Lord is My Shepherd (CH 23:1-6)

The Lord is my shepherd; I shall not want.
He makes me to lie down in green pastures;
He leads me beside the still waters.
He restores my soul;
He guides me in straight paths for His name's sake.
Yes, though I walk through the valley of the shadow of death,
I will fear no evil
For You are with me;
Your rod and Your staff, they comfort me.
You prepare a table before me in the presence of my enemies;
You have anointed my head with oil; my cup runs over.
Surely goodness and mercy shall follow me all the days of my
   life;
And I shall dwell in the house of the Lord forever.

The Earth is the Lord's (CH 24:1-5)

The earth is the Lord's in all its fullness;
The world, and they that dwell here.
For He has founded it upon the seas,
And established it upon the floods.
Who shall ascend into the mountain of the Lord?
And who shall stand in His holy place?

He that has clean hands and a pure heart;
Who has not taken My name in vain,
And has not sworn deceitfully.
He shall receive a blessing from the Lord,
And righteousness from the God of his salvation.

God's Omnipresence (CH 139:1-13)

Where shall I go from Your spirit?
Or how shall I flee from Your presence?
If I ascend up into heaven, You are there;
If I make my bed in the nether-world, You are there.
If I take the wings of the morning,
And dwell in the uttermost parts of the sea;
Even there would Your hand lead me,
And Your right hand would hold me.
And if I say: "Surely the darkness shall envelop me,
And the light about me shall be night;
Even the darkness is not too dark for You,
But the night shines as the day;
The darkness is even as the light."

Divine Providence (CH 145:4-21)

One generation shall laud Your works to another,
And shall declare Your mighty acts.
The glorious splendor of Your majesty,
And Your wondrous works will I rehearse.
And people shall speak of the might of Your tremendous acts;
And I will tell of Your greatness.
They shall utter the fame of Your great goodness,
And shall sing of Your righteousness.
The Lord is gracious and full of compassion;
Slow to anger and of great mercy.
The Lord is good to all;
And His tender mercies are over all His works.
All Your works shall praise You, O Lord.
The Lord upholds all that fall,
And raises up all those that are bowed down.
The eyes of all wait for You,
And Your give them their food in due season.

Your open Your hand,
And satisfy every living thing with favor.
You are righteous in all of Your ways,
And gracious in all of Your works.
The Lord is near to all who call upon Him,
To all who call upon Him in truth.
He also will hear their cry and will save them.
The Lord preserves all who love Him;
But all the wicked will He destroy.
My mouth shall speak the praise of the Lord;
And let all flesh bless His holy name for ever and ever.

PROVERBS

The Fear of the Lord (CH 1:7)

The fear of the Lord is the beginning of knowledge;
But the foolish despise wisdom and discipline.

The Way to Peace is God's Teaching (CH 3:1-4)

My son, do not forget My teaching;
But let your heart keep My commandments;
For the length of your days, and the years of your life,
And peace, they will add to you.
Bind them about your neck,
Write them upon the table of your heart;
In that way you will find grace and good favor
In the sight of God and humanity.

Wisdom (CH 3:17-18)

Happy is the person that finds wisdom,
And the one that obtains understanding.
Wisdom's ways are ways of pleasantness,
And all her paths are peace.
She is a tree of life to them that lay hold upon her,
And happy is everyone that holds her fast.

Fidelity (CH 5:5-20)

Drink waters out of your own cistern,
And running waters out of your own well,
Let your springs be dispersed abroad,
And streams of water in the streets.
Let them be only your own,
And not strangers' with you.
Let your fountain be blessed;
And have joy with the wife of your youth,
A lovely female and a graceful young woman,
Let her breasts satisfy you at all times;
With her love be ravished always.
Why then will you, my son, be ravished with a strange woman,
And embrace the bosom of an alien?

The Evil Person (CH 6:16-19)

There are six things which the Lord hates,
Yes, seven which are an abomination to Him:
Haughty eyes, a lying tongue,
And hands that shed innocent blood;
A heart that devises wicked thoughts,
Feet that are swift in running to evil;
A false witness that breathes out lies,
And one that sows discord among friends.

The Heart as the Voice of God (CH 6:20-21)

My son, keep the commandments of your father,
And forsake not the teaching of your mother;
Bind them continually upon your heart (the Soul),
Tie them about your neck.

The Soul (Wisdom) (CH 6:22)

When you walk, the Soul shall lead you,
When you lie down, It shall watch over you;
And when you awake, It shall converse with you.

Wisdom (CH 8:22)

The Lord made me as the beginning of His way,

The first of His works of old.

The Wise Woman (CH 14:1)

Every wise woman builds her house
But the foolish pluck it down with their own hands.

God is With the Lowly (CH 14:31)

Those who oppress the poor blaspheme their Maker
But those who are gracious to the needy honor God.

The Wise Person (CH 15:1)

A soft answer turns away wrath;
But a grievous word stirs up anger.

The Wise Word (CH 15:23)

A person has joy in the answer of his/her mouth;
A word in due season, how good is it!

Wonders of Creation (CH 30:18-49)

There are three things which are too wonderful for me,
Yes, four which I do not know:
The way of an eagle in the air;
The way of a serpent upon a rock;
The way of a ship in the midst of the sea;
And the way of a man with a young woman.

Woman of Valor (CH 31:10-12, 23, 25-31)

Who can find a woman of valor?
For her price is far above rubies.
The heart of her husband does safely trust in her,
And he has no lack of gain.
She does him good and not evil
All the days of her life.

Her husband is known in the community,
When he sits among the elders of the land.

Strength and dignity are her clothing;

And she laughs at the time to come.
She opens her mouth with wisdom;
And the law of kindness is on her tongue.
She looks well to the ways of her household,
And does not eat the bread of idleness.
Her children rise up and call her blessed;
Her husband also, and he praises her:
Many daughters have done valiantly,
But you excel them all.
Grace is sometimes deceitful, and beauty is often vain;
But a woman who respects the Lord, she shall be praised.
Give her of the fruit of her hands;
And let her works praise her in the community.

JOB

The Suffering of Job (CH 1:20-22)

Then Job arose and tore his coat; he shaved his head and fell down upon the ground to worship. He said:

Naked I came out of my mother's womb,
And naked shall I return there;
The Lord gave, and the Lord has taken away;
Blessed be the name of the Lord.
For all this—his loss of family, property and health—
Job did not sin or reproach God.

When Job's three friends heard of all the evil that had come upon him, they came, everyone from his/her own place—Eliphaz the Temanite, Bildad the Shuhite, and Zophas the Naamathite. They made an appointment together to come to see him and to comfort him. When they saw him from a distance, they did not recognize him, and they raised their voices and wept. They tore their garments and threw dust upon their heads. Then they sat down with him upon the ground for seven days and nights, and none spoke a word to him, because they saw that his grief was very great.

Job Speaks (CH 3:1-4)

Then Job opened his mouth and cursed the day. Job spoke and said:
> Let the day when I was born perish
> And the night when it was said:
> "A man-child is brought forth."
> Let that day be darkness;
> Let not God inquire after it from above,
> Neither let the light shine upon it.

Death-Wish (CH 3:20-22)

Why is light given to him that is in misery,
And life to the bitter in soul—
Who longs for death, but it does not come;
And digs for it more than for hidden treasures;
Who are the ones that rejoice in exaltation,
And are glad, when they can find the grave? –

Eliphaz Speaks (CH 4:1-8)

Then Eliphaz the Temanite answered and said:
Your words have supported those who are falling;
And you have strengthened feeble knees.
But now grief has come to you, and you are weary;
It touches you, and you are afraid.
Is not your fear of God your confidence,
And your hope the integrity of your ways?
Remember, I pray, who ever perished being innocent?
Or where were the upright cut off?
According to what I have seen, those who plow iniquity,
And sow mischief, reap the same.

Visions of the Night (CH 4:12-17)

A word was secretly brought to me,
And my ear received a whisper of it.
In thoughts from the visions of the night,
When deep sleep falls on everyone,
Fear and trembling came upon me,
And all my bones shook.

Then a spirit passed before my face,
That made my hair stand on end.
It stood still, but I could not discern its appearance;
A form was before my eyes;
I heard a still voice:
Shall mortal beings be just before God?
Shall people be pure before their Maker?

Trust in God (CH 5:8-9)

But as for me, I would seek God,
And to God would I commit my cause;
God does great things and unsearchable,
Marvelous things without number.

God Heals (CH 5:17-19)

Behold, happy is the one whom God corrects;
Therefore do not despise the chastening of the Almighty,
For He makes people sore and binds them up;
He wounds, and His hands make whole.
He will deliver you in six troubles;
Yes, in seven no evil shall touch you.

Optimism (CH 5:27)

We have searched for the world of God, and so it is;
We hear it and know it is for your good.

Job Replies to Eliphaz (CH 6:8-10)

Oh that I might have my request,
And that God would grant me the thing that I long for!
Even that it would please God to crush me;
That He would let loose His hand and cut me off!
Even then I would still have comfort;
Yes, I would exult in pain even though He does not spare me;
For I have not denied the words of the Holy One.
What is my strength, that I should wait?
What is my end, that I should be patient?
Is my strength the strength of stones?
Or is my flesh of brass?

Is it that I have no help in me,
And that sound wisdom is driven from me?

Job Speaks Out (CH 7:11-21)

Therefore I will not refrain my mouth;
I will speak in the anguish of my spirit;
I will complain in the bitterness of my soul.
Am I a sea, or a sea-monster,
That You set a watch over me?
When I say: "My bed shall comfort me,
My couch shall ease my complaint";
Then You scare me with dreams,
And terrify me through visions;
So that my soul chooses strangling,
And death rather than these bones of mine.
I loathe it; I shall not live forever;
Let me alone; for my days are vanity.
What is humanity, that You should magnify us,
And that You should set Your heart upon us,
And that You should remember us every morning,
And try us every moment?
How long will You not look away from me,
Nor let me alone till I swallow my saliva?
If I have sinned, what do I do to You, O watcher of all?
Why have You set me as a mark for You,
So that I am a burden to myself?
And why do You not pardon my transgression,
And take away my iniquity?
For now I shall lie down in the dust;
And You will seek me; but I shall not be.

Bildad's Argument (CH 8:1-3)

Then Bildad the Shuhite answered and said:
How long will you speak these things,
Seeing that the words of your mouth are as a mighty wind?
Does God pervert judgment?
Or does the Almighty twist justice?

Bildad Continues His Defense of God (CH 8:20-22)

Behold, God will not cast away an innocent person,
Neither will He uphold the evil-doers;
Till He fills your mouth with laughter,
And your lips with shouting.
They that hate you shall be clothed with shame;
And the home of the wicked shall be no more.

Job Responds to Bildad (CH 9:20-24)

Though I am righteous, my own mouth shall condemn me;
Though I am innocent, God shall prove me perverse.
I am innocent—I regard not myself,
I despise my life.
It is all one—therefore I say:
God destroys the innocent and the wicked.
If the scourge slays suddenly,
He will mock at the calamity of the guilty.
The earth is given into the hand of the wicked;
God covers the faces of the judges;
If it is not He, who then is it?

Job Continues His Protest (CH 10:18-22)

Why then have You brought me forth out of the womb?
I wish that I had perished, and no eye had seen me!
I should have been as though I had not been;
I should have been carried from the womb to the grave.
Are my days only a few? Cease then,
And let me alone, that I may take comfort a little,
Before I go where I shall not return,
Even to the land of darkness and of the shadow of death;
A land of thick darkness, as darkness itself;
A land of the shadow of death, without any order,
And where the light is as darkness.

Zophar Speaks (CH 11:1-6)

Then Zophar the Naamathite answered and said:
Should not the multitude of words be answered?
And should a man full of talk be accounted right?

Your boastings have made people hold their peace,
And you have mocked, with none to make you ashamed;
You have said: "My doctrine is pure,
And I am clean in Your eyes."
But oh that God would speak,
And open His lips against you;
And that He would tell you the secrets of wisdom,
That sound wisdom is manifold!

Job Answers Zophar (CH 13:2-24)

What you know, I know also;
I am not inferior to you.
Notwithstanding, I would speak to the Almighty,
And I desire to reason with God.
But you are plasterers of lies,
You are all physicians of no value.
Oh that you would altogether hold your peace!
It would be wisdom to do so.
Hear now my reasoning,
And hearken to the pleadings of my lips.
Will you speak unrighteously for God,
And talk deceitfully for Him?
Hold your peace. Let me alone, that I may speak,
And let come on me what will.
I will take my flesh in my teeth,
And put my life in my hand.
Though God slays me, yet will I trust in Him;
But I will argue my ways before Him.
Only do not do two things to me,
Then will I not hide myself from You:
Withdraw Your hand far from me;
And let not Your terror make me afraid.
Then call me, and I will answer;
Or let me speak, and answer me.
How many are my iniquities and sins?
Make me to know my transgression and my sin,
For what reason should You hide Your face,
And hold me for Your enemy?

Job's Sense of Immortality (CH 19:25-27)

As for me, I know that my Redeemer lives,
And that He will witness at the end upon the earth;
And when after my skin is destroyed,
Then without my flesh I shall see God;
Whom I, even I, shall see for myself;
My eyes, and not another's, shall behold Him.

Job's Refusal to Compromise With the Truth of Experience (CH 27:1-6)

Job again took up his parable and said:
As God lives, who has taken away my right;
And the Almighty, who has dealt bitterly with me;
All the while my breath is in me,
And the spirit of God is in my nostrils,
Surely my lips shall not speak unrighteousness;
Neither shall my tongue utter deceit;
Far be it from me that I should justify you;
Till I die I will not give up my integrity.
My righteousness I hold fast and will not let it go;
My heart shall not reproach me so long as I live.

Elihu the Interloper Argues with Job (CH 33:12-18, 29-30)

Behold, I answer you: In this you are not right,
That God is too great for humanity;
Why have you striven against Him?
Seeing that He will not answer any of his words.
For God speaks in one way,
Yes in two, though we do not perceive it correctly.
In a dream, in a vision of the night,
When deep sleep falls upon all,
In slumberings upon the bed;
Then He opens our ears,
And by our chastisement seals the decree,
That all of us may put away our limited purpose,
And that He may hide pride from us;
That He may keep back our lives from temptation,
And our lives from perishing by the sword.

All these things does God work,

Twice, yes three times, with a person,
To bring back his life from temptation,
That he may be enlightened with the light of the living.

God Speaks to Job (CH 38:1-4)

Then the Lord answered Job out of the whirlwind and said:
Who is this that darkens counsel
By words without knowledge?
Gird up your life like a man;
For I will demand that you be accountable to Me.
Where were you when I laid the foundations of the earth?
Shall those that reprove contend with the Almighty?
Those that argue with God, let him answer them.

The Acquiescence of Job (CH 40:3-5 and 42:2-6)

Then Job answered the Lord and said:
I am of small account; what shall I answer You?
I lay my hand upon my mouth.
Once I have spoken, I will not answer again;
Yes, twice, but I will proceed no further.

I know that You can do everything,
And that no purpose can be kept from You.
Who is it that hides counsel without knowledge?
Therefore I have uttered that which I did not understand,
Things too wonderful for me, which I knew not.
Hear, I beg You, and I will speak;
I will demand of You, and declare You to me.
I had heard of You by the hearing of the ear;
But now my eye sees You;
Therefore I abhor my words and repent,
Seeing that I am dust and ashes.
...and the Lord accepted Job and did compensate him in manifold ways.

THE SONG OF SONGS

The Divinity of Love (CH 1:1-3, 5-7, 15-17)

The song of songs, which is Solomon's.
   Let him kiss me with the kisses of his mouth –
   For your love is better than wine.
   I am black, but beautiful,
   O you daughters of Jerusalem,
   As the tents of Kedar,
   As the curtains of Solomon.
   Look not upon me, that I am of dark complexion,
   That the sun has tanned me;
   My mother's sons were incensed against me,
   They made me keeper of the vineyards;
   But my own vineyard I have not kept.
   Tell me, O you whom my soul loves,
   Where you feed, where you make your flock to rest at noon;
   For why should I be as one that veils herself
   Beside the flocks of your companions?

Behold, you are fair, my love; Behold, you are fair;
Your eyes are as doves.

Behold, you are fair, my beloved, yes, pleasant;
Also our resting place is leafy.
The beams of our houses are cedars,
And our panels are cypresses.

Love's Fever (CH 2:2-7)

As a lily among thorns,
So is my love among the daughters.
As an apple-tree among the trees of the wood,
So is my beloved among the sons.
Under its shadow I delighted to sit,
And its fruit was sweet to my taste.
He has brought me to the banqueting-house,
And his banner over me is love.
Keep me with dainties, refresh me with apples;

For I am love-sick.
Let his left hand be under my head,
And his right hand embrace me.
I adjure you, O daughters of Jerusalem,
By the antelopes, and by the animals of the field,
That you do not awaken, nor stir up love,
Until it pleases you.

Mutuality of Love (CH 2:13-14, 16-17)

The fig-tree puts forth her green figs,
And the vines in blossom give forth their fragrance.
Arise, my love, my fair one, and come away.
O my dove, who is in the cleft of the rock, in the shelter of the
    cliff,
Let me see your countenance, let me hear your voice;
For sweet is your voice, and your countenance is attractive.
My beloved is mine, and I am his,
That feeds among the lilies.
Until the day breathes, and the shadows flee away,
Turn, my beloved, and be like an antelope or a young deer
Upon the mountains of spices

Love's Fulfillment (CH 3:1-5)

By night on my bed I sought him whom my soul loves;
I sought him, but I did not find him.
I will rise now and go about the city,
In the streets and in the broad ways,
I will seek him whom my soul loves.
I sought him, but I did not find him.
The watchmen that go about the city found me:
Did you see him whom my soul loves?
Scarcely had I passed from them,
When I found him whom my soul loves.
I held him, and would not let him go,
Until I had brought him into my mother's house,
And into the chamber of her that conceived me.
I adjure you, O daughters of Jerusalem,
By the antelopes, and by the animals of the field,
That we do not awaken, nor stir up love, until it pleases us.

Longing (CH 5:2-6)

I sleep, but my heart wakes;
Hark! My beloved knocks:
Open to me, my sister, my love, my dove, my undefiled;
For my head is filled with dew,
My locks with the drops of the night.
I have put off my coat;
How shall I put it on?
I have washed my feet;
How shall I defile them?
My beloved put in his hand by the hole of the door,
And my heart was moved for him.
I rose up to open to my beloved;
And my hands dropped with myrrh,
And my fingers with flowing myrrh,
Upon the handles of the bar,
I opened to my beloved;
But my beloved had turned away and was gone.
My soul failed me when he spoke.
I sought him, but I could not find him;
I called him, but he gave me no answer.

I Am My Beloved's and My Beloved Is Mine (CH 6:1-3)

Where is your beloved gone,
O our fairest among women?
Where has your beloved turned,
That we may seek him with you?
My beloved is gone down to his garden,
To the beds of spices,
To feed in the gardens,
And to gather lilies.
I am my beloved's, and my beloved is mine,
That feeds among the lilies.

Love's Ecstasy (CH 7:2-14)

How beautiful are your steps in sandals,
O prince's daughter!
The roundings of your thighs are like the links of a chain,
The work of the hands of a skilled workman.

Your navel is like a round goblet,
Where no mingled wine is wanting;
Your belly is like a heap of wheat
Set about with lilies.
Your two breasts are like two fawns
That are twins of a gazelle.
Your neck is as a tower of ivory;
Your eyes as the pools in Heshbon,
By the gate of Bath-rabbim;
Your nose is like the tower of Lebanon
Which looks toward Damascus.
Your head upon you is like Carmel,
And the hair of your head like purple;
The king is held captive in your braids.
How fair and how pleasant you are, O love, for delights!
This your stature is like that of a palm-tree,
And your breasts to clusters of grapes.
I said: I will climb up into the palm-tree,
I will take hold of its branches;
And let your breasts be as clusters of the vine,
And the smell of your countenance like apples;
And the roof of your mouth like the best wine,
That glides down smoothly for my beloved,
Moving gently the lips of those that are asleep.
I am my beloved's,
And his desire is toward me.
Come, my beloved, let us go forth into the field;
Let us lodge in the villages.
Let us get up early to the vineyards;
Let us see whether the vine has budded,
Whether the vine-blossom is opened,
And the pomegranates is in flower;
There will I give you my love.
The mandrakes give forth fragrance,
And at our doors are all manner of previous fruits,
New and old,
Which I have laid up for you, O my beloved.

Love As Strong As Death (CH 8:6)

Set me as a seal upon your heart,

As a seal upon your arm;
For love is strong as death...

RUTH

Ruth and Naomi Are Bonded (CH 1:14-17)

The people raised their voices and wept again. Orpah kissed her mother-in-law, but Ruth held on to her. And she said: "Behold, your sister-in-law has gone back to her people and to her god; return after your sister-in-law." Ruth replied: "Do not ask me to leave you and to return from following after you, because where you go, I will go; where you lodge, I will lodge. Your people shall be my people, and your God my God; where you die, I will die, and there I will be buried. The Lord do whatever He chooses to me, if nothing but death parts you and me."

Naomi Sends Ruth to Boaz (CH 3:1-18)

Naomi, her mother-in-law, said to her: "My daughter, shall I not seek rest for you, that you may be well? There is Boaz, our kinsman, with whose young women you stayed? He will be working with barley tonight in the threshing-floor. Wash yourself therefore, and anoint yourself. Put on your raiment and get down to the threshing-floor. Do not make yourself known to the man until he has finished eating and drinking. It shall be that when he lies down, you shall mark the place where he is resting. You shall then go in and uncover his feet and lie down. He will tell you what you shall do."

So Ruth went down to the threshing-floor and did according to what her mother-in-law asked her. When Boaz had eaten and drunk, and his heart was merry, he went to lie down at the end of the heap of corn. Ruth came softly, uncovered his feet, and lay down. At midnight Boaz was startled and turned himself and discovered Ruth lying at his feet. And he said: "Who are you?" And she answered: "I am Ruth your handmaid. Therefore, spread your blanket over your handmaid, for you are a near kinsman." Boaz said: "Blessed are you of the Lord, my daughter. You have shown more kindness in the end than at the beginning, inasmuch as you did not follow the young men, whether poor or rich. Now, my daughter, do not fear. I will do to you all that you say, because all the men in our community know that you are a virtuous woman.

When Ruth came to her mother-in-law, she said: "Who are you, my daughter?" And Ruth told her all that Boaz had done for her. Ruth said: "These six measures of barley he gave me, and he said to me: "Do not go empty to your mother-in-law." Then Ruth's mother-in-law said: "Sit still, my daughter, until you know how the matter will fall, because Boaz will not rest until he has finished his work today."

Ruth Marries Boaz: Great Grandmother of David (CH 4:9-17)

Boaz said to the elders and to all the people: "You are witnesses today that I have bought all that was Elimelech's, and all that was Chilion's and Mahon's, of the hand of Naomi. Moreover Ruth the Moabitess, the wife of Mahlon, I have asked to be my wife, to raise up the name of the dead upon his inheritance, that the name of the dead shall not be removed from among his relatives and from his home. You are witnesses today."

So Boaz asked Ruth, and she became his wife. The Lord gave her conception, and she bore a son. The women said to Naomi: "Blessed is the Lord, who has not left you this day without a near kinsman, and may his name be famous in Israel. He shall be to you a restorer of life and a nourisher of your old age. Your daughter-in-law, who loves you, and who is better to you than seven sons, has borne him." Naomi took the child and laid it against her bosom and became its nurse. Her neighbors gave it a name, saying: "A son is born to Naomi"; and they called his name Obed. He is the father of Jesse, who in turn is the father of David.

LAMENTATIONS

Jeremiah Mourns Jerusalem (CH 1:1-7, 16-17)

How does the city sit solitary,
That was full of people!
How has she become as a widow!
She that was great among the nations,

And princess among the provinces,
How has she become tributary!
She weeps painfully in the night,
And her tears are on her cheeks;
She has none to comfort her
Among all her lovers;
All her friends have dealt treacherously with her,
They are becoming her enemies.
Judah is gone into exile because of affliction,
And because of great servitude;
She dwells among the nations,
She finds no rest;
All her pursuers overtook her
Within its narrow passages.
The ways of Zion do mourn,
Because none come to the solemn assembly;
All her gates are desolate,
Her priests sigh;
Her virgins are afflicted,
And she herself is in bitterness.
Her adversaries have become the head,
Her enemies are at ease;
For the Lord has afflicted her
For the multitude of her transgressions;
Her young children are gone into captivity
Before the adversary.

Jerusalem remembers
For these things I weep;
My eye, my eye runs down with water;
Because the comforter is far from me,
Even he that should refresh my soul;
My children are desolate,
Because the enemy has prevailed.
Zion spreads forth her hands;
There is none to comfort her;
The Lord has commanded concerning Jacob,
That they who are around him should be his adversaries;
Jerusalem is among them
As one unclean.

Supplication (CH 2:1, 18, 19)

Their heart cried to the Lord
"O wall of the daughter of Zion,
Let tears run down like a river
Day and night;
Give yourself no respite;
Let not the apple of your eye cease.
Arise, cry out in the night,
At the beginning of the watches;
Pour out your heart like water
Before the face of the Lord;
Lift up your hands toward Him
For the life of your young children,
That faint for hunger
At the head of every street."

Jeremiah in the Dungeon (CH 3:49-51, 52-54, 55-57)

My eye is poured out and does not cease,
Without any intermission,
Till the Lord looks forth
And beholds from heaven.
My eye affected my soul,
Because of all the daughters of my city.

They have chased me like a bird,
That are my enemies without cause.
They have cut off my life in the dungeon,
And have cast stones upon me.
Waters flowed over my head;
I said: "I am cut off."

I called upon Your name, O Lord,
Out of the lowest dungeon.
You heard my voice; hide not
Your ear at my sighing, at my cry.
You drew near in the day that I called upon You;
You said: "Fear not."

Edom – Arch Enemy of Israel (CH 4:22)

The punishment of your iniquity is accomplished,
O daughter of Zion,
He will no more carry you away into captivity;
He will punish your iniquity, O daughter of Edom,
He will uncover your sins.

Renew Our Days (CH 5:17-21)

For this our heart is faint,
For these things our eyes are dim;
For the mountain of Zion, which is desolate,
The foxes walk upon it.
You, O Lord, are enthroned forever,
Your throne is from generation to generation.
Why do You forget us forever,
And forsake us for such a long time?
Have us turn to You, O Lord, and we shall be turned;
Renew our days as of old.

ECCLESIASTES

Vanities of Vanities (CH 1:2-7, 9, 15, 18)

The words of Koheleth, the son of David, king in Jerusalem:
    Vanity of vanities, said Koheleth;
    Vanity of vanities, all is vanity.
    What profit have people of all their labor
    When they labor under the sun?
    One generation passes away, and another generation comes;
    And the earth abides forever.
    The sun also rises, and the sun goes down,
    And hastens to the place where it rises.
    The wind goes toward the south,
    And turns about and goes toward the north;
    It turns about continually it its circuit,
    And the wind returns again to its circuits.
    All the rivers run into the sea,
    Yet the sea is not full;

To the place where the rivers go,
There they go again.
That which has been is that which shall be,
And that which has been done is that which shall be done;
And there is nothing new under the sun.
That which is crooked cannot be made straight;
And that which is wanting cannot be numbered.
For in much wisdom is much vexation;
And those who increase knowledge increase sorrow.

A Striving After the Wind (CH 2: 12-17)

I turned myself to behold wisdom, madness, and folly. For what can the person do that comes after the king? Only that which has been already done. Then I saw that wisdom excel folly, as far as light excels darkness.

Wise people, their eyes are in their heads;
But fools walk in darkness.

I also perceived that one event happened to them all. Then I said in my heart: "As it happens even to me; and why was I then more wise?" Then I said in my heart that this also is vanity. For of the wise person, even as of the fool, there is no remembrance forever; seeing that in the days to come all will long ago have been forgotten. The wise person must die even as the fool! So I hated life; because the work that is wrought under the sun was grievous to me. All is vanity and a striving after wind.

To Everything There Is a Season (CH 3:1-8)

To everything there is a season, and a time to every purpose under the sun:
A time to be born, and a time to die;
A time to plant, and a time to pluck up that which is planted;
A time to kill, and a time to heal;
A time to break down, and a time to build up;
A time to weep, and a time to laugh;
A time to mourn, and a time to dance;
A time to cast away stones, and a time to gather stones together;
A time to embrace, and a time to refrain from embracing;
A time to seek, and a time to lose;
A time to keep, and a time to cast away;

A time to rend, and a time to sow;
A time to keep silence, and a time to speak;
A time to love, and a time to hate;
A time for war, and a time for peace.

Life's Portion (CH 9:9-12)

Enjoy life with your wife whom you love all the days of your life, which He has given you under the sun, all the days of your vanity. For that is your portion in life, and in your labor that you do under the sun. Whatever your hand does by your strength, that do; for there is no work, nor device, nor knowledge, nor wisdom, in the grave where you go.

I returned and saw under the sun that the race is not to the swift, nor the battle to the strong, neither yet bread to the wise, nor yet riches to people of understanding, nor yet favor to people of skill; but time and chance happen to them all. For humanity also does not know its time; as the fishes that are taken in an evil net, and as the birds that are caught in the snare, even so are children snared in an evil time, when it falls suddenly upon them.

Cast Your Bread (CH 11:1)

Cast your bread upon the waters,
For you shall find it after many days.

Remember Your Creator (CH 12:1-8)

Remember then your Creator in the days of your youth,
Before the evil days come,
And the years draw near when you shall say:
"I have no pleasure in them";
Before the sun and the light and the moon,
And the stars are darkened,
And the clouds return after the rain;
In the day when the keepers of the house shall tremble,
And the strong men shall bow themselves,
And the grinders cease because they are few,
And those that look out shall be darkened in the windows,
And the doors shall be shut in the street,
When the sound of the grinding is low;
And one shall start up at the voice of a bird,

And the daughters of music shall be brought low;
Also when they shall be afraid of that which is high,
And terrors shall be in the way;
And the almond-tree shall blossom,
And the grasshopper shall drag itself along,
Because people go to their homes,
And the mourners go about the streets;
Before the silver cord is snapped asunder,
And the pitcher is broken at the fountain,
And the wheel falls shattered into the pit;
And the dust returns to the earth as it was,
And the spirit returns to God who gave it.
Vanity of vanities, said Koheleth;
All is vanity.

Trust God (CH 12:13-14)

The end of the matter, all having been heard: trust God, and keep His commandments; for this is the whole person. For God shall bring every work into the judgment concerning every hidden thing, whether it be good or whether it be evil.

ESTHER

Haman – an Edomite (CH 3: 8)

Haman said to King Ahasaerus: "There is a certain people scattered abroad and dispersed among the peoples in all the provinces of your kingdom; and their laws are diverse from those of every people; neither do they keep the king's laws; therefore it does not profit the king to enforce them.

"If I Perish, I Perish" (CH 4:9-12, 13-16)

Hathach came and told Esther the words of Mordecai. Then Esther spoke to Hathach, and gave him a message to Mordecai: "All the king's servants, and the people of the king's provinces, do know that whoever, whether man or woman, shall come to the king into the inner court, who is not called, there is one law for them, that they be put to death, except such to whom the king shall hold out the golden sceptre, that they may live; but I have not been called to come in to the king these thirty days." And they told to Mordecai Esther's words.

Then Mordecai asked them to return his answer to Esther: "Do not think with yourselves that you shall escape the king's house more than all the Jews. For if you altogether hold your peace at this time, then will relief and deliverance arise to the Jews from another place, but you and your father's house will perish. Who knows whether you have not come to royal estate for such a time as this?" Then Esther asked them to return her answer to Mordecai: "Go, gather together all the Jews that are present in Shushan and fast for me. Neither eat nor drink three days, night or day. My maidens and I will fast in like manner; and so will I go in to the king, which is not according to the law. If I perish, I perish.

Mordecai vs. Haman: Purim (CH 9:20-22, 23-26)

Mordecai wrote these things and sent letters to all the Jews that were in all the provinces of King Ahasuerus, both near and far, asking them to keep the fourteenth day of the month Adar, and the fifteenth day of the same, yearly, the days when the Jews had rest from their enemies, and the month which was turned from sorrow to gladness, and from mourning into a good day; that they should make them days of feasting and gladness, and of sending portions one to another, and gifts to the poor.

The Jews took upon them to do as Mordecai had written to them. Haman, the son of Hammedatha, the Agagite, the enemy of all the Jews, had cast the lot to discomfit them and to destroy them. But when Esther came before the king, he commanded by letters that his wicked device, which he had devised against the Jews, should return upon his own head; and that he and his sons should be hanged on the gallows. Therefore they called these days Purim, after the name of Pur (lot).

Speaking Peace (CH 10:3)

Mordecai the Jew was next to King Ahasuerus and well accepted among the Jews and the multitude of his friends, seeking the good of his people and speaking peace to all his friends and relatives.

DANIEL

The Handwriting on the Wall (CH 5:1-7, 13-29)

Belshazzar the king made a great feast to a thousand of his lords and drank wine before the thousand. Behshazzar, while he tasted the wine, commanded his servants to bring the golden and silver vessels which Nebuchadnezzar his father had taken out of the temple which was in Jerusalem, so that the king and his lords, his consorts and his concubines, might drink from them. Soon the servants brought the golden vessels that were taken out of the temple of the house of God at Jerusalem, and the king and his lords, his consorts and his concubines, drank from them. They drank wine, and praised the gods of gold and silver, of brass, iron, wood, and stone.

In the same hour, fingers of a man's hand came forth and wrote on the wall plaster of the king's palace. The king saw the palm of the hand that wrote. Then the king's countenance changed, and he became fearful. He loosened his garments, and his knees hit one another. The king cried aloud to bring in the enchanters, the Chaldeans, and the astrologers. The king spoke and said to the wise men of Babylon: "Whoever shall read this writing, and declare to me the correct interpretation, shall be clothed with purple, have a chain of gold around his neck, and rule as one of three in the kingdom.

Then Daniel was brought before the king. The king spoke and said to Daniel: "Are you Daniel, who is of the children of the captivity of Judah, whom the king my father brought out of Judah? I have heard of you, that the spirit of the gods is in you, and that light and understanding are found in you. The wise men, the enchanters, have been brought before me, that they should read this writing, and make known to me its interpretation. But they could not declare the interpretation of the writing. But I have heard of you, that you can give interpretations. If you can read the writing, and make known to me the correct interpretation, you shall be clothed with purple, have a chain of gold about your neck, and rule as one of three in the kingdom."

Then Daniel answered the king: "Let your gifts be to yourself, and give your rewards to another. Nevertheless, I will read the writing to you, and make known to you the interpretation. O King,

God Most High gave Nebuchadnezzar your father the kingdom, its greatness, glory, and majesty. Because of the greatness that God gave him, all the peoples, nations, and languages trembled and were fearful. Whoever he chose he slew, and whoever he chose he kept alive. Whoever he chose he raised up, and whoever he chose he put down.

But when his heart was hardened, and his spirit was unaffected that he dealt ruthlessly, he was deposed from his kingly throne, and his glory was taken from him. He was driven from his home, his heart was made like the beasts, and his dwelling was with the wild animals. He was fed with grass like oxen, and his body was wet with the dew of the earth, until he knew that God Most High rules in the kingdom of the people, and that He sets up as ruler whomever He wills.

And you, O Belshazzar, have not humbled your heart, though you knew all this, but you have raised yourself against the Lord. Your servants have brought the vessels of His house before you, and you and your lords, your consorts and your concubines, have drunk the wine in them. You have praised the gods of silver and gold, of brass, iron, wood, and stone, which do not see or hear or know. The God in whose hand your breath is, and whose ways should be your ways, you have not glorified.

Then the palm of the hand was brought to him, and this writing was inscribed: MENE MENE, TEKEL UPHARSIN. This is the interpretation of the thing: MENE, God has numbered your kingdom and brought it to an end. TEKEL, you have been weighed in the balance and found wanting. PERES, your kingdom is divided and given to the Medes and Persians." Then Belshazzar commanded that Daniel be clothed with purple, he put a chain of gold about his neck and made a proclamation that he should rule as one of three in the kingdom.

Plot Against Daniel (CH 6:6-12)

Then some men who had been helping said: "We do not find anything against Daniel except with regard to the law of his God." Then these presidents and satraps came to the king and said to him: King Darius, live forever. All the presidents of the kingdom, the prefects and the satraps, the ministers and the governors, have talked together and recommend that the king establish a statute that whoever asks a petition of God or any person for thirty days except you, O king, shall be cast into the den of lions. Now, O king, kindly establish the interdict and sign the writing, so that it cannot be changed, according to the law of the Medes and Persians." Then Darius signed the writing and the interdict.

In the Lion's Den (CH 6:11-13, 17-24)

When Daniel knew that the writing was signed, he went into his home, with his windows open in his upper chamber toward Jerusalem. He kneeled upon his knees three times a day and prayed, giving thanks to God, as he had always done. Then these same men came and found Daniel making petition and supplication before God.

They then returned to the king: "Know, O king, that it is a law of the Medes and Persians, that no interdict or status which the king establishes may be changed." So the king commanded that Daniel be brought to him, and he cast Daniel into the den of lions. The king spoke and said to Daniel: "Your God, whom you serve continually, will deliver you." A stone was brought and laid upon the mouth of the den, and the king sealed it with his own signet, and with the signet of his lords, so that nothing might be changed concerning Daniel.

Then the king went to his palace and spent the night fasting. No diversions were brought before him, and he was unable to sleep. The king arose very early in the morning and went in haste to the den of lions. When he came near the den where Daniel was, he cried with a troubled voice. The king said to Daniel: "O Daniel, servant of the living God, is your God, whom you serve continually, able to deliver you from the lions?" Then Daniel said to the king: "O king, live forever! My God has sent His angel and has shut the lions' mouths, and they have not hurt me. Inasmuch as innocence before God was found in me; and also before you, O king, I have done no hurt." Then the king was exceedingly glad, and commanded that they should take Daniel out of the den. So Daniel was taken out of the den, and no manner of hurt was found on him, because he has trusted in God.

On the End of Days (CH 12:1-12)

At that time shall Michael stand up, the great prince who stands for the children of your people; and there shall be a time of trouble, such as never was since there was a nation even to that time. At that time your people shall be delivered, every one that shall be found written in the book. Many of them that sleep in the dust of the earth shall awake, some to everlasting life, and some to reproaches and everlasting abhorrence. Those that are wise shall shine as the brightness of the heavens, and those that turn the many to righteousness shall shine as the stars forever and ever. But you, O Daniel, save your words and seal the book, even to the time of the end. Many shall run to and fro, and knowledge shall be increased."

Then I Daniel looked, and there stood two others, one on the bank of the river on this side, and the other on the bank of the river on that side. One said to the man clothed in linen, who was above the waters of the river: "How long, shall it be till the end of the wonders?" And I heard the man clothed in linen, who was above the waters of the river, when he lifted up his hands to heaven, and swore by Him that lives forever, that it shall be for a time yet. And he added: "When they have made an end of breaking in pieces the power of the holy people, all these things shall be finished."

I heard, but I did not understand. Then I said: "O my lord, what shall be the latter end of these things?" And he said: "Go your way, Daniel, for the words are sealed till the time of the end. Many shall purify themselves and make themselves refined. But the wicked shall do wickedly; and none of the wicked shall understand. But they that are wise shall understand. From the time that the continual burnt-offering shall be taken away, and the detestable thing that causes dismay is set up, there shall be a thousand two hundred ninety days. Happy is the one who waits, and lives for many more days. But go your way till the end. You shall rest, and shall stand up to receive your verdict at the end of the days."

EZRA

The Proclamation of Cyrus (CH 1:1-8)

In the first year of Cyrus, King of Persia, in order that the word of the Lord by the mouth of Jeremiah might be accomplished, the Lord stirred up the spirit of Cyrus, so that he made a proclamation throughout his kingdom, and also put it in writing, saying: "Thus says Cyrus, King of Persia: All the kingdoms of the earth have the Lord, the God of heaven, given me. He has charged me to build Him a house in Jerusalem, which is in Judah. Whoever there is among you of all His people – his God be with him – let him go up to Jerusalem, which is in Judah, and build the house of the Lord, the God of Israel. He is the God who is in Jerusalem. Those who are left, in any place where they live, let the people of their places help them with silver and gold, with goods and beasts, beside the freewill-offering for the house of God which is in Jerusalem.

Then the heads of fathers' houses of Judah and Benjamin, and the priests and the Levites, arose, all whose spirit God had stirred to go up to build the house of the Lord which is in Jerusalem. All those who were around them strengthened their hands with vessels of silver, gold, goods, animals, and precious things, beside all that was willingly offered. Cyrus the King brought forth the vessels of the house of the Lord, which Nebuchadnezzar had taken from Jerusalem, and put them in the house of his gods. Cyrus, King of Persia, even brought forth those by the hand of Mithredath the treasurer, and numbered them for Sheshbazzar, the prince of Judah.

To Build a House of God in Zion (CH 5:1-3)

The prophets, Haggai the prophet, and Zechariah the son of Iddo, prophesied to the Jews that were in Judah and Jerusalem. In the name of the God of Israel they prophesied to the Jews. Then Zerubbabel the son of Shealtiel, and Jeshua the son of Jozadak rose up and began to build the house of God which is at Jerusalem; with them were the prophets of God helping them. At the same time Tattenia, the governor beyond the river, and Shethar-bozenai, and their companions came to them and said to them: "Who gave you a decree to build this house and to finish this structure?"

A Promise Fulfilled (CH 6: 1-5)

Then Darius the King made a decree, and search was made in the house of the archives, where the treasures were laid up, in Babylon. There was found at Ahmetha, in the palace that is in the province of Media, a scroll. On it was written: "A record. In the first year of Cyrus the King, Cyrus made a decree: Concerning the house of

God at Jerusalem, let the house be built, the place where they offer sacrifices, and let the foundations be strongly laid: the height being threescore cubits and the breadth threescore cubits; with three rows of great stone, and a row of new timber. Let the expenses be given out of the king's house, and also let the gold and silver vessels of the house of God, which Nebuchadnezzar took forth out of the temple at Jerusalem and brought to Babylon be brought back to the temple at Jerusalem, every one to its place in the house of God."

NEHEMIAH

A Prayer of Redemption (CH 1:1-6)

The words of Nehemiah, the son of Hacaliah:

In the month Chislev, in the twentieth year, as I was in Shushan the castle, that Hanani, one of my friends, came out of Judah, he and certain people. I asked them about the Jews that had escaped, that were left of the captivity, and about Jerusalem. They said to me: "The remnant that are left of the captivity there in the province are in great affliction and reproach. The wall of Jerusalem also is broken down, and the gates have been burned with fire."

When I heard these words, I sat down and wept; I mourned for several days. I fasted and prayed before God and said: "I beseech You, O Lord, the God of heaven, the great and awful God, who keeps covenant and mercy with those who love Him and keep His commandments. Let Your ear now be attentive, and Your eyes open, that You may hearken to the prayer of Your servant, which I pray before You at this time for the children of Israel, Your servants.

A Shovel, a Spear, and a Horn (CH 4:9-14)

When our enemies heard that it was known to us, and that God had brought their counsel to nothing, that all of us returned to the wall, every one to his work. From that time forth, half of my servants went to work, and half of them held the spears, shields, bows, and coats of mail. The rulers were behind all the house of Judah. Those that built the wall, and those that bore burdens loaded themselves, every one with one of his hands wrought in the work, and with the other held his weapon. The builders had their swords girded by their side and so continued to build the wall. The one who sounded the horn was by me. I said to the nobles, to the rulers, and to the rest of the people: "The work is great and large, and we are separated upon the wall, one far from another. In whatever place you hear the sound of the horn, come to us. Our God will fight for us."

Ezra Teaches the People Torah (CH 8:1-6, 9)

When the seventh month came, and the children of Israel were in their cities, all the people gathered themselves together into the broad place that was before the water gate. They spoke to Ezra, the scribe, to bring the book of the Law of Moses, which the Lord had commanded to Israel. Ezra, the priest, brought the Law before the congregation, both men and women, and all that could hear with understanding, upon the first day of the seventh month. He read from the Law in the broad place that was before the water gate from early morning until midday, in the presence of the men and the women, and the ears of all the people were attentive to the book of the Law.

Ezra, the scribe, stood upon a pulpit of wood, which they had made for the purpose. Beside him stood Mattithiah, Shema, Anaiah, Uriah, Kilkiah, and Maaseiah on his right hand. On his left hand stood Pedddaiah, Mishael, Malchijah, Hashum, Hahsbaddanah, Zechariah, and Meshullam. Ezra opened the book in the sight of all the people — for he was above them — and when he opened it, all the people stood up. Ezra blessed the Lord, the great God. All the people answered: "Amen, Amen," with the lifting up of their hands. They bowed their heads and fell down before the Lord, with their faces to the ground.

Nehemiah, who was the Tirshatha, and Ezra the scribe, and the Levites that taught the people, said to everyone: "This day is holy to the Lord your God. Do not mourn or weep." For all the people wept when they heard the words of the Law.

FIRST CHRONICLES

David Dedicates Ark of the Covenant to the Lord (CH 16:23-33)

Sing to the Lord, all the earth:
Proclaim His salvation from day to day.
Declare His glory among the nations,
His marvelous works among all the peoples.
For great is the Lord, and highly to be praised;
He also is to be feared above all gods.
For all the gods of the peoples are things of nought;
But the Lord made the heavens.
Honor and majesty are before Him;
Strength and gladness are in His place.
Ascribe to the Lord, you relatives of the peoples,
Ascribe to the Lord glory and strength.
Ascribe to the Lord the glory due His name;
Bring an offering, and come before Him;
Worship the Lord in the beauty of holiness.
Tremble before Him, all the earth;
The world also is established that it cannot be moved.
Let the heavens be glad, and let the earth rejoice;
And let them say among the nations: "The Lord reigns."
Let the sea roar, and the fullness thereof;
Let the field exult, and all that is therein;
Then shall the trees of the wood sing for joy,
Before the Lord, for He is come to judge the earth.

SECOND CHRONICLES

Solomon's Prayer Concerning the Stranger (CH 6:32-33)

Moreover concerning the stranger, that is not of Your people Israel, when he shall come out of a far country for Your great name's sake, and your mighty hand, and Your outstretched arm; When they shall come and pray toward this house; then hear You from heaven, even from Your dwelling-place, and do according to all that the stranger calls to You for; that all the peoples of the earth may know Your name, and respect You, as do Your people Israel, and that they may know that Your name is called upon this house which I have built.

MISHNAH

Ethics of the Fathers
(CH 1:2, 12, 14, 18)

Simeon the Just was one of the last survivors of the Great Assembly. He used to say: Upon three things does the world stand: upon the divine teachings, upon the divine worship, and upon deeds of loving kindness.

Hillel and Shammai received the Torah from (their teachers). Hillel said: Be of the disciples of Aaron, loving peace and pursuing peace, loving humanity and bringing them near to the Torah. Hillel used to say: If I am not for myself, who is for me? And being only for my own self, what am I? And if not now, when?

Rabban Simeon ben Gamaliel said: By three things is the world sustained: By truth, by justice and by peace, as it is said (Zechariah 8:16): "Render in your world judgments that are true and make for peace."

(CH 2:5, 13, 16, 20, 21)

Hillel said: Do not keep aloof from the community, and trust not in yourself until the day of your death, and judge not your fellow beings until you have been placed in the other person's position, and do not say anything that cannot be understood, in the hope that it will be understood in the end. Do not say: "When I have leisure I will study," because you may never have leisure.

Rabban Johanan ben Zakkai said to them: Go forth and see what is the best way to which a person should be devoted. Rabbi Eliezer said: A good eye. Rabbi Joshua said: A good companion. Rabbi Jose said: A good neighbor. Rabbi Simeon said: The one who considers what may result from his/her actions. Rabbi Eleazar said: A good heart. Thereupon he said to them, I approve the words of Elazar, the son of Arakh, rather than your words, for in his words, yours are included.

Rabbi Joshua said: The evil eye, the evil impulse, and hatred of humanity put a person out of this world.

Rabbi Tarfon said: The day is short, the task is great, the laborers are idle, and the wage is great, and the Master is urgent.

Rabbi Tarfon used to say: It is not your duty to complete the task, but niether are you free to desist from it.

(CH 3:2, 11-13, 18, 22)

Rabbi Hanina, the deputy High Priest, said: Pray for the welfare of the ruling power, since but for fear of it, people would swallow up each other alive.

Rabbi Hanina ben Dosa Said: The one whose fear of sin comes before his wisdom, his wisdom endures; but the one whose wisdom comes before his fear of sin, his wisdom does not endure.

He used to say: He whose deeds exceed his wisdom, his wisdom endures; but he whose wisdom exceeds his deeds, his wisdom does not endure.

He used to say: He in whom the spirit of humanity finds delight, in him the Spirit of the All-present finds delight; but the one in whom the spirit of humanity finds no pleasure, the Spirit of the All-present finds no pleasure.

Rabbi Akiba taught: Beloved is the human person, for s/he was created in the image of God; but it was by an exceedingly great love that it was made known to them that they were created in the image of God. Beloved is Israel, for they are called children of God (Makom). But it was by an exceedingly great love that it was made known to them that they were called children of the "Makom." And beloved are they that they were given a precious instrument and by an exceedingly great love was it made known to them that they were given this precious instrument by which the world was created, as it is written: "For I give you a good doctrine; do not forsake My law."

Rabbi Eleazar ben Azariah used to say: He whose wisdom exceed deeds, to what is he like? To a tree whose branches are many but whose roots are few, and the wind comes and uproots it and overturns it; as it is written (Jeremiah 17:6): "He is like a shrub in the desert and shall not see any good come. He shall inhabit the parched places in the wilderness." But he whose deeds exceed his wisdom, to what is he like? To a tree whose branches are few but whose roots are many; so that even if all the winds in the world come and blow against it, it cannot be moved from its place; as it is written (loco citato 8): "And he shall be like a tree planted by the waters, and spreads out its roots by the river, ands shall not fear when heat comes, and its leaves shall be green; and shall not be troubled in the year of drought, neither shall it cease from yielding fruit."

(CH 4:1, 14)

Ben Zoma said: Who is wise? He that learns from all beings, as it is written (Psalm 119:99): "From all my associates have I gained knowledge." Who is mighty? He who subdues his evil impulse, as sit is written (Proverbs 16:32): "He that is slow to anger is better than the mighty, and he that rules his spirit than he that takes a city." Who is rich? He that rejoices in his portion, as it is written (Psalms 128:2): "When you labor with your own hands happy shall you be, and it shall be well with you." Happy shall you be –in this world; and it shall be well with you—in the world to come. Who is honored? He who honors humanity, for it is written (I Samuel 2:30): "For them that honor Me I will honor, and they that despise Me shall be lightly esteemed."

Rabbi Johanan, the sandal-maker, said: Any assembly which is for the sake of Heaven shall in the end be established, but any assembly which is not for the sake of Heaven shall in the end not be established.

MISHNA

Covenant of Noah

Our Rabbis taught: Seven precepts were the children of Noah commanded: To establish courts of justice; to refrain from blasphemy, idolatry, adultery, bloodshed, robbery, and eating flesh cut from a living animal.[1]

---

[1] Mishna Sanhedrin 56. These seven laws of Noah represent seven categories of law from which are derived at least 66 specific laws constituting a system for a universal morality, (Lichtenstein, A.)

On the Sanctity of the Human Person

Therefore a single person was created in the world to teach that if anyone has caused a soul to perish, Scripture treats him as though he had caused a whole world to perish; and if anyone saves alive a single soul, Scripture treats him as though he had saved a whole world. Again, for the sake of peace among humanity, that none should say to his fellow, "My father was greater than your father"; also that the heretics should not say, "There are many ruling powers in heaven". Again to proclaim the greatness of the Holy One, blessed is He; for we stamp many coins with the one seal and they are all like one another; but the King of kings, the Holy One, blessed is He, has stamped everyone with the seal of the first person, yet not one of them is like his fellow. Therefore everyone must say, for my sake was the world created.[2]

TALMUD

The Soul and the Holy One

Rabbi Shimi bar Ukba said to Rabbi Shimon ben Pazzi:

What is the meaning of the passage in Psalms 103:1: "Bless the Lord, O my soul and all that is within me; bless His holy name." ... In reference to what did David recite this passage? He said it, replied Rabbi Shimon B. Pazzi, in reference to the Holy One blessed be He and in reference to the soul.

Even as the Holy One, blessed be He, fills the whole world, so does the soul fill the whole body.

Even as the Holy One, blessed be He, sees but is not seen, so does the soul see and is not seen.

Even as the Holy One, blessed be He, feeds the whole world, so does the soul feed the whole body.

Even as the Holy One, blessed be He, is pure, so is the soul pure.

And just as the Holy One, blessed be He, dwells in a hidden place, so does the soul dwell in a hidden place.

---

[2] Mishna Sanhedrin 4:5.

Therefore, let that (the soul) which possesses these five attributes come forth and praise Him who possesses these same five attributes.[3]

MIDRASH

Treatise on Peace

Rabbi Joshua ben Levi said: Great is peace, for peace is to the world as leaven is to dough. Had not the Holy One, blessed be He, given peace to the earth, the sword and the beast would have robbed the world of its children. Whence do we know this? From what is written, And I will give peace in the land ... and I will cause evil beasts to cease out of the land, neither shall the sword go through your land; and land means nothing else than Israel, as it is stated, All nations shall call you happy; for you shall be a delightful land. (And so Solomon declared,) One generation passes away, and another generation comes; and the earth abides forever. Solomon said: Although a generation passes away and another generation comes, one kingdom goes and another kingdom comes, one decree passes away and a new decree is imposed upon Israel, the earth abides forever, i.e., Israel will abide forever, they are not forsaken nor will they be forsaken, they are not destroyed nor will they be destroyed, as it is stated, For I the Lord do not change; and you, O children of Jacob, are not consumed—as I have not changed nor will I change, so you, the House of Jacob, are not destroyed and will not be destroyed, but (as it is stated), You that did cleave to the Lord your God are alive this day.

There they taught: Rabban Simeon ben Gamaliel used to say: By three things does the world endure: justice, truth, and peace. Rabbi Muna said: The three are one, because if justice is done, truth has been effected and peace brought about; all three are mentioned in one verse, as it is stated, Execute the judgment of truth and peace in your land, (indicating that) wherever justice is done peace is to be found.

---

[3] Berachot 10A.

Rabbi Joshua said: Great is peace, for the covenant with the priests was made with (the word) "peace," as it is stated, Behold, I give to him My covenant of peace.

Rabbi Joshua said: Great is peace, for the name of the Holy One, blessed be He, is called "peace", as it is stated, And he called it "Adonai—Shalom." Rabbi Hiyya ben Abba said: Hence it can be deduced that a person may not extend a greeting of peace to his fellow in a place of filth, because it is stated, And Gideon built an altar there to the Lord and called it "Adonai—Shalom." Now if an altar which does not eat, drink or smell and was erected only to make an atonement for (the sins of) Israel is called "peace", he who loves peace and pursues peace, who welcomes people with the greeting of peace and responds with peace, and who maintains peace between Israel and their God, how much more so! Rabbi Jose the Galilean said; Even the same of the Messiah is called "Peace", (as it is stated): And his name is called … Abi-ad-sar-shalom, "the everlasting prince of peace."

Rabbi Joshua said: Great is peace, for it is given (as a blessing) to the living and the dead. From what source is it to the living? (As it is stated): And Jethro said to Moses: "Go in peace." And from what source to the dead? (As it is stated): But you shall go to your fathers in peace.

Rabbi Joshua of Siknin said in the name of Rabbi Levi: Great is peace, for all benedictions and prayers conclude with "peace." In the case of the benedictions of the Shema one concludes with "peace": (Blessed are You, O Lord.) Who spreads the tabernacle of peace; in the case of prayers one concludes with "peace": (Blessed are You, O Lord) who make peace.

Rabbi Joshua ben Levi said: The Holy One, blessed be He, said to Israel, "You have brought about the destruction of My Temple and the dispersion of My children; pray, therefore, for the peace (of Zion) and I will give you peace"; as it is stated, Pray for the peace of Jerusalem, and it also declares, Peace be within your walls, and it is also stated, For my friends and companions' sakes, I will now say: Peace be within you.

As for those who love peace, pursue peace, and give the greeting of peace and respond with peace, the Holy One, blessed be He, will cause them to inherit life in this world and life in the world to come, as it is stated, But the humble shall inherit the land, and delight themselves in the abundance of peace.

CHRISTIAN SCRIPTURES

INTRODUCTION

OLD TESTAMENT

All of the Christian Scriptures are, directly or indirectly, of Hebrew origin. The Old Testament itself contains the basis of historic Judaism, particularly in the Pentateuch (or the first five books of the Bible). Christians have adopted the Old Testament as an essential part of their canon, but it is supplemented by the books of the New Testament.

Judaism traces its origin to the life and teachings of Moses around 1200 B.C., when he freed the Israelites from captivity in Egypt and established them in the worship of Jehovah. Their religion, which was called "the religion of Israel", eventually became so universal in its conceptions that it is still able to hold the Jews together, even though they are scattered throughout the world.

Christians see the Old Testament as essential to their faith because Jesus was a Jew, and because the roots of Christian faith come from many of the teachings and prophecies of the Hebrew Bible. Thus the same scriptural material is used by both religions though often seen in a different light.

The Life and Teachings of Jesus of Nazareth

This document contains a unified picture of the life and teachings of Jesus, as told in the four gospels, but interpreted in the modern light. Here, while Jesus is still the great figure of the Palestinian setting, he speaks in terms meaningful in the world of today, thereby showing the result of approximately two thousand years of slow, but eventually inevitable, progress in religious thought. The term "Christ" is used to mean the enlightened individual who is thought by Christians to have fulfilled the Jewish messianic prophecies; this interpretation makes the notion approximately parallel to the term "Buddha" in the Buddhist tradition.

Probably the most prominent single idea which Jesus taught was that of the Kingdom of God. To him it was conceived as a supernatural kingdom which would come at the expected end of the natural world. Although Jesus was incorrect in his notion that the world would end "within a generation," he did have many timeless insights about the Kingdom and about the people who would be part of it. However, instead of the Kingdom's being a social utopia on earth, as many modern Christians have concluded, it is much more adequate as an inner condition of lasting happiness, which should be apparent in the parables and other teachings.

Other New Testament Writings

The books of the Christian Bible (the "New Testament") that follow the gospels show the process of change which Christianity underwent in becoming adapted to the needs of many different kinds of people. Of course, most of the writings contain some doctrine suitable to this particular religion. Perhaps the best way to describe the essential worth which these books contribute to religion is to say that they express the perfectionist ethics of Jesus in a variety of ways which are more nearly attainable by the society than were the original ideals themselves. Relatively little mysticism is present, as compared with the Bhagavad Gita and the Tao-Te-Ching; rather, the stress is upon God's love as applied to daily living.

The section entitled "Paul the Apostle" gives a general picture of the towns and cities which Paul, the man most responsible for the establishment of the Christian Church, visited while on his missionary journeys. His teachings are given as speeches at these various locations, rather than as letters to them; also, two of Paul's co-workers are given advice as to what their own teachings should be. Whether modern scholarship finds all of these words to be Pauline or not makes no difference in this interpretation. The important item is the present worth of the teachings themselves.

Later sections are in letter form, and comprise those writings of other disciples and followers of Jesus which still have outstanding value for today.

OLD TESTAMENT

The Ten Commandments

You shall believe in no lesser ideal than union with God.

You shall not make yourself a graven image, or any likeness of anything that is eternal; you shall not bow down to them or serve them; for misery visits those who do not seek God, whereas happiness may be found by those who love God and keep its commandments.

You shall not make religion profane; for misery is sure to follow.

Remember to save time for meditation on holy ideas. Most of the time you shall labor, and do your work; but some time must be spent in solitude; in it you shall not do any exhausting work, you, or your son, or your daughter, or any of your acquaintances; for what was created by labor was first conceived in meditation; therefore this time is blessed above all other.

Honor your father and your mother; that your days may be happier than otherwise.

You shall not kill.

You shall not commit adultery.

You shall not steal.

You shall not bear false witness against your neighbor.

You shall not covet your neighbor's house; you shall not covet your neighbor's wife, or his children, or his pets, or anything that is your neighbor's.

Other Commandments

You shall not utter a false report. You shall not join hands with a wicked individual, to be a malicious witness. You shall not follow a multitude to do evil; nor shall you bear witness in a suit, turning aside after a multitude, so as to pervert justice; nor shall you be partial to a poor person in his/her suit.

If you meet your enemy's ox or donkey going astray, you shall bring it back to him. If you see the donkey of one who hates you weighed down by its burden, you shall help the donkey to lift it up.

You shall not pervert justice due to the poor. Keep far from a false charge, and do not slay the innocent and righteous, for the wicked will not be acquitted in the long run. And you shall take no bribe, for a bribe blinds the officials and subverts the cause of those who are in the right.

You shall not oppress a stranger; you know the heart of a stranger, for you were strangers yourselves at one time or another.

You shall not oppress your neighbors or rob them. The wages of a hired servant shall not remain with you even a night after they are due to be paid. You shall not curse the deaf or put a stumbling block before the blind.

You shall do no injustice in judgment; you shall not be partial to the poor or defer to the great, but in righteousness shall you judge your neighbor. You shall not go up and down as a slanderer among your people, and you shall not stand forth against the life of your neighbor.

You shall not hate your neighbors in your heart, but you shall reason with your neighbors, lest you bear sin because of them. You shall not take vengeance or bear any grudge against the children of your own people, but you shall love your neighbor as yourself.

And these words shall be upon your heart; and you shall teach them diligently to your children, and shall talk of them when you sit in your house, and when you walk by the way, and when you lie down, and when you rise.

When you rule justly over people, ruling in the awareness of the Spirit, you dawn on them like the morning light, like the sun shining forth upon a cloudless morning, like rain that makes grass sprout from the earth.

Elijah's Inspiration

And Elijah came to a cave, and lodged there; and behold, he was inspired to go forth and stand upon the mount before him. And behold, a strong wind tore into the mountains, and broke in pieces the rocks, but God was not readily to be found in the wind; and after the wind an earthquake, but God was not apparent in the earthquake; and after the earthquake a fire, but God was not in the fire; and after the fire a great calm followed. And when this occurred, Elijah heard the voice of God speaking to him. This is the inspiration which guides all great individuals and gives them courage.

The Story of Job

There was a man in the land of Uz, whose name was Job; and that man was blameless and upright, one who sought God and turned away from evil. There were born to him seven sons and three daughters. He had seven thousand sheep, three thousand camels, five hundred yoke of oxen, and five hundred donkeys, and very many servants; so that this man was the greatest of all the people of the east. His sons used to go and hold a feast in the house of each on his day; and they would send and invite their three sisters to eat and drink with them. And when the days of the feast had run their course, Job would send and sanctify them (as they did in those days); for Job said, "It may be that my sons have sinned." Thus Job did continually.

Now there was a day when his sons and daughters were eating and drinking wine in their eldest brother's house; and there came a messenger to Job, and said, "The oxen were plowing and the donkeys feeding beside them; and the Sabeans fell upon them and took them, and slew the servants with the edge of the sword; and I alone have escaped to tell you." While he was yet speaking, there came another, and said, "Fire has burned up the sheep and the servants, and consumed them; and I alone have escaped to tell you." While he was yet speaking, there came another, and said, "The Chaldeans formed three companies, and made a raid upon the camels and took them, and slew the servants with the edge of the sword; and I alone have escaped to tell you." While he was yet speaking, there came another, and said, "Your sons and daughters were eating and drinking wine in their eldest brother's house; and behold, a great wind came across the wilderness, and struck the four corners of the house, and it fell upon the young people, and they are dead. I alone have escaped to tell you."

Then Job arose and tore his robe, and fell upon the ground. He said, "Naked I came from my mother's womb, and naked shall I return; but I shall not turn aside from truth."

Job became afflicted with loathsome sores from the sole of his foot to the crown of his head. Then his wife said to him, "Do you still hold fast your integrity?"

He then said to her, "You speak as one of the foolish women would speak. Shall we receive good in life, and shall we not receive evil?"

Now when Job's three friends heard of all this evil that had come upon him, they came each from his own place—Elphaz the Temanite, Bildad the Shuhite, and Zophar the Naamathite. They made an appointment together to come to console with him and comfort him. And when they saw him from afar, at first they did not recognize him, and they raised their voices and wept. Then they sat with him on the ground seven days and seven nights, and no one spoke a word to him, for they saw that his suffering was very great.

After this Job opened his mouth and cursed the day of his birth. Job said:

Let the day perish wherein I was born, and the night which said,
'A man-child is conceived.'
Let that day be darkness!
Let gloom and deep darkness claim it.
Let clouds dwell upon it; let the blackness of the day terrify it.
That night—let thick darkness seize it!
Let it not rejoice among the days of the year; let it not come
into the number of the months.
Yes, let that night be barren; let no joyful cry be heard in it.
Let the stars of its dawn be dark; let it hope for light, but have
none, nor see the eyelids of the morning; because it did not

shut the doors of my mother's womb, nor hide trouble from
my eyes.

Why did I not die at birth, come forth from the womb and ex-
pire?
Why did the knees receive me?
Or why the breasts, that I should suck?
For then I should have lain down and been quiet;
I should have slept; then I should have been at rest, with kings
and counselors of the earth who rebuilt ruins for themselves,
or with princes who had gold, who filled their houses with sil-
ver.
Or why was I not as a hidden untimely birth,
As infants that never see the light?
There the wicked cease from troubling, and there the weary are
at rest.
There the prisoners are at ease together; they hear not the voice
of the taskmaster.
The small and the great are there, and the slave is free from
his/her master.

Why is light given to the one that is in misery, and life to the
bitter in soul, who long for death, but it comes not, and dig
for it more than for hid treasures; who rejoice exceedingly,
and are glad, when they find the grave?
Why is light given to one whose way is hid, whom Life has
hedged in?
For my sighing comes as my bread, and my groanings are
poured out like water.
For the thing that I fear comes upon me, and what I dread befalls me.
I am not at ease, nor am I quiet;
I have no rest; but trouble comes.

Then Eliphaz the Temanite answered:
"If one ventures a word with you, will you be offended?
Yet who can keep from speaking?
Behold, you have instructed many, and you have strengthened
the weak hands;

Your words have upheld the one who was stumbling, and you
have made firm the feeble knees.

But now it has come to you, and you are impatient; it touches
you, and you are dismayed.

Is not your awareness of God your confidence, and the integrity
of your ways your hope?

"Think now, who that was innocent ever perished?

Or where were the upright cut off?

As I have seen, those who plow iniquity and sow trouble reap
the same.

The roar of the lion, the voice of the fierce lion, the teeth of the
young lions are broken.

The strong lion perishes for lack of prey, and the offspring of
the lioness are scattered.

"Call now; is there any one who will answer you?

To which of the holy ones will you turn?

Surely vexation kills the fool, and jealousy slays the ignorant.

I have seen fools taking root, but suddenly I cursed their dwelling.

Their sons are far from safety, they are crushed in the gate, and
there is no one to deliver them.

Their harvest the hungry eat, and they take it even out of
thorns; and the thirsty pant after their wealth.

For affliction does not come from the dust, nor does trouble
sprout from the ground; but we are born to trouble as the
sparks fly upward."

And God said to Job:

"Shall a faultfinder contend with all this?

The one who argues with life, let that person answer it."

Then Job answered God:

Behold, I am of small account; what shall I answer you?

I lay my hand on my mouth.

I have spoken once, and I will not answer; twice, but I will proceed no further."

Then God answered Job out of the night:

"Gird up your loins like a man; I will question you, and you declare to me.
Will you even put me in the wrong:
Will you condemn me that you may be justified?

"Behold, the hippopotamus which was made as you were made;
he eats grass like an ox.
Behold, his strength in his loins, and his power in the muscles
of his belly.
He makes his tail stiff like a cedar;
The sinews of the thighs are knit together.
His bones are tubes of bronze, his limbs like bars of iron.

"He is one of the works of God,
For the mountains yield food for him where all the wild beasts
play.
Under the lotus plants he lies, in the covert of the reeds and in
the marsh.
For his shade the lotus trees cover him;
The willows of the brook surround him.
Behold, if the river is turbulent he is not frightened; he is confident though Jordan rushes against his mouth.

Can one take his fish hooks or pierce his nose with a snare?
"Can you draw out the crocodile with a fish hook or press
down his tongue with a cord?
Can you put a rope in his nose or pierce his jaw with a hook?
Will he make a covenant with you to take him for your servant
forever?
Will you play with him as with a bird, or will you put him on
leash for your maidens?
Will traders bargain over him?
Will they divide him up among the merchants?
Can you fill his skins with harpoons, or his head with fishing
spears?
Lay hands on him; think of the battle; you will not do it again!

"Behold, the people's hopes are often disappointed;
They are laid low even at the sight of the crocodile.
We are not so fierce that we dare to stir him up.

Who then are we that can stand before God?
Who has given to God that we should be repaid?
Whatever is in the universe is One."

Then Job answered God:
"I knew that only God can do all things, and that no purpose of
God can be thwarted.
Who is this that hides counsel without knowledge?
Therefore I have uttered what I did not understand, things too
wonderful for me, which I did not know.
Hear, and I will speak;
I will question you, and you declare to me.
I had heard of you by the hearing of the ear, but now my eye
sees you; therefore I humble myself, and I apologize."

After the prophet had spoken these words to Job, the prophet said
to Eliphaz the Termanite: "My wrath is kindled against you and
against your two friends; for you have not spoken what is right, as
Job has. Now therefore take some bulls and rams, and go to my
servant Job, and offer them to him as a gift. So Eliphaz the Termanite and Bildad the Shuhite and Zophar the Naamathite went
and did what the prophet had told them.

The fortunes of Job were restored, and he gained back twice as
much as he had before. Then all his brothers and sisters came to
him, and all who had known him before, and ate bread with him in
his house; they showed him sympathy and comforted him for all
the evil that had come upon him; and each of them gave him a
piece of money and a ring of gold. The latter days of Job were better than his beginning; he had fourteen thousand sheep, six thousand camels, and a thousand donkeys. He had also seven sons and
three daughters. After this time Job lived a hundred and forty years,
and saw his sons and his sons' sons, four generations. Job died as
an old but happy man.

THE PSALMS

The Righteous and the Wicked

Blessed are the ones who walk not in the counsel of the wicked
nor stand in the way of sinners nor sit in the seat of scoffers;
but whose delight is in the law of God, and on its law they
meditate day and night.

They are like a tree planted by streams of water, that yield its
fruit in its seasons and its leaf does not wither.

In all that they do, they prosper.

The wicked are not so, but are like chaff which the wind drives
away.

Therefore the wicked will not stand the test of Life, nor sinners
in the congregation of the righteous; for the way of the righteous is eternal, but the way of the wicked will perish.

The Folly of Trusting in Riches

Hear this, all people,

Give ear, all inhabitants of the world, both high and low, rich
and poor together!

My mouth shall speak wisdom; the meditation of my heart shall
be understanding.

I will incline my ear to a proverb; I will solve my riddle to the
music of the lyre.

Why should I fear in times of trouble, when the iniquity of my
persecutors surrounds me,

People who trust in their wealth and boast of the abundance of
their riches?

Truly, people can ransom themselves, or give to God the price
of their lives, for the ransom of their lives is costly, and can
never suffice, that we should continue to live on forever, and
never see death.

Yes, we shall see that even the wise die, the fool and the stupid
alike must perish, and leave their wealth to others.

Their graves are their homes forever, their dwelling places to all
generations, though they named lands their own.

We cannot abide in our pomp, we are like the beasts that perish.

This is the fate of those who have foolish confidence, the end of those who boast about their portion.

Like sheep they are appointed for death;

Death shall be their shepherd; straight to the grave they descend, and their form shall waste away; death shall be their home.

Do not be afraid when people become rich, when the glory of their homes increases.

For when they die they will carry nothing away; their glory will not go down after them.

Though, while they live, they count themselves happy, and though they get praise when they do well for themselves, they will go as all the generations before them, who will never more see the light.

A Profession of Uprightness

I will sing of loyalty and of justice;

I will give heed to the way that is blameless.

I will walk with integrity of heart within my house;

I will not set before my eyes anything that is base.

I hate the work of those who give up their ideals; it shall not cleave to me.

Perverseness of heart shall be far from me; I will know nothing of evil.

I will look with favor on the faithful in the land, that they may dwell with me; those who walk in the way that is blameless shall minister to me.

THE PROVERBS

That all may know wisdom and instruction, understand words of insight, receive instruction in wise dealing, righteousness, justice, and equity; that prudence may be given to the simple, knowledge and discretion to the youth—the wise ones also may hear and increase in learning, and the people of understanding acquire skill, to understand a proverb and a figure, the words of the wise and their riddles.

The awareness of God is the beginning of knowledge; fools despise wisdom and instruction.

Hear, my child, your father's instruction, and reject not your mother's teaching; for they are a fair garland for your head, and pendants for your neck.
My child, if sinners entice you, do not consent.
If they say, "Come with us, let us lie in wait for blood, let us wantonly ambush the innocent;"
My child, do not walk in the way with them, hold back your foot from their paths; for their feet run to evil and they make haste to shed blood.
For in vain is a net spread in the sight of any bird; for these people lie in wait for their own blood, and they set an ambush for their own lives.
Such are the ways of all who get gain by violence; it takes away the life of its possessors.

Wisdom cries aloud in the street; in the markets she raises her voice; on the top of the walls she cries out; at the entrance of the city gates she speaks:
"How long, foolish ones, will you love being ignorant?
How long will scoffers delight in their scoffing and fools hate knowledge?
Give heed to my reproof; behold, I will pour out my thoughts to you;
I will make my words known to you.
Because I have called and you refused to listen, have stretched out my hands and no one has heeded, and you have ignored all my counsel and would have none of my reproof, I also will laugh at your calamity;
I will mock when panic strikes you, when panic strikes you like a storm, and your calamity comes like a whirlwind, when distress and anguish come upon you.
Then they will call upon me, but I will not answer; they will seek me diligently but will not find me.
Because they hated truth and did not choose the way of God, would have none of my counsel, and despised all my reproof, therefore they shall eat the fruit of their way and be sated with their own devices.

For the ignorant are killed by their turning away, and the complacency of fools destroys them; but those who listen to me will dwell secure and will be at ease, without dread of evil."

My child, if you receive my words and treasure my commandments with you, making your ear attentive to wisdom and inclining your heart to understanding;

Yes, if you cry out for insight and raise your voice for understanding; if you seek it like silver and search for it as for hidden treasures; then you will understand the meaning of God and find the knowledge of Spirit.

For God gives wisdom; from God's mouth come knowledge and understanding; Spirit is a shield to those who walk in integrity, guarding the paths of justice and preserving the way of the saints.

Then you will understand righteousness and justice and equity, every good path; for wisdom will come into your heart, and knowledge will be pleasant to your soul; discretion will watch over you; understanding will guard you; delivering you from the way of evil, from people of perverted speech, who forsake the paths of uprightness to walk in the ways of darkness, who rejoice in doing evil and delight in the perverseness of evil; people whose paths are crooked, and who are devious in their ways.

You will be saved from the loose woman, from the adventuress with smooth words, who forsakes the companion of her youth and forgets the covenant of her virtue; for her house sinks down to death, and her paths to the shades; few who go to her nor do they regain the paths of life.

So you will walk in the way of good people and keep to the paths of the righteous.

For the upright will inhabit the land, and people of integrity will remain in it; and the treacherous will be rooted out of it.

My child, do not forget my teaching, but let your heart keep my commandments; for length of days and years of life and abundant welfare will they give you;

Do not let loyalty and faithfulness forsake you; bind them about your neck, write them on the tablet of your heart.

So you will find favor and good report in the sight of all true beings.

Happy is the one who finds wisdom and the one who gets understanding, for the gain from it is better than gain from silver and its profit better than gold.

Wisdom is more precious than jewels and nothing you desire can compare with it.

Eternity is in its right hand; in the left hand are true riches and honor.

Its ways are ways of happiness, and all its paths are peace.

Wisdom is a tree of life to those who lay hold of it; those who hold fast are called happy.

My child, keep sound wisdom and discretion; do not let them escape from your sight, and they will be life for your soul and adornment for your neck.

Then you will walk on your way securely and your feet will not stumble.

If you sit down, you will not be afraid; when you lie down, your sleep will be sweet.

Do not be afraid of sudden panic or of the ruin of the wicked, when it comes; for Spirit will be your confidence and will keep your foot from being caught.

Do not withhold good from those to whom it is due, when it is in your power to do it.

Do not say to your neighbor, "Go and come again, tomorrow I will give it"—when you have it with you.

Do not plan evil against your neighbor who dwells trustingly beside you.

Do not contend with people for no reason, when they have done you no harm.

Do not envy people of violence and do not choose any of their ways;

The wise will inherit honor, but fools get disgrace.

Hear, O children, a parent's instruction, and be attentive, that you may gain insight; for I give you good precepts: do not forsake my teaching.

When I was a child with my father, tender, the only one in the sight of my mother, they taught me, and said to me,

"Let your heart hold fast our words; keep our commandments, and live;

Do not forsake wisdom, and it will keep you; love wisdom, and it will guard you.

The beginning of wisdom is this: Get wisdom, and whatever you get, get insight.

Prize it highly, and it will exalt you; wisdom will honor you if you live it.

Wisdom will place on your head a fair garland; it will bestow on you a beautiful crown."

Hear, my child, and accept my words, that the years of your life may be many.

I have taught you the way of wisdom;

I have led you in the paths of uprightness.

When you walk, your step will not be hampered; and if you run, you will not stumble.

Keep hold of my instruction, do not let go; guard wisdom, for it is our life.

Do not enter the path of the wicked, and do not walk in the way of the evil ones.

Avoid evil; do not go on that path; turn away from it and pass on.

For the evil ones cannot sleep unless they have done wrong; they are robbed of sleep unless they have made someone stumble.

For they eat the bread of wickedness and drink the wine of violence.

But the path of the righteous is like the light of dawn, which shines brighter and brighter until full day.

The way of the wicked ones is like deep darkness; they do not know over what they stumble.

My child, be attentive to my words; incline your ears to my saying.

Do not let them escape from your sight; keep them within your heart.

For they are life to those who find them, and healing to all flesh.

Keep your heart with all vigilance; for from it flow the springs of life.

Put away from you crooked speech, and put devious talk far from you.

Let your eyes look directly forward and your gaze be straight before you.

Take heed to the path of your feet, then all your ways will be sure.

Do not swerve to the right or to the left; turn your foot away from evil.

My child, be attentive to my wisdom, incline your ear to my understanding; that you may keep discretion, and your lips may guard knowledge.

For the lips of a loose woman drip honey, and her speech is smoother than oil; but in the end she is bitter as wormwood, sharp as a two-edged sword.

She does not take heed to the path of life; her ways wander, and she does not know it.

And now, O children, listen to me, and do not depart from the words of my mouth.

Keep your way far from evil, and do not go near the door of its house; lest you give your honor to others and your years to the merciless; lest strangers take their fill of your strength, and your labors go to the house of an alien;

And at the end of your life you groan, when your flesh and body are consumed,

And you say, "How I hated discipline, and my heart despised reproof!

I did not listen to the voice of my teachers or incline my ear to my instructors.

I was at the point of utter ruin in the assembled congregation."

My child, if you have become surety for your neighbor, have given your pledge for a stranger; if you are snared in the utterance of your lips, caught in the words of your mouth; then do this, my child, and save yourself.

For you have come into your neighbor's power: go, hasten, and importune your neighbor.

Give your eyes no sleep and your eyelids no slumber; save yourself like a gazelle from the hunter, like a bird from the hand of the fowler.

Those who love purity of heart and whose speech is gracious will have the true ruler as their friend.
The sluggard says, "There is a lion outside! I shall be slain in the streets!"
Those who oppress the poor to increase their own wealth, or give to the rich, will only come to want.

Incline your ear, and hear the words of the wise, and apply your mind to understanding, for it will be pleasant if you keep them within you, if all of them are ready on your lips.
Make no friendship with people given to anger, nor go with a wrathful person, lest you learn those ways and entangle yourself in a snare.
Do not be one of those who give loans, or who become surety for debts.
If you have nothing with which to pay, why should your bed be taken from under you?

Do not remove the ancient landmark which your ancestors have set.
Do you see people skillful in their work?
They will stand before rulers; they will not stand before corrupt individuals.

When you sit down to eat with a society's leaders, observe carefully what is before you.
Do not desire their delicacies, for they are deceptive food.
Do not toil to acquire wealth; be wise enough to resist.
When your eyes light upon it, it is gone, for suddenly it takes wings, flying like an eagle toward the sky.
Do not eat the bread of ones who are stingy; do not desire their delicacies; for they are like people who are inwardly reckoning.
"Eat and drink!" they say to you; but their hearts are not with you.

Do not speak in the hearing of fools, for they will despise the
wisdom of your words.

Do not remove an ancient landmark or enter the fields of the
merciless.

Apply your mind to instruction and your ear to words of wisdom.

My child, if your heart is wise, my heart too will be glad.

My soul will rejoice when your lips speak what is right.

Surely there is a future, and our hope will not be cut off.

The wicked flee when no one pursues, but the righteous are
bold as a lion.

When a land transgresses, it has many rulers; but with people of
understanding, its stability will long continue.

Rich people who oppress the poor are a beating rain that leaves
no food.

Those who forsake the law praise the wicked, but those who
keep the law strive against them.

Better are poor people who walk in integrity than rich people
who are perverse in their ways.

Those children who keep the law are wise, but companions of
gluttons shame their fathers.

Those who mislead the upright into an evil way will fall into
their own pit; but the blameless will have a goodly inheritance.

Rich people are wise in their own eyes, but poor people who
have understanding will find them out.

What, my child? What, my child of my womb? What, child of
my vows?

Do not give your strength to harlots, your ways to those who
destroy kings.

It is not for kings to drink wine, or for rulers to desire strong
drink; lest they drink and forget what has been decreed, and
pervert the rights of all the afflicted.

Give strong drink to those who are perishing, and wine to those
in bitter distress; let them drink and forget their poverty, and
remember their misery no more.

Open your mouth for the hard of hearing, for the rights of all
who are left desolate.

Open your mouth, judge righteously, maintain the rights of the
poor and needy.

A good wife who can find? She is far more precious than jewels.

The heart of her husband trusts in her, and he will have no lack
of gain.

She does him good, and not harm, all the days of her life.

ECCLESIASTES OR THE PREACHER

The words of the Preacher, the son of David, king in Jerusalem.

Vanity of vanities, says the Preacher, vanity of vanities! All is vanity.

What do people gain by all that toil at which they toil under the
sun?

A generation goes, and a generation comes, but the earth remains
forever.

The sun rises and the sun goes down, and returns to the place
where it rises.

The wind blows to the south and goes round to the north; round
and round goes the wind, and on its circuits the wind returns.

All streams run to the sea, but the sea is not full; to the place
where the streams flow, there they flow again.

All things are full of weariness; a person cannot utter it; the eye is
not satisfied with seeing, nor the ear filled with hearing.

What has been is what will be, and what has been done is what
will be and there is nothing new under the sun.

Is there a thing of which it is said, "See, this is new"?

It has been already in the ages before us.

There is the remembrance of former things, nor will there be any
remembrance of later things yet to happen among those who come
after.

I the Preacher have been king over Israel in Jerusalem. And I applied
my mind to seek and to search out by wisdom all that is done
under the sun; it is an unhappy business that the people are busy
with. I have seen everything that is done under the sun; and be-

hold, all is vanity and a striving after wind. What is crooked cannot be made straight, and what is lacking cannot be numbered.

I said to myself, "I have acquired great wisdom, surpassing all who were over Jerusalem before me; and my mind has had great experience of wisdom and knowledge." And I applied my mind to know madness and folly. I perceived that this also is but a striving after wind. For in much wisdom is much vexation, and those who increase knowledge increase sorrow.

I said to myself, "Come now, I will make a test of pleasure; enjoy yourself." But behold, this also was vanity. I said of laughter, "It is mad," and of pleasure, "What use is it?" I searched with my mind how to cheer my body with wine—my mind still guiding me with wisdom—and how to lay hold on folly, till I might see what was good for people to do during the few days of their lives. I made great works; I built houses and planted vineyards for myself; I made myself gardens and parks, and planted in them all kinds of fruit trees. I made myself pools from which to water the forest of growing trees. I brought male and female servants, and had servants who were born in my house; I had also great possessions of herds and flocks, more than any who had been before me in Jerusalem. I also gathered for myself silver and gold and the treasures of kings and provinces; I got singers, both men and women, and many concubines for my delight.

So I became great and surpassed all who were before me in Jerusalem; also my wisdom remained with me.

And whatever my eyes desired I did not keep from them; I kept my heart from no pleasure, for my heart found pleasure in all my toil, and this was my reward for all my toil. Then I considered all that my hands had done and the toil I had spent in doing it, and behold, all was vanity and a striving after wind, and there was nothing to be gained under the sun.

So I turned to consider wisdom and madness and folly; for what can the person do who comes after the king: Only what he has already done.

Then I saw that wisdom excels folly as light excels darkness. Wise people have eyes in their heads, but fools walk in darkness; and yet I perceived that one fate comes to all of them. Then I said to myself, "What befalls the fool will befall me also; why then have I been so wise?" And I said to myself that this is also vanity. For of the wise person as of the fool there is no enduring remembrance, seeing that in the days to come all will have been long forgotten. Now the wise one dies just like a fool! So I hated life, because what is done under the sun was grievous to me; for all is vanity and a striving after wind.

I hated all my toil in which I had toiled under the sun, seeing that I must leave it to the ones who will come after me; and who knows whether they will be wise people or fools? Yet they will be master of all for which I toiled and used my wisdom under the sun. This also is vanity.

So I turned about and gave my heart up to despair over all the toil of my labors under the sun, because sometimes the one who has toiled with wisdom and knowledge and skill must leave all to be enjoyed by others who did not toil for it. This also is vanity and a great evil. What have people gained from all the toil and strain with which they toil beneath the sun? For all their days are full of pain, and their work is a vexation; even in the night their minds do not rest. This is also vanity.

There is nothing better for people than that they should eat and drink, and find enjoyment in their toil. For some people gain wisdom and knowledge and joy readily; others have only the work of gathering and heaping. This also is vanity and a striving after wind.

For everything there is a season, and a time for every matter under the sun:

a time to be born, and a time to die;
a time to plant, and a time to pluck up what is planted;
a time to kill, and a time to heal;
a time to break down, and a time to build up;
a time to weep, and a time to laugh;
a time to mourn, and a time to dance;
a time to cast away stones, and a time to gather stones together;
a time to embrace, and a time to refrain from embracing;
a time to seek, and a time to lose;
a time to keep, and a time to cast away;
a time to rend, and a time to sew;
a time to keep silence, and a time to speak;
a time for conflict, and a time for healing.

What gain have the workers from their toil?

I have seen the business that the people are busy with. Everything is beautiful in its time; also there is a bit of eternity in our minds, yet so that we cannot find out what life is from the beginning to the end. I know that there is nothing better for them than to be happy and enjoy themselves as long as they live; also that everyone should eat and drink and take pleasure in all their toil. I know that whatever is done endures forever; nothing can be added to it, not anything taken from it. That which is, already has been; that which is to be, already has been.

Moreover, I saw under the sun that in the place of justice, even there was wickedness, and in the place of righteousness, even there was wickedness. I said in my heart, the righteous and the wicked will somehow be judged. I said in my heart with regard to the people that they are being tested to show them that they are but beasts.

For the fate of people and the fate of beasts is the same; as one dies so dies the other. They all have the same breath, and people have no advantage over the beasts; for all is vanity. All go to one place; all are from the dust, all return to dust again. Who knows whether the spirit of the individual goes upward and the spirit of the beast goes down to the earth? So I saw that there is nothing better than that people should enjoy their work, for that is their lot; who can bring them to see what will be after them?

Again I saw all the oppressions that are practiced under the sun. Behold, the tears of the oppressed, and they had no one to comfort them! On the side of their oppressors there was power, and there was no one to comfort them. And I thought the dead who are already dead more fortunate than the living who are still alive; but better than both are those who have not yet been, and have not seen the evil deeds that are done under the sun.

Then I saw that all toil and all skill in work come from a people's envy of their neighbors. This also is vanity and a striving after wind.

Fools fold their hands and eat their own flesh.

Better is a handful of quietness than two hands full of toil and a striving after wind.

Again, I saw vanity under the sun: people who have no one, neither a child nor a sibling, yet there is no end to all their toil, and their eyes are never satisfied with riches, so that they never ask, "For whom am I toiling and depriving myself of pleasure?" This also is vanity and an unhappy business.

Two are better than one, because they have a good reward for their toil. For if they fall, one will lift up the other; but woe to those who are alone when they fall and have not another to lift them up.

Again, if two lie together, they are warm; but how can one be warm alone? And though people might prevail against one who is alone, two will withstand them. A threefold cord is not quickly broken.

Better is a poor and wise youth than an old and foolish king, who will no longer take advice, even though he had gone from prison to the throne or in his own kingdom had been born poor. I saw all the living who move about under the sun as well as the youth who was to stand in his place; there was no end of all the people, and he was over all of them. Yet those who come later will not rejoice in him. Surely this also is vanity and a striving after wind.

Guard your steps when you go to temple; to draw near to listen is better than to offer the gift of fools; for they do not know that they are doing evil. Do not be rash with your mouth, nor let your heart be hasty to utter a word; rather let your words be few.

For an idle dream comes with much business, and a fool's voice with many words.

When you take a vow, do not delay living it; for no one takes pleasure in foolishness. Do what you vow. It is better that you should not vow than that you should vow and not live accordingly. Let not your mouth lead you into sin, and do not say that it was a mistake; why should people be angry at your voice and destroy the work of your hands?

For when idle dreams increase, empty words grow many.

If you see in a province the poor oppressed and justice and right violently taken away, do not be amazed at the matter; for the high official is watched by a higher, and there are yet higher ones over them. But all in all, a king is an advantage to a land with cultivated fields.

Those who love money will not be satisfied with money; nor will those who love wealth be satisfied with gain: this also is vanity.

When goods increase, they increase who eat them; and what gain has their owner but to see them with his eyes?

Sweet is the sleep of laborers when they have done an honest day's work, but the excesses of the rich often will not let them sleep well.

A grievous evil have I seen under the sun. Riches were kept by their owner for his own selfish interests. Those riches were lost in a risky venture. He is father of a child, but he has nothing in his hand. As he came from his mother's womb he shall go again, naked as he came, and shall take nothing for his toil that he may carry away in his hand. This also is a grievous evil: just as he came, so shall he go; and what gain has he that he toiled for the wind, and spent all his days in darkness and grief, in much vexation and resentment?

Behold, what I have seen to be good and to be fitting is to eat and drink and find enjoyment in all the toil with which one toils under the sun. Every person also who has wealth and possessions and power should enjoy them modestly, and should accept his/her lot and find enjoyment in working—this is the gift of life.

There is an evil which I have seen under the sun, and it lies heavy upon individuals: people who have wealth, possessions, and honor, so that they lack nothing of all that they desire, yet do not have power to enjoy them, but a stranger enjoys them; this is vanity; it is a sore affliction. If people have a hundred children, and live many years, so that the days of their years are many, but they do not enjoy life's good things, and also have no burial, I say that an untimely birth is better off than they. For it comes into vanity and goes into darkness, and in darkness its name is covered; moreover, it has not seen the sun or known anything; yet it finds rest rather than they. Even though they should live a thousand years twice told, yet enjoy no good—do not all go to the one place?

All the toil of individuals is for their mouths, yet their appetite is not satisfied. For what advantage have the wise over the fool? And what do poor people have who know how to conduct themselves before the living? Better is the sight of the eyes than the wandering of desire; this also is vanity and a striving after wind.

Whatever has come to be has already been named, and it is known what humanity is, and that we are not able to dispute with one stronger than we. The more words, the more vanity, and what are we the better? For who knows what is good for us while we live the few days of our vain life, which we pass like a shadow? For who can tell us what will be after us under the sun?

A worthy name is better than precious ointment; and the day of death, than the day of birth. It is better to go to the house of mourning than to go to the house of feasting; for this can be the end of all balanced living. Sorrow can be better than laughter, for by sadness of countenance the heart is often made glad. The heart of the wise is in the house of mourning; but the heart of fools is in the house of mirth. It is better for people to hear the rebuke of the wise than to hear the song of fools. For as the crackling of thorns under a pot, so is the laughter of the fools; this also is vanity.

Surely oppression makes the wise person foolish, and a bribe corrupts the mind. Better is the end of a thing than its beginning; and the patient in spirit is better than the proud in spirit. Do not be quick to anger, for anger lodges in the bosom of fools.

Do not say, "Why were the former days better than those? For it is not from wisdom that you ask this. Wisdom is good with an inheritance, an advantage to those who see the sun. For the protection of wisdom is like the protection of money; and the advantage of knowledge is that wisdom preserves the life of those who have it.

Consider the work of God; who can make straight what has been made crooked? In the way of prosperity be modest. In the day of adversity consider that the one is as important as the other, so that we may find out something adequate about the meaning of life.

In my life I have seen everything. There are righteous people who perish in their righteousness, and there are wicked people who prolong their lives in their evil-doing. Do not be righteous overmuch, and do not make yourself overwise. Why should you destroy yourself? Be not wicked overmuch, neither be a fool. Why should you die before your time? It is good that you should take hold of this, and from that withhold not your hand; for those who are aware of God shall come forth from them all.

Wisdom gives strength to the wise more than ten rulers in a city.

Surely there is not a righteous person on earth who does only good and never sins.

Do not give heed to all the things that people say, lest you hear your associate cursing you; your heart knows that many times you have yourself cursed others.

All this I have tested by wisdom. I said, "I will be wise", but it was far from me. That which is, is far off, and deep, very deep. Who can find it out? I turned my mind to know and to search out, to seek wisdom and the sum of things, to know the wickedness of folly and the foolishness which is madness. I found more bitter than death the woman whose heart is snares and nets, and whose hands are fetters; he who is righteous escapes her, but the sinner is taken by her. Behold, this is what I found, says the Preacher, adding one thing to another to find the sum, which my mind has sought repeatedly, but I have not found. One person among a thousand I found, but a woman among all these I have not found. Behold, this alone I found, that most people are basically upright, but some individuals have sought out devices to deceive others.

Who are the wise ones?

And who knows the interpretation of a thing?

People's wisdom makes their faces shine, and the hardness of their countenances are changed.

Keep the divine commands, and because of your sacred oath, be not dismayed. Go from the ruler's presence. Do not delay when the matter is unpleasant, for the ruler may do whatever he/she pleases. For the word of the ruler is generally supreme in the land, and who may say, "What are you doing?" Those who obey a command will meet no harm, and the mind of the wise will know the time and way. For every matter has its time and way, although our troubles lie heavy upon us. For we often do not know what is to be, for who can tell us how it will be? No one has power to retain the spirit, or authority over the day of death; there is no discharge from war, nor will wickedness deliver those who are given to it. All this I observed while I was applying my mind to all that is done under the sun, when some rulers make demands of others to their disadvantage.

Then I saw the wicked buried; they used to go in and out of the holy place, and were praised in the city where they had done such things. This also is vanity. If a sentence against an evil deed is not executed speedily, the hearts of others can be fully set to do evil. Though some people commit evil deeds a hundred times and prolong their lives, yet I know that they will generally not prolong their days like a shadow.

When I applied my mind to know wisdom, and to see the business that is done on earth, how neither day nor night one's eyes see sleep; then I saw that we cannot find out the work that is done under the sun. However much we may toil in seeking, we will not find it out. Even though a wise person claims to know, he/she cannot find it out.

But all this I laid to heart, examining it all, how the righteous and the wise and their deeds are in the hand of God; whether it is love or hate we do not know. Everything before us is vanity, since one fate comes to all, to the righteous and the wicked, to the good and the evil, to the clean and the unclean, to those who sacrifice and those who do not sacrifice. As is the good person, so is the sinner; and those who swear are as those who shun an oath. This is an evil in all that is done under the sun, that one fate comes to all. Also the hearts of some people are full of evil, and madness is within them while they live; after that they go to death. But those who are joined with all the living have hope, for a living dog is better than a dead lion. The living know that they will die, but the dead know nothing, and they have no more reward. The memory of them is often lost. Their love, their hate, and their envy have already perished, and they have no longer any share in all that is done under the sun.

Go, eat your bread with enjoyment, and drink your wine with a merry heart.

Enjoy life with the wife whom you love, all the days of your life under the sun, because that is your portion in life and in your toil under the sun. Whatever your hand finds to do, do it with your might; for there is no work or thought or knowledge in death, to which you are going.

Again I saw that under the sun the race is not to the swift, nor the battle to the strong, nor bread to the wise, nor riches to the intelligent, nor favor to the people of skill. Time and chance happen to them all. For we do not know our time. Like fish which are taken in an evil net, and like birds which are caught in a snare, so people are shared at an evil time, when it suddenly falls upon them.

I have also seen this example of wisdom under the sun, and it seemed great to me. There was a little city with few people in it. A great king came against it and besieged it. But there was found in the city a poor wise one, and this person by his/her wisdom delivered the city. But I say that wisdom is better than might, though the poor people's wisdom is often despised, and their words are seldom heeded.

The words of the wise heard in quiet are better than the shouting of a ruler among fools. Wisdom is better than weapons of war, but one sinner can destroy such good.

Dead flies make the perfumer's ointment give off an evil odor. Likewise, a little folly often outweighs wisdom and respect.

If the anger of the ruler rises against you, do not leave your place, for deference will make amends for great offenses.

There is an evil which I have seen under the sun, as it were an error proceeding from the ruler. Folly is often set in high places, while the wise sit in a low place. I have seen fools on horses, and wise ones walking on foot like slaves.

Those who dig a pit will fall into it, and a serpent will bite those who break through a wall.

The ones who quarry stones are often hurt by them; and those who split logs can be endangered by them.

If the iron is blunt, and people do not whet the edge, they must put forth more strength; but wisdom helps one to succeed.

The words of wise people's mouths win them favor, but the lips of fools consume them.

The beginning of the words of their mouths is foolishness, and the end of their talk is madness.

Fools multiply words, though no one knows what is to be, and who can tell them what will be after them?

The toil of fools wearies them, so that they do not know the way to the city.

Woe to you, O land, when your king is a child, and your princes feast in the morning!

Happy are you, O land, when your king is the son of free people, and your princes feast at the proper time, for strength, and not for drunkenness!

Through sloth the roof sinks in, and through indolence the house leaks.

Even in your thought, do not curse the king, nor in your bedchamber curse the rich; for a bird of the air will carry your voice, or some winged creature will tell the matter.

Cast your bread upon the waters, for you will find it after many days.

Give a portion to seven, or even to eight, for you do not know what evil may happen on earth.

If the clouds are full of rain, they empty themselves on the earth; and if a tree falls to the south or to the north, there it will lie.

Those who observe the wind will not sow; and those who regard the clouds will not reap.

As you do not know how the spirit comes to the cones in the womb of a woman with child, so you do not know the work of Spirit.

In the morning sow your seed, and at evening do not withhold your hand; for you do not know which will prosper, this or that, or whether both alike will be good.

Light is sweet, and it is pleasant for the eyes to behold the sun.

Rejoice, O child, in your youth. Let your heart cheer you in the days of your youth. Walk in the ways of your heart and the sight of your eyes.

Besides being wise, the Preacher also taught the people knowledge, weighing and studying and arranging proverbs with great care. The Preacher sought to find appropriate words, and courageously he wrote words of truth.

ISAIAH

The word which Isaiah the son of Amoz saw concerning Judah and Jerusalem.

It shall come to pass in the latter days that the mountain of the house of the Lord shall be established as the highest of the mountains, and shall be raised above the hills; and all the nations shall flow to it, and many peoples shall come, and say:

"Come, let us go up to the mountain of the Lord, to the house of the God of Jacob; that he may teach us his ways and that we may walk in his paths."

For out of Zion shall go forth the Law, and the word of the Lord from Jerusalem.

He shall judge between the nations, and shall decide for many peoples; and they shall beat their swords into plowshares, and their spears into pruning hooks; nation shall not lift up sword against nation, neither shall they learn war any more.

Woe to those who call evil good and good evil, who put darkness for light and light for darkness, who put bitter for sweet and sweet for bitter!

Woe to those who are wise in their own eyes, and shrewd in their own sight!

Woe to those who are heroes at drinking wine, and valiant in mixing strong drink, who acquit the guilty for a bribe, and deprive the innocent of their rights!

The people who walked in darkness have seen a great light; those who dwelt in a land of deep darkness, on them has the light shined.

For to us a child is born, to us a son is given; and the government will be upon his shoulder, and his name will be called "Wonderful Counselor, Prince of Peace."

Of the increase of his government and of peace there will be no end; upon the throne of this land, and over the world, people will establish it, and uphold it with justice and with righteousness from this time forth and forevermore.

Woe to those who decree iniquitous decrees, and the writers who keep writing oppression, to turn aside the needy from justice and to rob the poor of their rights, that widows may be their spoil, and that they may make the fatherless their prey!

Ah, the thunder of many peoples, they thunder like the thundering of the sea!

Ah, the roar of nations, they roar like the roaring of mighty waters!

The nations roar like the roaring of many waters, but they will be rebuked, and they will flee far away, chased like chaff on the mountains before the wind and whirling dust before the storm.

At evening time, behold, terror!

Before morning, they are no more!

This is the portion for those who despoil, and the lot of those who plunder.

In returning and rest you shall be restored; in quietness and in trust shall be your strength.

And you would not, but you said, "No! We will speed upon horses, "therefore you shall speed away; and, "We will ride upon swift steeds," therefore your pursuers shall be swift.

A thousand shall flee at the threat of one, at the threat of five you shall flee, till you are left like a flagstaff on the top of a mountain, like a signal on a hill.

Behold, a king will reign in righteousness, and princes will rule in justice.

Each will be alike a hiding-place from the wind, a covert from the tempest, like streams of water in a dry place, like the shade of a great rock in a weary land.

Then the eyes of those who see will not be closed, and the ears of those who hear will hearken.

The mind of the rash will have good judgment, and the tongue of the stammerers will speak rapidly and distinctly.

The fool will no more be called noble, nor the knave said to be honorable.

Behold this servant, whom I uphold, the chosen, in whom my soul delights;

He will not cry or lift up his voice, or make it heard in the street; a bruised reed he will not break, and a dimly burning wick he will not quench; he will faithfully bring forth justice.

He will not fail or be discouraged till he has established justice in the earth; and the coastlands wait for his law.

For you shall go out in joy, and be led forth in peace; the mountains and the hills before you shall break forth into singing, and all the trees of the field shall clap their hands.

Instead of the thorn shall come up the cypress; instead of the briar shall come up the myrtle; and it shall be for a living memorial, for an everlasting sign which shall not be cut off.

JEREMIAH

Do not let the learned ones glory in their knowledge. Do not let the mighty ones glory in their might. Do not let the rich glory in their riches. But let those who glory do so in this, that they have understanding.

Woe to those who build their houses by unrighteousness, and their upper rooms by injustice; who make their neighbors serve them for nothing, who say, "I will build myself a great house with spacious upper rooms," and cut out windows for it, paneling it with cedar, and painting it with vermilion.

Do you think you are a king because you compete in cedar?

Did not your father eat and drink and do justice and righteousness?

Then it was well with him.

He judged the cause of the poor and needy; then it was well.

But you have eyes and heart only for your dishonest gain, for shedding innocent blood, and for practicing oppression and violence.

EZEKIEL

If people are honorable and do what is ethical and right—if they do not worship the idols of society, do not defile their neighbors' wives, do not oppress anyone, but restore to the debtors their pledges, commit no robbery, give their bread to the hungry and cover the naked with a garment, do not lend at excessive interest, withhold their hands from iniquity, execute true justice between one and another, walk in divine statutes, and are careful to observe divine ordinances—they are righteous; they shall surely live.

Repent and turn from all your transgressions, lest iniquity be your ruin. Cast away from you all the transgressions which you have committed, and get yourselves a new heart and a new spirit!

AMOS

Seek good, and not evil, that you may live; and so God will be a part of you.

Hate evil, love good; and establish justice in the gate. ... I hate, I despise your feasts; I take no delight in your solemn assemblies.

Take away from me the noise of your songs; to the melody of your harps I will not listen.

But let justice roll down like waters, and righteousness like an everflowing stream.

NEW TESTAMENT

The Birth of Jesus

In those days, a decree went out from Caesar Augustus that all the world should be enrolled. And all went to be enrolled, each to his/her own city. Joseph also went up from Galilee, from the city of Nazareth, to Bethlehem of Judea, to be enrolled with Mary, his wife, whose baby was about to be born. And while they were there, the time came for her to be give birth. As soon as her first-born son came, she wrapped him in baby clothes, and laid him in a manger, because there was no room for them in the inn.

And when they had performed everything according to the law, they returned into Galilee, to their own city of Nazareth. And the child, whom they named Jesus, grew and became strong, filled with wisdom.

The Childhood of Jesus

Jesus' parents went every year to Jerusalem at the feast of the Passover. It is said that when Jesus was twelve years old, they went up according to custom. When the feast was ended, and they began to return home, Jesus stayed behind in Jerusalem, and his parents did not know it. Supposing him to be in the company, they went a day's journey, seeking him among their friends and relatives. When they did not find him, they returned to Jerusalem, seeking him.

After three days they found him in the temple, sitting among the rabbi's, listening to them and asking them questions; and all who heard him were amazed at his understanding and his answers. When they saw him, they were astonished; and his mother said to him, "Son, why have you treated us so? Your father and I have been looking for you anxiously." He said to them, "How is it that you sought me? Did you not know that I must be here?" Then he went with them and came to Nazareth, and he was obedient to them. According to the story, his mother kept all these things in her heart.

Jesus continued to increase in wisdom and stature, and in favor with his fellow human beings.

After he met John the Baptist, who had been preaching about the coming of a man far greater than himself, Jesus withdrew into the wilderness for perhaps forty days, in order to seek further growth of the vision which he felt to be his. During this time Jesus had three major temptations to rise above: he could pretend to be a miracle-worker; he could try to defy the natural laws of the universe; or he could preach just what the people wished to hear, so as to please them, rather than revealing truth as he saw it. All of these temptations he overcame. Then Jesus returned to the world, strengthened by the power of his own prophetic vision, and determined to communicate this vision to others.

When Jesus began to preach, at about thirty years of age, he was walking by the sea of Galilee when he saw two brothers—Simon who is called Peter, and Andrew his brother—casting a net into the sea; for they were fishermen. He said to them, "Follow me, and I will make you fishers of people." Immediately they left their nets and followed him. Going on from there he saw two other brothers—James the son of Zebedee, and John his brother—in the boat with Zebedee their father, mending their nets; and he called them. Immediately they left the boat and their father, and followed him.

Jesus went from one end of Galilee to the other, teaching in the synagogues and preaching the good news. As a result, his fame spread throughout the land, and great crowds from Galilee and the surrounding areas followed him.

The Sermon on the Mount

Seeing the crowds, he went up on the mountain, and when he sat down his disciples came to him. He opened his mouth and taught them, saying:

"Blessed are the poor in spirit, for theirs is lasting happiness.

"Blessed are the meek, for they shall inherit the earth.

"Blessed are they that hunger and thirst after righteousness, for they shall be filled.

"Blessed are the merciful, for they shall obtain mercy.

"Blessed are the pure in heart, for they shall see God.

"Blessed are the peacemakers, for they shall be called the children of God.

"Blessed are those who are persecuted for righteousness' sake, for theirs is lasting happiness.

"Blessed are you when people revile you, persecute you, and utter all kinds of evil against you falsely in behalf of your adherence to truth. Rejoice and be glad, because they also persecuted the prophets who were before you.

"You are the salt of the earth; but if salt has lost its taste, how can its flavor be restored? It is no longer good for anything except to be thrown out and trodden underfoot.

"We must do the work God gives us to do while it is day, for the night comes, when no one can work.

"You are the light of the world. A city set on a hill cannot be hid. Nor do people light a lamp and put it under a bushel, but on a stand, and it gives light to all in the house. Let your light so shine before the world, that all may see your good works.

"For those who do evil hate the light, and do not come to the light, lest their deeds should be exposed. But those who do what is true come to the light, that it may be clearly seen that their deeds have been wrought in God.

"Do not think that I have come to abolish the law and the prophets. I have come not to abolish them but to fulfill them.

"You have heard that it was said to the people of old, 'You shall not kill.' But I say to you that everyone who is angry with a brother or sister is also at fault. So if you are offering your gift to God at your church or temple and there remember that your associate has something against you, leave your gift there and go. First be reconciled to your associate, and then come and offer your gift. Agree with your adversary quickly, while you are still able to be friends.

"You have heard that it was said, 'You shall not commit adultery.' But I say to you that everyone who looks at a woman lustfully has already committed adultery with her in his heart.

"You have heard that it was said, 'An eye for an eye, and a tooth for a tooth.' But I say to you, Do not resist one who is evil. If anyone strikes you on the right cheek, turn the other cheek also. If anyone would sue you and take your coat, let that person have your cloak as well. If anyone forces you to go one mile, willingly go two miles. Give to the one who begs from you, and do not refuse anyone who would legitimately borrow from you.

"You have heard that it was said, 'You shall love your neighbor and hate your enemy.' But I say to you, love your enemies, and do good to those who persecute you. For if you love only those who love you, what merit have you shown? And if you salute only your friends, what more are you doing than others?

"Beware of practicing your piety in public. When you do acts of charity, sound no trumpet before you, as the hypocrites do, that they may be praised by others. But when you do acts of charity, do not let your left hand know what your right hand is doing.

"When you pray, you must not be like the show people; for they love to stand and pray where they may be seen by others. But when you pray, go into your room and shut the door and pray in secret.

"If you would use certain words as in formal prayer, do not heap up empty phrases as many do, but pray in this general manner:

O Spirit of Love that dwells within us,
We would have You grow each day.
We strive, through You, to unite with the Eternal;
To come to know ourselves and our relation to the world;
To search always for lasting happiness.
May life take on new meaning as we overcome temptation by
  ever moving toward You,
Now and in all the days to come.

"Do not lay up for yourselves treasures of material worth, but rather keep for yourselves treasures of spiritual value; for where your treasure is, there will your heart be also.

"The eye is the lamp of the body. So, if your eye is sound, your whole body will be full of light; but if your eye is not sound, your whole body will be full of darkness. If then the light in you is darkness, how great is the darkness!

Other Teachings

"There was a rich man who had a steward, and charges were brought to him that this man was wasting his goods. So he called the steward and said to him, 'What is this that I hear about you? Turn in the account of your stewardship, for you can no longer be steward.' And the steward said to himself, 'What shall I do, since my master is taking the stewardship away from me? I am not strong enough to dig, and I am ashamed to beg. I have decided what to do, so that people may receive me into their houses when I am put out of the stewardship.' So, summoning his master's debtors one by one, he said to the first, 'How much do you owe my master?' That debtor said, 'A hundred measures of oil.' And the steward said to him, 'Take your bill, and sit down quickly and write fifty.' Then he said to another, 'And how much do you owe?' She said, 'A hundred measures of wheat.' He said to her, 'Take your bill, and write eighty.' The master commended the dishonest steward for his prudence; for people like him are sometimes wiser than the followers of truth. If you want to use money rightly, make friends for yourself through the honest use of money, and when they see you doing this, they will very likely receive you into their company.

"Those who are faithful in a very little are faithful also in much; and those who are dishonest in a very little are dishonest also in much. If then you have not been faithful in material things, who will entrust to you the spiritual things? And if you have not been faithful in that which is another's, who will give you that which is your own? No one can serve two masters; for either you will hate the one and love the other, or you will be devoted to the one and despise the other. You cannot serve both your highest ideals and your lowest desires.

"Therefore I tell you, do not be anxious about your life, what you shall eat or what you shall drink, nor about your body, what you shall put on. Is not life more than food, and the body more than clothing? Look at the birds of the air: they neither sow nor reap nor gather into barns, and yet they manage to survive. Are you not of more value than they? And which of you, by being anxious, can prolong your life a single moment? And why be anxious about clothing? Consider the lilies of the field, how they grow: they neither toil nor spin; yet I tell you, even the best of kings in all their glory are not arrayed like one of these. Therefore do not be anxious, saying, 'What shall we eat?' or 'What shall we drink?' or 'What shall we wear?' But seek first the moral and spiritual life, and all these things shall be yours as well.

"It is the Spirit that gives life, the flesh is of no avail. The words that I have spoken to you are Spirit and Life.

"Therefore do not be anxious about tomorrow, for tomorrow will be anxious for itself. Let the day's concerns be sufficient for the day.

"Do not judge others, that you may not be judged in return. For with the judgment you pronounce you will be judged, and the measure you give will be the measure you get. Why do you see the speck that is in your friend's eye, but do not notice the log that is in your own eye? Or how can you say to your friend, 'Let me take the speck out of your eye,' when there is the log in your own eye? First take the log out of your own eye, and then you will see clearly to take the speck out of your friend's eye.

"Do not give dogs what is holy; and do not throw your pearls before swine, lest they trample them underfoot and turn to attack you.

"Ask, and it will be given you; seek, and you will find; knock, and it will be opened to you. For everyone who asks receives, and those who seek will find, and to those who knock it will be opened. Which of you, if your daughter asks you for a loaf, will give her a stone? Or if she asks for a fish, will give her a serpent? So whatever you wish that others would do to you, do likewise to them.

"Enter by the narrow gate; for the gate is wide and the way is easy that leads to destruction, and those who enter by it are many. The gate is narrow and the way is hard that leads to life, and those who find it are few.

"The shepherd who does not enter the sheepfold by the door but climbs in by another way, is likely to be seen as a thief and a robber. But the shepherd who enters by the door is the shepherd of the sheep. To him the gatekeeper opens; the sheep hear his voice, and he calls his own sheep by name and leads them out. When the shepherd has brought out all his own, he goes before them, and the sheep follow him, for they know his voice. Strangers they will not follow, but they will flee from them, for the sheep do not know the voice of strangers.

"Beware of false prophets, who come in sheep's clothing but inwardly are ravenous wolves. You will know them by their fruits. Are grapes gathered from thorns, or figs from thistles? So, every sound tree bears good fruit, but the bad tree bears evil fruit. A sound tree cannot bear evil fruit, nor can a bad tree bear good fruit. Thus you will know them by their fruits.

"And to what shall I compare these people? They are like children sitting in the market place and calling to their playmates, 'We piped to you, and you did not dance; we wailed, and you did not mourn.' For one came neither eating nor drinking, and they say, 'He is crazy'. Another comes eating and drinking, and they say, 'Behold, a glutton and a drunkard.' Yet wisdom is supported by its deeds."

"Everyone then who hears these words of truth and does them will be like a wise person who built a house upon the rock. The rain fell, and the floods came, and the winds blew and beat upon that house, but it did not fall, because it had been founded on the rock. And everyone who hears these words of truth and does not do them will be like a foolish person who built a house upon the sand. The rain fell, and the floods came, and the winds blew and beat against that house, and it fell; and great was the fall of it."

When Jesus finished these sayings, the crowds were astonished at his teaching, for he taught them as one who had authority, and not as their scribes.

When he came down from the mountain, great crowds followed him. A scribe came up and said to Jesus, "Master, I will follow you wherever you go." Jesus said to him, "Foxes have holes, and birds of the air have nests; but I have nowhere to lay my head." Another person said to him, "Let me first go and bury my father." But Jesus said to him, "Follow me, and leave the dead to bury their own dead."

The Gathering of the Disciples

As Jesus passed by a tax office, he saw a man called Matthew sitting there. He said to him, "Follow me." Matthew rose and followed him. Similarly, Jesus found other people who wished to join him in his mission, until he had a total of twelve disciples.

Jesus went about all the cities and villages, teaching in their synagogues and preaching the good news. When he saw the crowds, he had compassion for them, because they were harassed and helpless, like sheep without a shepherd. Then he said to his disciples, "The harvest is plentiful, but the laborers are few; let us send out more laborers into the harvest."

Jesus sent out his disciples, charging them, "Go and preach the good news. You received freely; give freely. Take neither gold, nor silver, nor copper in your purses, neither beg for your journey, nor two coats, nor sandals, nor a staff; for the laborer deserves to be fed. And whatever town or village you enter, find out who are the worthy ones, and stay with them until you depart.

"I send you out as sheep in the midst of wolves; so be wise as serpents and innocent as doves. Beware of certain people; for they will deliver you up to councils, and deride you in their religious gatherings, and you will be dragged before government officials to bear testimony of your words. When they deliver you up, do not be anxious for your own safety; because those who endure to the end will find lasting happiness.

"So have no fear; for nothing is covered that will not be revealed, or hidden that it will not be known. What I tell you in the dark, utter in the light; and what you hear whispered, proclaim upon the housetops. And do not fear those who can destroy both soul and body.

"Those who love father or mother more than me are not worthy of me; and those who love son or daughter more than me are not worthy of me, and those who do not follow me are not worthy of me. Those who find their lives will lose them, and those who lose their lives for my sake will find them."

Relating to John the Baptist

Now when John the Baptist heard about the deeds of the Christ, he sent word by his disciples and said to him, "Are you he who is to come, or shall we look for another?" And Jesus answered John the Baptist, "Go and tell John what you hear and see: The people have good news preached to them, and their faith transforms their lives. And blessed are those who take no offense at me."

As they went away, Jesus spoke to the crowds concerning John the Baptist: "What did you go out into the wilderness to behold? A reed shaken by the wind? Why then did you go out? To see a person clothed in soft raiment? Behold, those who wear soft raiment are usually in luxurious homes. Why then did you go out? To see a prophet? Yes, I tell you, and more than a prophet. Truly, I say to you, among those born before John the Baptist there has risen no one greater than he; yet he who has really found lasting happiness is greater than John. From the day of John's birth, our movement has suffered violence, and people of violence attempt to take it over by force. For only the prophets of old and the law were consulted until John came. But if you are willing to accept it, he is the prophet of the one who is to come. Those who have ears to hear, let them hear."

Martha and Mary

Jesus entered a village; and a woman named Martha received him into her home. She had a sister called Mary, who sat at Jesus' feet and listened to his teaching. But Martha was distracted with preparing the meal; and she went to him and said, "Master, do you not care that my sister has left me to serve alone? Please ask her then to help me." But Jesus answered her, "Martha, Martha, you are anxious and troubled about many things. One thing is needful. Mary has chosen the good portion, which shall not be taken away from her."

Additional Teachings

At that time Jesus declared, "Come to me, all who labor and are heavy-laden, and I will give you rest. Take my yoke upon you, and learn from me; for I am gentle and lowly in heart, and you will find rest for your souls. For my yoke is easy, and my burden is light."

Knowing his disciples' thoughts, he said to them, "Every kingdom divided against itself is laid waste, and no city or home divided against itself will stand. How can one enter a strong man's home and plunder his goods, unless he first binds the strong man? Then indeed he may plunder his home.

"Make the tree good, and its fruit good; or make the tree bad, and its fruit bad; for the tree is known by its fruit. How can you speak good, when you are evil? For out of the abundance of the heart the mouth speaks. Good people out of their good treasure will bring forth good, and evil ones out of their evil treasure will bring forth evil."

Someone said to Jesus, "Teacher, please ask my brother to divide his inheritance with me." Jesus said to him, "My friend, who made me a judge over you? Take heed, and beware of covetousness; for people's lives do not consist in the abundance of their possessions."

And he told them a parable, saying, "The land of a rich man brought forth plentifully; and he thought to himself, 'What shall I do, for I have nowhere to store my crops?' And he said, 'I will do this: I will pull down all my barns, and build larger ones; and there I will store all my grain and my goods. And I will say to myself, You have ample goods laid up for many years; relax, eat, drink, be merry.' But God said to him, 'Fool! This night your life may be required of you; and the things you have prepared, whose will they be?' So it is with those who lay up treasures for themselves, and are not rich in their inner lives."

Then some skeptics said to him, "Teacher, we wish to see a sign from you." But he answered them, "A disbelieving generation seeks a sign, but no sign shall be given to it.

"When you see a cloud rising in the west, you say at once, 'A shower is coming'; and so it happens. And when you see the south wind blowing, you say, 'There will be scorching heat': and it happens. You know how to interpret the appearance of earth and sky; but why do you not know how to interpret what is happening spiritually?"

Very shortly thereafter, Jesus and his disciples broke several established religious practices. When Jesus' enemies saw this, they said to him, "Look, you and your disciples are doing what is not lawful." He said to them, "Human beings are more important than religious practice."

While he was speaking to the people, Jesus' mother and his brothers came, asking to speak to him. But he said, "Who is my mother, and who are my brothers?" Stretching out his hand toward his disciples, he said, "Here are my mother and my brothers! For those who truly believe my teachings are my brother, sister, and mother.

"A sower went out to sow. And as he sowed, some seeds fell along the path, and the birds came and devoured them. Other seeds fell on rocky ground, where they had not much soil, and immediately they sprang up, since they had no depth of soil, but when the sun rose they were scorched; and since they had no root they withered away. Other seeds fell upon thorns, and the thorns grew up and choked them. Other seeds fell on good soil and brought forth grain, some a hundredfold, some sixty, some thirty. Those who have ears, let them hear."

Then the disciples came and said to him, "Why do you speak in parables?" And he answered them, "To some it has been given to know the secrets of lasting happiness, but it has not been given to all. To those who have will more be given, and they will have abundance; but from those who have not, even what they have will be taken away. I speak in parables, because seeing some do not see, and hearing some do not hear, nor do they understand. But blessed are your eyes if they see, and your ears if they hear. Truly, I say to you, many prophets and righteous individuals longed to see what you see, and did not see it, and to hear what you hear, and did not hear it.

The disciples asked Jesus privately, "Why do we not have the power that you have?" He said to them, "Because of your little faith. For truly, I say to you, if you have faith as a grain of mustard seed, nothing will be impossible to you."

Jesus then said, "Lasting happiness is like treasure hidden in a field, which a man found and covered up; then in his joy he sold all that he had and bought that field."

"Lasting happiness is like a grain of mustard seed which people took and sowed in their fields; it is the smallest of all seeds, but when it has grown it is the greatest of shrubs and becomes a tree, so that the birds of the air come and make nests in its branches.

"Again, lasting happiness is like merchants in search of fine pearls, who, on finding one pearl of great value, went and sold all that they had and bought it."

"Lasting happiness is like leaven which a woman took and hid in three measures of meal, till it was all leavened."

"Lasting happiness is as if a person should scatter seed upon the ground, and should sleep and rise night and day, and the seed should sprout and grow. The earth produces of itself, first the blade, then the ear, then the full grain in the ear.

"Have you understood all this?" They said to him, "Yes.' And he said to them, "Every teacher of the law who has been trained to find lasting happiness is like a householder who brings out of his/her treasure what is new and what is old."

While eating at the house of a public official, Jesus noticed how they chose the places of honor. So he said to them, "When you are invited by anyone to an important dinner, do not sit down in a place of honor, or the host may ask you to give way to a more eminent guest, and you will be embarrassed. When you are seated, take a lower place, so that your host may invite you to a higher one, and you will be honored. Those who exalt themselves will be humbled, and those who humble themselves will be exalted."

"When you give a dinner or a banquet, do not invite your friends or your brothers or your kinsmen or rich neighbors, lest they also invite you in return, and you be repaid. But when you give a feast, invite the poor, the maimed, the lame, the blind, and you will be blessed, because they cannot repay you."

When Jesus ate with disreputable people, certain more reputable people asked, "Why does Jesus eat with such people?" When he heard this, Jesus said, "Those who are well have no need of a physician, but only those who are sick. I came to help those in need."

"If you were a shepherd and had a hundred sheep, what would you do if you lost one of them? Would you leave the ninety-nine in the wilderness, and go after the one which is lost, until you find it? And when you have found it, you would lay it on your shoulders, rejoicing. And when you come home, you would call together your friends and neighbors, saying to them, 'Rejoice with me, for I have found my sheep which was lost.' Even so, I tell you, there will be more joy to be had over one person who changes his/her ways than over ninety-nine persons who make no change.

"What woman, having many coins, if she loses one coin, does not turn on a light and sweep the house, seeking diligently until she finds it? And when she has found it, she calls together her friends and neighbors, saying, 'Celebrate with me, for I have found the coin which I had lost.' Even so, I tell you, there is joy among all over one person who sees his/her failings and is able to overcome them."

"There was a man who had two sons; and the younger of them said to his father, 'Father, give me the share of property that falls to me.' And he divided his living between them. Not many days later, the younger son gathered all he had and went to a distant land, where he spent his money carelessly. And when he had spent everything, a great depression came to that country, and he began to be in want. So he went to one of the citizens of that country, who sent him into his fields to feed the pigs. He would gladly have fed on the pods that the pigs ate, but no one gave him anything.

"When he came to himself, he said, 'How many of my father's hired servants have bread enough and to spare, but I perish here with hunger! I will go to my father, and I will say to him, 'Father, I have betrayed you; I am no longer worthy to be called your son; treat me as one of your hired servants.' And he went to his father. But while he was yet at a distance, his father saw him and had compassion, and ran and embraced him. And the son said to him, 'Father, I have betrayed you; I am no longer worthy to be called your son." But the father said to his servants, 'Bring quickly the best robe, and put it on him; and put a ring on his hand, and shoes on his feet; and bring the fatted calf and kill it. Let us eat and make merry; for this my son was dead, and is alive again. He was lost, and is found.' And they began to make merry.

"His elder son was in the field; and as he came and drew near to the house, he heard music and dancing. And he called one of the servants and asked what this meant. The servant said to him, 'Your brother has come, and your father has killed the fatted calf, because he has received him safe and sound.' The son became angry and refused to go in. His father came out and entreated him, but he answered his father, 'Alas, these many years I have served you, and I never disobeyed your command; yet you never gave me a kid, that I might make merry with my friends. But when this son of yours came, who has spent your money recklessly, you killed for him the fatted calf!' And the father said to him, 'Son, you are always with me, and all that is mine is yours. It was fitting to make merry and be glad, for your brother was dead, and is alive; he was lost, and is found.'"

When the disciples of John asked Jesus, saying, "Why do we fast so much, but your disciples do not fast?" And Jesus said to them, "Can the wedding guests mourn as long as the bridegroom is with them? The days will come, when the bridegroom is taken away from them, and then they will suffer. No one puts a piece of unshrunk cloth on an old garment, because the patch tears away from the garment, and a worse tear is made. Neither is new wine put into old wineskins; if it is, the skins burst, the wine is spilled, and the skins are destroyed; but new wine is put into fresh wineskins, and so both are preserved."

On the next day the people who remained on one side of the sea saw that there had been only one boat there, and that Jesus had not entered the boat with his disciples, but that his disciples had gone away alone. So when the people saw that Jesus was not there, nor his disciples, they themselves got into the boats and went in search of Jesus.

When people followed Jesus, he said to them, " You seem to seek me, not because you see real value in my teachings, but because you have nothing else to do, having eaten your fill of food. Do not labor for the food which perishes, but for the food of life, which is lasting happiness."

Jesus' Travels

Soon after Jesus finished these teachings, he left Galilee and traveled to many places so as to spread his message. Finally, however, he decided to return to Galilee, passing through Samaria. When he came to a certain city of Samaria, he saw a well; so, wearied as he was with his journey, he sat down beside the well to rest.

CHRISTIAN SCRIPTURES / 455

Shortly thereafter a woman of Samaria came to draw water. Jesus said to her, "Everyone who drinks of this water will thirst again, but anyone who drinks of the water that I shall give will never thirst; the water that I give will become a spring of water welling up to eternal life."

Coming to his own part of the country he taught them in their synagogues, so that they were astonished, and said, "Where did this man get his wisdom? Is not this the carpenter's son? Is not his mother called Mary? Are not his brothers James, Joseph, Simon, and Judas? Are not all his sisters with us? Where then did this man get all his wisdom?" And they took offense at him. But Jesus said to them, "A prophet is not without honor except in his own country and in his own house."

Who Is This Man?

Jesus went on with his disciples; and on the way he asked them, "Who do people say that I am?" They told him, "John the Baptist;" and others, "Elijah;" and others, "One of the prophets." And he asked them, "But who do you say that I am?" Peter answered him, "You are the Christ." And he charged them to tell no one about him.

He began to teach them that he must suffer many things, and be rejected by the elders, the chief priests, and the scribes, as well as to be killed; and he said this plainly. Peter took him aside and began to rebuke him. Turning and seeing his disciples, Jesus then rebuked Peter, saying, "You are betraying me yourself, because you are not on the side of adherence to truth, but of worldly success."

Further Teachings

Then various community leaders came to Jesus and said, "Why do your disciples eat without washing their hands?" He called the people to him and said to them, "Hear and understand: not what goes into the mouth defiles a person, but what comes out of the mouth, this is what defiles. Do you not see that whatever goes into the mouth passes into the stomach and out the bowels? But what comes out of the mouth proceeds from the heart, and this can truly defile a person. For out of the heart can come evil thoughts, murder, adultery, theft, false witness, and slander. These are what defile a person; but to eat with unwashed hands does not defile a person."

At that time the disciples asked Jesus, "Who has the greatest lasting happiness?" And calling to him a child, he put him in the midst of them, and said, "Truly, I say to you, unless you turn and become like children, you will never find lasting happiness. Those who can humble themselves like this child, they will have the greatest lasting happiness."

Then Peter asked him, "Master, how often shall my associates offend me, and I forgive them? As many as seven times?" Jesus said to him, "I do not say to you seven times, but seventy times seven.

"Lasting happiness may be compared to a political leader who wished to settle accounts with his people. When he began the reckoning, one was brought to him who owed him one hundred thousand dollars; and as he could not pay, the official ordered his possessions to be sold, with payment to be made. So the guilty individual fell on his knees, imploring him, 'Lord, have patience with me, and I will pay you everything.' And out of pity for him the official released him and forgave him the debt.

"But that same individual, as he went out, came upon one of his fellow workers who owed him one hundred dollars; and seizing him by the throat he said, 'Pay what you owe.' So his fellow servant fell down and pleaded with him, 'Have patience with me, and I will pay you.' He refused and went and put him in prison till he could pay the debt. When his fellow workers saw what had taken place, they were greatly distressed, so they went and reported to the official all that had taken place. Then the government leader summoned him and said, 'You unforgiving one! I forgave you all that debt because you asked me; and should not you have had mercy on your fellow worker, as I had mercy on you?' The official then delivered him to the jailers to imprison him till he could pay all of his debt. So also lasting happiness will escape you, if you do not forgive your associates from your heart."

Jesus also said, "No one who puts his hand to the plow and looks back is able to find lasting happiness."

Being asked how lasting happiness would come, Jesus answered, "Eternity does not come by means of signs to be observed; nor should you think, 'Here it is!' or 'There!' for behold, 'Eternity lies within you.'"

Now when Jesus had finished these sayings, he went away from Galilee and entered the region of Judea beyond the Jordan, and large crowds followed him.

When his disciples rebuked people who were bringing their children for a blessing, Jesus said, "Let the children come to me, and do not hinder them; for to such belongs the key to lasting happiness." And he then laid his hands on them.

A young man came up to Jesus, saying, "Teacher, what good deed must I do, to have eternal life? Jesus said to him, "If you would enter life, keep the Jewish commandments.' The young man responded, "Which ones?" And Jesus said, "You shall not kill, you shall not commit adultery, you shall not steal, you shall not bear false witness, honor your father and your mother, and, "You shall love your neighbor as yourself." The young man said to him., "All these I have observed ever since my youth; what do I still lack?" Jesus said to him, "If you would be perfect, sell your possessions and give the money to the poor; then you will find the secret of lasting happiness. Then come and follow me." When the young man heard this, he went away sorrowful, for he had great possessions.

Jesus said to his disciples, "Truly, I say to you, it will be hard for a wealthy person to find lasting happiness. Again I tell you, it is usually easier for a camel to go through the eye of a needle than for a rich person to find lasting happiness." When the disciples heard this, they were greatly astonished, saying, "Who then can find lasting happiness?" But Jesus looked at them and said to them, "with many people this is impossible, but with a person of faith all things are possible." Then Peter said to him, "Alas, we have left everything and followed you. What then shall we have?" Jesus said to them, "Truly, I say to you, everyone who has left houses, brothers, sisters, father, mother, children or lands, because of his/her faith, will receive a hundredfold and discover lasting happiness. But many that are first will be last, and the last first."

As he watched the rich giving to charity, Jesus also saw a poor widow put in everything she had. And he said, "Truly I tell you, this poor widow has put in more than all of them; for they all contributed out of their abundance, but she out of her poverty put in all the living that she had.

Jesus also told this parable: "Two people went up into a temple to pray, one an aristocrat and the other a day laborer. The aristocrat

stood and prayed thus. 'I am thankful that I am not like other people—extortioners, adulterers, thieves—or even like this day laborer.
I to go temple twice a week, and I give away part of all the money
that I get.' But the laborer, standing far off, would not even lift up
his eyes, but prayed, 'May a person like me obtain mercy!' I tell you,
this individual is far more of a person than the aristocrat.

"Will any one of you who has a laborer working in the field or
factory, say to him when he has returned, 'Come at once and sit
down at table'? Will you not rather say to him, 'Prepare supper for
me, and gird yourself and serve me, till I eat and drink; and afterward you shall eat and drink.' Do you thank the worker because he
did what was required? So you also, when you have done all that is
required, can say, 'We too can improve; we have done only what
was our duty.'"

Jesus Enters Jerusalem

As Jesus was going to Jerusalem, he took the twelve disciples aside,
and on the way he said to them, " We are now going to Jerusalem;
and I will be delivered to the chief priests and scribes. They will
condemn me to death, and deliver me to my enemies to be mocked
and scourged and crucified, but my spirit shall be with you always."

When they were close to Jerusalem and came to Bethphage, to
the Mount of Olives, then Jesus sent two disciples, saying to them,
"Go into the village nearby, and immediately you will find a colt
tied; untie it and bring it to me. If anyone says anything to you, you
shall say, 'The Master has need of it,' and he will send it immediately." The disciples went and did as Jesus had directed them; they
brought the colt, and put their clothes on it, and he sat on it. Most
of the crowd, which had come to Jerusalem with him, spread their
clothes on the road, and others cut branches from the trees and
spread them on the road. The crowds that went before him and
that followed him shouted, "Blessed is he who bears witness to
God!" When he entered Jerusalem, all the city was stirred, saying,
"Who is this?" The crowds replied, "This is the prophet Jesus from
Nazareth of Galilee."

When religious leaders asked Jesus about his teaching authority,
he answered them, "I also will ask you a question; and if you tell
me the answer then I also will tell you by what authority I do these
things. The message of John the Baptist, whence did it come?
From his inner self or from other people?" They argued with one

another, "If we say, 'From his inner self,' he will say to us, 'Why then did you not believe him?' But if we say, 'From other people,' we are afraid of the multitude; for all hold that John was a prophet." So they answered Jesus, "We do not know." And he said to them, "Neither will I tell you by what authority I do these things.

Lasting happiness is like a parent who had two children. He/she went to the first and said, 'My child, go and work in the vineyard today.' The child answered, 'I will not'; but afterward he/she repented and went. And the parent went to the second and said the same. The child answered, 'I will go,' but did not go. Which of the two did the will of his parent?" They said, "The second." Jesus said to them, "Truly, I say to you, the unenlightened public will find lasting happiness before you. For John came to you in truthfulness, and you did not believe him, but many others did believe him. Even when you saw that he was right, you did not afterward repent and believe him.

"Here is what seeking lasting happiness is like. There was a manager who planted a vineyard and set a hedge around it. He dug a wine press in it and built a tower. He then let it out to tenants and went into another region. When the season of fruit drew near, he sent his workers to the tenants to get his fruit. The tenants took his workers and beat one, killed another, and stoned a third. Again he sent other workers, more than the first; and they did the same to them. Afterward he sent his son to them, saying, 'They will respect my son.' But when the tenants saw the son, they said to themselves, 'This is the heir; come, let us kill him and have his inheritance.' So they took him, cast him out of the vineyard, and killed him. When the owner of the vineyard comes, what will he do to those tenants?" They said to him, "He will put those wretches out of the vineyard, and let it out to other tenants who will give him the fruits in their seasons."

Jesus said to them, "Have you read in the scriptures: 'The very stone which the builders rejected has become the head of the corner; this was the working of God, and it is marvelous in our eyes.'"

When the chief priests and the aristocrats heard his parables, they perceived that he was speaking about them. But when they tried to arrest him, they feared the multitudes, because the multitudes held him to be a prophet.

Being Tested

Some of Jesus' opponents said, "We know that you are truthful, and teach the ways of God, and care for no one because of position. Tell us, then, what you think. Is it lawful to pay taxes to the government, or not?" But Jesus said, "Why put me to the test? Show me the money for the tax." And they brought him a coin. And Jesus said to them, "Who minted this?" They said, "The government." Then he said to them, "Render therefore to the government the things that are the government's, but render to God the things that are God's." When they heard this, they marveled; and they left him and went away.

Later a lawyer asked him, "Teacher, what shall I do to follow the guidance of God?" He said to him, "What is written in the law? How do you read?" He answered, "You shall love God with all your heart, and with all your soul, and with all your strength, and with all your mind, and your neighbor as yourself." He said to him, "You have answered right; do this, and you will live fully."

The lawyer, desiring to justify himself, said to Jesus, " Who is my neighbor?" Jesus replied, "A man was going from Jerusalem to Jericho, and he fell among robbers, who stripped him and beat him, and departed, leaving him half dead. Now by chance a priest was going down that road; and when he saw him he passed by on the other side. So likewise a Levite, when he came to the place and saw him, passed by on the other side. But a Samaritan, as he journeyed, came to where he was; and when he saw him, he had compassion, and went to him and bound up his wounds, pouring on oil and wine; then he set him on his own beast and brought him to an inn, and took care of him. And the next day the Samaritan took out some money and gave it to the innkeeper, saying, 'Take care of him; and whatever more you spend, I will repay you when I come back.' Which of these three, do you think, proved neighbor to the man who fell among the robbers?" The lawyer said, "The one who showed mercy on him." And Jesus said to him, "Go and do likewise."

Jesus then said, "This is my commandment, that you love one another as I have loved you. Greater love has no one than this, that a person lay down his/her life in behalf of friends and faith."

Later, in the temple, Jesus said, "Religious leaders often sit in the seats of honor. Practice and observe what they tell you, but do not act as they do; for they preach, but do not practice. They bind together heavy burdens, hard to bear, and lay them on people's shoulders. They themselves will not move them with their finger. They do all their deeds to be seen by the people. They have meaningless prayers and endless sermons. They love the place of honor at feasts, the best seats in the places of worship, salutations in the market places, and being called teacher by their congregations. But you are not to be called teacher, for you in turn have a teacher and you are all brothers and sisters in your faith. Neither be called masters, for you have sworn loyalty to a master, the Christ. Those who are the greatest among you shall be your servers; those who exalt themselves shall be humbled, and those who humble themselves shall be exalted."

Speaking With the Disciples

Jesus left the temple and was going away, when his disciples came to point out to him the various buildings connected with the temple. He answered them, "You see all these, do you not? Truly, I say to you, there will not be left here one stone upon another that will not be destroyed."

As he sat on the Mount of Olives, the disciples came to him privately, saying, "Tell us, when will this be, and what will be the sign of the coming of the next prophet and the close of another age?" Jesus answered them, "Take heed that no one leads you astray. For many will come, saying, 'I am the prophet that was prophesied,' and they will lead many astray. You will hear of wars and rumors of wars. See that you are not alarmed; for this must take place, but the end is not yet. For nation will rise against nation, and kingdom against kingdom, and there will be famines and earthquakes in various places. All this is but the beginning of the sufferings.

"Then the people will deliver you up to tribulation and put you to death. You will be hated by all nations for my name's sake. Many will fall away, betray one another, and hate one another. Various false prophets will arise and lead people astray. Because wickedness is multiplied, most people's love will grow cold. But those who endure will find lasting happiness.

"From the fig tree learn its lesson. As soon as its branch becomes tender and puts forth its leaves, you know that summer is near. Watch therefore, for you do not know on what day an enlightened one is coming. But know this, that if householders had known in what part of the night the thief was coming, they would have watched and would not have let their homes be broken into. Therefore, you also must be ready.

"Then lasting happiness shall be compared to ten young women who dressed themselves and went to meet the bridegroom. Five of them were foolish, and five were wise. For when the foolish got dressed up, they took no light with them; but each of the wise took a light. As the bridegroom was delayed, they all slumbered and slept. But at midnight there was a cry, 'Awake, the bridegroom is here! Come out to meet him.' Then all these maidens rose and got ready. And the foolish said to the wise, 'Give us some of your lights, for we did not bring any.' But the wise replied, 'Perhaps there will not be enough for us and for you; go rather to the store and buy them for yourselves.' And while they went to buy, the bridegroom came, and those who were ready went in with him to the marriage feast; and the door was shut. Afterward the other young women came, saying to the doorkeeper, 'Please open to us.' But he replied, 'Truly, I say to you, I cannot, even though I sincerely desire to do so, because it is already too late. Watch, therefore, for you know neither the day nor the hour.'

"Again, lasting happiness is as when property owners going on a journey called their workers and entrusted to them their property. To one they gave five thousand dollars, to another two, to another one, to each according to his/her ability. Then the people in charge went away. The one who had received the five thousand dollars went at once and traded with them and made five thousand more. So too, the one who had the two thousand made two thousand more. But the one who had received the one thousand dollars, went and dug in the ground and hid the money.

"After a long time the owners came to settle accounts with their workers. The one who had received the five thousand dollars came forward, bringing five thousand more, saying, 'You delivered to me five thousand dollars; here I have made five thousand more.' The owners said, 'Well done, good and faithful worker; you have been faithful over a little, I will put you in charge of much.'"

The one also who had the two thousand dollars came forward, saying, 'You delivered to me two thousand; here I have made two thousand more.' The owners said to the second worker, 'Well done, good and faithful worker; you have been faithful over a little, I will put you in charge of much.'

The one also who had received the one thousand dollars came forward, saying, 'I knew you to be hard masters, reaping where you did not sow, and gathering where you did not winnow. So I was afraid. I went and hid your money in the ground. Here you have what is yours.' Their owners answered them, 'You irresponsible worker! You knew that we reap where we have not sowed, and gather where we have not winnowed? Then you ought to have invested our money with the bankers, and at our coming we should have received what was our own with interest. So take the one thousand from the third worker, and give it to those who have the ten thousand. For to all who have will more be given, and they will have abundance; but from them who have not, even what they have will be taken away.'

A man named Nicodemus came to Jesus by night and said to him, "Master, we know that you are an inspired teacher; for no one can say what you say unless he is certain within himself." Jesus answered him, "Truly, I say to you, unless you are born anew, you cannot find lasting happiness." Nicodemus said to him, "How can people be born when they are old? Can they enter a second time into their mothers' wombs and be born?" Jesus answered, "Unless we are born spiritually as well as materially, we cannot obtain lasting happiness." Do not marvel that I said to you, 'You must be born anew.' The wind blows where it will, and you hear the sound of it, but you do not know from where it comes or where it goes. So it is with everyone who is born of the spirit." Nicodemus said to him, "How can this be?" Jesus answered him, "Do you not understand this?"

"Similarly, when your life has been lived, and the day of evaluating your worth arrives, God will say to you on the one side, 'Enter into eternal life; for I was hungry and you gave me food, I was thirsty and you gave me drink, I was a stranger and you welcomed me, I was naked and you clothed me, I was sick and you visited me, I was in prison and you came to me.' Then the righteous will answer, 'When did we see you hungry and feed you, or thirsty and give you drink? And when did we see you a stranger and welcome you, or naked and clothe you? And when did we see you sick or in prison and visit you?' And God will answer them, 'Truly, I say to you, as you did it to one of the least of these my fellow human beings, you did it to me.' Then he will say to those on the other side, 'Depart from me; for I was hungry and you gave me no food, I was thirsty and you gave me no drink, I was a stranger and you did not welcome me, naked and you did not clothe me, sick and in prison and you did not visit me.' And they will pass away and be forgotten, but the righteous will blend into the Infinite."

When Jesus had finished these sayings, he said to his disciples, "You know that after two days the Passover feast is coming, and I am to be delivered up to be crucified."

The Beginning of the End

The chief priests and the elders of the people gathered in the palace of the high priest, and took counsel together in order to arrest Jesus by stealth and kill him. But they said, "Not during the feast, lest there be a tumult among the people."

Now once Jesus was dining at Bethany, a woman came up to him with an alabaster jar of very expensive ointment and poured it on his head. When the disciples saw this act, they were indignant, saying, "Why should you be so wasteful? This ointment might have been sold for a large sum and given to the poor." But Jesus said to them, "Why do you trouble the woman? She has done a beautiful thing to me. You will always have the poor with you, but you will not always have me. In pouring this ointment on my body, she has done the most she can do. Truly, I say to you, wherever the gospel is preached in the whole world, what this woman has done will be told in memory of her."

Seeing much disbelief, Jesus lamented, "Why do you kill the prophets and stone those who are sent to you? How often would I have gathered you together as a hen gathers her brood under her wings, and you would not have it so! Behold, your house is forsaken and desolate. For I tell you, you will not see me again until you say, 'Blessed is he who bears witness to God.' "

Jesus then said to the people who believed him, "If you abide in my word, you are truly my disciples. You will know the truth, and the truth will set you free."

Jesus said to his disciples, "The hour is coming, indeed it has come, when you will be scattered, everyone to his/her home, and will leave me alone. I have said this to you, that in me you may have peace. In the world you will always have tribulations; but be of good cheer, I have overcome the world."

Then one of the twelve, who was called Judas Iscariot, went to the chief priests and said, "What will you give me if I deliver him to you?" The priests paid Judas thirty pieces of silver. And from that moment Judas sought an opportunity to betray Jesus.

Observing Passover

Now as Jesus' last days approached, the disciples came to him, saying, "Where will you have us prepare for you to eat the Passover?" He said, "Go into the city to a certain man, and say to him, 'The Teacher says, My time is at hand; I will keep the Passover at your home with my disciples.'" The disciples did as Jesus had directed them, and they prepared the Passover.

When it was evening, Jesus sat at table with the twelve disciples; and as they were eating, he said, "Truly, I say to you, one of you will betray me." They were very sorrowful, and began to say to him one after another, "Is it I, Master?" He answered, "He who has dipped his hand in the dish with me will betray me. It would have been better for that man if he had not been born." Judas, who was to betray him, said, "Is it I, Master?" He said to him, "You have said so."

When Jesus and the disciples had sung a hymn, they went out to the Mount of Olives. Then Jesus said to them, "You will all fall away because of me this night." But Peter declared to him, "Though they all fall away because of you, I will never fall away." Jesus said to him, "Truly, I say to you, this very night, before the cock crows, you will deny me three times." Peter said to him, "Even if I must die with you, I will not deny you." So said all the disciples.

Meditating at Gethsemane

Then Jesus went with them to a place called Gethsemane, and he said to his disciples, "Sit here, while I go and pray." Taking with him Peter and the two young people, he began to be sorrowful and troubled. Then he said to them, "My soul is very sorrowful even to death. Remain here, and watch with me." And going a little farther he fell on his face and prayed. Afterward he came to the disciples and found them sleeping; and he said to Peter, "So, could you not watch with me one hour? Watch and pray, that you may not enter into temptation. The spirit indeed is willing, but the flesh is weak." Again, for the second time, he went away and prayed. And again he came and found them sleeping, for their eyes were heavy. So, leav-

ing them again, he went away and prayed for the third time. Then
he came to the disciples and said to them, "Are you still sleeping
and taking your rest? The hour is at hand, and I am betrayed into
the hands of my enemies. Rise, let us be going; see, my betrayer is
at hand."

The Betrayal

While he was still speaking, Judas, one of the twelve, came, and
with him a great crowd holding swords and clubs, from the chief
priests and the elders of the people. Now the betrayer had given
them a sign, saying, "The one I shall kiss is the man; seize him."
Judas came up to Jesus at once and said, "Hail, Master!" And he
kissed him. Jesus said to him, "Friend, why are you here?" Then
they came up and laid hands on Jesus and seized him. And behold,
one of those who were with Jesus stretched out his hand and drew
his sword, and struck the slave of the high priest, and cut off his
ear. Then Jesus said to him, "Put your sword back into its place;
for all who take the sword will perish by the sword." At that hour
Jesus said to the crowds, "Have you come out as against a robber
with swords and clubs to capture me? Day after day I sat in the
temple teaching, and you did not seize me." Then all the disciples
forsook him and fled.

Those who had seized Jesus led him to Caiaphas, the high priest,
where the elders and scribes had gathered. Peter followed him at a
distance as far as the courtyard of the high priest, and going inside
he sat with the guards to see the end. The chief priests and the
whole council sought false witness against Jesus, that they might
put him to death, but they found none, though many witnesses
came forward. The high priest then said to him, "I ask you to tell
us if you are the Christ." Jesus said to him, "You have said so."
Then the high priest tore his robes and said, "He has uttered blasphemy. Why do we still need witnesses? You have now heard his
blasphemy. What is your judgment?" They answered, "He deserves
death." Then they spat in his face and struck him. Some slapped
him, saying, "Prophesy to us, you Christ! Who was it that struck
you?"

Peter was sitting outside in the courtyard reflecting on what had
happened. A maid came up to him and said, "You also were with
Jesus the Galilean." But he denied it before them all, saying, "I do
not know what you mean." When he went out to the porch, an-

other maid saw him, and she said to the bystanders, "This fellow was with Jesus of Nazareth." And again he denied it with an oath, "I do not know the man." After a little while the bystanders came up and said to Peter, "Certainly you are also one of them, for your accent betrays you." Then he began to invoke a curse on himself and to swear, 'I do not know the man." And immediately the cock crowed. And Peter remembered the saying of Jesus. "Before the cock crows, you will deny me three times." He then went out and wept bitterly.

When morning came, all the chief priests and the elders of the people took counsel against Jesus to put him to death. They bound him and led him away, delivering him to Pilate the governor.

When Judas, his betrayer, saw that Jesus was condemned, he repented and brought back the thirty pieces of silver to the chief priests and the elders, saying, "I have sinned in betraying innocent blood." They said, "What is that to us? See to it yourself." And throwing down the pieces of silver in the synagogue, he departed. Shortly thereafter he went and hanged himself. But the chief priests, taking the pieces of silver, said, "It is not lawful to put them into the treasury, since they are blood money." So they took counsel, and bought with them the potter's field to bury strangers in. Therefore that field has been called the Field of Blood to this day.

Now Jesus stood before the governor; and the governor asked him, "Are you the King of the Jews?" Jesus said to him, "You have said so." But when he was accused by the chief priests and elders, he made no answer. When Pilate said to him, "Do you not hear how many things they testify against you?" Jesus gave Pilate no answer, not even to a single charge, so that the governor wondered greatly.

The Crucifixion

Now at the feast the governor was accustomed to releasing for the crowd any one prisoner whom they wanted. They had then a notorious prisoner, called Barabbas. When they had gathered, Pilate said to them, "Whom do you want me to release for you, Barabbas or Jesus?" For he knew that it was out of envy that they had delivered him up. Besides, while he was sitting on the judgment seat, his wife sent word to him, "Have nothing to do with that righteous man, for I have suffered much over him today in a dream." Now the chief priests and the elders persuaded the people to ask for

Barabbas and not Jesus. The governor again said to them, "Which of the two do you want me to release for you?" And they said, "Barabbas." Pilate said to them, "Then what shall I do with Jesus?" They all said, "Let him be crucified." Pilate said, "Why, what evil has he done?" But they shouted all the more, "Let him be crucified."

So when Pilate saw that he was gaining nothing, but rather that a riot was beginning, he took water and washed his hands before the crowd, saying, "I am innocent of this man's blood. See to it yourselves." All the people answered, "His blood shall be on us and on our children!" Then he released for them Barabbas, and having scourged Jesus, delivered him to be crucified.

Then the soldiers of the governor gathered the whole battalion before him. They stripped him and put a scarlet robe upon him, and plaiting a crown of thorns they put it on his head, and put a reed in his right hand. Kneeling before him they mocked him, saying, "Hail, King of the Jews!" And they spat upon him, and took the reed and struck him on the head. When they had mocked him, they stripped him of the robe, and put his own clothes on him, and led him away to crucify him.

As they were marching out, they came upon a man of Cyrene, Simon by name. This man they compelled to carry Jesus' cross. And when they came to a place called Golgotha, which means place of a skull, they offered him wine to drink, mingled with gall; but when he tasted it, he would not drink it.

When they had crucified him, they divided his garments among them by casting lots. Then they sat down and kept watch over him there. Over his head they put the charge against him, which read, "This is Jesus, the King of the Jews." Then two robbers were crucified with him, one on the right and one on the left. Those who passed by derided him. So also the chief priests, with the elders and teachers of the law, mocked him, saying, "He is the King of Israel; let him come down now from the cross, and we will believe him." The robbers who were crucified with him also reviled him in the same way.

Death and Its Aftermath

After about nine hours upon the cross, Jesus cried with a loud voice and yielded up his spirit.

When it was evening, a rich man named Joseph came from Arimathea, who also was a disciple of Jesus. He went to Pilate and asked for the body of Jesus. Then Pilate ordered it to be given to him. Joseph laid it in his own new tomb, which he had hewn in the rock. He rolled a great stone to the entrance of the tomb and departed.

Though Jesus died on the cross, yet he still lives in the hearts and minds of people everywhere, having become one with God. He appears individually to people throughout the world as they recall his words, "Peace I leave with you; my peace I give to you; not as the world gives do I give to you. Let not your hearts be troubled, neither let them be afraid. ... Behold, I am with you always, even to Eternity."

Beginning of the Resurrection

... On the first day of the week, at early dawn, (friends) came to the tomb, taking the spices that they had prepared. They found the stone rolled away from the tomb, but when they went in, they did not find the body. While they were perplexed about this, suddenly two men in dazzling clothes stood beside them. The women were terrified and bowed their faces to the ground, but the men said to them, "Why do you look for the living among the dead? He is not here, but has risen." Remember how he told you, while he was still in Galilee, that the Son of Man must be handed over to sinners, and be crucified, and on the third day rise again." Then they remembered his words, and returning from the tomb, they told all this to the eleven and to all the rest. Now it was Mary Magdalene, Joanna, Mary the mother of James, and the other women with them who told this to the apostles. But these words seemed to them an idle tale, and they did not believe them. But Peter got up and ran to the tomb; stooping and looking in, he saw the linen cloths by themselves; then he went home, amazed at what had happened.

Now on that same day two of them were going to a village called Emmaus, about seven miles from Jerusalem, and talking with each other about all these things that had happened. While they were talking and discussing, Jesus himself came near and went with them, but their eyes were kept from recognizing him. And he said to them, "What are you discussing with each other while you walk along?" They stood still, looking sad. Then one of them, whose name was Cleopas, answered him, "Are you the only stranger in Jerusalem who does not know the things that have taken place there in these days?" He asked them, "What things?" They replied, "The things about Jesus of Nazareth, who was a prophet mighty in deed and word before God and all the people, and how our chief priests and leaders handed him over to be condemned to death and crucified him. But we had hoped that he was the one to redeem Israel. Yes, and besides all this, it is now the third day since these things took place. Moreover, some women of our group astounded us. They were at the tomb early this morning, and when they did not find his body they had indeed seen a vision of angels who said that he was alive. Some of those who were with us went to the tomb and found it just as the women had said; but they did not see him." Then Jesus said to them, "Oh, how foolish you are, and how slow of heart to believe all that the prophets have declared! Was it not necessary that the Messiah should suffer these things and then enter into his glory?" Then beginning with Moses and all the prophets, he interpreted to them the things about himself in all the scriptures.

Recognizing Their Risen Lord

As they came near the village to which they were going, he walked ahead as if he were going on. But they urged him strongly, saying, "Stay with us, because it is almost evening and the day is now nearly over." So he went in to stay with them. When he was at the table with them, he took bread, blessed and broke it, and gave it to them. Then their eyes were opened, and they recognized him; and he vanished from their sight. They said to each other, "Were not our hearts burning within us while he was talking to us on the road, while he was opening the scriptures to us?" That same hour they got up and returned to Jerusalem; and they found the eleven and their companions gathered together. They were saying, "The Lord has risen indeed, and he has appeared to Simon!" Then they told what had happened on the road, and how Jesus had been made known to them in the breaking of the bread.

While they were talking about this, Jesus himself stood among them and said to them, "Peace be with you." They were startled and terrified, and thought that they were seeing a ghost. He said to them, "Why are you frightened, and why do doubts arise in your hearts? Look at my hands and my feet; see that it is I myself. Touch me and see; for a ghost does not have flesh and bones as you see that I have." And when he has said this, he showed them his hands and his feet. While in their joy they were disbelieving and still wondering, he said to them, "Have you anything here to eat?" They gave him a piece of broiled fish, and he took it and ate in their presence.

The Fulfillment of Prophecy

Then Jesus said to them, "These are my words that I spoke to you while I was still with you—that everything written about me in the law of Moses, the prophets, and the psalms must be fulfilled." Then he opened their minds to understand the scriptures, and he said to them, "Thus it is written, that the Messiah is to suffer and to rise from the dead on the third day, and that repentance and forgiveness of sins are to be proclaimed in his name to all nations, beginning with Jerusalem. You are witnesses of these things. And see, I am sending upon you what my Father promised; so stay here in the city until you have been clothed with power from on high."

The Ascension

Then Jesus led them out as far as Bethany, and, lifting up his hands, he blessed them. While he was blessing them, he withdrew from them and was carried up into heaven. And they worshipped him, and returned to Jerusalem with great joy; and they were continually in the temple blessing God.

In the first book, Theophilus wrote about all that Jesus did and taught from the beginning until the day when he was taken up to heaven, after giving instructions through the Holy Spirit to the apostles whom he had chosen. After his suffering he presented himself alive to them by many convincing proofs, appearing to them during forty days and speaking about the kingdom of God. While staying with them, he ordered them not to leave Jerusalem, but to wait there for the promise of the Father. "This," he said, "is what you have heard from me; for John baptized with water, but you will be baptized with the Holy Spirit not many days from now.

So when they had come together, they asked him, "Lord, is this the time when you will restore the kingdom to Israel?" Jesus replied, "It is not for you to know the times or periods that the Father has set by his own authority. But you will receive power when the Holy Spirit has come upon you; and you will be my witnesses in Jerusalem, in all Judea and Samaria, and to the ends of the earth." When he had said this, as they were watching, he was lifted up, and a cloud took him out of their sight. While he was going and they were gazing up toward heaven, suddenly two men in white robes stood by them. They said, "Men of Galilee, why do you stand looking up toward heaven? This Jesus, who has been taken up from you into heaven, will come in the same way as you saw him go into heaven."

Speaking in Tongues

Then they returned to Jerusalem from the mount called Olivet, which is near Jerusalem, a sabbath day's journey away. When they had entered the city, they went to the room upstairs where they were staying, Peter, and John, and James, and Andrew, Philip and Thomas, Bartholomew and Matthew, James son of Alphaeus, and Simon the Zealot, and Judas son of James. All these were constantly devoting themselves to prayer, together with certain women, including Mary the mother of Jesus, as well as his brothers.

When the day of Pentecost had come, they were all together in one place. And suddenly from heaven there came a sound like the rush of a violent wind, and it filled the entire house where they were sitting. Divided tongues, as of fire, appeared among them, and a tongue rested on each of them. All of them were filled with the Holy Spirit and began to speak in other languages, as the Spirit gave them ability.

Now there were devout Jews from every nation under heaven living in Jerusalem. And at this sound the crowd gathered and was bewildered, because each one heard them speaking in the native language of each. Amazed and astonished, they asked, "Are not all these who are speaking Galileans? And how is it that we hear, each of us, in our own native language? Parthians, Medes, Elamites, and residents of Mesopotamia, Judea and Cappadocia, Pontus and Asis, Phrygia and Pamphylia, Egypt and the parts of Libya belonging to Cyrene, and visitors from Rome, both Jews and proselytes, Cretans and Arabs—in our own languages we hear them speaking about God's deeds of power." All were amazed and perplexed, saying to one another, "What does this mean?" But others sneered and said, "They are filled with new wine."

But Peter, standing with the eleven, raised his voice and addressed them, "Men of Judea and all who live in Jerusalem, let this be known to you, and listen to what I say. Indeed, these are not drunk, as you suppose, for it is only nine o'clock in the morning. No, this is what was spoken through the prophet Joel:

'In the last days it will be, God declares,
That I will pour out my Spirit upon all flesh,
And your sons and your daughters shall prophesy,
And your young men shall see visions,
And your old men shall dream dreams.
Even upon my slaves, both men and women,
In those days I will pour out my Spirit;
And they shall prophesy.
And I will show portents in the heaven above
And signs on the earth below,
Blood, and fire, and smoky mist.
The sun shall be turned to darkness
And the moon to blood,
Before the coming of the Lord's great and glorious day.
Then everyone who calls on the name of the Lord shall be saved.'

"You that are Israelites, listen to what I have to say: Jesus of Nazareth, a man attested to you by God with deeds of power, wonders, and signs that God did through him among you, as you yourselves know—this man, handed over to you according to the definite plan and foreknowledge of God, you crucified and killed by the hands of those outside the law. But God raised him up, having freed him from death, because it was impossible for him to be held in its power. For David says concerning him,

'I saw the Lord always before me, for he is at my right hand so that I will not be shaken; therefore my heart was glad, and my tongue rejoiced; moreover my flesh will live in hope.
For you will not abandon my soul to Hades, or let your Holy One experience corruption.
You have made known to me the ways of life; you will make me full of gladness with your presence.'

"Fellow Israelites, I may say to you confidently of our ancestor David that he both died and was buried, and his tomb is with us to this day. Since he was a prophet, he knew that God had sworn with an oath to him that he would put one of his descendants on his throne. Foreseeing this, David spoke of the resurrection of the Messiah, saying,

'He was not abandoned to Hades, nor did his flesh experience corruption.'

Jesus as Lord and Messiah

This Jesus God raised up, and of that all of us are witnesses. Being therefore exalted at the right hand of God, and having received from the Father the promise of the Holy Spirit, he has poured out this that you both see and hear. For David did not ascend into the heavens, but he himself says,

"The Lord said to my Lord,

'Sit at my right hand, until I make your enemies your footstool.'

"Therefore let the entire house of Israel know with certainty that God has made him both Lord and Messiah, this Jesus whom you crucified."

Now when they heard this, they were cut to the heart and said to Peter and to the other apostles, "Brothers, what should we do?" Peter said to them, "Repent, and be baptized every one of you in the name of Jesus Christ so that your sins may be forgiven; and you will receive the gift of the Holy Spirit. For the promise is for you, for your children, and for all who are far away, everyone whom the Lord our God calls to him." And he testified with many other arguments and exhorted them saying, "Save yourselves from this corrupt generation." So those who welcomed his message were baptized, and that day about three thousand persons were added. They devoted themselves to the apostles' teaching and fellowship, to the breaking of bread and the prayers.

Awe came upon everyone, because many wonders and signs were being done by the apostles. All who believed were together and had all things in common; they would sell their possessions and goods and distribute the proceeds to all, as many had need. Day by day, as they spent much time together in the temple, they broke bread at home and ate their food with glad and generous hearts, praising God and having the goodwill of all the people. And day by day the Lord added to their number those who were being saved.

PAUL THE APOSTLE

Carrying on Jesus' Teachings

After the death of Jesus, the disciples, who from then on were called apostles, remained in Jerusalem for several years. They spent their time spreading the news about him, even to such an extent that they were persecuted and thrown into prison. Upon being released, they continued their work, and the number of disciples multiplied greatly. One of them, Stephen, was stoned for his convictions about the messages of Jesus.

At this time a man named Saul, who was leading the attacks, is said to have witnessed Stephen's death; and a great persecution arose against the church in Jerusalem, scattering it throughout the region to Judea and Samaria.

Now those who were scattered continued preaching the good news about Jesus. But Saul, still breathing threats and murder against the disciples, set off for Damascus, thinking that if he found any of those people along the way, he might bring them to Jerusalem. As he journeyed, he suddenly became aware through a vision of his folly in persecuting the followers of Jesus, and he decided to become one of them.

Saul, whose name then became Paul, felt himself called upon to spread the church throughout the rest of the known world; hence, he soon became the leader of this movement.

Those who were scattered because of the persecution that arose over Stephen traveled as far as Phoenicia, Cyprus, and Antioch. News of this came to the ears of the church in Jerusalem, and they sent Barnabas, a disciple, to Antioch. Barnabas went to Tarsus to look for Paul. When he found him, Barnabas brought Paul to Antioch. For a whole year they met with the church and taught a large company of people. In Antioch the disciples were for the first time called Christians.

Shortly thereafter Paul and Barnabas went down from there and sailed to Cyprus. Next they came to Perga in Pamphylia, and thence to Antioch of Pisidia. When Paul and his company were persecuted at Antioch, they went to Iconium and several other towns.

The Teachings of Paul

The following are teachings reputed to be those of Paul the Apostle at Colossae:

"Put to death what is evil in you: immorality, impurity, anger, evil desire, and covetousness, which is idolatry. Now put away also all these: malice, slander, and foul talk from your mouth. Do not lie to one another, seeing that you have put off the old nature with its practices and have put on the new nature, which is continually renewed in strength.

"Put on then, my beloved, compassion, kindness, lowliness, meekness, and patience, forbearing one another and, if one has a complaint against another, forgiving each other. Even as others have forgiven you, so you also must forgive. And above all those put on love, which binds everything together in perfect harmony.

"Managers, treat your workers justly and fairly, knowing that you also should be a servant to others. Let your speech always be gracious, seasoned with salt, so that you may know how you ought to answer everyone."

In the region of Galatia, Paul spoke as follows:

"For you were called to freedom, my friends. Only do not use your freedom as an opportunity for the flesh, but through love be servers of one another. For the whole law is fulfilled in one sentence, 'You shall love your neighbor as yourself.'

"But I say, walk by the spirit. Do not gratify the cravings of the flesh. The cravings of the flesh are against the spirit, and the cravings of the spirit are against the flesh. These two are opposed to each other, to prevent you from doing what you would. The works of the flesh are plain: immorality, impurity, licentiousness, idolatry, sorcery, enmity, strife, jealousy, anger, selfishness, dissension, envy, drunkenness, carousing, and the like. But the fruits of the spirit are love, joy, peace, patience, kindness, goodness, faithfulness, gentleness, and self-control. Against such there is no law.

"If we live by the spirit, let us also walk by the spirit. Let us have no self-conceit, no provoking of one another, no envy of one another.

"Friends, if a person is engaged in any wrongdoing, you who are spiritual should restore him/her in a spirit of gentleness. Look to yourself, lest you too be tempted. Help bear one another's burdens. For if any of you think you are something, when you are nothing, you deceive yourself. But let each of you test your own work, and then your reason to boast will be in yourself alone and not in your neighbor. For each of you will have also to bear your own load.

"Do not be deceived, for whatever a person sows, that he/she will also reap. Those who sow to their own flesh will from the flesh reap corruption. But those who sow to the spirit will from the spirit reap lasting happiness. Let us now grow strong in the spirit, for in due season we shall reap, if we do not lose heart. So then, as we have opportunities, let us do good to all beings."

After visiting several other towns, Paul and his company went to Troas, and from there set sail for Macedonia. When they reached Philippi, Paul gave further advice:

"If there is any encouragement in Christ, any incentive of love, any participation in the spirit, any affection and sympathy, complete my joy by being of one mind. Do nothing from selfishness or conceit, but in humility count others better than yourselves. Let all of you look not only to your own interests, but also to the interests of others.

"Also, friends, whatever is true, whatever is honorable, whatever is pure, whatever is lovely, whatever is gracious, if there is any excellence, if there is anything worthy of praise, think about these things. What you have learned, received, heard, and seen in me, do. May God be with you."

Now when they had passed through several towns, they came to Thessalonica, where Paul preached to the people in the synagogue:

"We beseech you, my friends, to respect those who labor among you and are your supervisors even if they admonish you, as well as to esteem them highly in love because of their work. Be at peace among yourselves. We exhort you, my friends, admonish the idle, encourage the fainthearted, help the weak, and be patient with them all. See that none of you repays evil for evil, but always seek to do good to one another and to all. Remain content, giving thanks in all circumstances. Do not quench the spirit, do not despise prophesying, but test everything. Hold fast what is good, and abstain from every form of evil.

"We ask you, friends, to keep away from any brother or sister who is living in idleness and not in accord with the tradition that you received from us. For you yourselves know how you ought to carry on. We were not idle when we lived among you. We did not eat anyone's bread without paying, but with toil and labor we worked night and day, that we might not burden any of you. It was not because we have not that right, but to give you in our conduct an example to follow. For even then we gave you this command: If anyone will not work, do not let him/her eat. We hear that some of you are living in idleness, mere busybodies, not doing any work. Such persons we command and exhort to do their work in quietness and to earn their own living. Friends, do not be weary in well-doing.

"If various people refuse to follow what we teach, note those individuals. Do not look on them as enemies, but help them as fellow human beings. Let us not sleep spiritually, as many others do. Rather, let us keep awake and be mindful."

Paul's visit caused quite a disturbance in Thessalonica, and as a result he was sent away by night to Beroea, and finally had to escape to Athens. There he was not too well received; hence, he soon left Athens for Corinth. At this place he was well received and delivered to them the essence of his whole message:

Paul, called to be an apostle of Christ Jesus by the will of God, and our brother Sosthenes,

To the church of God that is in Corinth, to those who are sanctified in Christ Jesus, called to be saints, together with all those who in every place call on the name of our Lord Jesus Christ, both their Lord and ours:

Grace to you and peace from God our Father and the Lord Jesus Christ.

I give thanks to my God always for you because of the grace of God that has been given you in Christ Jesus, for in every way you have been enriched in him, in speech and knowledge of every kind—just as the testimony of Christ has been strengthened among you—so that you are not lacking in any spiritual gift as you wait for the revealing of our Lord Jesus Christ. He will also strengthen you to the end, so that you may be blameless on the day of our Lord Jesus Christ. God is faithful; by him you were called into the fellowship of his Son, Jesus Christ our Lord.

Resolving Their Differences

Now I appeal to you, brothers and sisters, by the name of our Lord Jesus Christ, that all of you be in agreement and that there be no divisions among you, but that you be united in the same mind and the same purpose. For it has been reported to me by Chloe's people that there are quarrels among you, my brothers and sisters.

What I mean is that each of you says, "I belong to Paul," or "I belong to Apollos," or "I belong to Cephas," or "I belong to Christ." Has Christ been divided? Was Paul crucified for you? Or were you baptized in the name of Paul? I thank God that I baptized none of you except Crispus and Gaius, so that no one can say that you were baptized in my name. For Christ did not send me to baptize but to proclaim the gospel, and not with eloquent wisdom, so that the cross of Christ might not be emptied of its power.

For the message about the cross is foolishness to those who are perishing, but to us who are being saved it is the power of God. For it is written,

"I will destroy the wisdom of the wise, and the discernment of the discerning I will thwart."

Where is the one who is wise? Where is the scribe? Where is the debater of this age? Has not God made foolish the wisdom of the world? For since, in the wisdom of God, the world did not know God through wisdom, God decided, through the foolishness of our proclamation, to save those who believe. For Jews demand signs and Greeks desire wisdom, but we proclaim Christ crucified, a stumbling block to Jews and foolishness to Gentiles, but to those of you who are called, both Jews and Greeks, Christ is the power of God and the wisdom of God. For God's foolishness is wiser than human wisdom, and God's weakness is stronger than human strength.

Consider your own call, brothers and sisters, not many of you were wise by human standards, not many were powerful, not many were of noble birth. But God chose what is foolish in the world to shame the wise; God chose what is weak in the world to shame the strong; God chose what is low and despised in the world, things that are not, to reduce to nothing things that are, so that no one might boast in the presence of God. He is the source of your life in Christ Jesus, who became for us wisdom from God, and righteousness and sanctification and redemption, in order that, as it is written, "Let the one who boasts, boast in the Lord."

Now I would remind you, brothers and sisters, of the good news that I proclaimed to you, which you in turn received, in which also you stand, through which also you are being saved, if you hold firmly to the message that I proclaimed to you—unless you have come to believe in vain.

For I handed on to you as of first importance what I in turn had received: that Christ died for our sins in accordance with the scriptures, and that he was buried, and that he was raised on the third day in accordance with the scriptures, and that he appeared to Cephas, then to the twelve. Then he appeared to more than five hundred brothers and sisters at one time. Then he appeared to James, then to all the apostles. Last of all, as to one untimely born, he appeared also to me. For I am the least of the apostles, unfit to be called an apostle, because I persecuted the church of God. But by the grace of God I am what I am, and his grace toward me has not been in vain. On the contrary, I worked harder than any of them—though it was not I, but the grace of God that is with me. Whether then it was I or they, so we proclaim and so you have come to believe.

Supreme Importance of the Resurrection

Now if Christ is proclaimed as raised form the dead, how can some of you say there is no resurrection of the dead? If there is no resurrection of the dead, then Christ has not been raised; and if Christ has not been raised, then our proclamation has been in vain and your faith has been in vain. We are even found to be misrepresenting God, because we testified of God that he raised Christ—whom he did not raise if it is true that the dead are not raised. For if the dead are not raised, then Christ has not been raised. If Christ has not been raised, your faith is futile and you are still in your sins. Then those also who have died in Christ have perished. If for this life only we have hoped in Christ, we are of all people most to be pitied.

But in fact Christ has been raised from the dead, the first fruits of those who have died. For since death came through a human being, the resurrection of the dead has also come through a human being; for as all die in Adam, so all will be made alive in Christ. But each in his own order: Christ the first fruits, then at his coming those who belong to Christ. Then comes the end, when he hands over the kingdom to God the Father, after he has destroyed every ruler and every authority and power. For he must reign until he has put all his enemies under his feet. The last enemy to be destroyed is death. For "God has put all things in subjection under his feet." But when it says, "All things are put in subjection," it is plain that this does not include the one who put all things in subjection under him. When all things are subjected to him, then the Son Himself will also be subjected to the one who put all things in subjection under him, so that God may be all in all.

"Even to the present hour we hunger and thirst. We are ill-clad, buffeted, and homeless. We labor, working with our own hands. When reviled, we bless; when persecuted, we endure; when slandered, we try to conciliate; we have become, and are now, as the refuse of the world, the worst of all things.

"We are afflicted in every way, but not crushed; perplexed, but not driven to despair; persecuted, but not forsaken; struck down, but not destroyed. So, then, God is at work in us, and also in you.

"Therefore, we do not lose heart. Though our outer nature is wasting away, our inner nature is being renewed every day. This slight momentary affliction is preparing for us an eternal hardiness beyond all comparison, because we look not to the things that are seen but to the things that are unseen; for the things that are seen are transient, but the things that are unseen are eternal.

"We know that if the house we live in is destroyed, we have a spiritual home, a house not made with hands but eternal. While we are still in this house, we sigh with anxiety; not that we would be unclothed, but that we would be further clothed, so that what is mortal may be swallowed up in God.

"We are always of good courage. We know that while we are at home in the body we are away from the Spirit, because we walk by faith and not by sight. We are of good courage, and we would rather be away from the body and at home with the Spirit.

"Working together, then, we entreat you not to accept your gifts without appreciation. We put no obstacle in anyone's way, so that no fault may be found with our ministry. As servants of humanity we commend ourselves in every way: through great endurance, in afflictions, hardships, calamities, beatings, imprisonments, tumults, labors, and hunger. We seek purity, wisdom, forbearance, kindness, genuine love, truthful speech, and the power of inspiration with the weapons of righteousness for the right hand and for the left. We are treated as imposters, and yet are true; as unknown, and yet well known; as dying, and behold we live; as punished, and yet not killed; as sorrowful, yet always happy; as poor, yet rich in the Spirit; as having nothing, and yet possessing everything.

"Our mouth is open to you, Corinthians; our heart is wide. You are not restricted by us, but you are restricted in your own affections. In return—I speak as to children—widen your hearts also.

"I do all things for the sake of the gospel, that I may share in its blessings. Do you not know that in a race all the runners compete, but only one receives the prize? So run that you may obtain it. All athletes exercise self-control in all things. They do it to receive a perishable wreath, but we an imperishable. I do not run aimlessly, and I do not box as one beating the air. I consider my body and control it, lest after preaching to others I myself should be disqualified.

"Friends, do not be children in your thinking; be babes in evil, but in thinking be mature.

"Do not be deceived. Bad company can ruin good morals. Come to your right mind and sin no more. For some have no awareness of God.

Concerning Spiritual Gifts

"Now concerning spiritual gifts, friends, I do not want you to be uninformed. There are varieties of gifts, but the same spirit; and there are varieties of service, but the same ultimate goal; and there are varieties of working, but it is the same spirit which inspires them all in every one. To each is given the manifestation of the spirit for the common good. To one is given through the spirit the utterance of wisdom, and to another the utterance of knowledge according to the same spirit, to another faith by the same spirit, to another prophecy, to another the ability to distinguish between people, to another various kinds of languages, to another the interpretation of languages. All these are inspired by one and the same spirit.

"For just as the body is one and has many members, and all the members of the body, though many, are one body, so it is with the spiritual community.

"For the body does not consist of one member but of many. If the foot should say, 'Because I am not a hand, I do not belong to the body,' that would not make it any less a part of the body. If the whole body were an eye, where would be the hearing? If the whole body were an ear, where would be the sense of smell? If all were a single organ, where would the body be? As it is, there are many parts, yet one body.

The eye cannot say to the hand, 'I have no need of you,' nor again the head to the feet, 'I have no need of you,' nor again the head to the foot, 'I have no need of you.' On the contrary, the parts of the body which seem to be weaker are indispensable, and those parts of the body which we think less honorable we invest with the greater honor, and our unpresentable parts are treated with greater modesty, which our more presentable parts do not require. If one member suffers, all suffer together; if one member is honored, all rejoice together.

"Now you are body of the spiritual community and individually members of it. There are among you first spiritual leaders, second prophets, third teachers, then helpers, administrators, and speakers in various kinds of languages. Are all apostles? Are all prophets? Are all teachers? Do all speak with different languages? Do all interpret? But earnestly desire the higher gifts.

The Supremacy of Love

"I will also show you a more excellent way.

"If I speak with the language of the greatest of people, but have not love, I am a noisy gong or a clanging cymbal. If I have prophetic powers, understand all mysteries and all knowledge, and if I have all faith, so as to remove mountains, but have not love, I am nothing. If I give away all that I have, and if I deliver my body to be burned, but have not love, I gain nothing.

"Love is patient and kind; love is not jealous or boastful; it is not arrogant or rude. Love does not insist on its own way; it is not irritable or resentful; it does not rejoice at wrong, but rejoices in the right. Love bears all things, believes all things, hopes all things, endures all things.

"Love never ends. As for prophecy, it will pass away; as for languages, they will cease; as for knowledge, it will pass away. For our knowledge is imperfect and our prophecy is imperfect; but when the perfect comes, the imperfect will pass away. When I was a child, I spoke like a child. I thought like a child, I reasoned like a child. When I became an adult, I gave up childish ways. For now we see in a mirror dimly, but then face to face. Now I know in part; then I shall understand fully. So faith, hope, love abide, these three; but the greatest of these is love.

"Make love your aim, and earnestly desire the spiritual gifts, especially that you may prophesy. For those who prophesy speak to people for their upbuilding, encouragement, and consolation. Those who speak in another language edify themselves, but those who prophesy edify the spiritual community. I want you all to speak in various languages, if possible, but even more to prophesy. Those who prophesy are greater than those who speak in many languages, unless someone interprets, so that all may be edified.

"Now, friends, if I come to you speaking in an unknown language, how shall I benefit you, unless I bring some knowledge or teaching which you can understand? If even musical instruments, such as the flute or the harp, do not give forth familiar sounds, how will we know what is being played? If the bugle gives an indistinct sound, who will obey its summons? So with yourselves; if you in a language utter speech that is not intelligible, how will anyone know what is said? You will be speaking into the air. There are many different languages in the world, and none is without meaning. Yet if I do not know the meaning of the language, I will probably have difficulty communicating with the speaker and the speaker with me. So with yourselves; since you are eager for manifestations of the spirit, strive to find ways of transcending these barriers.

"So, my friends, earnestly desire to prophesy, and do not forbid speaking in different languages. However, all things should be done decently and in order.

Encouraging the Faithful

"Be watchful; stand firm in your faith; be courageous and strong. Let all that you do be done in love.

"If any have caused pain, they have caused it not just to me, but in some measure—not to put it too severely—to you all. For such people this punishment by the majority is sometimes enough. Therefore, you should rather turn to forgiving and comforting, so that others will not be overwhelmed by excessive sorrow. So I beg you to reaffirm your love for them.

"Many things are lawful, but they may not be helpful. Many things are lawful, but not all of these things build the spiritual community. Do not seek just your own good, but as well the good of your neighbor. Seek to give no offense to people of any ethnicity, religion, or culture, just as I try to help all beings in everything I do, not seeking my own advantage, but that of many.

"The point is this: those who sow sparingly will also reap sparingly, and those who sow bountifully will also reap bountifully. We must do as we have made up our minds, not reluctantly or under compulsion. If we do so, we will have enough of everything and in abundance for every good work. For it is not those who commend themselves that are accepted, but those whom others commend.

"We cannot do anything against the truth, but only for the truth. We are glad when you are strong. What we hope for is your improvement.

"Finally, my friends, farewell. Keep on improving your ways, heed my appeal, agree with one another, live in harmony, and the spirit of love and peace will be with you."

Paul Continues His Travels

Paul stayed many days longer at Corinth, and then took leave of the spiritual community and sailed for Syria, coming soon to Ephesus. There he said to them:

"I beg you to lead a life worthy of the calling to which you have been called, with all lowliness and meekness, with patience, forbearing one another in love, eager to maintain the bond of peace.

"Therefore, putting away falsehood, let all of you speak the truth with your neighbors, for we are members one of another. Do not let the sun go down on your anger, and give no opportunity for evil. Let the thieves no longer steal, but rather let them labor, doing honest work with their hands so that they may be able to give to those in need. Let no evil talk come out of your mouths, but only such as is good for edifying, as fits the occasion, that it may impart joy to those who hear. Let all bitterness, wrath, anger, clamor, and slander be put away from you. Be kind to one another, tenderhearted and forgiving.

"Thus immorality, all impurity and covetousness, must not even be practiced among you, as is fitting among saints. Let there be no filthiness, or silly talk, or levity, which is not fitting. Instead let there be thanksgiving. You may be sure of this, that no immoral or impure person, or one who is covetous (that is, an idolater), has any possibility of finding lasting happiness.

"We are not contending against flesh and blood, but against the principalities, against the powers, against the rulers of this present darkness, against the spiritual hosts of wickedness in the highest places. Therefore develop the strength of your character, that you can be able to show courage in the days of your greatest challenges, and having done so, to stand. Stand therefore, having girded your loins with truth, and having put on the breastplate of righteousness, and having covered your feet with the protection of the gospel of peace. Above all take the shield of faith, with which you can quench all the flaming darts of temptation. Take the helmet of perfection and the sword of the spirit, which is the awareness of God."

After many more days of travel, Paul and his community made ready and set out for Jerusalem. While on route, Paul wrote to Timothy, who was at Ephesus:

"We brought nothing into the world, and we cannot take anything out of the world. If we have food and clothing, with these we shall be content. But those who desire to be rich fall into temptation, into a snare, into many senseless and hurtful desires that can plunge us into ruin and destruction. For the love of money is a root of all kinds of evil; it is through this craving that some have wandered away from the faith and pierced their hearts with many pangs.

"But as for you, shun all this; aim at righteousness, faith, love, steadfastness, and gentleness. Fight the good fight of the faith. Take hold of the lasting happiness which may be found through religious living.

"As for the rich in the world, charge them not to be haughty, nor to set their hopes on uncertain riches but on the certain riches of the spiritual life. They are to be good, to be rich in good deeds, liberal and generous, thus laying up for themselves a firm foundation for the future, so that they may take hold of the life which is life indeed.

"O Timothy, guard what has been entrusted to you. Avoid the idle chatter and contradictions of what is falsely called knowledge, for by professing it some have missed the mark as regards faith."

When Paul reached Jerusalem, he was well received by the spiritual community there, but before long the Jews began stirring up trouble. Finally, Paul was tried before Festus, the governor, and he appealed his case to Caesar. Shortly, therefore, it was decided that he should sail for Italy.

While on the journey, his ship became wrecked on the island of Malta. After three months there, he and his companions set sail in another ship and came to Remo.

Titus, the disciple who had been left on Crete to take charge of the work of establishing churches there, received a letter from Paul containing these words of exhortation:

"To the pure all things are pure, but to the corrupt and unbelieving nothing is pure; their very minds and consciences are corrupted. They profess to know God, but they deny this awareness by their deeds; they are detestable, disobedient, unfit for any good deed.

"But as for you, teach what befits sound doctrine. Bid the elders to be temperate, serious, sensible, sound in faith, in love, and in steadfastness. Bid the older women likewise to be reverent in behavior, not to be slanderers or slaves to drink. They are to teach what is good, and thus train the young women to love their husbands and children, to be sensible, chaste, domestic, kind, and supportive of their husbands. Likewise urge the younger men to control themselves. Show yourself in all respects a model of good deeds, and in your teaching show integrity, gravity, and sound speech that cannot be censured, so that no one can have anything derogatory to say of you."

Paul the Prisoner

Paul was still held as a prisoner, even after reaching Rome. When his guard had appointed a day for him to talk with his disciples, the local leaders of the Jews came to him at his lodging in great numbers. He spoke with them from morning till evening, trying to convince them of his teachings and those of Jesus:

"If you are sure that you are a guide to the blind, a light to those who live in darkness, a corrupter of the foolish, a teacher of children, having the embodiment of knowledge and truth—you then who teach others, will you not teach yourself? While you preach against stealing, do you steal? You who say that one must not commit adultery, do you commit adultery?

"I appeal to you therefore, friends, to present our bodies as a living sacrifice, holy and acceptable to our highest ideals. Do not be conformed to this world but be transformed by the renewal of your spirit, that you may prove what is good and acceptable and perfect.

"I bid everyone among you not to think of yourself more highly than you ought to think, but to think with sober judgment, each according to the measure of faith which you have. Having gifts that differ according to our good fortune, let us use them: if prophecy, in proportion to our faith; if service, in our serving; we who teach, in our teaching; we who exhort, in our exhortation; we who contribute, in liberality; we who give aid, with zeal; we who do acts of mercy, with cheerfulness.

"Let love be genuine. Hate what is evil, and hold fast to what is good. Love one another with unconditional love. Outdo one another in showing honor. Never flag in zeal. Be aglow with the spirit. Serve humanity. Rejoice in your hope; be patient in tribulation; and be constant in prayer. Contribute to the needs of the spiritual communities. Practice hospitality.

"Bless those who persecute you; bless and do not curse them. Rejoice with those who rejoice; weep with those who weep. Live in harmony with one another; do not be haughty, but associate with the lowly. Never be conceited. Repay no one evil for evil, but take thought for what is noble in the sight of all. If possible, so far as it depends upon you, live peaceably with all. Beloved, never avenge yourselves; but if your enemies are hungry, feed them; if they are thirsty, give them drink. Do not be overcome by evil, but overcome evil with good.

"Let not sin therefore reign in your mortal bodies, to make you obey your passions. Do not yield your members to sin as instruments of wickedness, but yield yourselves to God as people who have been brought from death to life, and your members to the Eternal as instruments of righteousness. For sin will then have no dominion over you.

"But now we are discharged from the law, so that we serve not under the old written code but in the new life of the spirit. For those who live according to the flesh set their minds on the things of the flesh, but those who live according to the spirit set their minds on the things of the spirit. To set the mind on the flesh is death, but to set the mind on the spirit is life and peace. So then, friends, we are debtors, not to the flesh, to live according to the flesh—for if you live according to the flesh you will die, but if by the spirit you put to death the cravings of the body you will live.

"Besides this you know what hour it is, how it is time now for you to wake from sleep. The night is far gone; the day is at hand. Let us then cast off the works of darkness and put on the armor of light. Let us conduct ourselves becomingly as in the day, not in reveling and drunkenness, not in debauchery and licentiousness, not in quarreling and jealousy. Instead put on virtue, and make no provision for the flesh, to gratify its cravings.

"As for people who are weak in faith, welcome them, but not for disputes over opinions. One believes you may eat anything, while the weak person eats only vegetables. Let not those who eat despise those who abstain, and let not those who abstain pass judgment on those who eat. Who are you to pass judgment on someone else?

"Then let us no more pass judgment on one another, but rather decide never to put a stumbling-block or hindrance in the way of a disciple. I know that nothing is unclean in itself; but it is unclean for anyone who thinks it unclean. If your fellow seeker is being injured by what you eat, you are no longer walking in love. Let us then pursue what makes for peace and for mutual upbuilding. Do not, for the sake of food, destroy the work of God. Everything is indeed clean, but it is wrong for anyone to make others fall by what they eat; it is right not to eat meat or drink wine or do anything that makes your fellow stumble. Happy are those who have no reason to judge themselves for what they approve.

"We who are strong ought to bear with the failings of the weak, and not to please ourselves. Let all of us help our neighbors for their good, to edify them.

"Therefore we have no excuse, O friend, whoever you are, when you judge others. In passing judgment upon them you condemn yourself, because you, the judge, are doing the very same things.

"One person esteems one day as better than another, while another esteems all days alike. Let all of us be fully convinced in our own minds. We who observe the day, observe it for its highest good. We also who eat, eat reverently, since we give thanks. We who abstain, abstain through reverence and give thanks. None of us live to ourselves, and none of us die to ourselves. If we live, we live in God, and if we die we die in God; so then, whether we live or whether die, we are a fragment of the Eternal.

"Let every person be subject to the true authorities. For there is no authority except that of truth, which speaks through the inner self. Do that which is good; and if you do wrong, be afraid. Therefore one must be subject for the sake of conscience. Pay all your dues, taxes to whom taxes are due, revenue to whom revenue is due, respect to whom respect is due, honor to whom honor is due.

Owe no one anything, except to love one another, for love does not do wrong to a neighbor.

"Therefore, since we are supported by faith, we have found inner peace. More than that, we rejoice in our sufferings, knowing that suffering produces endurance, and endurance produces character, and character produces hope, and hope does not disappoint us, because love has filled our hearts.

"Who shall separate us from the love of our master? Shall tribulation, or distress, or persecution, or famine, or nakedness, or peril, or sword? No, in all these things we are more than conquerors through him who loved us. For I am sure that neither death, nor life, nor principalities, nor things to come, nor powers, nor height, nor depth, nor anything else in all creation, will be able to separate us from the love of God which was in our Master Jesus.

"I myself am satisfied about you, my friends, that you yourselves are full of goodness, filled with all knowledge, and able to instruct one another. For while your obedience is known to all, so that I rejoice over you, I would have you wise as to what is good and guileless as to what is evil."

Paul Continues in Rome

And Paul lived in Rome two whole years at his own expense, and welcomed all who came to him, preaching the good news and teaching about Jesus Christ quite openly and unhindered.

OTHER NEW TESTAMENT SPIRITUAL LEADERS

Hebrews

An anonymous letter to the Hebrews teaches:

"Now faith is the assurance of things hoped for, the conviction of things not seen.

"Therefore, since we are surrounded by so great a cloud of witnesses, let us also lay aside every weight and sin which clings so closely, and let us run with perseverance the race that is now before us, looking to Jesus the pioneer and perfecter of our faith, who for the joy that was set before him endured the cross, despising its shame.

"Consider him who endured from others such hostility against himself, so that you may not grow weary or fainthearted. In your struggle against sin you have not yet resisted to the point of shedding blood. It is for discipline that you have to endure. For the moment all discipline seems painful rather than pleasant; later it yields the peaceful fruit of righteousness to those who have been trained by it.

"Strive for peace with all, and for the consecration without which no one will discover God. See to it that no 'root of bitterness' springs up and causes trouble, and by it the many become defiled.

"Let unconditional love continue. Do not neglect to show hospitality to strangers. Remember those who are in prison, as though in prison with them; and those who are ill-treated, since you also are a human being and might be so treated. Let marriage be held in honor among all. Keep your life free from love of money, and be content with what you have.

"Do not be led away by false teachings. Do not neglect to do good and to share what you have, for such sacrifices help strengthen your character."

James

James, the Apostle, to the twelve tribes in the diaspora:

"Count it all joy, my fellow seekers, when you meet various trials, for you know that the testing of your faith produces steadfastness. Let steadfastness have its full effect, that you may be perfect and complete, lacking in nothing.

"Let the humble seekers boast in their exaltation, and the rich in their humiliation, because like the flower of the grass they will pass away. For the sun rises with its scorching heat and withers the grass. Its flower falls, and its beauty perishes. So will the rich people fade away in the midst of their pursuits.

Blessed are those who endure trials, because when they have stood the test they will receive the crown of life.

"Know this, my beloved ones. Let everyone be quick to hear, slow to speak, slow to anger, for one's anger does not spread righteousness. Therefore put away all filthiness and rank growth of wickedness, and receive with meekness the implanted word, which comes from inspiration and personal conviction.

"Be doers of the word, and not hearers only, deceiving yourselves. For those who are hearers of the word and not doers, they are like the ones who observe their natural faces in a mirror; they observe themselves and go away, at once forgetting what they were like. But those who look into the perfect law, the law of liberty, and persevere, being not hearers that forget but doers that act, they shall be blessed in their doings.

"If any of you think you are religious, and do not bridle your tongue but deceive your heart, your religion is vain. Religion that is pure and undefiled is this: to visit orphans and widows in their affliction, and to keep yourself unstained by the world.

"My friends, show no partiality as you hold the faith of Jesus Christ. For if a person with gold rings and in fine clothing comes into our assembly, and a poor person in shabby clothing also comes in, and you pay attention to the one who wears the fine clothing and say, 'Have a seat here, please,' while you say to the poor man, 'Stand there,' or, 'Sit at my feet,' have you not made distinctions among yourselves, and become judges with evil thoughts?

"What does it profit, my friends, if you say you have faith but have not works? When a brother or sister is ill-clad and in lack of daily food, and one of you says to them, 'Go in peace, be warmed and filled,' without giving them the things needed for the body, what does it profit? So faith by itself, if it has no works, is dead.

"But someone will say, 'You have faith and I have works.' Show me your faith apart from your works, and by my works I will show you my faith. Must you be shown that faith apart from works is barren? For as the body apart from the spirit is dead, so faith apart from works is dead.

"Let not many of you become teachers, my friends, for you know that we who teach shall be judged with greater strictness. For we all make many mistakes, and those of you who make no mistakes in what you say are perfect ones, able to bridle the whole body also. If you put bits into the mouths of horses that they may obey us, you guide their whole bodies. Look at the ships also; though they are so great and are driven by strong winds, they are guided by a very small rudder wherever the will of the pilot directs. So the tongue is a little member and boasts of great things. How great a forest is set ablaze by a small fire!

"The human tongue is a fire. The tongue can be an unrighteous world among our members, staining the whole body, setting on fire the cycle of human weakness and temptation. Every kind of beast and bird, reptile and sea creature, can be tamed and has been tamed by human beings, but no human being can tame the tongue—a restless evil, full of deadly poison. From the same mouth come blessing and cursing. My friends, this ought not to be so. Does a spring pour forth from the same opening as brackish? Can a fig tree yield olives, or a grapevine figs? Neither can salt water yield fresh water.

"Who is wise and understanding among you? By your good life may you show your works in the meekness of wisdom. However, if you have bitter jealousy and selfish ambition in your hearts, do not boast and be false to the truth. For where jealousy and selfishness exist, there will be disorder and other vile practices. Real wisdom is first pure, then peaceable, gentle, open to reason, full of mercy and good fruits, without uncertainty or insincerity. The harvest of righteousness is sown by those who make peace.

"What causes wars, and what causes fighting among you? Is it not your passions that are at war in your members? You desire and do not have; so you kill. You covet and cannot obtain; so you fight and wage war. You do not have, because you do not seek. You seek and do not find, because you seek wrongly, to spend it on your passions.

"Come now, you who say, 'Today or tomorrow we will go into such and such a town and spend a year there to trade and get gain'; whereas you do not know about tomorrow. What is your life? For you are a mist that appears for a little time and then vanishes."

Peter

"Peter, an apostle of Jesus Christ, to the exiles of the dispersion, and to those who have obtained a faith of equal standing with yours in the righteousness of our Master, Jesus Christ:

"Friends, put away all malice and all guile, all insincerity, envy and slander. Like newborn babes, long for the pure spiritual milk, that by it you may grow in character.

"Now who is here that really can harm you if you are zealous for what is right? Even if you do suffer for righteousness' sake, you will be blessed. Have no fear, nor be troubled, but in your hearts develop a reverence for life. Always be prepared to make a defense to anyone who calls you to account for the hope that is in you, yet do it with gentleness and reverence; keep your conscience clear, so that, when you are abused, those who revile your good behavior may be found at fault. For it is better to suffer for doing right than for doing wrong.

"For this very reason make every effort to supplement your faith with virtue, virtue with knowledge, knowledge with self-control, self-control with steadfastness, steadfastness with compassion, and compassion with love. For if these things are yours and abound, they keep you from being ineffective or unfruitful in understanding yourself and your relation to the world. Whoever lacks these things is blind or shortsighted, and has forgotten that we were supposed to have given up our former ways. Therefore, friends, be the more zealous to confirm your call and election, for if you do this you will never fall, and lasting happiness will be yours."

John

John, also a man having faith in Jesus Christ, writes to his friends:

"Those who say we are in the light and hate other beings are in the darkness still. We who love our fellow human beings are in the light, and in it there is no cause for stumbling. But those who hate our fellow humans are in the darkness and walk in the darkness, not knowing where we are going, because the darkness has blinded our eyes.

"My friends, let us not love just in word or speech, but also in deed and in truth.

"There is no fear in love, because perfect love casts out fear. For fear had to do with punishment, and those who fear are not perfected in love."

REVELATION OF JOHN

A New Heaven and a New Earth

Then I saw a new heaven and a new earth; for the first heaven and the first earth had passed away, and the sea was no more. And I saw the holy city, the new Jerusalem, coming down out of heaven from God, prepared as a bride adorned for her husband. And I heard a loud voice from the throne saying,

"See, the home of God is among mortals. He will dwell with them as their God; they will be his peoples, and God himself will be with them; he will wipe every tear from their eyes.

Death will be no more; for the first things have passed away."

And the one who was seated on the throne said, "See, I am making all things new." Also he said, "Write this, for these words are trustworthy and true." Then he said to me, "It is done! I am the Alpha and the Omega, the beginning and the end. To the thirsty I will give water as a gift from the spring of the water of life. Those who conquer will inherit these things, and I will be their God and they will be my children.

I saw no temple in the city, for its temple is the Lord God the Almighty and the Lamb. And the city has no need of sun or moon to shine on it, for the glory of God is its light, and its lamp is the Lamb. The nations will walk by its light, and the kings of the earth will bring their glory into it. Its gates will never be shut by day—and there will be no night there. People will bring into it the glory and the honor of the nations. But nothing unclean will enter it, nor anyone who practices abomination or falsehood, but only those who are written in the Lamb's book of life.

Then the angel showed me the river of the water of life, bright as crystal, flowing from the throne of God and of the Lamb through the middle of the street of the city. On either side of the river is the tree of life with its twelve kinds of fruit, producing its fruit each month; and the leaves of the tree are for the healing of the nations. Nothing accursed will be found there any more. But the throne of God and of the Lamb will be in it, and his servants will worship him; they will see his face, and his name will be on their foreheads. And there will be no more night; they need no light of lamp or sun, for the Lord God will be their light, and they will reign forever and ever.

And he said to me, "These words are trustworthy and true, for the Lord, the God of the spirit of the prophets, has sent his angel to show his servants what must soon take place."

"See, I am coming soon! Blessed is the one who keeps the words of the prophecy of this book."

I, John, am the one who heard and saw these things. And when I heard and saw them, I fell down to worship at the feet of the angel who showed them to me; but he said to me, "You must not do that! I am a fellow servant with you and your comrades the prophets, and who those who keep the words of this book. Worship God!"

And he said to me, "Do not seal up the words of the prophecy of this book, for the time is near. Let the evildoer still do evil, and the filthy still be filthy, and the righteous still do right, and the holy still be holy."

"See, I am coming soon; my reward is with me, to repay according to everyone's work. I am the Alpha and the Omega, the first and the last, the beginning and the end."

Blessed are those who wash their robes, so that they will have the right to the tree of life and may enter the city by the gates. Outside are the dogs and sorcerers and fornicators and murderers and idolaters, and everyone who loves and practices falsehood.

Let Everyone Come

"It is I, Jesus, who sent my angel to you with this testimony for the churches. I am the root and the descendant of David, the bright morning star."

The Spirit and the bride say, "Come."

And let everyone who hears say, "Come."

And let everyone who is thirsty come.

Let anyone who wishes take the water of life as a gift.

The one who testifies to these things says, "Surely I am coming soon." Amen. Come, Lord Jesus!

The grace of the Lord Jesus be with all the saints. Amen.

ISLAMIC SCRIPTURES

INTRODUCTION[1]

What is Islam?

The term Islam derives from the three-letter Arabic root s-i-m, which generates words with interrelated meanings, including "surrender," "submission," "commitment," and "peace." Commonly, Islam refers to the monotheistic religion revealed to Muhammad ibn (son of) Abdullah (pbuh)[2] between 610 and 632 of the common era. The name Islam was instituted by the Qur'an, the sacred scripture revealed to Muhammad. For believers, Islam is not a new religion. Rather, it represents the last reiteration of the primordial

---

[1] Adapted with permission from: Shaikh, Munir A. *Teaching About Islam and Muslims in the Public School Classroom*. Council on Islamic Education, Fountain Valley. 1995

[2] Out of respect Muslims say the words "peace and blessings be upon him" after mentioning the Prophet.

message of God's Oneness, a theme found in earlier monotheistic religious traditions.

Although Islam can be described as a religion, it is viewed by its adherents in much broader terms. Beyond belief in specific doctrines and performance of important ritual acts, Islam is practiced as a complete and natural way of life, designed to bring God into the center of one's consciousness, and thus one's life. Essentially, by definition Islam is a worldview focused on belief in the One God and commitment to His commandments. (Shaikh, 1995)

What does the term Allah mean?

The Arabic word Allah is a contraction of the words "al" and "ilah," and literally means The God. Believers in Islam understand Allah to be the proper name for the Creator as found in the Qur'an. The name Allah is analogous to Eloh, a Semitic term found in the divine scriptures revealed to Muhammad's predecessors Moses and Jesus (may peace be upon them all).

The use of the term Allah is not confined to believers in Islam alone. Allah means "God," like Dios and Dieu mean "God" in Spanish and French respectively. It is common to find many Arabic-speaking Christians and Jews also using the word Allah in reference to God (Shaikh. 1995)

How is God viewed in Islam?

The Qur'an, the divinely-revealed scripture of Islam, contains numerous verses describing the nature of God. The role of human beings as creations of God upon the earth and their relationship with God are also discussed extensively in the sacred text.

> Say: He is God, the One, the Eternal, Absolute. He does not beget, nor is He begotten, and there is nothing like unto Him. (112:1-4)

> It is He who brought you forth from the wombs of your mothers when you knew nothing and He gave you hearing and sight and intelligence and affections that you may give thanks. (16:78)

> No vision can grasp Him, but His grasp is over all vision. He is above all comprehension, yet is acquainted with all things. (6:103)

Muslims believe that God has no partners or associates who share in His divinity or authority. Muslims also believe that God is transcendent and unlike His creations, and thus has no physical form. Nor is God believed to exist in (or be represented by) any material object. A number of divine attributes or "names," which serve to describe God, are found in the Qur'an. Some commonly known attributes include the Most Merciful, the Most Forgiving, the Most High, the Unique, and the Everlasting, among others.

In Islam, human beings, like other creations, are seen as completely unlike God, though they may aspire to exhibit various attributes manifested by God, such as justice or mercy. Furthermore, even while God is believed to be beyond traditional human perception, the Qur'an states, "He is with you wherever you may be" (57:5). For Muslims, God's Oneness heightens the awareness that all life is ultimately bound by Divine Law emanating from a singular source and that life has a meaning and purpose which revolves around the consciousness of God's presence.

Moreover, belief in a singular Creator compels conscientious Muslims to view all humanity as one extended family, and treat others with justice and equity. Respect for the environment and natural resources also follows from the Muslim view of God. (Shaikh, 1995)

What is the Qur'an?

The word Qur'an literally means "the reading" or "the recitation," and refers to the divinely revealed scripture given to Muhammad. Since Muhammad is considered the last prophet of God, the Qur'an is believed to be the final revelation from God to humanity.

The Qur'an is considered by Muslims to be the literal Speech of God given to Muhammad in the Arabic language. The chapters and verses of the Qur'an were revealed throughout Prophet Muhammad's mission, over a span of close to twenty-three years, from 610-632 C.E. Contrary to common misconception, Muhammad is not the author of the Qur'an. Rather, he is viewed as the chosen transmitter of the revelation and the ideal implementer of principles and commandments contained therein. The personal sayings or words of Muhammad are known as hadith, which are distinct from the divine origin of the content of the Qur'an.

As verses of the Qur'an were revealed to Muhammad and subsequently repeated by him to companions and other fellow Muslims, they were written down, recited, and memorized. The Prophet also typically led the formal worship five times daily, during which he recited the revealed verses according to the procedure that he established. The verses were also recited out loud by designated Muslims in the early dawn hours and prior to the worship times and other important occasions. In short, the Qur'anic verses played an immediate and practical role in the spiritual lives of Muslims from the outset. Before he passed away, the Prophet arranged the 114 chapters into the sequence we find in the Qur'an. Scholars, both Muslim and non-Muslim, agree that the Qur'an has remained intact and unchanged to the present. The Qur'an as a scripture stands unique in this regard. (Shaikh, 1995)

Do Translations of the Qur'an exist in other languages?

Translations of the Qur'an exist in many languages throughout the world, including English, Spanish, French, German, Urdu, Chinese, Malay, Vietnamese, and others. It is important to note that while translations are useful as renderings or explanations of the Qur'an, only the original Arabic text is considered to be the Qur'an itself. As a consequence, Muslims the world over, regardless of their native language, always strive to learn Arabic, so they can read and understand the Qur'an in its original form. Muslims also learn Arabic in order to recite the daily formal worship (salah) and for greeting one another with traditional expressions. However, while almost all Muslims have some basic familiarity with the Arabic language, not all Muslims speak fluent Arabic. (Shaikh, 1995)

Who was Muhammad?

History records that a person by the name Muhammad was born into the tribe of Quraysh in the city of Makkah in 570 C.E. His father, Abdullah, fell ill and died before his birth. When Muhammad was six years old, his mother, Amina also became ill and died. Thus, at a very young age Muhammad was orphaned by the loss of both his parents.

For the next two years Muhammad was entrusted to his grandfather, Abd al-Muttalib, who also passed away of old age. His uncle Abu Talib, a well-respected member of the Quraysh tribe, took responsibility for young Muhammad. Muhammad grew up to become an honest and trustworthy businessman. Indeed, Muhammad's upright and dependable reputation earned him the designation al-Amin (the Trustworthy One) among his fellow Makkans, and even invited a marriage proposal from Khadijah, a businesswoman in Makkah for whom he worked.

At the age of twenty-five, Muhammad married Khadijah, a widow who was his elder by fifteen years. Their marriage lasted twenty-five years, until Khadijah's death. Muhammad and Khadijah had six children: two sons died in early childhood and four daughters lived to bless their household.

While most of his fellow Mekkans were polytheists, Muhammad refused to worship the traditional tribal deities and often retreated to meditate and worship the One God of his ancestor, Abraham. At the age of forty, while meditating in the cave of Hijra in the mountains above Makkah, Muhammad received the first of many revelations, beginning with the Arabic word Iqra, meaning "Read" or "Recite." Soon afterwards, he was commanded to convey the Divine message and thus became the last messenger of God, according to the Qur'an.

Read, in the name of thy Lord, Who Created—
Created man, out of clot (embryo).
Proclaim! And thy Lord is Most Bountiful,
He Who taught the use of the pen—
Taught man that which he knew not. (96:1-5)

Muhammad spent the remaining twenty-three years of his life receiving revelations from God and advocating the message of Islam among the peoples of the Arabian peninsula and working to implement the principles and teaching of Islam in human society. After suffering severe persecution from the polytheistic Mekkans for 11 years, he and his fellow Muslims emigrated to Yathrib, a city 200 miles north of Makkah, where he established Islamic rule. The city was renamed Madinah (short for Madunat an-Nabi, City of the Prophet). In the following years, the message of Islam brought more and more tribes in the Arabian Peninsula into the fold, creating a new community based on common religious principles, rather than tribal or other affiliations.

Muhammad died in 632 C.E. at the age of 63. His tomb is located adjacent to the Masjid an-Nabawi (Prophet's Masjid) in Madinah, Saudi Arabia, in what used to be his quarters next to the original masjid of the city. (Shaikh, 1995)

SCRIPTURE[3]

The Opening (1:1-7)

In the name of Allah the Compassionate the Merciful

Praise be to Allah, the Lord of the Worlds;
The Compassionate, the Merciful
Master of the Day of Judgment;
You alone do we worship, and to You alone we pray for help;
Guide us to the Straight Path;
The way of those whom You have favored;
Not of those who have incurred your wrath. Nor of those who
go astray.

ALLAH (THE EXALTED, THE MAJESTIC GOD)

From Al-Ikhlas (The Sincerity)

Say: "He is Allah, the One!
Allah the Everlasting Sustainer of all.
He begat none nor was He begotten.
And there is none comparable to Him." (112:1-4)

From Al-Hashr (Exile)

If We had caused this Qur'an to descend upon a mountain, you (O Muhammad) would have seen it humbled, rent asunder by the fear of Allah. Such are the parables We set forth to mankind, so that they may reflect.

He is Allah besides whom there is no other god; knower of the visible and the unseen. He is the Compassionate, the Merciful.

---

[3] Translations by: Ozek, Ali et al.: *The Holy Qur'an With English Translation*, Acar Matbaacilikyayincilik Hizmetleri: Istanbul, 1996

Irving, T. B.: *The Qur'an*. Amana Books: Brattleboro, Vermont, 1988.

Topics were adapted from: Osman, Fathi: Concepts of the Qur'an, A Topical Reading. MVI Publication: Los Angeles, CA, 1999.

He is Allah besides whom there is no other god. He is the Sovereign Lord, the Holy One, the Source of Security the Keeper of Faith; the Guardian, the Mighty One, the All-Powerful, the Proud! Exalted be He above the partners they ascribe to Him.

He is Allah, the Creator, the Originator, the Modeler. His are the most beautiful names. All that is in the heavens and the earth glorifies Him. He is the Mighty, the Wise. (59:21-24)

From Al-Baqara (The Cow)

Allah! There is no god but Him, the Living, the Eternal. Neither slumber nor sleep overtakes Him. His is what is in the heavens and what is in the earth. Who can intercede with Him except by His permission? He knows what is before them and what lies behind them, and they can grasp only that part of His knowledge which He wills. His Throne embraces the Heavens and the earth, and it tires Him not to uphold them both. He is the High, the Tremendous. (2:255)

From An-Nur (The Light)

Allah is the Light of the heavens and of the earth. The similitude of His light is as a niche wherein is a Lamp. The Lamp is in a glass, the glass is as it were a glittering star, lighted from a blessed tree, an olive, neither of the east nor of the west, whose oil would almost glow forth even if no fire touched it. It is light upon Light. Allah guides whom He wills to His light; and Allah sets forth parables to men, for Allah is knower of all things. (24:3 5)

THE CREATION

From Ya Sin

The dead earth serves as a sign for them; We revive it and bring forth the grain from it which they may eat. We have placed date groves and vineyards on it, and make springs flow forth from it so they may eat its fruit. Their own hands did not produce it. So, will they not give thanks? Glory be to the One Who has created every kind of species such as the earth grows, their own kind, and even some things they do not know!

Another sign for them is night; We strip daylight off from it so they are plunged into darkness! The sun runs along on a course of its own. Such is the design of the Powerful, the Aware! And We have designed phases for the moon so it finally appears again like an old palm frond. The sun dare not overtake the moon nor does night outpace the day. Each floats along in its own orbit. (36:33-40)

From Al-Furqan (The Criterion)

Blessed is He who sent down the Criterion unto His slave, that he may be a warner to the peoples (creatures).

His is the sovereignty of the heavens and of the earth! No partner has He in His sovereignty! All things has He created and He has decreed their destinies. (25:1-2)

From Al-Mulk (The Sovereignty)

Blessed is He in Whose hands there rests control; He is Capable of (doing) everything, the One Who created death and life, so He may test which of you is finest in action. He is the Powerful, the Forgiving, Who created seven matching heavens. You do not see any discrepancy in the Mercy-giving's creation. Look once again; do you see any flaws? (67:1-3)

From Al-Hijr (The Rocky Tract)

Earth have We spread out and cast headlands upon it, and planted a bit of everything to grow there (so it is) well balanced. We have placed various means of livelihood on it for (all of) you as well as anyone you do not have to provide for. There is nothing whose stores are not (controlled) by Us, and We send it down only according to a fixed quantity.

We send forth fertilizing winds and send down water from the sky and offer you something to drink from it. You are not the ones who store it up. (15:19-22)

From An-Nahl (The Bee)

Your Lord has inspired the Bees: "Set up hives in the mountains, and in trees and on anything they may build. Then eat some of every kind of fruit and slip humbly along your Lord's byways." (16:68-69)

God has granted you your houses as homes to live in, and granted you the skins of livestock (to make) houses which you find so light on the day you pack them up to move elsewhere and the day you come to a halt. From their wool, their fur and their hair come furnishings and commodities for a while. God has granted you shade out of what He has created, and granted you resorts in the mountains, and granted you garments with which to protect yourselves from the heat as well as garments to ward off your own violence. (16:80)

From Al-Anbiya' (The Prophets)

Have not those who disbelieve seen how the Heavens and Earth were once one solid mass which We ripped apart? We have made every living thing out of water. Will they still not believe? We have placed headlands on earth lest it should sway while they are on it, and have placed mountain passes on it as highways so they may be guided. We have placed the sky as a roof which is held up even though they shun its signs! He is the One Who has created night and daylight, and the sun and the moon, each floats along in an orbit. (21:30-33)

THE ANGELS

From Aal-'Imran (The Family of Imran)

The Messiah would never disdain to be God's servant, nor would the angels who are closest. He will summon anyone to Him who disdains to worship Him and acts too proud (for it). (3:80)

From Az-Zukhruf (Ornaments of Gold)

They even pretend the angels who are the Mercy-giving's servants are females! Were they present at their own creation? Their testimony will be written down and they will be questioned about it. (43:19-20)

From Al-An 'am (The Cattle)

Nothing prevents men from believing whenever guidance comes to them except that they say: "Has God dispatched a mortal as a messenger?" Say: "If there had been angels calmly walking around on earth, We would have sent an angel down from Heaven as a messenger for them."(6:8-9)

From Al-Baqara (The Cow)

Whenever a messenger from God has come to them to confirm what they already had, a group of those who were given the Book have tossed God's book behind their backs as if they did not know (any better). They followed whatever the devils recited concerning Solomon's control. Solomon did not disbelieve but the devils disbelieved, teaching people magic and what was sent down to Harut and Marut, two angels at Babylon. Neither of these would teach anyone unless they (first) said: "We are only a temptation, so do not disbelieve!" They learned from them both what will separate a man from his wife. Yet they do not harm anyone through it except with God's permission. They learn what will harm them and what does not benefit them. They know that anyone who deals in it will have no share in the Hereafter; how wretched is what they have sold themselves for, if they only knew! If they had only believed and done their duty, a recompense from God would have been better, if they had realized it! (2:101-103)

THE PROPHETS (ON WHOM BE PEACE)

From An-Nisa' (The Women)

We send revelation upon you (Muhammad), as We sent it upon Noah and the prophets after him, and as We sent revelation upon Abraham and Ishmael and Isaac and Jacob and the tribes, and Jesus and Job and Jonah and Aaron and Solomon, and as We gave David the Psalms.

And messengers We have mentioned to you before, and messengers We have not mentioned to you; and Allah spoke directly with Moses.

Messengers of good news and of warning, in order that mankind might have no argument against Allah after the messengers. And Allah was ever Mighty, Wise.

But Allah (Himself) bears witness concerning that which He has revealed to you; in His knowledge has He revealed it; and the angels also testify. And Allah is sufficient for a witness. (4:163-166)

THE INVISIBLE BEINGS

From Ar-Rahman (The Compassionate)

He created man from a ringing clay just as a potter does, while He created jinn (invisible beings) from the glow in fire. (55:15)

From Ar-Rahman (The Compassionate)

O company of jinn and humankind, if you can manage to penetrate beyond the realms of Heaven and Earth, then pass beyond them! Yet you will only penetrate them through some authority (from God). So which of your Lord's benefits will both of you deny? (55:33-34)

From Al-An'am (The Cattle)

They have set up jinn (invisible beings) as associates with God, even though He created them! They have even dared to impute sons and daughters to him without having any knowledge. Glory be to Him; Exalted is He over whatever they describe! Deviser of Heaven and Earth! How can He have a son while He has no consort? He created everything and is Aware of everything! (6:101-104)

HUMAN BEINGS

From Al-Baqara (The Cow)

So when your Lord told the angels: "I am placing an overlord on earth," they said: "Will You place someone there who will corrupt it and shed blood, while we hymn Your praise and sanctify You?" He said: "I know something you do not know."

He taught Adam all the names of everything; then presented them to the angels, and said: "Glory be to You: we have no knowledge except whatever You have taught us. You are the Aware, the Wise!" He said: "Adam, tell them their names."

Once he had told them their names, He said: "Did I not tell you that I know the Unseen in Heaven and Earth? I know whatever you disclose and whatever you have been hiding."

So We told the angels: "Bow down on your knees before Adam. "They (all) knelt down except Iblis. He refused and acted proudly, and became a disbeliever.

We said: "Adam, settle in the Garden, both you and your wife, and eat freely from it anywhere either of you may wish. Yet do not approach this tree lest you become wrongdoers."

Satan made them stumble over it and had them both expelled from where they had been (living). We said: "Clear out! Some of you will (become) enemies of others. You will have a resting place on earth and enjoyment for a while."

Adam received words (of inspiration) from his Lord and He turned towards him. He is the Relenting, the Merciful!

We said: "Clear out from it together! If you should be handed guidance from Me, then anyone who follows My guidance will have no fear nor will they be saddened; while those who disbelieve and reject Our signs will become inmates of the Fire; they shall remain in it!" (2:30-39)

There is a certain man whose talk about worldly life intrigues you (0 Muhammad). He calls God to witness whatever is in his heart. He is extremely violent in quarreling. Whenever he holds the upper hand, he rushes around the earth ruining it. He destroys (people's) crops and breeding stock even though God does not like ruination. When someone tells him: "Heed God," a (false) sense of importance leads him off to sin. He can count on Hell; what an awful couch!

Another type sells his own soul while craving God's approval, even though God is Gentle with (His) servants. You who believe, enter absolutely into peace! Do not follow Satan's footsteps; he is an open enemy of yours. If you should lapse after explanations have come to you, then know that God is Powerful, Wise. Are they only waiting for God as well as angels to come along to them under canopies of clouds, so the matter will be settled? Unto God do matters return. (2:204-209)

From An-Nisa' (The Women)

God wants to explain things to you (all) and to guide you in the customs of those who have preceded you. He turns to you; God is Aware, Wise.

God wants to turn to you while those who follow their passions want you to give in utterly. God wants to lighten things for you, since man was created weak! (4:26-28)

From Al-A'raf (The Heights)

When your Lord took their offspring from the Children of Adam's loins, and made them bear witness about themselves: "Am I not your Lord?"; they said: "Of course, we testify to it!" Lest you (all) might say on Resurrection Day: "We were unaware of this;" or lest you say: "It was only our forefathers who associated (others with God) previously; we are offspring following them. Will you wipe us out because of what futile men have done?" Thus We spell out signs so that they may repent. (7:172-174)

From Yunus (Jonah)

He is the One Who sends you traveling along on land and at sea until when you are on board a ship, and sailing along under a fair wind and they feel happy about it, a stormy wind comes upon them and waves reach from all sides and they think they are being surrounded by them. They appeal to God sincerely, (offering their) religion to Him: "If You will save us from this, we will be grateful!" Yet once He has saved them, they act willfully on earth without any right to (do so). Mankind, your willfulness falls only on yourselves to be enjoyed during worldly life; then to Us will be your return, and We will notify you (all) about whatever you have been doing! (10:22-25)

From Al-Hajj (The Pilgrimage)

0 men, if you have ever been in doubt about rising again We (first) created you from dust; then from a drop of semen; then from a clot; then from a lump of tissue either shaped or else shapeless, so

510 / WORLD SCRIPTURES

We might explain (things) to you. We cause anything We wish to rest in wombs for a stated period; then We bring you forth as infants; eventually you reach full growth. Some of you will pass away (early in life), while others of you will be sent back to the feeblest age of all, so that he will not know a thing after once having had knowledge.

You see the barren earth when We send water down upon it, stirring, sprouting and producing every sort of lovely species. That (comes about) because God is the Truth: He revives the dead and is Capable of everything! (22:5-6)

From Ar-Rum (The Romans)

Among His signs is (the fact) that He has created spouses for you from among yourselves so that you may console yourselves with them. He has planted affection and mercy between you; in that are signs for people who think things over. (30:21-23)

From Al-Ahzab (The Clans)

We offered the trust to Heaven and Earth, and to the mountains too, yet they refused to carry it, and shrank back from it. However man accepted it: he has been unfair (to himself), ignorant! (33:72)

From Luqman

Do you not see how God has harnessed whatever is in Heaven and whatever is on Earth for you? He has lavished His favor on you both publicly and privately. Yet some men will still argue about God without having any knowledge or guidance, nor any enlightening Book! Whenever they are told: "Follow whatever God has sent down," they say: "Rather we follow what we found our forefathers doing." Even though Satan has been inviting them to the torment of the Blaze? (31:20-21)

From Al- 'Asr (Time)

By (the token of) time (through the ages).
Surely man is in a state of loss.
Except those who believe and do good works, and exhort one another to truth, and exhort one another to steadfastness. (103:1-3)

SATAN

From Al-A'raf (The Heights)

Children of Adam, do not let Satan tempt you just as he turned your two ancestors out of the Garden, stripping them of their clothing in order to show them their private parts. He and his tribe watch you from where you do not see them. We have placed devils as patrons for those who do not believe. (7:27)

From Al-Anfal (The Spoils)

So Satan made their actions seem attractive to them, and said: "There will be no man who will overcome you today: I'll stand close by you." Yet as both detachments sighted one another, he wheeled around on his heels and said: "I am innocent of you; I see something you do not see! I fear God, and God is Severe in punishment." (8:48)

From Al-A'raf (The Heights)

If some urge from Satan should prompt you, seek refuge with God; He is Alert, Aware. The ones who perform their duty bear it in mind wherever some impulse from Satan bothers them, and so they are granted insight. Their brethren will trail off into aimlessness; therefore do not interfere with them. (7:200-202)

THE ETERNAL LIFE TO COME

From Al-Baqara (The Cow)

Yet there are some who set up equals with Allah and adore them with adoration due to Allah. Those who believe are stauncher in love of Allah. If only the unrighteous could see (on the day) when they behold the punishment, that might is His alone, and that Allah is severe in punishment!

Then would those who are followed declare themselves innocent of those who follow (them); they would see the punishment, and all that unites them will be broken asunder.

Those who followed (them) will say: "Would that we were given a chance to return (to life in the world); then we would disown them even as they have disowned us (since we are in Hell)." Thus will Allah show them their own deeds as anguish for them, and they will not emerge from the Fire. (2:165-167)

From Ibrahim (Abraham)

They shall all appear before Allah. Then those who were weak (in the world) will say to those who were arrogant: "We were your followers, can you now do anything to save us from the torment of Allah?" They will reply: "Had Allah guided us, we would have guided you. It is all the same whether we rage or patiently endure. We have no place of refuge."

And when the matter has been decided Satan will say: "It was Allah who gave you a promise of truth; I too promised, but failed in my promise to you. I had no power over you except to call you, but you listened to me. So do not blame me, but blame yourselves. I cannot help you, nor can you help me. I disbelieved in your making me a partner with Allah before this. The wrongdoers shall have a painful chastisement."

But those who have faith and do good works shall be admitted to gardens where running streams flow. They shall abide there forever by their Lord's permission. Their greeting shall be: "Peace (be upon you)!" ("Peace" is a greeting, and also the expression of a wish, that one's companion may be free of every difficulty and illness. Among believers, it is both a greeting and a prayer.) (14: 21-23)

From Al-An'am (The Ant)

And they say: "There is nothing save our life of the world, and we shall not be raised (again)."

If you could see when they are set before their Lord! He will say: "Is this not real?" They will say: "Yes, verily, by our Lord!" He will say: "Taste now the retribution for that you used to disbelieve."

They indeed are losers who deny their meeting with Allah until, when the hour comes on them suddenly, they cry: "Alas for us, that we neglected it!" They bear upon their backs their burdens. Ah, evil is that which they bear!

The life of the world is nothing but a pastime and a play. But best is the home in the Hereafter for those who keep their duty (to Allah). Have you then no sense? (6: 29-32)

From An-Nur (The Light)

Did you reckon that We only created you in jest, and that to Us you would not be returned?"

So, exalted is Allah, the King, the True. There is no god but He; Lord of the Noble Throne.

And whoever invokes another god with Allah, of which he has no proof, then his reckoning shall be with his Lord. Surely the unbelievers will be unsuccessful. (23:115-118)

From Az-Zumar (The Troops)

And they have not esteemed Allah as He has the right to be esteemed; when the whole earth is His handful on the Day of Resurrection, and the heavens will be rolled up in His right hand, Glory to Him! And High is He above the partners which, in their idolatry, they associate with Him.

And the Trumpet will be sounded, and all those who are in the heavens, and the earth will swoon, except those whom Allah may allow (to live). Then the Trumpet will be blown a second time, and they will all stand up, looking.

And the earth will shine with the light of her Lord, and the book will be placed open, and the Prophets and the witnesses will be brought, and the people will be judged with full equity, and none will be wronged.

And each soul will be paid in full for whatever it had done. And He is Best Aware of what they do.

(After this judgment) those who had disbelieved will be driven to Hell in groups, till, when they reach it, its gates will be opened, and its keepers will say to them: "Did not messengers of your own come to you, reciting to you the revelations of your Lord, and warning you of the meeting of this your Day?" They will say: "Yes, they did come, but the Decree of punishment has proved true against the disbelievers."

It will be said to them: "Enter the gates of Hell to dwell therein for ever. What an evil abode for the arrogant!"

And those who had feared their Lord will be led to the Garden in groups till, when they arrive there, and its gates will already have been opened, its keepers will say: "Peace be with you! You have done well. Enter here to dwell forever."

And they will say: Praise be to Allah, Who has fulfilled His promise to us, and has made us inherit the land; now we can dwell in the Garden wherever we like." How excellent a reward for the doers (of the right).

And you (0 Muhammad) will see the angels circling the Throne, glorifying their Lord with His praises; and the people will be judged with full equity, and it will be said: "Praise is for Allah, the Lord of the Worlds!" (39: 67-75)

From Ya Sin

It is but one Shout, and behold them brought together before Us!

This day no soul is wronged in aught; nor are you requited aught save what you used to do.

Surely the Garden's people this day are happily employed,

They and their wives, in pleasant shade on thrones reclining;

Much fruit (and enjoyment) will be there for them,

The word from a Merciful Lord (for them) is: Peace (salam). (36: 53-58)

WORSHIP

From Al-Hajj (The Pilgrimage)

O you who believe! Bow and prostrate yourselves, and worship your Lord, and do good, that perhaps you may prosper. (22:77)

From Adh-Dhariyat (The Scattering Winds)

I created the jinn and humankind only that they might worship Me.

I seek no livelihood from them, nor do I ask that they should feed Me.

Allah! He it is that gives livelihood, the Lord of unbreakable might. (51:56-58)

PRAYER

From Ibrahim (Abraham)

Tell my servants who have believed that they shall establish the Prayer and spend in charity of that which We have given them, secretly and openly, before the coming of a Day when there shall be neither bargaining nor friendship. (14:31)

Our Lord! I have settled some of my offspring in a barren valley near Your sacred house, in order, Our Lord, that they may establish the Prayer. So put in the hearts of some men kindness towards them, and provide them with fruits, so that they may give thanks. (14:37)

From Al-Baqara (The Cow)

And We made the House (the Holy Ka'ba at Makkah) a place of assembly for mankind and a place of safety, (saying): "Adopt the place where Abraham stood, as a place of worship." And We imposed a duty upon Abraham and Ishmael to purify Our house for those who walked around and those who meditate in it, and those who bow down and prostrate.

And when Abraham prayed: "Make this city a city of peace, and bestow fruits upon its people, such of them as believe in Allah and the Last Day", He answered: "As for those who disbelieve, I shall leave them in contentment for a while, then I shall compel them to the punishment of the Fire; and that is the worst abode."

And when Abraham and Ishmael were raising the foundations of the house, (they prayed): "Our Lord! Accept from us (this act); You are indeed the All-Hearing, the All-Knowing.

O our Lord! Make us submitters to You! And raise from among our offspring a community which will be submitters to You. Show us Your ways of worship, and relent towards us. You are indeed the Forgiving, the Merciful.

Our Lord! And raise up from among them a Messenger who shall recite Your revelations to them and teach them the Scriptures and the wisdom, and purify them (or: make them grow). You are the Powerful, the Wise.

Who but a foolish man would renounce the faith of Abraham?
We chose him in the world, and in the Hereafter he is among the
righteous. (2:125-130)

From Al-Ma'ida (The Table Spread)

O you who believe! When you rise up for prayer, wash your faces,
and your hands up to the elbows, and lightly rub your heads, and
(wash) your feet up to the ankles. And if you are unclean, purify
yourselves. And if you are sick or one a journey, or one of you
comes from the privy, or you have touched (had sexual relations
with) women, and you find not water, then go to clean earth, and
rub your faces and your hands with some of it. Allah would not
place a burden on you. But He would purify you, and would perfect His grace upon you, that you may perhaps give thanks.[4]

Remember Allah's favor upon you, and His covenant by which
He bound you when you said: "We hear and we obey"; and keep
your duty to Allah. Indeed Allah knows what is in the breasts (of
men). (5:6-7)

From Al-Muzzammil (The Enshrouded One)

Your Lord knows that you (Muhammad) sometimes keep vigil
nearly two thirds of the night and sometimes half or one — third
of it, and so does a party of those with you. Allah measures the
night and the day. He knows that you cannot count it, and turns to
you mercifully. Recite from the Qur'an as much as is easy (for you);
He knows that among you there are sick men and others traveling
the road in quest of Allah's bounty; and yet others fighting for His
cause. Recite from it, then, as much as is easy (for you). Attend to
your prayers, pay the Zakat, and give Allah a generous loan. Whatever good you do for your souls you will surely find it with Allah,

---

[4] Prayer for a Muslim is to commune intimately with the Lord. As is the
case before every important meeting, one must prepare for it in the
proper way. The practice of wudu', the minor ablution required before
most devotional acts, purifies the outward, symbolizes the purification of
the inward, and serves to wake us up, and redirect us towards Almighty
God. When water is not readily obtainable, clean earth may be used as a
temporary substitute.

better and richly rewarded by Him. Implore Allah to forgive you; He is Forgiving, Merciful. (73:20)[5]

ZAKAT (THE OBLIGATORY ALMS TAX)

From Aal-'Imran (The Family of 'Imran)

You will not attain to righteousness until you spend of what you love. And whatever you spend Allah is aware of it. (3:92)[6]

From At-Tawba (Repentance)

There are some among them who find fault with you (Muhammad) in the matter of alms. If a share is given them they are pleased but if they receive nothing, behold, they grow resentful.[7]

If only they had been content with what Allah and His messenger have given them, and would say, "Allah is Sufficient for us. He will provide us in abundance out of His Own bounty, and so will His messenger. To Allah we return our hopes."

---

[5] Some of the companions of the prophet were offering prayers a good part of the night and they would get tired and their feet would be swollen. Although the night prayer for the prophet was compulsory, it was not compulsory for the companions. So every person should offer (salah) prayers at night according to his physical condition.

[6] The word *birr* in this verse, here translated as "righteousness," denotes goodness and spiritual selflessness, the zenith of one 's maturity from the point of view of religion. This is also intimated in verse 177 of Surah Al-Baqara. In order to attain *birr* one has to spend the things that one loves most. According to the interpreters of the Holy Qur'an; these things might be wealth, belongings, status, knowledge, good health, and other material and spiritual gifts with which the Lord blesses us. Only work done against one's own worldly interests is in our spiritual interests, provided that this is not done to excess, and does not endanger our health or families.

[7] Sadaqa is alms which is given in God's name, mainly to the poor and needy, and for the associated purposes specified in verse 60 below. Zakat is the regular and binding charity in an organized Muslim community, usually one-fortieth of merchandise and one tenth of the fruits of the earth. Further details are given in the Hadiths of the Blessed Prophet, and in the classical works of Islamic law.

Alms are only for the poor and the needy, and those who collect them and for those whose hearts are to be reconciled, and for the ransom of captives and debtors and for the way of Allah and for (the hospitality of) the wayfarers. This is an obligatory duty from Allah, and Allah is Knowing, Wise. (9: 58-60)

FASTING

From Al-Baqara (The Cow)

O you who believe! Fasting is prescribed for you, as it was prescribed for those who came before you; that you will perhaps guard yourselves (against evil).

(Fast) a certain number of days, but if any of you is ill or on a journey, let him (break his fast, and) fast the same number of days later on. And for those who can afford it there is a ransom: the feeding of a man in need. But he that does good of his own accord, it is better for him, but to fast is better for you, if you did but know.

The month of Ramadan is when the Qur'an was revealed, a guidance for mankind, (a book of) clear proofs of guidance and the criterion (distinguishing right from wrong). Therefore whoever of you is present in that month let him fast; but he who is ill or on a journey shall fast (a same) number of days later on. Allah desires for you ease; He desires not hardship for you; and (He desires) that you should complete the period, and that you should magnify Allah for giving you His guidance, and that perhaps you will be thankful.[8]

When My servants question you about Me, (tell them) I am surely near. I answer the prayer of the suppliant when he prays to Me;

---

[8] There is no difficulty in the religion of Islam. While Allah has ordained an obligatory fast for men and women, those who are ill or on a journey for a period of time, which might render the fast difficult, are excused from fasting and permitted to make up an equivalent number of days at some later point in the year. Those who are unable to fast at all because of old age or chronic illness can feed the poor instead, if they can afford it.

therefore let them hear My call and put their trust in Me, that they may be rightly guided.[9]

It is made lawful for you to go unto your wives (in sexual relations) on the night of the fast. They are a garment for you and you are a garment for them. Allah is aware that you were deceiving yourselves in this respect, and He has turned in mercy toward you and pardoned you. Therefore you may now have intercourse with them and seek what Allah has ordained for you. Eat and drink until the white thread becomes distinct to you from the black thread of the dawn. Then resume the fast till nightfall, and do not approach them but stay at your devotions in the masjids. These are the limits set by Allah so do not approach them. Thus He makes known His revelations to mankind, that they may guard themselves (against evil). (2:183-187)[10]

HAJJ (PILGRIMAGE)

From Al-Baqara (The Cow)

Perform the Greater and Lesser Pilgrimage (Hajj and 'Umra) for Allah. If you are prevented, then send such offerings as you can afford. And do not shave your heads until the offerings have reached their destination. But whoever among you is ill or has an ailment of the head must pay a ransom, either by fasting or by

---

[9] The Prophet, peace be upon him, was once asked: "Is our Lord close to us or far away? If He is close we will whisper in our prayers; while if He is far away then we should shout!" A verse was thus revealed explaining that Allah promises to fulfill the prayers of those who believe and obey, and that He, being Omnipotent, can hear them even if they pray quietly. He surely accepts the prayers, as He promises, of those who are believers and His good servants.

[10] In the early days of Islam, the Muslims held to a strict rule of fasting from the evening meal of one day until the evening meal of the next. If they fell asleep before they had taken their meal they thought it necessary to abstain from it, with the result that some people fainted from hunger. Intercourse with their wives had been similarly restricted. By the revelation of this verse, the present, definitive practice of fasting from first light (as defined by the ability to tell between a white and black thread) until sundown, was established.

almsgiving, or by offering a sacrifice. And if you are in safety, then whoever combines the 'Umra with the Hajj (by relaxing the state of consecration in between) must offer such offerings as he can afford; but if he cannot find (such offerings) them let him fast three days while he is on pilgrimage and seven days when he has returned; that is, ten in all. That is for him whose family is not present (residents nearby) at the Inviolable Sanctuary. And fear Allah; and know that Allah is severe in punishment.

The Pilgrimage is (in) the appointed months. Whoever intends to perform it therein must abstain from sexual intercourse, obscene language, abuse and angry conversation while on the pilgrimage. And whatever good you do, Allah knows it. So make provisions for yourselves (for the journey to the hereafter) and the best provision is piety (fear of Allah and observance of His law); therefore keep your duty to Me, O people of understanding!

It is no sin for you to seek the bounty of your Lord (by trading during the Hajj season). When you come hastening from 'Arafat with the multitude, remember Allah at the Sacred Monument. Remember Him that gave you guidance, although before you were of those gone astray.[11]

Then hasten on from the place whence the multitude hastens onward, and ask forgiveness of Allah. Allah is Forgiving, Merciful.

And when you have completed your sacred rites, then (continue to) remember Allah as you remember your forefathers, or even more. Among mankind there are some who say: "Our Lord! Give us what is good in this world!" and in the Hereafter they have no share.

---

[11] 'Arafat and the Sacred Monument are two of the main ritual sites of the Pilgrimage ceremonies. Like the other forms of worship, Hail also benefits society in numerous ways, for instance: (1) The pilgrimage dress, or 'Ihram', comprising two seamless pieces of cloth, symbolizes the fact that the pilgrims have left behind all worldly things, their possessions, title, position, nobility and the like, and stand before Him Who created them equal. (2) The Ihram dress resembles the shroud in which the dead are interred. And the mass gathering at the plain of 'Arafat recalls the Day of Judgment. (3) People from all over the world, of every race and culture, gather together in order to exchange both material and spiritual things, and to seek solutions to their common problems. Thus are the divergences between mankind reduced.

And there are others who say: "Lord! Give us what is good in this world and in the Hereafter; and keep us from the fire of Hell!"

Remember Allah on the Appointed Days (the three days which close the Half). Whoever hastens (his departure) on the second day, there is no sin upon him. And whoever delays, there is no sin for him; for him who fears Allah. Have fear of Allah, then, and know that you will be gathered unto Him. (2:196-203)

SUPPLICATION (DU'A)

From Al-A'raf (The Heights)

Allah's are the most beautiful Names; so call on Him by them! And leave the company of those who blaspheme His names. They will be requited for what they do. (7:180)[12]

From Al-Isra' (The Night Journey)

Say: "Call upon Allah or call upon the Compassionate; by whatever name you call upon Him (it is well); for to Him belong the most beautiful Names." And don't be loud in your prayer, nor say it in too low a voice, but seek a way in between. (17:110)

From Aal-'Imran (The Family of Imran)

In the creation of the heavens and the earth, and in the alternation of night and day, there are signs for men of understanding.

Those that remember Allah standing, sitting, and lying down, and meditate upon the creation of the heavens and the earth: "Our Lord! You have not created this in vain. Glory be to You! Protect us from the punishment of the Fire.

---

[12] According to a hadith (narration from the Prophet [pbuh]), "Allah has ninety-nine names, and whoever memorizes them (or acts in awareness of them) will enter into Heaven. Examples of His names are The Compassionate, The Merciful, The Loving The Kind, The Guide, The Great, The Eternal, and others. But this hadith does not put a restriction on the number of Allah's names. There are many other beautiful names of Allah. The idolaters used to blaspheme His names by mutilating them, giving some to their idols like "al-'Uzza."

Our Lord! We have heard a caller calling to faith: "Believe in your Lord!" So we believed. Our Lord! Therefore forgive us our evil deeds, and take our souls in death in the company of the righteous!

Our Lord! And grant us what You did promise to us through Your messengers, and do not abase us on the Day of Resurrection. You never break the promise!"

And their Lord accepted (their prayers) "Never will I suffer to be lost the work of any of you, whether male or female; you are (the offspring) of one another. So those who emigrated, and were expelled from their homes, and suffered harm in My cause, and fought and were slain, assuredly, I will remit from them their sins, and admit them into gardens beneath which rivers flow; a reward from Allah, and with Allah is the best of rewards." (3:190-195)

GOOD CHARACTER
VIRTUOUSNESS

From As-Saff (Battle Array)

0 believers! Why do you say what you do not do?

It is most odious in Allah's sight that you should say that which you do not do. (61:2-3)

From Al-Baqara (The Cow)

Righteousness is not whether you turn your faces to the East or to the West; but righteous is he who believes in Allah and the Last Day and the angels and the Scripture and the Prophets; and gives his wealth for the love of Allah to relatives, orphans and the needy, and the wayfarer, and those who ask, and for (the liberation of) slaves; and establish the Prayer and pay the Zakat; and those who keep their pledges when they make them, and show patience in hardship and adversity, and the time of distress. Such are the true believers; and such are the Godfearing. (2:177)

From Aal-'Imran (The Family of Imran)

And vie with one another for the forgiveness of your Lord and for a garden as vast as the heavens and the earth, prepared for the Godfearing.

Those who spend (of that which Allah has given them) in ease and adversity, those who control their anger and are forgiving toward mankind; for Allah loves the good.

And those who, when they do an evil thing or wrong themselves, remember Allah and seek forgiveness for their sins—Who can forgive sins except Allah?—and will not knowingly persist (in their misdeeds).

The reward of such will be forgiveness from their Lord, and gardens beneath which rivers flow, where they will abide forever. Blessed is the reward of those who work! (3:133-136)

From An-Nisa' (The Women)

Have you not seen those who praise themselves for purity? Allah purifies whom He will, and they will not be wronged, even (in a measure as trivial as) the hair upon a datestone.

See how they invent lies about Allah! That of itself is a most flagrant sin. (4:49-50)

From Al-Ahzab (The Clans)

Behold; men who surrender to Allah, and women who surrender, and men who believe and women who believe, and men who obey and women who obey, and men who speak the truth and women who speak the truth, and men who persevere (in righteousness) and women who persevere, and men who are humble and women who are humble, and men who give alms and women who give alms, and men who fast and women who fast, and men who guard their modesty and women who guard (their modesty), and men who remember Allah much and women who remember, Allah has prepared for them forgiveness and a vast reward. (33:35)

From Al-Hujurat (The Private Apartments)

0 you who believe! If a wicked person brings you some news, inquire into it carefully lest you should harm others unwittingly and afterwards be sorry for what you did.

And know that the Messenger of Allah is among you. If he were to obey you in many matters, you would surely fall into distress. But Allah has endeared the Faith to you and beautified it in your hearts, making unbelief, wrongdoing and disobedience abhorrent to you. Such are they who are rightly guided.

From An-Nur (The Light)

Let not those endowed with dignity (grace) and means among you swear that they will not give to their kindred and to the needy and to emigrants in the cause of Allah; let them rather forgive and ignore the offence (show indulgence). Do you not wish that Allah may forgive you? And Allah is Forgiving, Merciful.[13]

Those who slander chaste women, ignorant even of sin, who are believers, are cursed in the world and the hereafter. And for them awaits a terrible torment.

On the day when their own tongues and their own hands and their feet shall bear witness against them as to what they used to do.

On that day Allah will give them the full recompense they deserve, and they will realize that Allah is the manifest Truth;

Vile women are for vile men, and vile men are for vile women. Good women are for good men and good men are for good women. Such are innocent of that which people say: for them is forgiveness and a generous provision. (24:22-26)

---

[13] The immediate reference is to Hazrat Abu Bakr, the father of Hazrat 'Aishah. He was blessed with spiritual grace from God and with ample means, which he always used in the service of Islam and the Muslims. One of the slanderers of Hazrat 'Aishah turned out to be Mistah, a cousin of Hazrat Abu Bakr, whom he had been in the habit of supporting. Naturally Hazrat Abu Bakr wished to stop that aid, but according to the highest standards of Muslim ethics he was asked to forgive and forget, which he did.

ADAB (APPROPRIATE MANNERS)

From An-Nisa' (The Women)

When you are greeted with a greeting, give a greeting better than it or return it. Surely Allah takes account of all things. (4:86)

From An-Nur (The Light)

O you who believe! Do not enter houses, other than your own houses, until you ask for permission, and salute those in them (greet their dwellers). That is best for you. Perhaps you will remember (observe this).

If you do not find anyone therein, do not enter until you have been given permission, and if it is said to you "Go back," then go back, for that is purer for you. And Allah has full knowledge of whatever you do.[14]

There shall be no harm in your entering uninhabited houses wherein is supply for your needs, and Allah knows what you do openly and what you hide.[15]

Say to the believers that they should restrain their eyes and guard their modesty. That will be purer for them. Allah is well aware of what they do. (24:27-30)

From Al-Hujurat (The Private Apartments)

(O Prophet), those who call out to you from behind the apartments, most of them have no sense.[16]

And if they had had patience until you came out to them, it had been better for them. And Allah is Forgiving, Merciful.[17]

---

[14] Entry into an empty house is not allowed unless permitted by the owner of the house.

[15] The phrase "uninhabited house" means places for public use which are not allocated to certain group of people, such as inns, hotels, shops marketplaces, baths, etc.

[16] A group of Bedouins came while the Messenger was sleeping in his room at noon. They shouted to him to come out. The verse was revealed on that occasion.

[17] Some of the people who came to see the Holy Prophet (pbuh) from different parts of Arabia were so uncouth and impolite that instead of informing him of their arrival through some attendant they would start

JUSTICE

From An-Nisa' (The Women)

O you who believe! Stand out firmly for justice, as witnesses to Allah, even though it may be against yourselves, or your parents or your kindred, and whether it be against rich or poor, for Allah is nearer to both (than you are). So follow not caprice, lest you lapse (from truth); and if you lapse or fall away, then surely Allah is ever Informed of what you do. (4:135)

From Al-Ma'ida (The Table Spread)

0 you who believe! Be steadfast witnesses for Allah in equity; and let not hatred of any people make you swerve from justice. Deal justly; that is nearer to Godfearingness. Observe your duty to Allah. Indeed Allah is Informed of what you do.

From An-Nahl (The Bee)

Allah commands justice, kindness and charity to one's kindred, and forbids indecency, wickedness and oppression. He admonishes you so that you may take heed. (16:90)

MODESTY

From Al-Furqan (The Criterion)

And the servants of the Compassionate God are they who walk on the earth in modesty. And if the ignorant address them, they say, "Peace!" (25:63)

---

shouting to call him from outside the apartments of his wives. This sort of behavior troubled the Holy Prophet (pbuh) much, but he was tolerant on account of his natural clemency. At last Allah intervened, reproving the people for their uncivilized behavior and gave them the instruction: Whenever they came to see the Holy Prophet and did not find him, they should wait for him patiently until he came out to them himself instead of shouting to call him out.

From Luqman

Turn not your cheek in scorn toward folk, nor walk with insolence in the land. For Allah loves not each arrogant boaster.

Be modest in your bearing (walk) and subdue your voice. Lo! The harshest of all voices is the voice of the donkey. (31:18-19)

EQUITY

From Al-Baqara (The Cow)

0 you who believe! When you contract a debt for a fixed period, record it in writing. Let a scribe write it down for you with equity. No scribe should refuse to write as Allah has taught him, so let him write; and let the debtor dictate, fearing Allah his Lord, and not diminishing the sum (he owes). If the debtor be a feeble minded or weak person, or unable to dictate, let his guardian dictate for him in fairness. Call in two witnesses from among your men, and if two men (are not at hand), then one man and two women of such as you approve as witnesses, so that if either of the (women) commit an error, the other will remind her. Witnesses must not refuse if called upon to do so. Do not fail to record (your debts) in writing, be they small or large, together with the date of the payment. This is more just in the sight of Allah; it ensures accuracy in testifying and is the best way to remove all doubt. But if the transaction in hand be a bargain concluded on the spot, it is no offence for you if you do not record it in writing. See that witnesses are present when you trade with one another, and let no harm be done to either scribe or witness. If you harm them it shall be a wickedness in you. Have fear of Allah. Allah is teaching you; and He is Knower of all things. (2:282)

From Al-Baqara (The Cow)

There is no compulsion in religion. True guidance is distinct from error. But whoever disbelieves in Taghut and believes in Allah has grasped the strong handhold that will never break. And Allah is All-Hearing, All-Knowing.[18]

TOLERANCE

From Al-Baqara (The Cow)

A kind word with forgiveness is better than charity followed by injury. Allah is Self-Sufficient, Clement. (2:263)

From An-Nahl (The Bee)

If you punish, then punish with the like of that wherewith you were afflicted. But if you endure patiently, this is indeed better for those who are patient. (16:126)

From Ash-Shura (The Counsel)

The way (of blame) is only against those who oppress mankind, and wrongfully rebel in the earth. For such people there is a painful doom.

However, for the one who practices patience and is forgiving, these indeed are works of great courage and resolution. (42:42-43)

THE LAWFUL AND THE PROHIBITED

From Al-Ma'ida (The Table Spread)

O you who believe! Fulfill your undertakings! It is lawful for you to eat the flesh of all beasts except that which is (here) announced to

---

[18] "Taghut" denotes anything worshipped rather than Allah. Man, being subject to the inner promptings of the devil, is easily misled. By self-discipline and restraint, and the assistance of a guide, man can teach himself to combat these promptings, and hence save himself from committing wrong actions. Life is thus a struggle against Taghut, for when we do not serve God, we are assuming that others are more worthy of service than the Maker.

you. Game is forbidden to you while you are in the state of conse-cration.[19]

O you who believe! Violate not the sanctity of the symbols of God, nor of the Sacred Month, nor of the animals brought for sac-rifice, nor the people resorting to the Sacred House, seeking of the bounty and good pleasure of their Lord. But when you leave the state of consecration (and the sacred precincts around the City), you may hunt. Let not the hatred of a people (who once) ob-structed you from the Sacred Mosque lead you to transgress (and hostility on your part). Help one another in goodness and piety, and help not one another in sin and transgression. And fear God, for He is strict in punishment.

Forbidden to you (for food) are carrion and blood and swine-flesh, and that which has been dedicated to any other then Allah, and the strangled, and the dead through beating, and the dead killed by (the goring of) horns, and the devoured of wild beasts, saving that which you make lawful (by slaughtering decently before they die), and that which has been sacrificed to idols. And (forbid-den) also is settling matters with gambling-arrows. That is an abomination. This day are those who disbelieve in despair of (ever harming) your religion; so fear them not, and fear Me! This day have I perfected your religion for you and completed my favor upon you, and chosen for you as religion al-Islam. Whoso is forced by hunger, not by will, to sin: (for him) Allah is Forgiving, Merciful.

They ask you (O Muhammad) what is made lawful for them. Say: "(All) good things are made lawful for you. And those beasts and birds of prey which you have trained as hounds are trained, you teach them that which Allah taught you; so eat of that which they catch for you and mention Allah's name upon it, and observe your duty to Allah. Indeed Allah is swift to take account.

This day are (all) good things made lawful for you. The food of those who have received the Scripture is lawful for you and your food is lawful for them. And so are the virtuous women of the be-lievers, and the virtuous women of those who received the Scrip-ture before you (lawful for you) when you give them their marriage portions and live with them in honor, not in fornication, nor taking

---

[19] Fulfillment of undertakings, promises and contracts, is a pillar of the Islamic social, legal and political order. Here it is proclaimed as an abso-lute obligation.

them as secret concubines. Whoso denies the faith, his work is in vain, and in the Hereafter he will be among the losers.

0 you who believe! When you rise up for prayer, wash your faces, and your hands up to the elbows, and lightly rub your heads, and (wash) your feet up to the ankles. And if you are unclean, purify yourselves. And if you are sick or on a journey, or one of you comes from the privy, or you have touched (had sexual relations with) women, and you find not water, then to clean earth, and rub your faces and your hands with some of it. Allah would not place a burden on you, but He would purify you, and would perfect His grace upon you, that you may perhaps give thanks.

Remember Allah's favor upon you, and His covenant by which He bound you when you said: "We hear and we obey"; and keep your duty to Allah. Indeed Allah knows what is in the breasts (of men). (5:1-7)

From Al-Ma'ida (The Table Spread)

0 you who believe! Intoxicants and gambling, and (occult dedication of) stones and divining arrows are only an infamy of Satan's handiwork. Leave them aside in order that you may succeed.

Satan seeks to cast among you enmity and hatred by means of strong drink and gambling, and to turn you from remembrance of Allah and from (His) worship. Will you not then abstain?

Obey Allah and obey the messenger, and beware! But if you turn away, then know that the duty of Our messenger is only plain communication (of the message).

There shall be no sin (imputed) to those who believe and do good deeds for what they may have eaten (in the past); so be mindful of your duty (to Allah), and believe and do good works; and once again: be mindful of your duty and believe; and once again: be mindful of your duty, and do good. Allah loves those who do good. (5:90-93)

THE FAMILY AND MARRIAGE

From Ar-Rum (The Romans)

And of His signs is this: He created for you helpmeets (wives) from yourselves that you might find rest in them, and He set between you love and mercy. Lo, herein indeed are portents for folk who reflect. (30:21)

From Ash-Shura (The Counsel)

To Allah belongs the Sovereignty of the heavens and the earth. He creates whatever He wills. He gives daughters to whom He wills, and sons to whom He wills;

Or He gives sons and daughters to whom He wills and He makes barren whom He wills. Indeed He is Knower, Powerful. (42:49-50)

From An-Nisa' (The Women)

0 you who believe! It is not lawful for you to inherit women against their will, nor to put constraint on them that you may take away a part of that which you have given them, unless they be guilty of open lewdness. Treat them with kindness, for if you hate them it may be that you hate a thing in which Allah has placed much good.[20]

If you wish to divorce a woman in order to wed another, and you have given her a (whole) treasure as dowry, take not the least part of it back. Would you take by way of calumny and open wrong?[21]

---

[20] Before Islam it was customary for the Arab tribes to treat women like chattel. If a woman's husband died she would be forced to marry against her will or would be sold as though she were a commodity or be used for any other material gain. With the revelation of this verse this practice came to an end, and women who were candidates for salvation too, were given the dignity and respect they deserved.

[21] It is an obligatory customary in Islamic marriage that when a man marries a woman, he gives her a certain amount as a "gift" in the form of gold, jewelry, currency or property, or other material good, as specified by her and her family This is called *mahr*. This can be given in advance before the marriage once they decide to get married; or alternatively it can be postponed, to be paid either in case of a divorce or on the death of the husband, the option being in the bride's hand under Islamic Law, it is

How can you take it back when one of you has gone in to the other, and they have taken a strong pledge from you?[22]

From An-Nisa' (The Women)

Men are the protectors of women, because Allah has given the one more than the other (strength), and because they spend of their property (to maintain them). So righteous women are the devoutly obedient, guarding in secret that which Allah had secretly guarded. As for those from whom you fear disloyalty, admonish them and banish them to beds apart, and beat them (lightly, without visible injury). Then if they obey you, seek not a way against them. For Allah is High, Sublime.[23]

And if you fear a breach between them (man and wife), then appoint an arbiter from his people and an arbiter from her people. If they desire reconciliation, Allah will make them of one mind. Allah is ever Knower, Aware. (4:34-3 5)

From Al-Ahkaf (The Wind-Curved Sandhills)

We have enjoined man to treat his parents with kindness. His mother bore him with trouble and she gave him birth with trouble, and his bearing and weaning took thirty months, until, when he attained to his full strength and became forty years old, he said: "O my Lord, grant me the grace to thank you for the favors You have bestowed on me and on my parents, and to do such good works as may please You. And be gracious to me in my progeny. I turn to

---

illegal for men to deprive their wives of this money, the purpose of which is to give her a degree of financial independence. All kinds of abuse, pressure, and harassment are prohibited, and are actionable in a court of law.

[22] A man who marries a woman and has sex with her, and later decides to divorce her, is obligated to give her *mahr* in full, however brief the marriage may have been. If the marriage contract has been completed but not consummated, then the woman takes half of the dowry, whatever it might be.

[23] It should be observed that the sanction in the case of the marriage is a last resort. The Blessed Prophet never hit any of his wives. In fact, he warned the Muslim community that it is a donkey who beats his wife. If a man has to administer physical correction to his wife, his strokes should be symbolic, as they must leave no bruises or other marks. A wife with a complaint against her husband's treatment may apply to a magistrate to deal with the problem.

You in penitence, and I am of those who have surrendered to You (as Muslims)." (46:15)

HUMAN DIVERSITY

From Ar-Rum (The Romans)

And of His signs is the creation of the heavens and the earth, and the difference of your languages and colors. Lo! Herein indeed are portents for men of knowledge. (30:22)

STORIES OF THE PROPHETS (ON WHOM BE PEACE) IN THE QUR'AN

The stories of the Prophets of God in the Qur'an are examples and sources of inspiration for Muslim believers. The depiction of the lives of the Prophets in the Qur'an is similar but also different in important ways from the account presented in the Old and New Testaments. These stories highlight some of those differences.

JESUS (SON OF MARY) (ON WHOM BE PEACE)

From Al-Baqara (The Cow)

And assuredly We gave Moses the Scripture, and after him We sent messenger after messenger. We gave Jesus son of Mary the clear miracles (to serve as proofs of Allah's sovereignty), and strengthened him with the Holy Spirit (the Angel Gabriel). Is it so, that whenever a Messenger whose message does not suit your desires, comes to you, you grow arrogant, denying some of them and slaying others? (2:87)

From Aal-'Imran (The Family of Imran)

Allah did prefer Adam and Noah and the Family of Abraham and the Family of 'Imran above His creatures.

They were descendants of one another. Allah is Hearer, Knower.

(Remember) when the wife of 'Imran said: "My Lord! I dedicate to your service that which is in my womb. Accept it from me; You alone are the Hearer, the Knower."

And when she was delivered of the child, she said: "My Lord, I have given birth to a female child." Allah knows best of what she was delivered: the male is not like the female; "and I have named her Mary. Protect her and her descendants from Satan, the outcast."

And her Lord accepted her with full acceptance, and vouchsafed to her a goodly growth, and entrusted her to the care of Zachariah. Whenever Zachariah went into the chamber where she was, he found that she had food. He said: "Oh Mary! Where is this food from?" She answered: "It is from Allah. Allah gives without stint to whom He will."

Then Zachariah prayed to his Lord, and said: "0 my Lord! Grant me of Your bounty, of upright descendants. You are the Hearer of prayer."

And the angels called to him as he stood praying in the mihrab: "Allah gives you the glad tidings of a son whose name is John (Yahya), (who comes) to confirm a word from Allah, princely and chaste, a Prophet of the righteous."

"Lord," said Zachariah: "How can I have a son when old age has overtaken me and my wife is barren?" "Such is the will of Allah," He replied, "Who does what He will."

He said: "My Lord! Vouchsafe unto me a portent!" The answer was: "For three days you shall not speak to any man except by signs. Remember your Lord much, and praise Him in the early hours of night and morning."

And when the angels said: "0 Mary! Allah has chosen you, and made you pure, and has preferred you above all the women of creation."

O Mary! Be obedient to your Lord, prostrate yourself, and bow with those who bow in worship."

This is of the tidings hidden, which We reveal to you (0 Muhammad). You were not present with them when they cast lots to see which of them should be the guardian of Mary; nor were you present when they argued (concerning this).

When the angels said: "O Mary! Allah gives the glad tidings of a word from Him, whose name is the Messiah, Jesus, son of Mary, illustrious in this world and the Hereafter, and one of those who will be brought near (to God).

He will speak to mankind in his cradle and in his manhood, and he is of the righteous.

She said: "My Lord! How can I have a child when no man has touched me?" He replied: "Such is the will of Allah. He creates what He will. When He decrees a thing He only says: Be! and it is."

And He will teach him the Scripture and wisdom, and the Torah and the Gospel.

And will make him a Messenger to the Israelites. He will say: "I bring you a sign from your Lord. From clay I will make for you the likeness of a bird; I shall breathe into it and, by Allah's leave, it shall become a (living) bird. By Allah's leave I shall give sight to the blind, heal the leper, and raise the dead to life. I shall tell you what you eat and what you store up in your houses. Surely that will be a sign for you, if you are believers.

Allah is my Lord and your Lord; so worship Him. That is the straight path.

But when Jesus became aware of their disbelief he said: "Who will be my helpers in God? The disciples said: "We will be Allah's helpers. We believe in Allah; and bear you witness that we have surrendered (ourselves to Him)!

Our Lord! We believe in that which You have revealed, and we follow him whom You have sent. Account us among those who witness" (the truth; i.e. the oneness of God, and the truth of the prophets He has sent, including Jesus).

And they (the disbelievers) schemed and Allah schemed (against them); and Allah is the best of schemers.

(And remember) when Allah said: "O Jesus! I am gathering you and causing you to ascend to Me, and am cleansing you of those who disbelieve, and am setting those who follow you above those who disbelieve until the Day of Resurrection. Then to Me you will all return, and I shall judge between you as to that in which you used to differ. (3:33-55)

From Al-Nisa' (The Women)

O People of the Scripture! Commit no excess in your religion, and say nothing but the truth about Allah. The Messiah, Jesus son of Mary, was only a messenger of Allah, and His word which He conveyed to Mary, and a spirit from Him. So believe in Allah and His messengers, and say not "three." Cease! (it is) better for you! Allah is only One God. Far is it removed from His transcendent majesty that He should have a son. His is all that is in the heavens and all that is in the earth. And Allah is sufficient as Defender. (4:171)

From Al-Ma'ida (The Table)

Indeed, We did reveal the Torah wherein there was a guidance and a light, by which the prophets who surrendered (to Allah) judged by such of Allah's Scripture as they were bidden to observe, and thereunto were they witnesses. So fear not men, but fear Me. And sell not My revelations for a miserable price. Whoever judges not by that which Allah has revealed, such are disbelievers.

And We ordained for them therein: The life for the life, and the eye for the eye, and the nose for the nose, and the ear for the ear, and the tooth for the tooth, and for wounds retaliation. But, if any one remit the retaliation (by way of charity), it is an act of atonement for himself. And whoever judges not by what Allah had revealed, such are the wrongdoers.

And in their footsteps We sent Jesus son of Mary, confirming that which was (revealed) before him, and We bestowed on him the Gospel wherein is guidance and a light, confirming that which was (revealed) before it in the Torah - a guidance and an admonition to the Godfearing. (5:44-46)

From Al-Ma'ida (The Table)

In the day when Allah will gather the messengers together and ask: "What was the response you received (from the people you were assigned to teach)? They will say: "We have no knowledge: it is You, only You, who knows in full all that is hidden."

Then will Allah say: "0 Jesus, son of Mary! Remember My favor to you and to your mother; how I strengthened you with the holy spirit (the archangel Gabriel) so that you spoke to mankind in the cradle as in maturity; and how I taught you the Scripture and Wisdom and the Torah and the Gospel; and how you did shape of clay as it were the likeness of a bird by My permission, and did blow upon it, and it was a bird by My permission, and you did heal him who was born blind and the leper by My permission; and how you did raise the dead, by my permission; and how I restrained the Children of Israel from (harming) you when you came to them with clear signs, and those of them who disbelieved exclaimed: "This is nothing but clear magic!"

And when I inspired the disciples (saying): "Believe in Me and in My messenger," they said: "We believe. Bear witness that we have surrendered" (to You as Muslims).

When the disciples said: "0 Jesus, son of Mary! Is your Lord able to send down for us a table spread with food from heaven?" He said: "Observe your duty to Allah, if you are true believers."

They said: "We wish to eat thereof, that we may satisfy our hearts and know that you have spoken truth to us, and that thereof we may be witnesses."

Jesus, son of Mary, said: "0 Allah, our Lord! Send down for us a table spread with food from heaven, that it may be a feast for us, for the first of us and for the last of us, and a sign from You. Give us sustenance, for you are the Best of Sustainers."

Allah said: "I will send it down for you. But if any of you disbelieves afterward, him surely will I punish with a punishment wherewith I have not punished any of my peoples."

And when Allah said: "0 Jesus, son of Mary! Did you say to mankind: "Take me and my mother for two gods beside Allah?" he said: "Be glorified! It was not mine to say that to which I had no right. If I used to say it, then You knew it. You know what is in my mind, and I know not what is in Your mind. Assuredly, You, only You, are the Knower of things hidden."

I spoke to them only that which You commanded me, (saying): "Worship Allah, my Lord and your Lord. I was a witness of them while I dwelt among them, and when You took me You were the Watcher over them. You are Witness over all things.

If You punish them, they are Your slaves, and if You forgive them, You, only You, are the Mighty, the Wise."

Allah will then say: "This is a day in which their truthfulness profits the truthful, for theirs are Gardens beneath which rivers flow, wherein they are secure for ever, Allah is well-pleased with them and they with Him. That is the great triumph."

To Allah belongs the sovereignty of the heavens and the earth and whatsoever is therein, and He is Able to do all things. (5:109-120)

From Maryam (Mary)

And make mention of Mary in the Scripture; when she had withdrawn from her people to a place looking east.

She placed a screen to seclude herself from them. Then We sent to her Our Spirit (Gabriel), and he appeared before her as a man without fault.

She said: "I seek refuge in the Compassionate God from you; (do not come near) if you fear the Lord."

He said: "I am only a messenger of your Lord (to announce) to you the gift of a pure son."

She said: "How can I have a son when no man has touched me; neither have I been unchaste?"

(The angel) replied, "So shall it be; your Lord says: 'This is an easy thing for Me. And We shall make him a sign for mankind and a blessing from Us.' It is a matter decreed."

Thereupon she conceived (the child); and (with it) she went away to a distant place.

And the pains of childbirth drove her to a trunk of a palm-tree. She said: "Would that I had died before this, and had become a thing of naught, forgotten!"

But (a voice) cried unto her from below her saying: "Do not be sad; your Lord has provided a rivulet at your feet.

"(As for your food) shake the trunk of the palm-tree towards yourself; you will cause ripe dates to fall upon you.

"So eat and drink, and be consoled; and if you meet any mortal say: 'I have vowed a fast (of silence) to the Compassionate God, and will not speak with any human being this day.'"

At length she brought the (infant) to her people carrying him. They said: "0 Mary! Truly an amazing thing you have brought."

O sister of Aaron! Your father was not a wicked man, nor was your mother unchaste.

She made a sign (to them, pointing to the child). But they replied: "How can we speak with a babe in a cradle?"

(Whereupon) he (the babe) spoke out: "I am indeed a servant of Allah. He has given me the Scripture and has appointed me a prophet."

And He has made me blessed wheresoever I may be and has commanded me to pray and to give alms to the poor as long as I live.

And (He) has made me dutiful to my mother and has not made me oppressive, wicked.

So peace be upon the day I was born and the day that I die and the day that I shall be raised up to life (again).

Such was Jesus, the son of Mary; a statement of the truth about which they (vainly) dispute.

It is not befitting to (the majesty of) Allah that He should beget a son. Glory be to Him! When He determines a matter, He only says to it "Be!" and it is.

(And Jesus had declared): "Assuredly Allah is my Lord and your Lord. Therefore serve Him. That is the straight path."

Yet the sects differed among themselves concerning Jesus; and woe to those who disbelieve because of the witnessing of a great Day.

On that day when they will appear before Us, how plainly will they see and hear; but transgressors are this day in manifest deviation. (19:16-37)

MOSES (ON WHOM BE PEACE)

From Al-Kahf (The Cave)

And when Moses said unto his attendant: "I will not give up until I reach the place where the two seas meet, though I march on for ages."

But when at last they came to the place where the two seas met, they forgot their fish which made its way into the water, as if through in a tunnel.

And when they had gone further, Moses said to his servant: "Bring us our breakfast, truly we have suffered much fatigue at this (stage of) our journey."

He replied: "Did you see that I forgot the fish when we took refuge on the rock. I forgot the fish and none but Satan caused me to forget to mention it. The fish made its way into the sea in a bizarre fashion."

"This is what we have been seeking," said Moses. So they retraced their steps again.

Then they found one of Our servants on whom We had bestowed mercy from Ourselves, and whom We had taught knowledge from Our own Presence.

Moses said to him: "May I follow you so that you may teach me the right-guidance which you have been taught?"

"You will not be able to have patience with me," said the other.

"For how can you bear with that which is beyond your knowledge?"

Moses said: "Allah willing, you shall find me patient; I shall not in anything disobey you."

He said: "If, then, you would follow me, then ask me no questions about anything until I myself speak to you concerning it."

So they both set forth but as soon as they were in the ship he made a hole in its bottom. "A strange thing you have done!" exclaimed Moses. "Have you made a hole in it to drown its passengers?"

"Did I not tell you." He replied "that you would not have patience with me?"

Moses said: "Forgive my forgetfulness and do not grieve me by raising a difficulty in my case."

They both journeyed on until, when they met a young man, he (Moses' companion) slew him. And Moses said: "What! Have you slain an innocent soul though he had killed nobody? Truly you have done a foul thing."

"Did I not tell you," he replied, "that you would not have patience with me?"

(Moses) said: "If I ever question you again about anything do not let me accompany you, for then you would have received (full) excuse from myself."

So they both journeyed on until when they came to the inhabitants of a town. They asked them for food, but they refused to make them guests. And they found there a wall on the point of falling down, and he restored it. Moses said: "Had you wished, you could have demanded payment for this."

He answered: "This is the parting between you and me. (But first) I will tell you the interpretation of that which you could not bear with patience.

As for the boat, it belonged to poor people working on the sea, and I wished to render it unserviceable, because in their rear, there was a king who was seizing every ship by force.

As for the youth, his parents were believers, and we feared that he would oppress them by rebellion and disbelief.

So we desired that their Lord would give them in exchange (a son) better in purity (of conduct) and closer in affection.

As for the wall, it belonged to two orphan boys in the city. There was beneath it a (buried) treasure belonging to them, and their father had been a righteous man. So your Lord desired that they should attain their age of full strength and bring out their treasure as a mercy from their Lord. I did it not upon my own command. Such is the interpretation of (those things) which you were unable to bear with patience. (18:60-82)

From Ta Ha

Has the story of Moses reached you (0 Muhammad)?

When he saw a fire and said to his family: "Stay here, for I can see a fire. Perhaps I can bring you a burning brand or find some guidance at the fire."

But when he reached that place a voice was heard: "0 Moses!

I am your Lord. So take off your sandals; for you are in the sacred valley of Tuwa.

(Know that) I have chosen you. Therefore, listen to what is revealed.

I, even I, am Allah; there is no god but Me. So serve Me and establish the Prayer for My remembrance.

The Hour is surely coming. But I choose to keep it hidden, so that every soul may be rewarded for its labors.

Therefore let not any person who does not believe in it and follows his caprice, turn you away from it, lest you perish.

What is that in your right hand, 0 Moses?"

He said: "It is my staff; upon it I lean and with it I beat down leaves for my flock, and I have other uses for it."

(Allah) said: "Throw it down, 0 Moses!"

So he threw it down, and lo! it was a snake, gliding.

He said: "Catch hold of it and do not fear. We shall return it to its former state.

"And put your hand under your armpit it shall come forth white, without harm. (This will be) another sign.

That We may show you (some) of Our greater signs.
Go to Pharaoh for he has indeed transgressed all bounds."
Moses said: "My Lord open my breast for me.
Ease my task for me,
And remove the impediment from my tongue,
So that they may understand me,
And appoint a minister for me from my (own) family.
Aaron, my brother;
Confirm my strength with him.
And make him share my task.
That we may glorify You much,
And remember You much,
Indeed, You are ever watching over us."
He said, "Your request is granted, O Moses.
And indeed another time already We have shown you favor,
When We revealed (Our Will) to your mother by inspiration,
(Saying): 'Place (the child) into the chest and throw (the chest) into the river, then the river should cast it up to the bank, where he shall be taken by an enemy to Me and an enemy to him. And I endued you with love from Me, so that you might be reared under My eye.'"

"When your sister went and said: 'Shall I show you one who will nurse him?' Thus We restored you to your mother that her eyes might be cooled and she should not grieve. Then you did kill a man but We saved you from trouble, and We tried you in various ways. You stayed among the people of Midian for many years, and at length came here as was ordained." (20:9-40)

ABRAHAM (ON WHOM BE PEACE)

Ash-Shu'ara' (The Poets)

Recite unto them the story of Abraham.
When he said unto his father and his people: "What do you worship?"
They said: "We worship idols, and we are ever devoted unto them."
He said: "Do they hear you when you cry?
"Or do they benefit or harm you?"

They said: "Nay but we found our fathers acting in this way."

He said: "Do you then see whom you have been worshipping?"

You and your forefathers!

Behold! They are (all) an enemy unto me, save the Lord of the Worlds.

Who created me, and who guides me.

And who feeds me and waters me.

And when I sicken, then He heals me.

And who causes me to die, then gives me life again.

And who, I ardently hope, will forgive my sin on the Day of Judgment.

My Lord! Bestow wisdom on me and unite me to the righteous.

And give unto me a good report in later generations.

And place me among the inheritors of the Garden of Delight.

And forgive my father, for he was one of those who go astray.

And abase me not on the day when they are raised.

The day when wealth and sons avail not any man.

Save him who brings unto Allah a whole heart." (26:69-89)

BAHA'I SCRIPTURES

INTRODUCTION AND BASIC TENETS

The Baha'i Faith is a religion that was founded in Persia (now called Iran) in the middle of the nineteenth century. It teaches that all people of the world are members of one human family. It also teaches that all religions are basically the same, and that all religions worship the same God. According to the Baha'i Faith, one day all the countries of the world will join together as one (planet earth) with one (community of religions).

The founder of the Baha'i Faith was called Baha'u'lla'h. He taught that all the great religions of the world are divine in origin, that their basic principles are in complete harmony, that their aims and purposes are (ultimately) the same, and that their teachings are aspects of one truth. He explained that a Messenger from God is sent about every 1,000 years to provide spiritual guidance to humankind in a continuous and progressive process. Their missions represent successive stages in the spiritual evolution of human society. The unity and oneness of humankind is the central point of the Baha'i Faith, and the point from which all of its other teachings grow.

The Baha'i Faith is (a widely disseminated) religion, and one which is growing rapidly. Its central religious figures are the Bab (1819-1850), called the forerunner; Baha'u'lla'h (1817-1892), the Prophet; Abdu'l-Bah'a (1844-1921), the Interpreter; and Shoghi Effendi, the Guardian of the Baha'i faith.

Baha'is believe in:

- the oneness of humanity. All peoples are members of the human family, all have the same Creator.

- the independent investigation of truth. Baha'u'lla'h teaches that each person must investigate truth for him/herself—that faith in this day must be built on knowledge and based on one's own decision.

- elimination of all prejudices. For example, gender, religious, age, nationality, racial, economic, appearance, cultural.

- agreement of science and religion. Baha'u'lla'h teaches that true religion and true science are in complete harmony.

- world peace. This is the time when all nations must seek, by every means in their power, to establish cooperation (among) all the nations (of) the world.

- equality of men and women. Both men and women are equal in the sight of God, and both have the same rights and responsibilities.

- universal education. Everyone, rich and poor, men and women, should receive an education.

- consultation. Truth and the best decisions emerge from a process of honest and open discussion by every member of the group.

- limitation of wealth and poverty. Society must not permit extremes of either wealth or poverty. The economic problem is essentially a spiritual one.

- universal language. Baha'u'lla'h recommended the adoption of a common second language for all peoples in order to promote greater understanding between nations and individuals.

- unity in diversity. The different languages and cultures of the world should maintain their individuality, but there must be a common link between them that can bring about understanding.

- a world commonwealth of nations. This is the time when the peoples of the earth should meet as equals. Their governments will be represented in a world parliament that will be concerned with the prosperity of all nations and the happiness of humankind.

- progressive revelation. God has unfolded divine truth in successive stages through the whole history of humankind. This means that religion is evolutionary—it develops and progresses over the ages. Baha'u'lla'h's mission is to help unite humankind into a global community. (1)

SPIRITUAL REALITY

What It Means to Be Spiritual

Wert thou to attain to but a dewdrop of the crystal water of divine knowledge, thou wouldst readily realize that true life is not the life of the flesh but the life of the spirit. For the life of the flesh is common to both men and animals, where the life of the spirit is possessed only by the pure in heart who have quaffed from the ocean of faith and partaken of the fruit of certitude. This life knoweth no death, and this existence is crowned by immortality. (2)

Be generous in prosperity, and thankful in adversity. Be worthy of the trust of thy neighbor, and look upon him with a bright and friendly face. Be a treasure to the poor, an admonisher to the rich, an answerer of the cry of the needy, a preserver of the sanctity of thy pledge. Be fair in thy judgment, and guarded in thy speech. Be unjust to no man, and show all meekness to all men. Be as a lamp unto them that walk in darkness, a joy to the sorrowful, a sea for the thirsty, a haven for the distressed, an upholder and defender of the victim of oppression. Let integrity and uprightness distinguish all thine acts. Be a home for the stranger, a balm to the suffering, a tower of strength for the fugitive. Be eyes to the blind, and a guiding light unto the feet of the erring. Be an ornament to the countenance of truth, a crown to the brow of fidelity, a pillar of the temple of righteousness, a breath of life to the body of mankind, an ensign of the hosts of justice, a luminary above the horizon of virtue, a dew to the soil of the human heart, an ark on the ocean of knowledge, a sun in the heaven of bounty, a gem on the diadem of wisdom, a shining light in the firmament of thy generation, a fruit upon the tree of humility. (3)

Be swift in the path of holiness, and enter the heaven of communion with Me. Cleanse thy heart with the burnish of the spirit, and hasten to the court of the Most High. (4)

Human Nature

In man there are two natures; his spiritual or higher nature and his material or lower nature. In one he approaches God, in the other he lives for the world alone. Signs of both these natures are to be found in men. In his material aspect he expresses untruth, cruelty and injustice; all these are the outcome of his lower nature. The attributes of his Divine nature are shown forth in love, mercy, kindness, truth and justice, one and all being expressions of his higher nature. Every good habit, every noble quality belongs to man's spiritual nature, whereas all his imperfections and sinful actions are born of his material nature. If a man's Divine nature dominates his human nature, we have a saint.

Man has the power both to do good and to do evil; if his power for good predominates and his inclinations to do wrong are conquered, then man in truth may be called a saint. But if, on the contrary, he rejects the things of God and allows his evil passions to conquer him then he is no better than a mere animal. (5)

Believing in God

This people, all of them, have pictured a god in the realm of the mind, and worship that image which they have made for themselves. And yet that image is comprehended, the human mind being the comprehender thereof, and certainly the comprehender is greater than that which lieth within its grasp; for imagination is but the branch, while mind is the root; and certainly the root is greater than the branch. Consider then, how all the peoples of the world are bowing the knee to a fancy of their own contriving, how they have created a creator within their own minds, and they call it the

Fashioner of all that is—whereas in truth it is but an illusion. Thus are the people worshipping only an error of perception. (6)

To every discerning and illuminated heart it is evident that God, the unknowable Essence, the Divine Being, is immensely exalted beyond every human attribute, such as corporeal existence, ascent and descent, egress and regress. Far be it from His glory that human tongue should adequately recount His praise, or that human heart comprehend His fathomless mystery. He is, and hath ever been, veiled in the ancient eternity of His Essence, and will remain in His Reality everlastingly hidden from the sight of men. (7)

Give ear to the sayings of the Friend and turn towards His paradise. Worldly friends, seeking their own good, appear to love one the other, whereas the true Friend hath loved and doth love you for your own sakes. ... Be not disloyal to such a Friend, nay rather hasten unto Him. Such is the daystar of the world of truth and faithfulness, that hath dawned above the horizon of the pen of the Lord of all names. Open your ears that Ye may hearken unto the word of God, the Help in peril, the Self-existent. (8)

Love and Unity

But there is need of a superior power to overcome human prejudices, a power which nothing in the world of mankind can withstand and which will overshadow the effect of all other forces at work in human conditions. That irresistible power is the love of God. It is my hope and prayer that it may destroy the prejudice... between you and unite you all permanently under its hallowed protection. (9)

How is it possible for men to fight from morning until evening, killing each other, shedding the blood of their fellow-men: And for what object? To gain possession of a part of the earth! Even the animals, when they fight, have an immediate and more reasonable cause for their attacks! How terrible it is that men, who are of the higher kingdom, can descend to slaying and bringing misery to their fellow-beings, for the possession of a tract of land! ...

I charge you all that each one of you concentrate all the thoughts of your heart on love and unity. When a thought of war comes, oppose it by a stronger thought of peace. A thought of hatred must be destroyed by a more powerful thought of love. Thoughts of war bring destruction to all harmony, well-being, restfulness and content. (10)

Be in perfect unity. Never become angry with one another. Let your eyes be directed toward the kingdom of truth and not toward the world of creation. Love the creatures for the sake of God and not for themselves. You will never become angry or impatient if you love them for the sake of God. Humanity is not perfect. There are imperfections in every human being, and you will always become unhappy if you look toward the people themselves. But if you look toward God, you will love them and be kind to them, for the world of God is the world of perfection and complete mercy. Therefore, do not look at the shortcomings of anybody; see with the sight of forgiveness. The imperfect eye beholds imperfections. The eye that covers faults looks toward the Creator of souls. He created them, trains and provides for them, endows them with capacity and life, sight and hearing; therefore, they are the signs of His grandeur. You must love and be kind to everybody, care for the poor, protect the weak, heal the sick, teach and educate the ignorant. (11)

Prayer and Meditation

Spirit has influence; prayer has spiritual effect. Therefore, we pray, O God, Heal this sick one!" Perchance God will answer. Does it matter who prays? God will answer the prayer of every servant if that prayer is urgent. His mercy is vast, illimitable. He answers the prayers of all His servants. He answers the prayers of this plant. The plant prays potentially, "O God! Send me rain!" God answers the prayer, and the plant grows. God will answer anyone. He answers prayers potentially. Before we were born into this world did we not pray, "O God! Give me a mother; give me two fountains of bright milk; purify the air for my breathing; grant me rest and comfort; prepare food for my sustenance and living"? Did we not pray potentially for these needed blessings before we were created? When we came into this world, did we not find our prayers answered? Did we not find mother, father, food, light, home and every other necessity and blessing, although we did not actually ask for them? Therefore, it is natural that God will give to us when we ask Him. His mercy is all-encircling. (12)

Intone, O My servant, the verses of God that have been received by thee, as intoned by them who have drawn nigh unto Him, that the sweetness of thy melody may kindle thine own soul, and attract the hearts of all men. Whoso reciteth, in the privacy of his chamber, the verses revealed by God, the scattering angels of the Almighty shall scatter abroad the fragrance of the words uttered by his mouth, and shall cause the heart of every righteous man to throb. Though he may, at first, remain unaware of its effect, yet the virtue of the grace vouchsafed unto him must needs sooner or later exercise its influence upon his soul. Thus have the mysteries of the Revelation of God been decreed by virtue of the Will of Him Who is the Source of power and wisdom. (13)

SERVICE

Service to Humanity

Service to humanity is service to God. (14)

Be kind to all peoples; care for every person; do all you can to purify the hearts and minds of men; strive ye to gladden every soul. To every meadow be a shower of grace, to every tree the water of life; be as sweet musk to the sense of humankind, and to the ailing be a fresh, restoring breeze. Be pleasing waters to all those who thirst, a careful guide to all who have lost their way; be father and mother to the orphan, be loving sons and daughters to the old, be an abundant treasure to the poor. Think ye of love and good fellowship as the delights of heaven, think ye of hostility and hatred as the torments of hell. (15)

Love ye all religions and all races with a love that is true and sincere and show that love through deeds and not through the tongue; for the latter hath no importance, as the majority of men are, in speech, well-wishers, while action is the best. (16)

Effort and Perseverance

From the exalted source, and out of the essence of His favor and bounty He hath entrusted every created thing with a sign of His knowledge, so that none of His creatures may be deprived of its share in expressing, each according to its capacity and rank, this knowledge. This sign is the mirror of His beauty in the world of creation. The greater the effort exerted for the refinement of this sublime and noble mirror, the more faithfully will it be made to reflect the glory of the names and attributes of God, and reveal the wonders of His signs and knowledge. (17)

We must strive with energies of heart, soul and mind to develop and manifest the perfections and virtues latent within the realities of the phenomenal world, for the human reality may be compared to a seed. If we sow the seed, a mighty tree appears from it. The virtues of the seed are revealed in the tree. ... Similarly, the merciful God, our Creator, has deposited with human realities certain latent and potential virtues. Through education and culture these virtues deposited by the loving God will become apparent in the human reality, even as the unfoldment of the tree from within the germinating seed. (18)

The Physical World

The temple of the world hath been fashioned after the image and likeness of the human body. In fact each mirroreth forth the image of the other, wert thou but to observe with discerning eyes. By this is meant that even as the human body in this world which is outwardly composed of different limbs and organs, is in reality a closely integrated, coherent entity, similarly the structure of the physical world is like unto a single being whose limbs and members are inseparably linked together. (19)

Nature is that condition, that reality, which in appearance consists in life and death, or, in other words, in the composition and decomposition of all things.

This Nature is subjected to an absolute organization, to determined laws, to a complete order and a finished design, from which it will never depart—to such a degree, indeed, that if you look carefully and with keen sight, from the smallest invisible atom up to such large bodies of the world of existence as the globe of the sun or the other great stars and luminous spheres, whether you regard their arrangement, their composition, their form or their movement, you will find that all are in the highest degree of organization and are under one law from which they will never depart. (20)

Evolution and Human Capacity

... Life on this earth is very ancient. It is not one hundred thousand, or two hundred thousand, or one million or two million years old; it is very ancient, and the ancient records and traces are entirely obliterated. (21)

Moses taught that the world was brought into existence in the six days of creation. This is an allegory, a symbolic form of the ancient truth that the world evolved gradually. ... We thus have a progressive process of creation, and not a one-time happening. Moses' days of creation represent time spans of millions of years. (22)

HUMANITY

The Nature of God

In the Word of God there is still another unity—the oneness of the Manifestations of God, Abraham, Moses, Jesus Christ, Muhammad, the Bab and Baha'u'lla'h. This is a unity divine, heavenly, radiant, merciful—the one reality appearing in its successive Manifestations. For instance, the sun is one and the same, but its points of dawning are various. During the summer season it rises from the northern point of the ecliptic; in winter it appears from the southern point of rising. Each month between, it appears from a certain zodiacal position. Although these dawning points are different, the sun is the same sun which has appeared from them all. (23)

The Relationship Between God and Humanity

Having created the world and all that liveth and moveth therein, He, through the direct operation of His unconstrained and sovereign Will, chose to confer upon man the unique distinction and capacity to know Him and to love Him—a capacity that must needs be regarded as the generating impulse and the primary purpose underlying the whole of creation. ... Upon the inmost reality of each and every created thing He hath shed the light of one of His names, and made it a recipient of the glory of one of His attributes. Upon the reality of man, however, He hath focused the radiance of all of His names and attributes, and made it a mirror of his own Self. Alone of all created things man hath been singled out for so great a favor, so enduring a bounty. (24)

Let God's beloved, each and every one, be the essence of purity, the very life of holiness, so that in every country they may become famed for their sanctity, independence of spirit, and meekness. Let them be cheered by draughts from the eternal cup of love for God, and make merry as they drink from the wine vaults of Heaven. Let them behold the Blessed Beauty, and feel the flame and rapture of that meeting, and be struck dumb with awe and wonder. This is the station of the sincere; this is the way of the loyal; this is the brightness that shineth on the faces of those nigh unto God. (25)

Immortality

All divine philosophers and men of wisdom and understanding, when observing these endless beings, have considered that in this great and infinite universe all things end in the mineral kingdom, that the outcome of the mineral kingdom is the vegetable kingdom, the outcome of the vegetable kingdom is the animal kingdom and the outcome of the animal kingdom is the world of man. The consummation of this limitless universe with all its grandeur and glory hath been man himself, who in this world of being toileth and suffereth for a time, with diverse ills and pains, and ultimately disintegrates, leaving no trace and no fruit after him. Were it so, there is no doubt that this infinite universe with all its perfections has ended in sham and delusion with no result, no fruit, no permanence and no effect. It would be utterly without meaning. They were thus convinced that such is not the case, that this great workshop with all its power, its bewildering magnificence and endless perfections, cannot eventually come to naught. That still another life should exist is thus certain, and, just as the vegetable kingdom is unaware of the world of man, so we, too, know not of the great life hereafter that followest the life of man here below. Our noncomprehension of that life, however, is no proof of its nonexistence. The mineral world, for instance, is utterly unaware of the world of man and cannot comprehend it, but the ignorance of a thing is no proof of its nonexistence. (26)

Suffering

… All the sorrow and the grief that exist come from the world of matter—the spiritual world bestows only the joy! If we suffer it is the outcome of material things, and all the trials and troubles come from this world of illusion. (27)

God alone ordereth all things and is all-powerful. Why then does He send trials to His servants?

The trials of man are of two kinds. (a) The consequences of his own actions. If a man eats too much, he ruins his digestion; if he takes poison he becomes ill or dies. If a person gambles he will lose his money; if he drinks too much he will lose his equilibrium. All these sufferings are caused by the man himself, it is quite clear therefore that certain sorrows are the result of our own deeds. (b) Other sufferings there are, which come upon the Faithful of God. Consider the great sorrows endured by Christ and by His apostles! (28)

If people only realized it, the inner life of the spirit is that which counts, but they are so blinded by desires and so misled that they have brought upon themselves all the suffering we see at present in the world. (29)

Evil

... The spiritual and divine world is purely good and absolutely luminous, but in the human world light and darkness, good and evil, exist as opposite conditions. (30)

Indeed the actions of man himself breed a profusion of satanic power. For were men to abide by and observe the divine teachings, every tract of evil would be banished from the face of the earth. However, the widespread differences that exist among mankind and the prevalence of sedition, contention, conflict and the like are the primary factors which provoke the appearance of the satanic spirit. Yet the Holy Spirit hath ever shunned such matters. A world in which naught can be perceived save strife, quarrels and corruption is bound to become the seat of the throne, the very metropolis, of Satan. (31)

The reality underlying this is that the evil spirit, Satan or whatever is interpreted as evil, refers to the lower nature of man. This basic nature is symbolized in various ways. In man there are two expressions: one is the expression of nature, the other the expression of the spiritual realm. The world of nature is defective. Look at it clearly, casting aside all superstition and imagination. ... God has never created an evil spirit; all such ideas and nomenclature are symbols expressing the mere human or earthly nature of man. It is an essential condition of the soil of earth that thorns, weeds and fruitless trees may grow from it. Relatively speaking, this is evil; it is simply the lower state and basic product of nature. (32)

Spiritual Progress and Material Means

What result is forthcoming from material rest, tranquility, luxury and attachment to this corporeal world! It is evident that the man who pursues these things will in the end become afflicted with regret and loss.

Consequently, one must close his eyes wholly to these thoughts, long for eternal life, the sublimity of the world of humanity, the celestial developments, the Holy Spirit, the promotion of the Word of God, the guidance of the inhabitants of the globe, the promulgation of Universal Peace and the proclamation of the oneness of the world of humanity! This is the work! Otherwise like unto other animals and birds one must occupy himself with the requirements of this physical life, the satisfaction of which is the highest aspiration of the animal kingdom, and one must stalk across the earth like unto the quadrupeds. (33)

Progress is of two kinds: material and spiritual. The former is attained through observation of the surrounding existence and constitutes the foundation of civilization. Spiritual progress is through the breaths of the Holy Spirit and is the awakening of the conscious soul of man to perceive the reality of Divinity. Material progress ensures the happiness of the human world. Spiritual progress ensures the happiness and eternal continuance of the soul. The Prophets of God have founded the laws of divine civilization. They have been the root and fundamental source of all knowledge. (34)

Sacrifice

In order to understand the reality of sacrifice let us consider the crucifixion and death of Jesus Christ. It is true that He sacrificed Himself for our sake. What is the meaning of this? When Christ appeared, He knew that He must proclaim Himself in opposition to all the nations and peoples of the earth. He knew that mankind would arise against Him and inflict upon Him all manner of tribulations. There is no doubt that one who put forth such a claim as Christ announced would arouse the hostility of the world and be subjected to personal abuse. He realized that His blood would be shed and His body rent by violence. Notwithstanding His knowledge of what would befall Him, He arose to proclaim His message, suffered all tribulation and hardships from the people and finally offered His life as a sacrifice in order to illumine humanity—gave His blood in order to guide the world of mankind. He accepted every calamity and suffering in order to guide men to the truth. Had He desired to save His own life, and were He without wish to offer Himself in sacrifice, He would not have been able to guide a single soul. There was no doubt that His blessed blood would be shed and His body broken. Nevertheless, that Holy Soul accepted calamity and death in His love for mankind. This is one of the meanings of sacrifice. (35)

Spiritual Potentialities Are Realized Through Education

Now reflect that it is education that brings the East and the West under the authority of man; it is education that produced wonderful industries; it is education that spreads great sciences and arts; it is education that makes manifest new discoveries and institutions. If there were no educator, there would be no such things as comforts, civilization or humanity. If a man be left alone in a wilderness where he sees none of his own kind, he will undoubtedly become a mere brute; it is then clear that an educator is needed.

But education is of three kinds: material, human and spiritual. Material education is concerned with the progress and development of the body, through gaining its sustenance, its material comfort and ease. This education is common to animals and man.

Human education signifies civilization and progress—that is to say, government, administration, charitable works, trades, arts and handicrafts, sciences, great inventions and discoveries and elaborate institutions, which are the activities essential to man as distinguished from the animal.

Divine education is that of the Kingdom of God: it consists in acquiring divine perfections, and this is true education; for in this state man becomes the focus of divine blessings, the manifestation of the words, "Let Us make man in Our image, and after Our likeness." This is the goal of the world of humanity. (36)

The Purpose of a New Religious System

The Prophets of God should be regarded as physicians whose task is to foster the well-being of the world and its peoples, that, through the spirit of oneness, they may heal the sickness of a divided humanity. To none is given the right to question their words or disparage their conduct, for they are the only ones who can claim to have understood the patient and to have correctly diagnosed its ailments. No man, however acute his perception, can ever hope to reach the heights which the wisdom and understanding of the Divine Physicians have attained. Little wonder, then, if the treatment prescribed by the physician in this day should not be found to be identical with that which he prescribed before. How could it be otherwise when the ills affecting the sufferer necessitate at every stage of his sickness a special remedy? In like manner, every time the Prophets of God have illumined the world with the resplendent radiance of the Day Star of Divine knowledge, they have invariably summoned its peoples to embrace the light of God through such means as best befitted the exigencies of the age in which they appeared. They were thus able to scatter the darkness of ignorance, and to shed upon the world the glory of their own knowledge. (37)

The City of Certitude

There is no paradise more wondrous for any soul than to be exposed to God's Manifestation in His Day, to hear His verses and believe in them, to attain His presence, which is naught but the presence of God, to sail upon the sea of the heavenly kingdom of His good-pleasure, and to partake of the choice fruits of the paradise of His divine Oneness. (38)

... O thou who hast surrendered thy will to God! By self-surrender and perpetual union with God is meant that men should merge their will wholly in the Will of God, and regard their desires as utter nothingness beside His Purpose. Whatsoever the Creator commandeth His creatures to observe, the same must they diligently, and with the utmost joy and eagerness, arise and fulfill. They should in no wise allow their fancy to obscure their judgment, neither should they regard their own imaginings as the voice of the eternal. In the Prayer of Fasting We have revealed: "Should Thy Will decree that out of Thy mouth these words proceed and be addressed unto them, "Observe, for My Beauty's sake, the fast, O people, and set no limit to its duration," I swear by the majesty of Thy glory, that every one of them will faithfully observe it, will abstain from whatsoever will violate Thy law, and will continue to do so until they yield up their souls unto Thee." In this consisteth the complete surrender of one's will to the Will of God. Meditate on this, that thou mayest drink in the waters of everlasting life which flow through the words of the Lord of all mankind. ... The station of absolute self-surrender transcendeth, and will ever remain exalted above every other station.

It behoveth thee to consecrate thyself to the Will of God. Whatsoever hath been revealed in His Tablets is but a reflection of His will. So complete must be thy consecration, that every trace of worldly desire will be washed from thine heart. This is the meaning of true unity. (39)

The Law of God

Since the Sanctified Realities, the supreme Manifestations of God, surround the essence and qualities of the creature, transcend and contain existing realities and understand all things, therefore, Their knowledge is divine knowledge, and not acquired—that is to say, it is a holy bounty; it is a divine revelation.

We will mention an example expressly for the purpose of comprehending this subject. ... The Prophets of God, the Supreme Manifestations, are like skilled physicians, and the contingent world is like the body of man: the divine laws are the remedy and treatment. Consequently, the doctor must be aware of, and know, all the members and parts, as well as the constitution and state of the patient, so that he can prescribe a medicine which will be beneficial against the violent poison of the disease. In reality the doctor deduces from the disease itself the treatment which is suited to the patient, for he diagnoses the malady, and afterward prescribes the remedy for the illness. Until the malady be discovered, how can the remedy and treatment be prescribed? The doctor then must have a thorough knowledge of the constitution, members, organs and state of the patient, and be acquainted with all diseases and all remedies, in order to prescribe a fitting medicine.

Religion, then, is the necessary connection which emanates from the reality of things; and as the supreme Manifestations of God are aware of the mysteries of beings, therefore, They understand this essential connection, and by this knowledge establish the Law of God. (40)

THE PROPHETS

A New Human Race

... The purpose for which mortal men have, from utter nothing-ness, stepped into the realm of being, is that they may work for the betterment of the world and live together in concord and harmony. (41)

"To build anew the whole world" is the claim and challenge of (Baha-u-llah's) Message. ... In this Revelation the concepts of the past are brought to a new level of understanding, and the social laws, changed to suit the age now dawning, and designed to carry humanity forward into a world civilization the splendors of which can as yet be scarcely imagined. (42)

O peoples of the world! The Sun of Truth hath risen to illumine the whole earth, and to spiritualize the community of man. Laud-able are the results and the fruits thereof, abundant the holy evi-dences deriving from this grace. This is mercy unalloyed and purest bounty; it is light for the world and all its peoples; it is harmony and fellowship, and love and solidarity; indeed it is compassion and unity, and the end of foreignness; it is the being at one, in complete dignity and freedom, with all on earth.

The Blessed Beauty saith: "Ye are all the fruits of one tree, the leaves of one branch." Thus hath He likened this world of being to a single tree, and all its peoples to the leaves thereof, and the blos-soms and fruits. It is needful for the bough to blossom, and leaf and fruit to flourish, and upon the interconnection of all parts of the world-tree, dependeth the flourishing of leaf and blossom, and the sweetness of the fruit.

... The Faith of the Blessed Beauty is summoning mankind to safety and love, to amity and peace; it hath raised up its tabernacle on the heights of the earth, and directeth its call to all nations. Wherefore, O ye who are God's lovers, know ye the value of this precious Faith, obey its teachings, walk in this road that is drawn straight, and show ye this way to the people. Lift up your voices and sing out the song of the Kingdom. Spread far and wide the precepts and counsels of the Loving Lord, so that this world will change into another world, and this darksome earth will be flooded with light, and the dead body of mankind will arise and live; so that every soul will ask for immortality, through the holy breaths of God.

Soon will your swiftly-passing days be over, and the fame and riches, the comforts, the joys provided by this rubbish-heap, the world, will be gone without a trace. Summon ye, then, the people to God, and invite humanity to follow the example of the Company on high. Be ye loving fathers to the orphan, and a refuge to the helpless, and a treasury for the poor, and a cure for the ailing. Be ye the helpers of every victim of oppression, the patrons of the disadvantaged. Think ye at all times of rendering some service to every member of the human race. Pay ye no heed to aversion and rejection, to disdain, hostility, injustice: act ye in the opposite way. Be ye sincerely kind, not in appearance only. Let each one of God's loved ones center his attention on this: to be the Lord's mercy to man; to be the Lord's grace. Let him do some good to every person whose path he crosseth, and be of some benefit to him. Let him improve the character of each and all, and reorient the minds of men. In this way, the light of divine guidance will shine forth, and the blessings of God will cradle all mankind: for love is light, no matter in what abode it dwelleth; and hate is darkness, no matter where it may make its nest. O friends of God! That the hidden mystery may stand revealed, and the secret essence of all things may be disclosed, strive to banish that darkness for ever and ever. (43)

The potentialities inherent in the station of man, the full measure of his destiny on earth, the innate excellence of his reality, must all be manifested in this promised Day of God. (44)

O Son of Man!

I LOVED Thy creation, hence I created Thee. Wherefore, do thou love Me, that I may name Thy name and fill Thy soul with the spirit of life.

If thou lovest Me, turn away from thyself; and if thou seekest My pleasure, regard not thine own; that thou mayest die in Me and I may eternally live in thee. (45)

The Manifestations of God—The Founders of the World's Great Religions

And since there can be no tie of direct intercourse to bind the one true God with His creation, and no resemblance whatever can exist between the transient and the Eternal, the contingent and the Absolute, He hath ordained that in every age and dispensation a pure and stainless Soul be made manifest in the kingdoms of earth and heaven. Unto this subtle, this mysterious and ethereal Being He hath assigned a twofold nature; the physical, pertaining to the world of matter, and the spiritual, which is born of the substance of God Himself. He hath, moreover, conferred upon Him a double station. The first station, which is related to His innermost reality, representeth Him as One Whose voice is the voice of God Himself. To this testifieth the tradition: "Manifold and mysterious is My relationship with God. I am He Himself, and He is I, Myself, except that I am that I am, and He is that He is." And in like manner, the words: "Arise, 0 Muhammad, for lo, the Lover and the Beloved are joined together and made one in Thee." He similarly saith: "There is no distinction whatsoever between Thee and Them, except that They are Thy Servants." The second station is the human station, exemplified by the following verses: (46)

"I am but a man like you. "Say, praise be to my Lord! Am I more than a man, an apostle?" These Essences of Detachment, these resplendent Realities are the channels of God's all-pervasive grace. Led by the light of unfailing guidance, and invested with supreme sovereignty, They are commissioned to use the inspiration of Their words, the effusions of Their infallible grace and the sanctifying breeze of Their Revelation for the cleansing of every longing heart and receptive spirit from the dross and dust of earthly cares and limitations. Then, and only then, will the Trust of God, latent in the reality of man, emerge, as resplendent as the rising Orb of Divine Revelation, from behind the veil of concealment, and implant the ensign of its revealed glory upon the summits of men's hearts. (47)

From the foregoing passages and allusions it hath been made indubitably clear that in the kingdoms of earth and heaven there must needs be manifested a Being, an Essence Who shall act as a Manifestation and Vehicle for the transmission of the grace of the Divinity Itself, the Sovereign Lord of all. Through the Teachings of this Day Star of Truth every man will advance and develop until he attaineth the station at which he can manifest all the potential forces with which his inmost true self hath been endowed. It is for this very purpose that in every age and dispensation the Prophets of God and His chosen Ones have appeared amongst men, and have evinced such power as is born of God and such might as only the Eternal can reveal. (48)

Can one of sane mind ever seriously imagine that, in view of certain words the meaning of which he cannot comprehend, the portal of God's infinite guidance can ever be closed in the face of men? Can he ever conceive for these Divine Luminaries, these resplendent Lights either a beginning or an end? What outpouring flood can compare with the stream of His all-embracing grace, and what blessing can excel the evidences of so great and pervasive a mercy? There can be no doubt whatever that if for one moment the tide of His mercy and grace were to be withheld from the world, it would completely perish. For this reason, from the beginning that hath no beginning the portals of Divine mercy have been flung open to the face of all created things, and the clouds of Truth will continue to the end that hath no end to rain on the soil of human capacity, reality and personality their favors and bounties. Such hath been God's method continued from everlasting to everlasting. (49)

The Person of the Manifestation

The Person of the Manifestation hath ever been the representative and mouthpiece of God. He, in truth, is the Day Spring of God's most excellent Titles, and the Dawning-Place of His exalted Attributes. If any be set up by His side as peers, if they be regarded as identical with His Person, how can it, then, be maintained that the Divine Being is One and Incomparable, that His Essence is indivisible and peerless? Meditate on that which We have, through the power of truth, revealed unto thee and be thou of them that comprehend its meaning. (50)

The purpose of God in creating man hath been, and will ever be, to enable him to know his Creator and to attain His Presence. To this most excellent aim, this supreme objective, all the heavenly Books and the divinely-revealed and weighty Scriptures unequivocally bear witness. Whoso hath recognized the Day Spring of Divine guidance and entered His holy court hath drawn nigh unto God and attained His Presence, a Presence which is the real Paradise, and of which the loftiest mansions of heaven are but a symbol. Such a man hath attained the knowledge of the station of Him

Who is "at the distance of two bows," Who standeth beyond the Sadratu'l-Muntahá'. Whoso hath failed to recognize Him will have condemned himself to the misery of remoteness, a remoteness which is naught but utter nothingness and the essence of the nethermost fire. Such will be his fate, though to outward seeming he may occupy the earth's loftiest seats and be established upon its most exalted throne. (51)

The Day Spring of Truth

He Who is the Day Spring of Truth is, no doubt, fully capable of rescuing from such remoteness wayward souls and of causing them to draw nigh unto His court and attain His Presence. "If God had pleased He had surely made all men one people." His purpose, however, is to enable the pure in spirit and the detached in heart to ascend, by virtue of their own innate powers, unto the shores of the Most Great Ocean, that thereby they who seek the Beauty of the All-Glorious may be distinguished and separated from the wayward and perverse. Thus hath it been ordained by the all-glorious and resplendent Pen. (52)

That the Manifestations of Divine justice, the Day Springs of heavenly grace, have when they appeared amongst men always been destitute of all earthly dominion and shorn of the means of worldly ascendancy, should be attributed to this same principle of separation and distinction which animateth the Divine Purpose. Were the Eternal Essence to manifest all that is latent within Him, were He to shine in the plenitude of His glory, none would be found to question His power or repudiate His truth. Nay, all created things would be so dazzled and thunderstruck by the evidences of His light as to be reduced to utter nothingness. How, then, can the godly be differentiated under such circumstances from the froward? (53)

This principle hath operated in each of the previous Dispensations and been abundantly demonstrated. ... It is for this reason that, in every age, when a new Manifestation hath appeared and a fresh revelation of God's transcendent power was vouchsafed unto men, they that misbelieved in Him, deluded by the appearance of the peerless and everlasting Beauty in the garb of mortal men, have failed to recognize Him. They have erred from His path and eschewed His company—the company of Him Who is the Symbol of nearness to God. They have even arisen to decimate the ranks of the faithful and to exterminate such as believed in Him. (54)

Each Bears a Distinct Message

The measure of the revelation of the Prophets of God in this world, however, must differ. Each and every one of them hath been the Bearer of a distinct Message, and hath been commissioned to reveal Himself through specific acts. It is for this reason that they appear to vary in their greatness. Their Revelation may be likened unto the light of the moon that sheddeth its radiance upon the earth. Though every time it appeareth, it revealeth a fresh measure of its brightness, yet its inherent splendor can never diminish, nor can its light suffer extinction. (55)

It is clear and evident, therefore, that any apparent variation in the intensity of their light is not inherent in the light itself, but should rather be attributed to the varying receptivity of an ever-changing world. Every Prophet Whom the Almighty and Peerless Creator hath purposed to send to the peoples of the earth hath been entrusted with a Message, and charged to act in a manner that would best meet the requirements of the age in which He appeared. God's purpose in sending His Prophets unto men is twofold. The first is to liberate the children of men from the darkness of ignorance, and guide them to the light of true understanding. The second is to ensure the peace and tranquillity of mankind, and provide all the means by which they can be established. (56)

Fostering the Well-being of All

The Prophets of God should be regarded as physicians whose task is to foster the well-being of the world and its peoples, that, through the spirit of oneness, they may heal the sickness of a divided humanity. To none is given the right to question their words or disparage their conduct, for they are the only ones who can claim to have understood the patient and to have correctly diagnosed its ailments. No man, however acute his perception, can ever hope to reach the heights which the wisdom and understanding of the Divine Physician have attained. Little wonder, then, if the treatment prescribed by the physician in this day should not be found to be identical with that which he prescribed before. How could it be otherwise when the ills affecting the sufferer necessitate at every stage of his sickness a special remedy? In like manner, every time the Prophets of God have illumined the world with the resplendent radiance of the Day Star of Divine knowledge, they have invariably summoned its peoples to embrace the light of God through such means as best befitted the exigencies of the age in which they appeared. They were thus able to scatter the darkness of ignorance, and to shed upon the world the glory of their own knowledge. It is towards the inmost essence of these Prophets, therefore, that the eye of every man of discernment must be directed, inasmuch as their one and only purpose hath always been to guide the erring, and give peace to the afflicted. These are not days of prosperity and triumph. The whole of mankind is in the grip of manifold ills. Strive, therefore, to save its life through the wholesome medicine which the almighty hand of the unerring Physician hath prepared. (57)

BAHA'U'LLA'H'S MESSAGE

The Purpose of Divine Revelation

And now concerning thy question regarding the nature of religion. Know thou that they who are truly wise have likened the world unto the human temple. As the body of man needeth a garment to clothe it, so the body of mankind must needs be adorned with the mantle of justice and wisdom. Its robe is the Revelation vouchsafed unto it by God. Whenever this robe hath fulfilled its purpose, the Almighty will assuredly renew it. For every age requireth a fresh measure of the light of God. Every Divine Revelation hath been sent down in a manner that befitted the circumstances of the age in which it hath appeared. (58)

Beware, 0 believers in the Unity of God, lest ye be tempted to make any distinction between any of the Manifestations of His Cause, or to discriminate against the signs that have accompanied and proclaimed their Revelation. This indeed is the true meaning of Divine Unity, if ye be of them that apprehend and believe this truth. Be ye assured, moreover, that the works and acts of each and every one of these Manifestations of God, nay whatever pertaineth unto them, and whatsoever they may manifest in the future, are all ordained by God, and are a reflection of His Will and Purpose.

Whoso maketh the slightest possible difference between their persons, their words, their messages, their acts and manners, hath indeed disbelieved in God, hath repudiated His signs, and betrayed the Cause of His Messengers. (59)

The Divine Springtime

The appearances of the Manifestations of God are the divine springtime. When Christ appeared in this world, it was like the vernal bounty; the outpouring descended; the effulgences of the Merciful encircled all things; the human world found new life. Even the physical world partook of it. The divine perfections were upraised; souls were trained in the school of heaven so that all grades of human existence received life and light. Then by degrees these fragrances of heaven were discontinued; the season of winter came upon the world; the beauties of spring vanished; the excellences and perfections passed away; the lights and quickening were no longer evident; the phenomenal world and its materialities conquered everything; the spiritualities of life were lost; the world of existence became like unto a lifeless body; there was no trace of the spring left. (60)

The Coming of Baha'u'lla'h

Baha'u'lla'h has come into this world. He has renewed that springtime. The same fragrances are wafting; the same heat of the Sun is giving life; the same cloud is pouring its rain, and with our own eyes we see that the world of existence is advancing and progressing. The human world has found new life. (61)

Our meaning is this: the religion of God is one, and it is the educator of humankind, but still, it needs must be made new. When thou does plant a tree, its height increaseth day by day. It pulleth forth blossoms and leaves and luscious fruits. But after a long time, it doth grow old, yielding no fruitage any more. Then doth the Husbandman of Truth take up the seed from that same tree, and plant it in a pure soil; and lo, there standeth the first free, even as it was before. (62)

Note thou carefully that in this world of being, all things must ever be made new. Look at the material world about thee, see how it hath now been renewed. The thoughts have changed, the ways of life have been revised, the sciences and arts show a new vigor, discoveries and inventions are new, perceptions are new. How then could such a vital power as religion—the guarantor of mankind's great advances, the very means of attaining everlasting life, the fosterer of infinite excellence, the light of both worlds—not be made new? This would be incompatible with the grace and loving-kindness of the Lord. (63)

The Day of the Awakening

Great indeed is this Day! The allusions made to it in all the sacred Scriptures as the Day of God attest its greatness. The soul of every Prophet of God, of every Divine Messenger, hath thirsted for this wondrous Day. All the diverse kindreds of the earth have, likewise, yearned to attain it. No sooner, however, had the Day Star of His Revelation manifested itself in the heaven of God's Will, than all, except those whom the Almighty was pleased to guide, were found dumbfounded and heedless. (64)

0 thou that hast remembered Me! The most grievous veil hath shut out the peoples of the earth from His glory, and hindered them from hearkening to His call. God grant that the light of unity may envelop the whole earth, and that the seal, "the Kingdom is God's", may be stamped upon the brow of all its peoples. (65)

The time foreordained unto the peoples and of the earth is now come. The promises of God, as recorded in the holy Scriptures, have all been fulfilled. Out of Zion hath gone forth the Law of God, and Jerusalem, and the hills and land thereof, are filled with the glory of His Revelation. Happy is the man that pondereth in his heart that which hath been revealed in the Books of God, the Help in Peril, the Self-Subsisting. Meditate upon this, 0 ye beloved of God, and let your ears be attentive unto His Word, so that ye may, by His grace and mercy, drink your fill from the crystal waters of constancy, and become as steadfast and Immovable as the mountain in His Cause. (66)

In the Book of Isaiah it is written: "Enter into the rock, and hide thee in the dust, for fear of the Lord, and for the glory of His majesty." No man that meditateth upon this verse can fail to recognize the greatness of this Cause, or doubt the exalted character of this Day—the Day of God Himself. This same verse is followed by these words: "And the Lord alone shall be exalted in that Day." This is the Day which the Pen of the Most High hath glorified in all the holy Scriptures. There is no verse in them that doth not declare the glory of His holy Name, and no Book that doth not testify unto the loftiness of this most exalted theme. Were We to make mention of all that hath been revealed in these heavenly Books and holy Scriptures concerning this Revelation, this Tablet would assume impossible dimensions. It is incumbent in this Day, upon every man to place his whole trust in the manifold bounties of God, and arise to disseminate, with the utmost wisdom, the verities of His Cause. Then, and only then, will the whole earth be enveloped with the morning light of His Revelation. (67)

The Revelation which, from time immemorial, hath been acclaimed as the Purpose and Promise of all the Prophets of God, and the most cherished Desire of His Messengers, hath now, by virtue of the pervasive Will of the Almighty and at His irresistible bidding, been revealed unto men. The advent of such a Revelation hath been heralded in all the sacred Scriptures. Behold how, notwithstanding such an announcement, mankind hath strayed from its path and shut itself from its glory. (68)

Say: O ye lovers of the One true God! Strive, that ye may truly recognize and know Him, and observe befittingly His precepts. This is a Revelation, under which, if a man shed for its sake one drop of blood, myriads of oceans will be his recompense. Take heed, O friends, that ye forfeit not so inestimable a benefit, or disregard its transcendent station. Consider the multitude of lives that have been, and are still being, sacrificed in a world deluded by a mere phantom which the vain imaginations of its peoples have conceived. Render thanks unto God, inasmuch as ye have attained unto your heart's Desire, and been united to Him Who is the Promise of all nations. Guard ye, with the aid of the one true God—exalted by His glory—the integrity of the Station which ye have attained, and cleave to that which shall promote His Cause. He, verily, enjoineth on you what is right and conducive to the exaltation of man's station. Glorified be the All-Merciful, the Revealer of this wondrous Tablet. (69)

The Coming of the Promised One

Behold, how the diverse peoples and kindreds of the earth have been waiting for the coming of the Promised One. No sooner had He, Who is the Sun of Truth, been made manifest, than, lo, all turned away from Him, except them whom God was pleased to guide. We dare not in this Day, lift the veil that concealeth the exalted station which every true believer can attain for the joy which such a revelation must provoke might well cause a few to faint away and die. (70)

He Who is the Heart and Center of the Bayan hath written: "The germ that holdeth within itself the potentialities of the Revelation that is to come is endowed with a potency superior to the combined forces of all those who follow Me." And, again, He saith: "Of all the tributes I have paid to Him Who is to come after Me, the greatest is this, My written confession, that no words of Mine can adequately describe Him, nor can any reference to Him in My Book, the Bayan, do justice to His Cause." (71)

Whoso hath searched the depths of the oceans that lie hid within these exalted words, and fathomed their import, can be said to have discovered a glimmer of the unspeakable glory with which this mighty, this sublime, and most holy Revelation hath been endowed. From the excellence of so great a Revelation the honor with which its faithful followers must needs be invested can be well imagined. By the righteousness of the one true God! The very breath. of these souls is in itself richer than all the treasures of the earth. Happy is the man that hath attained thereunto, and woe betide the heedless. (72)

"Now is the time! Now is the accepted time!

"Look ye at the time of Christ; had the people realized that the Holy Spirit of God was speaking to them through His divine mouth they would not have waited three centuries before accepting Him. And now is it meet for you that ye are sleeping upon the beds of idleness and neglect, while the Father foretold by Christ has come amongst us and opened the greatest door of bounteous gifts and divine favors? Let us not be like those in past centuries who were deaf to His call and blind to His beauty; but let us try and open our eyes that we may see Him, and open our ears that we may hear Him, and cleanse our Hearts that He may come and abide in our temples." (73)

True Liberty

True liberty consisteth in man's submission unto My commandments, little as ye know it were men to observe that which We have sent down unto them from the Heaven of Revelation, they would, of a certainty, attain unto perfect liberty. Happy is the man that hath apprehended the Purpose of God in whatever He hath revealed from the Heaven of His Will, that pervadeth all created things. Say: The liberty that profiteth you is to be found nowhere except in complete servitude unto God, the Eternal Truth. Whoever hath tasted of its sweetness will refuse to barter it for all the dominion of earth and heaven. (74)

The Critical Hour of the World

"How long will humanity persist in its waywardness? How long will injustice continue? How long are chaos and confusion to reign amongst men? How long will discord agitate the face of society? The winds of despair are, alas, blowing from every direction and the strife that divides and afflicts the human race is daily increasing. The signs of impending chaos and convulsions can now be discerned, inasmuch as the prevailing order appears to be lamentably defective. (75)

"Might there not emerge out of the agony of a shaken world a religious revival of such scope and power as to even transcend the potency of those world-directing forces with which the Religions of the Past have, at fixed intervals and according to an inscrutable Wisdom, revived the fortunes of declining ages and peoples? Might not the bankruptcy of this present, this highly-vaunted materialistic civilization, in itself clear away the choking weeds that now hinder the unfoldment and future efflorescence of God's struggling Faith? (76)

"To claim to have grasped all the implications of Baha'u'lla'h's prodigious scheme for worldwide human solidarity, or to have fathomed its import would be presumptuous on the part of even the declared supporters of His Faith. To attempt to visualize it in all its possibilities, to estimate its future benefits, to picture its glory, would be premature at even so advanced a stage in the evolution of mankind. (77)

"All we can reasonably venture to attempt is to strive to obtain a glimpse of the first streaks of the promised Dawn that must, in the fullness of time, chase away the gloom that has encircled humanity. All we can do is to point out, in their broadest outlines, what appears to us to be the guiding principles underlying the World-Order of Baha'u'lla'h, as amplified by Abdu'l Bah'a, the appointed Interpreter and Expounder of His Word." (78)

The Coming of the Golden Age

God's purpose is none other than to usher in, in ways He alone can bring about, and the full significance of which He alone can fathom, the Great, the Golden Age of a long-divided, a long-afflicted humanity. Its present state, indeed even its immediate future, is dark, distressingly dark. Its distant future, however, is radiant, gloriously radiant—so radiant that no eye can visualize it. (79)

"The winds of despair," writes Baha'u'lla'h, as He surveys the immediate destinies of mankind, "are, alas, blowing from every direction, and the strife that divides and afflicts the human race is daily increasing. The signs of impending convulsions and chaos can now be discerned, inasmuch as the prevailing order appears to be lamentably defective." "Such shall be its plight," He, in another connection, has declared, "that to disclose it now would not be meet and seemly." "These fruitless strifes," He, on the other hand, contemplating the future of mankind, has emphatically prophesied, in the course of His memorable interview with the Persian orientalist, Edward G. Browne, "these ruinous wars shall pass away, and the 'Most Great Peace' shall come. ... These strifes and this bloodshed and discord must cease, and all men be as one kindred and one family." "Soon," He predicts, "will the present-day order be rolled up, and a new one spread out in its stead." "After a time," He also has written, "all the governments on earth will change. Oppression will envelop the world. And following a universal convulsion, the sun of justice will rise from the horizon of the unseen realm." "The whole earth," He, moreover, has stated, "is now in a state of pregnancy. The day is approaching when it will have yielded its noblest fruits, when from it will have sprung forth the loftiest trees, the most enchanting blossoms, the most heavenly blessings." "All nations and kindreds," 'Abdu'l-Baha likewise has written, " ... will become a single nation. Religious and sectarian antagonism, the hostility of races and peoples, and differences among nations, will be eliminated." (80)

What we witness at the present time, during "this gravest crisis in the history of civilization," recalling such times in which "religions have perished and are born," is the adolescent stage in the slow and painful evolution of humanity, preparatory to the attainment of the stage of manhood, the stage of maturity, the promise of which is embedded in the teachings, and enshrined in the prophecies of Baha'u'lla'h. The tumult of this age of transition is characteristic of the impetuosity and irrational instincts of youth, its follies, its prodigality, its pride, its self-assurance, its rebelliousness, and contempt of discipline. (81)

A Universal and Lasting Peace

The ages of its infancy and childhood are past, never again to return, while the Great Age, the consummation of all ages, which must signalize the coming of age of the entire human race, is yet to come. The convulsions of this transitional and most turbulent period in the annals of humanity are the essential prerequisites, and herald the inevitable approach, of that Age of Ages, "the time of the end," in which the folly and tumult of strife that has, since the dawn of history, blackened the annals of mankind, will have been finally transmuted into the wisdom and the tranquility of an undisturbed, a universal, and lasting peace, in which the discord and separation of the children of men will have given way to the worldwide reconciliation, and the complete unification of the diverse elements that constitute human society. (82)

The Destiny of the Peoples of Earth

This will indeed be the fitting climax of that process of integration which, starting with the family, the smallest unit in the scale of human organization, must, after having called successively into being the tribe, the city-state, and the nation, continue to operate until it culminates in the unification of the whole world, the final object and the crowning glory of human evolution on this planet. It is this stage which humanity, willingly or unwillingly, is resistlessly approaching. It is for this stage that this vast, this fiery ordeal which humanity is experiencing is mysteriously paving the way. It is with this stage that the fortunes and the purpose of the Faith of Baha'u'llah are indissolubly linked. It is the creative energies which His Revelation has released ... that have instilled into humanity the capacity to attain this final stage in its organic and collective evolution. It is with the Golden Age of His Dispensation that the consummation of this process will be forever associated. It is the structure of His New World Order, now stirring in the womb of the administrative institutions He Himself has created, that will serve both as a pattern and a nucleus of that world commonwealth which is the sure, the inevitable destiny of the peoples and nations of the earth. (83)

Just as the organic evolution of mankind has been slow and gradual, and involved successively the unification of the family, the tribe, the city-state, and the nation, so has the light vouchsafed by the Revelation of God, at various stages in the evolution of religion, and reflected in the successive Dispensations of the past, been slow and progressive. Indeed the measure of Divine Revelation, in every age, has been adapted to, and commensurate with, the degree of social progress achieved in that age by a constantly evolving humanity. ... (84)

The Oneness of Humanity

"That which was applicable to human needs during the early history of the race can neither meet nor satisfy the demands of this day, this period of newness and consummation. Humanity has emerged from its former state of limitation and preliminary training. Man must now become imbued with new virtues and powers, new moral standards, new capacities. New bounties, perfect bestowals, are awaiting and already descending upon him. The gifts and blessings of the period of youth, although timely and sufficient during the adolescence of mankind, are now incapable of meeting the requirements of its maturity." "In every Dispensation," He moreover has written, "the light of Divine Guidance has been focused upon one central theme. .In this wondrous Revelation, this glorious century, the foundation of the Faith of God, and the distinguishing feature of His Law, is the consciousness of the oneness of mankind. (85)

He Who in such dramatic circumstances was made to sustain the overpowering weight of so glorious a Mission was none other than the One Whom posterity will acclaim, and Whom innumerable followers already recognize, as the judge, the Lawgiver and Redeemer of all mankind, as the Organizer of the entire planet, as the Unifier of the children of men, as the Inaugurator of the long-awaited millennium, as the Originator of a new "Universal Cycle," as the Establisher of the Most Great Peace, as the Fountain of the Most Great Justice, as the Proclaimer of the coming of age of the entire human race, as the Creator of a new World Order, and as the Inspirer and Founder of a world civilization. (86)

"How vast is the Revelation of Baha'u'lla'h! How great the magnitude of His blessings showered upon humanity in this day! And yet how poor, how inadequate our conception of their significance and glory! This generation stands too close to so colossal a Revelation to appreciate, in their full measure, the infinite possibilities of His Faith, the unprecedented character of His Cause, and the mysterious dispensations of His Providence." (87)

Mysteriously, slowly, and resistlessly God accomplishes His design, though the sight that meets our eyes in this day be the spectacle of a world hopelessly entangled in its own meshes. (88)

THE HEART OF BAHA'U'LLA'H'S MESSAGE

We desire but the good of the world and the happiness of the nations; yet they deem us a stirrer up of strife and sedition worthy of bondage and banishment ... that all nations should become one in faith all men as brothers; that the bonds of affection and unity between the sons of men should be strengthened; that diversity of religion should cease, and differences of race be annulled. (89)

... What harm is there in this? ... Yet so it shall be; these fruitless strifes, these ruinous wars shall pass away, and the "Most Great Peace" shall come. ... Is not this that which Christ foretold? (90)

... Yet do We see your kings and rulers lavishing their treasures more freely on means for the destruction of the human race than on that which would conduce to the happiness of mankind. These strifes and this bloodshed and discord must cease, and all men be as one kindred and one family. ... Let not a man glory in this, that he loves his country; let him rather glory in this, that he loves his kind. (91)

TRANSITION TO THE FUTURE

The Transformation of Humanity

Is not the object of every Revelation to effect a transformation in the whole character of mankind, a transformation that shall manifest itself, both outwardly and inwardly, that shall affect both its inner life and external condition? For if the character of mankind be not changed, the futility of God's universal Manifestation would be apparent. (92)

He Who is your Lord, the All-Merciful, cherisheth in His heart the desire of beholding the entire human race as one soul and one body. Haste ye to win your share of God's good grace and mercy in this Day that eclipseth all other created Days. How great the felicity that awaiteth the man that forsaketh all he hath in a desire to obtain the things of God! Such a man, We testify, is among God's blessed ones. (93)

0 Kama'l! The heights which, through the most gracious favor of God, mortal man can attain, in this Day, are as yet unrevealed to his sight. The world of being hath never had, nor doth it yet possess the capacity for such a revelation. The day, however, is approaching when the potentialities of so great a favor will, by Virtue of His behest, be manifested unto men. Though the forces of the nations be arrayed against Him, though the kings of the earth be leagued to undermine His Cause, the power of His might shall stand unshaken. He, verily, speaketh the truth, and summoneth all mankind to the way of Him Who is the Incomparable, the All-Knowing. (94)

An Ever-advancing Civilization

All men have been created to carry forward an ever-advancing civilization. The Almighty beareth Me witness: To act like the beasts of the field is unworthy of man. Those Virtues that befit his dignity are forbearance, mercy, compassion and loving-kindness towards all the peoples and kindreds of the earth. Say: 0 friends! Drink your fill from this crystal stream that floweth through the heavenly grace of Him Who is the Lord of Names. Let others partake of its waters in My name, that the leaders of men in every land may fully recognize the purpose for which the Eternal Truth hath been revealed, and the reason for which they themselves have been created. (95)

The Great Being saith: 0 ye children of men! The fundamental purpose animating the Faith of God and His Religion is to safeguard the interests and promote the unity of the human race, and to foster the spirit of love and fellowship amongst men. Suffer it not to become a source of dissension and discord, of hate and enmity. This is the straight Path, the fixed and immovable foundation. Whatsoever is raised on this foundation, the changes and chances of the world can never impair its strength, nor will the revolution of countless centuries undermine its structure. Our hope is that the world's religious leaders and the rulers thereof will unitedly arise for the reformation of this age and the rehabilitation of its fortunes. Let them, after meditating on its needs, take counsel together and, through anxious and full deliberation, administer to a diseased and sorely afflicted world the remedy it requireth. ... It is incumbent upon them who are in authority to exercise moderation in all things. Whatsoever passeth beyond the limits of moderation will cease to exert a beneficial influence. Consider for instance such things as liberty, civilization and the like. However much men of understanding may favorably regard them, they will, if carried to excess, exercise a pernicious influence upon men. ... Please God, the peoples of the world may be led, as the result of the high endeavors exerted by their rulers and the wise and learned amongst men, to recognize their best interests. How long will humanity persist in its waywardness? How long will injustice continue? How long is chaos and confusion to reign amongst men? How long will discord agitate the face of society? The winds of despair are, alas, blowing from every direction, and the strife that divideth and afflicteth the human race is daily increasing. The signs of impending convulsions and chaos can now be discerned, inasmuch as the prevailing order appeareth to be lamentably defective. I beseech God, exalted be His glory, that He may graciously awaken the peoples of the earth, may grant that the end of their conduct may be profitable unto them, and aid them to accomplish that which beseemeth their station. (96)

Beyond the Disturbances of Our Time

Behold the disturbances which, for many a long year, have afflicted the earth, and the perturbation that hath seized its peoples. It hath either been ravaged by war, or tormented by sudden and unforeseen calamities. Though the world is encompassed with misery and distress, yet no man hath paused to reflect what the cause or source of that may be. Whenever the True Counselor uttered a word in admonishment, lo, they all denounced Him as a mover of mischief and rejected His claim. How bewildering, how confusing is such behavior! No two men can be found who may be said to be outwardly and inwardly united. The evidences of discord and malice are apparent everywhere, though all were made for harmony and union. (97)

You Are the Fruits of One Tree

The Great Being saith: 0 well-beloved ones! The tabernacle of unity hath been raised; regard ye not one another as strangers. Ye are the fruits of one tree, and the leaves of one branch. We cherish the hope that the light of justice may shine upon the world and sanctify it from tyranny. If the rulers and kings of the earth, the symbols of the power of God, exalted be His glory, arise and resolve to dedicate themselves to whatever will promote the highest interests of the whole of humanity, the reign of justice will assuredly be established amongst the children of men, and the effulgence of its light will envelop the whole earth. The Great Being saith: The structure of world stability and order hath been reared upon, and will continue to be sustained by, the twin pillars of reward and punishment. ... In another passage He hath written: Take heed, 0 concourse of the rulers of the world'. There is no force on earth that can equal in its conquering power the force of justice and wisdom. ... Blessed is the king who marcheth with the ensign of wisdom unfurled before him, and the battalions of justice massed in his rear. He verily is the ornament that adorneth the brow of peace and the countenance of security. There can be no doubt whatever that if the day star of justice, which the clouds of tyranny have obscured, were to shed its light upon men, the face of the earth will be completely transformed. (98)

The Earth Is But One Country ...

The day is approaching when all the peoples of the world will have adopted one universal language and one common script. When this is achieved, to whatsoever city a man may journey, it shall be as if he were entering his own home. These things are obligatory and absolutely essential. It is incumbent upon every man of insight and understanding to strive to translate that which hath been written into reality and action. ... That one indeed is a man who, today, dedicateth himself to the service of the entire human race. The Great Being saith: Blessed and happy is he that ariseth to promote the best interests of the peoples and kindreds of the earth. In another passage He hath proclaimed: It is not for him to pride himself who loveth his own country, but rather for him who loveth the whole world. The earth is but one country, and mankind its citizens. (99)

World's Leaders Called to Counsel Together

0 ye the elected representatives of the people in every land! Take ye counsel together, and let your concern be only for that which profiteth mankind, and bettereth the condition thereof, if ye be of them that scan heedfully. Regard the world as the human body which, though at its creation whole and perfect, hath been afflicted, through various causes, ... Not for one day did it gain ease, nay its sickness waxed more severe, it fell under the treatment of ignorant physicians, who gave full rein to their personal desires, and have erred grievously. And if, at one time, through the care of an able physician, a member of that body was healed, the rest remained afflicted as before. Thus informeth you the All-Knowing, the All-Wise. (100)

A Catastrophic Tempest

A tempest, unprecedented in its violence, unpredictable in its course, catastrophic in its immediate effects, unimaginably glorious in its ultimate consequences, is at present sweeping the face of the earth. Its driving power is remorselessly gaining in range and momentum. Its cleansing force, however much undetected, is increasing with every passing day. Humanity, gripped in the clutches of its devastating power, is smitten by the evidences of its resistless fury. It can neither perceive its origin, nor probe its significance, nor discern its outcome. Bewildered, agonized and helpless, it watches this great and mighty wind of God invading the remotest and fairest regions of the earth, rocking its foundations, deranging its equilibrium, sundering its nations, disrupting the homes of its peoples, wasting its cities, driving into exile its kings, pulling down its bulwarks, uprooting its institutions, dimming its light, and harrowing up the souls of its inhabitants. (101)

"The time for the destruction of the world and its people," Baha'u'llah's prophetic pen has proclaimed, "hath arrived." The hour is approaching," He specifically affirms, "when the most great convulsion will have appeared." "The promised day is come, the day when tormenting trials will have surged above your heads, and beneath your fret, saying: 'Taste ye what your hands have wrought!'" "Soon shall the blasts of His chastisement beat upon you, and the dust of hell enshroud you." And again: "And when the appointed hour is come, there shall suddenly appear that which shall cause the limbs of mankind to quake." "The day is approaching when its (civilization) flame will devour the cities, when the Tongue of Grandeur will proclaim: 'The Kingdom is God's, the Almighty, the All-Praised!'" "The day will soon come," He, referring to the foolish ones of the earth, has written, "whereon they will cry out for help and receive no answer." "The day is approaching," He moreover has prophesied, "when the wrathful anger of the Almighty will have taken hold of them. He, verily, is the Omnipotent, the All-Subduing, the Most Powerful. He shall cleanse the earth from the defilement of their corruption, and shall give it for an heritage unto such of His servants as are nigh unto Him." (102)

Dear friends! The powerful operations of this titanic upheaval are comprehensible to none except such as have recognized the claims of both Baha'u'lla'h and the Bab. Their followers know full well whence it comes, and what it will ultimately lead to. Though ignorant of how far it will reach, they clearly recognize its genesis, are aware of its direction, acknowledge its necessity, observe confidently its mysterious processes, ardently pray for the mitigation of its severity, intelligently labor to assuage its fury, and anticipate with undimmed vision, the consummation of the fears and the hopes it must necessarily engender. (103)

This Judgment of God

This judgment of God ... is both a retributory calamity and act of holy and supreme discipline. It is at once a visitation from God and a cleansing process for all mankind. Its fires punish the perversity of the human race, and weld its component parts into one Organic, indivisible, world-embracing community. Mankind, in these fateful years, which at once signalize the passing of the first century of the Baha'i Era and proclaim the opening of a new one is, as ordained by Him Who is both the Judge and Redeemer of the human race, being simultaneously called upon to give account of its past actions, and is be purged and prepared for its future mission. It can neither escape the responsibilities of the past, nor shirk those of the future. God, the Vigilant, the Just, the Loving, All-Wise Ordainer, can, in this supreme Dispensation, neither allow the sins of an unregenerate humanity, whether of omission or of commission, to go unpunished, nor will He be willing to abandon His children to their fate, refuse them that culminating and blissful stage in their long, their slow and painful evolution throughout the ages, which is at once their inalienable right and their destiny. (104)

GLOBAL COMMUNITY

Earth In a State of Pregnancy

"The whole earth," Baha'u'lla'h, on the other hand, forecasting the bright future in store for a world now wrapped in darkness, emphatically asserts, "is now in a state of pregnancy. The day is approaching when it will have yielded its noblest fruits, when from it will have sprung forth the loftiest trees, the most enchanting blossoms, the most heavenly blessings." "The time is approaching when every created thing will have cast its burden. Glorified be God Who hath vouchsafed this grace that encompasseth all things, whether seen or unseen!' These great oppressions," He, moreover, foreshadowing humanity's golden age, has written, "are preparing it for the advent of the Most Great Justice." This Most Great Justice is indeed the Justice upon which the structure of the Most Great Peace can alone, and must eventually, rest, while the Most Great Peace will, in turn usher in that Most Great, that World Civilization which shall remain forever associated with Him Who beareth the Most Great Name. (105)

Beloved friends! Well-nigh a hundred years have elapsed since the Revelation of Baha'u'lla'h dawned upon the world—a Revelation, the nature of which, as affirmed by Himself, "none among the Manifestations of old, except to a prescribed degree, hath ever completely apprehended." For a whole century God has respited mankind, that it might acknowledge the Founder of such a Revelation, espouse His Cause, proclaim His greatness, and establish His Order. In a hundred volumes, the repositories of priceless precepts, mighty laws, unique principles, impassioned exhortations, reiterated warnings, amazing prophecies, sublime invocations, and weighty commentaries, the Bearer of such a Message has proclaimed, as no Prophet before Him has done, the Mission with which God had entrusted Him. To emperors, kings, princes and potentates, to rulers, governments, clergy and peoples, whether of the East or of the West, whether Christian, Jew, Muslim, or Zoroastrian, He addressed, for well-nigh fifty years, and in the most tragic circumstances, these priceless pearls of knowledge and wisdom that lay hid within the ocean of His matchless utterance. Forsaking fame and fortune, accepting imprisonment and exile, careless of ostracism and obloquy, submitting to physical indignities and cruel deprivations, He, the Vice-gerent of God on earth, suffered Himself to be banished from place to place and from country to country, till at length He, in the Most Great Prison, offered up His martyred son as a ransom for the redemption and unification of all mankind. "We verily," He Himself has testified, "have not fallen short of Our duty to exhort men, and to deliver that whereunto I was bidden by God, the Almighty, the All-Praised. Had they hearkened unto Me, they would have beheld the earth become another earth." And again: "Is there any excuse left for any one in this Revelation? No, by God, the Lord of the Mighty Throne! My signs have encompassed the earth, and My power enveloped all mankind, and yet the people are wrapped in a strange sleep!" (106)

The Most Great Peace

… in this marvelous cycle, the earth will be transformed, and the world of humanity arrayed in tranquility and beauty. Disputes, quarrels, and murders will be replaced by peace, truth, and concord; among the nations, peoples, races, and countries, love and amity will appear. Cooperation and union will be established, and finally war will be entirely suppressed. … Universal peace will raise its tent in the center of the earth, and the Blessed Tree of Life will grow and spread to such an extent that it will overshadow the East and the West. Strong and weak, rich and poor, antagonistic sects and hostile nations—which are like the world and the lamb, the leopard and kid, the lion and calf—will act towards each other with the most complete love, friendship, justice, and equity. The world will be filled with science, with the knowledge of the reality of the mysteries of beings, and with the knowledge of God. (107)

Universal Language

The tenth principle is the establishment of a universal language so that we shall not have to acquire so many languages in the future. In the schools they will study two, the mother tongue and the international auxiliary language. The use of an international auxiliary language will become a great means of dispelling the differences between nations. (108)

Every movement which promotes unity and harmony in the world is good, and everything which creates discord and discontent is bad. This is a century of illumination, surpassing all others in its many discoveries, its great inventions, and its vast and varied undertakings. But the greatest achievement of the age in conferring profit and pleasure on mankind is the creation of an auxiliary language for all. Oneness of language engenders peace and harmony. Oneness of language creates oneness of heart. It sweeps away all misunderstandings among peoples. It establishes harmony among the children of men. It gives to the human intellect a broader conception, a more commanding point of view. Today the greatest need of humanity is to understand and to be understood. (109)

Universal League of Nations

True civilization will unfurl its banner in the midmost heart of the world whenever a certain number of its distinguished and high-minded sovereigns—the shining exemplars of devotion and determination—shall, for the good and happiness of all mankind, arise, with firm resolve and clear vision, to establish the Cause of Universal Peace. They must make the Cause of Peace the object of general consultation, and seek by every means in their power to establish a Union of the nations of the world. They must conclude a binding treaty and establish a covenant, the provisions of which shall be sound, inviolable and definite. They must proclaim it to all the world and obtain for it the sanction of all the human race. (110)

Board of International Arbitration

When subjected to banishment by two kings, while a refugee from enemies of all nations and during the days of His long imprisonment, He wrote to the kings and rulers of the world in words of wonderful eloquence arraigning them severely and summoning them to the divine standard of unity and justice. He exhorted them to peace and international agreement, making it incumbent upon them to establish a board of international arbitration; that from all nations and governments of the world there should be delegates selected for a congress of nations which should constitute a universal arbitral court of justice to settle international disputes. He wrote to Victoria, Queen of Great Britain, the Czar of Russia, the Emperor of Germany, Napoleon III of France, and others, inviting them to world unity and peace. Through a heavenly power he was enabled to promulgate these ideals in the Orient. Kings could not withstand Him. They endeavored to extinguish His light but served only to increase its intensity and illumination. (111)

Unity of East and West

In the past, as in the present, the Spiritual Sun of Truth has always shone from the horizon of the East. In the East Moses arose to lead and teach the people. On the Eastern horizon rose the Lord Christ. Muhammad was sent to an Eastern nation. The Bab arose in the Eastern land of Persia. Baha'u'lla'h lived and taught in the East. All the great spiritual teachers arose in the Eastern world.

But although the Sun of Christ dawned in the East, the radiance thereof was apparent in the West, where the effulgence of its glory was more clearly seen. The divine light of His teaching shone with a greater force in the Western world, where it has made more rapid headway than in the land of its birth. (112)

In these days the East is in need of material progress and the West is in need of a spiritual ideal. It would be well for the West to turn to the East for illumination, and to give in exchange its scientific knowledge. There must be this interchange of gifts. The East and the West must unite to give to each other what is lacking. This union will bring about true civilization where the spiritual is expressed and carried out in the material. Receiving thus, the one from the other, the greatest harmony will prevail, all people will be united, a state of great perfection will be attained, there will be a firm cementing, and this world will become a shining mirror for the reflection of the attributes of God. (113)

We all, the Eastern and the Western nations, must strive day and night, with heart and soul, to achieve this high ideal, to cement the unity between all the nations of the earth. Every heart will then be refreshed, all eyes will be opened, the most wonderful power will be given, the happiness of humanity will be assured. ... This will be the Paradise which is to come on earth, when all mankind will be gathered together under the Tent of Unity in the Kingdom of Glory. (114)

Science and Religion

For every era hath a spirit; the spirit of this illumined era lieth in the teachings of Baha'u'lla'h. For these lay the foundation of the oneness of the world of humanity and promulgate universal brotherhood. They are founded upon the unity of science and religion and upon investigation of truth. They uphold the principle that religion must be the cause of amity, union, and harmony among men. They establish the equality of both sexes and propound economic principles which are for the happiness of individuals. They diffuse universal education, that every soul may as much as possible have a share of knowledge. They abrogate and nullify religious, racial, political, patriotic, and economic prejudices and the like. Those teachings that are scattered throughout the Epistles and Tablets are the cause of the illumination and the life of the world of humanity. (115)

Universal Education

Unto every father hath been enjoined the instruction of his son and daughter in the art of reading and writing and in all that hath been laid down in the Holy Tablet. He that putteth away that which is commanded unto him, the Trustees of the House of Justice are then to recover from him that which is required for their instruction, if he be wealthy, and if not the matter devolveth upon the House of Justice. Verily, have We made it a shelter for the poor and needy. He that bringeth up his son or the son of another, it is as though he hath brought up a son of Mine; upon him rest My Glory, My Loving-Kindness, My Mercy, that have compassed the world. (116)

REFERENCES

(1) Bridging our Faiths, prepared by the Interreligious Council of San Diego in conjunction with the National Conference of Community and Justice, published by Paulist Press (1997).

(2) Baha'u'lla'h, The Kitab-Iqa'n 120

(3) Baha'u'lla'h, Gleanings from the writings of Baha'u'lla'h 285

(4) Baha'u'lla'h, The Hidden Words 24

(5) Abdu'l-Bah'a, Paris Talks 60

(6) Abdu'l-Bah'a, Selections from Writings of Abdu'l-Bah'a 53f

(7) Baha'u'lla'h, Gleanings from the writings of Baha'u'lla'h 46f
(8) Baha'u'lla'h, The Hidden Words 40f
(9) Abdu'l-Bah'a, The Promulgation of Universal Peace 68
(10) Abdu'l-Bah'a, The Promulgation of Universal Peace 14f
(11) Abdu'l-Bah'a, The Promulgation of Universal Peace 93
(12) Abdu'l-Bah'a, The Promulgation of Universal Peace 247
(13) Baha'u'lla'h, Gleanings from the writings of Baha'u'lla'h 295
(14) Abdu'l-Bah'a, The Promulgation of Universal Peace 8
(15) Abdu'l-Bah'a, Selections from Writings of Abdu'l-Bah'a 244f
(16) Abdu'l-Bah'a , Selections from Writings of Abdu'l-Bah'a 68f
(17) Baha'u'lla'h, Gleanings from the writings of Baha'u'lla'h 262
(18) Abdu'l-Bah'a, The Promulgation of Universal Peace 90f
(19) Abdu'l-Bah'a, Huququlla'h 21
(20) Abdu'l-Bah'a, Some Answered Questions 3f
(21) Abdu'l-Bah'a, Some Answered Questions 160
(22) Abdu'l-Bah'a, quoted in Science and Religion 90
(23) Abdu'l-Bah'a, The Promulgation of Universal Peace 192
(24) Baha'u'lla'h, Gleanings from the writings of Baha'u'lla'h 65
(25) Abdu'l-Bah'a, Selections from Writings of Abdu'l-Bah'a 202f
(26) Abdu'l-Bah'a, Baha'i World Faith 340f
(27) Abdu'l-Bah'a, Paris Talks 110
(28) Abdu'l-Bah'a, Paris Talks 49f
(29) On behalf of Shoghi Effendi, Light of Guidance 113
(30) Abdu'l-Bah'a, Some Answered Questions 123
(31) Baha'u'lla'h, Tablets of Baha'u'lla'h 176f
(32) Abdu'l-Bah'a , Some Answered Questions 214-216
(33) Abdu'l-Bah'a, Tablets of Divine Plan 42f
(34) Abdu'l-Bah'a, The Promulgation of Universal Peace 142
(35) Abdu'l-Bah'a, The Promulgation of Universal Peace 450-52
(36) Abdu'l-Bah'a, Some Answered Questions 7f
(37) Baha'u'lla'h, Gleanings from the writings of Baha'u'lla'h 79f
(38) The Ba'b, Selections from Writings of the Ba'b 77
(39) Baha'u'lla'h, Gleanings from the writings of Baha'u'lla'h 338
(40) Abdu'l-Bah'a, Some Answered Questions 157f
(41) Baha'u'lla'h, Trustworthiness 5
(42) The Universal House of Justice, in The Kitab-I-Aqdas 1f
(43) Abdu'l-Bah'a, Selections from Writings of Abdu'l-Bah'a 1-3
(44) Baha'u'lla'h, Gleanings from the writings of Baha'u'lla'h 340
(45) Baha'u'lla'h, The Hidden Words – No. A4
(46) Baha'u'lla'h, Gleanings from the writings of Baha'u'lla'h 67
(47) Baha'u'lla'h, Gleanings from the writings of Baha'u'lla'h 67
(48) Baha'u'lla'h, Gleanings from the writings of Baha'u'lla'h 68
(49) Baha'u'lla'h, Gleanings from the writings of Baha'u'lla'h 69
(50) Baha'u'lla'h, Gleanings from the writings of Baha'u'lla'h 70

(51) Baha'u'lla'h, Gleanings from the writings of Baha'u'lla'h 70f
(52) Baha'u'lla'h, Gleanings from the writings of Baha'u'lla'h 71
(53) Baha'u'lla'h, Gleanings from the writings of Baha'u'lla'h 71f
(54) Baha'u'lla'h, Gleanings from the writings of Baha'u'lla'h 72
(55) Baha'u'lla'h, Gleanings from the writings of Baha'u'lla'h 79
(56) Baha'u'lla'h, Gleanings from the writings of Baha'u'lla'h 79f
(57) Baha'u'lla'h, Gleanings from the writings of Baha'u'lla'h 80f
(58) Baha'u'lla'h, Gleanings from the writings of Baha'u'lla'h 81
(59) Baha'u'lla'h, Gleanings from the writings of Baha'u'lla'h 59
(60) Abdu'l-Bah'a, The Promulgation of Universal Peace 10
(61) Abdu'l-Bah'a, The Promulgation of Universal Peace 10
(62) Abdu'l-Bah'a, Selections from Writings of Abdu'l-Bah'a 52
(63) Abdu'l-Bah'a, Selections from Writings of Abdu'l-Bah'a 52
(64) Baha'u'lla'h, Gleanings from the writings of Baha'u'lla'h 11
(65) Baha'u'lla'h, Gleanings from the writings of Baha'u'lla'h 11
(66) Baha'u'lla'h, Gleanings from the writings of Baha'u'lla'h 12f
(67) Baha'u'lla'h, Gleanings from the writings of Baha'u'lla'h 13f
(68) Baha'u'lla'h, Gleanings from the writings of Baha'u'lla'h 5
(69) Baha'u'lla'h, Gleanings from the writings of Baha'u'lla'h 5f
(70) Baha'u'lla'h, Gleanings from the writings of Baha'u'lla'h 9f
(71) Baha'u'lla'h, Gleanings from the writings of Baha'u'lla'h 10
(72) Baha'u'lla'h, Gleanings from the writings of Baha'u'lla'h 10
(73) Abdu'l-Bah'a, Selections from Writings of Abdu'l-Bah'a
(74) Baha'u'lla'h, Gleanings from the writings of Baha'u'lla'h 336
(75) Baha'u'lla'h, proclamation of Baha'u'lla'h 216
(76) Shoghi Effendi, World Order of Baha'u'lla'h 33
(77) Shoghi Effendi, World Order of Baha'u'lla'h 34
(78) Shoghi Effendi, World Order of Baha'u'lla'h 34
(79) Shoghi Effendi, Promised Day is Come 116
(80) Shoghi Effendi, Promised Day is Come 116
(81) Shoghi Effendi, Promised Day is Come 117
(82) Shoghi Effendi, Promised Day is Come 117
(83) Shoghi Effendi, Promised Day is Come 117f
(84) Shoghi Effendi, Promised Day is Come 118
(85) Shoghi Effendi, Promised Day is Come 119
(86) Shoghi Effendi, God Passes By 93f
(87) Shoghi Effendi, World Order of Baha'u'lla'h 24
(88) Shoghi Effendi, Promised Day is Come 116
(89) Baha'u'lla'h, proclamation of Baha'u'lla'h 1
(90) Baha'u'lla'h, proclamation of Baha'u'lla'h 1
(91) Baha'u'lla'h, proclamation of Baha'u'lla'h 1
(92) Baha'u'lla'h, The Kitab-Iqa'n 241
(93) Baha'u'lla'h, Gleanings from the writings of Baha'u'lla'h 214
(94) Baha'u'lla'h, Gleanings from the writings of Baha'u'lla'h 214

(95) Baha'u'lla'h, Gleanings from the writings of Baha'u'lla'h 215

(96) Baha'u'lla'h, Gleanings from the writings of Baha'u'lla'h 215-217

(97) Baha'u'lla'h, Gleanings from the writings of Baha'u'lla'h 218

(98) Baha'u'lla'h, Gleanings from the writings of Baha'u'lla'h 218f

(99) Baha'u'lla'h, Gleanings from the writings of Baha'u'lla'h 249f

(100) Baha'u'lla'h, Gleanings from the writings of Baha'u'lla'h 254f

(101) Shoghi Effendi, Promised Day is Come 3

(102) Shoghi Effendi, Promised Day is Come 3f

(103) Shoghi Effendi, Promised Day is Come 4

(104) Shoghi Effendi, Promised Day is Come 4f

(105) Shoghi Effendi, Promised Day is Come 5

(106) Shoghi Effendi, Promised Day is Come 6

(107) Abdu'l-Bah'a, Some Answered Questions 62

(108) Abdu'l-Bah'a,Compilations, Baha'i Scriptures 279

(109) Abdu'l-Bah'a,Compilations, Baha'i Scriptures 337

(110) Abdu'l-Bah'a, The Secret of Divine Civilization 64

(111) Abdu'l-Bah'a, Compilations, Baha'i Scriptures 336

(112) Abdu'l-Bah'a, Paris Talks 21

(113) Abdu'l-Bah'a, Paris Talks 21

(114) Abdu'l-Bah'a, Paris Talks 21

(115) Abdu'l-Bah'a, Selections from the Writings of Abdu'l-Bah'a 109

(116) Baha'u'lla'h, Tablets of Baha'u'lla'h 128

SCIENTOLOGY SCRIPTURES

INTRODUCTION
BY REVEREND WOLFGANG KELLER

In the introduction of his book, *Science of Survival*, L. Ron Hubbard[1] acknowledges fifty-thousand years of thinking scholars without whose speculations and observations the creation and construction of Dianetics[2] would not have been possible. He gives specific credit to twenty-three philosophers of Western civilization and his instructors in atomic and molecular phenomena, mathematics and humanities at George Washington University and at Princeton.

---

[1] American philosopher and humanitarian, 1911—1986, the founder of Scientology.

[2] That branch of Scientology that addresses what the soul is doing to the body, derived from the Greek *dia = through* and *nous = soul.*

The Scientology Cross is a trademark and service mark owned by Religious Technology Center and is used with its permission.

Scientology is the study and handling of the spirit in relationship to itself, universes and other life, codified and implemented into counseling procedures by the founder. Scientology offers a unique synthesis of scientific inquiry and religious philosophy, comprising traditional knowledge and modern discoveries and utilizing most recent developments in electronics. It is based on observation, a formulation of axioms with predictable results in their technological applications; while at the same time, it gives perspective as to purpose and evaluation in respect to ethics. As a religion, Scientology lives in the tradition of the great religions of the East, closest related in thought to Buddhism. Scientology is not dogmatic in regards to a Supreme Being, but encourages its followers to be inquisitive and to discover truth for themselves. It lays out a road and provides the tools to salvation which to a Scientologist is eternal spiritual freedom. Consequently, Scientology is non-denominational and open to everyone, independent of his or her religious background. In fact, Scientology incorporates the elements essential for a global religion that adequately serves all traits of ethnic and educational background.

In the following section, excerpts from Mr. Hubbard's writings are given from various Scientology scriptures; however, only a comprehensive study will enable the interested reader to acquire a real understanding of the philosophy and religious practice of Scientology. Born of his research in the field of study the following advice may be given: "The only reason a person gives up a study or becomes confused or unable to learn is because he or she has gone past a word that was not understood." This factor of study is also why you will find some new terms in Scientology. They are not new names for elements already understood. Vital to an understanding of Scientology is the realization that many elements necessary to an understanding of man have not been accurately defined. These elements have been precisely observed and those observations are then passed on to the student for his own verification from his own viewpoint. A fundamental premise common to all of Mr. Hubbard's teachings is that a datum is only true for you if you have observed it for yourself and find it to be so.

Scientology does not rely on revelatory writings to impart understanding. Scientology is a religion of self-deliberation without reliance on exterior forces. Beyond the communication of its basic philosophy and principles, the religious scriptures are devoted to the education of its disciples to acquire the knowledge and skill to apply these principles.

While L. Ron Hubbard's legacy comprises some 40 million words of recorded lectures, books and writings, none of the technical materials will be presented here. Rather, the arrangement of excerpts I have selected seeks to convey an overview of the philosophic ideas and principles on which the religion of Scientology is based. Grateful acknowledgment is made to L. Ron Hubbard Library for permission to reproduce selections of the copyrighted works from L. Ron Hubbard.

A final note: When we study the works of L. Ron Hubbard, we immediately recognize that his primary interest serves the spiritual aspects of humankind, without reference to body forms. The words *man* or *men*, as well as use of *he*, *his*, or even the terms *fellow* or *brother* are consistently understood to refer to spiritual beings, irrespective of gender.[3]

Reverend Wolfgang Keller[4]

---

[3] These terms are defined by all Scientologists according to definition 2 in: New World(TM) College Dictionary (Third Edition): *MAN*: the human race, mankind: used without *the* or *a*. Etymology: [ME < OE mann, akin to Germ mann, Goth manna < IE base *manu- (>Sans manu-, Russ muz): akin ? to *men-, to think > mind].

[4] Wolfgang Keller was born 1937 in Eisleben, Germany. He studied engineering sciences and received his masters and doctors degrees from the Technical University of Aachen, Germany. Including his research time at the university he worked nearly 20 years in the field of engineering. However, he never ceased feeling that his real calling was to improve the human condition, a desire reinforced by extensive travels that showed him a multitude of faces of human suffering. His discovery of the works of L. Ron Hubbard and the Scientology religion enabled him to pursue his calling by becoming a Scientology minister. After intensive study in advanced Scientology organizations in Copenhagen, Denmark, and Clearwater, Florida, he was awarded the highest level of ministerial training. For the last twelve years he has enjoyed helping people of every race and many faiths to overcome suffering by applying the precise procedures of Dianetics and Scientology counseling so that they may live happier lives in their own estimation.

L. RON HUBBARD
THE FOUNDER OF SCIENTOLOGY

As the founder of the Scientology religion and the sole author of its Scripture, L. Ron Hubbard is respected by Scientologists throughout the world, and he has no successor. He is remembered not as one to be idolized or worshiped but as a man whose legacy is the religion of Scientology which still lives on. Some understanding of his background serves to illustrate how he came to discover the truths of the Scientology religion.

"To know life you've got to be part of life," he wrote, "You must get down there and look, you must get into the nooks and crannies of existence, and you must rub elbows with all kinds and types of men before you can finally establish what man is."

He did exactly that.

Armed with a keen intellect, boundless energy, limitless curiosity and a unique approach to philosophy and science which emphasized workability and practicality over all else, Ron embarked upon his study of life and its mysteries while still in his teens. His subsequent travels and discoveries alone fill scores of pages.

It was his lifelong purpose to complete his research into the riddle of man and develop a technology that would bring him up to higher levels of understanding, ability and freedom—a goal which he fully achieved in the development of DIANETICS and SCIENTOLOGY. Ron always considered it was not enough that he alone should benefit from the results of his research. He took great care to record every detail of his discoveries so that others could share the wealth of knowledge and wisdom to improve their lives.

L. Ron Hubbard said in a 1965 essay, "I know no man who has any monopoly upon the wisdom of this universe. It belongs to those who can use it to help themselves and others. ... If things were a little better known and understood, we would all lead happier lives."

The greatest testimonies to Ron's vision are the miracle results of his technology and the millions of friends around the world who carry his legacy forward into the twenty-first century. Both continue to grow in number with each passing day.

MY PHILOSOPHY
BY L. RON HUBBARD

The subject of philosophy is very ancient. The word means: "The love, study of pursuit of wisdom, or of knowledge of things and their causes, whether theoretical or practical."

All we know of science or of religion comes from philosophy. It lies behind and above all other knowledge we have or use.

For long regarded as a subject reserved for halls of learning and the intellectual, the subject, to a remarkable degree, has been denied the man in the street.

Surrounded by protective coatings of impenetrable scholarliness, philosophy has been reserved to the privileged few.

The first principle of my own philosophy is that wisdom is meant for anyone who wishes to reach for it. It is the servant of the commoner and king alike and should never be regarded with awe.

Selfish scholars seldom forgive anyone who seeks to break down the walls of mystery and let the people in. Will Durant, the modern American philosopher, was relegated to the scrapheap by his fellow scholars when he wrote a popular book on the subject, *The Outline of Philosophy*. Thus brickbats come the way of any who seek to bring wisdom to the people over the objections of the "inner circle."

The second principle of my own philosophy is that it must be capable of being applied.

Learning locked in mildewed books is of little use to anyone and therefore of no value unless it can be used.

The third principle is that any philosophic knowledge is only valuable if it is true or if it works.

These three principles are so strange to the field of philosophy, that I have given my philosophy a name: SCIENTOLOGY. This means only "knowing how to know."

A philosophy can only be a *route* to knowledge. It cannot be crammed down one's throat. If one has a route, he can then find what is true for him. And that is Scientology.

Know thyself ... and the truth shall set you free.

Therefore, in Scientology, we are not concerned with individual actions and differences. We are only concerned with how to show man how he can set himself free.

This, of course, is not very popular with those who depend upon the slavery of others for their living or power. But it happens to be the only way I have found that really improves an individual's life.

Suppression and oppression are the basic causes of depression. If you relieve those a person can lift his head, become well, become happy with life.

And though it may be unpopular with the slave master, it is very popular with the people.

Common man likes to be happy and well. He likes to be able to understand things, and he knows his route to freedom lies through knowledge.

Therefore, for fifteen years I have had mankind knocking on my door. It has not mattered where I have lived or how remote, since I first published a book on the subject my life has no longer been my own.

I like to help others and count it as my greatest pleasure in life to see a person free himself of the shadows which darken his days.

These shadows look so thick to him and weigh him down so that when he finds they are shadows and that he can see through them, walk through them and be again in the sun, he is enormously delighted. And I am afraid I am just as delighted as he is.

I have seen much human misery. As a very young man I wandered through Asia and saw the agony and misery of overpopulated and underdeveloped lands. I have seen people uncaring and stepping over dying men in the streets. I have seen children less than rags and bones. And amongst this poverty and degradation I found holy places where wisdom was great, but where it was carefully hidden and given out only as superstition. Later, in Western universities, I saw man obsessed with materiality and with all his cunning; I saw him hide what little wisdom he really had in forbidding halls and make it inaccessible to the common and less favored man. I have been through a terrible war and saw its terror and pain uneased by a single word of decency or humanity.

I have lived no cloistered life and hold in contempt the wise man who has not *lived* and the scholar who will not share.

There have been many wiser men than I, but few have traveled as much road.

I have seen life from the top down and the bottom up. I know how it looks both ways. And I know there is wisdom and that there is hope.

Blinded with injured optic nerves, and lame with physical injuries to hip and back, at the end of World War II, I faced an almost nonexistent future. My service record states: "This officer has no neurotic or psychotic tendencies of any kind whatsoever," but it also states "permanently disabled physically."

And so there came a further blow ... I was abandoned by family and friends as a supposedly hopeless cripple and a probable burden upon them for the rest of my days. I yet worked my way back to fitness and strength in less than two years, using only what I know and could determine about man and his relationship to the universe. I had no one to help me; what I had to know I had to find out. And it's quite a trick studying when you cannot see.

I became used to being told it was all impossible, that there was no way, no hope. Yet I came to see again and walk again, and I built an entirely new life. It is a happy life, a busy one and I hope a useful one. My only moments of sadness are those which come when bigoted men tell others all is bad and there is no route anywhere, no hope anywhere, nothing but sadness and sameness and desolation, and that every effort to help others is false. I know it is not true.

So my own philosophy is that one should share what wisdom he has, one should help others to help themselves, and one should keep going despite heavy weather for there is always a calm ahead. One should also ignore catcalls from the selfish intellectual who cries: "Don't expose the mystery. Keep it all for ourselves. The people cannot understand."

But as I have never seen wisdom do any good kept to oneself, and as I like to see others happy, and as I find the vast majority of the people can and do understand, I will keep on writing and working and teaching so long as I exist.

For I know no man who has any monopoly upon the wisdom of the universe. It belongs to those who can use it to help themselves and others.

If things were a little better known and understood, we would all lead happier lives.

And there is a way to know them and there is a way to freedom.

The old must give way to the new, falsehood must become exposed by truth, and truth, though fought, always in the end prevails.

L. Ron Hubbard

THE AIMS OF SCIENTOLOGY
BY L. RON HUBBARD

A civilization without insanity, without criminals and without war, where the able can prosper and honest beings can have rights, and where man is free to rise to greater heights, are the aims of Scientology.

Nonpolitical in nature, Scientology welcomes any individual of any creed, race or nation.

We seek no revolution. We seek only evolution to higher states of being for the individual and for society.

We are achieving our aims.

After endless millennia of ignorance about himself, his mind and the universe, a breakthrough has been made for man.

Other efforts man has made have been surpassed.

The combined truths of fifty thousand years of thinking men, distilled and amplified by new discoveries about man, have made for this success.

We welcome you to Scientology. We only expect of you your help in achieving our aims and helping others. We expect you to be helped.

Scientology is the most vital movement on Earth today.

In a turbulent world, the job is not easy. But then, if it were, we wouldn't have to be doing it.

We respect man and believe he is worthy of help. We respect you and believe you, too, can help.

Scientology does not owe its help. We have done nothing to cause us to propitiate. Had we done so, we would not now be bright enough to do what we are doing.

Man suspects all offers of help. He has often been betrayed, his confidence shattered. Too frequently he has given his trust and been betrayed. We may err, for we build a world with broken straws. But we will never betray your faith in us so long as you are one of us.

The sun never sets on Scientology.

And may a new day dawn for you, for those you love and for man.

Our aims are simple, if great.

And we will succeed, and are succeeding at each new revolution of the Earth.

Your help is acceptable to us.

Our help is yours.

L. Ron Hubbard
Founder

SCIENTOLOGY FUNDAMENTALS
BY L. RON HUBBARD

What Is Scientology?

Scientology is an applied religious philosophy.

The term *Scientology* is taken from the Latin word scio (knowing in the fullest meaning of the word) and the Greek word logos (study of). In itself the word means literally *knowing how to know.*

Scientology is further defined as the study and handling of the spirit in relationship to itself, universes and other life.

Any comparison between Scientology and the subject known as psychology is nonsense. Early psychology such as that begun by St. Thomas Aquinas and extended by many later authors was, in 1879, interrupted severely by one Professor Wundt, a Marxist at Leipzig University in Germany. This man conceived that man was an animal without soul and based all of his work on the principle that there was no *psyche* (a Greek word meaning "spirit"). Psychology, the study of the spirit (or mind) then came into the peculiar position of being "a study of the spirit which denied the spirit." For the subsequent decades, Wundtian "psychology" was taught broadly throughout the world. It taught that man was an animal. It taught that man could not be bettered. It taught that intelligence never changed. This subject, Wundtian psychology, became standard, mainly because of the indifference or lack of knowledge of people in charge of universities.

Scientology can and does change behavior and intelligence, and it can and does assist people to study life. Unlike Wundtian pseudo-psychology, it has no political aspiration. Scientology is not teaching dialectical materialism under the heading of "psychology."

Scientology is a *route*, a way, rather than a desertion or an assertive body of knowledge.

Through its drills and studies one may find the truth for oneself. It is the only thing that can show you who *you* really are.

The technology is therefore not expounded as something to believe but something to *do*.

The end result of Scientology studies and drills is a renewed awareness of self as a spiritual and immortal being.

Only those who believe, as do psychiatrists and psychologists, that man is a soulless animal or who wish for their own reasons to keep man unhappy and oppressed are in any conflict with Scientology.

Scientology, used by the trained and untrained person, improves the health, ability, intelligence, behavior, skill and appearance of people.

It is a precise and exact science, designed for an age of exact sciences.

It is employed by an *auditor* upon individuals or small or large groups of people in their presence. The auditor makes these people, at their choice, do various exercises, and the exercises bring about changes for the better in intelligence, behavior and general competence.

Scientology is employed as well by business and government persons to solve problems and to establish better organization.

It is also employed by the average person to bring better order into life.

How Is Scientology Used?

Scientology is employed by an auditor as a set of drills upon the individual, and small or large groups. It is also employed as an educational subject. It has been found that persons can be processed in Scientology with Scientology exercises and can be freed from their major anxieties and can become brighter, more alert and more competent. *But* if they are *only* processed they have a tendency to be overwhelmed or startled and although they may be brighter and more competent they are still held down by an ignorance of life. Therefore it is far better to teach *and* process a person than only to process him. In other words, the best use of Scientology is through processing and education in Scientology. In this way there is no imbalance. It is interesting that people only need to study Scientology to have some small rise in their own intelligence, behavior and competence. The study itself is therapeutic by actual testing.

It is also used by business and government leaders to establish or improve organization.

It is used as well by the individual at home or at his work to make a better life.

Is Scientology Valid?

Tens of thousands of case histories, all sworn to, are in the possession of the organization of Scientology. No other subjects on Earth except physics and chemistry have had such grueling testing. Scientology in the hands of an expert can restore man's ability to handle any and all of his problems. Scientology is used by some of the largest companies on Earth. It is valid. It has been tested. It is the only thoroughly tested system of improving human relations, intelligence and character, and is the only one which does.

Basic Principles

Like engineering, Scientology has certain basic principles. These are necessary to a full understanding of the subject. It is not enough to know how to process people in Scientology. To be effective one must also know the basic principles. Scientology is very exact. The humanities of the past were full of opinions. Scientology is full of facts that work.

To study Scientology one should scan quickly through the basics and find something with which one can agree. Having found *one thing* with which he can agree, one should then skim through again and find another fact. One should continue to do this until he feels some friendliness to the subject. When one has achieved this, and *only* when one has achieved this, he should then study all the basic principles. There is no effort here to be authoritarian. No one will try to make the subject difficult.

You may have been taught that the mind is a very difficult thing to know about. This is the first principle of Scientology: It is possible to know about the mind, the spirit and life.

The Parts of Man

The individual man is divisible into three parts.

The first of these is the spirit, called in Scientology the *Thetan.*

The second of these parts is the *Mind.*

The third of these parts is the *Body.*

Probably the greatest discovery of Scientology and its most forceful contribution to the knowledge of mankind has been the isolation, description and handling of the human spirit, accomplished in July, 1952, in Phoenix, Arizona. I established along scientific rather than religious or humanitarian lines that that thing which is the person, the personality, is separable from the body and the mind at will and without causing bodily death or mental derangement.

In ages past there has been considerable controversy concerning the human spirit or soul, and various attempts to control man have been effective in view of his almost complete ignorance of his own identity. Latterly spiritualists isolated from the person what they called the astral body, and with this they were able to work for various purposes of their own. In Scientology, the spirit itself was separated from what the spiritualists called the astral body and there should be no confusion between these two things. As you know that you are where you are at this moment, so you would know if you, a spirit, were detached from your mind and body.

Man had not discovered this before because, lacking the technologies of Scientology, he had very little reality upon his detachment from his mind and body; therefore, he conceived himself to be at least in part a mind and a body. The entire cult of communism is based upon the fact that one lives only one life, that there is no hereafter and that the individual has no religious significance.

Man at large has been close to this state for at least the last century. The state is of a very low order, excluding as it does all self-recognition.

The Spirit

The thetan is described in Scientology as having no mass, no wave-length, no energy and no time or location in space except by consideration or postulate. The spirit, then, is not a *thing*. It is the *creator* of things.

The usual residence of the thetan is in the skull or near the body. A thetan can be in one of four conditions. The first would be entirely separate from a body or bodies, or even from this universe. The second would be near a body and knowingly controlling the body. The third would be in the body (the skull) and the fourth would be an inverted condition whereby he is compulsively away from the body and cannot approach it. There are degrees of each one of these four states. The most optimum of these conditions from the standpoint of man, is the second.

A thetan is subject to deterioration. This is at first difficult to understand since the entirety of his activity consists of considering or postulating. He uses, through his postulates, various methods of controlling a body. That he does deteriorate is manifest, but that he can at any moment return to an entirety of his ability is also factual. In that he associates beingness with mass and action, he does not consider himself as having an individual identity or name unless he is connected with one or more of the games of life.

The processes of Scientology can establish this for the individual with greater or lesser rapidity, and one of the many goals of processing in Scientology is to "exteriorize" the individual and place him in the second condition above, since it has been discovered that he is happier and more capable when so situated.

The Mind

The *mind* is a communication and control system between the thetan and his environment. The mind is a network of communications and pictures, energies and masses, which are brought into being by the activities of the thetan versus the physical universe or other thetans. A thetan establishes various systems of control so that he can continue to operate a body and through the body operate things in the physical universe, as well as other bodies. The most obvious portion of the mind is recognizable by anyone not in serious condition. This is the "mental image picture." In Scientology we call this mental image picture a *facsimile* when it is a "photograph" of the physical universe sometime in the past. We call this mental image picture a *mock-up* when it is created by the thetan or for the thetan and does not consist of a photograph of the physical universe. We call a mental image picture a *hallucination* or, more properly, an *automaticity* when it is created by another and seen by self.

Various phenomena connect themselves with this entity called the mind. Some people closing their eyes see only blackness, some people see pictures. Some people see pictures made by body reactions. Some people see only black screens. Others see golden lines. Others see spaces, but the keynote of the entirety of the system called the mind is postulate and perception. Easily ten thousand new, separate mental phenomena, not hitherto seen by earlier observers, have been classified in scientology and Dianetics.

The thetan receives, by the communication system called the mind, various impressions, including direct views of the physical universe. In addition to this he receives impressions from past activities and, most important, he himself, being close to a total knowingness, conceives things about the past and future which are independent of immediately present stimuli. The mind is not in its entirety a stimulus-response mechanism as old Marxist psychology, as once taught in universities, would have one believe. The mind has three main divisions. The first of these could be called the *analytical mind*, the second the *reactive mind* and the third the *somatic mind*.

The Analytical Mind

The *analytical mind* combines perceptions of the immediate environment, of the past (via pictures) and estimations of the future into conclusions which are based upon the realities of situations. The analytical mind combines the potential knowingness of the thetan with the conditions of his surroundings and brings him to independent conclusions. This mind could be said to consist of visual pictures either of the past or of the physical universe, monitored by, and presided over by, the knowingness of a thetan. The keynote of the analytical mind is awareness. One knows what one is concluding and knows what he is doing.

The Reactive Mind

The *reactive mind* is a stimulus-response mechanism, ruggedly built, and operable in trying circumstances. The reactive mind never stops operating. Pictures, of a very low order, are taken by this mind of the environment even in some states of unconsciousness. The reactive mind acts below the level of consciousness. *It* is the literal, stimulus-response mind. Given a certain stimulus it gives a certain response. The entire subject of Dianetics concerned itself mainly with this one mind.

While it is an order of thinkingness, the ability of the reactive mind to conclude rationally is so poor that we find in the reactive mind those various aberrated impulses which are gazed upon as oddities of personality, eccentricities, neuroses and psychoses. It is this mind which stores up all the bad things that have happened to one and throws them back to him again in moments of emergency or danger so as to dictate his actions along lines which have been considered "safe" before. As there is little thinkingness involved in this, the courses of action dictated by the reactive mind are often not safe, but highly dangerous.

The reactive mind is entirely literal in its interpretation of words and actions. As it takes pictures and receives impressions during moments of unconsciousness, a phrase uttered when a blow is struck is likely to be literally interpreted by the reactive mind and becomes active upon the body and analytical mind at later times. The mildest stage of this would be arduous training, wherein a pattern is laid into the mind for later use under certain given stimuli.

A harsh and less workable level is the hypnotic trance condition to which the mind is susceptible. Made impressionable by fixed attention, words can be immediately implanted into the reactive mind which become operable under restimulation at later times.

An even lower level in the reactive mind is that one associated with blows, drugs, illness, pain and other conditions of unconsciousness. Phrases spoken over an anesthetized person can have a later effect upon that person. It is not necessarily true that each and every portion of an operation is painstakingly "photographed" by the reactive mind of the unconscious patient, but it is true that a great many of these stimuli are registered. Complete silence, in the vicinity of a person under anesthetic or a person who is unconscious or in deep pain is mandatory if one would preserve the mental health of that person or patient afterwards.

Probably the most therapeutic action which could occur to an individual would be, under Scientology processing, the separation of the thetan from the mind so that the thetan, under no duress and with total knowingness, could view himself and his mind and act accordingly. However, there is a type of exteriorization which is the most aberrative of all traumatic actions. This is the condition when an individual is brought, through injury or surgery or shock, very close to death so that he exteriorizes from body and mind. This exteriorization under duress is sudden, and to the patient inexplicable, and is in itself very shocking. When this has occurred to an individual, it is certain that he will suffer mentally from the experience afterwards.

It could be said that when the reactive mind contains these sudden shocks of exteriorization under duress, attempts to exteriorize the individual later by Scientology are more difficult. However, modern processing has overcome this. The phenomenon of exteriorization under duress is accompanied at times by energy explosions in the various facsimiles of the mind, and these cross-associate in the reactive mind. Therefore, people become afraid of exteriorization, and at times people are made ill simply by discussing the phenomenon, due to the fact that they have exteriorized under duress during some operation or accident.

Exteriorization under duress is the characteristic of death itself. Therefore, exteriorization or the departure of the soul is generally associated with death in the minds of most people. It is not necessarily true that one is dead because he exteriorizes, and it is definitely not true that exteriorization not accompanied by a shock, pain or duress is at all painful. Indeed, it is quite therapeutic.

The Somatic Mind

The third portion of the mind is the *somatic mind*. This is an even heavier type of mind than the reactive mind since it contains no thinkingness and contains only actingness. The impulses placed against the body by the thetan through various mental machinery arrive at the voluntary, involuntary and glandular levels. These have set methods of analysis for any given situation and so respond directly to commands given.

Unfortunately the somatic mind is subject to each of the minds higher in scale above it and to the thetan. In other words, the thetan can independently affect the somatic mind. The analytical mind can affect the somatic mind. The reactive mind can affect the somatic mind. Thus we see that the neurons, the glandular system, the muscles and masses of the body are subject to various impulses, each one of a lower order than the next. Thus it is not odd to discover what we call "psychosomatic" illness. A condition exists here where the thetan does not have an awareness of burdening the somatic mind with various commands or derangements. Neither does the thetan have an awareness of his own participation in the analytical mind causing this action against the body.

In that the thetan is seldom aware of the reactive mind, it is possible, then, for the reactive mind, with its stimulus-response content, to impinge itself directly, and without further recourse or advice, upon the neurons, muscles and glandular system of the body. In that the reactive mind can hold a fixed command in place, causing a derangement in the somatic mind, it is possible, then, for illness to exist, for bizarre pains to be felt, for actual physical twists and aberrations to occur, without any conscious knowledge on the part of the thetan. This we call physical illness caused by the mind. In brief, such illness is caused by perceptions received in the reactive mind during moments of pain and unconsciousness.

Whether the facsimile in the mind is received while the thetan is awake or unconscious, the resulting mass of the energy picture is energy just as you see energy in an electric light bulb or from the flames of a fire. At one time it was considered that mental energy was different from physical energy. In Scientology it has been discovered that mental energy is simply a finer, higher level of physical energy. The test of this is conclusive in that a thetan "mocking up" [creating] mental image pictures and thrusting them into the body can increase the body mass and, by casting them away again, can decrease the body mass. This test has actually been made and an increase of as much as thirty pounds, actually measured on scales, has been added to, and subtracted from, a body by creating "mental energy." Energy is energy. It has different wavelengths and different characteristics. The mental image pictures are capable of reacting upon the physical environment, and the physical environment is capable of reacting upon mental image pictures. Thus the mind actually consists of spaces, energies and masses of the same order as the physical universe, if lighter and different in size and wavelength. For a much more comprehensive picture of the mind one should read *The Dynamics of Life* and *Dianetics: The Modern Science of Mental Health*. These were written before the discoveries of the upper levels of beingness were made and are a very complete picture of the mind itself, its structure and what can be done to it and with it.

The Body

The third part of man is the physical *body*. This can best be studied in such books as *Gray's Anatomy* and other anatomical texts. This is the province of the medical doctor and, usually, the old-time psychiatrist or psychologist, who were involved, in the main, in body worship. The body is a purely structural study, and the actions and reactions among its various structures are complex and intensely interesting.

When Scientology established biophysics, it did so because of the various discoveries which had accumulated concerning mental energy in its reaction against physical energy, and the activities which took place in the body because of these interactions. Biophysics only became feasible when it was discovered in Scientology that a fixed electrical field existed surrounding a body entirely independent of, but influenceable by, the human mind. The body exists in its own space. That space is created by *anchor points* [those points which demark (limit) the outermost boundaries of a space or its corners]. The complexity of these anchor points can cause an independent series of electronic flows which can occasion much discomfort to the individual. The balance structure of the body and even its joint action and physical characteristics can be changed by changing this electrical field which exists at a distance from, or within, the body.

The electrical field is paramount and monitors the actual physical structure of the body. Thus the body is not only influenced by the three minds, it is influenced as well by its own electrical field. An expert Scientologist can discover for the average person this field, and can bring about its adjustment, although this is very far from the primary purpose of the Scientologist.

The use of electrical shocks upon a body for any purpose is therefore very dangerous and is not condoned by sensible men. Of course, the use of electrical shock was never intended to be therapeutic, but was intended only to bring about obedience by duress and, as far as it can be discovered, to make the entirety of insanity a horror. Electrical shock deranges the electronic field in the vicinity of the body and is always succeeded by bad health or physical difficulties and never does otherwise than hasten the death of the person. It has been stated by people using electric shock that if they were denied euthanasia, they would at least use partial euthanasia in the form of electric shock, brain surgery and drugs. These treatments in some large percentage of cases, however, effected euthanasia as they were expected to do.

A knowledge of the mental and physical structure of the body would be necessary in order to treat the body, and this knowledge has not existed prior to Scientology. The medical doctor achieved many results by working purely with structure and biochemical products, and in the field of emergency surgery and obstetrics and orthopedics, he is indispensable in the society. Medicine, however, did not even contain a definition for *mind* and is not expected to invade the field which belongs properly to Scientology.

These three parts of man—the thetan, the mind and the body—are each one different studies, but they influence each other markedly and continually. Of the three, the senior entity is the thetan, for without the thetan there would be no mind or animation in the body, while without a body or a mind there is still animation and life in the thetan. The thetan *is* the person. You are *you, in* a body.

Many speculations in the field of para-Scientology have been made. Para-Scientology includes all of the uncertainties and unknown territories of life which have not been completely explored and explained. However, as studies have gone forward, it has become more and more apparent that the senior activity of life is that of the thetan, and that in the absence of the spirit no further life exists. In the insect kingdom it is not established whether or not each insect is ordered by a spirit or whether one spirit orders enormous numbers of insects. It is not established how mutation and evolution occur (if they do), and the general authorship of the physical universe is only speculated upon, since Scientology does not invade the eighth dynamic.

Some facts, however, are completely known. The first of these is that the individual himself is a spirit controlling a body via a mind. The second of these is that the thetan is capable of making space, energy, mass and time. The third of these is that the thetan is separable from the body without the phenomenon of death, and can handle and control a body from well outside it. The fourth of these is that the thetan does not care to remember the life which he has just lived, after he has parted from the body and the mind. The fifth of these is that a person dying always exteriorizes. The sixth of these is that the person, having exteriorized, usually returns to a planet and procures, usually, another body of the same type of race as before.

In para-Scientology there is much discussion about *between-lives areas* and other phenomena which might have passed at one time or another for heaven or hell, but it is established completely that a thetan is immortal and that he himself cannot actually experience death and counterfeits it by forgetting. It is adequately manifest that a thetan lives again and that he is very anxious to put something on the *time track* (something for the future) in order to have something to come back to, thus we have the anxieties of sex. There must be additional bodies for the next life.

It is obvious that what we create in our societies during this lifetime affects us during our next lifetime. This is quite different than the "belief," or idea, that this occurs. In Scientology we have very little to do with forcing people to make conclusions. An individual can experience these things for himself and unless he can do so no one expects him to accept them.

The manifestation that our hereafter is our next life entirely alters the general concept of spiritual destiny. There is no argument whatever with the tenets of faith since it is not precisely stated, uniformly, by religions that one immediately goes to a heaven or hell. It is certain that an individual experiences the effect of the civilization which he has had part in creating, in his next lifetime. In other words, the individual comes back. He has a responsibility for what goes on today since he will experience it tomorrow.

L. Ron Hubbard

ETHICS, JUSTICE AND THE DYNAMICS
BY L. RON HUBBARD

Every being has an infinite ability to survive. How well he accomplishes this is dependent on how well he uses ethics on his dynamics.[5]

---

[5] Dynamics: These are the eight urges (drives, impulses) in life. We call them the DYNAMICS. These are motives or motivations. These are the EIGHT DYNAMICS. The purpose of setting forth this division is to increase an understanding of life by placing it in compartments. Having subdivided existence in this fashion, each compartment can be inspected as itself and by itself in its relationship to the other compartments of life. In working a puzzle it is necessary to first take pieces of similar color or character and place them in groups. In studying a subject it is necessary to proceed in an orderly fashion. To promote this orderliness it is necessary to assume for our purposes these eight arbitrary compartments of life.

The First Dynamic: The FIRST DYNAMIC is SELF. This is the effort to survive as an individual, to be an individual. It includes one's own body and one's own mind. It is the effort to attain the highest level of survival for the longest possible time for self. This dynamic includes the individual plus his immediate possessions. It does not include any other people. It is the urge to survive as one's self. Here we have individuality expressed fully.

The Second Dynamic: The SECOND DYNAMIC is CREATIVITY. Creativity is making things for the future and the second dynamic includes any creativity. The second dynamic contains the family unit and the rearing of children as well as anything that can be categorized as a family activity. It also incidentally includes sex as a mechanism to compel future survival.

The Third Dynamic: The THIRD DYNAMIC is GROUP SURVIVAL. This is the urge to survive through a group of individuals or as a group. It is group survival, the group tending to take on a life and existence of its own. A group can be a community, friends, a company, a social lodge, a state, a nation, a race or in short, any group. It doesn't matter what size this group is, it is seeking to survive as a group.

The Fourth Dynamic: The FOURTH DYNAMIC is SPECIES. Man's fourth dynamic is the species of mankind. Meaning both men and women. This is the urge toward survival through all mankind and as all

Ethics tech exists for the individual.

It exists to give the individual a way to increase his survival and thus free himself from the dwindling spiral of the current culture.

Ethics

The whole subject of ethics is one which, with the society in its current state, has become almost lost.

Ethics actually consists of rationality toward the highest level of survival for the individual, the future race, the group, mankind and the other dynamics taken up collectively.

Ethics are reason.

Man's greatest weapon is his reason.

---

mankind. Whereas the white race would be considered a third dynamic for a white person, all the races of man together would be considered the fourth dynamic. All men and women because they are men and women seek to survive as men and women and for men and women.

The Fifth Dynamic: The FIFTH DYNAMIC is LIFE FORMS. This is the urge to survive as life forms and with the help of life forms such as animals, birds, insects, fish and vegetation. This includes all living things whether animal or vegetable, anything directly and intimately motivated by life. It is the effort to survive for any and every form of life. It is the interest in life as such.

The Sixth Dynamic: The SIXTH DYNAMIC is MEST or the PHYSICAL UNIVERSE. MEST stands for Matter, Energy, Space and Time. These are the component parts of the physical universe. We take the first letter of each of these words and coin a word, MEST. The sixth dynamic is the urge to survive of the physical universe, by the physical universe itself and with the help of the physical universe and each one of its component parts.

The Seventh Dynamic: The SEVENTH DYNAMIC is the SPIRITUAL DYNAMIC, the urge to survive as spiritual beings or the urge for life itself to survive. Anything spiritual, with or without identity, would come under the heading of the seventh dynamic. It includes one's beingness, the ability to create, the ability to cause survival or survive, the ability to destroy or pretend to be destroyed. A subheading of this dynamic is ideas and concepts and the desire to survive through these. The seventh dynamic is life source. This is separate from the physical universe and is the source of life itself. Thus there is an effort for the survival of life source.

The Eighth Dynamic: The EIGHTH DYNAMIC is the urge toward existence as INFINITY. The eighth dynamic is commonly supposed to be a Supreme Being or Creator. It is correctly defined as *infinity*. It actually embraces the allness of all.

The highest ethic level would be long-term survival concepts with minimal destruction, along all of the dynamics.

An optimum solution to any problem would be that solution which brought the greatest benefits to the greatest number of dynamics. The poorest solution would be that solution which brought the greatest harm to the most number of dynamics.

Activities which brought minimal survival to a lesser number of dynamics and damaged the survival of a greater number of dynamics could not be considered rational activities.

One of the reasons that this society is dying and so forth is that it's gone too far out-ethics. Reasonable conduct and optimum solutions have ceased to be used to such an extent that the society is on the way out.

By out-ethics we mean an action or situation in which an individual is involved, or something the individual does, which is contrary to the ideals, best interests and survival of his dynamics.

For a man to develop a weapon capable of destroying all life on this planet (as has been done with atomic weapons and certain drugs designed by the U.S.Army) and place it in the hands of the criminally insane politicians is obviously not a survival act.

For the government to actively invite and create inflation to a point where a depression is a real threat to the individuals of this society is a nonsurvival action to say the least.

This gets so batty that in one of the South Pacific societies infanticide became a ruling passion. There was a limited supply of food and they wanted to keep down the birthrate. They began using abortion, and if this didn't work, they killed the children. Their second dynamic folded up. That society has almost disappeared.

These are acts calculated to be destructive and harmful to the survival of the people of the society.

Ethics are the actions an individual takes on himself in order to accomplish optimum survival for himself and others on all dynamics. Ethical actions are survival actions. Without a use of ethics we will not survive.

We know that the dynamic principle of existence is Survive!

At first glance that may seem too basic. It may seem too simple. When one thinks of survival, one is apt to make the error of thinking in terms of "barest necessity." That is not survival. Survival is a graduated scale with infinity of immortality at the top and death and pain at the bottom.

Good and Evil, Right and Wrong

Years ago I discovered and proved that man is basically good. This means that the basic personality and the basic intentions of the individual, toward himself and others, are good.

When a person finds himself committing too many harmful acts against the dynamics, he becomes his own executioner. This gives us the proof that man is basically good. When he finds himself committing too many evils, then, causatively, unconsciously or unwittingly, man puts ethics in on himself by destroying himself; and he does himself in without assistance from anybody else.

This is why the criminal leaves clues on the scene, why people develop strange incapacitating illnesses and why they cause themselves accidents and even decide to have an accident. When they violate their own ethics, they begin to decay. They do this all on their own, without anybody else doing anything.

The criminal who leaves clues behind is doing so in hopes that someone will come along to stop him from continuing to harm others. He is *basically* good and does not want to harm others; and in the absence of an ability to stop himself outright, he attempts to put ethics in on himself by getting thrown in prison where he will no longer be able to commit crimes.

Similarly, the person who incapacitates himself with illness or gets himself in an accident is putting ethics in on himself by lessening his ability to harm and maybe even by totally removing himself from the environment that he has been harming. When he has evil intentions, when he is being "intentionally evil," he still has an urge to also stop himself. He seeks to suppress them, and when he cannot do so directly, he does so indirectly. Evil, illness and decay often go hand in hand.

Man is basically good. He is basically well intentioned. He does not want to harm himself or others. When an individual does harm the dynamics, he will destroy himself in an effort to save those dynamics. This can be proven and has been proven in innumerable cases. It is this fact which evidences that man is basically good.

On this basis we have the concepts of right and wrong.

When we speak of ethics, we are talking about right and wrong conduct. We are talking about good and evil.

Good can be considered to be any constructive survival action. It happens that no construction can take place without some small destruction, just as the tenement must be torn down to make room for the new apartment building.

To be good, something must contribute to the individual, to his family, his children, his group, mankind or life. To be good, a thing must contain construction which outweighs the destruction it contains. A new cure which saves a hundred lives and kills one is an acceptable cure.

Good is survival. Good is being more right than one is wrong. Good is being more successful than one is unsuccessful, along constructive lines.

Things are good which complement the survival of the individual, his family, children, group, mankind, life and MEST.[6]

Acts are good which are more beneficial than destructive along these dynamics.

Evil is the opposite of good, and is anything which is destructive more than it is constructive along any of the various dynamics. A thing which does more destruction than construction is evil from the viewpoint of the individual, the future race, group, species, life or MEST that it destroys.

When an act is more destructive than constructive, it is evil. It is out-ethics. When an act assists succumbing more than it assists survival, it is an evil act in the proportion that it destroys.

Good, bluntly, is survival. Ethical conduct is survival. Evil conduct is nonsurvival. Construction is good when it promotes survival. Construction is evil when it inhibits survival. Destruction is good when it enhances survival.

An act or conclusion is a right as it promotes the survival of the individual, future race, group, mankind or life making the conclusion. To be entirely right would be to survive to infinity.

An act or conclusion is wrong to the degree that it is nonsurvival to the individual, future race, group, species or life responsible for doing the act or making the conclusion. The most wrong a person can be on the first dynamic is dead.

The individual or group which is, on the average, more right than wrong (since these terms are not absolutes, by far) should survive. An individual who, on the average, is more wrong than right will succumb.

---

[6] MEST: a word coined from the initial letters of matter, energy, space and time, which are the component parts of the physical universe.

While there could be no absolute right or absolute wrong, a right action would depend upon its assisting the survival of the dynamics immediately concerned; a wrong action would impede the survival of the dynamics concerned.

Let us look at how these concepts of right and wrong fit into our current society.

This is a dying society. Ethics have gone so far out and are so little understood that this culture is headed for succumb at a dangerous rate.

A person is not going to come alive, this society is not going to survive, unless ethics tech is gotten hold of and applied.

When we look at Vietnam, inflation, the oil crisis, corruption of government, war, crime, insanity, drugs, sexual promiscuity, etc., we are looking at a culture on the way out. This is a direct result of individuals failing to apply ethics to their dynamics.

It actually starts with individual ethics. Dishonest conduct is nonsurvival. Anything is unreasonable or evil which brings about the destruction of individuals, groups or inhibits the future of the race.

The keeping of one's word, when it has been sacredly pledged, is an act of survival, since one is then trusted, but only so long as he keeps his word.

To the weak, to the cowardly, to the reprehensibly irrational, dishonesty and underhanded dealings, the harming of others and the blighting of their hopes seem to be the only way of conducting life.

Unethical conduct is actually the conduct of destruction and fear. Lies are told because one is afraid of the consequences should one tell the truth. Destructive acts are usually done out of fear. Thus, the liar is inevitably a coward, and the coward inevitably a liar.

The sexually promiscuous woman, the man who breaks faith with his friend, the covetous pervert are all dealing in such nonsurvival terms that degradation and unhappiness are part and parcel of their existence.

It probably seems quite normal and perfectly all right to some to live in a highly degraded society full of criminals, drugs, war and insanity, where we are in constant threat of the total annihilation of life on this planet.

Well, let me say that this is not normal and it is not necessary. It *is* possible for individuals to lead happy productive lives without having to worry about whether or not they are going to be robbed if they walk outside their door or whether Russia is going to declare war on the United States. It is a matter of ethics. It is simply a matter of individuals applying ethics to their lives and having their dynamics in communication and surviving.

Morals

Now, we have ethics as survival. But what of such things as morals, ideals, love? Don't these things go above "mere survival"? No, they do not.

Romantic novels and television teach us that the hero always wins and that good always triumphs. But it appears that the hero doesn't always win and that good does not always triumph. On a shorter view we can see villainy triumphing all about us. The truth of the matter is that the villainy is sooner or later going to lose. One cannot go through life victimizing one's fellow beings and wind up anything but trapped—the victim himself.

However, one doesn't observe this in the common course of life. One sees the villains succeeding everywhere, evidently amassing money, cutting their brother's throat, receiving the fruits of the courts and coming to rule over men.

Without looking at the final consequence of this, which is there just as certainly as the sun rises and sets, one begins to believe that evil triumphs, whereas one has been taught that only good triumphs. This can cause the person himself to have a failure and can actually cause his downfall.

As for ideals, as for honesty, as for one's love of one's fellow man, one cannot find good survival for one or for many where these things are absent.

The criminal does not survive well. The average criminal spends the majority of his adult years caged like some wild beast and guarded from escape by the guns of good marksmen.

A man who is known to be honest is awarded survival—good jobs, good friends. And the man who has his ideals, no matter how thoroughly he may be persuaded to desert them, survives well only so long as he is true to those ideals.

Have you ever seen a doctor who, for the sake of personal gain, begins to secretly attend criminals or peddle dope? That doctor does not survive long after his ideals are laid aside.

Ideals, morals, ethics, all fall within this understanding of survival. One survives so long as he is true to himself, his family, his friends, the laws of the universe. When he fails in any respect, his survival is cut down.

In the modern dictionary we find that *ethics* are defined as "morals" and *morals* are defined as "ethics." These two words are *not* interchangeable.

Morals should be defined as a code of good conduct laid down out of the experience of the race to serve as a uniform yardstick for the conduct of individuals and groups.

Morals are actually laws.

The origin of a moral code comes about when it is discovered through actual experience that some act is more nonsurvival than prosurvival. The prohibition of this act then enters into the customs of the people and may eventually become a law.

In the absence of extended reasoning powers, moral codes, so long as they provide better survival for their group, are a vital and necessary part of any culture.

Morals, however, become burdensome and protested against when they become outmoded. And although a revolt against morals may have as its stated target the fact that the code no longer is applicable as it once was, revolts against moral codes generally occur because individuals of the group or the group itself has gone out-ethics to a point where it wishes to practice license against these moral codes, not because the codes themselves are unreasonable.

If a moral code were thoroughly reasonable, it could, at the same time, be considered thoroughly ethical. But only at this highest level could the two be called the same.

The ultimate in reason is the ultimate in survival.

Ethical conduct includes the adherence to the moral codes of the society in which we live.

Justice

When an individual fails to apply ethics to himself and fails to follow the morals of the group, justice enters in.

It is not realized generally that the criminal is not only antisocial but is also antiself.

A person who is out-ethics, who has his dynamics out of communication, is a potential or active criminal in that crimes against the prosurvival actions of others are continually perpetrated. Crime might be defined as the reduction of the survival level along any one of the eight dynamics.

Justice is used when the individual's own out-ethics and destructive behavior begin to impinge too heavily on others.

In a society run by criminals and controlled by incompetent police, the citizens reactively identify any justice action or symbol with oppression.

But we have a society full of people who do not apply ethics to themselves, and in the absence of true ethics one cannot live with others and life becomes miserable. Therefore we have justice, which was developed to protect the innocent and decent.

When an individual fails to apply ethics to himself and follow the moral codes, the society takes justice action against him.

Justice, although it unfortunately cannot be trusted in the hands of man, has as its basic intention and purpose the survival and welfare of those it serves. Justice, however, would not be needed when you have individuals who are sufficiently sane and in-ethics that they do not attempt to blunt others' survival.

Justice would be used until a person's own ethics render him fit company for his fellows.

Ethics, Justice and Your Survival

In the past the subject of ethics has not really been mentioned very much. Justice was however. Justice systems have long been used as a substitute for ethics systems. But when you try to substitute ethics for justice, you get into trouble.

Man has not had an actual workable way of applying ethics to himself. The subjects of ethics and justice have been terribly aberrated.

We now have the tech of ethics and justice straightened out. This is the only road out on the subject that man has.

People have been trying to put ethics in on themselves for eons without knowing how. Ethics evolved with the individual's attempts at continued survival.

When a person does something which is out-ethics (harms his and others' survival), he tries to right this wrong. Usually he just winds up caving himself in. (Caved-in means mental and/or physical collapse to the extent that the individual cannot function causatively.)

They cave themselves in because, in an effort to restrain themselves and stop themselves from committing more harmful acts, they start withdrawing and withholding themselves from the area they have harmed. A person who does this becomes less and less able to influence his dynamics and thus becomes a victim of them. It is noted here that one must have done to other dynamics those things which other dynamics now seem to have the power to do to him. Therefore, he is in a position to be injured and he loses control. He can become, in fact, a zero of influence and a vacuum for trouble.

This comes about because the person does not have the basic tech of ethics. It has never been explained to him. No one ever told him how he could get out of the hole he's gotten himself into. This tech has remained utterly unknown.

So he has gone down the chute.

Ethics is one of the primary tools a person uses to dig himself out with.

Whether he knows how to or not, every person will try to dig himself out. It doesn't matter who he is or what he's done, he's going to be trying to put ethics in on himself, one way or the other.

Even with Hitler and Napoleon there were attempts at self-restraint. It's interesting in looking at the lives of these people how thoroughly they worked at self-destruction. The self-destruction is their attempt at applying ethics to themselves. They worked at this self-destruction on several dynamics. They can't put ethics in on themselves; they can't restrain themselves from doing these harmful acts, so they punish themselves. They realize they are criminals and cave themselves in.

All beings are basically good and are attempting to survive as best they can. They are attempting to put ethics in on their dynamics.

Ethics and justice were developed and exist to aid an individual in his urge towards survival. They exist to keep the dynamics in communication. The tech of ethics is the actual tech of survival.

An individual's dynamics will be in communication to the degree that he is applying ethics to his life. If one knows and applies ethics tech to his life, he can keep the dynamics in communication and continuously increase his survival.

That is why ethics exists, so that we can survive like we want to survive, by having our dynamics in communication.

Ethics are not to be confused with justice. Justice is used only after a failure of the individual to use ethics on himself. With personal ethics in across the dynamics, third dynamic justice disappears as a primary concern. That's where you get a world without crime.

A man who steals from his employer has his third dynamic out of communication with his first dynamic. He is headed for a prison sentence, or unemployment at best, which is not what one would call optimum survival on the first and second dynamic (not to mention the rest of them). He probably believes he is enhancing his survival by stealing, yet if he knew the tech of ethics he would realize he is harming himself as well as others and will only end up further down the chute.

The man who lies, the woman who cheats on her husband, the teenager who takes drugs, the politician who is involved in dishonest dealings, all are cutting their own throats. They are harming their own survival by having their dynamics out of communication and not applying ethics to their lives.

It may come as a surprise to you, but a clean heart and clean hands are the only way to achieve happiness and survival. The criminal will never make it unless he reforms; the liar will never be happy or satisfied with himself until he begins dealing in truth.

The optimum solution to any problem presented by life would be that which leads to increased survival on the majority of the dynamics.

Thus we see that a knowledge of ethics is necessary to survival.

' The knowledge and application of ethics is the way out of the trap of degradation and pain.

We can, each and every one of us, achieve happiness and optimum survival for ourselves and others by using ethics tech.

What Happens if the Dynamics Go Out-Ethics

It is important to remember that these dynamics comprise life. They do not operate singly without interaction with the other dynamics.

Life is a group effort. None survive alone.

If one dynamic goes out-ethics, it goes out of communication with (to a greater or lesser degree) the other dynamics. In order to remain in communication, the dynamics must remain in-ethics.

Let us take the example of a woman who has totally withdrawn from the third dynamic. She won't have anything to do with any groups or the people of her town. She has no friends. She stays locked in her house all day thinking (with some misguided idea of independence or individuality) that she is surviving better on her first dynamic. Actually she is quite unhappy and lonely and lives in fear of other human beings. To ease her misery and boredom, she begins to take sedatives and tranquilizers which she becomes addicted to and then starts drinking alcohol as well.

She is busy "solving" her dilemma with further destructive actions. You can see how she has driven her first, second and third dynamics out of communication. She is actively destroying her survival on her dynamics. These actions are out-ethics in the extreme, and it would not be surprising if she eventually killed herself with the deadly combination of sedatives and alcohol.

Or let us take the man who is committing destructive acts on the job. These acts need not be large; they can be as simple as showing up late for work, not doing as professional a job on each product as he is capable of, damaging equipment or hiding things from his employer. He does not have to be overtly engaged in the total destruction of the company to know that he is committing harmful acts.

Now, this man finds himself sliding more and more out-ethics as time goes along. He feels he must hide more and more and he does not know how to stop this downward spiral. Very likely it never even occurred to him that he could stop it. He is lacking the tech of ethics. He probably doesn't realize that his actions are driving his dynamics out of communication.

This may affect his other dynamics in various ways. He will probably be a bit miserable, and since he is basically good, he will feel guilt. He goes home at night and his wife says cheerily, "How was your day?" and he cringes a little and feels worse. He starts drinking to numb the misery. He is out of communication with his family. He is out of communication on his job. His performance at work worsens. He begins to neglect himself and his belongings. He no longer gets joy out of life. His happy and satisfying life slips away from him. Because he does not know and apply ethics tech to his life and his dynamics, the situation goes quite out of his control. He has unwittingly become the effect of his own out-ethics. Unless he gets his life straightened out by using ethics, he will undoubtedly die a miserable man.

Now I ask you, what kind of life is that? Unfortunately, it is all too common in our current times.

A person cannot go out-ethics on a dynamic without it having disastrous consequences on his other dynamics.

It is really quite tragic, the tragedy being compounded by the fact that it is so unnecessary. If man only knew the simple tech of ethics, he could achieve for himself the self-respect, personal satisfaction and success that he only believes himself capable of dreaming of, not attaining.

Man is seeking survival. Survival is measured in pleasure. That means, to most men, happiness, self-respect, the personal satisfaction of a job well done and success. A man may have money, he may have a lot of personal belongings, etc., but he will not be happy unless he actually has his ethics in and knows he came by these things honestly. These rich political and financial criminals ate not happy; they may be envied by the common man for their wealth, but they are very unhappy people who more often than not come to grief eventually through drug or alcohol addiction, suicide or some other means of self-destruction.

Let us look at the all-too-common current occurrence of out-ethics on the second dynamic. This is generally thought to be perfectly acceptable behavior.

It is easy to see how second dynamic out-ethics affects the other dynamics.

Let us say we have a young woman who is somewhat happily married and decides to have an affair with her boss, who happens to be a good friend of her husband. This is quite obviously out-ethics, as well as against the law, although an amazing number of people would find this sort of behavior acceptable or mildly objectionable at most.

This is quite a destructive act, however. She will suffer from guilt; she will feel deceitful and unhappy because she knows she has committed a bad act against her husband. Her relationship with him will certainly suffer and since her boss is experiencing much the same thing in his home, she and her boss will begin to feel bad towards each other, as they begin to target each other for their misfortune. Their dynamics end up quite messed up and out of communication. She will feel unhappy on her first dynamic as she has abandoned her own moral code. Her second dynamic will be out of communication and she may even begin to find fault with and dislike her husband. The situation at work is strained as she is now out of communication with her boss and her fellow workers. Her boss has ruined his relationship and friendship with her husband. She is so embroiled in these three dynamics that they go totally out of communication with her fourth, fifth and sixth dynamics. This is all the result of ethics going out on a single dynamic.

The repercussions spread insidiously to all the dynamics.

Our survival is assured only by our knowledge and application of ethics to our dynamics in order to keep them in communication.

Through ethics we can achieve survival and happiness for ourselves and for planet Earth.

L. Ron Hubbard

THE CREED OF THE
CHURCH OF SCIENTOLOGY
BY L. RON HUBBARD
[1954]

We of the Church believe:

That all men of whatever race, color or creed were created with equal rights;

That all men have inalienable[7] rights to their own religious practices and their performance;

That all men have inalienable rights to their own lives;

That all men have inalienable rights to their sanity;

That all men have inalienable rights to their own defense;

That all men have inalienable rights to conceive, choose, assist or support their own organizations, churches and governments;

That all men have inalienable rights to think freely, to talk freely, to write freely their own opinions and to counter or utter or write upon the opinions of others;

---

[7] *inalienable*: that may not be taken away or transferred.

That all men have inalienable rights to the creation of their own kind;

That the souls of men have the rights of men;

That the study of the mind and the healing of mentally caused ills should not be alienated[8] from religion or condoned[9] in non-religious fields;

And that no agency less than God has the power to suspend or set aside these rights, overtly or covertly.

And we of the Church believe:

That man is basically good;

That he is seeking to survive;

That his survival depends upon himself and upon his fellows and his attainment of brotherhood with the universe.

And we of the Church believe that the laws of God forbid man:

To destroy his own kind;

To destroy the sanity of another;

To destroy or enslave another's soul;

To destroy or reduce the survival of one's companions or one's group.

And we of the Church believe that the spirit can be saved and that the spirit alone may save or heal the body.

L. Ron Hubbard

---

[8] *alienated*: withdrawn or detached from.
[9] *condoned*: given tacit (implied or unspoken) approval.

BRAHMA KUMARIS SCRIPTURES

INTRODUCTION

The Speaker who answers the questions posed in the following pages is not of this world. He has entered this world for a short time to impart some very important information to humanity as a whole, and to you, the reader, in particular.

The Source of this information provides answers to fundamental human questions which have been asked throughout the ages. He speaks to us with an authority born of absolute certainty; with a complete picture of our past, present and future; with the unconditional love and compassion possible only when there is total detachment, from a place of seminal power, and with a peace that far surpasses human understanding.

The factual details about the origin of these materials are outlined in essence below. We have kept this description to a minimum so that your intellect may be stimulated to explore the text on its own merit without stumbling over the events that accompanied these revelations.

Divine revelations have occurred in various historical periods according to the need of the time. On their basis, various religions have been founded. The need of the present age is God's knowledge—presented outside of the framework of religious dialogue, presented freely and openly to all seekers after truth. Each and every one may believe it or not, and take whatever she or he wishes from it—from a single inspiration to complete understanding.

BACKGROUND

In 1936, in a country that is now called Pakistan., a being describing Himself as "The Supreme Soul Shiva"—"the Knowledgful, Luminous, and Blissful Self"—entered the 60-year-old body of a well-established Sindhi gentleman, a multimillionaire diamond merchant named Dada Lekraj.

In a short while, several hundred people began to gather on a regular basis to listen to the teachings of Shiva being spoken through Dada, whom Shiva renamed Prajapita Brahma (The Father of Humanity). The community of these people eventually became known as the Brahma Kumaris. The teachings, referred to by Shiva as the Ancient Raja Yoga of Bharat, became a daily morning discourse known as the Murli, which, literally translated, means "flute."

Now, for the first time in the history of the Brahma Kumaris organization, a direct translation of some of the major points of the Murlis is being presented. The extracts have been grouped under two main subject areas of the Brahma Kumaris curriculum, and within that they have been ordered according to linear logic. To present the Murlis in their entirety in the non-linear fashion in which they were spoken, and with sufficient annotation to make them coherent to the yogicly untrained, would have been a daunting task. However, for anyone who wishes to complete a basic introductory course in meditation and spiritual knowledge provided without charge at any of the more than 5000 Brahma Kumaris centers worldwide, the full Murlis are available for further study.

Translator's Note

Great care has been taken to maintain the style and authenticity of the original Hindi spoken word. As this is an oral rather than written text, words are used sparingly. Many words that are required for clear communication in English are simply not present in the Hindi versions; they are either left out or assumed. To show where this has happened in the discourse, we have relied on the use of brackets to indicate what is implied in the Hindi original.

Some Hindi words have been retained in the text, as there is no one adequate English word to explain them; or in some cases because they are defined in the text itself. These Hindi words are italicized and their meaning explained in the endnotes.

Stylistically, we have endeavored to keep as close to the Hindi construct as possible. We felt it was important to show which words were given the primary emphasis in each sentence syntax as a way of revealing important spiritual and poetic subtext. Oral Hindi reveals a rhythm and flow different from English, the former being more a language of the heart, the latter more a scientific language of the head. In this translation, we have attempted to balance the flow of love with the clarity and simplicity that the English language demands.

Verb tenses change often, even from one line to the next. This is due to the unique capability of the Speaker to be aware of the past, present and future all at once.

Please note that any reference to the Speaker in the masculine has been done as a convention, rather than as a gender bias. As well as using the pronoun "I", the Speaker often refers to Himself in the objective third person. The original Hindi word "Baba" means Father. It has been retained in the text to indicate the affection with which the Speaker is addressing (and is regarded by) His listeners. Because this term appears frequently, it has not been italicized. "Baba" also means Father in other languages such as Kiswahili and Arabic. Within the masculinity of the term Baba the feminine is also implied (In some cultures the grandmother or maternal aunt is referred to as "Ba"). When the Speaker has used the word Bap, we have sometimes literally translated it as 'Father,' and sometimes more poetically used the term 'spiritual Father'-- again to convey the sweetness of tone.

SCRIPTURES

SOUL

What is our spiritual identity?

First of all, human beings should know the soul, (but) the
   knowledge of the soul is not with any human being.
Father[1] sits and explains to the spiritual children that the soul is
   so very tiny.
It is so very tiny.

Compared to such a tiny soul, the body is so big.
When the tiny soul separates (from the body), then it is not able
   to see anything.
Such a tiny point performs so many activities!
Such a huge sky and earth are seen through these eyes.
Nothing exists (for the soul) when it leaves.
Such a tiny soul becomes pure and impure.
Think deeply about these aspects.

The first thing I say (to you) is:
Be soul conscious and sit (in this consciousness].
Not as a body, (but) understand yourself to be a soul and sit.
Only the soul activates these organs.
This is the first lesson

While living in the body, such a tiny soul creates so many
   things, sees so many things.
How it works is a wonder!

The soul is eternal

---

[1] The word *Father* is translated from the Hindi word *Bap*, which is not as
formal or as austere as the English word Father can sometimes sound. See
Translator's Notes.

The soul is not something that is created

You, the soul, are imperishable, the body is perishable ...
"I am a soul, not a body"—
Father teaches these words at this time.

Can the soul be seen?

No one can see the soul.
The soul sees the body.
The body cannot see the soul.
When the soul leaves, the body becomes inert.
The soul cannot be seen.
The body can be seen.

It is understood [that] the soul exists.
It can be seen through divine vision.
Baba[2] says: What will you understand by seeing it?
The soul is just a tiny point.
Doctors try so hard to see the soul, but they cannot see it.
The soul is realized.
Father asks: Now, did you realize the soul?

The soul cannot be seen with these (physical) eyes.
One 'feels' the soul is within.

Doctors remove human hearts, put them aside, then replace
   them.
But no one knows about the soul.

Just as the Soul is hidden and the body is visible, the soul can-
   not be seen through these eyes; it is hidden.
It is definitely there, but it is hidden by the body ...
The soul itself says: "I am incorporeal.
By coming into the corporeal, I have become hidden."

---

2 When the Speaker refers to Himself as "Baba," meaning Father, the
original Hindi word has been retained in the text because this term conveys the intimacy between the soul and the Supreme. See the Translator's
Notes for further information about the use of this term.

What is the form of the soul?

The form of the soul is zero, or one can also say that it is a
  point.
Now, one should think about this.
How subtle the soul is!

It is remembered that in the center of the forehead sparkles an
  amazing star.
It is also remembered that this body is the throne of the incorporeal soul.

The soul is like a point, the subtlest of forms, (and it) resides in
  the center of the forehead.

Not even one human being has the knowledge of the self, the
  soul.
"I am a soul, this is a body."
There are two things, are there not!
This body is made of the five elements.
The soul is imperishable, a point.
What can it be made of?
It is such a tiny point!

The soul is neither called male nor female.
The soul is unique.
A name is given to the male or female body.

People come in many different forms and shades, but there is
  no variation in the form and color of the soul; all are alike.
There is variation only in the role that each soul plays.
Whereas human beings grow in size, souls do not grow in size.
Souls are of just one size.

It is only the soul who talks, walks.
It is such a tiny, tiny point.
It never becomes smaller or bigger.
It is never destroyed.

The soul is immortal.
It never burns, it never splits, nor does it reduce (in size).

The intellect is now aware:
"I am a point."
This is called 'realization of the soul.'
Then in order to 'see' [the soul], one needs insight.
These are all aspects to be understood.

What is the relationship between soul and body?

The soul says, "This is my body."
The body would not say: "My soul."
The soul is in the body.
It says. "This is my body."

"My eyes, nose, ears"—the body does not say this either.
"These are organs.
I, the soul, am separate from them.
Through these organs, I perform action.
It is not that I am the organs which perform action!
I am separate from them,
I am a soul."

The material of the whole world is created from the five elements.
However, the soul is not created.
The soul exists eternally.

There is such a vast difference between the body and the soul.
The body becomes such a large puppet made of the five elements.
Even if it (the puppet) is small, it is still definitely larger than the soul.
To begin with, the foetus is very tiny.
When it becomes a little larger, the soul enters.
(The body) then continues to grow and becomes so big.

Until the soul enters a body, it cannot see through the eyes.
It cannot hear through the ears.
Without the soul, the body becomes inert
The soul is the conscious living being.

The foetus may be in the body, but if the soul has not entered it
is not active.
When the soul enters the body, there is movement and noise in-
side (the womb).
Then one knows the soul has entered.
The organs of the foetus begin to move.

The soul is separate from the body.
When the soul enters a body, it is called a human being.
One only receives a body in order to perform action.
The soul is called the life force.
When the soul leaves (the body), then it is said:
"The life force has departed."

Action has to be performed through the body.
By (the soul) becoming separate from the body, there is hushed
silence.

When the soul leaves (the body), neither the soul nor the body
can speak.
Without the soul, the body cannot do anything.
When the soul leaves the body, then no matter what is done to
the body, would the soul feel anything?
Only when the soul and the body are combined does the soul
feel.

When the soul leaves the body, the body is said to be dead.
It is then of no use.
When the soul leaves, an odor is created in the body.
Then, they go and burn the body ...
You children should have this pure pride: "I am a soul."

You need to become completely soul conscious.
It is the body which dies.
It is not that the soul dies.
The soul cannot die! To say (that it dies) is wrong.
"The soul left the body"—these words are right.
This is a matter of understanding.

When the soul is not in the body, the body does not have any
  consciousness.
The soul leaves one body and makes a connection with another
  body—then that body becomes alive.

The soul does not commit suicide.
Suicide of the body is committed.
The soul always exists.
It goes and adopts another life, meaning, another body.

When the soul leaves the body, then (it is said)
"When you die, (for you) the world is dead."
Then no relationships exist.
Until the soul enters the mother's womb again, no world exists
  for you.
You are separate from the world.

The soul is the master.
It leaves one body and enters another in order to play a part.
What a wonder!

What makes souls different from each other?

All souls are actors.
The (physical) features of one birth cannot compare with the
  features of another; the part of one birth cannot compare with
  that of another.
No one knows who one was in the past and what one will become in the future.

All souls have exactly the same form, but the bodies are differ-
  ent ...
You will never see two bodies exactly the same.
The part of each and every soul is recorded within itself.
A soul leaves one body, adopts another and plays its own part.
Each one's part is its own; one cannot be compared to another.
No actors are ever alike.

The part of some is that of a hundred years, some that of
  eighty, some that of two years, and some that of six months.
Some (souls) leave (the body) as soon as they are born.

While in the womb, some leave even before taking birth.

Each one has received a unique part; it is an eternal part.

One needs to understand the soul:
"I am a soul, this is my body.
I come here into this body and play my part ..."
All are souls anyway—some have this much part, some have
   this much.
This is a deep, unlimited drama.

Where do souls come from?

From Paramdham³, the incorporeal world ...
There, souls remain beyond happiness and sorrow.

The place where you reside as brothers is the original Home, or
   the land of Nirvana,⁴ which is also called the Incorporeal
   World.

Just as stars are seen in the sky, in the same way there also, souls
   are like tiny, tiny stars.
That (Home) is beyond the sky where there is not the brightness of the sun or the moon.

This (physical world) is not Home.
Only that (world) where God and you children, the souls, reside
   can be called Home.
This body does not exist there.

This body is created out of five elements.

---

³ *Paramdham* is the name given to the supreme region or incorporeal
world. In this text, it is also referred to as the Home, *Nirvana*, the world
beyond sound, the land of silence (*Shantidham*), the land beyond sound
(*Nirvandham*).

⁴ In this text, *Nirvana* is another name for the soul world, the land of silence. In Hinduism it generally means extinction, in the sense of extinguishing all worldly desire and attaining knowledge which is free from
illusion. In Buddhism, it means the transcendence of the ego-self and the
attainment of supreme knowledge.

So, these five elements draw the soul to come down and reside
here ...
The sky, ether—these elements do not exist there ...
The soul has adopted this property, this is why it has become
attached to the body.
However, we souls are residents of that place.
All souls are the residents of the supreme region.
The soul comes here to play a part.
Then it makes effort to return to its supreme region.

With great love, Father continues to explain to the children:
The one who plays a part is the soul.
It will definitely adopt a body, then play a part.
The soul's place of residence is the land of silence.
Children know souls reside in the great dimension of light.

In reality, all human souls [originally] reside there in the su-
preme region.
They have come here to play a part.
It is a long and complicated journey, but the soul reaches (here)
in a second.
Even aeroplanes, etc. could not travel that fast ...
Whether a soul leaves a body and takes another one, or whether
new souls come (down) from up above, the time taken (for
both) is the same.
New souls continue to come down, do they not!
The population continues to increase.
Nothing can travel as fast as the soul.

How does the soul take rebirth?

Again and again, your soul sheds one body and adopts another.
At the present time whatever is your present form will not re-
main in the next birth.
One (form) cannot be the same as another.
The soul sheds one body and adopts another, so its activity,
thoughts etc. everything changes.
The soul has to play such a variety of different parts.
It plays a part through a variety of names, forms, countries,
times and activities.
The activity continues to change;

sometimes it is that of a king, sometimes of a pauper.

However, it is not that the human soul becomes a cat or a dog.
Father says: Beloved children, a human being only becomes a
  human being.

It isn't that a male will take a male body again.
Souls continue to change their costumes.
Some (take) a male costume and some (take) a female costume.

All souls have sanskaras[5] within them.
Then by adopting a body, the sanskaras emerge.

Only the soul understands, only the soul listens through the or-
  gans.
Only the soul carries sanskaras with itself.
Baba gives the example of those who fight: they carry their san-
  skaras with them, do they not!
Then, in their next birth, they go back into battle again.
In the same way, you children also carry sanskaras (with you).

The soul says. "I shed one body according to my sanskaras, I
  then adopt another."
Rebirth definitely occurs.
Whatever part the soul has received it continues to play it, and
  according to its sanskaras continues to take another birth.
Good or bad sanskaras remain in the soul.
According to those sanskaras one also receives a body like that.
Everything depends on the soul.

The body is left in a second, and off the soul runs.
The next body is already prepared.
In one second, it leaves one body, and enters the womb of the
  next.
If someone has a karmic account[6] in London, in a second the
  soul will go to London and take birth there.

---

 [5] No one word is sufficient to translate *sanskaras*. The term refers to past
impressions left within the subconscious of the soul from previous actions. These include habits, personality traits and memories of the subconscious mind.

After playing a part through the body, one then separates from
   the body.
Those (physical) actors finish their parts and change their costumes.
You too remove your old costume and adopt a new costume.

How can one realize the soul?

When a soul enters a body, it is given a name because it is
   through the body that one needs to play a part.
So human beings then come into the consciousness of the
   body: "I am so-and-so."
The same soul continues to play its eternal part through its
   body.
Then it is this body which everyone continues to remember.
It is because this body is either good or bad that everyone is
   drawn to it.

Your love has become entwined with the perishable body, this
   is why you end up crying ...
Now that you understand yourself to be an eternal soul, there is
   no need to cry, because you are soul conscious.
The spiritual Father now makes you children soul conscious.
By being body conscious, there are tears.
People cry over a perishable body.
(Even though) they also understand that the soul does not die.
Father says. Understand yourself to be a soul, then there is no
   need to cry.
Why do you hold on to the attachment to the body? ...
Understand yourself to be an eternal soul.

So whom should one love?
The eternal soul!
One should only love that which is eternal.
It isn't that one should love a perishable body.
The entire world is perishable.

---

6 *Karma* means action. *Karmic account* refers to the connection or unset-
tled business of a soul which determines the relationships and location of
its next birth.

Each and everything is perishable.
The body is perishable.
The soul is imperishable.

Your vision should always go towards the soul.
The soul resides in the center of the forehead.
When one's vision falls on the body, obstacles come.
It is the soul that one should talk to.
It is only the soul that should be seen.
Renounce body consciousness.

Understand the self to be a soul, moment by moment.
"I, the soul, adopt this body.
The spiritual Father is now teaching us souls."
This is the spiritual knowledge which the spiritual Father gives.
The first and foremost thing is that children need to remain
    soul conscious.
To remain soul conscious is a very elevated destination.

What is the soul's religion?

The soul does not belong to any religion.
When the soul adopts a body it then says:
"I, so-and-so, belong to such-and-such a religion."
What is the religion of the soul?
Firstly, the soul is like a point, the embodiment of peace; it re-
    sides in the land of peace.

The soul needs to be shown its original religion.
Father also says:
I am Peace, (I am) the One who resides in the land of peace.
In reality, you are also a soul.
Your original religion is peace. ...
The phrase Om Shanti is good:
(It means) "I am a soul, my original religion is peace.
I, the soul, am a resident of the land of peace."
The meaning is so simple.

Inside of you is a current of peace.
When someone comes here, they say:
"There is a lot of peace here."

Real peace (occurs when) the soul becomes detached from the
body...
You now understand: "Our original religion is definitely that of
peace."

Our original religion is peace.
One would not say that the original religion of the body is
peace.
The body is a perishable thing, the soul is something eternal.

Human beings stumble around so much to attain peace.
They do not know that the original religion of us souls is peace.
Now you know about the religion of the soul.

GOD

Who is God?

The people of today don't know the Father.
They speak of God, but they don't know God.

Neither does anyone have the introduction of the soul.
Nor (does anyone have) the introduction of the Supreme Soul.
That is why Baba says: No one can know Me as I am, or what I
am.
It is only through Me that one can know Me and My creation.

God does not have His own body.
Just as you are a soul, He is also a soul.
However, the Supreme among souls is called the Supreme Soul.
He does not enter the cycle of birth and death.
A soul can only be called Supreme when it is beyond the cycle
of birth and death.

Only God is remembered as the Highest on High.
Whether one says "the Highest on High" or "the most elevated
of all," it is the same thing.
Only the One Father is the most elevated of all.

What is the soul?

If this in itself is not known, how will they know the Supreme
Soul?

It is only from the spiritual Father that you receive the understanding of the soul...

Father says: I am the seed of the human world, the Truth, the
Living Consciousness, the Embodiment of Bliss...

Originally, I have only one name, however, I have been given a
variety of names.

In fact, the name of the Incorporeal Soul is Shiva.[7]

This name is eternal.

It never changes.

I am the Supreme Soul.

My name is Shiva ...

There are numerous other names.

This one—Shiv Baba—is the accurate one.

Shiva means point.

The Father of all souls is One.

All beings with a living consciousness, who reside in a body,
remember that Father.

People of all religions definitely remember the Father, the Supreme Soul.

The Father of all souls is One.

All beings with a living consciousness, who reside in a body,
remember that Father.

People of all religions definitely remember the Father, the Supreme Soul.

What is the form of God?

First of all, one needs to have the complete introduction to
God.

It has never been known that, just as a soul is a star, in the same
way God is also a star.

---

[7] *Shiva* is a Sanskrit word for God which means the Point, the Seed, and
the Benefactor.

He is also a soul, but He is the Supreme among souls and is
  called the Supreme Soul.
It is not that He comes into rebirth.
It is not that he comes into the cycle of birth and death.
No. He does not take rebirth.

So the Supreme Soul does exist, but He is extremely subtle.
He is the subtlest of the subtle.
There is nothing as subtle as He is.
He is an absolute point.
It is because He is so subtle that no one knows him.

It is not possible to see His form ...
His form is not like that of a human being.
Everything definitely has a form.
The tiniest of all is the form of the soul ...

A soul is truly like a star.
The Supreme Father, the Supreme Soul, is also a Star.
But because He is knowledge-full, the Seed, there is power in
  Him ...
Human beings cannot be called the Ocean of Knowledge, the
  Ocean of Love.

Human beings do not know the soul accurately.
In the same way also, the Supreme Soul is not known accu-
  rately.
In the world, human beings have innumerable opinions.
Some say that the soul merges into the Supreme Soul.
Others say something else.
Saying that the soul merges with the Supreme Soul or that the
  soul is the Supreme Soul—to have this understanding is
  wrong.

Some then call Him the eternal, infinite element of light.
Others say that He is beyond name and form.

The Supreme Soul is not what human beings understand Him
  to be, is He!

Just as the soul cannot be seen, but can be realized, in the same
way, the Supreme Soul cannot be seen.
It can (only) be understood that God is the Father of souls.

What is the difference between the soul and the Supreme Soul?

Only the supreme among souls is the Supreme Soul.
You are not supreme.
See how great is the difference between you, the soul, and that
Soul!
You souls are now learning from the Supreme Soul.
God has not learned from anyone
This one is Father, is He not!
You call the Supreme Father, the Supreme Soul "Father," you
also call Him the Teacher and also call Him the Guru.
It is the (same) One.
No other soul can become the Father, Teacher and Guru.
There is only one Supreme among souls who can be called the
Supreme.

You are amazed: How is all the knowledge contained in God!
Where did the knowledge in Him come from that He explains it
to you?
He does not even have a father from whom He could have
taken birth or understood from ...
He sits and gives so much knowledge to the children ...
So the question would certainly arise, would it not:
"Baba, how did you find out?"
Baba says. Children, according to the eternal drama, this knowl-
edge which I teach to you is merged within Me from the be-
ginning.
This is why I am called the Highest-on-High God.

There is no difference between the forms of the soul and Supreme Soul,
however, there is a difference in the part and sanskaras.

Father explains what My sanskaras are and what the sanskaras
of you souls are.

Because of not knowing the form of the soul and the Supreme
Soul, human beings say that the soul and the Supreme Soul
are the same.
A lot of confusion has been created.
The soul of the Father is not larger.
The soul of the Father is the same [size] as that of you children.
It isn't that the children are smaller and the Father is larger. No.

This One is called the Supreme because He is the most knowl-
edgeable.
The Highest on High is God.
He is ever pure.
Children become pure and then become impure, whereas the
Father is always pure.
Father explains: You, the soul, are like a point.
"I, Shiva, am also like a point but I am the Supreme, the Crea-
tor, the Director.
I am the Ocean of Knowledge.
In Me is the knowledge of the beginning, the middle, and the
end of the world.
I am knowledge-full and Blissful.
I shower blessings on everyone. I take everyone into salvation.

No human being can be God.
God is the Ocean of Knowledge.

So now you are receiving this knowledge ...
God, the Father, is the Seed of the human world tree.
He is the unlimited Father of all.
He is the Truth, the Living Consciousness.
In God only is the true knowledge.
He is also called Truth.
No one else has true knowledge.
The Creator is the one Father in whom there is the knowledge
of the whole creation.

Father says:
There is no one who teaches Me.
Nor do I have a father.
Everyone enters a womb, takes sustenance from a mother;

whereas I definitely never enter a womb nor take sustenance
from a mother.
Only the souls of human beings enter a womb.

Only Father says.
I do not come into the cycle of birth and death.
You enter into the cycle of birth and death.
You call Me the Ocean of Knowledge, the Ocean of Happiness.
So I would definitely give knowledge to you.
I am giving it now!

'The Ocean of Mercy, the Ocean of Happiness, the Ocean of
Peace'—this praise has been given to God.
You are souls, but you cannot be called the Ocean of Knowl-
edge, the Ocean of Happiness, the Ocean of Peace.
This praise belongs only to the One Father ...
This praise of the Father is forever.
Shiv Baba is incorporeal and eternally pure.
God only comes for a short time in order to purify.
There is no question of Him being omnipresent.

Why do people say that God is omnipresent?

In fact, human beings do not know the Father at all.
They just say that He is omnipresent.
Some say He is the Infinite Light, and then they say that He is
beyond name and form.
Because of not knowing the Father, they have become impure.

They either say that God is beyond name and form, or that
God is omnipresent.
The difference between both of these concepts is like day and
night.
Nothing that exists is beyond name and form.

Then they say the Supreme Soul is in the dogs and cats, in everything.
Both these concepts are totally opposite.

Although Shiva is worshipped and remembered with a lot of
love, still human beings have said that the Supreme Soul is in
everyone.
So for whom can one have that love?
This is why intellects have become divorced from having love
for the Father.

This is definitely a world of blind faith.
Whatever they keep seeing, they will keep calling all of it God.
So it is blind faith to believe everything to be God, is it not!
They say that everything—the cats, the dogs, the pebbles and
the stones—is God.

The intellects of the devotees wander here and there thinking
about God.
Human beings do not understand anything because they under-
stand the Supreme Soul to be omnipresent.
So, where can the intellect go?
Because they understand God to be omnipresent, they say eve-
rything is a form of God.
They do call out, but the intellect does not have any aim.
Does the intellect go towards the Father, the Supreme Soul?
No!
It does not enter the intellect of any human soul:
"I am remembering that Being of Light, the Point of Light."

It is not that the Supreme Soul is (present) in everyone. No!
Otherwise what would be the point of taking an oath?
If the Supreme Soul is in everyone, then in whose name are
they taking an oath?
To believe in the Supreme Father, the Supreme Soul, to be om-
nipresent is the greatest mistake of all.

God does not experience any sorrow.
God is a separate entity ...
(To say God is omnipresent) is a mistake human beings make
due to which they continue to experience sorrow.
This concept of omnipresence has caused so much loss.

God Himself says, "I come and explain the essence of all the
Vedas[8] and the scriptures ...
The number one lie is to say that the Supreme Soul is omni-
present.
God is the Purifier."

Does God have a personality?

Baba is the Authority of Knowledge
Human beings cannot be authorities of knowledge.
You call Me the Ocean of Knowledge, the Almighty Authority.
This is the praise of the Father.
One should know the occupation of one's Father.

He is the Seed, the Truth, the Living Consciousness, the Em-
bodiment of Bliss, the Ocean of Knowledge and the Ocean of
Peace.
All the virtues are in Him.

God is also called the Incorporeal, the Egoless One.
No one can understand the meaning of this.

Such a spiritual Father has been found by the sweetest spiritual
children:
One who does not accept anything from them,
Who doesn't eat anything, nor drink anything.
He doesn't have any hopes or desires; whereas human beings
definitely have one or another desire—to become wealthy, to
be this or that—
Baba has no desires.
He is the One who does not partake of the elements or the
vices.
It should emerge from the heart:
"We have found such a Father who doesn't eat, drink, or take
anything."
Shiv Baba has no need of anything.
There cannot be anyone (else) like this.

---

[8] The *Vedas* are among the oldest of the Hindu scriptures comprising
four books containing hymns and psalms in praise of the gods.

This One is a wonderful Father who has no desire for Himself.
There is no human being like Him.
Human beings need food, clothes, etc.;
I do not need anything.
Shiv Baba says: I am selfless.
I make you into the masters of the world.
I do not become that Myself;
I have no desire for the fruit.
I am the altruistic Server.

Human beings cannot be altruistic.
Whatever one does, one definitely receives the fruit of that
    (deed).
I cannot accept any fruit.

Look how God, the Father, sits and teaches.
He does not say: "Bow at (My) feet."

Such a great Father relates Knowledge with such humility.
Father is so soft and gentle—just as soft and gentle as a little
    child.

Father sees that "My children are in great sorrow", and so He
    would definitely have mercy, would He not!
God is definitely the merciful Father.
At present, in the whole world there is peacelessness.
Except the One Father, no one can bestow peace.

No one can give peace and happiness here even for one birth,
    because no one has (peace or happiness).
The Bestower is only the One Father.
He is called the Ocean of Peace, Happiness, and Purity.
Only the praise of the Highest-on-High is sung ... (because)
    there is the understanding that peace will only be attained
    from God.

Baba says: I am beyond happiness and sorrow.
Yes, I come and make the children constantly happy.
Eternal Shiva is praised.
They say. Eternal Benefactor, the Bestower of Happiness.

When one experiences sorrow, one goes and seeks refuge with
someone who has greater strength.
This happens in a practical way here.
When one sees a lot of sorrow and can no longer tolerate it, in
desperation one then comes running and seeks refuge with
Baba.
After all, salvation cannot be granted by anyone except the Fa-
ther.

Father is the Lord of the Poor.
This means He is the Father of those in the world who become
. poor and unhappy.
What would be in His heart?
"I am the Lord of the Poor.
Everyone's sorrow and poverty should come to an end."

Where does God reside?

You children know that God resides in Paramdham, the Su-
preme Region.
That is the great dimension of light.
Father reveals such deep, subtle things.
Where has the spiritual Father come from?
From the spiritual world!
It is also called Nirvandham, the land beyond sound and Shan-
tidham, the land of silence.

You know that the Father will always remain up there.
Even when someone says, "Oh God, Father," his vision would
definitely go up above...
The Resident of the far-away land comes to a foreign land.
Only Father is the Resident of the far-away land.

You say "Om Shanti—I, the soul, am peace."
Father also says Om Shanti.
This means you souls are the embodiments of peace.
The Father is also the embodiment of peace.
The original religion of the soul is peace.
The original religion of the Supreme Soul is also peace.
You (once were) the residents of the land of peace.

I, too, am the Resident of that place.

Only pure souls can return Home.
Impure souls cannot return there ...
Maya[9] has made you impure.
Because of being impure, one cannot go to such a far-away,
  holy place.

Now it is time to go Home.
The entire world has love for that Home.
Everyone desires to go to the land of liberation.

Father says:
Understand yourself to be a soul and remember Me.
Then you will come to Me.
Maya has clipped everyone's wings.
No one is able to return (Home).
Otherwise, the soul is capable of flying so very fast.
But no one can go to the supreme region.
No one except the Purifier Father can take anyone to the pure,
  incorporeal world.

How can one experience a relationship with God?

Father says: Hey, sweet, sweet children!
He calls everyone sweet, sweet, because all are the children.
However many human souls there are, all are eternal children of
  the Father.
The body is perishable anyway, the Father is eternal.
The children, the Souls, are also eternal.

The Father's task is to sustain and love.
Such a Father should definitely be remembered.
He cannot be compared to anyone else...
Only the One—whom the Hindus, Muslims, and Christians
  definitely call God the Father—is the unlimited Father.
Children know that Baba is the Ocean of Love who teaches
  everyone with a lot of love.

---

[9] *Maya* is illusion, deception, or falsehood. In the Hindu *Upanishads*, *Maya* stands for false knowledge or the negative principle.

Baba never becomes angry.

Baba always gives understanding with love.
Baba says "child, child," to everyone because Father knows that
I am the Father of unlimited souls.
This unlimited Father is really very loving.
He fulfills all the pure desires of the mind.

There are many yogis in the world, but Baba says:
Not a single one of them has yoga with Me.
They have yoga with my place of residence—the dimension of
light—instead of with Me.

Previously, one used to say: "I am remembering God."
But (at that time), one considered the self to be corporeal while
remembering the Incorporeal.
One never understood oneself to be incorporeal while remembering the Incorporeal.
Now you need to understand yourself to be an incorporeal soul
as you remember the Incorporeal Father.

First of all, from body conscious become soul conscious.
Then, you will be able to inculcate (this knowledge) and remember the Father ...
Everyone is body conscious.
You also understand that if we do not become soul conscious
and do not remember the Father, we remain exactly as we
were previously.

How can we remember a point?
Something large is (more easily) remembered.
(Some ask), "The Supreme Soul, Whom you remember, what is
He?"
Then (others) say: "He is the embodiment of infinite light."
But it is not like this.
It is wrong to remember (the Supreme Soul as) the infinite light.
There needs to be accurate remembrance.
First, one needs to know accurately.

I am known by a rare few.

As I am, what I am—even among you children, only a few
know Me accurately.

Now, how can a point be remembered?.
A point would definitely remember a point, would it not!
The soul knows that I am a point.
Now, you children have this faith that the One whom we call a
Point is very subtle, yet His praise is so great.

(People sing His) praise:
"You are the Mother and You are the Father."
He is the One who gives the happiness of all relationships.
(They also say) "You are the Brother, You are the Friend."
The sweetness of all (relationships) is experienced with Him.

No one knows about the relationship between the soul and the
Supreme Soul.
The Mother and Father are definitely only One.
Father says: I alone am your Mother and Father.
These are extremely deep aspects.

The number one Friend who constantly gives happiness is God.
Human beings do say that God is the Friend.

There is a saying: "Let the hands do the work, let the heart remember the Friend." Continue to work through the physical
organs that perform action, but also remember the Father.

There is One Beloved of all the lovers.
Everyone only remembers the One.
How beautiful is that One!
The soul is beautiful, is it not?
That One is ever-beautiful.

Souls on the path of worship are also lovers of the Beloved, the
Supreme Father, the Supreme Soul but they do not know the
Beloved, nor do they know themselves as souls.
To the extent that Father is remembered, that much will one's
love increase.
So now your love is the spiritual love with the Father.

The fire of spiritual love is ignited inside you...
Now the love of you souls is with the Father.

There can only be real love with Father when one understands
the self as a soul.

God Shiva speaks: I, God Shiva, teach you children Raja Yoga
...
No human being can ever teach this Raja Yoga.
A human being is not teaching you.
The Supreme Soul is teaching you souls.
You must then teach others.

Father explains: Only I come and make you children pure.
You were completely pure, then again you became completely
impure.
Now, in order for you to become pure, I teach you to have yoga
with Me.
Do not say the word 'yoga". It is good to use the word "re-
membrance."
I teach you remembrance.

This is (what has been) called the "Ancient (Raja) Yoga of
Bharat."
In reality it should not be called yoga, but remembrance.
There is effort in this ...
Father says: Become soul conscious; this is the spiritual pilgrim-
age of remembrance; it is not a pilgrimage of knowledge.

You definitely have knowledge, but there is not the powerful
strength of yoga.
Power only comes through purity and staying in remembrance.

By staying on the pilgrimage of remembrance, it is as though
the body is forgotten. If you were to sit in this bodiless stage
for even an hour, how pure you would become!
"I am a soul, a soul."
Sit and study this lesson.
"I, the soul, am Shiv Baba's child."
Each aspect needs to be practiced, does it not!

When you understand yourself to be a soul very strongly, then
the spiritual Father will be remembered finally.
If there is body consciousness, one would not be able to remember the spiritual Father ...

When you understand yourself to be a soul and remember the
Father, then you will become pure ...
This remembrance involves true, incognito effort.
Whether someone remembers or not—it is not something that
is visible.

Your (power) is the power of yoga through which the organs
that perform action are brought under control.
As they continue to become controlled through the power of
yoga, they will definitely become cool.
The organs that perform actions will be brought under control
when you are strong in yoga.
They will become peaceful.

While continuing to remember, limitless happiness will be at-
tained.
Whatever past conflicts and sicknesses etc., existed—all that
will finish ...
You become free from disease ...
Father explains to you in a practical way:
Remember the Father and all your desires will be fulfilled and
you will become happy.

Your yoga is the ancient Raja Yoga.
No one, except the Supreme Father, the Supreme Soul, can
teach this.

What is the ultimate aim of this practice?

It has been explained to the children: "As are the final thoughts,
so is the destination."
When one leaves the body, at that moment, if the intellect wanders off somewhere, [the soul] will have to go and take birth
there.
If at the last moment, one sees the face of one's husband, then
the intellect goes there.

Whatever is the consciousness in which one stays will be of great influence at that end time.

At the end, only the One Father; the Supreme Soul is able to help us.
During the final moments, on the one side there is the limited, and on the other side the unlimited.
Father explains: if you continue to remember well, there will not be untimely death.
You are made immortal.
(But) first of all, one needs to have a loving intellect with the Father.

Father says: you are not to just say, "Baba, Baba," through your lips, but remember Baba internally in such a way that "the final thoughts lead (you) to the destination." Renounce body consciousness and understand oneself to be a soul.
To the extent that one understands oneself to be a soul and remembers the Father—to that extent one's sins will be destroyed.
There is no other solution.

You have been directed by Baba to give the message to everyone. Children know that this message has to be given to hundreds of thousands of people.
There will then be a time when many will come, and you will give the message to many.
Everyone has to receive Baba's message.
The message is very simple.
Just tell them "Consider yourself a soul and remember the Father."

BAWA MUHAIYADDEEN'S TEACHINGS

INTRODUCTION

Who Was M.R. Bawa Muhaiyaddeen?

Muhammad Raheem Bawa Muhaiyaddeen was a Sufi saint, a man of extraordinary wisdom and compassion. For over seventy years he selflessly shared his knowledge and experience with people of every race and religion, and from all walks of life.

Born well before 1900, Bawa Muhaiyaddeen spent his early years traveling throughout the Middle East and India, examining the world's religions and a myriad of spiritual practices. Our record of his life begins around 1914, when pilgrims traveling through the jungles of Sri Lanka first encountered him. Awed by the depth of his wisdom, they asked him to come to their village to be their teacher. Some time later he did so, thereby beginning a life of public service—feeding, healing, and uplifting the lives of all who came to him.

The name Muhaiyaddeen literally means "one who restores to life, faith and the path of purity." Indeed, Bawa did devote himself tirelessly to awakening faith within people's hearts. As a Sufi, he had that special gift of distilling and revealing the essential truth contained within all religions—the oneness of God. Thus, whenever he spoke, Buddhists, Hindus, Muslims, Jews, and Christians would sit together for hours listening to his wisdom.

In 1971 he was invited to come to Philadelphia, the 'City of Brotherly Love.' There, learned and unlearned, young and old responded to his message of unity. Over the next fifteen-year period, until his death in Philadelphia in December, 1986, he divided his time between the United States and Sri Lanka. He spoke on university campuses, in churches, meeting houses, and private homes, as well as on numerous radio and television programs. He reached audiences around the globe, from the United States and Canada to England and Sri Lanka. He was interviewed by Time Magazine, Psychology Today, Harvard Divinity School Bulletin, The Philadelphia Inquirer, and numerous other publications. Over twenty books of his discourses and songs were published, as well as scores of audio- and videocassettes, and artwork.

M.R. Bawa Muhaiyaddeen passed away on December 8, 1986 and is buried in a suburb outside of Philadelphia, at the Fellowship Farm, where a mazâr (place of visitation) is established.

Bawa's work is being continued at the main branch in Philadelphia of the Bawa Muhaiyaddeen Fellowship and at branches in various communities including greater Los Angeles. The headquarters serves as a meeting house and as a reservoir of wisdom materials.

BAWA MUHAIYADDEEN'S TEACHINGS

MEANING OF A TRUE HUMAN BEING

My God, may YOU protect us, sustain us, and give us Your grace. May You lead us on the straight path. May God protect us always, now and forever, and for all time. Ameen.

My precious brothers and sisters, we have to realize the most important thing in the world; we have to realize why we are here. In this world of God's creation, there is the one power and one vibration of the One God existing in all hearts. Every one of us should reflect upon this power. We should think, "What kind of thing is this power?" Only the discriminatory wisdom of humanity can understand, separate, and see what kind of treasure this power is. The knowledge of this wisdom is found only with us, and through this wisdom we can know the power of our God.

This wisdom has been created in the individual by God. It does not exist with such clarity in other beings. Other beings have five levels of consciousness or intelligence, but we have the sixth level of consciousness called divine wisdom. Within us is the power and the divine wisdom which can discriminate and the consciousness which can understand and explain about God. We need to have that consciousness and that wisdom. It is not a simple thing to develop; however, it is the most important thing that we must do. It is easy to talk about, but it is very difficult to act accordingly.

There are people with the qualities of a human being and people with the qualities of animals. The difference cannot be seen just by looking at their faces. It is said that monkeys evolved into human beings; but truly it is human beings who are changed into monkeys. Many may have the faces of people, but they are like beasts, or demons, or monkeys, or idols, or ghosts, or any of the four hundred trillion, ten thousand energies of the elements which form these things. Therefore, not all people can be called a true human being.

A true human being is one who knows this, one in whom wisdom has dawned, and who can use wisdom discriminatingly. A true person understands this wisdom and this consciousness. The tens of millions of beasts who have the faces of people have only the first three levels of consciousness, but a fully realized individual has seven levels: perception, awareness, intellect, judgment, wisdom, divine analytic wisdom, and divine luminous wisdom. We have to think about this. We have to use wisdom and think.

There are six kinds of lives in the creation of God: earth-lives, fire-lives, water-lives, air-lives, ether-lives, and the light-life of the divine ray of the soul which is the power that came from God. But only one kind of life contains the discriminatory wisdom which is the power of God and which contains the perfectly pure shadow-less perfection, and that is the individual, the light-life. God has no shadow, and the soul of the individual has no shadow. That soul is a shadowless, formless power. It is not like the lights which we see; there is no light or power like God. We, in our wisdom, need to think about this.

THE MIND

My sisters and brothers, anything that can be seen can be de-stroyed. There is only one treasure which cannot be seen by the mind, desire, or the physical eyes. That is God. The ray which came from God is the soul, and the light which explains within the soul is wisdom. That light is a power. We should think about this with wisdom.

What is known as God is not a sun, a moon, or a star. God is not a light, a glitter, or anything which can be seen. God is not a color or anything which has been born out of earth, air, fire, water, or ether. Whatever has dawned from the mind is not God. Only God is God, and the only One who can see God is God. The wisdom which sees God has to exist as God. The power and the light which see God have to exist as God.

Mantras, tantras (tricks), magic, and the intentions of our mind are given form by the mind. Once the mind gives form to these, it has to carry them. It makes statue forms and spirit forms. It is like a store. It is a shaker-maker company which shakes things and then makes them into forms. Once it makes the forms, it looks at them and then rejoices and dances. It cries or smiles at them. It praises them and desires them. And when the mind is afflicted by hunger, disease, old age, and death, it becomes sad and perishes. It disinte-grates by looking at its own self. We should think about this, my brothers and sisters.

Like the magnifying glass which can draw the power of the sun's heat and burn things, the mind looks at the objects of creation and draws the power from them. Then the mind converts them into many forms of other energies. Whatever science originates from the creations of God has a beginning and an end. Those scientific creations are subject to decay and destruction; they are not from the Source of God's power. God is the power which has no beginning, no change, and no end. My sisters and brothers, it is this power called God that we must reflect on with our higher states of wisdom.

The creations of God are the stories of God. The spiritual objects which are created by the five elements and which have shadows, and the four hundred trillion, ten thousand glitters of illusion have been created by external and mental visions. They are the things which are admired by the mind and desire. The creations of God are only signs of the existence of God. They are not the reality that is God. They were created in order that we could understand the Ultimate Reality that lies hidden within God's signs. You will be able to reach the Ultimate Reality only if you go beyond these signs. Please, my brothers and sisters, reflect upon this.

The mind creates forms and then bows down to them. It carries them to certain places, worships them, and then carries them back. All these things are carried out by the mind because of its lack of understanding of the reality of God. The thoughts of the mind, the burdens of the mind, the creations of the mind, the statues, the lights, the magic tricks, and the incense are all things which cannot move by themselves. The mind must carry them around, and it rejoices and weeps when worshiping them.

This aspect does not belong to God, nor will the mind and desire ever realize God. None of these mental powers is God, because God is One whom the mind and desire cannot see. When the storm of death strikes, all the things which the mind carried will disintegrate. My brothers and sisters, please reflect upon this with your discriminatory wisdom. We must think about this because we are born with human wisdom and because we are God's noble creations.

We exist as God's secret. With the wisdom which exists as the power of God, we have to extract Life's permanent essence. That essence is what can see God. It exists within everything, everywhere. It is the power which understands. We must think about this, my brothers and sisters.

All things which can be seen and which have been created will be destroyed. But God is a treasure which has no form nor shape; therefore, God can never be destroyed.

THE SHORE OF THE HEART

God is not a darkness, but is an ever-existent light. Spirit is not the sun or the moon, but is a light which fills all of the universes, everywhere. It has no torpor. Its power exists as wisdom within wisdom and gives all explanations. It is a treasure which explains all the universes, everywhere. That is God. That is the One. God is a great power, a wise power. My sisters, my brothers, I love you. We have to realize this. If we do not understand this, then we can never reach God. We have to think about and understand this. Here is a song:

> The good people who have seen
> The shore of the heart
> Will reach the shore.[1]
> The good people who have transcended the mind,
> Have reached the shore of God.

Those who are swimming in the sea of maya must cross that sea to get to the shore. They must reach the shore which is God. One who does not transcend the mind or desire will never reach the shore of the heart or know God. This sea of maya, this desire, this demon of the mind has to be transcended. It is easy to talk about, but it is very difficult to act accordingly. This must be understood.

All the physical visions must be pushed back. Everything the mind and the eyes see must be pushed back as you swim forward. Whatever desire thinks about must be pushed back, and you must go forward. What the ears hear must be pushed back, and wisdom must be heard. All of the words of the mouth must be pushed back and must become words spoken by the One. Everything the nose smells must be pushed back and God's fragrance must be inhaled. The visions seen by the eyes must be pushed back and Spirit's

---

[1] Explanation: One who transcends the mind will cross the ocean of *maya* (illusion). It is a huge ocean. We have to reach the shore of this ocean of the mind. Mind and desire can never see the shore of God. The mind is an ocean of *maya*.

sights must be seen. The music heard by the ears and the sixty-four
arts must be pushed back, and God's music must be heard.

Push back the words of the tongue and speak only God's words.
Push back the mental visions seen in the heart and look at Spirit's
vision. Push away all of these things. Push them back with wisdom
and the iman of faith, certitude, and determination. The prerequisites for iman are inner patience, contentment or gratitude, trust in
God, and giving all praise to God. You must go forward in this
way. You must reach the shore of the heart. You must cross the
ocean of maya. You must try to do this, my brothers and sisters.
This is easy to talk about.

It is possible to become a swami, a poet, a king, a beggar, or a
yogi. It is possible to do miracles and tricks. It is possible to study
all of these. But to control the thoughts and be still is very rare. It is
not something which can just be spoken about. It is not a title, a
beard, a mustache, a blanket, a trick, or long fingernails. It is a very,
very rare thing.

All people have faces. But to become a sage is very, very rare. A
true human being has the divine wisdom with which to discriminate. Whoever has the consciousness to know the difference between right and wrong is truly a sage. Anyone can look like a
swami, but to be a true swami is difficult. Anyone can become a
student, but to study about the supreme treasure of God which has
no studying is difficult. Everything can be explained, but to simply
be still is very rare. We must think about this. My brothers and sisters, if we do not realize this during our lifetime it will be a hopeless wonder.

THE PATH OF GOD

My sisters and brothers, I love you. You must know and understand everything which comes along on the path of God. We have
to understand God's story. As you go on understanding yourself,
you will find that God's story exists within you. You are God's
story, and God is your story. This is what you have to understand.

Those who are very learned are fools. The one who has learned
everything is mad. One who has learned everything about the
world is foolish. Satan knows everything but the Truth. Satan will
have completed the learning of everything but the Truth. But one
who has little formal learning is a wise person, and one who has no
such learning is a Gnostic, a Gnani.

The energy understood by the five senses, maya, is not the power which can explain. That power is the divine treasure which is wisdom within wisdom. It is the Original, Great Effulgence. This must be understood.

I love you, my sisters and brothers. Please think about this a little. May God protect us all.

TSALAGI TRADITIONS
(NATIVE AMERICAN)

INTRODUCTION

Dhyani Ywahoo is a member of the traditional Etowah Band of the Eastern Tsalagi (Cherokee) Nation. Trained by her grandparents, she represents the twenty-seventh generation to carry the ancestral wisdom of the Ywahoo linage. In 1969, after generations of secrecy, it was decided to share the teachings of the Tsalagi tradition with non-Native people, to help save the environment. Charged with the duty to rekindle the fire of clear mind and right relationship in these changing times, she has become a guide to all who walk the Beauty Road. She is the founder of Sunray Meditation Society in Bristol, Vermont. The selections are taken from her book *Voices of Our Ancestors: Cherokee Teachings from the Wisdom Fire* (Boston, 1987).

SCRIPTURES

The People of the Fire

TSALAGI ELO – our philosophy, our oral tradition—tells how the Principal People, the Ani Yun Wiwa, originated in the star system known as the Pleiades, whence first arose the spark of individuated mind.

From the mysterious void came forth a sound, and the sound was light, and the light was will, intention to be, born of the emptiness: "Creator Being," fundamental tone of the universal song, underlying all manifestation. Compassionate wisdom arose and well perceived the un-manifest potential of mind streaming forth. Will and compassion together gave birth to the fire of building intelligence, and thus was formed the sacred triangle from which all matter is derived, the Three in One. It is a Mystery, we say.

The first "thought beings," carriers of mind's pure light, existed like cells in one body, of one mind and purpose: to explore the mysteries of mind. Coalescing along twelve vortices of activity, elemental lines of energy or force, mind took form, the One became the many. Star Woman fell to Earth, opening the way for star beings to manifest upon Earth the light of pure mind. The Three Elders precipitated the planets and the animals, while the people were the dream children of the angels, their dreaming arising with the primordial sound.

The twelve original tribes of the Tsalagi Nation each exemplified a particular vortex of activity, a particular creative energy, all moving cohesively together.

Tribe Activity/Energy

Quality of will. Crystal caretakers, maintaining clear thought and rituals to keep form in order. Timekeepers, drummers.

The healers, caretakers, high teachers; the Peace Chief who never sheds blood.

Those with understanding of sacred geometry and astronomy, watchers of the skies, giving instruction on proper building.

Masons, builders of the form shaped by the Three. Local administrators, responsible for good clan and community relations. Craftspeople, creating objects of beauty for prayer, contemplation, and utility.

The scientists, mastering and teaching the wisdom of particulars; observing patterns and possible futures.

Great caretakers of the temples and holy gardens where the sacred food is grown for the communities. Keepers and manifesters of the ritual form.

Sacred warriors, warring on ignorance; the shakers, transformers, life force makers; guardians of correct action.

Ambassadors with other realms, having access to consciousness (this the Ani Gadoah are particularly known for, with their great accessibility to other realms). Planetary understanding; assisting in planetary weather system, distributing energy for the benefit of all beings.

Communicating with stars, creating inventions for clear communication. Bringing forth new plants to feed the people. Expressing a more ethereal manifestation of the conscious building seen in the third line of force.

Of the tenth, eleventh, and twelfth lines of force we do not speak, for their function is beyond words; it cannot be cognized.

Native religion is a whole way of life, based on everything being in relationship. The sacred rituals are to maintain harmonious balance of the energy currents of sun, moon, Earth, the entire universe, so that the seed's bounty can be brought forth. Contemplating this orderly, harmonious universe, ten thousand years ago our ancestors here in the Americas were able to develop a mathematics and an astronomy that reached the highest level. These are things that archaeologists are beginning to learn only now. And it is good that these truths be rediscovered and made known, for the wisdom of our ancestors is a gift to all the children of Earth, that we, too, may be wise and generous in creating a good future for those not yet born.

Three Fundamental Truths

From the Mystery all came forth. All manifestation is in harmony with the sacred Law; nothing is outside of it.

Wisdom is a stream put forth from the Great Mystery, beyond concepts, worlds, or form.

In the beginning was the emptiness. There came forth a sound as light, giving birth to all that we perceive in this and all worlds—the light-sound, the sacred Word, the un-manifest becoming real. The intention of Creator underlies all manifestation, and each human being is aligned with that sacred intention through the energy of will, shaping outcomes by thought, word, and deed.

Will to be, will to know—that sacred blue fire is a color, a tone reminding us of our life's purpose: to understand the nature of mind. As this light observed its flow, it noted intention to be. Its un-manifest potential generated a ray of wisdom. Compassionate wisdom, red fire of equanimity and generosity, in observing itself brought forth the seed of active intelligence, the means to make the un-manifest real, yellow fire of creative mind, wisdom to succeed.

From these Elder Fires Above come all phenomena, one mind exploring itself in myriad forms. This creative process is ongoing at all levels of life.

The triangle and three fires is a symbol of unity, the triune mind. The will to be is intention manifest as action, then beings swim in reaction. The lake is still, a pebble drops, cycles of energy radiate out. So life arises from intention and causes radiating out, becoming the dance around the wheel of life. Sleeping mind perceives the ripples as challenges of life; awakened mind sees them as ripples on a lake. Human beings have a particular opportunity to realize the arising nature of mind, mind's creative nature, and to generate those thoughts and actions which are beneficial to harmony and balance. In this lifetime we may know all worlds, transcend suffering, and transform conflict to manifest a world of peace and beauty.

The First Sacred Fire: Will, Intention to Be

Will is the underlying current, the fire that brings forth that which we perceive as our reality. Many may think of will as a force or energy used to control others, oneself, the environment; yet will is the first building fire, pure intention to do. We may affirm the will to do good, to live in harmony, or we may be unaware of the creative power of will in our lives.

To bring our will into harmony with the sacred Law is to understand our life purpose. Why am I here, what are my gifts? Human life is a great opportunity. Each one has particular gifts, a unique role in the circle. Conscious will becomes manifest as one dedicates one's gifts for the benefit of family, clan, nation, all beings.

From the emptiness spiraled forth the light and sound, and intention to be was the apex of the triangle, doorway through which all manifests. The wise practitioner cultivates the principle of will to overcome habits of conflict and discord, supplemented by the wisdom of compassion and the voice of affirmation. Child mind is aware, yet one may relinquish or lose touch with the sacred principle of will at an early time in life, through fear, lack of understanding, abuse, or whatever cause, and then choices of unconsciousness are made. When a young person hears adults say, "We will," and then in fact they won't, a sense may arise that outside forces are determining their reality, leading to a feeling of will-lessness, powerlessness. Faith in a sacred plan, divine law, is the wind that fans the flames of will power to manifest what is good. Through spiritual practice we reawaken clear relationship with the principle of light, conscientiously planting seeds of good cause for the benefit of all. Will combined with the wisdom of equanimity, seeing all things in right relationship, makes choices that manifest what is good for seven generations. So the sacred principle of will considers all, recognizing and affirming that all are in relationship to oneself, calling forth peace and harmony throughout the circle of life.

Wisdom of equanimity knows all things as relative to one's own thought and action and stirs the fire of generosity and good relations, in harmony with neighbors, friends, family, co-workers, and critters.

The Medicine Wheel of Life is a circle; all exists within that circle. The circle is named life—precious opportunity. The circle is 0 (zero), balance of positive and negative. All creatures walking about the circle experience birth, pain, old age, death; no one is above or below. When it comes to dying time all go alone without the comforts of wealth or friends. Birth of any form has its attendant struggle. All beings seek peace and the comforts of a secure home and healthy family. All young and aged beings require care and support. Here arise patterns of relationship giving order to what could be chaotic.

The circle teachings represent the cycle of all things that spiral in the ever-moving universe, in a process of constant movement and subtle change in harmony together. Thus each one of us, within the circle of our own time and space, is ever spiraling with our thoughts, words, and actions toward realization of the whole. The circle represents complete harmony and balance. It becomes our Medicine Wheel.

To transform any thought or activity that hides the perception of the circle is the duty of human beings. Where separation thoughts arise, thoughts of "them" and "us", recall that we are all in the circle of life together.

Each great religion has its prophecies of what may come. These prophecies serve as reminders to live in a harmonious manner lest destructive energies be loosed upon the Earth. The foundations of spiritual practice remind us to cultivate care for life and one another.

Many now sense the power of peace within ourselves, knowing that our consciousness does affect the stream of thought upon this world. As responsible human beings, let us affirm a world of complementary resolution. We may recognize the different parts of the whole, hear the different views and perspectives, and know that our view does not invalidate another's view. We are human beings and our perception of the same reality—the way the flame moves, the color of the grain—may be expressed differently based on our language, our culture, our experience. It is aqua, or is it blue? Familiarity, or habitual thought, is the screen through which the world is shaped. The congregation of thoughts and patterns that we think to be ourselves becomes the feelings of a city, the feelings of a nation. Each nation upon this planet has the heart of the people, the voices of the people, bringing it into form as a nation. Individuals make a group, individuals make states and nations.

Whatever our religious or philosophical views, we may each trace our roots to the Great Tree of Peace. Whatever we call ourselves the result is the same—we are people living together on planet Earth. In this time it is our duty to transform the obstacles of prejudice expressed as "isms." Let us put aside ideas of separation, for what occurs in one hemisphere will surely be carried on the winds to the other hemisphere.

The wondrous process of creation has brought forth the gift of human life, with limitless opportunities to explore its mysteries. We in turn have responsibility to cultivate seeds of good relationship, expressing joy for the opportunity of life. Some of the first lessons taught by my grandparents were: "You have a spiritual duty to be happy," and "Speak kindly of others, for you know not what they have suffered until you have walked ten thousand miles in their moccasins." See things as they are, in process of change, without fixation on imbalance; see the potential and call it forth. By acknowledging the inherent perfection, the crystal song singing within each one, we may bring forth the best in our family, nation, and planet.

When errors in thought, word, or deed are expressed, the result is like an ash-filled fireplace; wisdom becomes a dim ember buried in the ashes of confused thought and conflicting emotions. The appreciative fire-keeper purifies the mind as one sweeps a fireplace— sweeping it clear of doubt that the fire exists, fear that one may not keep it burning, envy that another fire burns more brightly, anger at the damp wood. Any thoughts, words, or actions that hinder the wisdom light are errors of unbalanced actions. Spiritual practice opens the flue, bearing the winds of inspiration and insight, renewing and maintaining balance.

An error of thought, word, or deed is that which takes one out of harmony, giving rise to anger, fear, envy, doubt in the orderly flow of universal love. Any human who feels that he or she is not "good enough" to cultivate peace and generosity is overlooking the wondrous gift of life. You live, therefore you are good enough. You live, therefore your merit is such that you can make a difference.

A young child expresses joy at seeing leaves shimmer as if dancing on the tree. An adult replies, "Leaves do not dance." Doubt may arise in the child's mind about the validity of feeling joy. The fire of joyful expression has been dampened by careless speech; the pattern of joy may be deeply altered, giving rise to imbalance. Through the heart meridian flows the river of joy, and this river can be dammed by harsh words, uncaring words.

Envy of another's success, good fortune, wealth, or good looks is an error because it disturbs the equilibrium of the mind and hinders the lover flow, disturbing synthesis and appreciation of one's life accomplishments. Envy poisons the group effort because "I wish" becomes bigger than "We can."

One may profess to be a Christian or a Buddhist, or this or that, and harbor angry seed thoughts at another's views. Sectarian views hinder peace. To live the great teachings is to see inherent truth underlying all great religions.

The Second Sacred Fire: Affirmation, the Wisdom Energy of Compassion

Positive affirmation and generosity arise from the wisdom of equanimity, seeing all things in relationship and choosing to articulate and live in a sacred manner. By affirmations one energizes one's vision of enlightened action.

Our elders taught that forgiveness was a great balm, the most great medicine that brings freedom from hurt. We may pray, do outward good works, yet they mean little without forgiving ourselves and others for what might have been, could have been, should have been.

Discipline, diligence, active intelligence make waves of grace for the land and the people for seven generations.

The Third Sacred Fire: Actualization, Skillful Means

The fire of actualization precipitates the ideal into reality in harmony with the sacred will and the energy of compassion. These three fires together become a triangle from which ideals are actualized through a process of strong intention, diligent action, and consideration for all beings.

Through the third fire the Creator's intention and individuals' relationship with that intention become real. For example, one of having strong faith, even in a challenging situation such as loss of job and income. Strong faith in a divine presence and ability to accomplish through diligent action, may bring into manifestation the desired goals. Skillful means is the perspiration, the diligent action, and one's willingness to apply clear thought and ethical and moral behavior to manifesting the ideal in one's life.

AFFIRMATION

To manifest fully, an affirmation needs to be unambiguous, a simple and clear statement of one's intentions. To make clear an affirmation, one first gives thanks for having a human life and the ability even to consider enlightened action. Then, in the sanctuary of mind, one assesses the skills of this time and considers the goals and objectives to be accomplished—in three days, three months, three years, one's lifetime—for the benefit of one's family, clan, nation, planet, and future generations. Affirmation enables one's un-manifest potential to become real through the following means:

Acknowledge the creative principle in yourself. Look at yourself in the mirror and greet yourself: "Hello, how are you?" Affirm, "I am alive, I am thankful, and I shall accomplish this day, for the benefit of myself, my family and all beings, these three specific things. ..." Repeat the affirmation three times. You may say, "On this day I shall respond with compassion to any anger or frustration," or "On this day I shall listen without interrupting." One states very clearly an objective of clear relationship.

Affirm, "I shall realize my creative gifts," repeating this affirmation also three times. And visualize in your mind's eye the accomplishment of such tasks. For example, if you wish to have a better relationship with your co-workers, visualize you and your co-workers seated in a circle, surrounded by rose light, talking heart to heart and accomplishing great works. It is important to believe your words and to cultivate faith that you will manifest your sacred gifts in this life. Another example: Suppose you are addicted to tobacco, alcohol, coffee, or unwholesome food. The first step is to acknowledge that this is something that will be put aside. Then affirm, "I am free from attachment to_____," repeating three times. And see yourself surrounded in light, happy, healthy, active, free from attachment, those objects of craving or attachment no longer present in your life, your mind-stream.

To actualize is to manifest the ideal, through sacred practice, great diligence, perseverance, and perspiration. To actualize is to make real a vision of peace for the people and the land. It is the happening and the doing. You bring your mind to stability with thankfulness, prayer, and meditation. The actualization of your idea—be it the idea to be free from drinking intoxicants or to build your home—is apparent in your actually putting aside that to which you were attached or beginning to create designs for your new home. This is the wakening of clear energy to bring forth your visualized goals and your creative potential. Another example: You hoped, you prayed to make your family relationships clearer. Your vision of family harmony, magnetized by your prayer, your affirmation, and your action in generating peace, is manifested as a family gathering free of previous negative patterns. Through the process of magnetizing and actualizing what is beneficial for all, patterns that have obscured clarity of thought and relationship become less and less grasping, they become more transparent until finally they disperse. The actualization is the beauteous results derived from the skillful means of the third sacred fire.

Will is the neutron, compassion the proton, and the energy of actualization the elections in the outer ring, wisdom that succeeds, bonding in good relationships. In your life, the clear intention to manifest your sacred gifts, to bring forth your creative potential and establish good relationships, is the neutron of will. So here we are, weaving patterns in a dream.

MEDICINE WHEEL, MANDALA
MIRROR CLEAR MIND.
LET THE SACRED HOOP
BE RENEWED IN THIS TIME.

Vigil

To hear the voice of wisdom one first stabilizes the mind. In the Tsalagi tradition the development of mental stability is called the vigil. The vigil begins as one observes the dancing fires throughout a given time period, usually outdoors. One may fast or take purifying baths before gathering the seven sacred woods for building the fire. Then one makes offering of tsalu (tobacco) to the fire and dedicates the vigil endeavor to aid all creatures, whether they walk crawl, swim, or fly. One gives thanks for the opportunity of life and "cries for vision" of life purpose and means of aiding the people. One's family, clan, co-workers, and nation are included in the circle of those whom one's actions are to benefit. The process of maintaining the fire through weather changes requires and develops determination to succeed. Lazy attitudes become transparent to one's sight, enabling transformation. As a rhythm becomes established the fire burns with ease, enabling the vigilant person to focus the mind on the flames. Many images may arise from the mind as one sits and watches.

The fire is a gateway to wisdom. By observing, one may see more clearly those thought patterns which hinder successful good relations. As thoughts of arrogance and fear arise, like a weaver one pulls those threads of discord and replaces arrogance with humility. See how small the concepts of self are in relation to the vastness of the sky. Replace fear of success, fear of life, with committed courage to succeed for the benefit of those you love. Should love not be apparent, cultivate appreciation for the gift of life. The greatest wealth is that of good relations with family, friends, and neighbors.

Should you have doubt of love, cultivate love for the child within your breast. In this way one begins to heal the illusion of separation.

We are the children of the light, we are the voice of creation, exclaimed as sound became light. We have come here through the illusion of separation to explore all the wonders of this creation. As we explore we recognize ourselves as co-creators in this universe, our thoughts and deeds shaping tomorrows. We see within our hearts a stream of wisdom ever aware of right action.

Right action is that which eases suffering, causes no harm, and inspires others to generous caretaking. Right action enables one to honor the fire of clear mind with one another without need to perceive one above or below, more or less than another. Right action perceives the cycles of relationships and creates order within one's own mind, putting forth disciplined action free from desire to dominate or be dominated. Mind dedicated to right action perceives that we are the ancestors to those yet unborn and considers the effects of thought, word, and deed for seven generations—each moment a holy moment, pregnant with tomorrow. Best to speak kindly, act with care, lest your tomorrow be filled with fear.

Spiritual Practice

It is our spiritual duty to pray in the morning, to pray in the evening, to call people together in joy, to eat together, to be happy human beings together. Many of us did these things in the past; we can recall how in our growing-up years when your neighbors needed aid, we were there. Now we are too busy. We have forgotten that the inventions are creations of our own minds and they have begun to gobble up our every moment. We must be disciplined and say again, "These machines have come from our minds; let us direct them with clear thought." Let us very carefully examine the wisdom of the day and nourish those ideas and inventions whose roots are deep in the soil of harmony. Let us recall that what each of us does will come around the sacred wheel and touch us again. As the pebble in the stream makes many ripples, so does each word and thought we hold in our minds.

This is the power of the voice: affirming that there shall be peace. Let us hold the thought of our planet's wholeness; let us honor the children, the future generation. This is how we make peace. As we look around us at events in the world, we see many things happening that stimulate fear, the thought of "Them" and "Us." But there is no "them." We are all together. What happens in the north, what happens in the south, it is happening in each of us. In the east the sun rises and I realize, "I am that I am. I am a human being with a gift, I am a human being with a purpose." The gift may be hidden, yet it shall become apparent. To be a friend to one person, to inspire one heart to clarity, that is a special gift. Too often we may think the gift is something else, something we must get from outside. The gift is in each of us to give. First we align with the perfection in ourselves, bring the mind, the body, the emotions into harmony with the creative principle of life. We may do it in many ways, through introspection, through making something with our hands, through community action. We cultivate peaceful thought, and soon we react less and less to the idea form of conflict. Then there arises the awareness that we are all relatives on Earth.

In the morning I sing a simple song of thanks, as my grandparents taught me. I am singing for all my relatives, everyone who lives and breathes, even the stones, for the crystals are alive and they grow just as we do. Through our experience with life, through our interactions with one another, we learn to put aside anger, we learn ways of communion, we find ways of resolution. The sacred spiral of light unites all beings. My grandparents said, "Remember that you come from the place of the Seven Dancers, the Pleiades star system; that is where your nation comes from." So, visualizing seven stars above my head and perceiving the three sacred fires deep within my spine, I sit and listen as they sing a very simple song. May you recall that sacred spiral of light, Asga Ya Galunlati, Great Spirit that unites us all. Through all of our cultures, all of our religions, there is one thread, there is one tree. Let us perceive that great tree, let us recognize that clear light of reason, the fire of wisdom through which we may all trace our roots to the Great Tree of Peace.

As a young child, that was a first step upon the Beauty Path. Just learning to sing a morning song of thanks, and sitting quietly and realizing that there truly is light moving through this body, made the words of my grandparents take on more meaning in my heart. I understood that there truly is light moving through each of our bodies as we breathe: we have mind, and it is carried on breath. Then another question arose as I recognized the light: "Does mind truly affect the plants, the crops, the environment? Will I be like my old people, calling forth what is needed just with a prayer in the heart?" A seed was planted that many would sing out a song of peace and abundance as the elders did. By the standards of life in these days it would seem a poor life that they led. If they wanted water they went out and pumped it; if they wanted butter they churned it. It was good. Many of us are looking again to simple ways of living, dignified ways that do not enslave us to wage labor in order to pay for things we don't really need, becoming ever more dependent on technology that pollutes the Earth. It is fine to chop our own wood, it is fine to make a cook-fire outside. To live simply is to see without attachment. Our status, our position, is determined not by the work we do outside but by the work in our hearts and how we assist others. The effort to recognize and speak the truth is the greatest work that any of us can do. It is to realize the power of our clear mind and to call forth the best from all the people with whom we walk along life's path. This is a gift of giving and receiving. Then one's heart feels it will burst with a sense of love and appreciation, free of confining fears.

Take time to pray with your children in the morning. It has far more power for your family and your planet than all your busy work. The power of our voices tuned to right action and the willingness to speak and live correctly and to hold our hearts in joyous balance—this is the path of harmony. Each of us seeks to come into union with the sacred wisdom. Communion, communication, community—words calling forth from the longing in our hearts the desire that we stand together around the sacred circle, that we honor the truth in ourselves and all our relations.

Ten Sacred Stones

As a teaching aid, my great-grandfather Eli Ywahoo would draw a triangle on the ground and place ten stones within it. He said, "The quartz is the will. This reminds us of the sacred flow. Those red stones, the petrified coral, are to remind you of love's wisdom. The yellow of the topaz is to remind you of the well-tuned mind, that you may actively bring forth with your thought what is good for all the people in this moment and in future generations." These are the stones of the sacred triangle, the three flames of most pure mind.

As that triangle is made strong, you recognize the sacred energy of the square, and you begin to put down roots for a holy place for people to meet as a family and as friends. The stone to remind you of this is the jasper, yellow and orange jasper. This stone removes swelling and pain from the body and reminds us that our feeling of being separate from the source of all nature is overcome in our right relationship with family and friends.

The fifth stone is green jadeite or emerald. It is the stone through which you make balance from the realm of ideal form into the present moment. Through knowing, through practice, you will find the medicines that best strengthen the people. The fifth stone represents the practice.

The rose quartz is the sixth stone, showing the open heart, the heart that gives and receives. In time people will recall the sacred power of that stone for strengthening the heart that has been overcome by grief.

Looking to uncover great beauty makes apparent the obscurations. It is then that you call upon the energy of the seventh stone, the amethyst, stone of transformation. That subtle purple quartz very quickly speeds up the process of transformation in ourselves, and what was an obstacle becomes the heart of the wisdom fire.

Looking inside, we call upon the pearly wisdom of the eighth stone, the simple pearl from the fresh water, to remind us of our perfection and our many layers, and of the light ever reflecting. We have a recognition, a remembrance of light whence we spring, and respect for all within Earth's dream. As we recall more and more of the light and see one another in interaction as co-creators, then we come to the wisdom of the opal. The opal is the ninth stone, a stone of universal mind, the awakened fire of mind precipitating thoughts revealing enlightened action. A door may be opened in our nature as our aura reflects that opalescent light.

And the tenth stone, it is being formed within each of us. It is somewhat like the lapis, but translucent. It is our will in alignment with the Creator's will and the purpose of this planet that shall manifest this stone in the Earth. The Earth is always producing new elements, which come to the surface as we transmute and transform. This stone of knowing shall unfold in our hearts as a flower of knowing. We must call forth the beauty. We must recognize that Earth herself is a holder of the form and we all share in the mind of that being. We might say that this is our planetary garden, and within this garden we develop a planetary mind.

Ten sacred stones, ten mirrors of the wisdom fire within.

There is a message in these stones, there is a message in our hearts. The symmetry of these crystal structures points to the symmetry of this universe. As in music, everything in creation is moving, and its flow is a song of jubilation. We are now in the process of changing from one key to another. The people are now awakening to the song of inherent joy, appreciation of life, recognizing that in this moment the song can fully resound. The sound of human thought and the planet's dance is changing. We are moving into the key of D, the only key that is a reciprocal of itself, that returns to itself. It is a note attuned to the sacred will, and it ever comes around the sacred circle. Many of the songs you have learned in churches and in sacred ceremonies are in the key of D. It is strengthening in you the will to do good.

In these times the crystal is the hub of our communications wheel, amplifying many thoughts, feeding desire, calling forth action. Crystals activate the "go buttons" in armament systems, and the sounds of desire are amplified through advertisements chanting, "Buy this, you need that." And yet it is the crystal networks that make apparent our neighbor's plight halfway around the world, the singing of crystals in radio and television that conveys that all humans share the same concerns, the same planet. Destruction or peace: it is your choice what message is amplified. Recognize the thoughts arising in your mind. Weed thoughts of greed and anger from the garden of your mind. Cultivate what is beneficial and generous. The crystal heart of the Earth sings, "Help me renew the waves and the atmosphere." You may assist by purifying your thought, word, and deed.

The crystal is a living being, vibrating faster than the speed of light. It is not a solid; it is sound, ether, concretized. The crystal is a conscious being that has taken a particular form to resonate the basic sound of creation. The clear quartz crystal is one of the deeper mysteries of the practice of the Tsalagi people. With the quartz one walks in all dimensions. It is also a key to healing, amplifying the proper tone so that the body may realize its resonance with the sound of creation.

The Rainbow Bridge

We are the rainbow, each of us. When we speak of "rebuilding the Rainbow Bridge," it is to bring again into harmony the left and right hemispheres of the brain, to renew the flow of our intuitive mind and the mind that has learned through repeated action. The body knows what is good for it, the body knows to inhale and exhale. It is our middle brain that oversees these functions. When we accept the innate wisdom of our middle brain, we integrate the wisdom of triune mind, right and left hemispheres, and limbic system functioning together in harmony.

My great-grandfather said to me, "When you see the rainbow, it is an indication that the holy spirit is strong in the people's bodies as a result of ceremonies done correctly." If there were no rainbows after the ceremony it would mean that somehow the connection was not complete between left and right, mother and father, moon and sun in ourselves. We can make it complete by honoring the beauty of our mothering nature if we are wearing a man's body and the power of our fathering nature if we are wearing a woman's body. Everything we are, every form, has within it the energy of the mother and the father, the seed of the rainbow.

Here in this new age, this changing of keys, it is we who determine the future. As we learn to work as families, as friends, as groups, united by sacred law, we will renew this planet and her waters. The creative elements of life have not been made impure. They are obscured by our impure thinking, and our thought can very easily make the transition. This is the question for each of us now: Are you one with creation? Do you want to come again to the sacred stream? Will you stand on the Beauty Path? Yes or no. We can't say "maybe." As my grandmother said, "You're either pregnant or you're not." And we are each pregnant with a new world. Each of us is carrying the seed of a planetary unity and a great peace that has not been seen for thousands and thousands of years. The seed of that peace is a child within us all.

To nourish that seed of peace we must nourish one another. To come again as friends, to sit, to pray, to offer food to one another, in this way we return something to the Earth. In your busy life, in the cities, you may wonder how you can return anything to the Earth. Remember the rivers of energy within your own body. The sacred meridians that carry subtle energy through your body also resonate with the energy of this planet. Earth, too, has meridians, sacred energy flows. Some of these places we know as holy places; others we feel for a moment and say, "Oh, is this a power spot?" What is the sacred flow? How do we recognize it? All around the Earth is a lightning grid through which the lightning energy of inspiration flows, quickening the seed that life may grow, drawing forth the waters of the Earth. The lightning grid is the nervous system of the Earth—and our thoughts affect the lightning grid. Our thought forms, how we feel about ourselves and one another, become collected in the grid-work around the planet. As we move through the process of resolution, the last fear, that last guardian of the threshold, shall give way and the Great Peace shall manifest.

We fill each area we live in with forms of our thoughts. Sometimes a thought becomes separated and one becomes fearful. We decided to live in communities long ago so that food could be easily gathered and we could care for one another. In that process of community development we also developed territorial mind. As the tribe became larger, this territorial mind sometimes felt scarcity. That thought form of scarcity is still hanging on around this planet. It is for us to recognize the abundance in our hearts so that the last illusion, that most fearful separation from the abundant wisdom of love, can be put aside.

Discipline the mind so that you see the best. Doubt is probably the greatest scourge of human nature. To doubt the divine order of things is to deny the dignity of humanity. A first step is to look within and extract the thought form of doubt. Realize what you can be sure of: you inhale, you exhale. Our actions are the seeds of tomorrow. The mind weaves a picture, one of many in the great tapestry of life. Inhale, exhale, sun rises and sets, of that there is no doubt.

Give and you shall receive. Share a smile; give alms and kind words. As our own generosity grows, we find that our family receives what is necessary for continued growth. It begins in our mind, it begins in our thought. Have the discipline to say each day, "I realize more and more the wisdom light. I am light, I cultivate thoughts of love and harmony." Something happens around you. When you first begin the process of affirmation, everything will test you. The children who were so well behaved will go wild when you sit down to meditate; everyone will want to speak to you on the phone. You listen and love and return to the quiet. Eventually the distractions will lessen. Our family, our friends, they reflect our inner life. If we see uncertainty around us, it is to remind us to cultivate certitude. We must come again to the only thing we can be sure of—the breath of life, that we inhale, we exhale. By exploring the breath and its movement through the body we can stay centered when many things are going on around us that may distract us from the quiet. We can be sure of this: we live in the present, in the moment. Our thoughts do become a reality. You think "hungry," then you eat.

We are always communicating, heart to heart, mind to mind. There is a universal language that all beings understand. Even these words on the page are just a carrier wave for the deeper communication that occurs within ourselves. To recognize our own thought and to take responsibility for the thought forms we create, to see that which we project and that which we receive and to make a discriminating choice, this is most important.

You are the ancestors of those yet unborn. You are the road of a great peace. May you observe the nature of mind, cultivate generosity and joy, and actualize peace on Earth. May you recognize the power of active intelligence integrated with love's wisdom and the ever-present will to be, that most beauteous triangle of creation. As one sits and stills the mind, subtle means of knowing are revealed in the mind, in the light, in the stars above the head. There is a way of knowing that passes through all realms: to be fully present in the moment, that what is above may manifest below. That is our choice.

How to make this choice when one has so many responsibilities in the world? How to come again to living as truly dignified human beings? God is in the marketplace, too. Everything is part of the sacred flow. To see our work as prayer and an opportunity to bring forth a flash of truth is a great gift. To know that even the busy world is a holy world is quite a change of heart. And as the years go on, perhaps the heart will say to many of us that it is time to go back to the land, or to make stronger and more sacred the flow of life in whatever business we are working in. As long as we are attentive and not reacting to the thought form of limitation, whatever we are doing is sacred. To be aware in the moment, recognizing past and future in the moment, is to be firmly rooted in the now. This is our gift and our bounty as human beings: to have an opportunity to live as individuals and to share in the planet's evolution.

In this time our sun is taking an initiation of great significance. For many of the Native people of the United States of America it has meant a great revival of our sun dances. The sun that feeds and sustains this planet is going through an initiation that will open the door for us to communicate with others in other worlds as we recognize the sun of reality in ourselves. So our thought process and our affirmation of our beauty are important for the Earth and for our entire solar system. A little over ten years ago the keepers of the lodge keys of Jupiter and other planets put out a great song of distress, calling on many of Earth's medicine people: "Are you going to do something about this planet? The experiment is not very good." What was being done here on Earth was polluting the whole solar system. Jupiter was upset because the anger coming from the Earth was interfering with the very beautiful flow of energy between it and its most important moon, Iona. People sat in kivas and longhouses and churches and prayed and listened. How will people hold the form? Do we believe in humanity's future? Are we willing to hold a thought form of peace and continued well-being, or do we have to say to those beings that Experiment Earth was a mistake?

The disarmament movement proves that people are able to call forth good medicine. Cultivate the essential good nature. Affirm that peace may prevail through complementary resolution. Trust that we shall come again as a human family, as beings of light, to live in harmony. You make a difference. I ask you, with the power of your voice affirm peace in yourself and beauty in one another. This is how Earth's beautiful song shall gladden all the universe.

Meditation on Clear Intention

Sitting easily, spine erect, breathing in, breathing out, allow your thoughts to slow down, your mind to become quiet. Visualize yourself surrounded in light, receiving heaven's light through the crown of your head, Earth's energy through the base of your spine. Be aware of these two spirals of light, one flowing up, one flowing down, dancing in the spine. Maintain the inner motion as you sit. Attune to the primordial force of life, will to be, cause of your living in this time. Will, born of the void, symbolized by egg or circle. Observe the ever-flowing stream of consciousness, light giving birth to sound and manifestation. Attuning to the light of clear mind leads to thought and action in harmony with divine will, enabling one to shape one's life in right relationship with others and with our planet. See that in a universe of abundance there is no scarcity. Dedicate your thought and action to peace. As our solar system moves into a higher vibration, humans shall realize a consciousness of planetary oneness. Perceive within yourself the silver cord that connects you with awakened mind, enlightenment a seed within you awaiting its glorious blossoming.

Completion Stage: Light is absorbed into your being, and a vision of a peaceful Earth resides in your heart. Rose light expands from your heart, reaching to all realms with thoughts of compassion for all beings. Maintain equanimity. Then your mind will become quiet.

Go through the day with peaceful thoughts, doing good things.

CAODAI SCRIPTURES

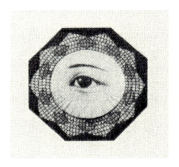

INTRODUCTION

In the earliest days of human existence on earth, direct contact with
the Creator was more common than it is today. The Creator spoke
in ways and symbologies relevant to each culture, for each tribe had
its own land, language, and customs distinct from the other. The
Magnanimous Force we know as God loved not one more than the
other and communicated directly, answering each in its own
tongue. Humanity's numbers were yet few, spread sparsely, mostly
isolated from one another. Glorious cultures and religions, all
springing from God who had created them, developed everywhere
independently. As time passed, humans more and more forgot how
to communicate directly with God, though they still held dear their
religions.

When the various tribes began to encounter one another upon
the earth, they were mystified, not understanding why these others
were so dissimilar, appearing and acting differently, worshiping
differently, and surely each thought the other must revere a different God! Because humans did not understand one another, they
had fear, and as children who are afraid and away from the guid-

ance of a parent will become bullies, humans created friction and war. They did not recognize each other as children of the same Creator. Even though there were further revelations from God to those who could still hear ("Love your neighbor as yourself."—Christianity; "There is no God but God."—Islam), rather than embracing diversity, people still preferred to resist the differences between themselves and continued to make war with one another. Separations became more and more minute, until even a single principle was allowed to splinter the mightiest of religions into sect upon sect.

Then, in the last century of the second millennium at a far corner of the earth, an as-yet unrenowned place we today call Vietnam, with the bodies of eight million victims of World War I still decomposing (a testimonial to the great evil of war), God spoke to an unrenowned esotericist practicing his self-cultivation (meditative arts).

Precisely, this contact occurred on the Vietnamese island of Phu Quoc, south of the mainland of Cambodia. There Ngo Van Chieu received messages directly from God relating to a great reconciliation which must take place between all religions. Chieu worshiped and vowed to obey God, Whom he knew by the name of Cao Dai. He asked if he might have permission to worship God in a representation he could view. God replied that the human form is too limiting to represent the essence of universality that God embodies, and that the Eye would be more apt, as it is the symbol for both Universal and Individual consciousness,

So the All-Seeing Eye of God (Thien Nhan, Divine Eye) became the symbol for CaoDai, for God, and for the ensuing religion which is called CaoDai.

God said:
The Eye represents the heart
From which twin pure lights beam.
Light and Spirit are One,
God is the Spirit's gleam.

As one who still hears the Original Call, I welcome the reader to this text.   Ngasha Beck.[1]

---

[1] The CaoDai Scriptures were presented by Hum Bui, M.D. in collaboration with Ngasha Beck.

CAODAI FAITH: A RELIGION OF UNITY

THE MESSAGE

What is CaoDai?

CaoDai is a universal religion which considers all religions One. Unique in its integrative approach, it originated in Southeast Asia in the 1920s. God, celebrated as Source of the Universe and all souls, and as the origin of all religions, is seen to have manifested differently in different epochs and be called by myriad Names. CaoDai teaches human beings, who all have sprung from the same Source, to live in harmony, love, justice and peace; to enjoy universal sisterhood and brotherhood; and to cultivate themselves to seek and be reunited with God in their hearts.

CaoDai propounds that God has come and expressed Himself in a new Way: The Third Revelation of The Great Way (Dai Dao Tam Ky Pho Do). Literally, CaoDai means roofless tower, Abode on High where God reigns. Figuratively, the phrase Cao Dai (two words) is used as God's symbolic name and CaoDai (one word) refers to the path being taught. At the heart of the CaoDai path is the recognition of oneness between the Supreme Being and the universe, including humanity and its religions.

What is the Goal of CaoDai?

The immediate goal of CaoDai is to increase human awareness that all religions have indeed one same origin and also one same fundamental: love and justice. As Christians put it: Do to others as you would have them do to you. If human beings were to stop discriminating against each other because of differences in religions and treat each other with true love and justice, there would soon be religious understanding and tolerance and subsequently harmony in the world and peace on earth. One way CaoDai moves toward this goal is to bring to the individual teachings of self-purification, both physical and spiritual, and self-cultivation through meditation with the goal of attaining of peace within.

Physical purification begins through making healthy choices about what is eaten. Vegetarianism is considered one way of purifying the body. Avoiding the influence of substances such as alcohol, cigarettes, opiates, or other drugs is also useful. Spiritual purification is accomplished through daily meditation, and mindfully practicing compassion, love and altruism in our lives, while eliminating greed, hatred, jealousy, and anger. As one progressively purifies, physically and spiritually, one finds inner peace and connects more easily to, eventually becoming unified with the Supreme Being.

From a moral point of view, CaoDai reminds a person of duties toward self, family, society (one's broader family) and humanity, the universal family.

From a philosophical point of view, CaoDai recommends forgoing honors, riches and luxury, emancipating oneself from servitude to materialism in order to attain spirituality and peace.

From the spiritual point of view, CaoDai recognizes the existence of the spirit and the soul, their survival beyond that of the physical body, and promotes self-cultivation as the way to return to oneness with The All That Is.

And from the initiates' point of view, by uniting Humanism, Christianity, Taoism and Buddhism, CaoDai provides teachings which encompass all stages of a person's physical, emotional and spiritual evolution. At a stage where one is still attached to many secular obligations—such as toward husband or wife, parents, children, brothers and sisters and humanity—CaoDai with its humanistic teachings can guide one through all activities of one's life. Later, whenever one wishes to achieve a deeper level of peace of mind and to be united with the Almighty deep in one's heart, CaoDai will provide guidance in self-cultivation through meditative practices.

Is there a Universal Religion?

CaoDai is a universal religion with the principle that all religions are one and of one origin. There are other religions and philosophical systems that adhere to this fundamental principle as well and with whom CaoDai finds easy alliance: Baha'i, Theosophy, Unitarian-Universalism, Unity Church and The Oomoto Foundation of Japan. Also many New Age teachings would agree that there is one

Truth and many paths to this Truth. The Hindu Vedas put it this way: Truth is One, but sages have given it different names.

Oneness of God, Humans and Universe

Among Eastern philosophies, this point stands out: The sky, the earth and ten thousand things are of one same constitution (Thien Dia Van Vat Dong Nhat The). Ten thousand things symbolically refers to the multitude of diverse forms of matter in the universe. A stunning assertion, but what does it really mean? What does it imply? In this universe, all things are comprised of atoms as a commonality, but a few situations would show how the sky, the earth and all the things in the universe can be of one same nature.

A pedestrian and his dog walk wearily in the heat looking for a respite, shade, water. A plant by the road wilts under the same fierce sun. Water would be the savior for the man, the dog and the plant. Without water, under the heat, man, animal and plant will dehydrate, die and decompose eventually into earth elements. It appears that the stones underfoot are unimpaired, but if the stone bakes at high enough temperatures it would also become dehydrated and decompose.

Thus the same effect from excessive heat is observed for the person, the animal, the plant and eventually the stone. If they don't have the same basic constitution, how is it that a common result occurs?

Stones appear quite solid on the physical plane, diamonds being the hardest. A wooden table, a steel filing cabinet, an insect and a human body all appear solid to varying degrees, but yet each of them, and the stone too, amazingly contain much more empty space between their spinning electrons than solid matter.

Regarding another aspect of life, a common law governs reproduction. A marigold plant gives seeds which if placed in appropriate conditions will produce marigold plants. A dog, after conceiving, will give birth to a dog. A similar law applies to the human being. The same rule of specific continuation of the line applies, whether human, or animal or plant. This common law of physical existence is reminiscent of this saying from ancient China:

Ta cung muon vat dong sinh;

Ta va muon vat su tinh chang hai.

Myself and ten thousand things are born together;

Myself and ten thousand things bear together the same condition.

Ten thousand things on this earth are part of the universe and of its smooth functioning. Lives on this earth rely on the sun and on the punctuality of the earth revolving around the sun to receive the narrow range of light and temperature needed.

Physical bodies of all lives on earth are part of the body and life of the universe. After death physical bodies turn to dust, also a part of the universe.

As to the emotional part of human nature, day-to-day life, with its wheel of fortune ups and downs, normally creates a similar feeling among all mortals. In a theater, most people watching a play feel the same emotions and thus laugh or cry at the same instant.

As to the spiritual, God has granted mortals and everything in the cosmos a part of That Spirit. And among humans the spirit is shared, which is why they have similar basic principles and the same conscience. This is why the world's great wisdom traditions have a common central essence and why, for example, the Latin motto on the U.S. dollar bill, E Pluribus Unum, would have a counterpart in Vietnamese:

Nhut Bon Tan Van Thu;
Van Thu Qui Nhut Bon.
From one, emanate many;
From many, emanates one.

Many times during this manifestation, the Supreme Being taught: "I, your Master, am you; and you, My children, are Me;" or "I divided My spirit to create materials, plants, animals and humans; I am the father of all lives; where there is life, there is Me." This teaching constitutes the most important principle of CaoDai and becomes the ultimate goal of all mortals on this earth: to return to complete oneness with the Supreme Being.

The Five Vows

We pray that the wisdom of the Great Tao be widely spread on Earth,
May peaceful existence manifest for all creatures of Nature's birth.
May all humanity be redeemed
And our whole world know peace.

And may the places we meet to worship You be granted safety's
  lease.

Prayers Before Sleep

All material desires consume me by day,
Leading my mind and my actions astray.
Holy One, I am prostrating here to pray
That Your lovingness will cause my mind to stay
Focused and clear on Your Divinity,
Taking no actions toward infidelity.
During my sleep, when my soul is at rest,
Superior Spirits, please guide me to what is best.
Toward my home in your Sacred Nirvana I yearn
So teach me the lesson which I need to learn.

Prayers Before Eating

Foremost to the multitude of living beings,
To eat is the most necessary of things.
Cereals, the Creator has brought to this need,
And gives to His children upon which to feed.
Our deep thanks go to Sen Nong King
Who taught in the ways of plants' upbringing.
Gratefully, I vow to borrow this physical body of man
In use for the spiritual quest of the Eternal land.

The Voyager's Prayer

For this is but the road of life;
Along its way may we be saved
By faith in teachings we embrace
Though we are as foam tossed on the wave.
I find my trustfulness oft shaken
So I retreat from early tide
But such happenstance is purification
along the soul's journey toward CaoDai.
I realize from that place of refuge in my soul
and repent for harm I have caused to others;
May the Almighty know of my good faith
and my dedication to serve others.
As I brave the thorns and brambles,

May I set out safe and return sane.
May the Almighty grant me protection as I pass
along Heaven's path and life's road the same.

Entering Divine Realms

Though arduous it may be to enter Divine realms,
Hesitate not to surpass your human kin,
Keep a peaceful heart to turn negative to positive and keep a
  plain mindset as your place to begin.
Keep practicing your miracles, and slowly, day by day,
Your tireless devotion will keep you from the fray.
The wicked flaunt their wickedness but the pure remain pure,
Practicing triple cultivation to assure their spirit's cure.

Cultivating Heart

And then you will see the outcome
Of the actions you have taken,
Yet complain not, for life is fraught
With opportunity forsaken.

In the cultivation of your heart,
Make wisdom's sharp blade steady
For cutting through the karma you
Have honed to make you ready.

Your suffering is fully seen
In the Eye of My compassion
Now hasten to rise and flee
Toward reunion in My Heaven!

And whoever has despised you,
My gentle female devotee,
Has disregarded Me and so will see
These deeds' remorse one day.

Perseverance and Sincerity in Self-Cultivation

I, your Master, grant you, the most sincere disciples, the Chi
To be pure, your true self should emanate bright energy.
To help others, heed closely the Tao's examination

Have no confusion, as you will find complete illumination.
As the moon shines brightly in the clear night,
In cultivating self, child, keep your heart and mind aright.
Be completely patient with your hardships year by year,
The blessing of your growth shall wipe clean your fears.

Child, you were taught to have compassion,
And blessed for your sincerity of cultivation,
The Huyen Quan Khieu (Crown chakra) will open through the
    clarity of your heart,
Which has been replete with My blessings from the start.

Tending your virtues and having mind toward cultivation,
Willing to pray to Superior Spirits in your contemplation,
They bless and grant you vision to their emanations bright,
Your name will be sanctified as a gentle being's birthright.

Being conscientious of the test of the Flower Convention Day,
You'll be elated to discover where your predestiny has lain,
But, for now, focus only on the growth of mind and virtue
Thereby your home in the divine abode will be well reserved for
    you.

Give deep thought to all that I have said,
Let your conscience give your reply,
Meanwhile My blessings all flow out to you
as you are held in My own eye.

How Does One Practice CaoDai?

A spiritual message from Cao Dai said:
Out of Love and Mercy, out of respect for life, I have founded
    the Great Way's Third Revelation to save the earthly human,
    to help the virtuous attain a world of peace and avoid reincar-
    nation to the earthly world of suffering.
The ultimate goal of CaoDaists is to be reunified with The All
    That Is, to be at one with the entirety of the universe—while
    still in a body. In the outer, exoteric practice of CaoDai, hu-
    manistic principles are important. A disciple or adept would:
Complete duties toward self, family, society, country, living be-
    ings and nature.

Practice good and avoid evil.

Show kindness to nature, plants, animals, and human beings, and avoid unnecessary destruction of any creature, recognizing that they all have the Supreme Being's spirit and are part of nature's cycle.

Observe five Precepts: Do not kill; Do not steal; Do not commit adultery; Do not get drunk; Do not sin by word.

Practice vegetarianism at least ten days per month. This is a way to purify one's body and spirit and to promote love by avoiding the killing of living beings.

Participate in ritual acts of devotion and worship to the Supreme Being.

CAODAI: THE INNER TEACHINGS THE VOYAGE INWARD

Esoterism, Cosmology, and Ethics

The entire universe proceeded from a single source, the Thai Cuc, or Monad, in the midst of the Khi Hu Vo, or The Invisible Void (called in Buddhism Chunyata). This is the Supreme Being. The Supreme Being then divided its spirit into two energies (Luong Nghi): Yin and Yang, or Am Quang and Duong Quang. Everything in the universe, therefore, has properties of Am and Duong. Generally, all Am (Yin) matter (which is darker, heavier and weaker) is seen as coming from the feminine aspect of the Supreme Being (the Mother Goddess, Kim Ban Phat Mau), and all Duong (Yang) matter (which is brighter, lighter, and stronger) is seen as coming from the masculine aspect of the Supreme Being (the Father God, Duc Chi Ton). Duong is the spiritual dimension and Am is the material dimension. As such, Duong is eternal and imperceptible by the physical senses. In contrast, Am is transitory and decaying.

This initial division then produced the Tu Tuong (Tetrad), which then produced the Bat Quai (Eight Trigrams). Finally, the Bat Quai produced the "ten thousand things," a Taoist euphemism for the entire universe in all its complexity.

In spiritual terms, the Supreme Being is the Dai Linh Quang, or Great Sacred Light, and the Human Being is the Tieu Linh Quang, or Little Sacred Light. What this means is that, while Human Beings have the divine spark (Duong aspect) within them, they are mixed with the darker Am aspect as well.

The Supreme Being is Duong aspect only. All created matter, as it descends on the great chain of being, becomes heavier and heavier, imbued with greater and greater Am aspect, culminating in minerals. Conversely, all created matter, as it ascends the great chain of being, becomes lighter and lighter, imbued with greater and greater Duong aspect, culminating in human beings.

The Duong aspect of Human Beings, the aspect identical with the Supreme Being, is known as the soul, or the conscience (the Than in Vietnamese). The Am aspect of Human Beings is known as the physical body (the Tinh in Vietnamese) and the emotional self (the Khi in Vietnamese).

"Cultivate Than, transform to Hu,
Cultivate Hu, transform to Vo."

In Chinese Taoist theory, Tinh is usually translated as Ching or Jing. This refers to the symbolic essence of the physical aspect of Humans: the reproductive elements of both sexes. Similarly, Khi is usually translated as Chi or Ji. This refers to the symbolic essence of the emotional aspect of Humans: breath, or, in a larger sense, the energy aspect. Than is usually translated as Shen, and means the spirit or soul. Hu and Vo are generally translated as Wu Chi, or Tai Chi, which mean, respectively No Chi (nothingness) or the Supreme Ultimate Chi. This ultimate state implies a full balance and purification of energies. Martial artists should find these terms quite familiar.

The goal of meditation, then is purification of the self to reach unification with the divine spirit. This is known as Thien Dinh, or "Calming Down and Concentrating." Buddhists refer to this as Shamatha Vipasana, respectively, while the Omotokyo Shinto Term is Chinkon Kishin, meaning calming down and returning to the Source. There is a striking parallel between this practice and those of Taoists (in directing Chi through the body), Buddhists (in the Completion Stage Highest Yoga Tantras), Hindus (in Kundalini Yoga and its Chakra system), and Jews (in meditation on the Kabbalah Tree of Life). It seems the same centers of energy are used for spiritual purification, except that in this case, the goal is divine union with the spirit of CaoDai.

The following is a fairly simple meditation technique designed to aid in the purification of Tinh and Khi through the path described in the poem above.

Sit with spine and head straight, eyes half open, not focused on anything, mouth closed and relaxed, with the tip of the tongue lightly touching the roof of the mouth.

Inhale gently, directing the breath past the Phach Cung Hoa: the fire center of the heart (where it is imbued with the fire principle) to the Phach Ha Dinh, the lower center at the navel (sacral plexus).

While holding the breath for two seconds, transfer the energy of the inhalation into the Phach Cuc Am, the extremely yin center at the base of the spine.

Exhaling, direct the energy from the breath up through the spine into the Phach Cuc Duong, the extremely yang center at the top of the head. Along the way the breath is imbued with the water principle, and the "steam" (from the fire principle) helps the third eye to begin to open (this is the spiritual principle knowledge center, typically shown in the middle of the forehead between the eyes).

The important point is that one's expectation should be humble at first and the key to success is absolute sincerity. One should be sincere in the goal of development of love, compassion, and understanding which will naturally lead to the True Self in one's heart and to the unification with the Supreme Being.

While a disciple performs duties toward humanity and is practicing vegetarianism for at least ten days per month, he or she may be guided to the practice of esotericism, with meditation a major component. The goal is to progressively eradicate the inferior self and develop the divine element within the self, reaching toward oneness with the Supreme Being.

Esoteric practices have become increasingly popular. The esotericist aspires to unite with the Supreme Being by concentrating on self-cultivation through meditation and self-purification, learning to simplify their needs, to become sincere, kind, loving persons and to expand their love to humanity and nature. Gradually, as neutrality and inner peace are gained, the practitioner or aspirant becomes free of the adverse emotions. At this point, a continual sense of loving openness with the Universe, the Supreme Being, becomes possible. Meditation quiets the mind, which otherwise constantly roams from one thought to another. Meditation often allows a person the first deep contact with the inner Self. It has value at whatever stage the meditator is, all the while laying the groundwork for the ultimate unification with the Creator, the Original Source.

It is not necessary to enter a temple to practice this form of CaoDai, for the esotericist realizes that the temple resides within. But, by coming together, esotericists can share, learn, firm up their thinking and practice together, all of which helps further their personal paths.

Spiritual Messages from Victor Hugo: Dialogue between the Ho Phap Pham Cong Tac and Victor Hugo's spirit, 1930

Ho Phap:
   When will the Earth progress to a higher state?
Victor Hugo:
   In order that you may comprehend the process of spiritual evolution,
   I have to use a spiritual expression you will understand.
   You must advance through stages of purgatory,
   Even the blessed have a long way to go to reach enlightenment.
   In order to comprehend the nature of the Highest Spirit,
   One must evolve to that same level to fully understand.
   No lesser spirit can even begin to comprehend;
   Even the Buddha could only make suppositions on the matter.
   I don't say you must comprehend all that I am telling you,
   What I say reflects thoughts from the spirits' vantage point.
   Suppose for a moment that the Holy of Holies,
   Also once had a life in one of these universes.
   Passing at length through the realm of matter,
   He became mortal; a sage;
   And therefrom advanced upward unto the Divine level,
   Entering at last into the mystery of Creation.
   Through successive lives, gaining in spiritual power,
   Finally transforming into the Master of wisdom and science.
   Attracting the best of spirits into a core of allegiance,
   And across the border of Infinity together they passed.
Ho Phap:
   (Referring to the Creator) He has a heaven of His own?
Victor Hugo:
   Yes, as each of us are within our own soul domain

Which is a product of our own spiritual life force.
Those of complementary karmic states to our own
Accompany us and populate our environs.
These are not necessarily trustworthy,
Having their own agendas to fulfill,
Thus it is upon our own shoulders to redeem ourselves.
Leaving ourselves impure invites evil into our lives.
This is whence the specter of Satan emerges,
If we face facts, we realize this,
For Satan has a place in God's plan.
By that element, our unpurified attributes cause all our strife,
Through jealousy, envy, or pure caprice.
You have, Ho Phap, a cramp in your hand,
Let us continue our talk tomorrow.

Ho Phap:
Pardon, if all comes from our Master, all must be perfect. Why
then do we observe imperfection in nature?

Victor Hugo:
What are these imperfections? Will you give some examples?

Ho Phap:
The wickedness and uselessness of beings, whether men, animals or vegetables. Sometimes their cause for being cannot be
reasonably appreciated.

Victor Hugo:
Nothing is wicked or useless in nature.
To stay alive, all must receive nourishment.
The Good Lord ardently loves His Children,
And through this great love, they are provided with the means.
For their progress, He creates for them sufferings,
But they're also given means of defense.
Have you seen in this world a man truly devout?
Though they be wicked to us, they are useful to them!
How did our great sages become as they are
As revealed by the pages of human history?
A fierce struggle between the weak and the strong,
Those of greatest fortitude are more often the victors.
The struggle between the two polarities
Leads to an upward march
Of ideas and wise realizations.
Our dear world is purely relative;

Wicked and useless are only qualifications.
On this globe, each of us has a place;
All worlds, all lives are but classrooms,
The universe is therefore a school for our spirits,
Who attend it for erudite study.
Those who fail their courses,
Must repeat them, and study the lessons again.
All spirits hope to read the eternal book
That holds the wisdom that should make them immortal.
The goal is to accomplish the task before us
Which takes time and effort on our parts.
From the material world to divine purity
Is a road leading into Eternity.
The result is the realization of true self,
And through conscience, to know how to be.
The difference in characteristics has its reason;
'Tis an aid in making comparisons.
Make room for great tolerance in your studies;
Classify the spirits according to their aptitude.
Simply separate those who are human
From those already a little divine.
Recruit the best of these to the task of uplifting humanity.
Use all means to teach the spiritually unenlightened
Without showing distaste for any shortcomings you may per-
    ceive in them;
Think only of the advancement of their souls!
Love always in order to give humanity
These two verities: Love and Eternity.

Life, Death, Reincarnation, Karma

CaoDai propounds that each human has two lives: a spiritual one which is everlasting, and a physical life which is temporary. The spiritual life is everlasting because a human being's spirit is part of the Supreme Being. The physical body, being comprised of matter, is only temporary and suffers wear and tear and, with time, death. Physical life, the life of the body, is used by spirit for its evolution toward unification with the Supreme Being.

The earth is considered as a school of life where human beings' spirits learn to progress by means of education, knowledge, and experiences through the physical body. The physical body, being comprised of matter, is only temporary and suffers wear and death with time. The spirit has to leave this physical body sometime via physical death and to use another body via rebirth to continue its evolution. All education, knowledge, and experiences of this life would be factors of influence upon the person's intelligence, knowledge, and experiences in the next life and would explain early knowledge and experiences of ingenious individuals such as Beethoven, Mozart, Einstein, et cetera, in the West, and Nguyen Binh Khiem, Le Qui Don, et cetera, in Vietnam. Striking examples of "déjà vu" described by many authors and of the experiences from the lives of the Dalai Lama, such as recognizing objects they used in previous incarnations, is attributable to the reincarnation phenomenon.

To CaoDai, death is the gateway to live another life for spiritual progression. Depending on one's level of spiritual evolution, a human spirit may have to reincarnate on earth to learn more or to progress on to other dimensions.

As the divine law is love and justice, this law is the golden rule for the spirit to follow in order to progress. Justice is: "Do unto others as you would have them do unto you," or, "Do not do to others what you do not want others to do to you." This rule of justice is also called Karma, and the results of one's actions, wise and kind or nasty and ignoble, take on Karmic meaning. As the Bible states: "As ye sow, so shall ye reap." Karma explains why perfectly wonderful humans on this earth may sustain great sufferings: they may be reaping the result of misdeeds, unfavorable actions, sins, not from this life but from previous lives.

The two ways to detach from sufferings without losing your compassion or feeling nature, are to practice love and justice with others and to practice self-cultivation. True love and justice are not only the foundation for individual spiritual liberation but lead to harmony on earth. CaoDai's diverse spiritual teachings allow all persons in all spiritual states to find refuge.

Exotericism and Esotericism

CaoDai always promotes exoterism and esoterism to be practiced at the same time. Exoterism is a path to do good works for humanity in order to pay off one's debt.

Esoterism is a way to make oneself purer and purer in order to be more unified with the Supreme Being. You may also find in the

Tibetan book CAP B of the Dead that the soul is just a form of Light. The Supreme Being is also composed of Light. In CaoDai, the Supreme Being is called Dai Linh Quang, Great Sacred Light; and the soul of a human being is called Tieu Linh Quang, little sacred light. The difference between human beings (Tieu Linh Quang) and the Supreme Being (Dai Linh Quang) is that the Supreme Being is purely Yang, invisible, absolutely pure, absolutely good, omnipotent, omniscient, omnipresent, has no beginning and no end; while the human being consists of Yin and Yang. The Yang part (the Than or the spirit) in a human being has exactly the same characteristic as the Supreme Being's Yang and is called consciousness; but it is covered by the Yin part, the visible part created by the Mother Goddess, which is the Tinh and Khi represented respectively by the physical body and the emotions.

Self-cultivation consists of bringing one's Tinh and Khi to purer and purer levels so that the Than may get closer and closer to The Supreme Being and finally become one with the Dai Linh Quang. As the result of self-cultivation, one's second body becomes purer and lighter and subsequently assimilates with higher and purer dimensions (heavens).

A PRACTICAL WAY

Religions' Unity

A thorough study of all religions leads to the conclusion that all are indeed one, not necessarily in their historical accuracy and certainly not in their varying customs, but in their essential spiritual messages: All of humanity is one common family; All religions come from one divine source; All ethics are essentially contained in the Golden Rule; good deeds are rewarded, evil deeds corrected. Divinity can be experienced and realized in the individual through prayer/meditation/contemplation.

CaoDai's highest, most honorable goal is to unite all of humanity through a pure understanding of the Supreme Being and to thus promote peace and understanding on the planet. With shared understanding and vision, people and religions could set aside minor differences that now cause much separation. A decorous ordered world where all religions nicely match up is not the desire of Cao-

Dai. The true intent is to create a more tolerant, unbiased world where all can accept each other as family from a common, divine source.

Holy messages from the Supreme Being:

Formerly, people lacked transportation and therefore did not know each other. I then founded at different epochs and in different areas, five branches of the Tao: Humanism, Shintoism, The Way of Saints, The Way of Immortals and The Way of Buddhas, each based on the customs of the respective race. In present days, transportation has been improved and people have come to know each other better but do not live in harmony because of the very multiplicity of their religions. That is why I have deigned to unite all of the religions back into one, to return them to the primordial unity.

A Final Message

In the 1920s, new hope was quietly bestowed upon the world in the form of a message, delivered to a secluded mystic, from God. This message, thereafter called the Third Revelation of the Ultimate Way (Tao), or CaoDai, teaches the unity of purpose behind all religions.

That this flower of peace took seed in a land destined for war may seem a contradiction, but once understood, the CaoDai path simply transcends all contradiction and leads the world to tranquility. Within these teachings is found the revelation of a unique yet all-encompassing path to God.

SCIENCE OF MIND SCRIPTURES

INTRODUCTION

Ernest Holmes, founder of the Religious Science movement, was born on a farm in Maine in 1887. He grew up in a poor but very literate family and was an especially curious youngster who read avidly but found school dull. Before finishing high school, he abandoned formal education and set out on a lifetime of independent study. Early on he discovered Ralph Waldo Emerson, with whose teachings he immediately felt a deep identification. While living in Boston, Holmes was introduced to Christian Science and soon developed a mental healing technique similar to that practiced in Christian Science. In 1912 he moved to Los Angeles, and after coming across the works of a leading New Thought writer, Thomas Troward, Holmes began lecturing on metaphysics. Growing demand led him in 1927 to establish the Institute of Religious Science and Philosophy, which later became the Church of Religious Science. Its first formally organized congregation was Founder's Church in Los Angeles, which at one period had more than 10,000 members. By the time Holmes died in 1960 there were 85 Religious Science churches nationwide as well as hundreds of licensed Religious Science ministers and practitioners. Holmes was a student of all the world's religions and philosophies, and believed they were all pointing to the unity found in one ultimate, universal Truth. [1]

SCIENCE OF MIND SCRIPTURES

The Meaning of Freedom

Freedom of will means the ability to do, say and think as one wishes; to express life as one personally desires. To be able only to think and dream of freedom would not be liberty. To imagine, without the power to manifest that imagination, would be to remain in a sort of dream world which would never come to complete self-realization. This is not the world in which we live at all, for our world is one of self-expression, even though that expression appears at times to destroy us.

Sin and Punishment, Righteousness and Reward

We do not wish to enter into theological discussions, but we do wish to make the thought clear to those who care to study it. There is no sin but a mistake and no punishment but an inevitable consequence. Wrongdoing must be punished, for the Law of cause and effect must be eternally operative. Right doing must be rewarded for the same reason.

Science of Mind does not say that people cannot sin; what it says is, that we do sin or make mistakes and that we are thereby automatically punished, as long as we continue to make mistakes. This does not mean that there is an evil power in the Universe; but it does mean that there is an immutable Law of cause and effect running through everything. Sin is its own punishment and righteousness its own reward.

The age-long discussion of the problem of evil will never be answered until we realize that it is not a thing of itself but is simply a

---

[1] Excerpts are taken from: Ernest Holmes, *Can We Talk to God?* (Science of Mind Publishing, 1934, 1992).

misuse of the Law of freedom. The problem of evil will be met only to the degree that we *cease doing evil and do good,* for evil will disappear when we no longer indulge in it. When the whole world sees the right and does it; then, and not until then, will the problem of evil be solved for the entire race.

The Incarnation of Spirit

To return to individuality; it is that which distinguishes us from the mere brute creation; it is the greater Incarnation of God in the human; the Indwelling Spirit of the Most High.

We are created and left to discover ourselves, and on the road to this self-discovery we experience the creations of our own imaginations which ultimately show us the Truth and lead to real freedom.

There is an interesting myth in regard to the human creation which may serve to point out this fact. It is said that when the gods decided to make human beings and make them Divine Beings, they held a long discussion as to where would be the best place to hide our Divinity. Some of the gods suggested that it be hidden in the earth, but others argued that some day we would penetrate the earth and so discover ourselves; it was then suggested that it be hidden in the depths of the sea, but this idea was rejected, for we would go under the sea and there discover our true nature; it was next suggested that our real nature should be deposited somewhere in the air, but this also was rejected, for we would surely fly through the air and find ourselves. After a long discussion it was finally agreed that the best place to hide our Divinity would be in the innermost nature of ourselves—this being the last place we would look to find it!

This discovery would not be made until we had had all the experience necessary to complete a well-rounded life. "The Word is very close to you in your mouth, and in your heart, that you may do it."

Of course, this is a fable, but how clearly it sets forth the reality of the case! The word is really in our own mouths, and every time we say, "I am" we are repeating it; for "I am" is the secret of nature and the emblem of Eternity.

The story of "The Prodigal Son" is the story of our return to "His Father's House." How truly the poet puts it when he says that "Trailing clouds of Glory do we come from Heaven which is our home." This is the mystical meaning of that marvelous poem of

Robert Browning's, called "Saul." Saul had lost his sense of real life and lay in a stupor in his tent when David came to sing to him, to awaken him to the realization of his true nature. At first David sings of the wonders of Creation and of the delights of life; he tells Saul of his power and glory as a human being; and, as the song expands, he touches the secret spring of Saul's being—"He is Saul ye remember in glory, ere error had bent the broad brow from the daily communion." Then, he plainly tells Saul of the Christ. This revelation finally awakens Saul to "His old motions and attitudes kingly." The healing has taken place and the realization of the Truth has freed Saul from the thralldom of false belief.

Different Viewpoints

Some take the viewpoint that human beings were cast forth to discover themselves; and others contend that we decided to do this for ourselves. It makes no difference what the case may be; we are certainly on the pathway to self-discovery, and everything in our experience points to the truth of this fact. We know that the forces of nature wait on our discovery of them and our willingness to obey them. We certainly have freedom enough when we understand how to use that freedom. The Pilgrim Fathers might have had steam cars if they had understood the nature of steam. It was not pushed into our experience by any autocratic power, but served us only after we had discovered how to use it. We might say the same of any and all of the laws that we now understand and utilize.

The Lesson of Nature's Laws

If we find this to be true of the laws of the mechanical world, why should we not also find it true of those Mental and Spiritual Laws which transcend the mechanical world? No doubt, we shall find latent powers and capacities of which we have never dreamed; powers and abilities waiting to be understood and used. "Behold I stand at the door and knock." It certainly will pay us to spend much time and thought in the study of our own nature; for we will discover things about ourselves that will cause us to "Arise and shine." We are today more than ever before, awakening to the real facts of the case, and from now on our evolution will become very rapid. Nothing is impossible; all things are possible to the Great Whole, and we are a part of that Whole.

Our Experience

Let us assume that we are on the road to self-discovery. What are we to discover?—That we are really free, but that, in order to be free, we must first go through experiences which will teach us how to use our freedom properly; and, after the lesson is learned, we will be free indeed. Everything seems as if this were true. We have traced the progress of humans carefully through our journey on this planet from time when the first face "Was turned from the clod," to now, and what have we discovered? That all nature waits upon our self-discovery and is ever ready to serve us and do our bidding. Laws and forces undreamed of by our ancestors are now being employed; powers and forces which to prehistoric human beings would have seemed as gods, are today called nature's forces, and we consciously make use of them. Human beings have gradually merged with nature and its laws, and today stand forth as new beings so far as the mechanical world is concerned. It seems as if we had conquered nature and compelled her to serve us.

Nature Waits on Us

Nowhere on this path have we found nature opposed to us. She has silently waited for our recognition and has silently done our bidding. She will never contradict herself nor operate contrary to her inherent laws; but she will serve whoever comes to understand and use them along the lines of her way of working. We never created any of these laws but simply use them, and we can do this only as we first obey them. "Nature obeys us as we first obey it" is an old saying and a true one. We learn the fundamental principle of a law, obey its mode of operation and then have conscious use of it. It would be absurd to say that nature punished us because we did not make proper use of her laws. She simply will not work harmoniously for us until we harmonize with her; she will obey us only after we have obeyed her. This is, of course, true of any and all law. If we obey, it serves; if we disobey, it seems to punish us.

Mental and Spiritual Laws

It is the same with those great Mental and Spiritual Laws of our Being. We must come to discover and utilize the inner forces of Mind and Spirit, for they are the highest powers.

We will be delivered from sin, sickness and trouble in exact proportion to our discovery of ourselves and our relationship to the whole.

Law is law wherever we find it, and we shall discover that the Laws of Mind and Spirit must be understood if they are to be consciously used for definite purposes. *The Spirit knows and the Law obeys.*

Hidden away in the inner nature of the real person is the Law of His life, and some day we will discover it and consciously make use of it. We will hear ourselves, make ourselves happy and prosperous, and will live in an entirely different world; for we will have discovered that *life is from within and not from without.*

God and Human Beings

We are made out of and from Life; and, as effect must partake of the nature of its cause, so we must partake of the Divine Nature from which we spring.

Human Beings Reenact the Nature of God

If we realize that God is "Triune" and that we are made in the Image and Likeness of God, we shall see that the whole scheme of Life and the whole nature of the Divine Being is reenacted through us. This, of course, does not mean that we are God; It means that, in our small world of individual expression, our nature is identical with God's. This is what Jesus meant when he said, "As a Father has Life within himself, so has He given to the children to have Life within themselves."

A single drop of water is not the whole ocean, but it does resemble the ocean and does contain within itself the same qualities and attributes. We might say that we are in God and that God works through us. "I and The Father are One," "The Kingdom of God is within you;" and we might add, "God's in His Heaven; all's right with the world."

The Two Ways to Reason

There are but two processes of reasoning known to the human mind: inductive and deductive; and from these two ways of reasoning all our knowledge of life has come. Inductive reasoning is the systematic process of reasoning from a part to the whole. Deductive reasoning is the process of accepting certain conclusions as truths and drawing other conclusions from them; it is reasoning from the whole to a part. For instance, in inductive reasoning we would say that everything happens just as if there were what we call electricity and that it is everywhere present. Deductive reasoning says that since electricity is everywhere present, it is always where we are and can always be generated from any center.

Using these two methods of reasoning to deduce the nature of God, we may start with the assumption that God *is*, drawing all our conclusion from this premise; or we may carefully study human nature and the Universe and so draw the conclusion that a God must exist. Whichever method we use will lead to the same conclusion; namely, that there is a Divine Being and that humans are made in this image and must reenact and portray the same attributes as the Life from which we came.

Nothing happens by Chance

Nothing in the Universe happens by chance. All is in accordance with Law, and the Law of God is as Omnipresent as is the Spirit of God. This Law is a Law of Mind, but back of the Law is the Word. "All things were made by God and without God was not anything made that was made."

Back of our lives is the Law of our Being; and through that Law runs the word which we speak; for "Whatever things the children (the Son) see the Parent do, these will they do also."

Many Are Waking up to The Facts

Thousands of people today are beginning to realize this and put it into operation, and the results attained would fill more books than one person could read in a lifetime. Thousands today are using the silent power of Mind to heal their bodies and bring prosperity into their affairs; and the Law is always working in accordance with the belief of those seeking to use It. As the Universe is run by an Infinite Mind, so our lives are controlled by our thinking; ignorance of this keeps us in bondage; knowledge will free us.

One by one, people will investigate the Truth and put It into operation, and the time will come when disease and poverty will be swept from the face of the earth, for they were never intended to

be. They are simply the by-products of ignorance, and enlightenment alone will erase them.

The Time Has Come to Know the Truth

The hour of freedom has struck, the bell of Liberty is ringing, and
"Let those that are athirst come." Let us, then plunge more deeply
into our own natures and into the nature of the Universe and see if
we shall not find treasures undreamed of, possibilities never imagined and opportunities which the fond thought—yearning for freedom—has often, in our vision of the greater Life, given us.

"Prove me now, herewith, says the Lord of hosts, if I will not
open you the windows of heaven, and pour you out a blessing that
there shall not be enough to receive it."

A Wonderful Experiment

It would be a wonderful experiment for anyone to make to begin
to live as if this promise were true; to talk, think and act as though
there were a Limitless Power attending us on our journey through
life; as though our every act were directed and guided into expressions of peace, health, happiness and harmony. It is surely worth-
while, and understanding will make the way so clear before us that
we shall some day come to see the logic of it; and then, indeed,
shall we really begin to live. Our lives, fortunes and happiness are
in our own hands to mold as we will—provided we first obey the
Law and learn how to make conscious use of It. "With all your getting get understanding"—an old adage—but today as true as ever.

It has been the teaching of all times that we reproduce the Divine
Nature; and if we do, we shall expect to find in our nature the same
qualities that we suppose must be in the Nature of Life Itself.

What Psychology Teaches about Human Nature

A study of our psychological nature verifies the belief in "The Trinity" running through all Life. We are self-conscious; of this we are
sure, for we can say, "I am." This fact alone proves our claim to
immortality and greatness. In psychology we learn that humanity is
threefold in its nature; that is, we have a self-conscious mind, a
subconscious mind and a body. In metaphysics we learn that the
three are but different attributes of the same life. Our self-
conscious mind is the power with which we know; it is, therefore,

one with the Spirit of God; it is, indeed, our only guarantee of conscious being.

The Self-Knowing Mind

It is from this self-knowing mind that we are able to realize our relationship with the Whole; for without it we would be un-human and most certainly not Divine; but since we are it, we must be Divine.

It is the self-knowing mind alone that constitutes reality, personality and individuality. It is the "image of God," the essence of Life, and the "Personification of the Infinite."

Our Unity with the Whole

We recognize, then, in our self-knowing mind our Unity with the Whole. For while a drop of water is not the ocean, yet it does contain within itself all the attributes of the limitless deep.

Our self-knowing mind is the instrument which perceived reality, and cognizes or realizes Truth. All illumination, inspiration, and realization must come through the self-knowing mind in order to manifest in us. Vision, intuition and revelation proclaim themselves through our self-knowing mind; and the Saints and Sages, the Saviors and Christs, the Prophets and Seers, the Wise and Learned, have all consciously perceived and proclaim this fact. Every evidence of human experience, all acts of kindness and mercy, have interpreted themselves through our self-knowing mind. All that we know, say or think, feel or believe, hope or long for, fear or doubt, is some action of the self-knowing mind. Subjective memories we have, and inner unexpressed emotions we feel; but to the self-knowing mind alone does realization come. Without this capacity to consciously know, we would not exist as an expressed being; and, so far as we are concerned, would not exist at all. The self-knowing mind proclaims itself in every thought, deed or act, and is truly the only guarantee of our individuality.

We Are a Center of God-Consciousness

With this vast array of facts at our disposal it would be foolish to suppose that our self-knowing mind is any other than our perception of Reality. *It is our Unity with the Whole, or God, on the conscious side of life, and is an absolute guarantee that we are a Center of God-Consciousness in the Vast Whole.*

Unity with Law

We will say, then, that in Spirit we are One with God. But what of the great Law of the Universe? If we are really One with the Whole we must be one with the Law of the Whole, as well as One with the Spirit. Again, psychology has determined the fact to be more than a fancy. The characteristics of the subconscious mind determine our Subjective Unity with the Universe of life, Law and Action.

The Subjective Obeys the Objective

In the Subjective Mind we find a law obeying our word, the servant of our Spirit. Suggestion has proved that the subconscious mind acts upon our thought without question or doubt. It is the mental law of our Being and the creative factor within us. It is unnecessary, at this point, to go into all the details of the Subjective Mind and its mode of action; it is enough to say that within us is a mental law, working out the will and purposes of our conscious thoughts. This can be no other than *our individual use of that greater subjective mind which is the seat of all law and action, and is "the servant of the eternal spirit through all the ages."*

Marvelous as the concept may be, it is nonetheless true that we have at our disposal, in what we call the subjective mind, a power which seems to be Limitless. This is because it is One with the Whole, on the subjective side of life.

Our thought, falling into our subjective mind, merges with the Universal Subjective Mind and becomes the law of life, through *the one great law of all life.*

There are not two subjective minds. *There is but one subjective mind; and what we call our subjective mind is really only the use that we are making of the one law.*

Individuals maintain their identity in Law through their personal use of It; and all are drawing *from* Life what *they think into it.*

To learn how to think is to learn how to live, for our thoughts go into a Medium that is Infinite in Its ability to do and to be.

We, by thinking, can bring into our experience whatsoever we desire, if we think correctly and become a living embodiment of God's thoughts. This is not done by holding thoughts but by knowing the truth.

The Body

But what about our body? Is that, too, one with the Body of the Universe? Let us briefly analyze matter and see what it really is. We are told that matter is not a solid, stationary thing; but is a constantly flowing, formless substance which is forever coming and going. Matter is as indestructible as God, as eternal as Timeless Being; nothing can be either added to or taken from it. The very bodies we now have were not with us a short time ago. As Sir Oliver Lodge says, we discard many of them on the path through this life, for the material from which our bodies are composed is in a constant state of flow. Vistas of thought open up along the line of mental healing when we realize this fact; later we will thoroughly discuss and work out a definite technique for the purpose of healing.

Matter is not what we thought it to be; it is simply a flowing stuff taking the form that Mind give it. How about the matter from which other things than the body are made? It is all the same—*one substance in the universe takes different forms and shapes and becomes different things.*

Last Stages of Matter

The last analysis of matter resolves it into a universal ether and leaves nothing more than a stuff which may be operated upon.

Matter, in the last analysis, is composed of particles so fine that they are simply supposed to be. In other words, it disappears entirely, and the place where it once was is again "without form and void." Matter, as we know it, is only an aggregation of these particles arranged in such order as to produce definite forms, which are determined by something *which is not material.*

There is no difference between the particles which any one form takes and the particles which all forms take; the difference is not in the minute particles but in their arrangement.

The Unity of all Body

Our bodies are One with the Whole Body of the Universe. Seeds, plants, cabbages and kings are made of the same substance; minerals, solids and liquids are made from *the primordial substance which is forever flowing into form and forever flowing out again into the void.*

The Formless and the Formed

Nothing could form a formless stuff, which has no mind of its own, except Intelligence operating upon it. Again we come back to the Word as the starting point of all Creation—God's Word in the Great World, our word in the small world.

One *Spirit, one Mind, and one Substance; one Law but many Thoughts; one Power, but many ways of using it; one God in whom we all live, and one Law which all operate; one, one, one. No greater unity could be given than that which is already vouchsafed to humankind.*

But why are we so limited? Why are we still poor, sick, afraid and unhappy? Because we do not know the Truth—that is the only "Why." But why were we not so made that we would have to know the Truth? The answer is that even God could not make a real person, that is, a real Personified Expression of Itself, without *creating us in freedom and leaving us to discover Ourselves.* This is the meaning of the story of the Prodigal Son and the whole meaning of it.

Individuality Means Self-Choice

Individuality means real individualized being and real personified self-choice. We could not imagine an individuality without self-choice; but what would be the use of self-choice unless the ability to choose were backed with the power to externalize that choice? It would remain simply an idle dream, never coming into real self-expression. A little thought will make it clear that, if we are created to express freedom, we must be left to discover ourselves. Of course, during the process we will have much experience, but in the end we will come out a real being.

The day of our discovery of ourselves marked the first day of the record of human history on this planet; and from the day when we first made this discovery we have constantly risen and continuously progressed. All the forces of nature attend us on our way but we much first discover them in order to make use of them.

The Greatest Discovery Ever Made

The greatest discovery that humankind ever made was, that our thought has creative power; that is, that it uses creative power. This thought, of itself, would have no power unless it were operative through a creative medium. We do not have to compel Law to operate; all that we have to do is to use it. The Law of Mind is just like any and all other laws of Being. It simply Is.

A Complete Unity

We have now discovered a Unity with the Whole on all three sides of life or from all three modes of expression. We are One with all matter in the physical world, One with the Creative Law of the Universe in the Mental World, and One with the Spirit of God in the Conscious World.

What more could we ask or hope for? How would it be possible for more to be given? We could ask for no more, and no greater freedom could be given. From now on we will expand, grow and express, only to the degree that we consciously cooperate with the Whole.

Limitless Medium

When we realize that as we deal with our own individuality we are dealing with Self-Conscious mind, and when we realize that as we deal with subjective mind we are dealing with the Universal Subjectivity, we see at once that we have at our disposal a Power compared to which the united intelligence of the human race is as nothing; because the Universal Subjective Mind, being entirely receptive to our thought, is compelled by reason of Its very being to accept that thought and act upon it, no matter what the thought is. Since we are dealing with an Infinite Power, which knows only Its own ability to do, and since It can objectify any idea impressed upon It, there can be no limit to what It could or would do for us, other than the limit of our mental concept. Limitation could not be in Principle or in Law but only in the individual use that we make of It. Our individual use of It can only equal our individual capacity to understand It, to embody It. *We cannot demonstrate beyond our ability to mentally conceive, or to mentally provide, an equivalent.* We must have a mental equivalent of the thing we want, in order to demonstrate.

Subjectivity is entirely receptive and neutral, as we have learned, and It can take our thoughts only the way we think them. There is no alternative. If I say, "I am poor," and keep on saying, "I am poor," subconscious mind at once says, "Yes, you are poor," and keeps me poor, as long as I say it.

This is all there is to poverty. It comes from impoverished thinking. We deal only with thoughts, for thoughts are things, and if the thought is right the condition will be right. An active thought will produce an active condition. Suppose I have thought poverty year after year, I have created a law, which keeps on perpetuating this condition. If the thought be un-erased, the condition will remain. A law has been set in motion which says, "I am poor," and sees to it that it is so. This is, at first, auto-suggestion; then it becomes an unconscious memory, working day and night. This is what decides the law of attraction, because the laws of attraction and repulsion are entirely subjective. They may be *conscious to start with, but they are subconscious as soon as they are set in motion.* Now suppose I did not say I was poor, but came into the world with an unconscious thought of poverty; so long as that thought operated, I would be poor. I might not have understood the Law, but it would have been working all the time.

There is also a race-suggestion which says that some people are rich and some are poor, so we are all born or come into this world with a subjective tendency toward negative conditions. But we are also dealing with a subjective tendency toward ultimate good; because, in spite of all conditions, the race believes more in the good than in the evil; otherwise, it would not exist. It believes that everything will come out all right, rather than all wrong. This is the eternal hope and sense of all life.

No matter what may be in the soul, or subjective state of our thought, the conscious state can change it. This is what treatment does. How can this be done? Through the most direct method imaginable—by consciously knowing that there is no subjective state of poverty, no inherited tendency toward limitation, no race-suggestion operating through subjectivity; nothing in, around or through it that believes in or accepts limitation in any way, shape, form or manner. The conscious state must now provide a higher form of thought. What does it do? It supplies a spiritual realization, a self-conscious realization, and says, "I partake of the nature and bounty of the All Good and I am now surrounded by everything which makes life worth while." What happens then? This Soul side of life, this Universal Medium, at once changes Its thought (because Its thought is deductive only) and says, "Yes, you are all of these things." *Whatever is held in consciousness until it becomes a part of the subjective side of thought must take place in the world of affairs. Nothing can stop it.* The reason we do not demonstrate more easily is that the objective state of our thought is too often neutralized by the subjective state. There is more fear of poverty than there is belief in riches. As long as that fear remains it is sure to produce a limited condition. *Whatever is subjective must objectify.* Matter is immaterial, unknowing, unthinking, and plastic in the hands of Law or Mind; and Law or Subjective Mind, which is entirely un-volitional, but not unintelligent, is compelled by its own subjectivity to receive the thought of the conscious mind, which alone can choose and decide. It follows then that whatever the conscious mind holds long enough is bound to be produced in external affairs; nothing can stop it, because we are dealing with Universal Law. This is called Divine Principle. It is the Medium in which we all live, move and have our being on the subjective side of life; our atmosphere in Universal Subjectivity; the medium through which all intercommunication takes place on every plane.

It follows from what we have said that any suggestion held in Creative Mind would produce its logical result, no matter what that suggestion might be. If it were a suggestion of destruction, it would destroy; for this is a neutral field. If it were a suggestion of good, it would construct.

Christ and Antichrist

The Spirit of Christ means that mentality which recognizes the Law and uses It for constructive purposes only. The spirit of Antichrist is the spirit of the individual, or class of individuals who, understanding the Law, use It destructively. The meaning of the Flood or Deluge (which is recorded in every sacred scripture we have read or heard of) is that a race of people were upon the earth who came to understand psychic, or subjective law as being the servant of the Spirit. They understood themselves to be Spirit, but they did not understand the harmonious Unity of Spirit. They had arrived at an intellectual concept of the Law—a very clearly defined mental concept; but that knowledge and wisdom were not used for constructive purposes. They used it destructively, and what happened? The confusion which took place in the psychic world (or the psychic atmosphere of this planet) caused its physical correspondence in the form of the Deluge or Flood.

Psyche also means "sea," and it was into this psychic sea that Jonah fell. This is the meaning of the story of Jonah and the whale and is also why, in Revelation, it says: "There was no more sea." It does not mean that Law shall be eliminated, but that the time will come when It will be used for constructive purposes only. The misuse of this Law today is called "Malpractice." We have no fear of malpractice, because it can be practiced only upon the person who believes in it. If we say to Mind: "There is no such thing as malpractice," there being only One Ultimate Reality, as far as we are concerned, we are free from it." Against such there is no law." We recognize Subconscious Mind as the Great Servant of our thought. It is the Medium through which all treatment operates. How do we contact this Universal Subjective Mind, which is the Medium through which healing and demonstration take place? *We contact It within ourselves and nowhere else.* It is in us, being Omnipresent. Our use of It, we call our subjective mind: but It is Universal Subjectivity.

Humanity Is Identified in Mind

Spiritual mind recognizes that individuals have their identity in mind and are known in a Mind by the name they bear. This Subjective Law knows there is a John Smith and a Mary Jones. Why? Because John Smith and Mary Jones know that there is a John Smith and a Mary Jones. *But It only knows about them what they know about themselves.* Being subjective to their thought, It could not know anything else, consequently, whatever John Smith and May Jones say, It says, accepts and does. This is a marvelous concept. Unless we have thought it out, it may seem rather startling. But it means this: —that *the Law absolutely accepts us at our own valuation.* Now this does not mean that it accepts us at an *assumption* of *valuation,* but at the *actual valuation.* It can reflect to us only the actual embodiment of ourselves. *It is the deep inner conviction that we carry which decides what is going to happen.* So we are each known by the name we bear, and each is daily making some statement about that name. When we say "I am this or that," we are involving in mind statements which Mind in turn produces as conditions.

Treatment

In treatment we turn entirely from the condition, because so long as we look at a condition we cannot overcome it. That is why the mystic said: "Behold my face forevermore." "Look to me and be saved, all the ends of the earth." That is, look up and not down. It is useless to treat one's business, because business is an immaterial thing. It is an unthinking, unknowing thing—a lot of stuff in form, a lot of forms in stuff. That which decides what the business shall be is in Consciousness or Mind. Consequently, we must involve in Mind a correct concept of the business, seeing it as we want it to be; and when we have seen it that way long enough, it will be so. How long will it take? *Until the subjective side of thought accepts the new concept as true, or until we have neutralized the old concept.*

Jesus had a great understanding, and He gave a clue to that understanding when He said: "The Prince of this world comes and finds nothing in me." He meant that race-suggestion found no mental correspondence or equivalent in Him. His consciousness was so clear that it operated directly from the Spirit.

The Aim of Evolution

The aim of evolution is to produce people who, at the point of their objective thought, may completely manifest the whole idea of life—i.e., bring the concept of Unity to the point of particularization, finding nothing in the Law to oppose it. The reason Jesus was able to become the Christ was, that at the objective point of His thought there was a complete realization of the Unity of the Spirit and the Absoluteness of his word. His spiritual and psychical faculties, his objective and subjective mind, were completely poised and perfectly balanced.

It is evident that if this took place in any individuals, their word would be manifested likewise. It would have to be, because behind the word is Universal Soul, Omnipotent Law. Divine Principle is Limitless, but *It can only be to us what we believe It is.* Why must we believe It is? Because until we believe It is, we are believing It is not. The reason some people cannot demonstrate the Truth is, they do not realize It. The whole thing is a matter of belief; *but belief is scientifically induced into a subjective state through conscious endeavor and effort.* Treatment is the science of inducing within Mind concepts, acceptances, and realizations of peace, poise, power, plenty, health, happiness and success, or whatever the particular need may be.

What do practitioners do? They set the Law in motion in Universal Mind. Let us suppose that Mary is sick, and that John is a practitioner. She comes to him, saying, "I am sick." He, being a metaphysician, understands that Mind is all; she does not understand this. She feels that she is sick. But he knows that all sickness is mental. He does not try to hold a thought over her, nor does he try to suggest anything to her; for that is not mental treatment. He simply declares the Truth about her; he speaks her name and says: "This word is for her; she is perfect; she is well." In other words, he contradicts what appears to be and declares the Truth about her. What happens? A law is being enacted on the subjective side of life. His word, operative through the Universal Sea of Mind (in which both live), sets in motion a law which objectifies through her body as healing.

Mary thinks a miracle has been performed. She exclaims: "I am healed. I did not have a bit of faith, but John healed me." No miracle has been performed. He used a law which all may use if they will. Suppose Mary were perfectly well, but wanted a position, — what would the treatment be? It would be the same. John would state in Mind what should be done for Mary. There is only One Law, and Mary could demonstrate just as well for herself if she understood It, but she must first see It demonstrated to realize it. This is the state of mind of most people who come for healing. They do not know what ails them; they think their condition is due to some external cause. Nevertheless, they are healed and exclaim: "This is a marvelous thing, though I do not understand what it is all about." Often they become superstitious about it, as people do about the things they do not understand; once they understand the law, however, healing is no longer a mystery.

The only reason people have difficulty in throwing off some weakness of character, while believing in Spirit implicitly and having faith that they are going to overcome their limitations, is because they have not induced the necessary mental images in Mind. If they had, they would have overcome their troubles; thinking of their weakness keeps the image of it before them.

In treating, turn entirely away from the condition. Disease and limitation are neither person, place nor thing; they are simply images of thought. Turn entirely

*from the condition, or the limited situation, to its opposite, that is, to the reali-
zation of health, happiness or harmony.*

Methods of Treatment

Although several methods of treatment are used, there are but two
distinct methods; one is called argumentative, and the other realization. The argumentative method is a process of mental argument in
which the practitioner argues to himself about his patient. He is,
consequently, presenting a logical argument to Universal Mind, or
Divine Principle; and if that argument carries with it a complete
evidence in favor of his patient, it is supposed that the patient will
be healed.

The method of realization is one whereby practitioners realize
within themselves perfect state of their patient; it is purely a spiritual and meditative process of contemplating the Perfect Being;
and if the embodiment of the idea is really made, it will at once
produce a healing.

Treatment is for the purpose of inducing an inner realization of
perfection in the mentality of the practitioner, which inner realization, acting through Mind, operates in the patient.

Between John and Mary there is One Universal Medium which is
also in John and Mary; It is not only between them, but in them. As
John knows right where John is (since there is only *One*), he is at
the same time knowing right where Mary is, because his work is
operative though a field which is not divided but which is a complete Unit or Whole, i.e., Universal Subjectivity. As he knows
within or upon himself, he is setting in motion the Law, which operates through the person whom he mentions in his treatment, no
matter where the patient may be. There is no such thing as an absent treatment, as opposed to a present treatment.

Mary must have a consciousness of health before the healing can
be permanent. It will have to become a part of her subjective
thought. If the consciousness did not change, we would perpetuate
the old thought images and would get sick again; and that is why, in
treating, people get well for a while and then become sick again.
They are not permanently healed unless the consciousness is
healed.

*A treatment begins and ends within the thought of the one giving it. The
practitioners must do the whole work within themselves. They must know the
Truth, and as they do that, they set in motion the Law. A thing which is*

known by any part of the Universal Mind is known by every part of It, for It is an Undivided Whole. When you know in one place you know everywhere. When you give a treatment you do not send out a thought, or hold a thought, or give suggestion. A treatment is a positive thing.

If you are treating a certain John Smith, you say (if he is not present), "I am treating John Smith of such and such a place." Then you forget all about him as a personality and give your treatment. It is not necessary to specify the trouble. Once in a great while, you might find yourself mentioning a thing in order to make some statement against it, but probably that is not the best way. Of course there are certain thoughts back of certain things, and a knowledge of the disease might enable you to know better what thought to destroy.

It is like this: Mary Jones comes to John Smith and says, "I have tuberculosis." In answer to this he declares, "This word is for Mary Jones. She is a perfect and complete manifestation of Pure Spirit, and Pure Spirit cannot be diseased; consequently she is not diseased." This is an argument, trying to bring out the evidence in favor of perfection. It is an argument which produces a certain conclusion in the mentality of John Smith, and, consequently, it sets in motion a certain law for Mary Jones. As John does this, day after day, he gradually becomes convinced of her perfection and she is healed. If he could do it in one minute, she would be healed in one minute. *There is no process in healing. It is a revelation, an awakening, a realization of Life.* Humankind exists in Divine Mind as a Perfect Image; but it covers itself with the distorted images of its own thought along the pathway of its mental experience.

If using the method of realization, say, "This word or this thought is for Mary Jones." Then begin to realize the Perfect Presence, the *Only* Perfect Presence. "God is all there is; there is no other Life"; very little argument, but more and more a complete realization. This is very powerful, although it makes no difference which method you use, as they produce the same result. It is a good idea to combine both.

In the case of a child, the treatment should be the same. *It would have an effect commensurate with the absolute conviction that the practitioner has.* But in the case of an infant, who is subjective to the conscious thought of the people around it, you must teach those people how to think about the child, and see that they do think that way; else you might heal the child and their thought might make it sick again.

In case of failure, it is probable that the trouble is more with John than with Mary, as far as the immediate healing is concerned. However, diseases are the direct results of certain habitual mental attitudes which people entertain, and unless those mental attitudes are changed, there will be no permanent healing. It is the business of the practitioner to discover what those attitudes are and to change them. It is also the business of the practitioner to show people why they are as they are, and to teach them how to overcome undesirable attitudes.

In giving a treatment, you talk to yourself about somebody else.

We must grasp the idea of Universal Subjectivity, the Potentiality of all things, the Divine Creative Medium. This is the Principle through which we are to demonstrate the healing of the body or of the condition; and It acts accurately and mathematically, because It is the Law of cause and effect.

Subjective Law

When we think, we think from conscious intelligence, or Spirit. We will say that the thought becomes subjectified; i.e., it goes into the subconscious mind. But what is our subconscious mind? It is our atmosphere or mental vibration in Universal Subjectivity. There is no such thing as your subjective mind and my subjective mind, meaning two, for this would be duality. But there is such a thing as the subjective state of your thought and of my thought in Mind. This should be made very clear, for here is where psychology and metaphysics separate; i.e., their understandings are different. When we think, we think into a Universal Creative Medium, a receptive and plastic substance which surrounds us on all sides, which permeates us and flows though us. We do not have to think that we are thinking in It or upon It; for when we think we do think into and upon It; there is no other place that we could think, since It is Omnipresent.

As we subjectify ourselves in consciousness we are building around ourselves a mental atmosphere; and nothing can enter this unless we allow it to, through the avenues of our own thought; but this thought might be conscious or unconscious; in most cases it is unconscious, but students of Truth are learning to consciously control the stream of thought that we allow to enter our inner and creative mentality.

Thought and the Creative Medium

Thought is an inner movement which is the result of our perception of life and our reaction to it. Every time this movement takes place it takes place within Mind, upon Cause, according to law. We are, without question, dealing with the same Power that molds the planets and all that is upon them; and the limit of our ability to prove this is not in Principle, but is in our understanding of It; in our ability to incorporate within ourselves an embodiment of our ideals.

Each is the Logical Result of Our Own Thinking

We are dealing with a neutral, creative power, just as we would be in the case of electricity or any other natural force. It is on a higher plane; for it is the power of intelligence. As we think into this Universal Mind, our thought, in its externalization, will reach its own level, just as water will reach its own level by its own weight and without effort. This is in line with necessity; for the Universe, in order to be at all, must be Self-Existent.

What is meant by the Self-Existence of the Universe? This means a Universe which is Its own reason for being; a Universe which exists by virtue of Itself, being All.

All of us are today the result of what has gone before, either consciously or unconsciously, no matter what kind of a condition we may be in. As soon as we realize this we shall be better off, because we shall see that since what we now are, or what we now have and experience, is the result of what we have thought; the answer to what we shall be is contained in what we now are; for we *can change* out thinking.

We think and suppose that we let go of the thoughts we think. But such is not the case; for thought becomes subjectified in mind, like a seed planted in the soil; it stays there, unless neutralized, and decides the attraction and repulsion in the experience of the one thinking. There is a constant action on the subjective side of life; and it is this unconscious process which decides what is going to happen in the outer expression. Whatever we think, act, believe in, feel, visualize, vision, image, read, talk about, in fact, all processes which affect or impress us at all, are going into the subjective state of our thought, which is our individualized use of Universal Mind.

Whatever goes into the subjective state of thought tends to return again as some condition.

A Law of Belief

Jesus said, "As you have believed so be it done to you." Knowing the nature of the law, He did not say, "It is done unto you as you wish." He announced the universality of law when He said, "As you have believed so be it done to you."

We Are Dealing with Law

Someone may say, "I can't imagine God not caring." I cannot either; but we are dealing with law. Does the law of electricity care whether it cooks the dinner or burns the house down? Whether it electrocutes a criminal or warms the feet of a saint? Of course it does not care at all! Does the urge, which impels people to express, care whether a person kneels in ecstasy or lies drunk in the gutter? We are dealing with law. And it follows that, since we are dealing with law, it will ultimately bring back to us the results of the forces which we set in motion through it. Consequently, no person who is enlightened would seek to use this law destructively; for we would know that, sooner or later, the very power set in motion by ourselves would ultimately destroy us." All they that take the sword shall perish with the sword." The Spirit of Christ is the spirit which constructively uses the law. The spirit of Antichrist is the destructive use of law. The Spirit of Christ, being in line with the Cosmic Life, will always transcend, neutralize, destroy, and utterly obliterate the spirit of Antichrist; and ultimately only the Spirit of Christ can succeed. "Those that have an ear, let them hear."

The Cycle of Necessity and Karmic Law

The cycle of necessity means that those things which individuals set in motion through the law must ultimately swing back to them again. This is the Karmic Law; "The law that binds the ignorant but frees the wise." This law has been announced by every great teacher who has ever lived. Jesus referred to this law when He said, "As you have believed so be it done unto you"; and when He said, "Heaven and earth shall pass away: but my words shall not pass away." It is the law to which Isaiah referred when he said, "So shall my word be that goeth forth out of my mouth; it shall not return unto me void, but it shall accomplish that which I please." This is the law which today is called "Divine Principle," or the law of cause and effect; it means that once a tendency is set in motion through law, it is bound to objectify at the level of the subjective concept which entertains it. There is nothing fatalistic about this, for we may consciously change the currents of subjectivity with the conscious thought. Indeed, this is what treatment does.

The Law of Action and Reaction

This is simply the law of cause and effect, and instead of getting too occult or mystical a concept of it we would better think of it simply as something into which we think, and which returns to the thinkers what we think into it. This law can be applied for concrete purposes, and once it is set in motion the rest works automatically. This is why we may absolutely trust Principle when we understand how it operates. It knows everything and can do anything; but in order to work for us, we must let it work though us. This is the power that Jesus used when He withered the fig tree and when He raised Lazarus from the dead.

We Argue in Mind

So we argue in Mind; and if we argue toward a belief in health, we will be healed. It isn't a question of suggestion or of the power of thought making us well, for this is but a limited sense of will power. It isn't something over which we must clinch our teeth and will to be; it is something which we have to know. Water doesn't have to will to be wet, it is wet; and if we go into it we will get wet. Life doesn't have to claim to be Life; It simply announces Itself to be what It knows that It is. So we argue in Mind, not to convince Mind that It is or can accomplish, but to convince ourselves that we are *now* perfect.

Wrong Use of Mind

There have been many controversies about the use and the misuse of this power. Some claim that we cannot misuse this power, since there is but One Mind, and It cannot act against Itself. Mind cannot act against Itself; and any individuals who know this, and who know that there is no human mind to destroy, or to be destroyed, are immune from malpractice. But let people believe in malpractice, and they will open mental avenues of receptivity to it; for we can receive only that to which we vibrate.

Malpractice is the ignorant use of something which of itself is good. It is the wrong use of mental power and will never be indulged in by any one who understands the Truth; neither can one who understands the Truth be affected by it. There could be innocent, ignorant and malicious malpractice. Innocent malpractice, in the form of sympathy with disease and trouble, thereby accentuating these conditions, is often prolific of dire results. Ignorant malpractice would be about the same thing; for instance, when one sees a criminal, thinking of him/her as such helps to perpetuate the state in which he/she is manifesting. Malicious malpractice would be an act of centering thought for destructive purposes. When Jesus said, "The prince of this world comes and has nothing in me," He meant that he had neutralized all race thought about destruction and so was immune to all false suggestion. This we should all try to do.

Subjective But Not Unconscious

The subjective mind can deduce only; it cannot, of itself, initiate anything; but this does not mean that it is unintelligent. We must be very careful not to labor under the delusion that because the subjective mind cannot reason it is unintelligent, for it is infinitely more intelligent than our present state of conscious mind, but is, nevertheless, controlled by it. If our subjective consciousness were always clear, that is, if it never received any false impressions, the Spirit would always flow to the point of objectivity and we would never make mistakes; we would never be sick, poor, or unhappy.

How Habits Are Formed

Back in the subjective are the images of thought surrounding us, all acting as living intelligences. It is here that habits are formed; for when we have a habit that we cannot seem to break we are hypnotized by the thought and desire back of that habit; the thought force has grown too strong to be controlled. Habits are healed by neutralizing the thought forces behind them.

Law Is Mind in Action

There is One Infinite Life acting through Law, and this Law is mental; Law is Mind in action. We are surrounded by an Infinite, Subconscious, Impersonal, Neutral, Plastic, Creative, Ever-Present, Thinking Stuff from which all things come, which, in Its Original State, permeates and penetrates all things. By impressing our thought upon this Substance we can cause It to produce for us that which we think, to the limit of our ability to mentally embody the idea. Impressing our thought upon It is not an external act, for when we impress our thought upon ourselves, we are thinking into It; this is because of the Unity of all Mind. This is one of the great lessons to learn; we do not know anything outside ourselves. This is what Jesus meant when He said, "You shall know the Truth, and the Truth shall make you free." When we know within ourselves we are knowing at the point of that Individualized Spirit which we are; upon the very Heart of the Infinite, the Ever-Present Substance, which is ever responsive to Itself.

We Are Bound by Our Own Freedom

We are all bound, tied hand and foot, by our very freedom; our free will binds us; but, as free will creates the conditions which externally limit us, so it can un-create or dissolve them. The universe, being deductive only, cannot refuse us anything. The very force that makes us sick can heal us; the force that makes us poor can make us rich; and the power that makes us miserable can make us happy. If this were not true there would be duality in the Universe, and this is impossible.

Oneness with All Law

When we know of our Oneness with God and Law, what a great burden will be removed which otherwise would cause us to struggle in making a demonstration! The sense of opposition must forever be removed from the consciousness which perceives Unity. Instead of saying, "Here is a sick person to heal and I shall have to work hard on this case," we should realize that there is nothing but concept in the Universe and, therefore, say, "I am going to conceive of this person as being absolutely perfect," then the same power which made the individual sick will also heal. This is the reversal of thought.

That which we call our subjective mind is but a point in Universal Mind where our personality maintains its individualized expression of Spirit. If we think of ourselves as being separated from the Universe we will be limited by this thought; for it is a belief in separation from Good which binds and limits; we are bound by nothing except belief. "They could not enter in because of unbelief," and because they "limited the Holy One of Israel."

There is but One Mind. Here is the point: everything we experience, touch, taste, handle and smell: environment, bodies, conditions, money, happiness, friends; all are effects. Is it clear that the infinite and limitless possibilities of that One of which we are a part depend, in our expression, upon our own concepts? If we are a point of personality in limitless Mind, which we are, and if all of our life must be drawn from this One Mind, which it must, there cannot be anything else, can there? And if there is nothing else, if there is nothing to move but Mind, and if we are a thinking center in Mind, nothing is going to happen to us that does not happen through us, whether this is the result of our own erroneous conclusions, those of our grandfathers, or the race to which we belong. It is impossible to conceive of anything ever happening to any one unless the force back of it was set in motion by ourselves sometime or somewhere. But this is not fatalistic, for we may change the chain of causation which we have set in motion.

Everything comes from Intelligence; there is nothing but Unity; there is nothing but freedom; there is nothing but completeness; there is nothing but Totality. Begin at the beginning and reason this out time after time till doubt disappears; for you will be neutralizing that subjectivity which rises to slay you. It is necessary that all of us do this for ourselves.

Demonstration

As far as making a demonstration is concerned, when we get the correct consciousness this is the easiest thing in the world; but we cannot demonstrate beyond our ability to mentally embody an idea. The argument is between our experience, what the world believes, and what we are convinced is the Truth.

It should be understood that we can demonstrate in spite of our own selves, in spite of all weakness, in spite of every fear, in spite of all that is in us, because such is the power of the Truth. If we waited to be good before demonstrating, the wheel might turn a million times; but law is neither good nor bad; law is and responds.

The possibility of demonstrating does not depend upon an incident, conditions, location, personality or opportunity, It depends upon ourselves and upon nothing else. The Universe will never deny us anything, unless we conceive that it is possible for us to think of something that it is impossible for the universe to produce. Every one who asks receives according to his/her belief.

Karmic Law

Annie Besant said of Karma, "It is the law that binds the ignorant but frees the wise." That which is called Karma in the Orient, we call cause and effect. The subjective state of consciousness is our Karma; this is the result of the thinking that has gone before, and of the race-suggestion operating through us. Karma is not fate; it is mental law; and it can be changed by right thinking and right action. Karma is not Kismet.

Thought Force

Thought force is the movement of consciousness which sets law in operation. The movement of consciousness upon itself creates a motion or vibration in Intelligence and upon Substance, the force of which is equal to the reality of the thought set in motion. For everything that happens in the objective world, there must be something in the subjective world to perfectly balance it. Just suppose for a moment that the Universe is nothing but water, permeated by an Infinite Intelligence. Imagine that every time this Intelligence moves or thinks an icicle is formed in the water, exactly corresponding to the thought. We might have countless numbers of icicles of different forms, colors and sizes; but these icicles would still be water. If we could heat the whole mass, it would melt, and all the forms would again become fluent; nothing would have changed but form. This is all there is to matter; it is Spirit in Form; and as such is perfectly good; to deny matter is poor logic.

First is Intelligence; then the Word, the vision, the image, the concept; then the movement to the thing. Remember, thought is an actual working power; otherwise there would be nothing with which the Universe could be run.

Choosing Thought

We have a right to choose what we shall induce in Mind. The way that our thoughts are to become manifested we cannot always see; but we should not be disturbed if we do not see the way, because effect is potential in cause; "I am Alpha and Omega." And all that comes between cause and effect. Cause and effect are really One, and if we have a given cause set in motion the effect will have to equal this cause. One is the inside and the other the outside of a concept or idea.

Practitioners' work begins and ends within themselves. If, in doing mental work, the thought should come that the thing cannot be done, you must treat this thought as not having power, but only as an impersonal suggestion trying to gain entrance to your mentality. Realize that there is nothing in you that can hinder you from demonstrating the Truth.

If we say to ourselves, "I am filled with life, heart, strength and vigor," and then we go down the street saying, "I see a poor blind beggar, a criminal and a sick person," we are still treating ourselves just as much as when we affirmed that we were perfect. We are only as perfect as we perceive others to be. This does not mean that we shut our eyes to those who are in trouble; for we may have sympathy with the one having trouble without having sympathy with his trouble. We must have sympathy with all, for, as one of the great prophets of the new age said, "The Divinity of Christ was made manifest through the humanity of Jesus."

A certain, specific, intelligent form, or idea in Mind, will produce a certain, specific, concrete manifestation in matter, equal to itself. There is one Infinite Principle, One Infinite Thought-Stuff, One Infinite Creative Power and countless numbers of forms, which appear and disappear as the definite, specific, concrete thought behind them changes.

Practitioners are ones who change the false thought and build on the Principle of Truth, which executes and manifests the truth that practitioners embody. They can demonstrate to the limit of their mental ability and their spiritual capacity to conceive of the Truth.

If you wish to demonstrate prosperity, you must first have a consciousness of prosperity; if you wish health, you must embody the idea of health. A consciousness of health, happiness and prosperity can be induced within through right mental and spiritual practice. By consciousness is meant the inner embodiment of an idea; the

subjective image of the idea; the mental and spiritual equivalent of
the idea.

Inducing Thought

While a certain consciousness may be mechanically induced, of
course, the more spontaneity put into the mechanical word, the
more power the word must have. Since we all must begin right
where we are, most of us will be compelled to begin with a mechanical process. This is more than faith, for it is a sure knowledge
that we are dealing with Law.

Principle is Changeless Reality. That which we call personality is
the instrument through which Principle operates, but It can operate
for the individual only by operating through them. It is never
bound by the form that It takes, but is forever free. Principle is all
form, and not only fills all forms, but surges around them, and is in
and through them. Ice is water and water is ice; so God and humankind exist in an Eternal state of Unity.

When we realize that we are depending upon Principle, we should
educate ourselves to the point of realization of our ability to use It.

We should always be impersonal in mental work. We do not have
to be impersonal in life, for we are brought to the point of personality in order that we might enjoy each other. But in mental work
we are dealing with an impersonal Principle. It will operate for one
just as quickly as for another, because It is Law. Dare to speak and
to know that what you speak is the law to the things spoken. One,
alone in consciousness with the Infinite, constitutes a complete
majority.

Knowing this in your own thought, work in perfect peace and
calm; always expect; have enthusiasm; and have a consciousness of
love; that is, a radiant feeling flowing through the personality at all
times. If you do not have this, you should treat yourself until you
do have it; for without it, you are diseased in mind. Treat until you
feel an inner sense of Unity with the all Good. There is One Mind,
and the moving impulse of this Mind is Love.

In choosing words in treatment, say anything that will induce the
right mental attitude. Giving formulas is a mistake, for how can any
one put a spontaneous thought into the mind of another? Any one
can stand in front of a dead person and say, "Arise," but who is
going to have the consciousness to make this happen?

Place No Limit on Principle

Know your own mind; train yourself to think what you wish to think; be what you wish to be; feel what you wish to feel; and place no limit on Principle. The word which you speak would be just as powerful as the words which Jesus spoke, if you knew it; but know this within and not only without.

After all, all there is, is mental action and reaction. If you have reached the point where the inner consciousness produces all things, then your word is simply an announcement of reality. There will come a time when demonstration will no longer be necessary.

Know that when you give a treatment, the act takes place in Infinite Mind. Infinite Mind is the Actor and you are the announcer. If you have a vague, subtle unconscious fear, get still and think, "Who am I? What am I? Who is speaking? What is my life?" Think right back to Principle until your thought becomes perfectly clear again.

Such is the Power of right thinking that It cancels and erases everything unlike itself. It answers every question, solves all problems, is the solution to every difficulty. It is like the sunlight of Eternal Truth, bursting through the clouds of obscurity and bathing all life in glory. It is the Absolute with which you are dealing and nothing less.

About the Compiler

LELAND P. STEWART grew up in Detroit, Michigan, and attended the University of Michigan in Ann Arbor, where he obtained two Bachelor of Science degrees—one in mathematics and the other in mechanical engineering. While working as a test engineer for the General Electric Company and planning to study further at the Harvard Business School in preparation for administrative work in industry, he suddenly came to the realization that his life was to be headed in another direction. Rev. Stewart then applied and was accepted at the Harvard Divinity School, where he graduated with a S.T.B. degree in 1953. He was ordained by the Universalist Church of America at Little Falls, New York, in 1954.

Since his entry into the life of world spiritual and community leadership, Rev. Stewart has served, and continues to serve, as the Founder and Central Coordinator of the Unity-and-Diversity World Council (UDC), bringing high energy to the practice of universal cooperative co-existence. The Council began during 1965, when the General Assembly of the United Nations declared International Cooperation Year. The Council has its headquarters in Los Angeles.

SOURCES

Ballou, Robert O. *Bible of the World*. New York: Viking Press, 1939.
Source for: Taoism, Confucianism, Hinduism (except Upanishads), and Buddhism.

Holmes, Ernest. *Can We Talk to God?* (Science of Mind Publishing, 1934, 1992).
Source for: Science of Mind.

Holy Bible. Revised Standard Version. New York: Thomas Nelson and Sons, 1952.
Source for: Old and New Testament writings.

Prabhavananda, Swami, and Frederick Manchester. *Upanishads*. Hollywood: Vedanta Press: 1947.
Source for: Upanishads.

Scientology.
See footnotes.

Ywahoo, Dhyani. *Voices of Our Ancestors: Cherokee Teachings from the Wisdom Fire*. Boston: Shambhala Publications, 1987.
Source for: Tsalagi traditions.

All interpretations upon these and other sources are the responsibility of the editor alone.

CONTENTS

TAOIST SCRIPTURES 17
THE TAO-TE-CHING... 18
THE WORKS OF CHUANG TZE... 49

CONFUCIANIST SCRIPTURES 91
ANALECTS OF CONFUCIUS 92
THE GREAT LEARNING... 107
THE DOCTRINE OF THE STEADFAST MEAN................ 108
THE WORKS OF MENCIUS 115
THE BOOK OF FILIAL PIETY 130

HINDU SCRIPTURES 133
THE UPANISHADS... 135
THE BHAGAVAD-GITA (OR "THE SONG OF THE LORD").......... 164
SANKACHARYA'S ATMA BODHA (KNOWLEDGE OF THE SOUL).......... 179
THE YOGA SUTRAS OF PATANJALI.............................. 180
THE WORKS OF SRI RAMAKRISHNA 184
THE PARABLES OF SRI RAMAKRISHNA 195

BUDDHIST SCRIPTURES................................ 203
BUDDHIST SCRIPTURES 205
THE LIFE OF THE BUDDHA 205
THE DOCTRINE OF THE BUDDHA............................... 223
THE DHAMMAPADA.. 252
THE DIAMOND SUTRA.. 260
ASVAGHOSHA'S DISCOURSE ON THE AWAKENING OF FAITH.......... 265
THE TIBETAN DOCTRINE.. 268
JAINA SUTRAS.. 272
A MANUAL OF MAHAYANA AND ZEN BUDDHISM 275

ZOROASTRIAN SCRIPTURES 293
ZOROASTRIAN SCRIPTURES 296
ZARATHUSHTRA'S PHILOSOPHY................................. 316
BASIC OVERVIEW BY SHAHRIAR SHAHRIARI............. 316

THE HEBREW SCRIPTURES AND OTHER SACRED
JEWISH WRITINGS...................................... 321
GENESIS.. 323
EXODUS... 334
LEVITICUS... 336
NUMBERS.. 337
DEUTERONOMY 338
JOSHUA... 341
JUDGES... 342
FIRST SAMUEL... 346
SECOND SAMUEL... 347
FIRST KINGS... 349
SECOND KINGS.. 350
ISAIAH.. 351
JEREMIAH 355
EZEKIEL.. 357
HOSEA.. 358

JOEL... 358
AMOS.. 359
OBADIAH... 359
JONAH.. 360
MICAH.. 362
HABAKKUK... 363
ZEPHANIAH.. 364
HAGGAI... 364
ZECHARIAH.. 364
MALACHI.. 365
PSALMS.. 365
PROVERBS... 370
JOB... 373
THE SONG OF SONGS... 381
RUTH.. 385
LAMENTATIONS.. 386
ECCLESIASTES.. 389
ESTHER... 392
DANIEL... 394
EZRA... 397
NEHEMIAH.. 399
FIRST CHRONICLES.. 401
SECOND CHRONICLES... 401
MISHNAH... 402
MISHNA.. 404
TALMUD... 405
MIDRASH.. 406

CHRISTIAN SCRIPTURES...................................... 409
OLD TESTAMENT... 411
THE PSALMS.. 419
THE PROVERBS.. 420
ECCLESIASTES OR THE PREACHER...................................... 428
ISAIAH.. 438
JEREMIAH.. 440
EZEKIEL.. 441
AMOS.. 441
NEW TESTAMENT.. 442
PAUL THE APOSTLE.. 475
OTHER NEW TESTAMENT SPIRITUAL LEADERS................. 490
REVELATION OF JOHN.. 495

ISLAMIC SCRIPTURES 497
SCRIPTURE.. 502
ALLAH (THE EXALTED, THE MAJESTIC GOD)..................... 502
THE CREATION.. 503
THE ANGELS.. 505
THE PROPHETS (ON WHOM BE PEACE)............................... 506
THE INVISIBLE BEINGS.. 507
HUMAN BEINGS.. 507
SATAN.. 511
THE ETERNAL LIFE TO COME.. 511
WORSHIP.. 514
PRAYER.. 515
ZAKAT (THE OBLIGATORY ALMS TAX)............................... 517

FASTING.. 518
HAJJ (PILGRIMAGE)... 519
SUPPLICATION (DU'A) 521
GOOD CHARACTER VIRTUOUSNESS.. 522
ADAB (APPROPRIATE MANNERS) 525
JUSTICE... 526
MODESTY.. 526
EQUITY.. 527
TOLERANCE... 528
THE LAWFUL AND THE PROHIBITED.. 528
THE FAMILY AND MARRIAGE 531
HUMAN DIVERSITY 533
STORIES OF THE PROPHETS (ON WHOM BE PEACE) IN THE QUR'AN............ 533
JESUS (SON OF MARY) (ON WHOM BE PEACE).............................. 533
MOSES (ON WHOM BE PEACE)... 539
ABRAHAM (ON WHOM BE PEACE)... 542

BAHA'I SCRIPTURES **545**
SPIRITUAL REALITY... 547
SERVICE.. 551
HUMANITY.. 553
THE PROPHETS 560
BAHA'U'LLAH'S MESSAGE 566
THE HEART OF BAHA'U'LLAH'S MESSAGE...................................... 575
REFERENCES.. 585

SCIENTOLOGY SCRIPTURES **589**
L. RON HUBBARD THE FOUNDER OF SCIENTOLOGY..................... 592
MY PHILOSOPHY BY L. RON HUBBARD.. 593
THE AIMS OF SCIENTOLOGY BY L. RON HUBBARD........................ 596
SCIENTOLOGY FUNDAMENTALS BY L. RON HUBBARD................. 597
ETHICS, JUSTICE AND THE DYNAMICS BY L. RON HUBBARD 609
THE CREED OF THE CHURCH OF SCIENTOLOGY BY
  L. RON HUBBARD [1954] 622

BRAHMA KUMARIS SCRIPTURES................................. **625**
BACKGROUND.. 626
SCRIPTURES.. 628
SOUL.. 628
GOD.. 639

BAWA MUHAIYADDEEN'S TEACHINGS...................... **655**
BAWA MUHAIYADDEEN'S TEACHINGS... 657

TSALAGI TRADITIONS (NATIVE AMERICAN) **663**
SCRIPTURES.. 664

CAODAI SCRIPTURES **683**
CAODAI FAITH: A RELIGION OF UNITY.. 685
THE MESSAGE 685
CAODAI: THE INNER TEACHINGS THE VOYAGE INWARD 692
A PRACTICAL WAY.. 699

SCIENCE OF MIND SCRIPTURES.................................**701**
SCIENCE OF MIND SCRIPTURES.. 702